Russell Scott retired from business in 1838 with a capital said to be worth
£38,000. He and Robert Scott both lent money to the firm during the
crisis described in chapter 10

Russell Scott was the executor of his brother-in-law's will and trustee for
his young children. During the minority the copyright was registered in
his name.

Russell **SCOTT**
1760-1834
Unitarian Minister
at Portsmouth

m. 1832
Russell **SCOTT** = Isabella **Prestwich**
1801-1880   1813-1894
Coal Merchant
in London

TAYLOR
1905

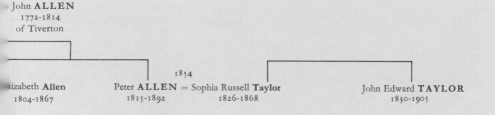
Names are given only of those connected with the paper or where
necessary to show inter-relationships. Others are indicated by
symbols – 's' (son) and 'd' (daughter)

John **ALLEN**
1772-1814
of Tiverton

lizabeth **Allen**   Peter **ALLEN** = Sophia Russell **Taylor**   John Edward **TAYLOR**
1804-1867   1815-1892   1826-1868   1830-1905
                    1854

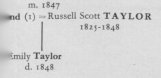

m. 1847
nd (1) = Russell Scott **TAYLOR**
        1825-1848

Emily **Taylor**
d. 1848

Peter Allen, like the Boyces, came from Tiverton. He was a
posthumous son, was apprenticed to a chemist, and came to
London in 1837 with £10 to last for three months. He found
employment with a big chemist's with whom he remained until
he was brought to Manchester to succeed his cousin Henry
Boyce in 1851. He was admitted a partner in 1854.

On Emily Taylor's re-marriage (to a Frenchman), her brother-
in-law, John Edward Taylor arranged to buy her half share in
the copyright.

GUARDIAN
Biography of a Newspaper

THE MANCHESTER

Guardian.

Biography of a Newspaper

DAVID AYERST

CORNELL UNIVERSITY PRESS
ITHACA, NEW YORK

First published 1971

International Standard Book Number 0-8014-0642-0
Library of Congress Catalog Card Number 78-150425
Printed in Great Britain

FOR

THE MANCHESTER GUARDIAN

S'il gagne bataille
Aura mes amours.
Qu'il gagne, ou qu'il perd
Les aura toujours.

Perhaps the nymph was a prophetess, with such
a paper in her mind.

Richard Whiteing (1915)
echoed by
David Ayerst (1971)

The quotation is from Whiteing's autobiography,
'My Harvest.' Whiteing was on the staff of the
Manchester Guardian 1873-1875.

Contents

PART THREE: *The Guardians*

List of Illustrations

Preface

WHEN the *Guardian* was a hundred years old Haslam Mills wrote its first biography –' The Manchester Guardian: A Century of History', an exquisite and evocative volume tailored to the needs of a special supplement. In 1932 C. P. Scott died. Two years later J. L. Hammond published his life of 'C. P. Scott of the Manchester Guardian' which concentrated on Scott as a politician, A dozen years later the centenary of Scott's birth brought 'C. P. Scott and the Making of the Manchester Guardian,' a symposium by members of the staff, edited by A. P. Wadsworth. Wadsworth had it in mind to mark the centenary of the *Guardian* as a daily by a more substantial work but his illness and death prevented this.

The present book, which coincides with the paper's third jubilee, has been six years in writing. The *Guardian*. which became my first employer forty-two years ago to-day, kindly took me back on to its staff to undertake it after thirty years' absence. Its whole records have been at my disposal and I have been left entirely free to form and to express my own conclusions. As one would expect of the *Guardian*, there has been no censorship. Clearly, then, neither the paper nor the company has any responsibility for the opinions I have expressed. This essential freedom has been possible because at the beginning we decided that the history should stop short in 1956, a date of as much significance in the little world of the *Guardian* because of the death of its editor, A. P. Wadsworth, as in the great world because of Suez.

When I think of the very large number of past and present members of the staff of the *Guardian* and of others connected with it who have so generously helped in the preparation of this book, I realise that one might almost as well print an historical staff list as attempt to thank them here individually by name. Obviously this book could not have been written without their help. Collectively it is theirs just as the paper is. I hope they will pardon my reversion to the time before by-lines and accept my thanks to the *Manchester Guardian* for sitting so patiently for its portrait. The publishers with their long experience of Bedside Guardian books will perhaps for this occasion accept the same collective thanks. Others will pardon me if I mention by name –

J. E. Mossey, C. P. Scott's secretary who joined the staff in 1898, the first man to whom I turned to for help; Frank Singleton, and the *Guardian* librarians in Manchester and London and all who work with them. Tom Kirkham's professional eye as head reader in Manchester has detected much that I would not have seen. I want also to include in my short list my secretary, Mrs. Crang, who has struggled all this time not only with my handwriting but with others' more difficult than mine such as J. L. Hammond's and A. P. Wadsworth's.

DAVID AYERST

Burford
January 1, 1971

NOTES ON ILLUSTRATIONS

The line blocks on pages 40, 48, 55, 74 and 88 show the kind of pictures, usually advertisements, which appeared in the paper in its first decade. After that the pressure of news and advertisements on a fixed number of pages determined by taxation, cut out illustrations. They were resumed in 1886. The illustrations between pages 336 and 337, 464 and 465, 496 and 497, and also those facing pages 576, 577 and 608 have been chosen to show the development of illustrations in the *Guardian* from that time on. Half tone blocks were first used in the paper in 1905, and in 1908 the first staff photographer, Walter Doughty, was appointed. The gothic lettering on the title page is reproduced from the masthead of the first issue of the paper.

The illustrations are drawn either from the files of the paper itself or from its records with the following exceptions. The picture of Market Street on page 24 is reproduced from a set of drawings in the Manchester Central Library. The illustrations facing pages 64 and 65 are from paintings in the possession of Canon R. R. Allen; that facing page 192 of W. T. Arnold from a photograph lent by Mrs. Mary Trevelyn; the Lowry painting between pages 304 and 305 and that of C. E. Montague between pages 432 and 433 from originals in the possession of R. S. Scott and Andrew Montague respectively. The graphs on pages 79 and 300 were drawn by A. P. Wadsworth for his paper to the Manchester Statistical Society on 'Newspaper Circulations'. The line drawing on page 6 comes from the same source; that on page 168 from the jubilee history of the Manchester Press Club. The cartoons of C. P. Scott on pages 268 and 269 appeared in *Punch* and the *Westminster Gazette* respectively in 1899. The drawings on pages 419 and 585 are by Birger Lundqvist and come from 'Engelska Mil' (Wahlstrom & Widstrand, Stockholm). To all these thanks are due as also to the *Guardian* photographers in London and Manchester who took great trouble to provide the prints from which the blocks have been made.

PART ONE
Before Agamemnon

Vixere fortes ante Agamemnona
HORACE

*

BOOK ONE

The Founder 1821-1844

*

CHAPTER ONE

Glad Confident Morning

I

'IT is now plain you have the elements of public work in you. Why don't you start a newspaper?' John Childs, a radical printer of Bungay in Suffolk, made this suggestion to John Edward Taylor on March 30, 1819 and followed it up with practical details of what this would involve. Their conversation, to which the *Guardian* traces its origin, took place in a coach on the way back to Manchester from Lancaster Assizes. Taylor had just been acquitted on a charge of criminally libelling John Greenwood, the Manchester Tory leader.[1]

The case had been a deliberate trial of strength between the two parties. Its origin went back to 1812, a year when potatoes and oatmeal, the main items in the Lancashire working class diet, were dearer than ever before. Once, when the French Revolution was new, the Manchester mob had been Tories to a man and had enjoyed sacking the offices of the new radical *Manchester Herald* and driving its proprietor, Matthew Falkner, to flee to America. By 1812 hunger and the long war had turned them against the Establishment and they set fire to the Exchange, the centre of Manchester's business life. Who put them up to it? A placard had been posted on the walls with the title 'Now or Never.' Rumour said that the authors were 'eloquent, intellectual and bold' John Shuttleworth and twenty-one year old John Edward Taylor.

> Ye weavers what's a *Shuttle worth?* Ye *Taylors*, quit your goose, Sirs.
> Come up and head the mob you've raised, for Bedlam's now broke
> loose, Sirs.
> And you, ye two great Jacobin placarders, learn'd and clever,
> Come up and gain the prize you've gain'd: Come forward *Now or*
> *Never.*

Six years later this old unsubstantiated rumour was revived and indignantly denied. Neither Manchester nor Salford had an elected town council, but there were a number of special committees for various purposes. In 1818 the police commissioners had to appoint assessors

for Salford. John Edward Taylor was put forward as a moderate reformer. John Greenwood objected: 'Moderate indeed – he was the
author of the handbill that caused the Manchester Exchange to be set
on fire in 1812.' He was not selected.

He twice demanded an apology from Greenwood, but his letters
were ignored. He then asked his next door neighbour, Archibald
Prentice, to take a third note to Greenwood and personally to obtain
an answer. 'Things began to look serious. I said, "Will you fight,
Taylor, if he should refer to that kind of satisfaction?" "Certainly I
will," he said. "Have you ever fired a pistol in your life?" I asked. "I
have not," was the reply. "Then you shall not have me for your second,
for you could be as likely to wing me as to shoot Mr Greenwood." '
Taylor sent another letter in which he described Greenwood as 'a liar,
a slanderer and a scoundrel.' He put a copy of the whole correspondence
on public view in the offices of the *Manchester Gazette*. He was then
prosecuted for criminal libel.

The trial was before Baron Wood. Leading counsel for the prosecution was James Scarlett, later Lord Abinger. The judge was hostile,
but Taylor, who conducted his own defence, got permission to call
evidence contrary to the then practice of the courts, and thus to justify
the libel. The evidence showed that in reality it was he and not Greenwood who was the aggrieved party. But this would have been useless
but for the foreman of the jury, 'honest, firm, conscientious' John
Rylands of Warrington.* When the jury retired at 11.15 a.m. there was
a majority for conviction. After a long discussion the foreman declared,
' "If you will insist upon the verdict, I will go to sleep and consider it
in the morning; there is my bed", throwing his coat into one corner of
the room and lying down upon it . . . John Rylands stretched himself
in his corner and lay in sober thoughtfulness, munching his crust
quietly to conceal his possession of it from those with whom he was
locked up.' At last at 10.20 p.m., eleven hours after they had retired,
the cold and hungry jury reached agreement, were escorted by the
beadle carrying a lantern through the dark narrow streets to the
Judge's Lodgings and taken upstairs to a bedroom 'where with drawn
curtains, bolt upright, in his night-cap and bed clothing, sat Baron
Wood.' When the foreman 'pronounced with a triumphant emphasis,
"He is *not* guilty," there rose a burst of exultation, notwithstanding
the privacy of the place, which made the whole house ring.'[2]

---

* Rylands was a member of what became one of the great Lancashire cotton
families. Fifty years later his son and Taylor's son stood together as Liberal candidates for the county. See p. 176.

2

Taylor's father, a Lancashire man from a farming family at Stand, had been one of two Presbyterian ministers who shared a church at Ilminster in Somerset. There John Edward Taylor was born in 1791. The French Revolution divided the two ministers. Both gave up their charge. Mr Noon became a Jacobin; Mr Taylor a Quaker. For many years he was headmaster of a Quaker school in Manchester. He took his son as a pupil, though he sent him to John Dalton for lessons in mathematics. At 14 young Taylor was apprenticed to a cotton manufacturer, Benjamin Oakden. In 1811 Oakden was in financial difficulties and Taylor senior had to come to his assistance. The next year Oakden did well and was so anxious to retire that he made young Taylor a partner as soon as his apprenticeship was up. Soon after this Taylor left the manufacturing side of the trade and became a merchant. He was in partnership with John Shuttleworth until the end of March 1823.

Taylor's interest was from the beginning more in public affairs than in business. Before he was out of his apprenticeship he became secretary of a Lancasterian school, the dissenting form of educational provision for the working classes. His political views were those of a reformer at a time when reform was dangerous talk. In 1813 a friend took him to visit Leigh Hunt in the prison in Horsemanger Lane where he was serving a sentence of two years for a libel on the Prince Regent. He found Leigh Hunt 'a very interesting and agreeable young man, and all things considered quite as comfortable as can be expected in prison.' Hunt, who was in fact seven years older than Taylor, was then editing the *Examiner* from his cell. This was just the kind of example, combining the glamour and the perils of political journalism in an age of reaction, which an earnest young man who was just starting to write for the press would find irresistible. 'Mr Taylor (then scarcely 21 years of age) . . .' so his obituary ran, 'wrote many articles, distinguished for their earnestness and intelligence, in the newspapers of the town as well as in London journals and other periodicals.'[3] The writer was almost certainly his partner, Jeremiah Garnett, who would have known. Most of Taylor's journalistic work was done, unpaid, for Cowdroy's *Manchester Gazette*. By 1819 Cowdroy had, in fact, come to rely on Taylor and his friend and neighbour Archibald Prentice for the paper's more serious political articles.[4]

3

John Childs's suggestion was, therefore, by no means a hasty shot in the dark. He had reason to think that his listener was likely to be receptive. Taylor's experiences during the next few months settled the matter. Eighteen-nineteen was a year of intense political agitation throughout the manufacturing districts of the Midlands and the North. Manchester, like other important towns, had no separate members of parliament. Its merchants and manufacturers clamoured for direct representation. The workers, who had no votes anywhere, joined in the agitation. There were secret drillings on the moors. Revolution was in the air.

The radical plan was to elect what we should call 'shadow MPs' for the unrepresented manufacturing towns. Birmingham chose Sir Charles Wolseley. In the North a meeting on Hunslet Moor resolved that 'as soon as an eligible person can be found to represent the un-represented part of the inhabitants of Leeds in the House of Commons another meeting shall be called for the purpose of electing him to the situation.' A similar meeting was announced in Manchester for August 9 but called off in view of the action threatened by the magis-trates, country gentlemen or parsons to a man, and 'the committee to strengthen the Civil Power.' But on August 19 the great popular orator, Henry Hunt, came to Manchester. Manchester's workers turned out in force and large contingents marched in from the neigh-bouring towns. A meeting took place in St Peter's Fields. In prepara-tion the magistrates called out the special constables, the regular cavalry and the Yeomanry, who were virtually the younger members of the Tory party in arms.

Of course the Manchester newspapers arranged to cover the meet-ing. So did the reforming press of other towns. John Tyas was there for the London *Times*; Edward Baines, the owner's son, for the *Leeds Mercury*, and John Smith for the *Liverpool Mercury*. Taylor and Prentice naturally were there. It was expected to be a significant occasion. But nobody could have guessed that Peterloo* would have as profound an effect on English sentiment as Sharpeville has had in our own time. What happened is not in dispute. The Yeomanry and the 15th Hussars went into action. Orator Hunt was arrested. Eleven people were killed, hundreds wounded. Just how it happened is still not clear. Was it the Battle of Peterloo or the Peterloo Massacre? Both titles have been used. Robert Walmsley, whose 'Peterloo: The Case Reopened' (1969) is the latest addition to the debate, would incline to the former.

* The name was a lucky invention of the extremist *Manchester Observer*.

Fortunately we are not concerned to establish precisely how a peaceable meeting became a battlefield, but to see what Taylor made of it. In the normal way he would probably have gone quietly back either to his office in Toll-lane Buildings or his home in Islington Street, Salford. It was only Monday afternoon and the *Gazette* was not published until Saturday. There would have been no need to hurry with his article. But John Tyas, the reporter of the London *Times*, had been arrested. Prentice, who had gone home earlier, and Taylor were both anxious that the London newspapers should have as accurate a report as they could give of what had happened. The magistrates were bound to send off their account to the Home Office. It ought not to go uncorrected. Prentice and Taylor sat down that afternoon and wrote separate reports for two London newspapers. Prentice, who told the story, does not name the papers, but it was clear that the same hand wrote the reports which the *Times* carried on Thursday the 19th and the *Manchester Gazette* on Saturday the 21st. Given the slow travelling of those days, the *Gazette*'s article could not have been copied from the *Times*. Either Taylor or Prentice was responsible for the report which, by catching the attention of the *Times* leader-writer, turned a Manchester demonstration into a national atrocity story. The report by Tyas reached London in time for the later editions, but the leader itself had been written earlier on the strength of the free-lance message from Manchester.[5]

In the autumn and winter Taylor devoted much time to the careful case work on which the 'committee for the relief of the sufferers of the 16th August 1819' insisted. These enquiries were often troublesome – not only because there were, no doubt, some applicants who were not entitled to relief, but because a good many of the injured and their families were reluctant to come forward lest their employers should victimise them. When Taylor wrote a pamphlet that winter 421 cases of injury had been 'authenticated by the strictest personal investigation.' Ten had died of wounds.

This pamphlet by an anonymous member of the committee was Taylor's major contribution to the rapidly growing literature of Peterloo – a name which he himself only used in a quotation in a footnote. He was also careful to write 'tragedy' where others already shouted 'massacre.' His 'Notes and Observations,' published early in 1820, dealt first with what would now be called the Government's White Paper on the disturbances, which he reprinted verbatim with his own running comments. He went on to reply to the 'Exposure of the Calumnies' upon the magistrates, which Francis Philips had published in November 1819. The significance of his controversy with

Philips is that it was a dialogue between a moderate reformer and a moderate Tory. Philips had been at pains to explain that he was not a high 'Church and King' Tory. Like most cotton men he was a Pittite, and it was to lobby a cotton grievance against the Tory landed interest that he had gone to the House of Commons in 1812 on the day when the Prime Minister was assassinated. Spencer Perceval, he recalled, 'breathed his last with his head reclining on my breast.' 'The first bumper toast I ever drank,' he wrote in the preface, 'was to "the glorious and immortal memory of the great King William, who delivered us from popery, slavery, arbitrary power, wooden shoes, etc., etc., etc." . . . When a schoolboy, though I trust not of a quarrelsome turn, I would have fought for Lord Chatham against any lad of my standing who would have said a word in favour of Lord North . . . the attempted taxation on our colonies I reprobated, and I gloried in the independence of the United States . . .' [6]

Taylor, for his part, was out of sympathy with the extreme radical leaders. Whether or not an article in the *Gazette* published just before Peterloo was written by Taylor – and on stylistic grounds it probably was – it certainly represents his point of view about the extremists:

'We do not mean to apply hard terms to any of our countrymen, and shall not therefore accuse them of wishing for tumult and revolution, but . . . they have appealed not to the reason but the passions and sufferings of their abused and credulous fellow-countrymen, from . . . whose ill-requited industry they extort for themselves the means of a plentiful and comfortable existence. "They toil not, neither do they spin," but they live better than those that do . . .' [7]

And when Taylor came to give his considered opinion of what happened at Peterloo he refused to make a blanket condemnation of all on the other side. There were good magistrates and 'men of the most violent political character . . . who . . . sometimes use language on the bench more fit for the orgies of a Pitt Club.' The greater part of the Yeomanry were 'incapable of acting with deliberate cruelty', but in its ranks were 'individuals whose political rancour approaches to absolute insanity.' This willingness to discriminate made his condemnation the more telling.

The 'Notes and Observations' contain many touches which were to be characteristic of the *Guardian*'s early manner. The way in which Taylor cut down to size Philips's boast about the size of a Tory meeting foreshadows the later reporting of Chartist meetings where enthusiasm or fear tended to magnify numbers beyond probability: 'The large room, where this delectable assembly took place, measures about 26 ft by 14 ft and more than one-sixth of its space was occupied by furniture. My informant assures me that he could have walked with ease to any part of it. There could not, therefore, have been more than one hundred persons present.'[8]

In another passage Taylor noted that Wheeler, the editor of the Tory *Manchester Chronicle*, fancied the weavers' sticks to be 'clubs and bludgeons', 'shouldered as representative of muskets' as they marched to the meeting. To Taylor, they were nothing but common walking-sticks. He did not see any shouldered, 'nor if I had, should I have considered it of importance, any more than if they had been bestrode, "as representative" of horses.' His account of Peterloo is for the most part a dry, salty narrative, but towards the end a note of passionate, moral anger breaks in. After the charge the Yeomanry reassembled and burst into cheering as for a famous victory. 'That waving of swords I saw, those cheers I heard, and the sight and the sound smote heavy on my heart.' This combination of much cool, deprecating observation with occasional, vehement protest was also to be characteristic of the *Guardian*.

While Taylor was preparing his 'Notes and Observations', which he finally finished on December 14, 1819, the extremist *Manchester Observer* was publishing 'The Peterloo Massacre' in fourteen weekly parts at twopence each.[9] It has been customary for the last fifty years to attribute the editing of this tract to Taylor. No direct evidence supports this view. It is rejected on convincing grounds by Robert Walmsley, the latest historian of Peterloo. Considering Taylor's close association with the *Gazette* it would indeed be strange that he should refer to 'the puerile and unmanly tirade of the Editor of *Cowdroy's Gazette*.' Nor is he likely to have described the plan of the authorities as 'a plot which had for its object the inhuman and indiscriminate murder of at least 100,000 men, women and children . . . yet such was the deadly purpose which rankled in the bosoms of those dastardly minions of power . . .' The point is important because, if Taylor was really prepared to subscribe to statements such as this, he must either have been completely unscrupulous in his journalism or remarkably fickle in his opinions. But all the evidence shows him to have been a man of complete moral integrity and rather obstinate convictions. Between moderate Tories, like Francis Philips, and moderate reformers like John Edward Taylor, there was sufficient common ground on which to build the Taylor family fortune and the reputation of the *Guardian*. This common ground, however, did not extend to the 'Peterloo Massacre.'

It was the custom of those days to print a more or less appropriate

Latin motto on the title page of a book or pamphlet. Taylor chose for his 'Notes and Observations' three lines from Terence. They are lines which a hundred years later C. P. Scott might have been proud to adopt for a collection of his leading articles:

> *Et errat longe mea quidem sententia*
> *Qui imperium credat gravius esse aut stabilius*
> *Vi quod fit, quam illud quod amicitia adiungitur.*

A rough English equivalent might be:

> He greatly errs who thinks
> Force floats, but friendship sinks
> The ship of state.

4

Meanwhile Taylor and his friends were looking to the future. They were determined to play their part in the reform movement, and this in their view would best be done by regular and purposeful use of the opportunities which Manchester, even though it had no town council, already offered for effective political activity. If the borough-reeve, the manorial officer, was unwilling to act, it was possible to turn to the churchwardens, the parish officers, or vice versa. The technique of public town's meetings was already well developed. The Six Acts which followed Peterloo ruled out for the time being mass demonstrations. Political activity of a different kind was still possible.

For this purpose the reformers needed a powerful newspaper. Cowdroy's *Manchester Gazette* was feeble. Some of the reformers, like 'Radical Dick' and his brother Thomas Potter, had money to finance a paper; others, like Taylor and Prentice, had the gift of effective political writing. They took their time and sought advice. Prentice talked to his kinsman, David Prentice of the *Glasgow Chronicle*, and consulted the *Scotsman*. Others sounded Edward Baines of the *Leeds Mercury* and Egerton Smith of the *Liverpool Mercury*.[10]

At first their idea was to take over an existing paper, but this could not be arranged. John Edward Taylor then decided to start a new paper of his own with the financial backing of his friends. Ten men put up £100 each and an eleventh contributed £50. These sums bore interest at 5 per cent. They were to be repaid if and when the paper was in a position to do so; if it failed, there was to be no claim against Taylor, who was to be not only editor but sole proprietor. It was a singularly generous method of financing the venture. It seems probable that more capital would have been available had it been needed. At any rate, one man who was certainly associated with the launching of the paper does not figure in the Account Book. He was John Chessborough Dyer, an American settled in Manchester, who before he left the United States had been associated with the founding of the *North American Review*. The eleven who contributed were Edward Baxter, William Duckworth, Thomas Johnson, George Philips, Robert Philips, Richard Potter, Thomas Potter, Samuel Pullein, B. W. Sanderson, Thomas Wilkins and George Wm. Wood.* The total amount lent was £1,050 and the amount actually paid over in cash before the first issue was only £400.

Taylor's first concern was to find a manager with practical experience of printing and newspaper work. Here he was undoubtedly lucky. There was on the *Manchester Chronicle* a young man named Jeremiah Garnett, Taylor's junior by two years. He moved to the *Guardian* on April 1, 1821, just five weeks before the first issue was due to appear. His salary was to be £120 a year. But Garnett was not only a journalist. He had learnt and practised every branch of newspaper production. As soon as Miss Sophia Scott, who was engaged to marry John Edward Taylor, received the first issue of the *Guardian* she wrote to her brother that the paper would 'not at all interfere with his (Taylor's) business as there is a person to take the labour of it.' This was neither a polite nor an entirely accurate account of the matter since Taylor from the start played a full part in editing and managing his paper, and soon devoted his whole time to it. But certainly Garnett did take a great deal of 'the labour of it', and was to do so for the next forty years.[11]

The prospectus showed that the *Guardian*'s readership was intended to be 'amongst the classes to whom, more especially, Advertisements are generally addressed' and who might be expected to value the trade reports which 'the commercial connections and knowledge of the conductors of the *Guardian*' would enable them to provide 'with accuracy and effect.' This would make good a deficiency 'which is often so obviously apparent both amongst public men and those connected with the press.' The proprietors of the other Manchester papers were all primarily either printers or booksellers, rooted in these trades. Taylor and his friends between them had experience in many branches of the textile trade. Taylor himself was a cotton and twist dealer and had originally been a manufacturer. The Potters were in the fustian section of the trade; Baxter in ginghams and shirtings; Brotherton was a spinner, the American Dyer was in textile machinery, and Prentice in muslins.

* Robert Philips and Wood were in partnership with Taylor and Shuttleworth as cotton merchants.

The *Guardian* was first printed from an office just below the cutler's shop

But what were the politics of the newspaper to be? 'It will', the public were told, 'zealously enforce the principles of civil and religious Liberty . . . it will warmly advocate the cause of Reform; it will endeavour to assist in the diffusion of just principles of Political Economy; and to support, without reference to the party from which they emanate, all serviceable measures.' In foreign affairs the *Guardian* would follow 'with intense anxiety' the 'magnificent experiments' which various states in Europe and Latin America were making in trying to replace 'antiquated and despotic Governments . . . by institutions conformable to the increased intelligence of the age.' Particular attention was promised to the fair reporting of both sides in parliamentary debates and to the provision of full and accurate reports of important public meetings in Manchester and neighbouring towns.

There is no date on the prospectus, but it cannot have been earlier than April because Garnett's name is given as printer and publisher. Taylor's does not appear though, as Miss Scott told her brother, 'it is generally known that he is the editor, and indeed it was thought that no one could establish a paper with equal prospects of success.' A month later he stated in the *Guardian* that he was its sole proprietor.[12]

The *Manchester Guardian* had its staff and its capital ready; but, as yet, no premises. The prospectus had to content itself with stating that 'the Place of Publication will be announced when the necessary arrangements are completed.' Accommodation was found at 29 Market Street at a rental of £31. 10. 0 a year, and from this address the first number appeared on May 5, 1821.

This first number did what the prospectus promised. There was a long article on gold and currency and a sad list nearly a column long of bankruptcies in all parts of the kingdom. The grain markets of London and Liverpool were reported. Much space was given to the week's parliamentary debates; there was a good summary of European news; and a special article denounced the police for using in an ordinary criminal case tainted evidence obtained from police spies who had been exposed as long ago as 1812. The leading article naturally was devoted to the policy which the paper would follow. 'For ourselves' Taylor wrote, 'we are enemies of scurrility and slander . . . we hope so to deliver them (pointed animadversions on public questions) that even our political opponents shall admit the propriety of the spirit in which they are written, however fundamentally they may differ from their own principles and views.' This was, of course, to expect too much and to promise more than would always be fulfilled. 'We believe,' he went on, 'that by industry and attention, by displaying a wish to cater judiciously for the public improvement, the success of our undertaking may be assured – that we shall obtain that support, which we do not expect, and in fact ought not to wish for, on any other terms.'

This is a moderate but confident note. It is the outlook of a man who believed that, in spite of Peterloo and police spies, reason was great and would prevail. Taylor felt that in his own recent experience there was solid ground for this belief. The *Guardian* may claim to be the most durable and, to the partial, not the least valuable outcome of the Battle of Peterloo.

CHAPTER TWO

Running a Country Newspaper

THE top right-hand corner of the first page of the first *Guardian* sums up the economics of running a weekly newspaper in the 1820s. Clear print gives the price as sevenpence; the embossed stamp, like the stamp on a cheque, shows that fourpence of this went straight to the government, though it also served to cover postage when needed, and there was a discount of 20 per cent. There were other 'taxes on knowledge' to charge against income – a flat rate duty of three shillings and sixpence for each advertisement and a duty of 3d a lb on paper – but the stamp duty was the major burden. It was the stamp duty, levied on each sheet of four pages, that in practice limited papers to this size and made them so expensive that there was no possibility of finding sufficient readers to support a daily paper outside London. Short-lived attempts were made to test the market – in Liverpool in 1803, in Manchester in December 1821, where the *Northern Express* had a life of about three months – but with those exceptions the rest of England got not only its reports of local events but its national news mainly from weekly newspapers until the middle of the nineteenth century, when the final end of the stamp duty made it possible for the *Guardian* and other provincial papers to publish daily. Even after that there were many people who continued to rely on a weekly paper.

Problems of distribution as well as taxation shielded the country weeklies from effective competition by the London dailies until well into the railway age. In the North of England at least the *Times*, the *Morning Post* or the *Morning Chronicle* could be read in reading rooms and no doubt in some large business houses, but they would rarely be found in people's homes. In 1836, for instance, W. H. Smith sent some 600 London papers daily to Manchester; by 1846 the number was about 1,500, and these were 'a large proportion' of all the London papers reaching Manchester, where even ten years later they were not available until mid-day.[1]

For the first couple of years of the *Guardian*'s existence the net revenue from sales of the paper, after payment of stamp duty, cannot have averaged more than about £15 or £16 a week, to which must be added payments for advertisements and general printing. Most of the existing country newspapers had started as by-products of a general printer's or bookseller's business. Many were still primarily advertising sheets. The *Guardian* from the start was a political newspaper; that was its owner's sole interest, but, like his competitors, he could not live by newspaper work alone. He had also to be a jobbing printer.

Newspapers, then, were expensive for the public to buy, but they were basically cheap and simple to establish. Printing in 1821 had hardly been touched by the industrial revolution.[2] Both the two basic processes were still hand crafts. There had been little fundamental change in composing (or type-setting) since Gutenberg invented movable type in the fifteenth century. New founts of type were still punched and cast by hand. The compositor still picked the individual letters by hand from the case in which they were kept and placed them in the composing stick which he held in his left hand. When a line was full or nearly full, the compositor's next duty was to 'justify' it, or see that the words were so spaced that the right-hand edges were as even as the left. This he did by varying the space between words. When his stick was full, the compositor placed the lines in a long shallow tray called a galley from which rough proofs could be printed. Finally, the separate galleys were assembled in correct order on a hard flat surface called a 'stone' from its usual material. The whole page or sheet was firmly fixed together in a 'chase' or iron frame and, when finally tightened, the two separate 'formes', corresponding to the two sides of the sheet of paper, were ready to be carried to the press. The compositor's work was now done until the printing was finished and the 'formes' returned. Then he had to 'distribute' the type back to the type cases – capitals to the 'upper case' and the remainder to the 'lower case', an expression still in more common use in the trade than small letters, just as a certain length of 'copy' is still commonly referred to in newspaper offices as 'two sticks.' Printing, even of newspapers, is a traditional and conservative craft.

It is not known how many compositors Taylor employed at the start, but in 1825 he had six, and would on the current trade union practice of ten years later have been entitled to three apprentices. There was a seven-year apprenticeship to letterpress printing and the 'stab rate' (for staff men) in 1825 was 30/– a week in Manchester compared with 26/– in Leeds and 48/– on London daily newspapers.

The second fundamental process in all kinds of book or newspaper production is the actual printing itself. For this purpose Taylor bought Stanhope presses. In 1825, in an apology for its bad printing, the *Guardian* explained that its 'presses have been rather insufficient in power for the very large quantity of matter which the pages of the

PRINTING OFFICE OF HARROP'S "MERCURY." 1752.

Guardian have latterly contained.' The use of the plural suggests that two presses were employed – one for the outer 'forme' (pages 1 and 4) and one for the inner (pages 2 and 3). The Stanhope was a printing machine invented in 1798 by the third Lord Stanhope. Its main advantage was the greater and more even pressure that could be applied by its system of geared levers in place of the old screw press. A better impression could be obtained and a bigger size sheet printed. What had occurred by 1825 in the *Guardian* was that more news and advertisements had been accommodated by using a slightly larger sized page – a little too large for the Stanhope on which it was printed. The difficulty was overcome for the time being by the purchase of 'a new and superior Columbian press', an American improvement on the original Stanhope design.[3]

Two men, working together as 'partners', ran a press. One was responsible for inking the 'forme'; the other for placing the sheet in position, running in the carriage, applying the levers to make the impression and removing the printed page. But the press printed on one side only of the paper. The process of 'perfecting', or printing the other side, required another impression on either the same or a different press, doubling the time in man hours to produce a finished paper. The output of the original *Guardian* presses was a little over 200 pulls an hour. The usual print in the first year was about 1,000 copies, a large circulation at a time when most country journals printed no more than six or seven hundred. To run this number off would take ten hours' work, or a total of five if two presses were in operation.

As long as its presses were hand-operated, a newspaper which wanted to increase its print much beyond 1,500 or 2,000 copies and at the same time to give its readers reasonably up-to-date news, was driven to the ruinously expensive process of setting its copy twice over so that two or more sets of presses could be simultaneously employed. The *Times* reached this position in the early years of the century. By 1814 it found a practicable solution through the introduction of Koenig's steam driven press. This was capable of printing 1,000 sheets an hour – a five-fold improvement which made it possible for the *Times* to give up duplicate composition and to go to press later. By 1828 the rising sales of the *Guardian* – it was by then selling about 3,000 copies per issue – justified Taylor in installing a 'machine.' This was almost certainly a steam-driven press capable of producing about 1,500 impressions an hour. There was, naturally enough, a moment of hesitation among the workers. The minutes of the Manchester Typographical Society record that it was decided to 'make a trial of the machine for a week or so' before coming to a decision. Apparently the experience was satisfactory. No further entry was made.

The two fundamental processes of composing and printing were, of course, distinct from the beginning of the trade, but the account given above rather anticipates a division of labour between compositors and press-men or machine men. In 1821 this had hardly yet taken place anywhere in the provinces; it was the introduction of steam-driven presses which brought this about. Even after that the Manchester Typographical Society, the compositors' trade union, tried and for some time succeeded in enforcing a rule that journeymen employed on press or machine work should have served their time as apprentices and belong to the Society. But in 1821 there was as yet very little rigid differentiation of function, and there were no demarcation disputes. A man's main job was of one kind, but that did not prevent him helping out with other jobs.

Even the editorial, managerial and technical staffs were not at all rigidly separated. John Edward Taylor was no doubt the proprietor and certainly to begin with the principal, if not the sole, leader writer. But he acted as reporter as well. On one early occasion he attended an inquest from which the coroner wanted to exclude the Press. He reported not only the substance of the enquiry, but his brush with the coroner.[4] Jeremiah Garnett used to recall that in the early days he would attend a meeting, take a shorthand note of the proceedings, return to the office, set up in type his report straight from his notebook without transcribing his note, give a hand with the press work – a heavy manual job – and then help with the distribution.[5] By 1830, when the *Guardian* appointed its first full-time reporter, these primitive days of an interchangeable staff were passing away; but John Harland, described in the 'Dictionary of National Biography' as 'reporter and antiquary', had served his time as a letter-press printer on the *Hull Packet*. Only in the more developed world of the *Guardian* of the 1830s did he become solely a reporter.

Taylor thought of the *Guardian* primarily as a means of political expression and communication. His aim, and the aim of his paper, was to serve the cause of reform. But it is doubtful if he would have found sufficient readers for his paper if that was all it had to offer. From the beginning, some bought the *Guardian* because of its politics; some in spite of its politics; but very few read it only for its political opinions. It had to satisfy its readers' demands for international, national and local news of all kinds.

There were three main sources of foreign news on which the *Guardian* could draw – foreign papers, either direct or as quoted in the London press, private letters which reached Manchester business houses from their correspondents overseas, and information collected from ships docking in Liverpool. The following examples are taken from two months in 1822. The hardships of the 1820 settlers in South Africa were recounted from private letters (28 September). The *Royal Gazette* of Kingston, Jamaica, provided the story of how a London ship's captain was made to walk the plank and then shot as he struggled in the sea, and how his 14-year-old son was knocked on the head and thrown in after him (5 October). The arrival of a captured French slave trader with 343 slaves on board at Portsmouth was reported (10 August). 'An authority of very high respectability' stated that in the first six months of the year, Virginia had exported 12,000 slaves to Louisiana; the planters were probably making bigger profits from breeding slaves than from growing tobacco, or so the *Guardian* thought (31 August). In a French treason trial a sub-prefect gave evidence that one woman had said to another woman that there would soon be a dance without a fiddle: 'The *importance* and *applicability* of this testimony,' wrote the *Guardian*, 'reminds us of some which was let in on the part of the defence in the trial of Redford v. Birley,' the case in which a weaver unsuccessfully summoned a Yeomanry officer for assault at Peterloo (3 August). But the *Guardian* was not only interested in French politics. In Paris, English actors found that 'Othello' was made inaudible by cat-calls and the 'School for Scandal' was pelted off the stage with rotten eggs: a French paper was quoted as saying, 'Shakespeare must not be compared with Corneille, but it is just to admit that there are in the English tragedian some rays of genius which pierce through the darkness of his age.' (10 August).

Foreign news was, of course, often sadly delayed. The *Guardian* gave good coverage to the revolutionary risings in Latin America against Spanish and Portuguese colonial rule; but the news it received was commonly two months old. The issues of 21 and 28 September 1822 contained a long private letter from Brazil written on 14 July; a letter from Kingston, Jamaica, about republican successes on the mainland, dated 25 July; and news about the readiness for revolt of Cuba, quoted from a message of 29 July to the Charlestown *City Gazette* of South Carolina. From the Far East news took even longer. The 21 September issue had news in letters sent from Bombay five months before, containing messages a month older still from Penang about Siamese aggression in Malaya. Even from the Near East news was often over a month old. Week after week news of the Greek revolt was given; hopes rose and fell. Most news came from Vienna. The *Guardian* recognised that this was pro-Turkish and hoped that the Greeks were doing better than the messages suggested. A message from Constantinople itself was published on 21 September 1822; it had been dispatched on 11 August.

Both the *Guardian* and its readers were keenly concerned about the improvement of communications. Both had world-wide interests. Both had well founded grievances. The *Guardian* pointed out that the mails from St Petersburg could reach London in ten days instead of twenty-one if the Government would use steam packets, calling 'at Lübeck or some central place to examine the machinery.' The London–Rotterdam steam ship service was so dependable that agents would sometimes save time by meeting the incoming steamer down the river. Similar economies in time could be made in mails from South-western Europe if they were routed to Lisbon or Ferrol and then sent by steamer in sixty hours to Falmouth. There certainly ought to be a daily mail service to and from Paris. It was quite inexcusable that there should be two days on which business letters had to be sent by private express because there was no public mail.[6] Until regular mail services by steam ship were established there was no possibility of planning a time-table of newspaper production in relation to the receipt of foreign news, except from the nearer parts of the Continent. News might come any day; there might be weeks without news. It had to take its chance.

But this was not true of home news. By 1821 there was a reasonably reliable network of main roads with established stage-coach services. London and Manchester, Manchester and Leeds, and Manchester and Liverpool were all connected by regular lines. Manchester and Liverpool, indeed, were serviced not only by stage-coach, but also by passenger boats on the canal by way of Wigan. New turnpike roads were still being built. In 1822, for instance, the church bells of Glossop, Mottram and other villages and small towns rang peals to celebrate the opening of the new direct road from Manchester to Sheffield over the Pennines by way of Glossop, Woodhead and Penistone, the route later followed by the Great Central Railway.[7] The first years of the *Guardian* coincided with the short high summer of the coaching age. There is a modern sound about the beginning of an early Letter to the Editor: 'Sir, it is a lamentable fact that one can scarcely take up a newspaper without the pain of meeting with an accident that has arisen from a stage-coach . . .'[8]

The most important mail coaches from the newspaper point of view were those which ran to and from London. It was in the evening that the mails left London and Manchester for what in the later 1820s was normally about a twenty-four-hour journey. In 1827 Mrs J. E. Taylor took her young children to visit her parents at Portsmouth. She left Manchester a little before six p.m. and reached London about five the next day. Soon after the *Guardian* was founded the Postmaster-General took powers to start an experimental fast express, carrying only mail, which, travelling at 11 miles per hour, would cut the journey time by 13 hours and reach Manchester at 10.20 a.m.[9] The mail brought to Manchester the London morning and evening papers of the same day. The ministerial papers were largely bought by the government and sent free to country papers with certain articles ready marked in the hope that they would be used. 'This is a thing', the *Guardian* said, 'within our own knowledge.'[10] It was the only form of assistance that the country newspapers received at a time when London papers, which supported the government, could hope for direct subsidy or heavy official advertising.

With the London mail there would come a selection of country papers, though some of the more important came directly from Leeds and Liverpool, which also supplied the Irish papers. Irish news took a considerable amount of space, whether it was used for reports of famine or for accounts of political repression, or for comment on the Archbishop of Armagh's estate of £220,000 personal property – 'certain spiritual graziers there seem to have no cause of complaint . . . and the text "feed my sheep" corruptly read "feed on my sheep".'[11]

The greater part of the home news from beyond the paper's own circulation area was quoted with or without acknowledgment from other newspapers. On the whole, the *Guardian* gave its sources, especially when they could be significant. It even gave credit, when credit was due, to papers with which it strongly disagreed. Cobbett's *Political Register*, for instance, had unearthed a decision of the Hampshire justices to arrange for poor relief in such a way as to discourage men from seeking seasonal work outside their own parishes. In quoting this, the *Guardian* adds, 'We think it right to observe that the foregoing extraordinary manifesto was first noticed by Mr Cobbett; and it is tolerably evident that certain journals in which it has been adverted to have derived their knowledge of it from his *Register*; a circumstance which they ought, in common candour, to have stated.'[12] The introduction of a co-operative newsagency covering the whole country and serving all papers, a step forward in which the *Guardian* played a leading part, was still nearly half a century off. Until then most news like this was copied from paper to paper.

Internal evidence suggests that until 1829 the two outside pages of the *Guardian* were finally 'made up' and printed by Thursday night or Friday mid-day, ready for publication on Saturday. The first page was normally entirely devoted to advertisements, though occasionally in the early days these were insufficient completely to fill it. When this happened, no doubt the page was 'left open' to the last possible moment in the hope of more advertisements being available. The back page normally contained a high proportion of what may be called magazine material – poetry, literary or historical anecdotes, Letters to the Editor and other miscellaneous matter, much of which could be held over without damage if there was unexpected pressure on space. There was, of course, some hard news on the back page. It always contained, for instance, the list of bankruptcies taken from the *London Gazette* of Saturday or Tuesday.

Friday was the heavy day for the *Guardian* staff because of news arriving by the London mail. For this purpose the two inside pages were kept open until late in the evening. When Parliament was in session there were Thursday's debates to be recorded. Usually there could only be a summary of the later stages of the sitting; but on occasion a full report was given. On Thursday, 5 March 1829 Peel gave the Commons the details of the Catholic Emancipation Bill. He started speaking at 6.10 p.m. and sat down at 10.15. The first leading article in the *Guardian* on 7 March begins, 'By an extraordinary exertion of the very spirited proprietors of the *Sun* newspaper, we were, at six o'clock last (Friday) evening, put in possession of a full report of Mr

Peel's speech.' The *Guardian*'s summary was two-and-a-third columns long, and a leader supported Peel's proposal. The staff of the *Guardian* as well as the *Sun* were entitled to credit for their 'extraordinary exertions.'

There was often late foreign news to be included, and always there was a stock exchange report giving the prices of government stocks up to mid-day on Thursday. Sometimes the market report was very brief, but on occasion it was considerably extended. One day, for instance, 'the market was in a great bustle this morning' because a private express had reached Mr Rothschild's with favourable news from Paris where Spanish funds were reported to have risen 14 per cent in the last few days. 'It is just stated on 'Change,' the report continued, 'that a courier has arrived early this morning to Government from Lord Wellington who left him at Verona on the 6th instant. It is reported the dispatches are favourable.'[13]

The inside pages also contained reports of the Liverpool Cotton Market, carrying the dealings down to Friday mid-day, and of various commodity markets. These market reports do not give the impression of being scissors and paste work taken from other newspapers, but of being specially commissioned. The surviving account books give some evidence for this – there are regular payments of eight shillings and sixpence a week in 1832 for reporting the Wakefield corn market, a service which at one time at any rate was shared with Wheeler's *Manchester Chronicle*. Differences in politics did not stop sensible business relations. The *Guardian* was determined to serve the business community well. The account books show that both Taylor and Garnett paid their £2. 2. 0 subscription to the Manchester Exchange, and Garnett was long a familiar figure there, gathering news and assessing opinions and trends.

The leading articles were printed in the inside pages. There was nearly always at least one dealing with national or international politics, and often others discussing local issues. Their position on an inside page made it possible for them to be written on Friday night, or at least brought up to date if they had been written earlier. Thus in the issue which contained the postscript of news from Verona there was an optimistic addition to Taylor's earlier pessimistic leading article.

The *Guardian* prospectus had promised full reporting of local news, a promise that was faithfully kept even when it meant a rush on Friday night. Thus a compensation case arising out of the Market Street improvements was fully reported up to the time the court rose at half-past six on Friday evening. The following week there was another long, hotly disputed case which was fully reported in the *Guardian*. This time it concerned watered milk. The complainant's case was weakened when it turned out that it was the price and not the strength of the milk to which he objected since he had gone on buying milk and water from the same supplier.[14]

The latest news appeared under the headline 'Postscript', the equivalent of to-day's Stop Press. Very occasionally even later news justified a second edition. The first time this happened was at the beginning of George IV's state visit to Scotland from which so much of the revived Highland mystique stems. The royal yacht arrived at Leith on a Wednesday afternoon, and that evening an *Edinburgh Gazette Extraordinary* (the equivalent of the official *London Gazette*) announced that the king would land at noon on Thursday. This news was dispatched from Edinburgh on Thursday morning, but did not reach Manchester until the following night, when some of the week's *Guardian* had already been run off. The press was stopped, the inner pages re-opened and the third column of page three was proudly headed 'Second Edition – Safe Arrival of His Majesty at Leith.' Below, under an Edinburgh date line, was a quarter of a column of news about the visit.[15]

Most of the news, of course, could be treated in a more leisurely fashion, though there can have been little free time for either Taylor or Garnett, who did a good deal of travelling. During the four years 1828–1831, the accounts show that he claimed expenses for visits to thirty-eight different towns on 118 different occasions besides various unspecified journeys. Sometimes these journeys involved prolonged absence as, for example, his twice yearly visits to Lancaster Assizes. Their total cost to the paper averaged £60 a year, though sometimes there was a £5. 5. 0 fee from a private client to set off against this. For the most part Garnett's visits were to the nearer Lancashire and Cheshire towns, the paper's own circulation area, but on occasion he went farther afield on the paper's business. He was, for instance, three times in London during these years, twice in Shrewsbury and Leeds, once in Skipton and once in St Asaph. In 1829 he spent several days in Oxford to report Peel's unsuccessful candidature for the university seat which he had just resigned in order to fight it again at a by-election. The issue on which Peel wanted to test the electors' opinion was Catholic Emancipation, a cause dear enough to the *Guardian* and newsworthy enough to justify the very substantial sum of £12. 3. 6 in expenses. The account books too show that it is to Garnett we owe the vivid description of the fatal accident when Huskisson was killed at the opening of the Liverpool and Manchester Railway. Some of his journeys, however, were certainly managerial, as when he went to

Hull in 1830 to engage a reporter. For this journey he claimed £4. 17. 6 in expenses.

Much of the paper in the early days was taken up by a long succession of town's meetings, whose resolutions were published as advertisements, but which received full reports in the news columns. Some idea of the scale of reporting may be gained from a dinner of the Whig Club at Chester, which was considered worth rather more than the whole of one of the paper's four pages. All the toasts were given in full, including the rather admonitory form in which the King's health was drunk – 'The Royal family, and the principles which seated them upon the throne.' A speech by Canning at Liverpool opposing parliamentary reform got a two-column report and three and a half columns of hostile comment.[16]

There were special articles to be prepared as well as straightforward reports to be written. The new incumbent of Astley, near Leigh, was forced to call in the aid of the 7th Dragoon Guards to disperse a hostile crowd before he could be inducted into the possession of his benefice. The *Guardian*'s account bears the marks of careful investigation, and the incumbent's case was fully given although the paper did not accept it. Nearer home there was a watch to be kept on other papers. There was, for instance, the matter of forged signatures to a petition against allowing Roman Catholic peers to sit in the House of Lords. 'The petition was originally placed for signature in the *Mercury* and *Volunteer* office, where a boy belonging to the establishment superintended the process of signing. Urged by curiosity to watch the mode of proceeding, a friend of ours went into the office and saw a man subscribe two names to the petition. He enquired of the boy in attendance whether he might do the same, and was told he might, but he had better *vary his handwriting for fear it should be found out.*'[17]

A good deal of attention was paid to sport. Garnett had a taste for most varieties of field sports and a passion for fishing. He it was, no doubt, who saw to it that important race meetings were reported and that walking races were described, including one in which a thousand miles were covered in a thousand hours and, by contrast, a four-mile foot race between champions of Yorkshire and Lancashire, won by Yorkshire in twenty minutes thirty-five seconds. Half a column was devoted to a round-by-round account of a boxing match (the result had been given the previous week), 'because of the extraordinary language' in which it was described. A main of cocks between Lord Dudley and Thomas Leigh was recorded without comment, but the vicar and churchwardens of a Derbyshire parish were blamed when they set out to choose a suitable bull for baiting. Advice was given on how to behave if challenged by a gamekeeper. Such a challenge was then a more serious matter than it has been in this century. The *Guardian* was worried, for instance, by the sentence of transportation for seven years passed by the Staffordshire magistrates on a farmer 'of considerable means' for stealing by finding a net: 'the severity of the sentence may probably excite a feeling of surprise; but the feeling will be a good deal diminished on learning that Lee was suspected by the magistrates of *poaching*.'[18]

There was the theatre to be visited and concerts attended. Praise and blame were distributed with Olympian detachment. The critic, for instance, found fault with the choice of Colley Cibber's 'She Would and She Would Not', for the author's lack of characterisation, but lavishly praised the actors, for 'we were treated not to a single star but to a whole constellation.'* Especially good was Mr Dowton who made Don Manuel a most effective character, although the author had done 'little more for him than keep him almost always on the stage.' A month later John Braham, a tenor with an international reputation, was engaged for one night only to sing Henry Bertram to Mrs Bunn's Meg Merilees in a musical version of Walter Scott's 'Guy Mannering.' The house was utterly crowded. 'All this, no doubt, was very flattering to Mr Braham, and very profitable to the managers; but it has incapacitated us from giving any thing like a *critique* of the performance. It was our fate to be in the rear and therefore almost unable to obtain even a sight of the *dramatis personae*.' When Mr Braham's songs *were* audible the critic noted the same beauties and the same faults as in the past, 'the same power and compass, the same sweetness and flexibility of voice and the same profusion of unnecessary and injurious ornament.' Interpolated into the play were such songs as 'The Death of Nelson' and 'Scots wha' hae' which drew two encores but provoked a Tory in the audience to start 'God Save the King' as a counterblast. But, thought the *Guardian*, Mr Braham's indignant tone as 'he demanded "wha' sae base to be a slave?" with the descending in semi-tones to the contemptuous "let him turn and flee" was the finest thing we ever heard.'[19]

The *Guardian* was first and foremost a Manchester paper, but Manchester was already in 1821 the capital of an economic region which certainly extended to a radius of a dozen miles. Inside this radius there was a cluster of growing towns, all engaged in different branches of the textile industry. Not only did their manufacturers and professional people have business and social interests in Manchester, but, when

* This use of the word 'star' is two years earlier than the first reported in the Oxford English Dictionary.

there was occasion for political agitation, the weavers and spinners and other workers were brought in to demonstrate in Manchester. The great political demonstrations there were regional rallies. Between the towns there was still open country, and the *Guardian* could not afford to forget agricultural interests. Prentice, writing of the Manchester of 1826, could say that 'thousands and tens of thousands avail themselves of the right of footway through the meadows and cornfields and parks in the immediate neighbourhood. There are so many pleasant footpaths that a pedestrian might walk completely round the town in a circle, which would seldom exceed a radius of two miles from the Exchange, and in which he would scarcely ever have occasion to encounter the noise, bustle and dust of a public cart road or paved street.'[20] But then, as now, there were those who would block footpaths, and in 1826 the *Guardian* was active in the formation of a 'Society for the Preservation of Ancient Footpaths.'

Beyond this immediate region there was still a recognisable community of interest extending northwards at least to Preston, westwards to Liverpool and eastwards into the nearer towns of the West Riding. Manchester certainly did not hold a metropolitan status in regard to this wider area, but it was interested in what went on there, and people in those towns were interested in Manchester news. The list of towns with agents from whom the *Guardian* could be obtained, published regularly at the head of the paper during its first year, included Huddersfield, Liverpool, Preston, Blackburn, Clitheroe, Halifax, Warrington and Wigan as well as the nearer towns.

It was not, of course, necessary to buy the *Guardian* in order to read it. The public libraries of to-day had their fore-runners in the numerous newsrooms to be found in every part of the country. These subscribed to a large variety of papers and often bought large numbers of copies of the more popular. Some newsrooms served mainly the business community; others had a strong political bias. The early account books show that the *Guardian* was bought by newsrooms outside its immediate circulation area as far apart as Glasgow, Hull and Exeter.

The *Guardian* started with a circulation of about 1,000 an issue. By the end of 1823 it had reached 2,000, and two years later 3,000, at which figure it remained for some time. About 500 copies were sold in the shop and about 1,000 through local 'newsmen.' Presumably the rest were posted – the government stamp covered this. Outside Manchester and Liverpool 'returns' appear to have averaged 2.4 per cent over the whole period 1828–1830.

Advertising was, then as now, of two kinds – national and local. The great standby of country newspapers in the national field was patent medicines, for the cure of venereal disease. Compare the news item that forty-five whores had been discharged with the warning that 'there is a treadmill in the prison and another one on order.'[21] Country newspapers and patent medicine manufacturers could not do without one another. Indeed, one London vendor went so far as to finance a Lancashire paper. Next to patent medicines as far as the *Guardian* was concerned came advertisements of new books and lotteries. There was very little other national advertising unless one counts the sailings (the word was still literally correct, of course) of ships from Liverpool to Baltimore and New York, and other shipping announcements which appeared every week. Occasionally some novelty would be advertised such as a fountain pen, but this was rare. Local advertising was mainly of house property, usually inserted by solicitors. A large number of private schools were steady advertisers. Plays and concerts were, of course, regularly announced and there were occasional advertisements of a different kind. Thus an absconding tailor's apprentice was sought by his master, and Salford offered rewards for the recovery of eight runaway husbands.

This account may end with descriptions of work on a country paper in the 1820s by two of the men who made the *Guardian*. The first comes from John Harland, and refers to his earlier days on the *Hull Packet*. It is about any Monday night – the *Hull Packet* was a Tuesday paper. 'We worked all through the Monday night and (save mealtimes) the labour continued from 9 a.m. on Monday to 7 or 8 a.m. on Tuesday, when the paper went to press. Proprietor, Editor, Reporter, Overseer, Compositors, Pressmen and Errand boys all sat down in the lower printing office to a hot joint and potatoes and cheese with plenty of ale at 11 p.m. on Monday. About two or three in the morning Mr Arnutt (the Editor) and I had coffee or tea in the counting house, next the shop, which was my ordinary post. Then Mr Arnutt would say, "I'll give you a *toon* on the horn," and taking his French horn from its box "wakes the echoes" to some soft, sweet melody . . . I used to say to my parents when I came home on Tuesday morning, "Please to ask me no questions nor try to talk with me; for I cannot bear it." I got some breakfast and then went to bed till one or two o'clock when I went to the office again.'*

The second is by John Edward Taylor in a letter to Miss Sophia Scott to whom he was engaged to be married. It is about a very special Friday night – the *Guardian* was a Saturday paper. 'You would

* Harland: Annals (under 1828). Readers of Francis Williams's 'Nothing so Strange' (1970) p. 42 will recall the head printer of the *Bootle Times* who a century later used to enliven publication night with his violin.

be astonished last week at the advertisements, weren't you, dear? I was at any rate. They kept pouring in so that I soon found there would be no more room to spare for me, and therefore as my men were forward at their work, I did what I have not done before on a Friday since I have had the *Guardian*. I went out to a five o'clock dinner, and stayed till ten enjoying myself; then returned to the office, and left it for home at half-past two. The profit that week was upwards of £86, and there was so little room for news that I wrote off on the Friday night about a quantity of smaller type to enable me to compress the advertisements into smaller compass. This will be an expense of £150 or £170 which I did not intend incurring at present: however, I cannot really say that I regret being obliged to do so.' The date was 28 December 1823.[23]

R EDUCED FARES to LEEDS.—A New COACH called the DOCTOR, carrying Four Insides only, sets out every day from the Swan and Flying Horse, Market-Street, at eleven o'clock, through Rochdale, Halifax and Bradford to the White Horse, Boar-lane, LEEDS, where it meets the Harrowgate and Hull Coaches daily.
ABRAHAM DEARDIN and Co. Proprietors.

SWAN INN COACH OFFICE, Market-street, Manchester, from whence the following ROYAL MAILS and POST COACHES leave as under:
B UXTON, SHEFFIELD, and LIN-COLN,—*Royal Mail*, at a quarter before ten, daily, through Stockport, Disley, Whalley Bridge, Buxton, Ashford, Bakewell, Totley, and arrives at a

CHAPTER THREE

The Rivals

WAS there room for the *Guardian*? The going was likely to be hard. 'We are entering on a course,' Taylor's first leading article admitted, 'not only new, but to a considerable degree preoccupied, and where our progress is impeded at least by the number of our competitors.' There were already six Manchester papers, some of them old, well-established journals. They were all, of course, weeklies. One against six sounds foolhardy; but, looked at another way, the six could be reduced to two. Four were published on Saturday; only two on Tuesday, which was then and for a hundred years to come known as 'High Change', the principal day of business when cotton merchants and manufacturers from the whole of East Lancashire and Cheshire met to transact business.

There was another way of reducing the six to two. Four of the six were Tory, only two represented the reformers – one, the moderates; the other, the radical reformers who bordered on revolutionaries. The two Tuesday papers were Tory; the two Reform papers were Saturdays. Whichever way one looked at it, however, Taylor's venture was something of a gamble.

But he had a sporting chance. To begin with, Manchester was a rapidly expanding town. Fifty years before its population was probably about 30,000. Ten years ago it had been 107,000. The sixth issue of the *Guardian* would show that by the latest census it had grown to 153,000. Thirty years on it would be nearly twice that figure.[1] Not only were there each year more people wanting newspapers but, Taylor thought, some people wanting a different kind of newspaper. 'There has been,' he wrote, 'in the last few years a great change in the manner in which much of the business of Manchester is conducted. We were formerly a community of manufacturers; we have now . . . become also a community of merchants' with a serious, world-wide interest in raw materials and in the products of countries which bought from Britain.[2] The Manchester Saturday papers were selling at the rate of one copy to every nineteen or twenty inhabitants, which at sevenpence a copy might have been near saturation point. But this is a misleading calculation because many were sold outside the immediate neighbourhood.

And in 1821 a determined and business-like newcomer to the trade had a fair chance of success because of the small capital needed to start a paper and the small staff needed to run it. A free press was possible in spite of the much abused 'taxes on knowledge.' If Taylor could identify a new or a badly served section of the community and meet its needs there was no reason why he should not make good. But what was the competition like?

Oldest of the papers and in the Tory interest was Harrop's *Manchester Mercury*, a Tuesday paper, which was owned and edited by James Harrop, then aged 64. His father, Joseph Harrop, had founded the paper as long ago as 1752, promising that, 'those who intend me the favour of their subscriptions shall have the paper delivered at their house with all due care and expedition.' Joseph was clearly an energetic newspaper man who must have put this side of his business quite as high as his general printing and book-selling, making the one support the other. In 1764, for instance, he gave away *A New History of England*, a book of 778 pages, as a free supplement to the *Mercury* at a cost to the firm of a hundred guineas. Very early in his career he arranged with the King's printer to be allowed to publish the whole text of the highly controversial Jewish naturalisation bill in which there was widespread national interest. From the start the *Mercury* had been in rivalry with the Whig *Manchester Magazine*, to whose editor, Henry Whitworth, Harrop had been apprenticed.[3] Whitworth was so timid in his approach to possibly dangerous topics, but yet so anxious to show himself well-informed, that after the Young Pretender's march through Manchester in the Forty-five he cautiously wrote in his paper, 'I have received some intelligence relating to Manchester which I am not willing to be the first in publishing.' It was, in fact, the arrest of the two Manchester constables for treason.[4] It was not perhaps surprising that the *Mercury* soon beat its rival in circulation and influence. In 1760 the *Manchester Magazine* stopped publication.

Joseph Harrop had been determined to get the news first. He arranged, for instance, to meet the night mail at Derby and bring the London papers to his office by private express. In 1793 when a penny post was established in Manchester his son James was appointed deputy postmaster, the head of the local office responsible directly to London, a job usually held by inn-keepers who found it a useful way of attracting custom. Manchester at that time was the most valuable of the country offices, producing a revenue of £15,000 a year, but the salary of its deputy was only £200. It seems likely that the attraction of the post to the Harrops was the opportunity it provided for the receipt of news and distribution of papers. James held the appointment

continuously from 1793 until he was removed in 1806 when Charles
James Fox and the Whigs came into power. James Harrop, however,
seems to have been more energetic as a newspaper manager than as
an editor. He had the reputation, like many others, of leaving the
compositors to decide what extracts from other papers they should
use.

Six months after Joseph Harrop died in 1804 his son James started
a new Saturday paper, the *British Volunteer*, designed to appeal to the
patriotic enthusiasm which Napoleon's projected invasion of England
had roused. That was the year the Duke of Gloucester reviewed more
than 6,000 Volunteers on Sale Moor near Manchester, but the enthusiasm was relatively short-lived and the *British Volunteer* never
acquired anything like the standing or success of the *Mercury*.[5] By 1821
it was perhaps the least serious of the Manchester papers, devoting a
quite inordinate amount of space to reporting every detail of public
executions. Thus nearly a sixth of the total space available for news in
one issue was devoted to the execution of a murderer and the dissection
of his body.

The oldest paper after the *Mercury* was the *Manchester Chronicle*, a
Saturday paper, Tory in politics, which was nearing its fortieth birthday when the *Guardian* was first published. Its founder, Charles Wheeler,
was the son of the manager of the Manchester theatre and had served
an apprenticeship with Joseph Harrop before starting a paper of his
own when he was 25. He seems to have been a kindly man, leaving by
his will £4 to every journeyman and £1 to every apprentice in his
employment.[6]

In 1821 Charles Wheeler was assisted by his son John, a harmless
eccentric who was known in Manchester as 'the veiled prophet' from
his habit of riding on horseback through the streets with a veil over
his face because he suffered from the wind.[7] The *Chronicle* had built up
the biggest circulation in Manchester – it sold 3,000 copies a week –
largely, it would seem, by being careful to offend as few people as
possible. Even the Manchester Constitutional Association, a highly
suspect radical organisation of the French revolutionary period, described the paper as 'generally moderate' in spite of the fact that it
would not print their propaganda.[8] It was in 1821 easily the dullest,
the worst arranged and most badly presented of the Manchester papers,
but it was undeniably the leading one. It could afford to send two
reporters to a fairly ordinary town's meeting,[9] and it was extremely
rich in advertisements. It was not that Wheeler went out of his way to
canvass for them (indeed, he refused to accept any handed in after 1 p.m.
on Friday); but, as Prentice put it, 'it was the custom to send advertise-

ments to Wheeler, and few had the courage to break through the custom.' More weeks than not, more than half the paper was taken up with advertisements. Wheeler, to quote Prentice again, 'did not think that his paper needed improvement.'[10]

The *Exchange Herald; Aston's Commercial Advertiser*, started in 1809, was the youngest of the Tory papers. Like the *Mercury*, it came out on Tuesdays. Joseph Aston was 60 in 1821 and, as he wrote in a farewell leader a few years later, the paper he had founded had 'as far as its capabilities extended, done its duty – through a long, a bloody, an expensive but a brilliantly successful war – through the sickening lassitude which the sudden arrest of the car of war occasioned by reaction . . . through the days when political incendiaries were putting firebrands in the hands of Ignorance . . . and during the time of commercial difficulties which followed the hardy days of mad speculation.'[11] It was not surprising if it had become a little wearied and set in its ways. It remained a good-looking paper with its single stamped sheet folded into eight small pages, each carrying three broad columns of type, instead of the customary four large pages each with six columns. Although it was published on Tuesday and might have been expected to cater especially for business interests, it was, in fact, the most literary of the Manchester papers. In 1817 it had published an anthology of original contributions which had appeared in it under the formidable title of Bibliographiana. There was more than a streak of laziness, laced perhaps with modesty and honesty, in Aston's attitude to politics. If there was no real news – but can there have been many whole weeks without any? – he saw no point in writing a leader. One January evening he put down just what he thought of the business:

'The King of France, with 30,000 men,
March'd up the hill – and then – march'd down again'

'To just as much purpose might we pretend to write a leading article this week.'[12] It was not likely that he would take kindly to the bustling, meddling ways of the young political journalists who would not let things be.

Still the *Exchange Herald* cannot have been a bad property. It could not touch the *Chronicle* for advertisements, but it often collected enough to fill a quarter of its space. Its editorial expenses must have been low. Joseph Aston would go to a town's meeting himself, 'without attempting to bring away the exact *words*', as he explained, 'but to secure the *sentiments*.' When he felt it necessary to include a full report of what had happened, he used what the Saturday papers had printed. Thus in 1823 – to anticipate a little – he contrived to give an eight and a half column report of a meeting, lifting Taylor's speech from the *Guardian* and his opponent's from the *Chronicle*.[13]

These four papers were all on the opposite side in politics to Taylor and his radical backers; but there were two papers which were roughly on the same side. The older was Cowdroy's *Manchester Gazette*, founded in 1795 by William Cowdroy who came to Manchester from the *Chester Chronicle*, where he had combined the duties of editor and compositor, composing his paragraphs, whether prose or verse, in type without first writing them. They had quality and were revived and put back into circulation time and again by other papers. He left the reputation of being 'a man of rare genius; a poet, a wit, a facetious companion, an unshaken patriot, a kind father, a firm friend and a truly honest man.'[14] But not, alas, even a moderately good editor. His paper was bought because it was the only non-Tory paper in Manchester, not because it was otherwise worth buying. William Cowdroy's four sons were all partners. The eldest, another William, took over the paper when his father died in 1814. Before long he began to accept regular contributions from Archibald Prentice and John Edward Taylor. The circulation went up four-fold – but only to a trifle over a thousand. As we have seen, Taylor and his backers made an offer for the paper which Cowdroy not unnaturally turned down since he was only 46. The *Guardian* was started. Ten months later Cowdroy died. Had this happened the year before there might never have been a *Guardian*, at least under that name, for his widow might well have been willing to sell. Would Taylor have followed the same policy with the *Gazette* that he was to adopt in the *Guardian*? This is by no means certain. He would not have had to choose between being to the right or to the left of the *Gazette*; there would have been only one paper for the middle class Manchester reformers.

Certainly of all the Manchester papers the *Gazette* had most to fear from the coming of the *Guardian*, which had the same politics; was published on the same day; and had carried off the *Gazette*'s most accomplished writers. The *Gazette* had never been a good paper; it became a worse one, affected by a deplorable tendency to devote its columns to interminable Letters to the Editor, or printer as he was then described, on the private whims of public bores. One issue, for instance, contained two long letters of heated religious controversy. One was by a Protestant who 'disproved' the doctrine of transubstantiation by mixing arsenic with a wafer and challenged the priest to eat it; the other debated whether an infidel could be a good man.[15]

The *Gazette* might differ fiercely in politics from the other Manchester papers, but it was written by men who mingled freely in business

and social life with their political opponents. Even the puritanical
Prentice was a member of the Scramble Club, which met at Froggatt's
Inn for a meal ('food usually 10d; potations 6d') and discussion in
which politics of all sorts were broached, from budding radicalism to
downright 'Church and King' Toryism.[16]

There was another Manchester, articulate but distinct from the
world of Taylor, Prentice, Harrop, Wheeler and their readers. A writer
on the provincial press in the *Westminster Review* described Manchester
as 'that extraordinary town . . . a place where the population is in a very
marked way divided between the governing and the governed, between the employers and their workmen; or, as some have unjustly said,
the task-masters and their slaves – there must be more of party violence
among the conductors of newspapers in Manchester than in Liverpool.'[17] This other Manchester had in 1821 its own printers, reading
rooms and newspaper – its own 'culture', to use the modern jargon,
which found its expression in the *Manchester Observer*, a Saturday paper
which was, as the stipendiary magistrate described it in a report to the
Home Office, 'the organ of the lower classes' designed 'to inflame their
minds.' It was the only Manchester newspaper regularly sent to the
Home Office, number by number, in the hope, no doubt, that 'something could be done about it' by the Government. Local action apparently was not enough, though in the end it proved effective. The
Manchester Observer suspended publication a month after the *Guardian*
began.

For three and a half years the *Manchester Observer* had lived a precarious life. It lacked advertisements – sometimes it could only muster
one column out of its total of twenty-four. It was frequently driven to
change editors and publishers. Rogerson, Wardle, Chapman, Wroe,
T. J. Evans and Service all appeared as publishers. Wroe and Chapman
were both sent to prison for political libels, and T. J. Evans, who had
been imprisoned during the suspension of the Habeas Corpus Amendment Act in 1817, was held to bail for an article charging soldiers with
outrages committed in Oldham. The *Observer* had regularly to appeal
for funds for the defence of James Wroe in some of the numerous
actions brought against him. The one thing the *Observer* did not lack
was readers – its circulation rose to a peak of 4,000 a week in the
month of Peterloo, and for a longer period was probably 3,000, as
many as the *Chronicle*, the leader of the Manchester press. The *Observer*
was the successor to 'Citizen' Howarth's short-lived *Courier* of 1817,
and was itself revived in 1822, in conjunction with Wooler's London-
based *British Gazette*, but it lasted in this new form for only a year. The
demand for a literate working class paper was genuine enough, and the

Observer went some way towards meeting it. In layout and style it was the equal of the best of the Manchester papers, and its mast-head with its arresting eye had a touch of distinction. What was lacking – and this was fatal – was sufficient financial backing and some defence against vicious prosecutions. When Taylor referred in the *Guardian*'s first leading article to the danger of criminal libel and the fact that an editor's 'duty to his conscience and himself will often be at variance', he probably had in mind not only his own experience at the Lancaster Assizes two years before, but the disasters that were overtaking the *Observer*.

As the law stood and was administered, that other Lancashire, the Lancashire of the two handloom weavers who were also writers, Samuel Bamford and Robert Walker, had only a precarious footing in the newspaper press.* It found an easier and in some ways a more natural outlet in the topical and political ballads which a gifted family of Scottish immigrants, the Wilsons, made and sang in Manchester pubs. In 1815 Michael Wilson's theme had been how

> 'Great Caesar's actions are tenfold
> Outdone by Soldier Jack so bold'

but four years later Alexander Wilson had turned to topics nearer home:

> Bob, lets ta'e a peep o' these Peterloo chaps,
> 'At ma'es sich a neyse abeawt cullers an 'caps,
> See what they'm composed on, and then we may judge,
> For it runs i' mi moind 'ot ther loyalty's fudge.

In these and similar songs Manchester working-class folk told each other what they felt, but their good-humoured, gently satirical voices did not carry across the chasm which cut off their life from that of the mill-owners and business men of the town, let alone the polite society of London. It was not, in fact, until half a generation later that middle-class Manchester got to know these ballads as John Harland began to collect them and publish them in the *Guardian*.† Ballads could not be a substitute for newspapers.

This survey of the Manchester press in 1821 suggests that there were

---

* Samuel Bamford was the author of 'Passages in the Life of a Radical.' Walker's 'Plebian Politics' was a response to Burke's scorn for 'the swinish multitude.'

† Harland started the series in the M.G. in 1839 under the title 'Songs of the Working Classes.' The quotations are from his 1865 edition 'The Songs of the Wilsons.'

two possible openings for the *Guardian*. Both offered a fair prospect of
success. But Taylor would have to choose. There was an opening
towards the centre because the four Tory papers were in the hands of
elderly men, set in their ways, wide-open to attack from a newcomer
with something definite to offer the business community. Manchester
business men, even the Tories among them, were not normally of the
Church and King variety to whom the landed aristocracy's interests
ought to remain law. They shared a whole host of economic grievances
with Taylor and his fellow-reformers. They would buy the *Guardian* if
he provided for their needs.

To the left the situation was superficially even more promising.
The *Gazette*, the one existing middle-class reforming paper, had come to
depend on the men who were now establishing the *Guardian*. It was
difficult to see how it would manage without their help. Farther left
the *Manchester Observer* was tottering to its fall in spite of a circulation
second to none in Manchester. Working-class and middle-class radicals
might keep to opposite sides of the road, and one might run while the
other walked, but at least they were going in the same direction.

There was then a reasonable prospect of success for the *Guardian*
if Taylor declared himself either a moderate reformer or a moderate
radical.

JAMES COWLAN, in addressing the inhabitants of Liverpool, Manchester, and their vici-
nities, cannot but return his sincere acknowledgements
for the great encouragement and decided preference

CHAPTER FOUR

The Lost Leader

'I WOULD respectfully suggest that the *Manchester Guardian*, combining principles of complete independence, and zealous attachment to the cause of reform, with active and spirited management, is a Journal in every way worthy of your confidence and support; and any favours conferred by my friends upon the paper, I shall acknowledge as given to myself.' This handsome invitation to the readers of the dead *Manchester Observer*, given by its last editor, appeared in the ninth issue of the *Guardian*. It seemed evident that Taylor had decided that the place of his new paper was to the left of the *Gazette*. Although he had not bought the copyright of the *Observer*, he had, according to Prentice, paid something for the goodwill as indicated by this puff.

There was a good deal to be said from both sides in favour of this link of the *Guardian* with the *Observer*. The dust of Peterloo had not yet settled. It was still the main item of home news, and one on which there was no difference of opinion between middle-class and working-class reformers. *Observer* readers would have thoroughly agreed with the *Guardian* that no 'terms of reprehension are too severe to be applied to (the) conduct' of the church organist who greeted the Manchester Yeomanry at a parade service with 'See the conquering hero comes.' They would have welcomed, and perhaps found useful, the description quoted from the *Times* of an *agent provocateur* 'about five foot six inches high, mooned-faced, dark eyebrows, pallid, sickly-looking complexion and a mincing mode of speaking, with a dandified, quadrilling sort of gait' and relished the *Guardian*'s tentative identification of his accomplice, 'this *gentleman with a cast in his eye*', with 'our late *worthy* and *most respectable* townsman Alfred M . . . n who, we understand, is one of the agents of this unconstitutional crew!' This was the kind of writing to which they were accustomed. Where prosecutions for selling seditious literature were concerned, the *Guardian* was as outspoken as the *Observer* in its opposition to the Establishment with its Constitutional Association and its Orange Lodges 'knowing, as we do, that the Orange Lodges in this part of the country are the hot-beds in which the spy system has been generated.'[1]

It was possible to attract readers by a radical policy though probably not enough of them, given the newspaper stamp duty, to make a paper pay on sales alone. A circulation big enough for that was possible only to the unstamped press, which had to take care by one device or another to avoid becoming a newspaper. Papers which really gave their readers news as well as views needed additional income. In 1815, for instance, the London *Morning Chronicle* had calculated that the income from the sale of 4,000 copies a day would be insufficient to keep it going. But for its advertisements the price would have had to be a shilling instead of 6½d. If Taylor wanted to provide a good all-round newspaper, he could not avoid the tax and he must have advertisements. Could he do this and run a paper well to the left of centre? The *Observer* had failed; the *Gazette* was failing; the *Guardian*'s first eight months were not encouraging, but there was a marked improvement from the beginning of 1822. What Edward Baines had done in Leeds might very possibly succeed in Manchester. Instead the *Guardian* went on another tack.

Looking back in later years, Prentice felt sure that the decisive event which turned the *Guardian* into Manchester's most profitable newspaper took place at Shrewsbury. There on 29 March 1823 John Edward Taylor lost a libel case but won the confidence of Manchester's business community. Ten days later at noon there arrived at the *Guardian* office a parcel containing a gift of £211. 5. 0 towards the costs of the action with the promise of more to follow. The covering letter to the editor, simply signed 'A Townsman', spoke of the 'valuable services you have rendered the town' and the wish of the subscribers, regardless of 'their diversity of opinion respecting the general politics of the *Guardian*', 'to testify their approbation of your conduct.'[2] In his editorial footnote Taylor underlined his pleasure in the fact that the subscribers had not been confined to members of any one party. Those who thought well enough of the paper to give it money were likely to think well enough of it to read it. Thus began one of the characteristic marks of the *Guardian* as a newspaper. It gradually became a paper with which many of its most careful readers disagreed. It had to temper its style to this new situation. Argument had to replace or reinforce exhortation or denunciation. The *Guardian* had to try by reasoning to convince the sceptical or the hostile; it had a genuine chance to do this because at least they bought the paper. This dialogue with its readers suited Taylor's temperament and was to suit most of his successors.

The precipitating event, the libel case at Shrewsbury, was a by-product of England's desperately unsound banking and currency system. In 1822 the traders of Manchester were worried by the introduction of insecurely backed local bank notes, and a town's meeting was held to protest against it. As a result, two of the leading banks which had been planning to print their own notes decided not to. The week after this meeting the *Guardian* carried a long article 'from a correspondent' under the headline 'Paper Money-Makers: Local Notes.' The notes were issued by the insignificant firm of Williams and Dicas of Holywell in Flintshire, who were not, however, named in the article. Although the firm was still small – its total note circulation was only £1,900 in pound notes – one of the partners was notorious. John Dicas had been an attorney in Manchester where he had been convicted of perjury in arranging a fraudulent bankruptcy to suit a client. He had been sentenced to two years' imprisonment. After his release he remained in Manchester until, harassed by rates which he could not pay, he made in the words of the libel ' "a moonlight flit" and went immediately to commence "banking", and is now beginning to avenge himself for the treatment he experienced here, by indirectly drawing away our solid valuables in exchange for the dirty rags which present no security but *his* or his partner's integrity and wealth.'[3]

The case would naturally have been heard at St Asaph near Holywell, but Dicas got it transferred to Shrewsbury. Taylor asked that it should be heard at Lancaster but, when he was over-ruled, was quick to pillory the plaintiffs' reluctance to put their case before jurors from their own county or from the county in which the libel had been published. Since no names had been given in the *Guardian* article, Dicas had to identify himself with the perjured lawyer described in the libel. The jury, helped by skilful cross-examination, found little difficulty in holding that, although the libel was proved, the damage could be put at £10 instead of the £5,000 for which the plaintiffs asked.

The action cost the *Guardian* a good deal of money. The amount contributed by Manchester business men finally reached £307, but the total expenditure was £483, leaving a net balance against the firm of £176. It was money prudently invested. There was a good deal of favourable publicity. Counsel for the plaintiffs, for instance, seeking to magnify the damage his clients had suffered from 'as foul a libel as was ever published', spoke of the *Guardian* as a paper conducted with considerable talent, which was certainly true, and having probably the most extensive sale of any provincial paper in the kingdom, which in 1823 was certainly untrue.[4] This particular puff was a passing advantage; the lasting benefit which Taylor earned was the conviction of Manchester business men that his was a paper which would stand up for their interests. In Prentice's sour words, 'the paper had the advantage from that time of being considered as the guardian of the commercial interests of the town and neighbourhood – a reputation much more valuable, in a pecuniary point of view, than the fame of being the advocate of popular rights.'[5] It was not for nothing that in 1826 when a society was set up to help business men to establish the credit worthiness of customers it was called the 'Manchester Guardian Society for the Protection of Trade.'

Of course, confidence in business matters between Taylor and the traders and manufacturers of Manchester had been growing for some time. Dicas v. Taylor merely set the seal on it. In 1821 Taylor had been appointed one of the commissioners for the Market Street improvement which brought him into close contact with Tories and neutrals as well as with the Whigs and Radicals he had known before. Taylor was obviously pleased that Tories found him 'a reasonable gentleman and not a rough radical bear' and bothered to tell him so. This did not bring them close together in religion or politics, but it did mean that Taylor was breaking out of the rather narrow dissenting world in which he had been brought up.* It meant too that Tory business men came to read with care what he had to say.

Advertisers, therefore, found that the *Guardian* was a paper worth using because it reached a wide range of readers – virtually the whole of the Manchester business community, not only the reformers among them. The way in which newspapers at that time most commonly estimated their success in attracting advertisements was by their number rather than their length. This was because the tax on advertisements was calculated in the same way. The graph opposite shows how the *Guardian* had established itself during the first two years of its life. The progress continued. At Christmas 1823 Taylor passed the immediate advertising mark that he had set himself – one hundred advertisements in a single issue – 'at a hand canter', as he put in a letter to his fiancée.† During the same period the circulation rose from about a thousand to 1,865; by Easter 1824 it was 2,400.

The *Guardian*'s discovery of common ground with political opponents was not at all to the liking of many of Taylor's backers. They were not interested in the *Guardian*; all they wanted was a paper in which to attack the Tories. Any opportunity missed was almost a treachery. But there was little they could do. The copyright was Taylor's. If the paper made losses, they had agreed to stand the loss;

---

* Taylor's father had become a Quaker and as a youth his son wore the distinctive Quaker dress. He had, however, been a Unitarian for some time. (Prentice: *Historical Sketches*, p. 210; A Brief Memoir of John Edward Taylor, p. 16.)

† I. & C. Scott: *A Family Biography*, p. 198.

A normally careful man may be granted a little licence in a love letter: the actual total seems to be ninety-nine, but one of these was for the sale of a print works in Perthshire: an encouraging sign of widening influence.

if it made profits they were entitled to their five per cent and that was all. They had no control over what Taylor did. In fact, Taylor was making the paper pay and steadily reducing his indebtedness to the eleven men who had financed him. On 14 May 1824 Taylor had paid off the last instalments of the original capital. The only thing the discontented among his backers, notably the Potter brothers and Edward Baxter,

Average No. of Advts. per Issue	1821			1822				1823	
	May-June	July-Sept.	Oct.-Dec.	Jan.-Mar.	Apr.-June	July-Sept.	Oct.-Dec.	Jan.-Mar.	Apr.-June
70									69
65									
60								61	
55									
50							50		
45									
40					41				
35	36			37		39			
30		31	32						

could do was to try their luck elsewhere and subsidise another paper. They thought they had the right man in Prentice. They knew that he could write – his style was simpler, less pompous than Taylor's, though it lacked the latter's occasional imaginative illustration that still makes a difficult subject lively and lucid.* They knew too that Prentice shared their dissatisfaction with the way the *Guardian* was going. 'I was often advised to purchase *Cowdroy's Gazette*', Prentice recalled, 'and offered assistance if I found that it required more capital than I could command.'[6]

Prentice was unlikely to resist these tempting offers. The better the *Guardian* became as a newspaper, the less satisfactory it seemed to him. He must have thought that it was a pity for 'the cause' – he was by nature a panacea man – that he had not become editor instead of Taylor

* Thus in an article on labour-saving machinery: 'It must be admitted,' says the pamphlet writer, 'that machinery can be multiplied to such an extent as to produce more goods than can be found consumers for.' 'It must be admitted,' say we, 'that, if the sky were to fall, we might catch larks' . . . It is quite as reasonable to dread the growth of more corn than can be eaten than to apprehend the manufacture of more clothes than can be worn.' *M.G.* 12 March 1823.

whose cast of mind was essentially empirical. Now he was being given the opportunity to do the job for which the *Guardian* had been intended. Besides this, he was afraid that a trade recession would ruin his textile business. He had better get out of the muslin trade. By 1824 Cowdroy's widow was willing to sell the *Gazette* to him and he decided to buy. The price was £1,600, of which half had to be paid at once and the remainder by eight annual instalments. If it was to compete with the *Guardian*, and that was the purpose of the deal, it needed new type and a new press on which Prentice had to spend £300. His outlay, therefore, was considerably greater than Taylor's had been when he started the *Guardian*. Prentice took over in June 1824. He made the *Gazette* an anti-*Guardian*. Taylor was not only himself moving slightly towards the centre, but was being firmly pushed there from the left.

From this time on, or a little before, real political differences were made worse by personal antipathy. It was Taylor who had first introduced Prentice, a newcomer from Scotland, into Manchester reforming circles, but their nine years' friendship was followed by twenty years of increasing acidity on the part of Prentice – indeed, by more than twenty years, since Taylor's death in 1844 in no way softened Prentice's asperity. When he wrote his reminiscences in 1851 he still thought it proper to describe the Taylor of 1830 as a man whose 'repeatedly detected falsehoods had deprived him of all claim to credence.'[7] Prentice was certainly a just man, but his unyielding brand of uprightness seemed to find particular joy over those sinners who were not, in his opinion, brought to repentance.

The vendetta which Prentice carried on against Taylor and the *Guardian* week by week was so much a part of *Guardian* life that it is worth trying to get as clear a picture as possible of the man who waged it. To John Childs, the dissenting printer of Bungay, Prentice was, as we have seen, a faithful, earnest man who never forfeited a principle. Bentham found him 'juggical,* Calvinistic, well-intentioned, serious, generous, zealous and disinterested', which squares well enough with Cobden's verdict in a private letter at the time of his death:

'I never knew a more honest politician. He was poor as Job when I first became intimate with him nearly twenty-five years ago and I often had to help him out of his straits, but anything like swerving from his innate convictions never I believe entered his thoughts. I doubt if he would have sold his poor beggared paper to the enemy for all the wealth of Rothschild.'

But Prentice was susceptible to flattery, or so Cobden thought. One

* ' "Jug" (short for Juggernaut) with its derivatives, a conveniently unintelligible synonym for orthodox Christianity.' (Wallas: Francis Place 1951 p.82)

night at dinner, discussing a parliamentary election, he remarked to Absalom Watkin, 'Prentice should have been bought over. Not that I mean to say that our friend is on sale, but he should have been won over – such things are to be done – *he should have been consulted; that would have been enough.*' 'Now,' Watkin's diary continues, 'Mr Prentice eulogizes Mr Cobden in the *Manchester Times* and, I have no doubt, has been consulted.'[8]

To Prentice, as to the politicians who used him, a newspaper was essentially a means of propaganda, more concerned with advocacy than with presenting the news. He felt this so strongly that in the end by excess he ruined his own paper as an effective instrument for his purpose. He filled it to the point of boredom with free trade politics, giving them, as he boasted, 'more space probably than any weekly newspaper ever devoted to a single object . . . I was often told that it would be more to my interest if I made the *Manchester Times* more of a newspaper. It mattered not. If journalism was not to effect public good, it was not the employment for me.'[9]

While Prentice was negotiating for the purchase of the *Gazette*,

Taylor was setting up house as a married man. He married into the Scott family like his father before him. Like his father too, he had had to face a deplorably long engagement. In November 1817 Taylor's uncle, Russell Scott, a Unitarian minister at Portsmouth, agreed to his daughter's engagement, warning Taylor to consider well the fact that he had no dowry to give Sophia: 'to a man of business a wife without money cannot be desirable, at least not so desirable as one with money.' It was May 1824 before the man of business was in a sufficiently strong financial position to marry Sophia Scott. The day chosen for the marriage was the third anniversary of the *Guardian*'s first going to press – 'I have a fondness', Taylor admitted '(perhaps not a wise one) for such coincidences.'[10] One wonders whether he also saw significance in the fact that at the same time he moved away from Islington Street, Salford, where he and Prentice had been neighbours.

Taylor's marriage was important for the *Guardian* in three ways. He now had responsibilities which he was not the man to take lightly. He must develop the profitability of the *Guardian*; he was not free to undertake quixotic campaigns. On a matter of conscience, he would still run risks with the paper; but unless he felt himself morally committed to swim against the tide, he would in future be inclined towards the prudent course. This is, of course, a subjective judgment, but it seems to square with the known facts and with what survives of his private correspondence.

The second way in which Taylor's marriage affected the *Guardian* was the close friendship it brought him with Russell Scott, Sophia's eldest brother who had the same Christian name as her father. Russell Scott was politically to the right of Edward Taylor, though he tended to take his politics from the *Guardian* whenever he could bring himself to do so. At the same time his influence with Taylor was considerable and at the very least reinforced that of the non-political, or even Tory, business men with whom Taylor was now beginning to associate in Manchester. Even more important was the fact that Russell Scott, starting like Taylor with nothing, had made a success of business and was in a position to put money into the *Guardian*. Money derived from the same source was also to play a vital part in saving the paper in its desperate need eighty years later.

The third consequence of the marriage was the most important. Nearly fifty years later, Taylor's son decided that the time was ripe for him to give up active newspaper work and to withdraw into the role of proprietor. The man he chose to succeed him was his cousin, Russell Scott's youngest surviving son, Charles Prestwich Scott, probably the most honoured name in the history of British journalism.

The success of the *Guardian* angered Manchester's Tories as well as its Radicals. It angered them so much that they decided to start a new Tory paper to compete with it. It was not that the existing ones were politically unreliable, but that they were becoming politically ineffective – the *Guardian* was enticing their readers away and giving them so much of what they wanted that they felt they could do without the true blue Tory politics which the *Guardian* still abominated. The average man in the Exchange was not only being lured away from the *Chronicle* or the *British Volunteer* but lured away from Toryism. And so on New Year's Day 1825 Thomas Sowler published the first number of the *Manchester Courier*, which for ninety years was to be the *Guardian*'s main conservative rival. Sowler was 'a good-looking, rather portly, well-dressed, gentlemanly-looking man, who being short-sighted generally wore his spectacles in the street.' It is also clear that he was by nature quarrelsome. His father had been a letterpress printer and he himself was a bookseller in St Ann's Square. But he realised that the day was passing when newspapers could be trusted to run themselves as side-lines to printing or bookselling. A professional journalist was needed. Alaric Watts, an old Manchester Grammar School boy who was now the editor of the Tory *Leeds Intelligencer*, became editor of the *Courier* and took a half-share in the paper. He was something of a literary man (he published a translation of Tasso) and established during the very short period of his editorship professional standards which were much nearer to the *Guardian*'s than the older Tory papers had reached. But by the end of March 1826 he sold his half-share in the copyright to Sowler for £500 and moved to London.[11]

It was the *Guardian*'s response to the change in Westminster politics that angered Manchester Tories and Radicals alike. In 1826 the *Guardian* published a very long leader by way of justification of the political line that it had taken for the past three years. It was written in an effort to mend the gap which had increasingly separated Taylor from his former personal and political friends who had begun to cold-shoulder him. Its theme was that Castlereagh was dead and Sidmouth, the Home Secretary of Peterloo, out of office; while Canning had 'called into existence a new world to redress the balance of the old' and Peel was busily humanising the savage penal code. 'Mr Huskisson's . . . efforts in favour of free trade, and the reliance which we place upon his determination to effect a complete alteration in the corn laws . . . secure for him all the support . . . which it is in our power to render.' Naturally the *Guardian*'s support for ministers was eclectic. It greatly regretted Canning's opposition to parliamentary reform and Peel's to Catholic emancipation – still – 'we are ignorant by whom, among the present race of public men, their places might advantageously be supplied.' Indeed, 'the old names of Whigs and Tories no longer give an idea of the state of parties in the House of Commons . . . the independent support, freely afforded from the left benches to the most important measures of the government, proves the present opposition to be . . . the least self-seeking of any' within memory. But, Taylor continued, there was a faction in the country 'who are the enemies of all improvement . . . and that faction regards the present administration . . . with the most complete and bitter hatred. We can scarcely conceive a political event which would be more to be deplored than that the reins of government should fall into the hands of men who would act on those principles which the organs of the old Tories make no scruple to avow. If this contingency is to be averted, the frank, unbought support of the independent section of the public, and of the press as the organ of the public, will be of much avail.' He might well have quoted in his defence the promise in the original prospectus 'to support, without reference to the party from which they emanate, all serviceable measures.'[12]

Taylor clearly hoped that his retrospective editorial would lead his former political allies to think less hardly of him. He was bitterly disappointed when Thomas and Richard Potter continued publicly to snub him. He wrote them a dignified and rather pathetic letter asking what evil he had done. The answer came from 'Radical Dick' who flatly denied the argument in the *Guardian*'s leader because he considered 'the country to be in a more critical and alarming condition than it was when your paper commenced, owing, as I think, principally if not entirely to misrule.' He continued: 'As my acquaintance and friendship with you arose from a similarity of feeling on political and municipal affairs, can it be wondered at that . . . I should not feel so cordially towards you as formerly.' Taylor's reply shows the depth of his feeling. 'I should never have thought', he wrote, 'of making an honest difference of opinion on the part of a friend, the ground for a breach of cordiality . . . I have heard you, for instance, advocate measures of which I thoroughly disapproved . . . but I should have been ashamed of myself if . . . I could for a moment have suffered the difference of our views to have the slightest tendency in producing on my part coldness and personal estrangement.'[13]

But there was plainly nothing more to be done. The breach with his old friends was complete. His former partner, John Shuttleworth, who had contributed concert notices and articles on the cotton trade to the *Guardian*, was as much alienated as the Potters. To them he was now the lost leader. But it was ridiculous to claim, as Prentice did, that there was no real difference between the politics of the *Courier* and the *Guardian*, that theirs was fundamentally a sham battle. The Tory Party of those years was deeply split. Taylor was right in insisting that there was much common ground between Whig Reformers and liberal Tories and that there was a real risk of an overthrow of the new Tories by the old. The *Courier* stood for the old Tories. The *Guardian* stood in the middle, using its influence to support the liberal wing of the Government and to try to make it more liberal still. At Westminster, the *Guardian* was entirely without influence; in Manchester, Taylor could claim with justice in his final letter to Richard Potter that the Tory Party was much less intolerant and overbearing than it had been and that this was to a considerable extent due to his exertions. And if the *Guardian* less frequently criticised the decisions of the Manchester magistrates – Tories to a man – it was not because the *Guardian* had changed, but because 'a considerable check has been imposed by my paper (on them) . . . and because they less frequently deserve it.'

It is against this background of infiltration into Tory territory that some further developments in Manchester journalism are to be understood. The *Guardian* and the *Gazette* gave both wings of the middle-class Reformers a big share in the Saturday press. Neither was represented on Tuesday, the main business day in Manchester. The *Exchange Herald* and the *Mercury* had this field to themselves. Then there was a change. In 1825 Aston moved the publishing day of his *Exchange Herald* to Thursday, Manchester's second most important day on 'Change. Taylor saw his opening. He had to move quickly because Prentice had the same idea. Taylor's *Manchester Advertiser* and Prentice's *Manchester Commercial Journal* both appeared for the first time on Tuesday 30 August 1825. Their names indicate the kind of readers they hoped to secure.

Four mid-week papers, three on Tuesday and one on Thursday, were more than Manchester was likely to be able to support. Competition was brisk. James Harrop of the *Mercury* had died in 1823. Taylor heard that Harrop's son wanted to sell. He offered to buy both the *Mercury* and the *British Volunteer*. Harrop asked £2,000. In the end he accepted £1,100 and on 30 November Taylor took over and produced that week's paper under the style of the *Manchester Mercury and Tuesday's General Advertiser*. He thus became the proprietor of Manchester's oldest surviving newspaper. In effect, it became a Tuesday edition of the *Guardian* with a better make-up but set in the same office, printed on the same presses, and written by the same team. The *British Volunteer* was amalgamated with the *Guardian* and for a few years its name appeared as a secondary part of the title.

It looks as if Taylor had borrowed from his brother-in-law to help him buy Harrop's papers and the 'new and superior Columbian press' which was used for the first time on 3 December. A few days after the purchase there was a run on the London bankers, Lubbock & Co, in which Russell Scott was a considerable depositor. Taylor wrote apologetically to Scott on 18 December: 'I could scarcely help reproaching myself at times during the last week for having diminished your resources at such a period to the amount of £600, but if, as we may surely believe, the hurricane has spent its force, I am willing to flatter myself the loan will not prove seriously inconvenient to you.'

From Taylor's point of view the loan was certainly justified and the purchase worth while. Mrs Taylor wrote to her brother, 'Edward has no doubt that in the present calm state of political feeling he should secure the bulk of the subscribers.' Edward was right. The *Guardian* circulation went up to 3,000, adding about 500 of the *British Volunteer*'s 800 subscribers – the proportion that Taylor had expected. Possession of the *Mercury* gave Taylor a firm footing in the mid-week market. No more was heard of Prentice's *Commercial Journal* after December.[14]

The reaction on the Right was a similar concentration of mid-week and Saturday papers under the same management. Aston sold his *Exchange Herald* to Sowler, the owner of the new *Courier*, and went off to start another paper in Rochdale. When the deal was complete, the *Exchange Herald* piously remarked, 'It may be satisfactory to the present subscribers to be informed that the change of property does not in this case involve a change of principles . . . and that, therefore, this change which has been a reproach to other papers . . . will not be imputable to the *Herald*.'[15]

On the Left the fury was louder. Prentice thought Taylor's 'apostasy' so notorious that nobody would remember that the *Guardian* had ever been the advocate of popular rights were it not 'for the occasional fits of absurdity . . . in which he sallies forth calling heaven and earth to witness that there is no difference between the *Guardian* which purchased and printed the recommendation of the "Hunt and Liberty" men of the *Observer* and the *Guardian and Volunteer* which defends and eulogises the individuals whom that said *Observer* . . . incessantly denounced as public malefactors.'[16]

CHAPTER FIVE

Property and Poverty

I

THE period of 'Tory men and Whig measures',* which Taylor had found acceptable, came to a rapid end after Roman Catholic emancipation in 1829. There were to be a dozen years of pure Whig government before the experiment was repeated. One reason for the split between Taylor and his fellow-reformers had been removed, but the differences had become too deep to be overcome. They often acted together; they continued to distrust each other.

At the end of July 1830 a revolution in Paris put Louis Philippe on the throne, excited English radicals and gave the *Guardian* sober satisfaction. By the end of November the Whigs were in power with a programme of far-reaching parliamentary reform. At once they found themselves faced not only by resolute opposition from Tory back-woodsmen but by virtually uncontrollable mob pressure from radicals who wanted to set a headlong pace that would carry the country well beyond the Government's programme to the distant goal of the secret ballot, annual parliaments and manhood suffrage. Because the political pressure from working-class radicals was rooted in the poverty of the people and was exerted with maximum force when trade was bad, wages low and unemployment high, it was accompanied by much violence. The long period of endemic labour troubles lasted until the collapse of Chartism in 1848, that mildest ripple in the year of revolutions which convulsed Europe. In the North of England the working-class agitation only stopped short of revolution because the army was there in sufficient force to keep the peace. Sometimes the agitation in Lancashire was directed to secure reforms, as in the pressure for a more representative parliament; and sometimes against them as in the fight against the New Poor Law of 1834 with its workhouse Bastilles and those 'three Bashaws' in Whitehall, the Poor Law Commissioners.

Property owners in the north felt with some reason in those years that their lives as well as their possessions were in danger. Those men

* Tadpole's description of 'a sound Conservative Government' in Disraeli's 'Coningsby.'

of property, such as Taylor, who wanted to see considerable political and economic reforms, were often more scared of their working-class allies than grateful to them. Looking back, many historians are now inclined to believe that the threat of mob violence was needed to induce the rulers of old England to give way. At this time, however, middle-class reformers thought that mob violence had the opposite effect. Rightly or wrongly, that was the consistent opinion of the *Guardian*.

Within a few days of Lord Grey taking office the *Guardian* defined its position in terms to which it was to adhere for the rest of Taylor's life and for a good many years afterwards. The qualification for a vote ought to be low enough, he wrote, 'to put it fairly within the power of members of the labouring classes by careful, steady and persevering industry to possess themselves of it, yet not so low as to give anything like a preponderating influence to the mere populace . . . The right of representation is not an inherent or abstract right, but the mere creation of an advanced condition of society. Its single object is to promote good government.' While this expresses the paper's aims, its fears were set out three weeks later in a New Year's message from the 'conductors' of the *Guardian* to its readers: 'They deprecate hurried and extreme changes because they regard them as dangerous to the maintenance of public order . . . But, it may be asked, why speak of this? The answer is, because at present there is a degree of excitement . . . which . . . has evidently a revolutionary tendency . . . It is . . . impossible . . . that changes of the character, which too many people nowadays not obscurely hint at, should ever be carried into effect without a civil war.'[1]

This line could not be to the taste of the working-class leaders. Their anger was deepened by the additional grievance that the *Guardian* often strongly opposed the economic measures which the working class demanded as a way out of the intolerable distress which each of the frequent trade recessions brought. It was at these moments of despair that agitation was most vigorous and violent. At such a time the *Guardian* seemed to these men to be not only pusillanimous in its politics but heartless in its economics. When Sadler's Ten Hours Bill was under consideration in 1832, for instance, the *Guardian* doubted whether in view of foreign competition 'the framing of a law positively enacting the gradual destruction of the cotton manufacture would be a much less rational procedure.' Taylor's attitude on social reforms was of a piece with his attitude on political – he would move forward, but only gradually. He would prohibit truck, or compulsory payment in kind. Instead of ten hours, he would settle for eleven and a half, which was all the advance he thought the country could afford over the existing twelve. He did not defend existing conditions as good, but only as better than the alternative – 'though child labour is evil, it is better than starvation.' This is pretty certainly an expression of genuine concern, but it was natural at the time to think it hypocritical. This kind of reasoning kept up year after year in the *Guardian* provoked an accompanying flow of abuse from the left-wing papers of which one example must suffice. To the *Manchester and Salford Advertiser*, a working-class radical paper of the 'Tory radical' type, founded in 1828, the *Guardian* of 1836 was 'The common heap in which every purse-proud booby shoots his basket of dirt and falsehood . . . the foul prostitute and dirty parasite of the worst portion of the mill-owners.'[2]

More lastingly important than the battle of the leader-writers was the effect of the struggles of those years on the job that newspapers, and in the North especially the *Guardian*, set out to do. The great reform meetings, the agitation against the Poor Law, the campaign for shorter working hours and for Free Trade made news. Their reporting was a major challenge. From the beginning the *Guardian* had determined to set a new standard of accuracy and thoroughness. To keep to it required a strengthening of the paper's staff. For nearly ten years Jeremiah Garnett had carried the main burden of news gathering as well as printing and publishing. Latterly he had had a rather unsatisfactory assistant as reporter. It was now necessary to find a man of equal calibre to his own who would devote his whole time to the reporting work. The opportunity came in the same month that Earl Grey formed his reform bill Cabinet.

Dr J. R. Beard, the minister of the Salford Unitarian Chapel, had been to preach at Hull. On the Monday morning he was flattered to receive from a young reporter a long account of his Sunday sermon, and, as he read it, he became astounded at the accuracy of this verbatim note. When he got home, he told Taylor the story. Taylor acted quickly. Jeremiah Garnett made a winter journey across England to enlist the young man on the *Hull Packet* as 'chief, and only, reporter on the *Guardian*' at a salary of £90 a year, £15 more than he was getting on the *Hull Packet*.[3]

The young man was John Harland, who rapidly made himself indispensable. Taylor, Garnett and Harland were the three men who, working closely together at first as employer and employed and then as partners, made the *Guardian* first among the newspapers of the area which was doing much to give England its mid-century commercial leadership of the world. To friend and foe alike their *Guardian* was 'the cotton lords' bible' – the phrase was coined in anger by Richard Oastler, the Tory-radical leader of the Ten Hours agitation, but it might have been proudly adopted by these three men who were making the paper just that. They would only have needed to add that the *Guardian*, like the Bible, had plenty to say against unjust weights and similar sharp practices. Thus Engels in his 'Condition of the Working Class in 1844' was able to build up a considerable part of his case against this kind of dishonest exploitation from the files of the *Manchester Guardian*. The paper was willing also to speak out against rather bigger villains. Reporting that whole districts were evading the provisions of Hobhouse's act limiting child labour, the *Guardian* characterised this as shameless, adding that it was 'excessively foolish work and somewhat wicked withal.'[4] Taylor we have already got to know; Garnett and Harland have only been mentioned in passing. It is time to say more about these two remarkable men.

2

Jeremiah Garnett's father owned and worked a small paper mill at Otley in the Yorkshire dales. In this countryside the son went to school until he was nearly 16, and there in the Wharfe he learned to fish, which remained his favourite relaxation all his life. He was tall and strong, devoted to all kinds of field sports, but also a wide reader with a catholic taste. This was perhaps natural in one whose elder brother, an Anglican clergyman, was a distinguished philologist and whose nephews and their descendants form one of the few examples of a family in which literary talent seems to extend through many members and many generations. To the end of his life, Jeremiah Garnett continued to read most of the important new books of travel, history, biography and fiction.

He left school to become apprenticed to a printer at Barnsley in south Yorkshire, at that time a small weaving town well known for its radical working class. As soon as he was out of his apprenticeship he crossed the Pennines to seek work in Manchester with his fellow-apprentice, Thomas Forrest. Both men were first employed on Wheeler's *Manchester Chronicle* as journeymen printers. Before long Garnett was employed by the *Chronicle* as a reporter as well as a printer, and in that capacity he was sent to Peterloo. He went back to the office and wrote his report, but most of it was not used, presumably because it did not suit Charles Wheeler's Tory opinions. Within a week Garnett had left the paper. He went straight to Huddersfield where there was a bookseller called William Garnett, later an agent for the *Manchester Guardian*, who may well have been a relative. Three weeks after Peterloo the first issue of the *West*

John Edward Taylor, founder of the *Manchester Guardian*. The article
he is writing is headed Peterloo

Jeremiah Garnett. The *Guardian's* first printer, publisher and reporter; later its editor

Red-headed John Edward Taylor the younger at the age of 19; proprietor for over fifty years

Yorkshire Gazette was published under Jeremiah Garnett's editorship –
the first Huddersfield newspaper. Garnett held the position for about
six months, after which the paper migrated to Wakefield and its editor
returned to Manchester and apparently for a time to Wheeler's *Chronicle*.
According to Garnett's obituary in the *Guardian*, he spent some of that
winter drawing up for a committee a 'memoir' on the disturbances in
the industrial districts for submission to the Home Office. It looks as
if this may have been associated with Taylor's pamphlet, published in
1820, of which the first part was a detailed commentary on what would
be called the Government's White Paper. At any rate, Garnett joined
Taylor on the *Manchester Guardian* the following year. About the same
time his old fellow-apprentice, Thomas Forrest, set up as a bookseller
in Manchester, the only one at the time who would put Unitarian
publications on the counter.[5]

When the Manchester reformers made their last vain effort to bring
home to the Yeomanry the responsibility for the casualties at Peterloo,
they relied to a considerable extent on Garnett's evidence in the action
they brought against H. H. Birley, the Yeomanry commander. Other
reporters also were called. John Smith of the *Liverpool Mercury*,
Baines of the *Leeds Mercury*, and Tyas of the *Times* were all men of
national reputation; but it was Garnett who was put first into the box
and on whose testimony the reformers' counsel seemed mainly to rely.
It is clear from the way in which Garnett behaved under cross-examination that he was a decided and careful witness, not to be provoked or
eased into giving answers damaging to the reformers' case. He confined
his evidence strictly to what he had seen and heard and could accurately
report. Its quality justifies counsel's decision to rely on the Press as
observers of integrity. The reasons counsel gave for relying so much
on the evidence of reporters show that he understood the nature of
their work then and now. He told the judge and jury that he was calling
the reporters because:

'those are a class of persons most likely from their experience and from the
number of things of the same kind they have attended, to give an accurate
account of the proceedings that take place: to them it is of the greatest
importance, that no one should observe any particular fact that has not been
remarked by themselves, for it is to their accuracy of observation they owe
the means of giving correct accounts of what passes at a public meeting;
they are the persons who, of all others, are the most likely to give a correct
account of what did take place.'

That this was not only the view of the reformers is suggested by the
fact that a special constable had taken the precaution at Peterloo of
confiscating Garnett's notebook. This had an unexpected consequence

to the reformers' advantage. Its disappearance enabled Garnett to refuse to tell the court what Henry Hunt had said, which counsel for the Yeomanry was anxious to elicit.[6]

Both Taylor and Garnett, 'the fat boy and the lean lad' to the hostile *Manchester and Salford Advertiser*, were well-known figures on 'Change, in the streets and at the public meetings in which Manchester life abounded. Garnett described himself in 1839 as having been 'joint editor' of the *Guardian* since its establishment and, though the term was loosely used at that time, there is no doubt that from the beginning his was a position of great responsibility and that at least by the later 1830s he wrote leading articles as well as managing the paper. One of his leaders had consequences which 'Jerry' Garnett (that was how he was known to his friends) liked to tell to the end of his life. It illustrates not only the manners of the time but the level of the political controversy in the country and between *Guardian* and *Courier*.

Before Queen Victoria became the devoted adherent of Mr Disraeli and the object of ostentatious Conservative loyalty, she had been the darling of the Whigs and the despair of the Tories. There was fierce political fighting over the sad story of Lady Flora Hastings who was thought to be with child by Sir John Conroy, the master of the household of Victoria's mother. She was in consequence suspended from court; but when the doctors discovered that she was not pregnant, she was reinstated. Shortly after she died from the disease which had wrongly been diagnosed as pregnancy. The young Queen's humanity was in question – 'nobody cares for the Queen, her popularity has sunk to zero, and loyalty is a dead letter', according to Greville. This was a disaster to the Whigs, but also a difficulty for the Tories who approved of the monarchy but disapproved of the Queen.

Mr R. S. Sowler, the young barrister who edited the Tory *Manchester Courier* for his father, wrote a leading article in which he said that 'the malice of the highest in the land gloated' over a meeting between Sir John Conroy and Lady Flora Hastings. Garnett assumed that the 'highest in the land' was the Queen and wrote strongly in her defence and against the *Courier*. Sowler denied that he had referred to the Queen. The 'highest in the land' were 'those vicious slanderers and intriguers in petticoats by whom our young Queen is unhappily surrounded,' the Whig ladies of the bedchamber; and for good measure he described the editor of the *Guardian* as a blockhead, a defender of national infidelity and a person of a degraded standard of morality. Garnett called Sowler's explanation 'a crawling, cowardly lie that would not be believed if he swore it a thousand times.' The Sowlers consulted a Tory barrister who advised them that 'the laws of society were peremptory and that prompt demand must be made of recantation or of the satisfaction by which wounded honour can alone be healed.' The barrister was delighted to act as Robert Sowler's second and sought out Garnett at the Exchange. Garnett did not take the same line about the peremptory laws of society and declined to give Sowler satisfaction.

Two hours later Garnett was walking in St Ann's Square when he saw the Sowlers run out of their shop and cross the street towards him. What followed may be described from Garnett's evidence in the borough court.

'Mr Sowler seized my right arm, with both his hands and called out, "Now, Robert!" Mr Robert Scarr Sowler then struck me over the head with a horsewhip. I then broke loose from Mr Sowler, and struck Mr Robert Scarr Sowler on the head with my umbrella, which I had in my hand. Mr Sowler made two or three efforts to get hold of me again, and he did succeed in catching hold of my arm again, and Mr Robert Scarr Sowler then struck me over the shoulders with his whip. I defended myself with my umbrella as best I could, and broke it over Mr Robert Scarr Sowler's head.'

The case was adjourned at the Sowlers' request to the Assizes where both father and son were sentenced to three months' imprisonment, a penalty which Mr Justice Erskine remitted the next day at Garnett's request.

Two things may be said about the conduct of the case in the magistrate's court. Counsel on both sides attacked each other as if they were themselves the parties to the case and not their professional advisers. Counsel for the Sowlers, who was, in fact, the 'friend' who took Robert Sowler's challenge to Garnett, started his cross-examination by proving that Garnett had been a mere journeyman printer and, therefore, as he claimed in his speech for the defence, no gentleman. Garnett's replies to the first three questions he was asked in cross-examination sufficiently state his view of his own position and of the newspaper industry in 1839.

> Q. What is your calling in life?
> A. I am a printer.
> Q. Anything else?
> A. I call myself a printer always.
> Q. Anything else?
> A. I am one of the editors of a newspaper.

The case, of course, made news. The *Courier* gave the court proceedings four columns under the heading: 'Affair of Honour: The Joint Editor of the *Guardian* publicly horsewhipped', and a leader entitled 'The Queen and the *Manchester Courier*.' The *Guardian* report was even longer but, characteristically, the only headline was 'Manchester Borough Court', and its leader note was labelled 'Assault on Mr J. Garnett.' The *Manchester and Salford Advertiser* thought the case worth about a column and a leg-pulling leader under the heading 'War in the Republic of Letters', of which 'Some of the causes . . . lie too deeply hidden in the mysteries of editorial statesmanship to be profaned by the popular gaze.' It ends by quoting Oliver Goldsmith: 'The great have their foibles as well as the little . . . These two great men are now at variance . . . like mere men, mere common mortals.' Prentice in the *Manchester Times* allowed three columns under the heading 'Belligerent Newspaper Editors.' He commented, 'We have sometimes seen lads sparring at play, who continued to receive hits in perfect good humour, till one of them hit rather harder than was palatable to the other, and then a contest began in good earnest. The *Guardian* and the *Courier* have been at this sort of play for some time . . . Those who were in the secret knew that it was only a sham fight. The object was to convince folks that there were only two parties . . . Whig and Tory . . . and that people should believe there was not a party of *The People*.'[7]

3

The third of the makers of the *Guardian*, John Harland, was a tremendous man; in some ways even more remarkable than Taylor or Garnett. His father was a hopeless drunkard, and the family's consequent poverty forced John to leave school at 11. He did a number of routine clerical jobs for three years, during which he taught himself an elementary form of shorthand. At 14 he went to the *Hull Packet* as an apprentice to learn the printer's trade. He spent his first year largely in the shop selling papers and the patent medicines advertised in them such as Balm of Gilead. Gradually he made himself a capable journalist as well as a printer. He practised his shorthand diligently on Sundays by taking down sermons, careless of denominational allegiance. Choosing his ministers for their speed of speech, he started with Mr Morley, the Baptist at Hope Street Chapel as the slowest. His sermon-sampling finally led him in 1828 to change his allegiance from the Church of England, in which he had been baptised, to the Unitarians.

In his boyhood Harland developed two other important interests which lasted throughout his life and greatly enriched the *Guardian*. One was his love of music. In Hull in the summer he would go out into the fields with two or three friends and, using a hedge or a bush as a music stand, they would play a duet or a trio and 'return home with a sharpened appetite for breakfast.' The other was his antiquarian passion. Just before his death he told the son of a boyhood friend that, since he left Hull when he was only 23, he had not by then made much progress in local antiquities, but he had acquired a smattering of Anglo-Saxon. Before he died he had edited fourteen volumes for the Chetham Society, revised the standard history of Lancashire, published collections of Lancashire folk-lore and ballads in his own name and other antiquarian works under the pseudonyms of Monkbarns, Jonathan Oldbuck and Crux. Much of this work was first published in the *Manchester Guardian*. It has stood the test of time and in this century Professor Tait recorded that Harland's work 'first made possible the study of the early history of the manor and town' of Manchester.[8]

But it was for his unsurpassed skill as a reporter that Harland had been engaged. For this, tireless energy and insatiable curiosity were necessary as well as technical efficiency. His journey to Manchester to join the *Guardian* shows the measure in which he had both these qualities. He sent his furniture by canal and travelled with his mother. They stayed the night in Leeds after what must have been an excessively tiring day, but Harland spent the evening helping a friend report a meeting for the *Leeds Mercury*. The next day he went on to Manchester by coach. At the toll bar at the top of Blackstone Edge Harland picked up 'a good ghost story, quite recent' which duly appeared in the next number of the *Guardian*. The place where the ghost had been seen, high up on the moors, had been the scene of many robberies two years before, '*ergo*', wrote Harland, 'someone had been murdered there this autumn and thrown into the reservoir which they seriously talked of drawing off for the purpose of finding the body . . . It is to be hoped, however, that they have not carried this scheme into execution. Ghosts have grown so very scarce of late that, when one does turn up, we think the most ought to be made of it.'[9]

But there were sterner things than ghosts to worry England in the 1830s. There was a series of turbulent meetings in Manchester, to some of which men came armed or with the promise of arms if they had none of their own. After a morning's regular work at court at the New Bailey, Harland covered most of the meetings for the *Guardian* unless they fell during the Lancaster or Liverpool Assizes which he regularly attended. Are his reports worth reading to-day? How much reliance can be placed on them as historical evidence? This can be settled by looking at his report, not of a major meeting but of one which for those angry days of 1831 was relatively unimportant. There were, John Harland thought, only about 1,500 or 1,600 present, and in this number too, apart from the genuine agitators, there were 'many females of the class who are usually to be seen on such occasions, and, amongst other groups, one which was sedulously occupied during the greater part of the proceedings in the amusement of pitch and toss, heedless of the great and important discussion on natural rights, national conventions, poverty and property which was going on within a few yards of the gamblers. We also noticed, close under the hustings, a more than usually numerous squad of lads, many of whose faces are well known at the New Bailey.' There were the usual inflammatory speeches which on this occasion only got one and a half columns in the *Guardian*. This was short measure for those days, but far more than even prime ministers receive to-day in any newspaper except on unusually important occasions.

Four months later there was a sequel at Lancaster Assizes when a number of the speakers were prosecuted. The principal witness for the Crown was John Harland, who had been subpoena'd while reporting at the New Bailey. He produced his shorthand notebook and read to the court verbatim for four hours the whole of the speeches made by the defendants at the November meeting and his notes of what was said at a January meeting. These latter were not made at the time, but put down at home half an hour after the meeting. The *Courier* reporter and a Manchester freelance reporter, who appears to have had a retainer for the London *Sun*, also attended the January meeting, but they too took no notes at it since they were frightened of the hostile crowds. They put down their recollections, one of them on the next day, the other three hours later. It was only about the precise words used at the January meeting that there was any doubt, and Harland made no difficulty in distinguishing between what he could and could not positively swear to. In his summing up, the judge said that 'Mr Harland was by no means a willing witness, but exactly what a witness ought to be. He had not proffered himself to the one side or to the other, but had clearly shown no zeal for the prosecution, or he would have communicated to them the nature of his evidence, which would have saved him and the court a great deal of labour.'

It is not clear whether it was this or a similar occasion that is referred to in his obituary notice. Harland, it recalled, once read out a passage from his notebook slowly to the judge who took it down in longhand. 'Defending counsel whispered to his neighbour, "I'll turn this fellow inside-out." "You profess to give the exact words?" "Yes." "You say the prisoner said so and so. Now read what immediately follows." Mr Harland turned to the place in his notes and read off without hesitation, and without waiting for the evidence to be taken down, a passage of a hundred words or more. He did the same from

another passage. Defence counsel, who knew that this was what the
man had said, turned to his neighbour: "I don't think there's another
man in England who could do that".'[10]

It is reasonable to conclude that the *Guardian*'s reporting of the
agitation in Lancashire and Cheshire during the 1830s and 1840s can
be accepted as first-class evidence.

However reluctant Harland may have been to give evidence for the
Crown, the radical workers could not forget that it was on his and the
Courier reporter's testimony that their leaders had been sent to prison.
When a meeting in St Peter's Fields was held to protest against the
defeat of the Reform Bill in the Lords great care was taken to draft
resolutions which both working-class radicals and middle-class reformers could support. In spite of this, and of the presence of leaders
of both wings on the hustings, it was difficult to secure a hearing for
the moderate reformers. At one point somebody on the hustings protested against the meeting being reported, shouting, 'We have had
enough of these reporters.' The *Courier* reporter hastily withdrew to
the back of the hustings and soon after discreetly left the meeting;
objection was then taken to Harland's presence who moved out of
sight to the back of the hustings, but not out of ear-shot since he
managed to fill three full columns with his report. This was the meeting
at which a banner with William IV's portrait was carried upside down,
and another with the words 'The King, his ministers and reform' had
had the first two words blacked out. Significant, too, was the banner
which read: 'We will not eat potatoes – those that will not work shall
not eat.'[11]

It was against this constant hostility on the part of the radical
workers that a *Guardian* reporter had to work throughout this period.
By January 1838 Taylor was worried enough to write privately to
Poulett Thompson, a Manchester MP and a cabinet minister, to tell
him what the *Guardian* had been doing and was proposing to do about
reporting meetings and to ask his advice about possible government
intervention which, on the whole, he would have favoured. Poulett
Thompson passed the letter on to the Home Office, but there is no
clue to the action taken. 'For some time,' Taylor wrote, 'it has been
almost a service of danger for my reporters to attend these meetings;
they have been insulted and threatened. Independent of this, however,
I have really doubted whether by giving publicity to the speeches and
proceedings that there take place, even with a strongly expressed dis-
approbation, I am not doing more harm than good. From this feeling
I have suppressed all mention of several recent meetings in this neighbourhood. I fear, however, that there is among the journeymen

spinners here an organisation very similar to that which has been exposed in Glasgow; and I have thought that we ought at least to know what is said. Consequently, we have applied to a Liverpool reporter to come over and attend the meeting for us, but have not yet had his answer. Do you not think it is time that government should take means to get authentic and trustworthy information of what takes place at these meetings? I confess I think the meeting on Monday is likely to be such that you ought to have somebody there, who is qualified to report, or take down at least any peculiarly objectionable passages . . .'[12] It is a far cry from the Taylor of 1821 to the Taylor of 1838.

4

Later that year seven men, six of them Scots, met at the Queen's Hotel in Manchester and founded the Anti-Corn Law Association (later League). Three weeks later a provisional committee was appointed, with John Bright as one of its members. The following week additional members were recruited, among them Richard Cobden and Jeremiah Garnett. Early in 1839 the Association set up two committees – a large council, of which both Taylor and Garnett were members, and a smaller executive to which Prentice was elected. The great days of the Manchester School had begun. The Anti-Corn Law League rapidly developed into the first really organised, effective political machine that England had ever had. George Wilson, the Manchester business man who was its chairman, was a marvellously successful political boss, the organising force behind Cobden's and Bright's advocacy. When the League was finally wound up its members voted Wilson £10,000 as a testimonial. During the League's seven years' struggle he had attended 1,361 committee meetings; Prentice was his runner-up with 1,117.

But both sides of Wilson's campaign tactics – moral fervour and slick electioneering – were distasteful to Taylor and Garnett, although they shared his objective. They saw Free Trade as a prudent, sensible way of organising the nation's economic life, not as a gospel. The *Guardian* and the League drifted far apart. An open split occurred in 1841 over the League's 'escapade', as the *Guardian* called it, when it intervened in a by-election at Walsall, forced the Whig candidate to retire because he was not a total repealer and secured the nomination of its own president. Shortly afterwards Peel formed his great ministry. The early 1840s repeated the pattern of the later 1820s – 'Tory men and Whig measures.' Once again the *Guardian* had no objection and gave Peel more support each year. It welcomed his sweeping tariff reductions in 1842, even though they had to be paid for by the strictly 'temporary' income tax which is still with us. But to Cobden 'the greatest evil' was 'a bona fide concession; the middle classes are a compromising set.' Prentice agreed with him and considered the *Guardian* people 'Tories who are pleased to call themselves reformers,' men 'with a horror of a too rapid march of improvement.' Taylor, on the other hand, was convinced that 'if a coachman who regulated his conduct by principle and scorned expediency were to endeavour to drive in a straight line from Manchester to London, his plan would end very much like most of the schemes of our political philosophers; he would either upset the coach or stick fast in a ditch.'[13]

The purist Free Traders found it impossible to forgive the *Guardian* for providing Peel with evidence that he used effectively in the House of Commons. A London merchant said when he saw the offending passage, 'If Peel had paid a million of money for this report, it would not have been misspent.' 21 July 1842 was probably the first time that a Prime Minister quoted the *Guardian* in the House of Commons:

'The paper from which I am about to quote, *The Manchester Guardian*, is one opposed to the policy of Her Majesty's Government. The article, which is dated July 19th, runs thus: ". . . the improvement which manifested itself last week has continued down to the present time, and a more healthy feeling prevails in the market than for some time past . . . It is not very probable that any substantial improvement in prices can take place until, by the result of a good harvest or by a change of the Corn Law, the great bulk of the working classes of the country, whose entire earnings are now absorbed in the purchase of food, shall be enabled to procure those supplies of clothing of which they stand in so much need." (Cheers)

'I understand that cheer, and I can only say that I should feel it unfair to suppress that passage, and I refer to the whole article with greater satisfaction, because it shows, upon the testimony of a disinterested witness, that a great improvement has taken place. Coming, as it does, from a quarter which would altogether repeal the Corn-Laws, it is gratifying to find a candid admission made that the improvement spoken of a week previously continues from the last week up to the present.'[14]

There does not seem to be much wrong with what the *Guardian* wrote or with the use the Prime Minister made of it. It is not the duty of a newspaper to suppress inconvenient facts, or of a politician to garble quotations. Indeed it is the duty of both to play fair. It is Prentice and the League, not Peel and the *Guardian* who come badly out of the episode.

Garnett and Prentice (and, behind Prentice, Cobden and Bright) quarrelled about personalities and about tactics. All of them were cut off from radical working-class leaders by deeper differences. The

Chartist agitation was, in practice, anti-government; but the Free Trade agitation brought employers and employed into the same organisation and enjoyed ever-increasing parliamentary support. For that very reason it was especially suspect to the more radical working-class leaders who saw in it largely a means by which employers hoped to be able to pay lower wages because the cost of living would fall.

To these men there seemed sometimes to be nothing to choose between Taylor's *Manchester Guardian* and Prentice's *Manchester Times*. At one of the Reform Bill meetings in 1831 the procession which escorted Henry Hunt on his way gave three groans as he passed the *Manchester Times* office; in 1839 three cheers were given for Oastler and Stephens and three groans for Archibald Prentice by the rowdy crowd which took over the Anti-Corn Law meeting and put Pat Murphy in the chair, 'a drunken and very dirty fellow' whose clogs bruised the reporters' hands as he climbed up on to the platform. Sometimes even these ungrateful working men (for so they must have seemed to the 'reformers') preferred the *Manchester Courier*, the Church and State Tory paper, to either the *Guardian* or the *Times*. R. S. Sowler, the editor of the *Courier*, was a member of the north-western committee of the Liberation Fund for Richard Oastler, the Tory radical, who was in prison for debt. He spoke from the same platform as John Fielden and J. R. Stephens. It was at this meeting that Ferrand anticipated Disraeli, denouncing the Anti-Corn Law League in the memorable words: 'Are the masses of England to be destroyed for ever? . . . We are now divided as nearly as possible into two classes – the very rich and the very poor.'[15]

MR. GEORGE WOMBWELL, proprietor of the ROYAL BRITISH GRAND MENA-GERIE of WILD BEASTS, BIRDS, begs leave to inform the Nobility, and Public in general, that both his extensive COLLECTIONS are joined to-

CHAPTER SIX

The Legacy of John Edward Taylor

I

TAYLOR had been in poor health for many years. His wife thought it began in 1829 with 'his whisking through the air at an immense velocity, on the Liverpool railroad, without a great coat, which Mr Whatton (the doctor) called "a very young trick" ' for the convalescent that he was at the time. In 1831 his friend Absalom Watkin had complained that the walks he took with Taylor were 'not exercise, only sauntering; neither fast enough nor far enough for me.' Yet in 1833 Taylor kept the national fast day against the cholera epidemic by taking John Harland and a party of friends for an eighteen-mile walk followed by a dinner party. From 1829 on, however, Taylor seems to have suffered periodically from the 'affection of the throat' from which he died in January 1844 at the early age of 52. For the last eighteen months of his life his lengthy correspondence with his brother-in-law, Russell Scott, came to an end; he played less and less part in the firm; and Jeremiah Garnett became virtually sole editor. Taylor's two sons, Russell Scott and John Edward, were respectively only 18 and 13 at his death. What was to happen to the paper?[1]

Taylor had begun to lay his plans for the future at least as far back as 1835. In that year he asked his brother-in-law, Russell Scott, if he would undertake to hold the copyright of the paper as trustee for the children. 'At one time,' he wrote, 'this might have been an affair of some difficulty and danger to you, but with the present feeling in regard to the libel law, I do not think it is . . . There would be no occasion whatever for your name to appear on the paper as proprietor. It need only be given in at the Stamp Office.' Presumably Russell Scott agreed and a will was executed. Taylor's last will, however, was not made until 1842, and the final decisions affecting the future of the paper were left until two days before his death, when a codicil was added to the will. Under the terms of the will Russell Scott became sole proprietor with 'full power and authority to carry on the said newspaper as shall seem most advantageous to him' or to sell it if he and his partners found it 'disadvantageous or deem it unadvisable' to continue to publish it. The will thus clearly envisaged the continuance of the existing partnership, though it left Russell Scott free to do what he thought best. When Taylor's two sons reached the age of 22 they were each to be offered a half-share in the paper. The codicil fixed the price at which the half-shares were to be offered at £3,000 each. For the next eight years Russell Scott, C. P. Scott's father, was thus directly concerned with the affairs of the paper, and his signature appears on the annual partnership accounts. Family letters show how close and affectionate was the interest he took in the young Taylors.

The point of putting a price of £6,000 on the copyright and plant of the *Guardian* was that Russell and Edward, the names by which the sons were known in the family, were not Taylor's only children. They had a sister, Sophia, and three half-sisters, for Taylor re-married shortly after his first wife's death. Taylor's second wife was Harriet Boyce of Tiverton who came to Taylor as a governess for his children early in 1835, about two years after his wife's death.* 'I think I may regard her,' Taylor wrote to his brother-in-law, 'as perhaps even peculiarly qualified, both morally and as an instructress, to superintend my children. She is a decided and zealous Unitarian and has been accustomed to give that sort of direction to the minds and pursuits of her pupils which my poor Sophia would have wished that her children should have.'² A year later Taylor married her. She soon brought her sister to live with them and help with the children. Taylor felt bound also to provide for this sister-in-law by his will and to add that 'knowing as I do that she is highly esteemed and regarded by my children by my first marriage and that these latter warmly love their younger sisters, it is my earnest wish and desire that in case of the loss of their parents they will all live together as a united family until and unless any of them may be removed from their home by marriage.'

It has been necessary to go into this detail about Taylor's private life because, like so many family events in the Taylor and Scott families, it had immediate and long-lasting public effect on the *Guardian*. Taylor not only enlisted his new sister-in-law as a governess but a new brother-in-law, Henry Boyce, to help with the office management of the paper. Nor was this all: two of Taylor's three children by his first wife married into his second wife's family. Russell Scott Taylor married a cousin of his step-mother's and Sophia Russell Taylor married another cousin of the Boyces, Peter Allen, who in time took

---

* In the interval he had been engaged to Miss Gaskell, a cousin of the novelist's husband, who finally refused him partly because he wanted to retain his existing governess in charge of the children. Taylor was not sensitive in personal relations and this affected his public life.

over the business management from Henry Boyce. Thus Taylor's first marriage brought in the Scotts, his second the Allens, two families which sometimes in friendship and sometimes in disagreement dominated the fortunes of the *Guardian* for over a century. The history of the paper is deeply dynastic.

The form which the business took, and which it was to retain until 1907, was a partnership usually renewable for terms of seven years. Originally Taylor had been in business solely on his own account with Jeremiah Garnett as his employee. In 1826 Garnett had been admitted into partnership with a third share in the profits, but with Taylor retaining the sole copyright. From the beginning of July 1839 two new junior partners, Henry Boyce and John Harland, were admitted. Boyce, who does not seem to have been a particularly good business man, owed his partnership to his status in the family; Harland his to the fact that he was indispensable.

Harland tells the story in his 'Annals', the manuscript jottings towards an autobiography which he put together towards the end of his life. He seems from internal evidence to have had a diary to consult.

'Sunday, February 17. Mr Eckersley proposed to me to join an intended new liberal paper in Manchester of "more advanced politics" than the *Guardian*. Tuesday, March 14. Mr William Evans made a more formal proposal. He said Mr Whittle of Liverpool was to find the capital and be the Editor. As Mr Evans pressed me for an answer, I told Mr J. E. Taylor, who said I had better consult my friends. I did so, and decided to decline Mr Evans' offer. May 31 (the day Mr Robert Sowler assaulted Mr Jeremiah Garnett in St Ann's Square*). Mr Garnett, Mr Boyce and I dined at Mr Taylor's and, after dinner, Mr Taylor said that he had for some time been much gratified with my exertions to promote the prosperity of the *Guardian*, and had thought of admitting me as a junior partner, but he could say nothing till I had decided about a rival offer. He now said that from the 1st of July, he proposed to take H. Boyce (his brother-in-law who managed the financial department) and myself into partnership, and stated the terms; the period seven years.'

If, like a good deal in newspaper history, Harland's promotion was an extorted concession, and had something about it of the nature of a forced marriage, it was at least a marriage of true minds. Harland was one of those men of whom one can reasonably be sure that they would not have been happy on any other paper than the *Guardian*; but in his case, as one of the founding fathers, it is right to add that this was partly at least because of what he made it.

---

* But for once Harland failed to 'verify his references.' The assault was on 24 July.

2

What was the financial position of the paper when Taylor made his will? The accountancy system of the partnership was primitive. No distinction was made between expenditure on capital and current account, nor was any allowance made for depreciation. The partners bought what they needed when they could afford it and the profits for that year were accordingly reduced. When money was likely to be needed for major projects no doubt the partners arranged to leave a substantial amount of their accumulated profits in the firm, but from 1838 to 1840 both Taylor and Garnett were investing large sums in railways. The books, however, show clearly enough that the paper was in a strong position and that the valuation under the codicil was as conservative as one would expect from the staunch advocate of sound money.

For the five years from midsummer 1839 to midsummer 1844 the annual profits of Taylor, Garnett & Co from all sources, including general printing, averaged £6,777. Of this, nearly £4,000 was Taylor's share and nearly £2,000 Garnett's. The two junior partners, Harland and Boyce, each received well over £400. This was four times as much as Harland had been getting. The figure which Taylor finally put on the value of the copyright and his share in all the plant and stock was not much more than the equivalent of eighteen months' profit. In addition to this, there was, of course, the value of the freehold property.

Taylor's record as a newspaper owner was one of consistent and increasing success. He was, of course, helped by the doubling of Manchester's population during the twenty-two years of his proprietorship, but he always had to meet fierce competition and to live through periods not only of generally bad trade but of frequent bankruptcies and deep distress. But it was other papers that went to the wall or had to be rescued by injections of new capital. Of the rivals described in Chapter 3, the *Chronicle* dwindled steadily to an end which came in 1838. It was briefly revived from 1839 to 1842, but never re-established itself. In its later days it distinguished itself mainly by inflating its sales figures in a curious way. It bought more stamps than it needed and printed several hundredweight of unnecessary copies which it sold to grocers for wrapping paper.[3] In this bit of odd economics it was caught out by the *Manchester Times* which put these unused copies on display in its shop window. The *Herald*, which Aston had sold to Sowler, stopped publication in 1836. The *Courier* survived, but from 1839 to 1841 it had to be published by assignees because Sowler was bankrupt.

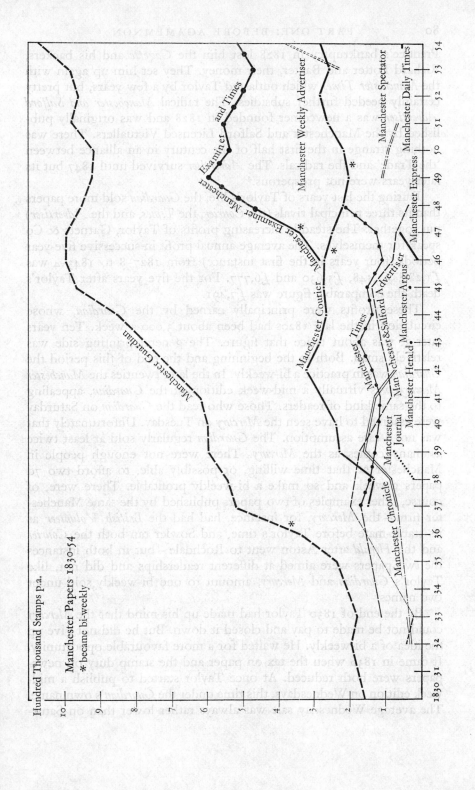

Prentice's bankruptcy in 1828 lost him the *Gazette* and his backers, Richard Potter and Baxter, their money. They set him up again with the *Manchester Times* which outlasted Taylor by a few years, but pretty certainly needed further subsidies. The radical *Manchester and Salford Advertiser* was a newcomer founded in 1828 and was originally published by the Manchester and Salford Licensed Victuallers. There was nothing strange in the first half of the century in an alliance between 'the Trade' and the radicals. The *Advertiser* survived until 1847 but its later years were not prosperous.[4]

During the last years of Taylor's life, the *Guardian* sold more papers than its three principal rivals (the *Courier*, the *Times*, and the *Advertiser*) put together. The steadily increasing profits of Taylor, Garnett & Co speak for themselves. The average annual profit in successive five-year periods (four years in the first instance) from 1827–8 to 1843–4 was £1,288, £2,548, £5,630 and £6,777. For the five years after Taylor's death the comparable figure was £7,491.

These profits were principally earned by the *Guardian*, whose circulation in the late 1820s had been about 3,000 a week. Ten years later it was about twice that figure. The general printing side was relatively small. Both at the beginning and the end of this period the *Guardian* was in practice a bi-weekly. In the later twenties the *Manchester Mercury* was virtually a mid-week edition of the *Guardian*, appealing to the same kind of readers. Those who read the *Guardian* on Saturday were assumed to have seen the *Mercury* on Tuesday. Unfortunately that was not a safe assumption. The *Guardian* regularly sold at least twice as many copies as the *Mercury*. There were not enough people in Manchester at that time willing, or possibly able, to afford two 7d papers a week and so make a bi-weekly profitable. There were, of course, other examples of two papers published by the same Manchester firm – the *Mercury*, for instance, had had the *British Volunteer* as its stable-mate before Taylor's time, and Sowler ran both the *Courier* and the *Herald* after Aston went to Rochdale – but in both instances the two papers were aimed at different readerships and did not, like Taylor's *Guardian* and *Mercury*, amount to one bi-weekly sold under two names.

By the end of 1830 Taylor had made up his mind that the *Mercury* could not be made to pay and closed it down. But he did not give up the idea of a bi-weekly. He waited for a more favourable opportunity. It came in 1836 when the tax on paper and the stamp duty on newspapers were both reduced. At once Taylor started to publish a mid-week edition on Wednesdays, this time under the *Guardian*'s own name. The average Wednesday sale was always rather lower than on Saturdays, but the difference was never anything like as great as the gap between the *Guardian*'s sale and the *Mercury*'s had been. What had been uneconomic at 7d was profitable at 4d. The high rate of newspaper duty had indeed been an effective tax on knowledge.

One other fiscal reform had helped to make a bi-weekly practicable. In 1833 the flat rate duty on advertisements had been reduced from three shillings and sixpence to eighteenpence. In Chapter 4 we saw the hard work the *Guardian* had in its first three years to reach Taylor's target of a hundred advertisements in an issue. In 1838-9 the corresponding figure was 179, and for 1839-40 it rose to 186. Moreover, the *Guardian* was now a bi-weekly. If the comparison is made on a weekly basis instead of per issue the comparison is between a bare hundred at the end of 1823 and nearly four times that number fifteen years later. As far as the *Guardian* was concerned, the Government as well as the paper did well out of the lower rate of duty. The amount paid in advertisement tax in 1822-3 was nearly £500; in 1839-40 it was nearly £2,000. And 1839 was a year of very bad trade and deep distress.

The *Guardian*'s expenditure was also increasing. In 1825 it probably employed about half a dozen journeymen; in 1838 there were fifteen under the head printer, T. Mayor, whose wages were £2. 5. 0 a week – three shillings more than Harland got whose pay was genteelly expressed in guineas. The journeymen received £1. 12. 0 or £1. 11. 6 plus some occasional small additional sums, presumably for overtime in excess of the fifty-nine-hour working week. There seem also to have been four apprentices earning weekly amounts varying from 14/– down to 5/–, again with occasional overtime. The bill for printers' wages in 1839 was round about £40 a week. The account books show another group of six employees, which was headed by Harland until his promotion to a partnership. These men usually drew their pay monthly and this amounted in total to between £35 and £36. Some of the men besides Harland were certainly reporters. Below Harland there was another reporter drawing £8 a month, two men at £7, and one at £4 who seems to have been something like a personal assistant to the partners since there are frequent disbursements to him by both Taylor and Garnett for 'sundries.' One man in this group was receiving only 7/– a month in 1838, but this was increased to £1. 8. 0 in the first half of 1839 and £1. 10. 6 in the second. He was probably an apprentice reporter. Harland records in his 'Annals' for 1843 that Hamilton Ballantyne, a nephew of Thomas Ballantyne, a senior member of the staff, 'was bound apprentice to me for six years to learn shorthand reporting. He was to receive at the end of the 4th, 5th and 6th years respectively £40, £60 and £80.' A group of about fifteen newsmen (distributors) and seven 'lads' drew weekly sums varying between £2 and £3 in total.

Quite considerable sums were paid out in linage* to reporters in Manchester and other towns in South-east Lancashire. The total amount for 1839 seems to have been £104. Some of the men concerned were people of real quality. Among them, for instance, was Samuel Bamford, the hand-loom weaver poet who led the Middleton contingent to Peterloo and was sent to prison for his pains. Two other local correspondents appear in Sutton's 'List of Lancashire Authors' as antiquarians and local historians. Is it fanciful to associate this historical interest with Harland's ruling passion? Certainly he was in later years a friend of Bamford's, and it may well be that Harland collected likeminded men as the paper's local correspondents.

The better the *Guardian* was doing, the more unreadable it became. Smaller type more closely set was the obvious way to fit more into a paper whose size was virtually fixed by taxation. It was also possible to extend the area of each page and this the *Guardian* had done from time to time in common with other Manchester newspapers. The last increase in size was made in 1839, after which the paper, though still confined to four pages, was nearly twice as large in area as it had been in 1821. In 1843 new machinery and new type were introduced at a cost of more than £1,200. The number of pages was doubled but their size reduced. The result was a paper nearly a third bigger than the *Guardian* of 1839. The new machinery, however, did not differ in kind from the old but only in speed and efficiency. After the introduction of steam-driven presses in 1828, there were no major technological changes affecting the newspaper industry in Taylor's lifetime. The coming of the railways was, of course, to have a marked effect, but it was not really felt until later.

3

There were three main ways by which the *Guardian* and other newspapers were distributed. There was free postal distribution – free, that is, once the newspaper duty had been paid since the stamp printed on the paper covered postage anywhere in the country up to 1840, outside its home town from that time on. The duty, of course, had to be paid whether the paper went through the post or not. The stamp, moreover, covered more than one transmission of the same paper so that a town reader often sent his paper on to a friend in the country and agreed to divide the price with him. Not long after Taylor's death, W. H. Smith reckoned that each London daily paper was transmitted on an average

* Payments for each line of copy used. Hence the term 'penny a liner.'

three times through the post so that the Post Office revenue per copy was only one-third of a penny.[5]

The second method of distribution was by agents in neighbouring towns or by newsmen employed directly by the paper. The third was by sales over the counter. The surviving account books make it

COWPERS' PATENT STEAM PRINTING MACHINE.

The *Manchester Courier*'s new press 1839

possible to study the distribution by the firm's own newsmen and through shop sales. These two methods seem regularly to have accounted for about half of the total sale in 1830, 1839 and 1845, years for which figures have been analysed. The proportion sold in the shop seems to have dropped from 10 or 11 per cent of the total circulation in 1830 to about 5 or 6 per cent in 1845.

There were striking fluctuations in the number of copies sold over the counter week by week. Eighteen times out of 167 consecutive issues between 1838 and 1840 the shop sales were more than 25 per cent above the average for the quarter. The newsmen's sales were also up on the same dates, though not in the same proportion. The news that sold so many more papers than usual is given in the following table (in three instances there does not seem to have been anything special in the paper):

Increase over Quarterly Average

315 per cent   Anti-Corn-Law League Gatherings (23 cols). (15 January 1840)

176 per cent   Hurricane in Manchester neighbourhood (9 January 1839)

100 per cent   Fire at Macintosh's waterproof works. (29 August 1838)

84 per cent   'National Holiday' (General Strike) disturbances (9 cols.) (14 August 1839)

62 per cent   Anti-Corn-Law Gatherings (5½ cols.) (15 December 1838)

61 per cent   Arrest of Chartists for illegal drilling: 2nd Edition with fall of Melbourne Government. (8 May 1839)

55 per cent   Meeting of Creditors of Imperial Bank. (6 November 1839)

47 per cent   District Bank Meeting. (31 January 1839 – two editions)

45 per cent   Fall of Melbourne Government. (11 May 1839)

45 per cent   Anti-Corn-Law dinner. (26 January 1839 – two editions)

43 per cent   Anti-Corn-Law dinner. (23 January 1839 two editions)

37 per cent   Manchester by-election result. (7 September 1839)

34 per cent   Queen Victoria's Wedding. (12 February 1840)

29 per cent   Editor of *Manchester Chronicle* challenges Chief Constable to a duel. (9 November 1839)

26 per cent   Manchester by-election. (4 September 1839)

Manchester readers certainly liked reading about themselves and liked seeing their names in print. The 'best seller' in this list was the paper which not only reported the interminable speeches in praise of free trade but listed the names of many who attended them. Probably some of those who normally would have been content to read the *Guardian* in a newsroom decided to buy a copy, and some regular subscribers probably bought a second copy. It is notable, too, that reports of Anti-Corn Law League gatherings sold more copies than accounts of Chartist meetings and conspiracies. It was not that the *Guardian* ignored these demonstrations but that middle-class Manchester was not inclined to buy more copies than usual to read about them. The great meeting on Kersal Moor which Feargus O'Connor addressed in September 1838 took up eight and a half columns of the *Guardian*, but the shop sales were up by only 13 per cent.

Only two of the issues which attracted extra large sales depended for their success on London news stories. The *Guardian* was a local paper; its readers wanted local news, enjoyed local controversies and were given what they wanted. The same could probably be said of provincial papers and their readers throughout England. London was far off. What happened there was important, and one must know what was going on. Parliament was generally better reported in 1840 than in 1960. But what happened in Whitehall was not as exciting as what happened at home. The Manchester papers used stronger language about each other and about local politicians than they employed about national leaders. It was stronger because it was more personal; it could be effectively more personal because those who wrote could rely on those who read picking up the references. When George Condy, Irishman, barrister, dramatist and editor of the radical *Manchester and Salford Advertiser*, referred in a leading article to Taylor's 'peach-tinctured and juvenile visage,' his readers knew what he meant.[6] They knew Taylor by sight. They had probably never seen a Cabinet Minister except Poulett Thompson, who happened to be a Manchester MP.

Local patriotism and local antagonism was common to all parts of England. There was something more than local interest, however, in Manchester and Lancashire news round about 1840. What happened was often of national importance: its trade mattered greatly to the whole country; it was a dominant centre of Chartist activities, the possible scene of revolutionary disturbances; and it was the headquarters of England's first modern political machine, the Anti-Corn Law League. While remaining essentially a local paper, the *Guardian* was in the course of its ordinary duties necessarily beginning to play a significant part in national life. Taylor had given it the means and the will to see that this was a worthy part.

Before Taylor died he could reflect that almost all he had wished to see happen in politics had come about and that he had played a part in securing it. He had longed to see religious discrimination ended, a sound banking system established, Manchester and other great towns self-governing and represented in parliament by their own members, elected by responsible men who could feel they had a stake in the country. The last of his wishes – the removal of the remaining trade barriers – was on the way to being accomplished. Two years later his old partner, Jeremiah Garnett, sat down on the day the royal assent was given to the abolition of the corn laws and wrote:

'the editor of the *Guardian* has witnessed and recorded the completion of that category of reforms which, at the commencement of his labours, he considered absolutely essential to the good government and well-being of his fellow-countrymen, and from the pursuit of which he has never deviated. (They) . . . have all been effected, almost precisely in the form in which they had been advocated in the columns of this journal.'[7]

4

Three marks honourably distinguish the *Guardian* as Taylor left it. First, it had set an entirely new standard of accurate and full reporting. Public men could and did, as we have seen, vehemently complain of what the *Guardian* said about them; they rarely complained that they had been misreported.

Secondly, the *Guardian* continued to be vigilant in looking after the business interests of the community it served. It was quick to detect and courageous to expose swindlers. The Dicas affair of 1823 did not stand alone. In 1834, for instance, the *Guardian* published a full and detailed exposure of a gang of London criminals who had set up an elaborate system for obtaining large quantities of textiles on false pretences, using well known and respectable Manchester business men as innocent agents. This involved the firm next year in an action for libel (Clark v. Taylor) which Taylor successfully defended, pleading justification. He then had to face a motion for retrial on the ground that he had not specifically proved Clark's fraudulent acquisition of goods in Leeds to which the *Guardian*'s exposure had referred, as well as in Manchester. The motion was refused. Almost certainly to-day it would not have been left to private persons at their own risk and expense to defend Manchester traders.[8]

If the *Guardian* was to be the effective and enquiring monitor of the business community, Taylor himself had to be above suspicion. This forced him into the one action for libel in which he was himself the plaintiff. It was brought against the proprietors of the *Manchester and Salford Advertiser*. The count which attracted great public attention, and which caused the judge to advise ladies to leave the court to avoid embarrassment, was the *Advertiser*'s accusation that Taylor had sent obscene pamphlets to Mrs Fildes, the woman who took the part of the Goddess of Liberty in Orator Hunt's procession to Peterloo. The story was so preposterous that it was, one may think, unlikely to have been believed. The second count was much more serious. It was that Taylor had made an unjustified claim for compensation against the Market Street Improvement Commissioners, of whom he was one. This touched his personal commercial honour and, if substantiated, would have seriously damaged the *Guardian* in its most valuable asset – its reputation for honest dealing. The case was heard in 1833 before a special jury, the majority of whose members were drawn from Liverpool and district. The defendants did not seriously attempt to justify the allegations, but relied rather on their pretended ignorance of what was in their own paper. They objected to the action being brought against them rather than the editor, or the publisher. But the editor was not necessarily the author of the libel; and the publisher was in a lunatic asylum by the time of the action. The libels charged were only the last in a continuous series of personal attacks extending over more than two years, many of which no doubt would have been actionable. This, and the refusal of the defendants to accept liability or to apologise, caused the judge to sum up strongly in Taylor's favour and the jury took only ten minutes to find the defendants guilty and to award Taylor £450 damages.[9]

This action, Taylor v. Curran and others, confirmed Taylor's reputation for honesty in business. He never again had to defend his personal honour. But it does not dispose of the objections which his political opponents felt to his record in public affairs. Prentice, it will be remembered, wrote of his 'repeatedly detected falsehoods.' It would be tedious, and perhaps ultimately impossible, to disentangle all the charges and counter-charges on such remote and curious by-ways as a controversy over a footpath at Pendleton. The likelihood seems to be that Taylor's position often seemed disingenuous to anybody who unhesitatingly followed (as most people did) a straight party line. Taylor's was increasingly a cross-bench mind, not tepid and Laodicean – that would never have sold a newspaper – but hot and cold, provoking both to right and left, interesting but annoying to readers of all parties. Added to this was the fact, which must be admitted, that Taylor's was also a priggish mind. Moral condemnation came easily to him, and he could be infuriatingly patronising. Those who disagreed with him, and almost everybody did over something, were apt to take particular pleasure in finding, if they could, cause to disapprove as well as to disagree. He himself disapproved so often that retaliation in kind was bound to be popular.

There was also, of course, a large dose of pure envy behind the attacks on Taylor. He was, after all, a highly successful rival. He had built up for himself and the paper a position of unqualified independence. This independence was the third honourable distinction of the *Guardian* as Taylor left it. He had borrowed money to start the paper; he had repaid it. From then on he was free, and he used his freedom to say what he thought and not what the political leaders of various parties thought he ought to say. Just as Manchester people enjoyed jokes about his personal appearance because they knew him, so they felt satisfaction at reading his views because they knew him to be writing just precisely what he thought and believed, and not what somebody else told him to write. Many times when he took an unexpected line, Taylor must have wondered whether he was risking his paper and his family's livelihood. He found that independence paid.

What Taylor gained when he paid off his original backers and became a free man is perhaps best expressed in a reflection of his friend, Absalom Watkin. The Potters and the Baxters wanted to set up Watkin as a newspaper editor. They had failed to get what they wanted

out of Taylor because he no longer shared their views; they were failing
to get what they wanted out of Prentice because it was plain that he
cared too much for pamphleteering and too little for making newspapers pay. They asked Watkin to take over; he demanded full editorial
freedom. Five days later,

'Potter told me that the idea of making me editor of the *Gazette* was given
up. "You know," said he, "it would be a terrible thing if somebody got
hold of it that was not decided in his opinions, and they think you would not
be decided enough." I expected the matter to end in this manner: by *decided*
they mean *decidedly of their opinion*, and my resolute demand of entire liberty,
and giving my own sentiments in my own way, has convinced those who
were most anxious to put me in possession of the paper that I am not the
man for their purpose.'[10]

That servitude is what Taylor and the *Guardian* had escaped from once
and for all. The *Guardian* owes its founder both life and liberty.

NEW METHOD OF CARRYING TIMBER.
EAGLE QUAY, OXFORD ROAD, MANCHESTER, AND QUEEN'S DOCK, LIVERPOOL.
DAVID BELLHOUSE and SONS, beg leave most respectfully to inform the Public, that they have commenced CARRIERS OF TIMBER, by Water,
betwixt LIVERPOOL and MANCHESTER. Their means consist of a Steam Boat, THE EAGLE, and a number of Vessels, built upon a new construction,
for the express purpose of carrying Timber. These vessels after reaching Runcorn, by the Steam Boat, are forwarded upon the Duke's Canal, to Manchester, where they arrive the day after they are shipped at Liverpool.

BOOK TWO

Garnett and the Young Taylors
1844-1871

CHAPTER SEVEN

Trains and Telegraphs

I

THE general election in July 1847 brought the Liberals back to power. Sir Robert Peel had served the country by his repeal of the Corn Law but split his party. The future lay with Russell and Palmerston, a man greatly to Garnett's taste, or, possibly, with Cobden and Bright, a man for whom Garnett had little liking. How long Garnett's preferences would determine the paper's policy was, however, a matter of considerable doubt.

John Edward Taylor's will had left the copyright of the *Guardian* equally between his two sons. In February 1847 Russell Scott Taylor reached the age of 22, which his father had fixed for his business majority. He was clearly an able, anxious and ambitious young man, and one who was much loved by his family. In a letter written when Russell was five, his mother records that he brought home the first prize in the junior school 'with a degree of ecstasy which I think you cannot conceive. He seemed as if he could think of nothing else all day . . . when he laid down in bed he said . . . "I shall sleep to-night – I shall not have to think".' When he was nearly 14 he went to stay with his uncle, Russell Scott, who reported that it had been a great pleasure to have him. 'I think this is saying a good deal,' he continued, 'considering that he is at an age at which almost all boys are positively troublesome . . . he appears to me to possess the combined cheerfulness and contentedness of disposition which almost always ensures happiness to its possessor.'[1]

Russell Taylor was the first graduate member of the *Guardian* staff. He had been admitted to Manchester New College at the age of 15 to work first for matriculation and then for his degree.* At the age of 17

---

* This was primarily a theological college for dissenters, but it had art and science departments and prepared men for London University degrees. The establishment of the much more richly endowed Owens College (now the University of Manchester) led to the removal of Manchester New College in 1856. It is now in Oxford where it is known as Manchester College. I am indebted to the Principal, the Rev. H. L. Short, for particulars of Russell Taylor's academic career.

he read a public oration at the summer 'examination' of the college on 'The English and French Revolutions compared in their causes, character and effects', which at least shows that his mind had a political cast. The next year, 1843, he took a second in his degree and started work on the *Guardian*. His sister, who was still at boarding-school, could only hope that when she came home for Christmas 'he will not be too immersed in politics and types to think of me.' The year after his father's death, when Russell was 20, his step-mother hoped to send him for a tour of six months on the Continent to see 'more of the world, and something of the governments, institutions and manufactures of other countries, before he is called on to take the important situation he must one day fill in Manchester.' But continental travel, she thought, might injure his character if he travelled alone. Russell and Sophia, however, were 'both anxious to share the pleasure together, and a sister, I think, must be a safe companion.' But even that was not safety enough and Mrs Taylor's own sister was to be included as chaperon.[2] It seems probable, however, that the heir never went on this heavily escorted tour. His step-mother died early in August, leaving three daughters, the eldest of whom was only 8. The ledger shows Russell receiving £70, 'year's salary', from the *Guardian* for the year ending 30 June 1846 as well as for the previous year. In 1847 he took up an active partnership. In the summer he married his step-mother's cousin, Emily Acland.

Edward Taylor was five years younger than his brother, but it was tolerably certain that he too would take up his share in the copyright and play an active part on the paper. He spent the autumn of 1847 working on the *Guardian* but taking time off from business to attend James Martineau's lectures on philosophy and economics at Manchester New College and to do a little reading in the office. The following year he went with his sister Sophia to Germany to learn the language and to attend university lectures. Garnett, who was still only 54, had to expect that long before he reached retiring age he would have become very much the third, instead of the second, partner in the firm of Taylor, Garnett & Co.

2

But there were more immediately pressing problems for Garnett. There were new opportunities open to the provincial press and at the same time new dangers facing it because of the development of the railways and telegraphs. The implications of the new situation were vital for the future of the *Guardian*; for British journalism in general, and for the cultural balance between London and the provinces.

A new session of parliament began in November 1847. In those days papers stood or fell by their parliamentary news. It was, therefore, a feat of some importance that Wednesday's *Guardian* contained in its third edition a three-column report of Tuesday night's debate on the Address. A short paragraph at the foot of the third column explains how it was done. 'We have received copies of the *Times* and of the *Daily News* of this (Wednesday) morning,' it ran, 'containing the whole of the parliamentary debate of last night, by W. H. Smith & Son's special express, at twenty minutes after ten o'clock.' Immediately afterwards another newsagent delivered the *Herald* and the *Morning Post*.[3] W. H. Smith was determined to get the London morning papers to the provinces in time to secure a good sale. That week he chartered special trains, or rather engines, to take them to Manchester, Liverpool and Birmingham. Shortly afterwards he added Carlisle and in 1848 Edinburgh and Glasgow. It showed some journalistic judgment and considerable technical efficiency on the *Guardian*'s part to turn W. H. Smith's enterprise to its advantage by getting a special *Guardian* on the streets with a full report of the debate by the early afternoon.

But W. H. Smith's initiative in exploiting the railway's power of quick, long-distance distribution was a suspended threat to the provincial newspapers. As long as news could only travel at the same speed as newspapers London had a decided advantage over the provinces because London was the source of the most important news. Its advantage was the time that it took to set the news in type after its arrival in a provincial newspaper office. This was considerable. Improvements in printing presses had by the middle of the century made it possible to print quickly as many copies of a paper as could then be sold. The machine room of the *Guardian* in its new building was vastly different from the simple hand-press which Garnett had helped to work when the paper was first started. But composing rooms were not to be mechanised for another generation. Type-setting was little changed since Caxton's day.

In 1846 W. H. Smith was selling more than twice as many London papers in Manchester as in 1837, the first year after the stamp duty had been reduced from 4d to a penny. This was also more than twice the rate of growth in the sale of Manchester papers in the same period – about 140 per cent compared with about 60 per cent. But the threat, though real and potentially dangerous, was still small. The total number of London papers sold each day in Manchester by W. H. Smith was still only some 1,500 (other wholesalers supplied a few hundreds more) compared with the *Guardian*'s sale of about 9,000 an issue. The London papers were making relatively little use of their real advantage.

More important was the change in the nature of the London competition. In 1837 the *Times* accounted for only about 16 per cent of the London dailies sold in Manchester; in 1846 for 48 per cent. These were the days when the *Times* enjoyed (the word is chosen with care) an undisputed ascendancy in the newspaper world. Its total sale that year was equal to that of all the other five London morning papers put together. The *Manchester Guardian*'s sale per issue in 1846 was more than that of any London dailies except the *Times* and the newly established *Daily News*. The *News* cost 2½d, half the price of the *Times* and the other London papers and 2d less than the *Guardian*. At this price it was selling four times as many copies as its nearest competitor except the *Times*. It accounted in its first year for about a fifth of the whole sale of all the London morning papers and for the same proportion of their sales in Manchester. For a brief period it touched 22,000 copies a day. There were then two dangers to the *Guardian* – from the *Times*, as the unrivalled national daily paper, and from the *Daily News*, as the first cheap daily newspaper. But the *Daily News* had miscalculated its finances. It had to double its price and its circulation fell away. And so correspondingly did the sale of London morning papers in Manchester. By 1851 the sale of the *Times* had gone up by one-seventh; the sale of the other London morning papers was virtually halved.[4]

There were perhaps three main reasons why throughout the 1840s and the first half of the 1850s the threat to Manchester papers from London remained largely latent. The first was the nature of the London news which gave them their start over the Manchester papers. Two main kinds of London news were important to *Guardian* readers – city news and parliamentary news. It was the timing of the parliamentary day which in effect deprived the London papers of their advantage over the Manchester papers. The House of Commons sat late and the winding up speeches were then much more important than they are now. To-day the Prime Minister and the Leader of the Opposition are apt to speak early enough to be reported in the evening news bulletins on radio and television and in the first editions of the morning papers which are printed by 10.30 p.m. or earlier. In the nineteenth century they frequently liked to have the last word – speeches then not only made news but could still sway votes. Members of Parliament were more like jurymen than voting machines; and political leaders, like Queen's counsel, knew that last impressions were important. They knew, too, that the London morning papers would hold up their editions, if necessary, in order to report the whole debate. The *Times*

on occasion even missed the morning mail trains if the House sat
especially late. Few papers regularly ran more than one edition, but their
normal time of going to press was 4 a.m. This meant that in 1851, for
instance, the normal time by which London papers were on sale in
Manchester was 2 p.m. The Manchester papers on their days of publication took pains to be available on people's breakfast tables. Much of
the advantage to be gained from the Londoner's privilege of being first
with the news was, therefore, lost. But a change in edition times and an
acceleration in railway timings could quickly have altered the position.
W. H. Smith's newspaper specials of 1847 showed what could be done.
When he extended his service in 1848 to reach Edinburgh and Glasgow
his specials actually arrived up to two hours earlier than the *evening*
mail from London of the previous day. The potential advantage enjoyed
by London newspapers over the provinces remained.

The second reason why in spite of the railways the London daily
newspapers did not sell more copies in Manchester was that relatively
few people could afford to buy them at the 1847 price. It was only just
worth while for London newsagents to advertise in Manchester their
subscription rates for the principal morning papers. Thus Henry
Clarke offered readers of the *Manchester and Salford Advertiser* (10 July
1847) the *Times*, the *Herald*, the *Chronicle* or the *Post* for £1. 12. 6 per
quarter, if sent by the morning mail; or for £1. 6. 0 if sent by the evening mail and, therefore, delivered a day late. But this was more than
half a week's wages for most working provincial journalists. Many
other educated men were in a similar position. As late as 1900 C. P.
Scott, worried by competition from the *Daily Mail*, thought that 'the
halfpenny makes a great difference to small clerks and the like who
think twice or thrice before they spend a penny a day on their newspaper.'[5] In 1847 it was not lack of desire but lack of purchasing power
which made Manchester an unprofitable market for a daily newspaper.

With wages and prices as they were, there was nothing for it but
co-operative readership. The newsrooms still flourished. The Manchester Exchange, for instance, was now buying many copies of all the
London dailies and took, all told, 130 papers a day from Monday to
Friday, 186 on Saturday and 36 on Sunday. Nor was this the only kind
of co-operative ownership. Small syndicates were formed to spread
the cost of, for example, the *Times* over a wide circle of readers. Thus,
one Norfolk clergyman got his *Times* for a penny instead of 5d. It
started its career in a Norwich newsroom, was posted on to a Norwich
householder, thence to a village eight or nine miles away, and eventually
after one or two other wayside stops to the clergyman. And all this
journeying was accomplished on the strength of the single penny paid

in newspaper stamp duty. Certainly the Norfolk clergyman was not up-to-date in his news, but this was not as important for him as for the business men who were the majority of direct subscribers to the papers.[6]

Taxation in 1847 still made newspapers dear, and thus acted as a form of protection for the provincial weekly and twice weekly newspapers against the London daily papers. There was then only a halfpenny difference in price between the *Times* and the *Guardian*, but the *Times* cost half-a-crown a week and the *Guardian* only 9d. And for this 9d the reader got a complete national newspaper in the sense that the whole week's national and international news was included, and not only that of the day of issue. It was not surprising that the abolition of the remaining 'taxes on knowledge' was not one of the good causes which the *Guardian* was active in promoting. The advertisement duty lasted until 1853, the stamp duty to 1855 and the paper duty to 1861. Protection by taxation had by then continued long enough to save provincial papers from the threat of suffocation by the London papers delivered by special express newspaper trains. Had the *Daily News* been able to hold its price at 2½d the story might have had another ending. The difference between buying the *Times* and the *Guardian* was 1/9d a week; between the *Daily News* and the *Guardian* it would have been only sixpence.

The third reason why the competition from the London daily papers was strictly limited in the 1840s and 1850s was that they did not give, and indeed could hardly have given, sufficient Lancashire news to satisfy Manchester readers. Manchester was neither an island backwater nor a cultural dependency of London. It was a strange world of its own which stirred the imagination, often the highly distorting imagination of intrepid southern visitors like Disraeli. There was, of course, a grim side to Cottonopolis with its almost savage hordes of starving Irish immigrants. This was the Manchester of *Sybil* and of Engels's *Condition of the Working Class in 1844*, published in Germany in the same year. But Manchester was not only that, nor were its ill-paid, hungry, diseased workers without leaders of their own, men of perceptive mind and sensitive imagination. It did not need strangers to point out this grandeur and this misery. Mrs Gaskell, the wife of a minister at Cross Street Unitarian Chapel where the Taylors had sittings, was busy writing *Mary Barton* in 1847. And there was a good deal of literary and artistic life for *Guardian* readers positively to enjoy. That winter Emerson was speaking twice weekly in Manchester, giving the lectures later published as *Representative Men*, Jenny Lind was to be heard in opera, and Rachel in a series of French tragedies.

In 1879 a new building was begun on an enlarged site. The editorial
and printing offices were moved to a Salford mill during reconstruction. Demolition was well advanced by 1881 as the bills announcing
'Death of Beaconsfield' show

The new building in Cross Street was completed in 1886. The site, bought in four lots between 1860 and 1867, cost £23,000

The *Guardian* thought comedy might have been more appreciated and that an English synopsis would have helped. Still, 'Rachel was called for and loudly cheered, and was "bouqueted" as the London papers style it, which, as well as the calling before the curtain, we humbly conceive to be a silly and most theatrical custom.' To the readers and writers of the *Guardian* the social news of London rarely seemed national, and for the most part appeared to them just as distinctly local as Manchester news did to Londoners. Newspapers might come every day from London to Manchester, but Manchester men still rarely went to London and their wives even less often. Russell Taylor, for instance, was only in London four times in 1847.

Manchester was no more an economic than a cultural dependency of London. Its trade was becoming world-wide and it was itself the place where the ultimate decisions of the international cotton industry were made. American news, therefore, had an especial importance for Manchester, and here the Manchester papers were at no disadvantage. The Mersey was closer to Manchester than Southampton Water to London. The movements of the mail steamers were closely watched and the *Guardian* staff were always ready to produce a special edition if there was any chance of late news. Thus on 16 October 1847, when the royal mail steamer *Britannica* arrived in the Mersey at 2.15 a.m., the *Guardian* contrived in a third edition to give three-quarters of a column of closely printed news covering the Mexican war, the potato crop and the cotton crop. Again on 24 December the paper reported:

'The Packet Ship, *Isaac Wright*, arrived off Liverpool last evening after the last train had left. We have, however, received a telegraphic dispatch from Liverpool, stating that a steam tug from the *Isaac Wright* had brought into the port files of the New York papers to the 3rd instant inclusive; but their contents are not important. There was no further news from Mexico. Cotton and corn were both quiet. The *Isaac Wright* is said to have brought a large amount of specie; no less than £250,000.'

3

It is doubtful whether the late arrival of the London papers, their high cost and their lack of local news, the three defences of the provincial press against the London morning papers, would have held firm but for the coming of the telegraph. This totally changed the situation. News could now travel faster than newspapers. Wherever there was a telegraph, distance could be disregarded. London might still be the source of the most important news, but the London papers had lost their natural start over Manchester and other provincial papers in making the news known. Competition was possible on equal terms. Indeed, the London papers were quick to complain that the terms were now unfair to them since news which had cost them large sums to collect was now available free of cost to the provincial press before the London papers reached their doorsteps.[7] But this controversy belongs to the next decade when the telegraph was a more developed instrument.

The first use to which the telegraph was put in England was for railway signalling. Gradually the lines, which were run beside the railway tracks, began to be used for private messages and for the trans-mission of news. By 1847 the system was extensive enough to be of real help to newspapers. The trans-Pennine lines were in position by the time of the general election, but the connections had not been com-pleted and there was no public service. But, thanks to the initiative of the Manchester Superintendent of the Electric Telegraph Co., the *Guardian* was able to give details which it could not otherwise have done of the nominations and the progress of the poll at Leeds, Halifax and Wakefield.* But the telegraph instruments were primitive and un-reliable, and telegrams expensive and slow in transmission. At first they were only normally used for news flashes, such as the volume of cotton sales, racing at Newmarket or election results.[8]

Newspapers had to learn to keep pace with the speed with which the telegraph could spread news and rumours. Editors had to make up their minds more quickly and be ready to think and think again in the course of a single night. News no longer came to Manchester from London all at one time when the coach or the train arrived, but con-tinuously. An early example of the problems this posed occurred in August 1847. There were strong rumours in London that Louis Philippe, the King of the French, had been murdered. Passengers by the 5 p.m. train from Euston brought the story to Manchester on Tuesday night. On Wednesday morning the same story was trans-mitted by telegraph from Rugby and 'a very powerful sensation was created in this town.' Garnett had to decide whether to issue a second edition of the *Guardian* that afternoon, as he did when important news broke too late for the morning issue. Tuesday's London evening papers came down by the night mail and contained no mention of the story. This looked suspicious. Then at 11.15 a.m., four hours before the London morning papers reached Manchester, there was a second message from the telegraph clerks at Rugby cancelling their earlier story. The telegraph company was already beginning to gather news

---

* Voting at elections was still, of course, in public, and hour by hour reports could therefore be given of how the candidates stood.

as well as transmitting messages. If the Rugby telegraph clerks had by their zeal nearly led the paper into reporting a non-event, they had been prompt enough on discovering their error to prevent this indiscretion. Some people, the *Guardian* said, blamed the Electric Telegraph Co's clerks for spreading rumours. 'We think, however, that those censures are altogether unfounded.'[9]

Occasionally the newspapers attempted longer messages even in 1847 and 1848. Thus the *Guardian* hoped to carry a full report of Lord John Russell's budget speech – a budget on Friday and the Prime Minister to open it in place of the Chancellor of the Exchequer was a sufficiently remarkable occasion. Moreover, a new form of transmission was to be used. This was Bain's system, a kind of primitive teleprinter recording the message in the form of dots and dashes which, the *Guardian* explained, was not only quicker than Cooke and Wheatstone's machine but more accurate since 'the printed sheets remain . . . so that mistakes may be detected and corrected.' Lord John Russell got up to speak at 5 p.m.; at 7.15 the message began to be received in Manchester. But Saturday's *Guardian* contained only a quarter of a column report which ended abruptly before the most important part of the speech was reached. The last words were in brackets '(At one o'clock the telegraph was left working)'; presumably it had broken down for there were still three hours to press time.[10]

The *Manchester Examiner* had had better luck with its report of the Queen's speech at the opening of the session. It had announced the previous week that it would give the text in Tuesday's paper by using the telegraph. There was no hitch. An editorial note records that transmission started at 2.15 p.m. and was complete by 6.10 p.m., which gives a speed of about three words a minute for the 750-word speech. The *Examiner*'s normal Tuesday edition time was 3 p.m., but on this occasion a special evening edition was printed.[11] Wednesday's *Guardian*, of course, also had the Queen's speech in full, but it had no need to use the telegraph and, equally, no opportunity to beat the *Examiner*. But if the *Examiner* had not paid for the telegram, its readers would either have had to wait for Saturday to find out what the Government proposed, or else to buy the *Guardian* or one of the London papers. Competition between twice weekly papers with mid-week editions appearing on different days was bound to be a limping affair.

4

This *Manchester Examiner* was a new paper. It was to be for forty years the *Guardian*'s most formidable rival. The competition from London papers, with which this chapter has been mainly concerned, was a general danger to all provincial newspapers. And it was a future threat rather than a present experience. The competition of the *Examiner*, however, was immediate and specific. It was aimed at the *Guardian*. This was its real enemy; but its victim was Archibald Prentice's *Manchester Times*. Indeed, the reason why the *Examiner* was started was the growing incompetence of the *Manchester Times* as an effective exponent of left-wing Liberal politics. No editor could have been more devoted to the cause than Archibald Prentice; the trouble was that nothing else interested him. His readers were not so single-minded and took to other papers. The *Guardian* flourished; the *Times* languished. John Bright, William McKerrow and Edward Watkin resolved to start the *Examiner* to do just what the *Times* was failing to accomplish.

The prospectus mentioned neither the price nor the day of publication of the new paper, but it clearly underlined the special interests of the three backers. 'Free trade without sham, mistake or compromise' – the *Examiner* was to be Bright's organ. 'The promoters . . . have a deep and serious conviction that religion is far too sacred to be stayed by the hands of cabinets and parliaments' – William McKerrow was a Presbyterian minister. 'To a great practical subject, the railway system, the *Examiner* will be found devoting its careful attention, supporting all that is safe and advantageous to the public; and yet exposing the delinquencies of sordid speculation' – 26-year-old Edward Watkin was already secretary to a railway company and was to become the last of the great railway promoters, the man who turned the Manchester, Sheffield and Lincolnshire line into the Great Central Railway and brought it to London. He was the son of Absalom Watkin whom the Potters had once thought of making editor of the *Manchester Gazette* in place of Prentice.* All three men were united in their belief that Manchester was 'the nucleus of the most enterprising and active district in the Empire', and held that 'its vast manufacturing labour – its great stores of capital – its extensively ramified commercial connections make its prosperity or adversity to be felt in the remotest corners of the British Empire.'

Probably the only sentiment in the whole prospectus from which Garnett would have dissented was the promoters' view that 'the spirit of Manchester is unrepresented' and in need of a journal which 'must cease to be a mere newspaper – a mere speculation in principles for the sake of pecuniary profit – and must raise itself to the elevation of the energy it should emulate, the benevolence it should rival, and the

---

* See p. 88. Edward Watkin was a left-wing radical, but had contributed a series of articles to the *Guardian* in 1844 on 'Public Walks'.

progress it should preach.' All this and a great deal more appeared in the advertisement columns of the *Guardian*,[12] and indeed may well have been drafted inside the office since the promoters of the *Examiner* went to the *Guardian* for their first editor. The man they chose was 40-year-old Thomas Ballantyne, who had been born in Paisley but had for a good many years been active in Lancashire journalism. He had been on the *Guardian* staff since 1841 and before that had been editor of the *Bolton Free Press*. He was associated with the Anti-Corn Law League and had written for it *The Corn Law Repealer's Handbook*. He joined the *Guardian* when John Edward Taylor's health was failing and there was room for a new senior man on the editorial side. He left it when it was clear that Russell Scott Taylor was going to take his father's place. He had no prospect of promotion on the *Guardian* and he took a sensible course in moving to the *Examiner*. His nephew, Hamilton Ballantyne,* remained with the *Guardian* for another two or three years.

Ballantyne gave the *Examiner* a cleaner and more attractive appearance than the *Guardian*, but it did not provide as good a news service. He was editor for not quite three years. In 1846 George Wilson, the great political boss of the Anti-Corn Law League, and Rawson had bought the *Manchester Times* from Prentice and installed as editor A. W. Paulton, who had been running the League's own paper. Two years later Wilson and Rawson bought the *Examiner* and amalgamated the *Times* with it. Paulton became editor of the combined paper. Ballantyne had carried on lively arguments with the *Guardian* on such subjects as the price of corn and the prospects of famine, remarking how sorry he was to perceive that 'the beautiful weather which has lately been diffusing universal gladness throughout the land has had a most unhappy effect upon the tone and temper of the *Manchester Guardian*.' But neither Garnett nor Ballantyne seem to have harboured hard thoughts about one another, and before long Ballantyne, now established in London as a newspaper editor, was again undertaking regular work for the *Guardian*.

What really separated the *Examiner* and the *Guardian* was not their differences about particular political measures, but the fact that they stood for opposed conceptions of the role of a newspaper. The *Examiner* was in effect the mouthpiece of the Liberal political machine. It was the duty of the editor to support the party line. This was the truth of the matter, but it sounded better to explain the position as a duty owed to readers rather than proprietors. 'A newspaper,' wrote the *Examiner*, 'enters upon certain relations with its readers, who "adhere" to it in the faith that it will steadily advocate defined and recognised principles.

* See p. 81.

A certain contract has been entered into . . . no newspaper has any right or privilege suddenly to outrage the sympathies of its readers, by advocating the contrary to-day of that which yesterday it pronounced to be essential to the well-being of the community.' The next day the *Guardian* replied: 'Some men seem to think that the editor of a newspaper is under some obligation to shape his course by that of parties or individuals with whom he may previously have acted, however much that may be at variance with his own convictions. That some newspapers are compelled to submit to this necessity, we are all aware . . . Anybody who learns what has been decided on in Newall's Buildings* may predict, to the nicest shade, the future opinions of the *Manchester Examiner* . . . Now, we have no fault to find with this particular connection between a journal and an organised party. It may be desirable that some journals should be tools and instruments; and, if they refuse to obey the word of command, of course they do violate the contract . . . But we object to be judged by the rules applicable to such cases. We have not undertaken to obey, and we will not obey, any man or set of men whatever . . .'[13]

For a long time both editors were able freely to express their own deeply held views. The editors of the *Examiner* were such good party men that they did not feel restricted by the necessity to please the proprietors. Forty years later conflict did arise. When that happened, the editor of the *Examiner* sought, and found, refuge on the staff of the *Guardian*.

* The headquarters of the Anti-Corn Law League.

CHAPTER EIGHT

Russell Scott Taylor: The *Guardian* in 1848

I

WHEN the first news came – by telegraph – of the revolution in France and the fall of Louis Philippe, Russell Taylor had been senior partner in Taylor, Garnett & Co. for just over one year. Jeremiah Garnett had completed more than a quarter of a century on the paper, and for the last five years certainly he had been in undisputed control of its policy. The revolutions that followed fast in one European capital after another and their pale reflection in the British Isles made it likely that a middle-aged man and a very young one would find themselves frequently at loggerheads both over the best way of handling the news and over the right line to take in comment on it. There is, however, no trace of difficulties of this kind having arisen. Garnett was still in spirit a pretty young man, and Russell Taylor seems to have been born with many of the qualities of middle age. 'In him the judgment and the reasoning powers were as fully developed at 21 years of age as in most men at 30 or 35; and with this early maturity of judgment, he combined a degree of prudence and forethought rarely acquired without a long acquaintance with the world.'[1] That was the judgment of an admiring friend: it explains how it was possible for the new partnership to work smoothly through a period of revolution; and how the *Guardian* came to take the line it did.

Fortunately the *Guardian* was much better able to rise to the occasion than it would have been a few years before. It now had for the first time good political commentators both in London and Liverpool. Whether this was Garnett's doing or Russell Taylor's one does not know, and perhaps it does not really matter. It had begun in London in the exciting summer of 1846 when the Corn Law was repealed. Russell Taylor at that time was still learning the job at a salary of 27/– a week. But when the London arrangement was extended to Liverpool in the autumn of 1847 Russell Taylor had taken up his partnership and must have agreed with what was being done since the cost was considerable – an additional £200 a year in 1847 and more than twice that sum in 1848.

Liverpool was important because it was the principal British

Atlantic port, England's window on the New World. Up to this time, however, the *Guardian* had relied on Liverpool only for cotton and commodity reports and as the place through which American newspapers reached Manchester. Now it began to use Liverpool as a listening post where an intelligent correspondent could hear much informed comment on the New World. For £100 a year the *Guardian* got, in addition to the prospects of the cotton crop, letters dealing with the end of the Mexican war; the half-million emigrants who left for America; the diversion of cargoes from France to Liverpool because of the revolution; the unreliability of the *New York Herald* with its Scottish editor whose 'sentiments should no more be taken as an index to public opinion than those of a chartist newspaper'; the appalling level of taxation in the United States, where one Baltimore man had to pay 20 per cent of his £15,000 income in taxes so that 'after all, we have not so much cause of complaint,' and, of course, the presidential election and the effect of the gold rush on the value of money. Earlier in the year, when the United States had just acquired California from Mexico, the Liverpool correspondent had thought it 'rather singular, considering the importance of our China trade and the value of San Francisco as a port that the British government had not years ago treated for the purchase which might have been effected without attracting attention.'[2] Normally the *Guardian* regarded colonies as burdens which free trade would make it unnecessary to bear much longer, but it allowed its trusted correspondents a reasonable latitude, though they must expect to be answered, if they transgressed, in a leading article. On this occasion there was no correction. Consistency can be carried too far.

The first, and for ten years the principal, London correspondent of the *Guardian* was James Wilson – principal, that is to say, for his importance and by the salary he commanded (£300 a year), but by no means the most regular or voluminous. In 1848, for instance, more of the work was done by J. B. Hewitt, whose contributions, when Wilson was writing, appear in second place with the by-line 'from another London correspondent' and are initialled 'H.' Generally speaking, 'H''s contributions appeared in every issue, except in the depth of the recess when the London correspondence entirely disappeared, while Wilson's, described as 'by a private correspondent', appeared only on Saturdays, and not always then. It seems likely from internal evidence that Wilson also supplied a good deal of material which was worked into leading articles. He may have written some as he certainly did a little later.

James Wilson had founded the *Economist* in 1843 and entered parliament in 1847, where early next year, as his London correspondence records, he heard Lord George Bentinck make 'the longest and dreariest speech ever delivered in the memory of the oldest member.' He spoke about the duty on West Indian sugar, but also in its three and a half hours about 'almost every imaginable object connected or not connected with the topic of his motion.' The new member was soon busily concerned in the Schleswig Holstein question. In April Mr Wilson, as London private correspondent, reported that Mr Wilson, as a member of Parliament, was to ask Lord Palmerston what he could do to reconcile Denmark and Prussia, and added, 'I have reason to know that special agents are now in London from the Danish Government and also from Hamburg and that they have already had a long interview with Lord Palmerston on the subject.' A fortnight later the new member became a junior minister, dealing with Indian affairs – a *Guardian* leader explained why he was not going to the Board of Trade, as the *Times* had imagined. Wilson continued to write for the *Guardian*: describing the repeal of the Navigation Laws, for instance, or forecasting that the cabinet would commute the death sentences on 'the silly and infatuated traitors in Ireland,' to which he added a characteristic aside, 'with this exception we have no other political news of a domestic kind; of foreign – unfortunately, too much.'[3]

For the first time the *Guardian* had close and regular contact with somebody at the centre of affairs, but without any suggestion of patronage or obligation to follow a party line. Wilson's writing for the *Guardian* was, of course, very much a side-line as far as he was concerned, but what he wrote showed the qualities for which Bagehot praised him: his 'business imagination' which enabled him to see 'what men did' and 'why men did it'; his instinctive mastery of statistical selection, picking out of a mass of figures those which would tell the most and leaving the rest alone; and his 'singular gift of *efficient* argument – a peculiar power of bringing home his opinions by convincing reasoning to convincible persons.'[4]

By the end of 1848 this double 'London correspondence' had been supplemented by a series of weekly 'Letters from London' which were more discursive and less concerned with business details. They gave Manchester readers something of the flavour of London life and a sense of taking part in it. The first few contributions were initialled 'R' (probably for F. Ross), but this identification was soon dropped though the same distinctive hand seems still at work. 'R's' elaborate style is out of fashion, but the relish with which he wrote persists. He still takes us back to the London of 1848 as truly as he took Manchester readers up to the capital:

where the railway from York is coming in like the great sea-serpent, throwing up prodigious embankments, pitching enormous bridges over the roads, passing close under houses that totter over the excavations, and ploughing its way into the intended terminus;

where Cockney John Bull, meaning nearly two millions of people, makes fearful efforts in his attempts to pronounce Windischgraetz and Jellalich; but nevertheless has some idea of who these personages are and what they are about; while as for the pope, he does not know what to say about him; he thinks that the old gentleman was wrong in running away from his business, but is inclined to think that matters may be made up;

where a year ago the fashion of drinking the queen's health at little private entertainments would have been voted pedantry, an impertinence, and a bore; but is now becoming quite fashionable, and the name of the sovereign is received in that emphatic way which conveys a certain significance;

where, at the Egyptian Hall a visit to Banyard's three mile long, revolving painted panorama of the Mississippi made one realise how important to each other are England and America, and how war between the two countries would be 'mutual suicide';

where the *Fonetic Nuz* was hoping, despite the vagaries of English pronunciation, to succeed in a market in which Mr Dilke had just failed to make a success of the *Daily News*, a newspaper which was as excellent in character as it was low in price.[5]

2

Garnett and Russell Taylor had thus given their paper a lively and thoughtful special news service from beyond its own immediate district. But for national and international news, apart from the all-important market prices, the *Guardian* was still in 1848 largely dependent on the London, the Irish and the continental newspapers. A series of snippets from various papers, often contradicting one another and requiring careful comparative study to make sense was no longer good enough. It was necessary to give readers a coherent and connected story. The first news of the French Revolution came to Manchester by telegraph from special late editions of the London papers. It took up a whole boldly displayed column of the *Guardian* – one of the very few occasions at this period when the paper used typographical display to draw special attention to important news. It was accompanied by a leading article. The two issues of the following week both contained two whole pages of French news put together from a variety of newspapers, mainly French but some English. Several London newspapers had their own Paris correspondents whose reports were useful. From these sources the *Guardian* wove a connected narrative, carefully weighing the known bias of each paper. It would be pleasant to know whom to praise. One cannot be certain. Russell Taylor may have had a hand in it, but it is likely that Robert Dowman, Thomas Ballantyne's successor, was the capable sub-editor. This was, perhaps, the first important occasion when a sub-editor's unobtrusive, constructive hand, invisible to the reader, was used by the *Guardian* to explain a tangled situation. The connected narratives compiled in the office were kept up issue after issue. It is an indication of the tremendous prestige of parliament at that time that reports of what happened in the French Chamber took the same form and stood apart from the general news story.

There were private sources in Manchester by which the *Guardian* could check other newspapers. Manchester had a great European trade, and the leading houses had close connections with their continental customers. It was possible for an observant man to pick up a good deal of information on 'Change. After Garnett's death a writer in the *Sphinx*, a short-lived Manchester literary quarterly, described how 'when, in his own office, he had the run of all the newspapers in England that were worth reading; he would come down to the stands on 'Change and wait for the man already there to turn over the leaf which he wanted to see. His pacings to and fro between his office and the Exchange were something marvellous, and had a dreamy monotony about them very characteristic of the man.' He may, as this writer re-called, have wandered about on 'Change 'as if he knew nobody, and as if nobody knew him'; but, for all that, he was quick enough to follow up a hint which might be useful to the paper. In the 1850s Engels, who was not only a business man but a considerable freelance journalist, noticed how Garnett at once pricked up his ears at any mention of a business scandal and started a series of probing questions.[6]

The *Guardian* had its own contacts too in France and Germany, though it made surprisingly little use of them in the news columns. Among them was Richard Potter, son of 'Radical Dick,' and an intimate friend of Russell Taylor. The quarrel between their fathers had not been passed on. Richard Potter was rich, farmed a little, and often took a house in Paris for a few months. During 1848 he wrote a number of very long Letters to the Editor[7] which brought together the experience of France and Britain in their common 'labour question.' He believed that democracy was likely to fail in France because she lacked the con-ditions which had helped it to succeed in the United States – universal education and 'the open frontier' to relieve distress. Neither in France nor in England could the labour question be solved except by educa-tion, emigration and public health legislation: 'The laisser-faire scheme of government will never provide such means.' This was constructive thinking, but Potter also shared the fears of less thoughtful British capitalists. In the same letter he agreed that socialism was robbery and that the wild and imbecile acts of the French provisional government were the work of men who were the puppets of the worst portion of the Parisian mob. Sandwiched in time between these signed Letters to the Editor from English addresses were a few unsigned news letters 'from a private correspondent, Paris,' who may well have been Richard Potter. They are more descriptive, less argumentative, but they show the same attitudes. From them readers learned how French capitalists, fearing a Chartist revolution in England, had sold out English investments and brought their money home in gold; and how the 'higher classes' in Paris were reducing their establishments. Thus M. Thiers had sold three carriage horses and discharged a coachman. He had also lost four of the finest trees from his 'English garden' which had been taken for Trees of Liberty. A fifth would have gone, but his wife, 'who knew how nearly demanding is to taking under the present system, arose precipitately from under the hand of her lady's maid and, with a part of her hair hanging about her shoulders, went to the gate to expostulate . . .'[8]

We know that Potter was writing for the *Guardian* on France in 1848 and would have liked to write more, probably leading articles. Sophia Taylor told Russell Scott in the autumn that Potter had offered 'a permanent supply' of articles but that Garnett had refused because he could not take liberties with them.[9]

Certainly *Guardian* leaders were occasionally contributed by outsiders, though this was a carefully guarded secret. The paper held strictly to the rule of anonymity which preserved its corporate personality. Taylor and Garnett were the *Guardian*; they took responsibility for the whole paper, for its news and its views, the credit and the blame. They felt that this was the paper's strength, and it would be weakened if individual articles were assigned to various authors. As Russell Taylor put it in a letter, to his uncle, 'the plan of allowing persons not connected with the office to write leaders has some advantages *provided that you can rely on their holding their tongues*; but in this respect there is considerable risk.'[10] The precautions which were taken to preserve anonymity were at any rate effective enough to make it difficult to-day to discover who even the principal contributors were and virtually impossible to discover who wrote precisely what.

3

Besides the occasional letters from a private correspondent in Paris, there were later in the year similar contributions from Germany. A few appear at full length in the news columns; others are quoted extensively in the leading articles. Like the Paris letters, these were background matter. One, for instance, contrasts the Prussian officers, who were devoted to the Hohenzollern monarchy and favoured the armistice with Denmark, with the rank-and-file who were pan-German national-ists and were correspondingly bellicose.[11] Manchester, of course, already had strong ties with Germany through the textile industry and the considerable German colony it had brought to the city. When the National Assembly, the first all-German representative body in the modern sense, met at Frankfurt the *Guardian* gave a two-column report of a meeting, 200 strong, of the Manchester German colony to send the National Assembly a message of support. A huge flag in the white, red and gold of Germany (as opposed to the separate states) hung over the platform and rosettes or sashes in the same colours were worn by all the committee members who included Dr Delius, the father of the composer.[12]

There was, therefore, no difficulty in securing contributors from Germany or in arranging for young Edward Taylor to spend 1848 as a student at Bonn. He attended the lectures of Professor Rinkel, the democratic deputy who was sent to prison for slandering the troops. He went to the National Assembly at Frankfurt with intro-ductions from a 'red hot democrat' and a sound conservative. He visited Berlin and delayed his return in order to be there when the imperial crown was offered to the King of Prussia. He and his family party – his sister, his young half-sisters and his step-mother's sister – stayed on while Bonn was in military occupation. 'In theory I am no democrat,' wrote his sister, 'but really the people here have been trifled with past bearing. The conduct of the soldiers after the late insurrections would leave one to believe that Christianity was unheard of. The King sends them into all parts, eight or ten boat-loads go past sometimes in a day.' But by this time it was the summer of 1849. In August Edward Taylor returned to England and went to London to read for the bar. He had had a good education for his partnership even though his Italian journey had to be abandoned because of the state of the country.[13]

With the exception of France and Germany the *Guardian* had no regular private correspondents from abroad. Even Ireland, which occupied a great deal of space both in the news and the leader columns, was covered almost entirely by extracts from the Irish papers. The treason trials which followed the feeble insurrection in the south-west were fully reported in the *Guardian*, but neither Harland nor any of his reporters seem to have been sent out to cover them. There were no special enquiries and investigations into the actual situation of the kind that later made the *Guardian*'s Irish reputation stand so high.

4

What line did the *Guardian* take on the new movements which convulsed Europe in 1848? The best starting point is its attitude on domestic English affairs. Manchester had long been in the front line of English industrial troubles. These troubles were by no means over, and they were now increasingly complicated by overtones of Irish political turbulence, the product of the massive flight from famine in that over-populated island. In the summer there was a three-day police alert in Manchester while the mobs waited in vain for sufficiently encouraging news from Ireland before they joined the rising. Yet at no time did the *Guardian* panic about the home situation: it was more inclined to ridicule than to fear Feargus O'Connor who claimed personally to have injured ninety-three people at one rough Manchester meeting – 'the heroes of the Trojan war, the paladins of Charlemagne, and the worthies of knight errantry must all look small before him.'[14]

At the beginning of the year the *Guardian* had, it is true, felt that these dangerous times were not suitable for another instalment of parliamentary reform. It was bitterly opposed to the Birmingham proposals for a 'room and pigstye' franchise. But by July the *Guardian* had decided that the emergency was past; that there ought to be a redistribution of seats to give the industrial North better representation; that there might be an experiment with the secret ballot (which would probably make little difference to election results); and that all ratepayers, though not all men, might get the vote.[15] This was its confident verdict on the political health of the nation. It was as glad to agree with Cobden as it was always reluctant to side with Bright.

To judge by its leading articles, the *Guardian* was more worried about the economic than the political situation. It kept up a steady campaign in favour of a gold-based currency free from political manipulation. It was against this background that it judged the news of the California gold rush. Those who feared a ruinous inflation were likely to be misguided because gold was so indestructible that the new discoveries could only fractionally increase the world's total stock – 'there is no difficulty in believing that portions of the sacred vessels that Nebuchadnezzar carried away from Jerusalem are now circulating as English sovereigns.' The value of gold would not be as much affected even by rich mining discoveries as, for instance, the price of corn was by a good harvest. No doubt nominal prices would rise; but there might be no great harm in this and even those with fixed incomes 'would much rather run the risk of any deterioration of the standard which is likely to arise from the exuberant produce of the Californian mines than trust to the consequences of those schemes of inconvertible paper which find favour with the *Liverpool Standard*.'[16]

After its worries about a paper currency, the *Guardian* was most concerned about the icy aftermath of the great railway boom. Several long leaders were devoted to railway amalgamation – in particular to the proposed merger, which miscarried, between the London and North-Western, the Great Western and the London and South-Western Railways. This would be all very well, but what the public needed was a halt to further capital expenditure financed by ruinous calls on shares which were not fully paid up. New railways were not needed in England, but in India. It was there that the development of an alternative source of cotton supply and the raising of the deplorably low standard of living alike demanded a tolerable system of communications and the infusion of English capital.[17]

The *Guardian* approached the chronic problem of Ireland from the same economic angle. There could be no future worth living for most of her people unless the country could be developed and freed from its complete dependence on a few crops. But capital would not be forthcoming without political stability. This was the true Irish problem. 'Martial law is better than the midnight legislation of Tipperary; and, if nothing else can secure the peace of the country, even that must be resorted to for that purpose. Of course we are perfectly aware that measures of coercion and repression must be accompanied by measures calculated to stimulate industry, and to give Irishmen some better employment than shooting landlords.' This severe leader called forth a 'rather orderly' protest meeting of the Manchester Irish at which the concluding speaker observed that 'if the editor of the *Manchester Guardian* were placed in the situation of many Irishmen, and had the feelings of a man, he would, had he courage enough, murder Jesus Christ and the twelve apostles' – which remark was received with loud laughter and applause.'[18]

In leader after leader throughout 1848 three themes recur. First, there was a need for majority verdicts since both repealers and Orangemen were equally disqualified as jurors by prejudice.* Next, Roman Catholic priests in Ireland should be given fixed salaries which would enlist their sympathies on the side of law and order – as witness the anxiety of the Archbishop of Tuam to prevent any such system being introduced. The third theme was the frivolity of the revolutionary leaders. 'If Mr Duffy and Mr Mitchell would turn out into the streets with pikes or muskets, or even with ginger-beer bottles filled with gunpowder and rusty nails, somebody would probably think they were in earnest.' As it was, the Irish people were 'like men who have become so accustomed to high seasoning that even cayenne pepper has lost its power upon their palates.' This point is made so frequently that the leading articles read almost like a schoolboy's 'dares.' And when, at last, a rising was attempted, the *Guardian*'s comment ran 'although we never expected any very serious consequences from the treasonable conspiracy in which so large a number of Irishmen were known to be engaged, we scarcely expected so ridiculous a burlesque of insurrection as that which Mr Smith O'Brien and his friends have just been acting.'[19]

What is missing is any realisation of the spiritual force of national feeling, which was manifesting itself in Ireland and throughout Europe. It was a curious blindness in a paper whose editor, commenting on the Oregon dispute with the United States three years before, had threatened 'a bloody and desperate war (since), though not caring much for the subject of the dispute, England will not permit her national honour to be outraged by any government or people under the sun.'[20]

Nationalism was associated with democracy in 1848, and democracy was still suspect in the *Guardian* circle. One reason for this suspicion was the belief that democracy was likely to lead to the destruction of property in such a way as to make it impossible to build up the developed capitalist society on which the prosperity of all depended. This was not a selfish concern for the interests of one class at the expense of another (though in practice this might be involved), but a genuine concern for the preservation of the welfare of society as a whole. When Garnett looked at the France of Louis Blanc, it was with eyes long accustomed to English industrial agitation. Louis Blanc would probably not have disputed the accuracy of the *Guardian*'s diagnosis:

---

* 'A Conservative' in a letter to the editor reminded readers that but for the rule of unanimity 'honest John Rylands' would have been unable in 1819 to save John Edward Taylor from conviction for criminal libel in 1819 (see p. 16). It is tempting to identify the anonymous correspondent with John Rickards's eldest son with whom Russell Taylor was 'very friendly' and who was an active member of the Manchester Board of Guardians. (Leader: 20 May; Letter 3 June 1848.)

'If the obvious intentions of the government were fully accomplished, the influence of property would be destroyed . . . and to the good will or forbearance of those who have nothing to lose but their lives, must all other classes be hereafter indebted . . . Now this is a change of relative positions to which men of property will not willingly submit; . . . When a civil conflict results from an antagonism of classes, it always engenders feelings of more deadly hostility than mere political differences can ever inspire; and there is no distinction of classes more formidable than that of people with and people without property.'[21]

When Louis Napoleon was finally elected president, the *Guardian* doubted his ability but welcomed his overwhelming majority as a pledge of stability.

Back in March the *Guardian* had thought the Germans in every respect better qualified than the French for self-government. Not only were they more calm and reflective in character, but they had experience with local institutions and voluntary associations. 'We think that the recent movement in that country is likely to be attended by consequences highly beneficial not only to the German people but also to the cause of freedom and government all over Europe.' But by the end of June the *Guardian* thought differently. 'Can any rational man see in any part of Germany the slightest hope of tranquillity and prosperity as the result of popular wisdom and popular control? . . . there is scarcely a hope for the protection even of life and property, except that which is to be found in a restoration of something like despotic authority. All this is, doubtless, very melancholy . . .'[22]

5

All this is, indeed, very melancholy reading for those readers who take a pride in the *Guardian*'s past akin to family pride. They must admit that in 1848 the *Manchester Examiner* would have been more to their taste: 'Granted, a thousand times, that the price is a heavy one – we would ask, is there no value in what it is paid to obtain?'[23] The *Guardian*'s leader makes melancholy reading too, in the light of the hopes with which the *Guardian* had set out in 1821 'to watch with intense anxiety the magnificent experiments being made in Europe and the New World to establish institutions conformable to the increased intelligence of the age, and calculated for the promotion of public happiness and the security of popular rights.' But the deep-seated pessimism of the *Guardian* about the continental revolutionaries must not be ascribed entirely to lack of vision. It saw the ineptitude and incapacity of the democratic leaders.

The things for which the *Guardian* stood in 1848 were sensible, worthy, necessary; the methods it advised were prudent, cautious, defensible even when wrong. Its concern for public health and public education was admirable and eminently reasonable – it produced convincing figures to show that schools were cheaper than prisons and that 'the alternative is between school-rates and poor-rates.'[24] It cared deeply for individual liberty, and was outspoken in its defence. When the future Lord Shaftesbury said that if he and his friends failed in their attempt to defend a Christian parliament, they would soon find themselves having to stand out for a *white* parliament, the *Guardian*, as zealous for Jewish emancipation as it had been for Roman Catholic, was quick to reply. 'An attempt to distinguish between different coloured races, however natural across the Atlantic, is unworthy of the British legislature; and we are happy to say that the noble lord's knowledge is not less at fault than his good feeling, and that the House of Commons does not keep an officer to inspect the colour of its members' faces.'[25] But this was a relatively rare moment of passionate perception. In a world overcrowded with abuses, the *Guardian* of 1848 too rarely experienced the impetus of indignation.

If Jeremiah Garnett took time that summer to compare the *Guardian* as a newspaper with what it had been five years before at the end of his long partnership with John Edward Taylor, he must have found reason for satisfaction. It was clearly a better newspaper. The new partnership was working well. But the autumn brought tragedy. In September Russell Taylor caught typhus fever; four days later he was dead. 'With great firmness of character', as his obituary records, 'he combined great modesty, purity of mind and delicacy of feeling, and was so uniformly gentle and courteous in his personal deportment, that he never gave pain or offence, even to the most sensitive mind, by his mode of refusing a request, or by the expression of a difference of opinion.'[26] It would be stupid to pretend that the *Guardian* in Russell Taylor's time fully reflected these amiable characteristics, but it was distinctly less censorious than it had been in his father's days. Now Jeremiah Garnett was alone again. It would be four years before Edward Taylor was old enough to take up his partnership.

CHAPTER NINE

Every Morning

I

'To-day the press, from duty free,
Appears on every side;
Whilst competition reigns around,
And news is scattered wide,
A perfect flood of papers rise,
Like breakers in the storm,
Of every size – of every price –
And every make and form.

This advertisement, which

'tells of Hyam's warehouse vast,
His efforts and success,
And does it not expatiate
Upon his wondrous dress?'

appeared on Saturday, 30 June 1855, the day after that on which the
bill abolishing the newspaper stamp duty received the royal assent.
Two days later, in the first Monday *Guardian* ever published, a leading
article made the same points more ponderously.

'The public will assuredly have, as candidates for their support, all sorts of
journals, professing to advocate all shades of opinion; and the various success
of each will be a curious barometer of public intelligence. For ourselves we
have but few words to say. We have felt compelled to move forward . . .;
In doing so we have considered it necessary to make arrangements both at
home and abroad, to enable us to furnish our readers with the latest and most
accurate intelligence. We feel that in such a conjuncture, we must act with
vigour and energy, . . . We may regret that it was not reserved to us to give
the first daily sheet to the public of Manchester; but we must acknowledge
that we have been outstripped by competitors whose zeal to serve the public
has been greater than their desire to obey the law.'

This curiously defensive tone reflects the anxiety which the partners
in Taylor, Garnett & Co. felt about the future and their chagrin at
being beaten by their rivals. There was no doubt about the demand

for daily papers that would be readily available in the North. There were now people enough who could read to support daily papers, but not enough who could afford fivepence every morning. But the public was hungry for news. England was fighting a European war after the longest period of general peace in her history. Trains and telegraphs had made the news from the Crimea available in England with reasonable speed and regularity. It was politically impossible to retain a barrier of taxation between the public and the news from the front.

In fact, a way was first found round the law. The definition of a newspaper had always been unsatisfactory. In 1851 the Inland Revenue had explained that papers confined to one class of news to one class of readers, such as religious articles for the clergy or legal gossip for lawyers, were not newspapers and need not pay the tax. But if, for example, a legal journal included a list of church appointments, it would become a newspaper and have to pay duty. Astute business men quickly turned this legal nicety to their advantage. The public wanted war news and wanted it cheaply. The public should have war news and have it cheaply, but they would have to have nothing but war news if they were to escape the tax. Within months of the declaration of war, and weeks of the landing in the Crimea, there appeared, first in Edinburgh and then a few days later in Manchester, unstamped daily war newspapers selling at one penny. Manchester, indeed, had two: the *Daily War Telegraph* and the *War Express*.[1]

The established papers lodged a righteous protest. They virtuously paid the duty; why should these newcomers escape? The pirates had a legal case, but it was not watertight. The type of news they printed might be restricted, but their papers were designed for the general public, not for a particular class of readers. They met half the Inland Revenue's test of when a newspaper was not a newspaper, but only half. A deputation from the established Manchester papers went to London to lobby the Government. The Chancellor of the Exchequer, Mr Gladstone, and the Attorney-General interviewed the proprietor of the *Daily War Telegraph*; they were not convinced by his case and it was decided to issue writs against the pirate papers. Their owners paid up and raised their price to 2d. A few weeks later the *Telegraph* decided that it had little to fear and went back to a penny unstamped paper; the *Express* drew in its horns and became a 2d twice weekly paper until the tax came off. Then it boldly reverted to a daily paper, selling at a halfpenny on three days and twopence on the other two on which it was published – there was no Saturday *Express*. But both the *Telegraph* and the *Express* had miscalculated. The public proved less anxious to read about the tortuous peace negotiations than about the fall of

Sebastopol, and by the end of 1855 both the *Telegraph* and the *Express* were dead. But they had played a notable part in securing the abolition of the newspaper stamp duty.

The three principal Manchester newspapers, the Tory *Courier*, the Radical *Examiner and Times*, and the Liberal *Guardian*, were united in their protest against the unstamped press, but there their agreement stopped. The *Courier*, whose circulation seems to have been largely in the country districts, decided to remain a weekly paper and did not change its mind until 1864. The *Examiner and Times* defended itself against the war newspapers by itself becoming in effect a daily newspaper. Early in December 1854 it began to issue the *Manchester Daily Times* at 3d on Mondays, Tuesdays, Thursdays and Fridays, while retaining the price of 5d for its Wednesday and Saturday issues which kept the old name of the *Examiner and Times*. This was clearly only an interim measure until the stamp duty was repealed. On 2 June the proprietors announced that they would publish the *Manchester Daily Times* every morning at 1½d and the *Manchester Evening News*, 'a daily Paper for the People,' every afternoon at 1d. A week later they changed their mind and decided to concentrate on a penny morning paper called the *Manchester Daily Examiner and Times*. Publication began on 18 June, as soon as the repeal of the duty was through the Lords but before it had become law, provoking the *Guardian*'s wry comment that its rival's zeal to serve the public was greater than its desire to keep the law.

2

The *Guardian* remained a twice weekly paper for another fortnight. It had, of course, been planning for some time to become a daily: it had no alternative. There was a considerable overlap between the potential readership of the *Guardian* and the *Examiner*. Men bought one rather than the other because they preferred the opinions of the *Guardian* or the *Examiner*, but they expected to find the same hard news in both – reports of the commodity markets, the state of the cotton trade, the price of stocks and shares. Both gave racing results and betting, though the fact that the *Examiner*'s custom extended lower socially than the *Guardian*'s is perhaps indicated by the fact that the *Examiner* carried tipsters' advertisements while the *Guardian* at first confined itself to a single bookie's discreet announcement. The same social distinction may be the reason why the *Guardian* gave a regular list of 'hunting appointments' and the *Examiner* did not.

Certainly, once the *Examiner* became a daily paper, the *Guardian* had to do the same. The only question was whether it would have to charge the same price. Its readers could no doubt afford to pay twopence if the paper was worth it; that is to say, if it contained news that they could not obtain for a penny elsewhere. On the other hand, if the *Guardian* brought its price down to a penny a day it was doubtful whether it could afford to provide as good a service as it had formerly done for a net eightpence a week. The basic calculation was something like this. The *Guardian* would, in future, have to produce six papers a week instead of two. Each issue could, of course, be smaller; but, even so, it was necessary to budget for a 40 per cent increase in newsprint. It would need more staff; distribution costs would be increased; and more of the news would have to be sent by telegraph. Additional revenue would have to be found; more money from advertisers and subscribers. Recently the *Guardian*, like its principal rivals, had been selling at 5d a copy, of which one penny went in tax. If the price of the *Guardian* was fixed at a penny, there would be a loss of net revenue of 2d per subscriber a week. The circulation would have to go up by a third to break even – but more money was needed, not the same amount.

If the price was 2d there would be a net gain per subscriber of 2d a week. How elastic was the demand? How much could the *Guardian* hope to enlarge its circulation by selling at a penny, given the character which it had developed in its thirty-four years? On the other hand, could it hope at 2d to keep its existing circulation in competition with the penny *Examiner*? The owners of the *Guardian* could certainly provide the North with a 'quality' newspaper, to use the modern phrase, but were there enough people prepared to pay for one? The partners decided to find out. For the first time the price of the *Guardian* was decidedly out of step with its competitors. In future it would not be enough just to prefer the *Guardian*; the reader had to prefer it sufficiently to pay twice what the other paper cost.

The decision was no doubt made by the two senior partners, Jeremiah Garnett and Edward Taylor, a handsome young man of 25 with a shock of red hair. He had enjoyed as privileged an upbringing as a rich young Unitarian could be given. Oxford and Cambridge were still closed to dissenters, but he had lived long enough in Germany to master the language and to get to grips with the troubled political situation of 1848 and 1849. He knew the great picture galleries of Europe and had started his own art collection which was ultimately sold in 1912 for £358,000. He had lived in London and been called to the bar by the Inner Temple. He had travelled extensively – in 1852 he sent his sister 'a hasty note by express dromedary from Akabah' as he was on his way back to Manchester to take up work on the *Guardian*. He had inherited a half share in the copyright, and he was soon to acquire the other half from his brother's widow. In 1854 she married a Frenchman, M. Delbrück, after some family opposition and went to live in France.[2] By 1858 Edward Taylor completed the purchase of her share in the copyright and became, as his father had been, sole proprietor of the *Manchester Guardian*.

By fixing the price of the *Guardian* at 2d, the partners had virtually undertaken to sell not only a more frequent but a better supply of news. The most marked change was in the development for the first time of a regular foreign news service of its own. It seems likely that this was Edward Taylor's contribution, for in later years he was to egg on a sometimes reluctant C. P. Scott into finding suitable foreign correspondents. Moreover, Garnett, who continued as principal editor, was perhaps too much an old-fashioned North countryman to think this kind of extravagance justified. 'If one of his literary staff consulted him upon an important political topic,' wrote one who knew him in the 1850s, 'he would maintain a stolid imperturbability of countenance and go on reading his paper as if he had no concern in the matter – suddenly remarking that Buckstone was about to visit the Theatre Royal or that there had been a bloody murder at West Bromwich which reminded him of a similar tragedy at Heckmondwike five-and-twenty years ago.' It does not sound as if he would have been the man to suggest enlisting foreign correspondents.

3

The first, and certainly the best, of these *Guardian* foreign correspondents was the regular Paris contributor, whose identity was hidden even in the business ledger under the symbol M.X. His first letters appeared while the paper was still a twice weekly; from July onwards he contributed a regular half column or column daily. Sometimes there was a second contributor from Paris and occasionally a third – the international exhibition of 1856 was covered by J. O. Murray, and the peace conference which ended the Crimean War was separately reported. But, while we have notes of payments to Francis, Clifford, Murray and G. Haller, by far the biggest sums went to M.X. – nearly £470 in the fifteen months from March 1855 to June 1856. The total cost of the Paris service for this period was over £700.

This Paris service was gradually reinforced by the appointment of correspondents in other European capitals. The *Guardian* was represented in Belgium by C. White who sent letters each day and fairly frequent telegrams. Brussels, with its uncensored press, was a good listening post for European affairs during the Crimean War. The Russian Embassy established in Brussels its own paper, *Le Nord*, while the *Independance Belge*, perhaps the leading European paper of the time, followed a pro-French but anti-English line. Almost as regular and long were the letters from Vienna, where Lambert was the correspondent, and from Berlin; a little less frequent and shorter were those from Hamburg and Frankfurt. By the autumn there were regular weekly letters from Naples and early in 1857 from New York, where the correspondent, although 'a thorough-bred American', congratulated the *Guardian* on the *Persia* regaining the blue ribbon of the Atlantic with a crossing in 9 days 12 hours and 40 minutes – 'Britannia again rules the waves.' There were less frequent messages from Raikes at Danzig, from Marseilles and Lisbon. All these articles were described as 'from our own correspondent.' This phrase did not mean, as it would to-day, a full-time member of the paper's staff, but it did imply that the writer was regularly retained to write special articles for the *Guardian*.

It is not possible to say exactly how much this foreign service cost because of the inconsistent way in which the ledgers were kept. There are headings which show the Paris, Brussels, Vienna and Hamburg services for 1855–6 and, for part of 1856 only, the Naples correspondence. But the Berlin, Frankfurt, New York and other costs cannot be determined. The known total amounts to £2,120. 19. 11, of which about a quarter is specifically assigned to telegrams. Perhaps £2,500 would be a fair estimate of the cost of the *Guardian*'s own foreign service in its first year as a daily.

There was one obvious gap – there was no special *Guardian* news from the front. This had still to be taken from the London papers. *Guardian* readers enjoyed the dispatches of W. H. Russell, the first of the great Victorian war correspondents, but they were, of course, copied from the *Times*. What they got from the paper's own correspondents was a stereoscopic view of the war as it looked from the different countries. Beyond this, they were provided with a good deal of information about political, social and economic conditions in a variety of European countries, a fair dose of heavy moralising, a certain amount of literary and artistic news and, especially from Paris, a rich store of political anecdote much of which is still entertainingly fresh to-day. Marx and Engels, at least, found the *Guardian*'s foreign correspondence well worthwhile as a source for their weekly articles for the *New York Tribune*. One story which particularly caught Engels's fancy was about the music critic of the *Monde* who, in spite of the law which forced all articles to be signed with the writer's true name, was allowed to use a pseudonym for his work for the official *Moniteur*. On the strength of this double identity he managed to extort two salaries from the prima donna at the opera for guaranteeing her favourable notices from himself and from his colleague on the *Moniteur*. Marx asked Engels to send him X's articles from time to time, remarking, 'Your *Manchester Guardian* has the special honour of being regarded as the immediate occasion for Bonaparte's declaration against the English press.' M.X. had been drawing attention to the misery of the poor and attacking Napoleon III's morals.[3]

These messages from the European capitals recall a vanished Europe which was half-strange and half-familiar to the merchants of the equally vanished mid-nineteenth century Manchester. Their writers tried to interpret for Lancashire readers something of the feel of the cities in which they lived:

the *Paris* in which M.X. with his own ears 'heard colonels and generals, tolerably forward in the Emperor's favour, say "The war is all very well; for that matter as good as, or better than Algeria; but it is difficult for the life of one to see what France has to do with it" ' (3 July 1855);

in which, so M.X. believed, the censor had deleted from General Pelissier's dispatch its opening sentence: 'I have followed your order and plans, as you commanded me to do, and, as I foresaw, have failed entirely' (7 July 1855);

and the *Paris* in which Prince Napoleon, the Emperor's nephew, gave a small party to intellectuals of the left – George Sand, Proudhon, Rostand among them – and invited them to vote on the existence of God: all voted 'Non' except the host who put in a blank paper (6 February 1856);

the *Naples* in which the fraudulent Finance Minister 'was never known to confer a favour and, that he might never learn to say "yes", had always avoided marriage' until he was forced to marry a peasant girl on his death-bed in order to get absolution (19 December 1855);

and where 'as usual we have been praying and peddling; where the King has been to Monte Cassino and back, as also to Monte Vergine, where he left a silver lamp worth 9,000 ducats – a monument to his devotion, and a bribe for protection' (5 May 1856);

the *Brussels* where 'the day may come when Englishmen, one and all, may say, "Let France take Belgium if she pleases!" What has Belgium done for us that we should draw our purse strings or our swords in her defence? Our allies have shared our dangers and our triumphs. Let their reward be taken at their own door' (3 July 1855);

the *Vienna* from which army reservists had to go home to gather the harvest but also the *Vienna* from which the *Guardian* correspondent sent a description of a fancy dress ball at the Hofburg with the names and costumes of the Bavarian and Austrian nobility who took part (2 February 1856);

and the *Berlin* which was so annoyed by Queen Victoria's visit to Paris that 'all the anti-bilious pills consumed by Queen Victoria's lieges, added to those engulfed by the free and dyspeptic citizens of the United States, would fail to disperse the gall stirred up in the gastric organs of the Prusso-Russians by the new rivet added to the anti-Muscovite alliance' (23 August 1855).

4

The home news service was not neglected. There was little need to do anything to the news gathering side in Manchester, where tireless John Harland continued to combine pioneering historical research with the superintendence of a Unitarian Sunday School and an inflexible pursuit of perfection in reporting. He knew how to collect a team of able men. He inspired affection in some; fear in others: 'His love of verbal accuracy amounted almost to a passion, this, and the severe discipline he considered necessary . . . created an admiration for Mr Harland's character which in the minds of some deepened into affection, while upon those less soldierly in disposition it produced the impression . . . of an austere and iron rule.'[4] Twenty years after Harland's retirement a friend recalled that Harland 'in his profession was of the *Ursa Major* constellation . . . but at supper the gentle, genial host stood revealed.' Perhaps that was why his rule was effective.

The problem was to secure a London news service of equal calibre. Part of this had already been achieved. The 'letters from private correspondents' had for some years provided a combination of the arts of the lobby correspondent, the parliamentary sketch writer and the general columnist. These were, and indeed often still are, good reading. But mid-nineteenth-century readers wanted in addition as good a straight report of what was said in parliament as of what was said in Manchester. They were not getting it. Readers knew they would get strong comment from the leading articles; they wanted to be in a position to make up their own minds whether what the *Guardian* said was justified. It was in a sense a bargain between the paper and its readers. In the old days of twice weekly publication it was possible to rely on the London newspaper reports for most of the parliamentary news. The only trouble was the Tuesday and Friday sittings – and then, as now, Friday was a light day for MPs. Daily publication, however,

meant that every day's reports, if they were to get into the next morning's paper, had to be sent by telegraph and this was a costly business.
The telegraph companies were quick to see that there was money in
supplying news as well as in sending it. They established their own
news agency and sold its products as a package deal. Unfortunately it
was a thoroughly bad package. The reports of parliament were little
better than most papers carry to-day, and that was not nearly good
enough for our ancestors.

The only solution was for the *Guardian* to have its own parliamentary reporters. Each day from the beginning of the 1856 session two
to five columns of parliamentary news was proudly headed 'from our
own reporters; by the Electric Telegraph Company.' Except for late
night sittings they covered the whole proceedings. The payments to
the four or five reporters amounted to about £22 a week during the
session. Long special reports were also given of the Crimean War
enquiry.[5] Manchester readers got their fill of serious London news
competently reported by the *Guardian* staff. They also had their full
complement of more popular news: thirty-four columns were given
up to 'our own reporter's' account of Madeline Smith's trial at Edinburgh.[6] The sums paid to the telegraph companies were becoming
substantial. The total cost, excluding foreign telegrams, for the first
year of the *Guardian* as a daily seems to have been a little over £1,200.

The one field in which no progress was made was in the appearance
of the paper. Its arrangement was orderly enough. But the foreign
messages from the *Guardian*'s own correspondents were grouped together with headlines no more illuminating than the invariable opening,
'The Continent', followed in smaller type by 'France', 'Prussia',
'Belgium', or even, though a faint double rule separated the hemi-
spheres, by 'The United States.' The leading articles now carried no
titles at all, a step backwards; and, though the home news headings
were a little more informative than the foreign, the smaller type used
and the intolerable compression of the lines make reading difficult and
unattractive. The *Guardian* had more to say than its rival the *Examiner*;
it had basically the same space. It therefore looked a good deal worse.

There were two levels of comment in the *Guardian* as well as
straightforward factual reporting. The editor took full responsibility
for the leading articles. These were now often the work of H. M. Acton,
who joined the staff in 1848. If he sometimes set about him with a
bludgeon, it was with the full approval of Jeremiah Garnett. Sophia
Taylor might privately whisper to her uncle that 'such expressions as
raw-head and bloody-bones are very little to my taste', but she came to
the sensible conclusion that 'with regard to Mr Acton, I suppose the

less we grumble the better.'* It was a man's world, and a rather rough man's world. But there was now also in the paper a second level of comment – perhaps commentary is a better word – from the regular London and foreign correspondents. They were, of course, chosen by the editor; and were chosen partly at least because they were in general sympathy with his outlook. But they had a freedom of expression which a leader-writer in Manchester did not enjoy. On occasion, what they wrote was taken up, corrected or even contradicted in the leader columns; but it was still printed. They seem, indeed, to have been given a greater latitude of expression than they would get to-day, but then they were not, of course, full-time members of the staff.

Sometimes, no doubt, they were deliberately used for flying a kite without committing the paper. In 1856 one of the London private correspondents reported a rumour that the illness which kept John Bright out of the House of Commons was 'diplomatic.' The *Examiner* was full of righteous indignation and the *Guardian* defended itself in a leader which sets out clearly the relation between the paper and its 'private correspondents':

Of the story we did not, and do not, believe a single word. We have not the slightest doubt about the reality of Mr Bright's illness . . . we have, on more than one occasion, warned our readers against accepting the statements of our correspondents with implicit faith. Perhaps it would have been as well if we had repeated our caution in reference to the letter of our London correspondent, but at the time we did not think it worth while . . . Of course with the usual amount of honesty and candour which governs the lucubrations of the *Examiner*, the writer . . . treats (the statement) all through his column of verbiage as if we made it editorially.'[7]

5

It follows that the *Guardian*'s own line is only safely to be inferred from its leading articles. The paper under Garnett was genuinely concerned to defend the cause of individual liberty, even the liberty of unpopular

---

* Sophia Scott-Russell Scott 12 October 1848: 'Raw-head and bloody bones,' were perhaps traditional *Guardian* expressions. They occur, for instance, in leading articles ten years before Acton's appointment. Acton mellowed:

'Gentle as Galahad, he sought
The dusty corners of our hearts
And quaintly there the sunshine brought
With dear, imaginative arts.'

(Memorial verses in the Papers of the Manchester Literary Club, 1907.)

minorities such as Roman Catholics. On this it had a better record than the *Examiner*. It supported the grant to Maynooth, the Irish Roman Catholic seminary. It defended a Roman Catholic customs officer whom the *Liverpool Journal* had denounced as a 'traitor' and 'villain' because he belonged to a society for the conversion of England. It maintained that an Irish friar who had publicly burned Protestant bibles ought not to have been prosecuted for an offence against religion, but merely for conduct likely to cause a breach of the peace: 'The Bible can vindicate its own claims to respect; or, if it cannot, no assistance from attorney-generals will help it.' It strongly supported the 1857 Divorce Bill; but was still convinced that murderers should hang, condemning the extreme reluctance of juries to convict and 'the far more criminal lenity of the Home Office' in advising reprieves. It opposed Sabbatarian restrictions on Sunday trading and bands in the royal parks, and regretted Lord Palmerston's 'surrender to puritanical clamour': 'It is all nonsense to pretend that such a man as Lord Palmerston has been diverted from the current of his humour by a pastoral expostulation from the Archbishop of Canterbury . . .'[8]

Lord Palmerston could be wrong, then, in Garnett's eyes, but very seldom. There was a natural affinity between them. That side of Garnett's character which was devoted to field sports, and his love of a glass of wine and a bawdy story on which Engels remarked* – this made it natural that he should find 'the most English minister' a sympathetic character. Garnett's views on foreign affairs stand clearly out in a leader written in the middle period of the Crimean War. He denounced the pledge we had given that Russia should not suffer territorially from the war because it underwrote 'the gigantic crime of subjugated Poland, annexed and blotted out in defiance of the treaties of 1815, filled with a restless, indignant and warlike population,' and 'lost us the moral support of the popular party throughout Europe.'[9]

A man who thought like this was not likely to be happy with John Bright, the Quaker pacifist, as a member for Manchester. Their mutual dislike was an old story. It went back to the time when the Anti-Corn Law League first became a political machine. It was sharpened in 1846 when Garnett had tried to prevent Bright becoming the Liberal candidate for Manchester. 'I met Garnett, the editor of the *Guardian*, yesterday,' Bright noted in his diary. 'He was dining at the Club and I sat almost close to him. We had some conversation and I told him what I thought of him. He was subdued and felt most awk-

* 'ein weiser Mann in his own mind eine Art Orakel bei einigen Philistern, in übrigen ein Zotenreiser und gemässigter Kneipeier.' Engels-Marx 12 December 1855 (Gemsamtausgabe III 2 (1930)).

wardly situated.'[10] Reluctantly, Garnett had supported Bright in 1852 because free trade could not yet be regarded as safe if the Tories won.

But the situation was different in 1857 when Bright and Milner Gibson, the sitting members, stood again, though Bright was sick in Italy and took no part in the campaign. Garnett took the lead in finding two Palmerstonian Liberals to oppose them, and young Edward Taylor joined their finance committee. Garnett had two objectives – first to see that Bright 'did not misrepresent Manchester and thereby cause the state of opinion prevalent here to be misconceived throughout Europe';[11] and, secondly, to put an end to the influence of the Anti-Corn Law League. This had been kept alive as a radical political machine operating in Manchester and district, long after the purpose for which it had been founded by, among others, Jeremiah Garnett, had been achieved. The electors agreed with Garnett on both points. Bright and Milner Gibson, who in 1852 had been top of the poll in every ward but one, were bottom in every ward in 1857 on a very much higher poll.

Milner Gibson and Cobden, who took an active part in Bright's campaign, both went out of their way to make strong, personal attacks on Garnett and the *Guardian*. In the Free Trade Hall, Milner Gibson, who had chaired the Select Committee on Newspaper Stamps in 1851, put down part of Jeremiah Garnett's hostility to him to the part he had taken in getting rid of the stamp duty – 'he was a free trader who did not like free trade in newspapers.' But it was Cobden who was really vitriolic:

'The vermin of your Manchester press, the ghouls of the *Guardian*,' he said 'are preying upon this splendid being (Bright), and trying to make a martyr of him in the midst of his suffering. (Applause) What are the motives by which these men are actuated? Are they public motives? (No, no) . . . where is the public ground? (Hear, hear) Where is there one fact? What have you had alleged against this man? No; it is a vile, dirty, contemptible – (applause) – a nasty, vile fireside jealousy (Applause). I will deal very candidly with you in this respect . . . I believe that the hostility is a personal one (Hear, hear).'[12]

The day after this report in the *Guardian*, Garnett played it cool. He referred to Bright as a manly and straightforward antagonist, and indeed he had been careful to take this line throughout the campaign. He was magnanimous too in victory. No sooner was the poll over than the *Guardian* hoped that when Bright recovered he would find another seat. In 1857 it still mattered what place a man sat for. The members for a few great constituencies – the West Riding and Manchester, for instance – had more influence than the members for small constituencies not far removed from pocket boroughs. Much of the *Guardian*'s opposition to Bright was on the ground that he sat for the wrong seat; that it was a reflection on the whole country when the 'second city of the Empire,' as the *Guardian* frequently described Manchester, was represented by so unrepresentative an Englishman as a Quaker pacifist.

The Manchester election of 1857 was a triumph for the *Guardian*. Of course the coalition of Disraeli, Lord John Russell and Richard Cobden which had defeated the Government was united only in its opposition to Palmerston. But the election came unexpectedly; there was less than four weeks between the government's defeat and polling in Manchester. The Anti-Corn Law League had an unrivalled reputation for 'managing' elections, and the *Examiner* provided strong newspaper support for Bright. Bright's opponents had neither organisation nor until a week before polling day had they found a second candidate to fight the two-member constituency. Their principal assets were the support of the *Guardian* and the determination of Garnett. Manchester was one of the few boroughs to poll on the first day of the election. What Manchester thought on Saturday, 27 March proved to be what England was thinking. It was what Garnett had been saying for the past three years. He used to look back on the 1857 election as the most satisfying moment of his forty years on the paper.

CHAPTER TEN

'A Damned Close Run Thing'

I

GARNETT's triumph over the Manchester election of March 1857 was
followed almost at once by a period of great peril in the affairs of the
Guardian. For some time things looked so black that the partners
wondered whether they could survive, and Garnett certainly might
well have applied to the struggle with the Manchester *Examiner* what
the Duke of Wellington said about Waterloo – 'a damned close run
thing.'

Both the twopenny *Guardian* and the penny *Examiner* had an
extensive circulation throughout the North as well as an intensive
circulation in Manchester and district. For the first half-dozen years
after the repeal of the stamp duty the only other English daily newspapers published to the north and east of Manchester, apart from two
short-lived ventures, were the *Sheffield Daily Telegraph*, which started
daily publication in 1855, and, from 1858, the *Newcastle Chronicle*. It
was not until 1861 that the *Leeds Mercury* and the *Newcastle Journal*
became dailies. Birmingham was without a daily paper until 1857.
The *Guardian*'s extensive circulation was of particular value commer-
cially because it was among 'men of substance' and therefore it helped
to make the *Guardian* a successful advertising medium for the sale of
property over a very wide area. A typical summer week in 1855, for
instance, produced advertisements for the sale of property in Anglesey,
Cumberland, County Durham, Denbighshire, Glamorgan, Ireland, the
Isle of Man, Lincolnshire, Radnorshire, Scotland, Shropshire, and all
three Ridings of Yorkshire besides all parts of the *Guardian*'s home
counties of Lancashire and Cheshire. (It also incidentally included an
announcement of the forthcoming auction at Liverpool of a male and
female rhinoceros fresh from Assam, to be followed shortly by the sale
of two young elephants still in transit; but that is by the way.)

No doubt Manchester merchants might be interested in buying a
castle in Wales, but they would hardly be concerned to know week by
week where distant packs of fox hounds were meeting. But in the late
1850s and early 1860s the *Guardian* regularly gave under the heading of

'The Chase' a list of 'hunting appointments', including, to the north and east, those of the Bedale Foxhounds, the Bramham Moor, the Craven and the Craven Harriers, the Easingwold Harriers and the York and Ainsty; to the south and west, those of the Albrighton, the Atherstone, the Bosworth, the Cheshire, the Meynell, the North Staffordshire, the Earl of Stamford's, and Sir W. W. Wynn's. These lists indicate a widely dispersed and moneyed readership which was important both in its own right and for the sake of advertisers.

The *Guardian* and the *Examiner* were published almost next door to one another – the site of the *Examiner* building was included in the 1929 extension to the *Guardian* office. This must have made it easy to keep an eye on each other's purely local sales. What the other paper was doing farther afield was more difficult to find out. During its first two years as a daily the *Guardian* circulation remained between nine and ten thousand on Wednesdays and Saturdays and was between five and six thousand on other days. But early in 1857 Peter Allen, the business manager who was also Edward Taylor's brother-in-law, began to suspect that his paper was being seriously outsold beyond Manchester by the *Examiner*, whose daily print he estimated to be 18,000 to 20,000. Accordingly, as he wrote to Henry Boyce, his kinsman and predecessor as manager:

'In September I set out to take a long journey through Yorkshire and the North, resolving to collect particulars respecting the position of the two papers from town to town. This investigation afforded me conclusive evidence that the *Guardian* was fast losing its claim to be *the* Lancashire paper. I found generally that where we were sending dozens, the *Examiner* sent hundreds; having hurried home I communicated these facts to the firm, the result was an unanimous conclusion that a reduction in price was necessary and we were fully persuaded too that a fight *on their own terms* was inevitable. The question of time was discussed. I advocated immediate change in which view Edward Taylor concurred, and after a day or two's hesitancy it was resolved upon, the greatest secrecy was preserved, not a soul in the office but the firm had an idea of the change until the announcement was sent up for composition to appear in the paper on Saturday, October 3. Although the *sudden* change was accompanied by many inconveniences in the printing department, it gave us an immense advantage in other ways. It prevented the *Examiner* people from "setting their house in order" to meet the new competition by improvements in their paper, and enabled us to create a sudden demand for the best penny paper, the result was a circulation of 15,000 the first day, October 5th., since that day there has been (and still is) a gradual and steady upward tendency. The *every day* sale is now 20,000 which frequently rises to 23,000 or 24,000 and on Saturdays a steady 33,000, showing perhaps an average circulation of 23,000 a day.'[1]

Peter Allen had made his discoveries in time to prevent the *Guardian*'s advertising revenue being affected as it would have been, he felt, had the *Examiner*'s lead in circulation been left long unchallenged. In the two and a half years of the *Guardian*'s daily publication each quarter's advertising had shown an improvement over the corresponding quarter of the previous year:

COLUMNS OF ADVERTISING

	1855	1856	1857
Jan.-March	575*	692	747
April-June	627*	677	845
July-Sept.	711	748	834
Oct.-Dec.	639	709	792**

* Bi-weekly only
** Price reduced to penny

The decline quarter by quarter in the last six months of 1857 was a reflection of the profound economic depression of that winter.

2

It was a pity that Peter Allen had not made his discovery six months before. He and his partners had ordered new plant and equipment suitable only for a daily paper with a small circulation. 'It became immediately necessary for the proprietors to obtain new and swifter machinery. This they did, but it is in getting their new machinery to work, under the pressure of an increasingly urgent demand, that the proprietors have been embarrassed by constant delays in the course of publication and by the fact that new machinery will not normally produce satisfactory work.'*

Three months later the firm was still having to bring into use and to pay for additional American machinery which was already unsuitable before it was introduced. This was a new four-feeder Hoe press, that is to say, a press which was simultaneously fed by hand with sheets of paper at four different points. It could print 8,000 impressions an hour – adequate for the *Guardian*'s sale in September 1857; quite inadequate for its sale in March 1858 when it was brought into use. But the machine

* M.G. 16 November 1857. But the 'new machinery' cannot be held responsible for that collector's piece, the leader page of the *Guardian* of Friday, February 12, 1858, which though correctly dated at the top, bore the date line Friday, February 11 immediately above the leading article. What half Manchester thought to-day, England knew was yesterday.

was already on board ship before the decision to reduce the price of the *Guardian* had been made. At the end of its trial run, Peter Allen reported that it was working well, but admitted that its purchase had been a mistake and that a six- or eight-feeder was 'looming in the distance.' A six-feeder must, in fact, have been ordered almost at once, for in December 1858 Edward Taylor was already negotiating the terms on which two new Hoe eight-feeders, costing £10,000, were to be purchased. Taylor wanted his existing six-feeder to be taken in part exchange at its full cost price, less depreciation for wear and tear at 10 per cent per annum, and a discount of 15 per cent on the new machines.[2]

Running costs inevitably rose in the effort to raise circulation. Delivery arrangements in the city were improved so that in February 1858 the *Guardian* was able to announce that subscribers living within four miles of the centre of the city would get their copies delivered before eight o'clock and, if they wanted to take advantage of the discount for cash, they had only to let the office know and the collector would call. A month after the *Guardian* became a penny paper an evening edition with a market report was started on Tuesdays, 'high 'Change' day. From the beginning of 1858 there was an evening edition every day at 3.30 p.m. This took the place of the occasional late editions which had long been produced when especially important news was received. Although it remained possible to buy a special stamped edition, for the post, this was decreasingly used and by 1864 the average number of stamped copies sold per day was under 250.[3] The country circulation of the *Guardian* had to be reorganised on the basis of train parcels and an extensive network of newsagents. A vigorous circulation campaign was carried on in outlying districts which required at least some additional staff on a temporary basis – one of the very few business letters surviving from this period is a 'reference' for a man who had been employed in this work in the northern counties.

3

The money needed to finance the new penny *Guardian* had to be found at a difficult time for the partners. Edward Taylor had just withdrawn all his liquid capital from the partnership, and indeed had borrowed from the firm in order to pay off his sister-in-law's capital and to buy her share in the copyright, thus becoming 'sole proprietor.' Emily Taylor, Russell Scott Taylor's widow, had married M. Jules Delbrück in 1854 – at first the family had thought he was after her money, but before the marriage took place they found his conduct to have been 'most proper and honourable' and were 'convinced of his unselfish attachment.' Nevertheless, there were difficulties about the financial transactions. Madame Delbrück's capital had been paid out in 1856, but in the summer of 1858 it was necessary to strike a special half-year's balance to determine how much was owing to her under the arrangement for the transfer of copyright. This showed a debit balance of £150 compared with a profit of £6,000 six months before and of over £12,500 on the eve of daily publication. Letters from Taylor to his London solicitor show that the Delbrücks were quite naturally pressing for access to the firm's books for purposes of verification. Taylor had told Garnett and Peter Allen about this family difficulty but had kept his other partners, John Harland and Robert Dowman, in the dark. Their consent, however, would be necessary before a scrutiny of the books could take place. How the difficulty was solved we do not know, but the Allens, Taylors and Delbrücks remained on friendly terms.[4]

The money needed for the new developments could not therefore be provided by Edward Taylor. It came from the senior of his partners and from his relations. In 1857 two of Peter Allen's relations provided an additional thousand pounds, and the next year Garnett put in two thousand pounds of new capital, and Taylor's two Scott uncles, Robert Scott of Bath and Russell Scott, the father of C. P. Scott, lent five hundred pounds each. The partners practised and enforced the most rigid economies. During the whole of the crisis year of 1858 Peter Allen, whose wife had a little money in her own right, drew nothing from the firm, and Jeremiah Garnett, who had other investments, drew only £275. The partners as a group took from the firm that year only half the average sum for the six years from 1855 to 1860. When the final balance for 1858 came to be struck the first half-year's loss of £150 had been turned into a profit of £2,179. 9. 2 – a small enough margin, but certainly better than the cost of 'a champagne dinner at the Albion', which at the beginning of the year Peter Allen had thought would swallow up the firm's profits. 'It is fortunate that the *Guardian* has made money' (in the past), to quote him further, 'and as Sharpe of St Helen's expresses it, "driven a tenpenny nail through it", or where should we be now, eh?'[5]

The need for new capital had come not only at the wrong time personally for the partners in Taylor, Garnett & Co., but when trade was very bad. Engels reported in December 1857 that business men could not bear to go home to their wives and families, but stayed drinking in their clubs to keep their courage up.[6] But by the early spring of 1858 the general business picture was better. The partners in Taylor,

Garnett & Co. found that they had weathered the storm. They made new arrangements and for the next few years the profits were distributed equally between them instead of the old arrangement by which the two senior partners took 70 per cent of the profits in approximately equal shares. The new arrangement was presumably a recognition of the equality of sacrifices that all had made.

There can be no doubt about the severity of the crisis. Something of its impact can still be felt and its progress traced in the letters of Sophia Allen to her uncle, Russell Scott:

11 December, 1857: 'Your letter seemed so refreshing. It turned my thoughts from their everlasting round of business and anxiety and economical plans ... We are so unwilling to part with our pretty home that we are advertising* to let it furnished for two or three years, intending to go to lodgings . . . Of course, Moor End will also be too expensive; indeed Edward means I believe to go into lodgings himself . . . The *Examiner* people are fighting desperately and I sometimes think success is a matter of the longest purse. The loss on the Saturday's publication is very serious, more than £2,000 a year. I assure you we are all rather down-hearted; it is trying to break up two happy homes and both Edward and my husband are often sadly overdone.'

16 December, 1857: 'Our home is not let, but I have just written answers to three answers . . . Moor End is also advertised . . .'

26 January, 1858: 'The newspaper battle goes better, I think. Edward keeps up his spirits wonderfully, and it is really almost amusing to see his strict economy. I could scarcely have believed in such a sudden change. The want of capital will be the greatest stumbling block, I fear . . .'

9 March, 1858: 'At Moor End things are not very comfortable as they have only one servant and a girl, and are living in a kind of transition state . . . The circulation increases and perhaps things altogether look rather brighter. The new advertising office is very convenient and *aristocratic* looking . . .'

2 April, 1858: 'Moor End is almost let.'

20 April, 1858: 'Edward himself is practising very strict economy, and all his alterations in the business tend that way more and more, so that I expect there will be a profit next year, if not this . . .'

18 June, 1858: (Moor End obviously let and the Taylors gone but) 'I really think we may hope to remain as long as we like; advertisements are improving wonderfully and this and a careful reduction in unnecessary expenditure will ensure some profit . . .'

* To Let: Dwelling Houses: Furnished house to let in a healthy situation 2½ miles from Exchange, contains three sitting and five bedrooms. Address Y 86 at the printer's (*Manchester Guardian* 12 December 1857).

9 June, 1859: 'Edward is not looking at all well. I hope he will contrive to get more assistance with the night work . . .'

1 December, 1859: 'Are not the advertisements grand?' 'There is life in the old dog yet" . . .'

And when the 1859 balance was struck the profit was back to over £6,000.

There can be little doubt that Sophia Allen was right in pointing to lack of capital as the *Guardian*'s main problem in 1857 and 1858. The *Examiner* was a good, straight party paper. It had very wealthy men behind it. The *Guardian* was a paper with a cross-bench mind which, however well adapted to the fluid politics of the 1850s, was exasperating to professional politicians and unlikely to attract their financial support. Nor would its almost pathologically independent-minded partners have accepted support which had any suggestion of strings attached to it. The *Examiner* pretty certainly had the deeper purse, but the *Guardian*'s proved just deep enough to keep it going while it was adapting itself to the new conditions of newspaper production. There was no doubt of its ability in the long run to attract sufficient readers and advertisers. In fact, the 1860s were to be a period of great prosperity for the paper, but it had been 'a damned close run thing.'

4

Fortunately the need to increase circulation to the point at which a penny paper would pay coincided with a renewed public interest in news. The news-hungry readers fascinated by the Crimean War had carried the *Guardian* easily through the transition from a twice weekly fivepenny to a twopenny daily paper. Then interest lessened and sales fell a little. But by the time Peter Allen was becoming afraid of the *Examiner*, the Indian mutiny – or, as the *Guardian* insisted more correctly in writing, the Indian mutinies – made men once again anxious for all the news they could get. It was a reasonable moment to cut the price and multiply the sales of a newspaper.

The *Guardian* had a line of its own on Indian affairs. Back in 1855 its London correspondent had welcomed 'Clemency' Canning's appointment as Governor-General because he would gain 'the confidence of the natives of India by cultivating a friendly, social intercourse with the educated classes of Hindoo.'[7] When the mutiny began, the *Guardian* commented:

'The English officer, from being the friend, the comrade and the adviser of his native followers, has become in too many instances, haughty, insolent and vain . . . looking at his military profession only as a stepping stone to dignified civil employment, and the speedy acquisition of wealth . . .' (1 August, 1857)

A fortnight later the *Guardian* was still temperately looking for the causes of the trouble. It found one in the fear of proselytising:

'Statesmen are not much given to proselytising; it is a task for which they have no leisure, and possibly no peculiar inclination. Col Wheeler seems to have forgotten that he acted as Caesar's servant . . . The calling of a missionary is a high and sacred one; but it is wholly incompatible with the duties of an officer commanding a native regiment.' (14 August, 1857)

These two themes recur as, for instance, in the following extracts.

' "Are the gentlemen who now come out to India of a different caste from those of former days?" was the question of a Sepoy to a European officer who preserved the confidence of his men – a question of the gravest significance.' (25 August 1857)

'England has governed in India well, tenderly and justly; as no nation of ancient or modern times ever yet governed a distant dependency . . . we regard as the most striking merit of our representatives in India that, while bringing English earnestness and Christian enlightenment to guide them in their work, they have consistently remembered that the people over whom they had to rule were not, and did not desire to be, either English or Christian.' (7 October, 1857)

A little later another note comes in:

'The principle which should preside over every arrangement . . . is that of unfaltering confidence in our right to rule over the native population by virtue of our inherent superiority. We believe ourselves to have received this great commission from the hand of nature . . . if we have begun to admit any doubts in our own minds as to the validity of our title, the attempt to retain our sovereignty will be equally culpable and vain.' (9 December, 1857)

And when all was nearly over:

'We have no motive for sparing the city of Lucknow, and have a sufficient park of artillery to crush it into dust. Let us hope that none but the guilty will suffer . . . It will be difficult to discriminate . . . Still we have great confidence in our troops and their leader. As they are strong, so may they be merciful.' (1 April, 1858)

These extracts, of course, are all from leading articles. Readers could expect characteristic and individual comment in the *Guardian* but they could not expect an independent news service. These were the days, before there was a cable to India, of great competition between London newspapers to be the first with the news from the East. Rival papers spent immense sums on developing rival routes. The *Guardian* did not, and could not, compete in these struggles. Nor had it any need to. The slowness of hand composition – the linotype was still many years away – and the slowness of trains, coupled with the speed of the telegraph, meant that the *Guardian* could not be beaten by the London newspapers in its own northern market. In their own area the *Guardian* and the *Examiner* were equally well placed to receive and use the Indian news of the London papers. To the provincial dailies, the Indian mutiny brought a great demand for news without a great expense in providing it.

5

It was just as well that it did. There was no money to spare in the *Guardian* office in 1857-8 for fresh news-gathering ventures, although both circulation and advertising were up. 'We have maintained, as you will doubtless see, all the mercantile advertisements and the current events of the day intact,' Peter Allen wrote, 'although the *Examiner* have posted this town for months that they will insert "wanted" advertisements twenty words for sixpence and so on.' Only the shops were lacking: they found the *Guardian* rates too high.[8] The table below, which carries on the story from that on page 130, shows how well-founded Allen's confidence was:

COLUMNS OF ADVERTISING

	1857	1858
Jan.-March	747	769
April-June	845	923
July-Sept.	834	
Oct.-Dec.	792*	

* Price reduced to a penny

One can understand Allen's plaintive question and answer. 'Where you will ask is the profit? The answer is nowhere. All the fine revenue from advertisements is swallowed up in expenses.' Certainly economies were necessary. Nothing could be done about the size of the paper – the four-page issues from Monday to Friday could not be further reduced and, although Saturday's paper was twice the size, the pressure of advertisements was so great that in two weeks out of three there was less space for news on Saturday than any other day. Indeed, on 12 June 1858, when over two columns of advertisements had to be held over, there were less than ten columns of news out of the forty-eight. And yet it was on the Saturday issues that the loss was especially high – £2,000 a year according to Sophia Allen. The main factor was the price of paper which after a steady fall through the first half of the century had risen steadily in the 1850s, partly because of the increased import of rags into the United States and partly because cotton mills which used to give away their waste were selling it for £8 a ton by 1860. There was also still a duty on paper, which constituted a heavy burden. Its repeal in 1861, for instance, saved the *Daily Telegraph* £12,000 a year.

The obvious and easy way to economise was to reduce editorial expenses. This was probably put in hand at once to judge from the letters of Peter Allen and his wife, but the effects were not immediately visible, presumably because of existing contracts. The messages from the *Guardian*'s own foreign correspondents withered faster away. Taylor first tried to spread the cost of his special parliamentary reports by getting other like-minded papers at a safe distance from Manchester to share the service. He approached the *Birmingham Daily Post*, which suggested forming a wider group than Taylor had suggested and would apparently have brought in the *Manchester Examiner*. This, of course, was unacceptable: 'You cannot expect for a moment I should concur in any scheme to enable . . . my opponents to get for nothing what I have to pay for handsomely . . . but as your objections are solely those of expense . . . I will for a time take the risk of cost myself and you shall tell me what expense per week you think would be within your means.'[9] The answer to this letter of Taylor's has not survived. In the end the *Guardian* dropped its special reports at the end of the 1861 session, probably because of increased telegraph rates. The messages from the *Guardian*'s own foreign correspondents withered faster away.

COLUMNS OF SPECIAL FOREIGN NEWS

1857 October	25	1858 January	20	1858 April	10
November	29	February	15	May	8
December	27	March	11	June	7

There were no messages from New York, Berlin or Hamburg after 20 April. There is no means of knowing how much ordinary readers missed these informed commentaries. Few can have changed newspapers in consequence. But other journalists, of course, noted the change. Engels, who valued the *Guardian* as a source for his own and Marx's journalism, was both annoyed professionally and, one suspects, delighted politically. In April he wrote to Marx: 'Seit das Blatt auf 1d herabgesetzt ist, lassen die Kerle alle Unkosten also Korrespondenzen etc reduzieren. Ihr Versuch, ein first-class provincial paper zu machen, scheiterte total.'* He was right about the economy drive, and his inference was reasonable enough. But mercifully it proved to be wrong. 'There was life in the old dog yet.'

* 'Since the price of the paper was reduced to a penny the (Guardian) chaps have reduced all expenses, correspondents' contributions, etc. Their attempt to produce a first-class provincial paper has completely collapsed.' (Engels-Marx 9 April 1858: Marx-Engels Gesamtausgabe III. 2. p. 313.)

CHAPTER ELEVEN

Edward Taylor and the Fight Against News Monopolies

I

THE surviving founders were growing old. At Christmas 1860 John Harland retired from the firm of Taylor, Garnett & Co., in which he had been a partner for twenty-one years, and from the staff of the *Manchester Guardian* which he had served as a reporter for thirty years. His impeccable shorthand has left us authentic records of the public speaking of William Cobbett, Feargus O'Connor, John Bright, Richard Cobden, old Lord Palmerston and young Mr Disraeli. Looking back, however, Harland thought that the hardest note he ever took was his almost verbatim account of a conversazione on the undulating theory of light, a report which earned him this cherished compliment, 'considering the abstruse subject, I was marvellous.' Latterly he had been driven to rely on crutches by a crippling lameness, but this immobility and his retirement from journalism served merely to give him more time for the antiquarian and historical work which was his chief love and with which he had filled many columns of the *Guardian* over the years. His last work was a revised edition of Baines's classic *History of Lancashire*. As the final sheets of the first volume were sent to press he was taken seriously ill. The first copy of the book, which he had eagerly awaited, was sent up to his house on 24 April 1868, but Harland had died during the night.[1]

A few weeks after Harland's retirement Jeremiah Garnett quietly withdrew from the firm and from the editorship of the *Guardian*. No reference was made to this either in the leading articles or in the news columns. On 16 January 1861 the formal imprint shows the paper was 'printed and published for Taylor, Garnett & Co. by Jeremiah Garnett'; the next day it was 'printed and published by Peter Allen.' That is all. As a young man Garnett had been a frequent speaker at public meetings, but it was characteristic of his later years that he should withdraw so unobtrusively.

'Old J— as the people loved to call him – . . . hated bother and fuss . . . his urbanity . . . was very conspicuous and embraced the humblest as well as the most trusted of his people – the gentlemen who wrote the leaders not more than the printer's devil who waited for the proofs. He was accused of small-ness in public matters, I think unjustly; but in his conduct towards his subor-dinates he was as fine an old cock as any village squire in a modern novel. He had many of the characteristics of a village squire – notably in the unstudied carelessness of his costume, which combined the qualities of a head game-keeper or a stud-groom, with an utter detestation of glossy hats . . . (But) Our old Editor never looked dirty or dingy. Everything about him was wholesome and healthy and in strict conformity with a bright blue eye, that was always clear, but which yet had no particular twinkle . . . He was occasionally as hard to draw as a reluctant badger, but it was never because he was afraid of the dogs. He was afraid of nothing in a general way; and whether he was justified in the sentiment or not, I feel satisfied that when properly roused – which was precious seldom – he would have grimly defied the stark-naked opinion of a world in arms against him.'

This, thanks to his own shy reticence, is probably as near as we can get to 'the kindly father; the open-handed, charitable, unostentatious, fast friend; the considerate master; the frugal, honest citizen' whom the anonymous writer in the *Sphinx* described in the year that Jeremiah Garnett died.[2]

Once at least in his ten years of retirement, Garnett appeared in public with Edward Taylor on an occasion that must have given him great pleasure and brought back many memories. In March 1861 the *Guardian* had published vitriolic attacks on the dealings between Jacob Behrens & Co. and the bankrupt firm of Dalton, Brothers & Heap which had been buying calico one day on credit and selling it at a lower price the following day to Behrens for cash. The *Guardian* thought this was flagrantly dishonest and said so. Messrs Behrens brought an action for libel and assessed their damages at £5,000. The case was heard in London at the request of the plaintiffs – 'a monstrous pretence has been advanced to the effect that the influence of the *Manchester Guardian* in this district was so much to be dreaded by the opposing party as to render it necessary that he should resort to the unusual and obviously inconvenient course of seeking an imperfectly qualified tribunal at the other end of the country.' That was how the *Guardian* leader put it after the jury had returned a verdict for Messrs Behrens and fixed damages at £1,000. It was a fair excuse for defeat because the complexities of the Manchester trade were such that the case really needed to be tried by 'men who knew what a calico printer is in the habit of doing, and what he ought to do, and who had the same general comprehension of the practice and duties of a Manchester commission agent.'

Garnett must surely have allowed himself a wry smile over the shortness of human memory as he read another sentence in the leader which claimed that this was 'the first time this journal had met with any misadventure of the kind in a career of upwards of forty years.' Did nobody now on the paper recall how its trembling fortunes had revived in 1823 after it lost the verdict in Dicas v. Taylor* but had been rewarded by a public subscription which covered the greater part of its expenses? Still it was good to read the way the other papers now supported the *Guardian* in the action it had taken. The *Examiner* was blunt: 'That their (Messrs Behrens) transactions with Messrs Dalton and Heap have not been compatible with sound commercial morality is an opinion which the commercial community of Manchester endorses with unmistakable unanimity.'

How true this was, and how grateful Manchester was to the *Guardian* for its exposure of the fraudulent transaction, was seen six months later when the Mayor, supported by a committee, of which Jeremiah Garnett was a member, presented Edward Taylor with an illuminated address and a cheque for £1,457 which had been subscribed by 1,100 merchants, manufacturers and bankers, of whom 600 were members of the Exchange.[3]

The retirement of Garnett and Harland made a new partnership necessary. The copyright of the paper, and therefore its ownership, had always been in the hands of the Taylor family; but, since the formation of the firm of Taylor, Garnett & Co. in 1826, there had always been partners who were on the staff of the paper, but not members of the family. Under the new deed the partnership was confined to the family – Edward Taylor and his brother-in-law, Peter Allen. Robert Dowman dropped out, though he continued to be what would now be called deputy editor. His salary was fixed at £500 for 1861 but rose gradually to £900 by 1868. Taylor paid himself £800 as editor and took thirteen-sixteenths of the profits. The arrangement continued substantially unaltered for a dozen years, though Taylor reduced his salary as editor to £750 in 1864 and to £700 the next year as Dowman's salary increased. A minor alteration in the distribution of profits to Peter Allen's benefit was made in 1868. These twelve years were highly prosperous. The average annual profit was more than £16,000.

A young man who joined the staff in 1862 put down nearly sixty years later his recollections of Taylor at this time. He recalled 'a sparely built man, with striking features and notably dark, piercing eyes which

* See p. 50-1.

saw everything.' But he was taciturn. At one time the young man worked at a desk in his editor's room. Sometimes a whole night would pass without a word between them. Such silence was bound to become legendary. A new hand was reported to have asked who the boss was. 'Boss? Why that thin, pale man who just passed through the room. He's a gentleman he is. He never speaks to nobody.' Taylor's imperturbability also gave rise to stories. A half-mad Greek merchant eluded the doorkeeper, bounded into the office, and sought to shoot the editor for having described him as a long-firm swindler. Without betraying the slightest excitement Taylor went on writing. After a time he turned to his clerk and said, 'This has gone on long enough. Just get a policeman to see this wild man home.'

Taylor might be remote, but he was just and could be generous. When a trade union deputation asked him to accept a new rate of wages he refused to deal with them, but he went into his existing scale with the head printer and decided to raise it above the level for which the deputation had asked. Those dark, piercing eyes which saw everything were quick to notice and encourage promising young men. T. S. Townend, the author of these recollections, was one such. Taylor promoted him to be London manager in 1868. He had been given a strict training. When he was sent to Blackpool for the opening of the town's first pier he wrote, anticipating a later *Guardian* manner, of the Freemasons marching 'in their white aprons as though their dinner napkins had slipped over their stomachs.' Next day he was 'called into the Presence, and informed in very solemn tones that the Editor strongly objected to flippancy. The lesson was not forgotten.' Taylor's *Guardian* would have been a livelier paper if the lesson had not been given.[4]

2

Taylor, like Allen, was primarily a newspaper manager. It was in this direction that initiative was most needed in the 1860s. The great problem was the relation of newspapers to the telegraph companies, which were privately owned. The telegraph was the safeguard of the provincial press against being overrun by the London dailies; but in the later part of the 1850s and throughout the 1860s the companies that owned the telegraphs exploited their monopoly position in a way that was as contrary to the public interest as it was to that of the provincial newspapers.

At first the companies had accepted, and sometimes supplied, news messages on normal commercial terms. The relation between the papers and the companies was friendly and often warm – the *Guardian*, for example, sometimes went out of its way to praise the telegraph officials for their initiative.* But before long the companies realised that the supply of news could be made a profitable side-line and each established its own 'intelligence department.' The three main companies, the Magnetic, the Electric and the United Kingdom, combined to set up one central intelligence department. They offered the papers a package deal, take it or leave it; and, by raising their charge for independent reports to a prohibitive figure, they made it virtually impossible for newspapers to by-pass this service. Its quality was deplorable. Newspapers could not rely on receiving the information for which they paid – on occasion, for instance, the *Guardian* had been carelessly left out of the distribution of a particular item; nor could they count on the accuracy of what was transmitted – serious errors occurred in Mr Gladstone's 1860 budget speech. This poor quality was, perhaps, inevitable in a service on which only a little over a third of the cost was attributable to reporting and editing the news and nearly two-thirds to its transmission. The charges, moreover, varied both according to distance and, latterly, also according to the pressure which the Intelligence Department could exert on a particular newspaper. The *Northern Whig*, for instance, was told that it might lose the service altogether because it had supported the nationalisation of telegraphs. What the newspapers, and the public, needed was access to the telegraph system on the same equal terms for all as had applied to the mails since Rowland Hill's reform.[5]

The chambers of commerce, which were vitally concerned in market reports, and the leading provincial newspapers joined forces to secure this. Most of the twelve hundred provincial newspapers were small weekly papers only marginally concerned, but 163 subscribed to the Intelligence Department. A handful of daily papers among them took the lead. The London papers were on the whole not interested or hostile. Provincial news was not as important to them as London news was to the provinces. And they wanted to stop the provincial papers getting free use of news which had cost them money. The bill for the repeal of the Newspaper Stamp Duty had originally been drafted to give a newspaper 'copyright in every original article, letter, paragraph, communication and composition which shall be for the first time published in such newspaper in this country.' This clause was deleted largely as a result of the efforts of the Provincial Newspaper Society.

* See p. 99.

For ten years Taylor was the leader in the fight against the Intelligence Department's monopoly. He argued the case publicly in leading articles and privately in business correspondence. As early as 1858 he took the matter up with John Pender, the Manchester business man who was the mainstay of the Atlantic Telegraph Company, in a letter written only a fortnight after the first trans-Atlantic messages were exchanged.[6] Taylor was capable of looking forward constructively even when he was forced to make the most drastic economies.

'The first question which you wish to have settled,' he wrote, 'is whether you propose to follow the example of the British and Electric companies who employ persons to supply them with news both commercial and political and after transmitting it along their lines sell it at a distance to newsrooms, hotels, journalists, and others. I most earnestly hope that the Directors of the Atlantic Telegraph Co will not act in the same way . . . Of course it must be pretty obvious to you that if once you do commence the system of conveying news and selling it on your account you put it out of our power to do any telegraphing over your line on our private account. This has been the result of the course pursued by our Inland Telegraph Companies; for the private business we now do with them is a mere bagatelle compared with what it would be if they did not interfere with our function . . . The Public too, in the end, will gain if it be left to the Press to obtain for themselves and transmit the news they publish; inasmuch as the active competition amongst newspapers will constantly urge the Proprietors of newspapers to strive to obtain the earliest, most correct, and fullest information. . . Should you decide then to leave the press and the public to obtain all news for themselves we are ready to negotiate with you immediately for a daily message and I feel sure that it is to your interest to treat us liberally . . .'[7]

The reply does not survive and in any event the enquiry remained academic. The line went dead only two months after it had started to work for, though the cable had been successfully laid, a mistake by the electricians ruined its insulation. It was 1866 before regular telegraphic communication was established across the Atlantic.

By that time the campaign against the telegraph companies was in full swing. In 1865 a number of the provincial daily papers decided to set up their own co-operative news agency, and a meeting for this purpose was held in Manchester on 1 November with Taylor in the chair. The Provincial Newspaper Society sent a deputation to see that the interests of the weekly papers were not overlooked, as it clearly feared they would be. The Press Association Co. Ltd. was formed, but could not function because the telegraph companies were unwilling to do business with it. It is worth stressing that the campaign of the provincial newspapers was not one in favour of nationalisation, though that was its outcome, but against the news monopoly. They would have been quite content if the telegraph companies had confined themselves to carrying messages entrusted to them by others.

But since the telegraph companies would not do so, the pressure continued. At last in December 1867 the Government announced its intention of taking over the inland telegraphs next year. On what terms as far as the supply of news was concerned? At first the Post Office merely promised 'to make arrangements for the transmission of intelligence to the press which, if not identical with those at present in force, shall be at least as satisfactory to the proprietors of newspapers.' This was not good enough for the papers, which found no satisfaction in something only 'at least as satisfactory' as the existing quite unsatisfactory system. It would need to be a great deal better. The leading provincial dailies held another meeting at Manchester with Edward Taylor again in the chair, but without any representatives of the weekly press. This upset the Provincial Newspaper Society. A deputation was appointed by the Society to interview Taylor. It was agreed to hold a joint meeting in London of the new Manchester committee and the Provincial Newspaper Society. This went off well and a further meeting was held in Manchester on 29 June 1868 at which agreement was reached on the details of the new Press Association, the provincial papers' news agency which was to replace both the telegraph companies' Intelligence Department and the abortive 1865 co-operative agency which was still nominally in existence. A committee was set up to work out detailed arrangements and to negotiate with the Post Office. On this committee there served, under Taylor's chairmanship, Clifford of the *Sheffield Telegraph*, Harper of the *Huddersfield Chronicle*, Jaffray of the *Birmingham Daily Post*, and Ireland of the *Manchester Examiner*. Representatives of the Scottish and Irish papers served on a consultative committee.[8]

A week later Taylor and others gave evidence to the Select Committee of the Commons on the Electric Telegraphs Bill. Relations with the Newspaper Society were now correct, but an echo of the clash of interests that had persisted from 1865 onwards can be heard in the following questions and answers:

Mr Leeman: Do you belong to the Provincial Newspaper Society?
Mr Taylor: Yes.
Mr Leeman: Were you at a meeting at the Crystal Palace a short time ago?
Mr Taylor: I never attended a meeting of it in my life. I am a sleeping member.
Mr Leeman: But I suppose you receive the communications of the Society?

Mr Taylor: I believe I receive them.
Mr Leeman: Will you look at that? Did you get a copy of it?
Mr Taylor: I cannot say. I take no concern in the society.

This testiness on Taylor's part did not prevent his carrying through a highly successful negotiation with the Post Office. The telegraph system in future confined itself to the transmission of messages, leaving the newspapers themselves to supply the news. Their co-operative news agency, the Press Association, run by journalists for journalists, was an instantaneous success. The quality of its work from the beginning showed how needlessly incompetent the old Intelligence Department had been. Soon the London papers were glad to use its services, and to-day the entire English press and the radio and television news services rely on the PA network as a primary source of home and foreign news.*

But no newspaper could be content to rely on receiving only the same news as all other papers had. The terms worked out between Taylor's committee and the Post Office allowed for competition as well as co-operation between papers. The *Times* objected strenuously but in vain. The tariff for press messages made great reductions for identical messages sent simultaneously to several newspapers. It was this that made possible the economical service to the Press Association. It provided a basic rate, irrespective of distance, for an individual message to a particular newspaper. It worked out at less than half the charge made by the private companies for distances up to 100 miles, less than a third of that for distances between 100 and 200 miles and less than a quarter of the old rate for greater distances.

This cheap rate was available from any place to any other place in the United Kingdom. But most general home news originated in London and an enterprising provincial daily needed, so to speak, to place a standing order for telegraphing so many words a night. The form in which this was done was the renting of the exclusive night-time use of one or more private lines from the paper's London office to its headquarters. This service had been available from the private telegraph companies but on a rental which varied with distance, and cost £675 to Manchester, £750 a year to Scotland, and £1,000 to Ireland. Only nine private wires were, in fact, rented, five of them by Scottish newspapers. As soon as it became known that the fixed rental throughout the United Kingdom would be £500, one Irish newspaper rented a private wire in order to get in first with an improved news

---

* Since 1925 Reuter's and the Press Association have been run in double harness.

service, a step which at £1,000 a year it could not have afforded except for a short period. By 1876 on a conservative reckoning of the average amount of copy transmitted each night (8,500 words), the rate for private wire messages worked out at 3/6½d per thousand words. This compared with 23/– per thousand words at the ordinary press night rate for a single, unduplicated message. It was, so Taylor told the committee, about what he had been paying to the private telegraph companies in 1856 for transmitting the *Guardian*'s own parliamentary report; but the three major companies were then still in competition with one another for newspaper business and had not yet combined to establish a monopoly.[9]

The rates negotiated between the Post Office and Taylor's committee were based on the principle that newspapers were a public service and entitled to be treated as such. This view was accepted by Mr Scudamore, the secretary of the Post Office, in his reply to a letter from Taylor. 'It seems to me, indeed,' Scudamore wrote, 'that the transmission of news to the press throughout the kingdom should be regarded as a matter of national importance and that charge for such transmission should include no greater margin of profit than would suffice to make the service fairly self-supporting.'* In fact, the rates charged were not high enough and had to be revised in 1876. Even so, in 1893 it was calculated that the annual loss on press telegrams was over £300,000. This was not for lack of traffic. The number of words transmitted to newspapers was three and a half times as great in 1870, the first year of Post Office telegraphs, as it had been in 1868. The use made of the telegraph service by individual newspapers for their own independent messages, as opposed to agency service, was twice as great in 1872 as it had been in 1870 and three times as great by 1875.[10]

Garnett lived just long enough to see his young partner's triumph, and doubtless he was glad at it, but the triumph was in a technological cause for which he had little real liking. 'I am not sure,' to quote once again the writer in the *Sphinx*, 'that he had any shares in the Electric and International Telegraph Co. or that his urbane manner to all men in his employ extended to the youthful "buttons" who brought in the wire messages for his official use.'[11] Edward Taylor, on the other hand,

* Select Committee on Post Office (Telegraph Dept) 1876. Evidence of J. E. Taylor (Scudamore–Taylor 15 May 1868). Compare Treasury Minute in Accounts and Papers (XL) 1860 on postal charges: 'If the free circulation of newspapers in general is an object of importance, and one which ought to be attained even at a disproportionate cost to the Post Office (which is the assumption on which the whole of the present system rests) . . .'

grew up with the telegraph. He came on to the paper at the time when it was first beginning to be regularly used for news. He knew that newspapers could never rest satisfied until they had unrestricted access to it. It was well for the *Guardian* that at the time when this battle had to be fought it had at its head a young, determined and confident proprietor. Taylor was only 28 when he wrote the letter to John Pender already quoted; two days after his fortieth birthday the Post Office took over the telegraphs and the Press Association began to supply news. He had already made his major personal contribution, and it was a substantial one, to the prosperity and welfare not only of the *Guardian*, not only of the provincial daily papers, but of the whole British newspaper industry. He was the father of the Press Association.

3

The provincial papers now had unrestricted access to the fastest method of transmitting news. But they had still no proper access to the most important regular source of news. There was another monopoly to be fought: the monopoly by the London newspapers of the reporters' gallery of the House of Commons. They owed this monopoly to the fact that they had been there before there were any provincial daily newspapers. There were then enough seats to go round though, since one must have a grumble, it was usual to complain of the tiresome weekly papers which attended on Fridays – 'as the accommodation is very limited, they trespass upon it' – was how the head of the *Morning Post* parliamentary reporting staff put it to a Select Committee in 1868. Leader writers too were a nuisance in his eyes, men who 'trespassed' upon the legitimate occupants of the gallery, though there was no objection to their coming if they did not take up the room the reporters required. One gets the impression of an exclusive club of gallery reporters, largely self-governing, unfriendly to newcomers, rather contemptuous of members of parliament even to their faces. Wemyss Reid, for instance, got into trouble with the old hands on his first night in the gallery because the proprietor of his paper, the *Leeds Mercury*, who was also a member of parliament, came upstairs to speak to him: 'Some of the old hands positively snorted at me in their indignation,' Reid wrote. And Charles Ross of the *Times*, the oldest of the old hands, who had joined the gallery in 1820, told a Select Committee nearly sixty years later that if there were to be, as some had suggested, an official report of what they said in parliament, the public would turn from it 'with feelings of extreme disgust'; and that, if he had his way, he would cut the length of the *Times* report by half and probably save his paper £20,000 to £30,000 a year: 'but it is not my business and I never interfere.'[12]

The *Guardian*, of course, had had its own corps of reporters from 1856 to 1861. It is not clear what their status then had been, but probably they had been engaged in the same unsatisfactory way that the *Guardian*, the *Leeds Mercury* and the Scottish and Irish papers had to adopt in 1868 when the Second Reform Act brought into existence many new voters who wanted to know what their MP's were doing. The Serjeant-at-Arms was the authority for allocating seats, and he issued tickets only to London newspapers. In a lordly way he told a Select Committee that that was that:

Question: You have no knowledge whether the newspapers themselves make use of the whole of these tickets?
Answer: No, I have not the slightest knowledge of it. I give them as they are asked for.[12]

This left two methods open to the provincial papers. They could acquire an unused seat or ticket from the paper to which it had been issued as Wemyss Reid of the *Leeds Mercury* did from the *Morning Star* in 1867; or they could pay reporters from London papers for providing a separate, additional report as the *Guardian* and the *Freeman's Journal* certainly did; or they could no doubt combine both methods as the *Guardian* probably did. It seems to have had an arrangement with the *Morning Advertiser*. Only the *Times* forbade its reporters to work for other papers, and E. D. Gray, the MP who owned the *Freeman's Journal*, told the committee that even the *Times* had not always been able successfully to enforce the ban. The other London papers regarded the payments made to their men by provincial papers as a useful subsidy which saved them paying the wages they would otherwise have had to do. It was in fact a racket which London papers were able to operate because of the refusal of the Serjeant-at-Arms to recognise that some provincial papers had better claims to a seat in the gallery than some London papers.

For ten years Taylor and his friends had to make the best of this very bad job. In 1868 the *Guardian* opened a London office at Charing Cross, rented two private lines, and resumed the independent reporting of parliament on terms which involved living from hand to mouth at the mercy of the London papers. In spite of this, the *Guardian*'s report was once again a solid, workmanlike affair.* In 1878 there was a Select Committee on Parliamentary Reporting. The excluded papers were

* There were five or six *Guardian* reporters under T. J. Dunning, who had earlier been a reporter in Manchester. At the Select Committee Mitchell Henry, M.P., the

able to show that although they were not supposed to be in the gallery, they covered the debates better than half the London papers which were officially there. The Irish, Scottish and north country MP's were determined to have their speeches reported in papers their constituents could read. They got their way and a profitable racket came to an end.

_____

founder of the *Manchester Evening News,* who had a grudge against the *Guardian* pressed T. S. Townend, the paper's London manager, for the name of the *Guardian's* sketch writer. This Townend refused to give and was backed up by the Committee in refusing (T. S. Townend: *Manchester Guardian House Journal,* December 1919).

CHAPTER TWELVE

The Tunnel

I

'A VERY bad paper (which) needed pulling up. It was also, alas, extremely profitable' – so A. P. Wadsworth once described the *Guardian* of the 1860s. This was the time when Edward Taylor was busy struggling with the telegraph companies and founding the Press Association, efforts on behalf of all provincial newspapers. They must have distracted his attention from his own paper which, however, continued to make large profits under Peter Allen's management. Editorially, Taylor allowed it to go on as it had been recently doing – not at the high level of its early period as a daily, but at the jog-trot, parsimonious pace which was the result of the financial crisis of 1858. News was received rather than diligently sought, and it was cobbled together in a ramshackle fashion. Business took Taylor increasingly to London. His deputy in Manchester, Robert Dowman, seems to have been content just to carry on. Reading the files, one feels one has passed into a long dark tunnel. Only after three-quarters of Taylor's time as editor was past does the *Guardian* begin to emerge again into the sunlight where, thanks to Taylor's successful campaign against the news monopolies, it was able to compete for the first time as a newspaper of equal quality with the great London papers. The record of the last three years of Taylor's active editorship shows that he could be as capable in running his own paper as he had proved himself in the politics of the newspaper industry as a whole.

The years in the dark tunnel were a time of missed opportunities. There were especially great opportunities for a Lancashire paper which had the resources of the *Guardian* to draw on. The American Civil War was a matter of intense interest all over England, one in which passionate feelings were roused and sides strongly taken. But it was more than that to Lancashire. The cotton famine brought bread famine to the workers of the Lancashire mills. The *Guardian* might have been expected to recognise both a moral duty and a journalistic need to provide a really good service of news of what was going on across the Atlantic.

It was in this respect at no great disadvantage to the London papers.

The cable which had been completed in 1858 had broken down after only a few weeks of work, and throughout the war there was no quicker source of news than the letters and papers which the steamships brought. A constant supply of messages could be guaranteed; there were sixteen steamer sailings from the United States to England during January 1862. The news they brought was, of course, up to a fortnight old by the time they reached Liverpool or Southampton, though a day could be saved by telegraphed summaries from the Irish ports – Queenstown (Cobh) or even on occasion Crookhaven on the southern route, and Greencastle on the northern. Thus in 1863 the *Guardian* used a Reuter telegram from Greencastle recording that 'Mr Lincoln, Mr Seward and the *corps diplomatique* were present at the dedication of the Gettysburg Cemetery. Mr Edward Everett delivered an oration.' Next day the *Bohemian* reached Liverpool and the *Guardian* gave the text of Lincoln's speech as the last item in a miscellaneous batch of American news. It was not thought worth a leading article. Fifteen months later the *Guardian* gave Reuter's version of Lincoln's Second Inaugural which omitted its best known words, 'with charity towards all . . .' Next day the full text was available and published, but again there was no leader. One cannot blame Edward Taylor for Reuter's lack of news sense, but the *Guardian's* failure to pick out for comment either the Gettysburg oration or the Second Inaugural is its own sad misjudgment.[1]

In the 1850s, before the paper's economic crisis, there had been a thorough and regular American correspondence. Now there were only Reuter telegrams and quotations from American and London papers plus a very occasional article from across the Atlantic. The paper must, in fact, have spent much more on its racing than on the American war: in 1862 there were twelve long articles on the previous year's 2-year-olds by 'Rataplan.'[2] No doubt Taylor was wise to keep out of the race between Reuter and the London papers to be first with the American news relaid from Ireland. Reuter was early enough for the *Guardian's* protected market. But he was certainly wrong not to provide his own coverage by ocean mail. He could not plead poverty. Between 1862 and 1865 the *Guardian* made £20,000 a year.

The *Guardian* was barely worth reading for its American news – the *Examiner* was better – but its views deserved attention. Above all, it hated slavery, and always had. But this did not imply whole-hearted support for the North. The Union had condoned slavery; the existence of the free states within the Union shielded the slave states from the universal condemnation which they would otherwise have suffered. The success of the Confederacy might even paradoxically bring nearer the end of slavery, as Mr Gladstone had suggested, because it would leave the South exposed to the full force of world public opinion.[3]

The *Guardian* made no bones of its belief that the South would succeed in establishing its independence, and that it had a perfect right to do so if it could. 'There is not the slightest pretence for investing a republic with privileges which have been repeatedly denied to monarchies. If the South can conquer their independence, they are just as well entitled to it as the Hungarians, whose "secession" from Austria the United States were in so much haste to recognise in 1849.' In this the *Guardian* merely said what most people in London felt, but it parted company with them when it opposed British intervention to break the Federal blockade of the South. If Lancashire had followed its own selfish economic interest and supported the campaign to let the cotton through, war could hardly have been avoided.[4]

It was this fear that brought Henry Adams, the son of the American minister in London, on a private visit of enquiry to Manchester in November 1861. What followed produced a passing and trivial diplomatic incident which is worth recording because of the devastating effect it had on Henry Adams. 'There was not a man of position in Manchester', he was told, 'who would venture to say to Lord Palmerston "interfere for the cotton", not a man.' All this he put down in his diary and forwarded to his brother who sent it to the Boston *Daily Courier* for publication. The Manchester *Examiner* picked up the story and used a short extract dealing exclusively with the intervention issue.

Four days later the *Guardian* published much fuller extracts. These caused the trouble. In Manchester Adams had been to a party and been happy at it; in London he went to parties and was miserable. 'In Manchester, I am told,' he wrote, 'it is still the fashion for hosts to see that their guests enjoy themselves. In London the guests are left to shift for themselves, and a stranger had better depart at once as soon as he has looked at the family pictures.' The Boston paper had published the diary under the author's name. The *Times* reprinted the *Guardian* article and next day complained that 'a document which evidently purports to be in the nature of a State paper contains a smart comparison between London and Manchester society greatly to the disadvantage of the former.' It objected to the idea that a visit to Manchester was necessary to 'bring its hidden opinion to light.' The idea that Manchester had an opinion of its own which it was worth going north to investigate was obviously as distasteful to the *Times* as the idea that Manchester had a society which was more friendly than that of the great houses of the capital. The London *Examiner* too took up the cudgels for London hostesses; 'He was regaled with hard seed cake and thimblefuls of ice-cream,' it wrote. 'That hard seed cake runs through and embitters all the young gentleman's reports of us.' Henry Adams's trouble was not only that his father had as tricky a diplomatic mission to carry out as any American diplomat has ever had, but that Henry was in a semi-official position as his father's secretary. He felt obliged to abandon the regular political correspondence which he did anonymously for the *New York Times* lest its authorship should be discovered. He had, as he wrote to his brother, 'to take in every spare inch of canvas and run under double-close-reefed mizzen to' gallant skysails before a tremendous gale' – a gale which had not blown itself out of his head over forty years later when he wrote *The Education of Henry Adams.*[5]

There was one feature of the *Guardian*'s attitude to American affairs which makes uncomfortable reading to-day. It is its utter inability to see the greatness of Abraham Lincoln. This blindness even increased as the years passed:

10 October 1862: 'It is impossible to cast any reflections upon a man so evidently sincere and well-intentioned as Mr Lincoln but it is also impossible not to feel that it was an evil day both for America and the world, when he was chosen President of the United States.'

2 January 1863: 'We have it from Mr Lincoln's own lips and pen that he does not desire to abolish slavery except as a means of extrication from the difficulties of government, and that he would willingly maintain it, if for no other reason, for the accomplishment of his own political ends.'

22 November 1864: 'Nor is Mr Lincoln's re-election by fraud, violence, and intimidation rendered a matter of comparatively small importance solely by the fact that it reveals nothing with respect to the real wishes and thoughts of the majority of his fellow-countrymen.'

On 27 April 1865 (*on the news of Lincoln's assassination*): 'Of his rule we can never speak except as a series of acts abhorrent to every true notion of constitutional right and human liberty; but it is doubtless to be regretted . . . that he had not had an opportunity of vindicating his good intentions.'

The *Guardian* objected to Lincoln partly at least because he stood for the maintenance of the Union at all costs. The paper thought this was negotiable. But it would have nothing to do with slavery while Lincoln was forced to treat emancipation as negotiable because it stood in the way of unity. The *Guardian* agreed that the North had the better cause in that Lincoln was pledged to prevent the expansion of slavery beyond the existing slave States, but the better cause fell far short of being 'the good cause.' The *Guardian* was indeed convinced that the majority of Northerners, so far from having any antipathy to slavery, considered it to be the natural condition of the Negro and were content to profit by it. The same reserve was felt by the Manchester *Examiner* which put the dilemma even more simply and directly: 'White men will not work in the same shop or on the same soil as the Negro. They won't acknowledge him as their equal; they won't shake hands with him as a man and a brother. Hence, above and beyond slavery, there remains the question of the enfranchised black man. How is he to be got out of the way? By what timely precaution shall this inferior race be prevented from some day numbering forty million?'[6] The hundred years since Henry Dunckley put this ironical question has only underlined its pertinence.

There was point, then, in the reserve of the two Manchester Liberal papers. But the *Guardian* might surely like the *Examiner* have supported the cotton operatives who, in spite of their hunger, filled the Free Trade Hall on the last day of 1862 to adopt an address to Lincoln recording their 'detestation' of the attempt of the South 'to organise a nation having slavery as its basis.' The *Guardian* complained that 'the chief occupation, if not the chief object of the meeting, seems to have been to abuse the *Manchester Guardian*' because it had objected to the meeting being held, and still more to the Mayor's unofficial presence in the chair, as a breach of the non-intervention policy. But perhaps too 'the working men of Manchester' had some reason to feel let down by the *Guardian* and a need, as they quaintly put it, 'to set themselves right with the world.' Next day the London correspondent of the *Guardian* reported that 'the current opinion in all classes . . . runs strongly with the South, and . . . it would hardly be possible to get up in London such a meeting of working men as I see you have had in Manchester.' Abraham Lincoln showed a true appreciation of the position in the letter of thanks he wrote three weeks later to 'the working men of Manchester.' 'Through the action of our disloyal citizens, the working men of Europe have been subjected to a severe trial . . . I cannot but regard your decisive utterances upon this subject (slavery) as an instance of sublime Christian heroism which has not been surpassed in any age or country.' The *Guardian* gave the letter; it made no comment on it.[7]

2

A few years later a revolution in English political life was accompanied by a revolution in the world of newspapers. The Reform Act of 1867 gave a rather bigger share in the Commons to the great industrial and commercial centres of provincial life. More importantly it gave working men in towns the vote. Five years later the Ballot Act removed one of the most effective ways of influencing elections by fear. The larger number of electors and the secrecy in which they now voted made members of parliament much more responsible to their constituents than most of them had been before. Far fewer constituencies were dominated by the kind of people who had town houses as well as country houses and who did the season in London and got their opinions there. Of course the old régime did not disappear overnight as readers of Trollope's political novels written in the 1870s will recognise; but there was a significant and continuous shift in the balance of power of which contemporary writers were well aware.

Only mass media, of which newspapers were as yet the only example, could reach the new mass electorate. Outside London and the south-east, and especially in Scotland and northern England, the papers that counted were the regional newspapers. Until the London papers started printing also in Manchester a generation later, and thus became for the first time national newspapers, the great provincial dailies continued to enjoy a protected market. In their own regional capitals they both shaped public opinion and expressed it. National politicians needed to read them to discover what was being thought in the England beyond London, and to use them to make their views known. The thirty years after 1867 were to be the golden age of the provincial press. But the papers had to become worthy of their new opportunities. The *Manchester Guardian* of the first half of the 1860s would not do, and Edward Taylor knew this.

In another sense the *Manchester Guardian* could never be made to do. There were many men who could not afford sixpence a week for a newspaper. There were many others who needed a more popular paper. There were openings in Manchester and the other great towns for two levels of journalism. Manchester got its second level about the same time as other towns, but in an unusual way as part of the general election campaign of 1868. One of the Liberal candidates, Mitchell Henry, fought the campaign as an interloper in search of the Irish vote.* He was dissatisfied with the publicity which Manchester's three daily papers provided and started the *Manchester Evening News* to give him what he wanted. On polling day he dramatically withdrew his candidature to avoid splitting the Liberal vote. He had no further use for the *Manchester Evening News*, which he sold to Edward Taylor for exactly what it had cost him. Its imprint shows that it was printed at 3 Cross Street, Manchester, by William Evans, who was an employee of Taylor, Garnett & Co. At first its editorial offices were a few streets away, but after two months they were moved to the next-door building.

* He subsequently sat for Galway.

It sold at a halfpenny and the first edition was published at 3 p.m. A note in the issue of 23 June 1869 sufficiently indicates one of the main interests of the paper and its readers: 'When our racing intelligence,' it read, 'does not arrive in time for the five o'clock edition, it will be printed on a separate slip (about half-past five o'clock) and presented gratutitously with the *Evening News*.'

From the beginning, then, the *Evening News* was in very close business association with the *Guardian*, though without an editorial link. Edward Taylor was the owner of both papers but he ran them as two separate partnerships – Taylor, Garnett & Co. for the *Guardian*, and Wm. Evans & Co. for the *Evening News*. They were destined to be both a strength and a trial to each other, as we shall see.

The *Guardian* itself published a third edition at 3 p.m. in the early 1870s. This was not in competition with the *Evening News* but probably to provide new postal subscribers with late news and prices. The introduction of a halfpenny postage rate for newspapers in 1870 had a considerable effect. On the first day over 10,000 papers were posted in Manchester.

3

The Franco-Prussian War of 1870 provoked much the same sudden appetite for news that the Crimean War had done half a generation before. The *Guardian* set out to provide for a thorough foreign news service of its own, covering every aspect of the war. It was badly placed at the start. M.X., the distinguished Paris correspondent of the 1850s and early 1860s, had not been replaced. During the last days of peace and the first days of war it relied as much on agency messages, scissors and paste as during the American Civil War. There were a few instructive articles 'From a military correspondent' comparing the rival armies and estimating their problems, articles of the kind that Engels had contributed during both the Schleswig-Holstein and the Seven Weeks wars. They virtually disappeared as front-line war reporting took over. One wonders whether Engels, who had only just moved from Manchester to London, wrote some of them.

By 6 July Solly was in Berlin beginning a regular series of articles which, if on the dry side, were both perceptive of German opinion and well informed. He was allowed, too, to spend considerable sums in telegraphing the full text of important diplomatic documents. Thus one day the *Guardian* proudly remarked that 'By the activity of our own correspondent in Berlin we were enabled to publish yesterday, in advance of any other English journal, Count Bismarck's dispatch to the Luxemburg Government respecting the alleged violations of the neutrality of the Grand Duchy.'[8]

It was not until 19 August that C. B. Marriott arrived in Paris and sent his first message describing a picket of the Garde Mobile who 'will doubtless fight like lions, but they looked far more to me like lambs going to be slaughtered.' He was in Paris through the September revolution, the siege and the Commune, with the exception of a short period when he toured the main towns of the South of France. He had an easy narrative style, a power of graphic description, considerable physical courage and a rather unexpected degree of sympathy with some of the revolutionary leaders. Mitchell, the second string in Paris, whose messages were usually described as 'from an occasional correspondent,' had a more conservative outlook. During the siege messages were sent by pigeon post or balloon. Some were lost, many got through quite promptly, though one which was washed up at the Lizard only reached Manchester after it had been forwarded by the vicar of St Ruan.[9]

By the time of the Commune communication was much easier, and the *Guardian* received a good service both of telegrams and messages by post. Marriott managed to get an 'interview' – the word was still enclosed in quotation marks – with the Communist leaders. He and a colleague determined to visit the revolutionary headquarters. They armed themselves with an introduction, which they wrote themselves, to 'the citizen members of the *République Democratique Française*.' It worked better than they dared to hope. They were passed from sentry to sentry and at length found themselves in the presence of the twelve members of the Central Committee in council. The chairman rose to welcome them as the first Englishmen who had cared to give them the title which they claimed, and deputed citizen Moreau to grant them a private interview of which the *Guardian* gave a full, objective account. The same issue contained a short interview with Thiers by an occasional correspondent in Versailles. Thiers spoke freely of the members of the Central Committee and 'did not conceal his contempt for those unknown men, as he called them, who were, perhaps, the agents of Bismarck or of Bonaparte.'[10]

Besides its correspondents in Berlin and Paris – and later at Tours and Bordeaux with the refugee government – the *Guardian* had war correspondents with the forces. A naval officer, Lt R. H. Armit, reached German headquarters by the middle of August and remained with them until the end of the war, apart from occasional expeditions with forward troops, usually in the company of a British Volunteer ambulance. He enjoyed a good deal more liberty than correspondents have had in later wars, riding across country in a battle-zone alone by night, 'navigating' by his pocket compass and the light of his cigar, in search of reinforcements for a desperately overworked advanced dressing station. Another sidelight on the relative freedom of movement in those days is given by his story of travelling in a railway compartment with a country parson, identifiable as an Englishman by the Murray's Guide sticking out of his pocket. He spoke neither French nor German and his only 'passport' was his parchment deed of institution to his Yorkshire living, complete with the Archbishop's seal. He had found it quite sufficient to satisfy both French and German sentries as he journeyed in search of a parishioner whose mother was seriously ill.

In one of Armit's early messages is a characteristic and endearing touch – 'I am heartily sick of war and carnage; I have never before seen it as a looker-on, and the feeling is very different in this case to that where you are yourself actively engaged.' This strong humanitarian concern marks nearly all his messages which are on the whole precise, detailed descriptions of troop movements, the lie of the land and the conduct of battles which would have enabled readers to follow operations with a clear understanding, if only the *Guardian* had ever provided a map. His descriptions indeed are clear enough almost to enable one to construct the missing map for oneself. His messages usually took ten to fourteen days in transit.[11]

There was another correspondent, probably D. Eaton, with the German eastern army at the siege of Strasbourg. He then followed von Werder's army right through until Bourbaki's men took refuge in Switzerland. His work had not quite Armit's sureness of touch, and he did not succeed in getting as far forward, but his descriptions of forced marches in bitter weather – seventy miles in two days, for instance – are vivid enough. In the later stages of the campaign, the *Guardian* arranged to use the messages of one of the official German correspondents, Dr Horn, 'in anticipation of their appearance in the German newspapers.'[12]

Two correspondents on the French side covered the war, or rather bits of the war, for the *Guardian*. Arthur Ory was with the French army on the Loire until he overslept in Vendome on 15 December. He was woken up by a great deal of running and rushing about, hurried into his clothes but got into the street only in time to see the bridge over which the French had retreated blown up and, turning round, 'a regiment of Prussian soldiers rushing towards me to whom I surrendered with the magnanimity of a Spartan.' He was, of course, arrested and taken, courteously and with opportunities of sight-seeing, to army headquarters where he was released and put on the way to Versailles, where he joined Armit on Christmas Eve.[13]

Much more satisfactory was the enterprising G. T. Robinson. He was an architect in St Peter's Square, Manchester, and the *Guardian*'s art critic. When he reached Paris on 9 August he was advised to go home or at least to stay in Paris. ' "You know, of course, that all the English correspondents have been sent out of Metz." That decided the question . . . Go I must. Having swept their house clean, the authorities at Metz would look no more for these noxious animals.' So it happened that Robinson was the only English correspondent in Metz during the siege. He was arrested at one time by the French as a spy. He made two efforts to cross the Prussian lines. First he tried openly in daytime, showing his Prussian visa to the outposts: 'they gave me beer, they gave me dinner, they gave me cigars; but they would not give me leave to pass.' He tried again, disguised as a very stupid peasant, but was caught by the Prussians. They gave him dark rye bread, excellent cheese, beer to wash it down with, and a delicious bundle of clean straw to lie down on. Before daybreak, they turned his face Metz-ward and told him to march or they would put a bullet into him.

With a French engineer officer he organised the manufacture of balloons and established a short-lived field post which brought a few brief messages to the *Guardian* before it was stopped by Marshal Bazaine. Some of Robinson's letters had been found by the Germans and sent back to Bazaine. For the last part of the siege the *Guardian* was entirely cut off from its correspondent.

When Metz fell after seventy days, the *Times* correspondent entered with the German army. That night he shared Robinson's room and saw his old straw hat hanging on the wall. ' "By George, to think it should have been you," ' the *Times* man said. 'It turned out that my old straw hat was well known . . . and that the Prussian marksmen had honoured it with much attention. Nay, I am by no means sure . . . that my welcome guest had not tried to bring down that hat . . . I was considered to be a personage of much more importance than your correspondent, from the fact that I always had so many officers around me . . . but my staff arose from the fact that my fieldglass was so much better than most of those at Metz that they always wanted to use it.' Early next morning Robinson got away from Metz, having been told privately that his name was on the list of dangerous persons which Bazaine handed over to the Prussians. For the next few weeks the *Guardian* carried extensive messages describing his experiences in the siege, which were republished as a book, dedicated to J. E. Taylor. It went to a second edition in 1874.[14]

A rough note survives in which the main items of expenditure on reporting the Franco–Prussian war and the Commune are given. The total comes to £4,775, but this seems to be a considerable under-estimate because it makes no allowance as far as can be seen for the frequent telegrams from an occasional correspondent at Brussels and for various other messages which can be traced in the files. When James Grant, who had been editor of the *Morning Advertiser*, published his *History of the Newspaper Press* in 1872, he wrote, 'The *Manchester Guardian* is conducted . . . "regardless of expense." During the late Franco–Prussian war it had correspondents at the headquarters – and subordinate ones too of importance – of both armies, who distinguished themselves by the earliness, the accuracy and the fullness of the information they furnished to the paper they represented. In fact, the *Manchester Guardian* proved itself, on repeated occasions, more than a successful competitor with some of our metropolitan daily journals.'

4

At the other end of the tunnel the country had an unfamiliar look. Lord Palmerston had died in 1865. Lord John Russell had retired from politics in 1866. Mr Gladstone and Mr Disraeli each became Prime Minister for the first time in 1868. Gladstone had already completed the work of the great Free Traders in budgets which the *Guardian* had welcomed with enthusiasm. Now he was turning to a new set of problems. In the end he would split his party as decisively as Peel had split the Tories. The *Guardian* had followed Peel; it would follow Gladstone, but that would be under another editor.

Meanwhile the paper was beginning to make discoveries of its own which in time made that decision inevitable. It was turning a compassionate, enquiring eye on the 'condition of England' problem. In 1864 it published a series of articles by Edward Brotherton on Manchester's educational provision. He showed that in many parts of the town a poor child had a poor chance of any education at all. What he found out about a child's prospects in the slums of Deansgate, the site of the *Guardian*'s new Manchester office, others would find elsewhere. His articles, and the backing they received in leaders, set men thinking in the way that led to Forster's Education Act of 1870. That is why H. A. Bruce, the Minister in charge of education at the time they were published, described them as 'the thunderclap from the North.' A little later there came a notable series of articles on the slums themselves. The first instalment appeared in 1870, but the series had to be broken off until the spring of 1871 because 'our own Observer' caught a serious illness in the course of his investigations.[15] They were followed by other investigations in depth into similar social problems which in the end edged a sometimes reluctant paper inexorably forward to Radicalism. The first decisive steps were taken while Edward Taylor was still editor as well as proprietor.

But Taylor was getting tired of editing his own paper. He moved from Manchester to London and gave more time to his splendid art collection. The paper suffered. Its individual leaders often made good reading, but they sometimes seemed to be written by different men arguing with one another, or by the same man who on different nights harboured contradictory thoughts. Taylor needed an editor who would give the paper the unity and direction that it lacked. By 1870 he had found his man; before the Germans entered Paris he had sent him to Manchester. When the *Guardian* celebrated its fiftieth birthday Taylor was still editor as well as proprietor; but, as C. P. Scott wrote to his mother, 'I am installed in Edward Taylor's old room which has been cleared out for the occasion.'[16]

PART TWO:

The Age of C. P. Scott

Just as he was a great man without any of the
airs of a great man, so he sought to create a
great paper without any of the airs of a great
paper. *C. E. Montague*

I never knew a happier man.
L. T. Hobhouse

From unsigned appreciations in the *Manchester Guardian* 1 January 1932

*

BOOK THREE:

The Silver Spoon 1872-1895

*

CHAPTER THIRTEEN

A Young Man with a Conscience

I

EVEN in the Victorian heyday of the family business it must have been unusual for a second-year undergraduate to be offered the editorship of a flourishing newspaper on the strength of being the owner's cousin. But this is what happened to C. P. Scott in 1867. And the paper was not just a successful provincial daily but 'the most valuable newspaper property outside London.'[1] Edward Taylor, of course, knew Russell Scott well, but he had had very little to do with his son Charles, who at that time had written nothing more relevant to newspaper work than letters to his family and essays for his tutor. Taylor was not looking for new capital, though, had this been needed, Russell Scott would no doubt have provided it as he had done in the past. Taylor was looking for something more elusive and valuable; for somebody to take his place, to pull the *Guardian* together journalistically (though no doubt he did not tell young Scott this), to give it the consistent distinction which he knew it still lacked. Of course, Taylor did what he could to check on the young man's capacity. Very likely he wrote to his tutor; if he did, he was probably told, like another correspondent, that Scott was 'in every respect one of the most satisfactory young men we have ever had in the college', though he might not get the highest honours.[2] Certainly Taylor read some of Scott's essays; they made a favourable impression, though he knew it was difficult to estimate promise at all accurately from such *juvenilia*. Twenty years later Taylor was to remind Scott of his 'little essay on "Is loyalty possible under a republic?" and of all the splendid fruit that lay only indistinctly germinant in that manifestation of a youth's faculties.'[3]

Still, indistinct or not, Taylor saw sufficient promise to make the offer. Scott accepted it, though not without a hesitation which he asked his father to pass on. 'Perhaps you will contrive to express my meaning for me to Edward better than I myself have been able. It would greatly relieve my mind if you would endeavour to do so.' The point was that Scott did not want to commit himself to the *Guardian* for life; in time other openings might arise and he wanted to feel free to take them.

This was a simple and sensible precaution which in later years Scott would have put perfectly plainly. But at 21 he expressed it in theological terms typical of mid-Victorian England, which throw light on the pedigree of that secular evangelism which marked the *Guardian* in Scott's time. Taylor had told Scott that he wished him to take part in 'public matters', but added that of course his duty to the *Guardian* would always come first.

'I said "yes",' Scott wrote to his father, '. . . But I ought to have added that the time might come when for this very reason the path of duty would lie the other way, and that should it ever be God's pleasure to give me power and opportunity to do better service in a fresh field, to that service I must be free to devote myself . . . hand and will must be always ready to obey the call, should it ever come. On the other hand, by binding myself down to a certain definite course of life, I should fall into the very sin of Ananias, and while professing to give all to God, I should be making a private stipulation in my own favour. The practical result is this – I would gladly go and work at the *Guardian* on any terms and with any prospects – . . . but it must be on the distinct understanding that . . . I am yet freely at liberty to go, should duty call me elsewhere. It follows that certainly at no time must my salary exceed the value of my actual services – possibly also that I am unfit for the very responsible position to which apparently Edward ultimately destines me.'[4]

If Russell Scott passed on his son's reservations to Taylor, they do not seem to have worried him. After all, Taylor was not binding himself by any legal contract. He was offering a job with unusually attractive prospects.

What other 'call' had Scott in mind when he wrote this letter to his father? Was he harking back to his boyhood inclination to the Unitarian ministry? Perhaps, but Seeley's *Ecce Homo*, which was a new book in Scott's first year at Oxford, had settled his mind about Christianity in a way that was unlikely to lead to ordination. Before he read Seeley, he had been much concerned with problems of doctrine; thenceforward he put theological speculation on one side. He wanted a platform, not a pulpit. Was Scott thinking of parliament? This seems more likely. The second Reform Bill had just received the royal assent, and few Liberals doubted that Mr Gladstone would soon become Prime Minister. Possibly Scott was considering a career in one of the new social services, such as housing. But whatever 'call' Scott half awaited, he overcame his scruples and accepted Taylor's offer.

He had not, however, yet recognised – how could he? – that his life's vocation was to be editor of the *Guardian*. His immediate aim, naturally and rightly, was to do well in the Schools. He had obtained a second-class in Honour Moderations, the first part of the classical degree course at Oxford. He was determined to get a First in Greats. He was due to sit for this examination in the summer of 1869 and, indeed, he did take the papers. But he was dissatisfied with his work and cautiously decided to withdraw his name and try again in the Michaelmas term as men were then able to do. He duly got his First. Nothing in the rest of his life could weaken his conviction that the difference between even the shakiest First and the best Second was one of kind rather than of degree. For a moment he was apparently tempted to think that his 'call' might be to academic life. He stood for a fellowship at Merton. It is difficult in retrospect to be sufficiently grateful to the Fellows of that college. Had they elected young Mr Scott of Corpus, Oxford would have gained a competent don; England might have lost a uniquely great editor.

In the summer of 1870 Scott went north to Edinburgh where Edward Taylor had arranged for him to have six months' training on the *Scotsman*, then at the height of its fame as a great Liberal newspaper under Sir Alexander Russel. While he was there he wrote on 2 November to his sister Sarah: 'There is some talk of my going to France as a correspondent of the *Manchester Guardian* if the war lasts on into next year. I hope and believe, however, that it is not likely to do so. The untimely fall of Metz is a crushing blow and may well make resistance seem very hopeless.' It is a pity that nothing came of the proposal. Scott's greatest weakness as an editor was probably his lack of first-hand experience of news-getting. He lacked in consequence an in-grained appreciation of the fact that newspapers were read first for news, and only secondly for views. Throughout almost the whole of his working life they were the only source from which news could be obtained.

On 9 February 1871 Scott joined the *Guardian* for duty in Man-chester. He was not yet 25, a strikingly handsome young man with piercing brown eyes which could signal with equal force both absorbed interest and inflexible determination. Perhaps it hardly needed the beard, which he had recently grown, to remind his colleagues – most of them many years his senior – that they should treat with respect the young man who now occupied Edward Taylor's old room and who clearly would soon become their employer. From the beginning C. P. Scott was a monarchial man. This is perhaps surprising. He had been brought up in a gentle, cultured household and educated in quiet private schools and by a private tutor. At Oxford he had been a member of a small, hard-working college. His early life had been sheltered from the great world by his membership of a rather isolated religious minority. There had been nothing in his upbringing to develop those

powers of leadership which British public schools prided themselves
on producing. The instinct to command and the unhesitating
expectation that others would obey were all his own.

Scott spent his first nights in Manchester with his cousin by
marriage, Peter Allen, the business manager of the paper and Edward
Taylor's partner. Allen's wife, Sophia, had looked forward to welcoming Charles Scott whom she 'had seen only once since he wore frocks',
but she had died in childbirth in 1868. She had been the main link
between the Scott, Taylor and Allen families, and she clearly hoped that
their alliance would be happily continued into the next generation. 'If
it should be,' she wrote to her uncle when she heard the news of his
son's appointment, 'that either of my boys should ever be connected
with him (C. P. Scott) in business I shall rejoice that they have an elder
cousin of high principle and good feeling to take an interest in them.'[5]
The Allens and Scotts did, in fact, have close business relations for
many years to come. They were often stormy. Had Sophia lived, a good
deal of unhappiness might have been avoided and the history of the
Guardian have been smoother – and less interesting.

That first evening in Manchester, however, disagreements were far ahead. Allen put himself out for his young guest. The first night he invited H. M. Acton from the office to meet Scott at dinner. Next day they played billiards with a neighbour till nearly midnight. Allen lost two shillings and Scott sixpence – 'a bore', as he told his mother, though whether he referred to the game or its outcome is not clear. Parsimony and generosity were both in Scott's character from the beginning. The same letter that records the loss of sixpence mentions that he is giving his first week's wages to the fund for relieving the famine in Paris after the siege.[6]

Before Scott had been four months on the paper, Taylor confirmed his appointment and speeded up the arrangements for handing over the editorship. It was decided that Robert Dowman, who had been acting as editor in Manchester, was to retire at the end of 1871 after twenty-one years' service on the paper.* Scott would then take over, some two or three years earlier than he had expected. Taylor himself continued nominally as non-resident editor for another year – at least the accounts for 1872 show that he paid himself a salary as editor that year for the last time – but to all intents and purposes C. P. Scott succeeded on New Year's Day 1872.

2

Soon after Scott reached Manchester he was greatly moved by the disclosures in the paper's articles on slum housing. He planned a holiday for the last week before he took over the editorship to be devoted wholly to personal canvassing for subscriptions for a housing society. He wanted to fix his own contribution at £500 if his father would allow him to draw to that extent on his future share in the family fortune. Housing, like education, had long been both a *Guardian* and a Scott interest. As early as 1845 the *Guardian* had argued that 'a landlord has no more right to let an insalubrious house than a butcher has to sell unwholesome meat', while C. P. Scott's father was the unpaid director of the 'Metropolitan Association for Improving the Dwellings of the Industrial Classes.'[7]

Scott himself at once extended the *Guardian*'s social investigations. In the first five months of 1873, for instance, he published five long

* 'a giant in stature with the voice of a babe . . . a bookworm, a linguist and a classical scholar,' he dealt with Letters to the Editor and Answers to Correspondents but wrote nothing except the foreign news summary. (T. S. Townend in the *Manchester Guardian House Journal*, January 1921.)

articles on the need for law reform, four on the working of the schemes for medical help for the poor by means of 'hospital letters', and another two describing seven case studies of family health in working-class homes. Two articles analysed the 'Emigrant Stream' from Liverpool to the New World. The protracted strike in the mines and iron works of South Wales was described in six special articles which gave balanced expression to the views of both employers and men and to the social consequences of the strike. This was followed by full coverage of the 'Miners' Parliament,' their trade union conference in Newport, Monmouthshire. A fortnight later there appeared the first of twelve detailed studies by 'a roving correspondent' of wages, living and working conditions in the various mining districts of the North of England.[8]

This is a remarkable record. The *Guardian* was no longer confining itself, as it had tended to do, to reporting what public men said and commenting on it, or to describing events which happened in the public eye or led to actions in the courts. It was now itself making news out of the hidden occurrences of ordinary life, bringing out dark things which the enlightened conscience of middle- and upper-class England ought to have known but did not. It was some years, however, before leader writers drew what now seem the obvious conclusions from the *Guardian* special correspondents. This is specially true in the key matter of the relations of employer and employed. Meanwhile the fact that this disturbing evidence was presented in a newspaper whose success belonged to the safe world of Samuel Smiles's *Self Help* (1859) secured it an attention from the ruling class of industrial England which the working-class movement could not yet command for itself.

An example may make clear the nature and extent of this gap between news and comment. First, the news from South Wales:

'. . . Even the pawnbrokers, who you would think were flourishing, say . . . that if the strike does not end immediately they must put up the shutters and depart as ruined men. My informant showed me in a room above his shop thirty feather beds, innumerable bundles of bedding, and said he had below lamps and tools enough to stock a large colliery . . . From Lancashire, Durham, Newcastle, Staffordshire and other mineral districts; even from the Welsh colonies in the coalfields of Pennsylvania and Ohio, there have come sums of money from sympathising working men for distribution among the unfortunates who are not "in union." But you may as well try to allay a tempest with a flask of salad oil as seek to assuage the troubled sea of sorrow by the sums of money which have reached these poverty-stricken people . . .'

and the writer went on to describe in terrifying detail the misery he found in the homes he visited:

'You will notice that the broken stone floor has no carpet, and is full of holes; that a turned-up box does duty as a table, and that a three-legged stool and an arm-chair are the only articles of furniture in the room. The paperless walls are begrimed and greasy. The shelves that serve as a cupboard in the corner are empty, but for two plates (one broken), a jug which has lost its handle, and a small tin saucepan. Above the chimney-piece is a sheet almanack of an advertising grocer, and on the ledge, which your eyes will see is thick in dust, are a medicine bottle, and, *mirabile dictu*, a champagne bottle doing duty for a candlestick, albeit the piece of candle is hardly long enough to last while a man wound his watch up . . . The arm-chair is drawn close to the grate, in which lingers the expiring embers of what originally could have been but a very small wood fire, for fuel, I need not say, is as scarce as food. A woman sits in the chair, and is gazing moodily, fixedly, into the dull red of the slow-burning wood – a thin, pinched, scantily clad woman, whose ragged cotton dress is as frouzy and dirty as the little woollen shawl which is drawn over her head to protect her neck from the draught that comes through the broken window pane at the back. At her breast is a two month baby . . . as thin and pinched as its haggard nurse. There is a little girl of ten or twelve kneeling before the fire, and shivering, as she tries to toast a slice of bread, which I learn has been begged of a neighbour, and is the only food in the house. A young man sits on the other side of the fire upon another box – not the table. He is a lodger; out of work, of course. He is smoking – mark that; he can buy tobacco, and the woman has to beg bread . . . "Yes, indeed, it was hard times, you see; there's all my clothes gone, and John's black, and Ellen there, she can't go to Sunday school 'cause her best things is sold." The clock that stood in the corner there, the chest of drawers that faced the clock, chairs, table, bed upstairs, everything moveable and saleable had been disposed of to find provisions; and last of all – she almost shrieked this out as if in pain – last week she sold her wedding ring to get the first food she had taken for two days and to buy milk for her tortured infant . . .'
(4 March 1873)

Another day the writer went off for a drink with a union official who 'is evidently not the demagogue I had imagined as my ideal union agent'; they discussed the three causes of the strike:

'You see, sir, the men had three causes – leastwise they had one cause and two reasons, – they did not like the reduction, and thought it was unjust; then they wanted to get arbitration 'stablished here, like 'tis in Staffordshire; and then, agen, they thought the ironmasters would give in almost directly, looking at the way in which iron was going up.' He explained that the union had not wanted the strike, indeed, the general secretary had appealed to the men not to do anything so rash: 'Their first step should be to join the union, then strike if they had just cause to do so . . . we can show a gain of nearly five thousand members since last December. That's the best answer we can

give to Mr Fothergill and such as he, who say they'll "crush the union" . . .
(10 March 1873).

The warmth and sympathy of these descriptive articles is in
marked contrast with the aloof, uncomprehending tone of such leading
articles as these:

'. . . it is impossible not to remember that if an accommodation can be
effected the occupation of the agents of the Union is gone. They live on strife.
. . . The temptations to which they are exposed would be too strong perhaps
for many consciences as yet untried. But it cannot be wondered at if employers of labour often discern in the obligation to resist such intervention
a matter of even greater importance than the pecuniary questions in
dispute . . .' (26 February 1873)

'We are strongly disposed to think that these last (Wigan miners earning
7/- to 9/- a day) would be richer men if they earned less money; and, considering what is the degree of culture, and what are the approved pleasures
of their class, we doubt greatly whether higher wages would be any benefit
to them. It cannot, of course, be expected that they should think so . . .'
(10 April 1873)

3

A newspaper cannot live on its special interests. It fails if it does not
cover the general news of the day thoroughly and clearly. This is its
primary function. Scott soon had a chance to show whether he could
improve on his predecessor's handling of a general election. He joined
the *Guardian* halfway through Gladstone's first great ministry. The
reporting of the general election of 1868, which gave Gladstone his
tremendous majority, seems old-fashioned compared with that of 1874,
which rejected him almost as decisively. The two elections have an
added interest in that these were the first in which the urban working
class had the vote, while the election of 1874 was the first at which
the secret ballot replaced the ordeal of standing up and being counted
in the presence of employers, landlords or their agents.

In Manchester, Marsh, who had been chief reporter in 1868, had
been succeeded by R. W. Spencer shortly before the 1874 election, but
four of the team of seven were with the paper on both occasions.
Four of them – Spencer, Cash, Biggs, E. J. Burton – were to serve on
until the present century, a fifth, John Turner, until his death in 1888.
Spencer ultimately became chief sub-editor and was succeeded by John
Cash, long-bearded, silent, 'not a brilliant man but a wonderful chief
reporter.' Burton was transferred to the London office in 1880, where

he worked with T. S. Townend, the manager, whom he succeeded a few years later. Burton retired in 1901. They were by any standards a strong team as well as a long service one, 'giants, at their game, most of them . . . something fine and high in the minds of the reporting staff did more than anything else to give the *Guardian* its special quality.' That at least was how Buchanan Taylor remembered these men a whole generation after they had gone. He doubted whether James Agate to whom he had been talking 'quite understood how much of the *Manchester Guardian*'s power and prestige came from the reporting staff.'[9] It is pretty certain that Scott would have been surprised by this judgment. At any rate, between Harland's time and Wadsworth's reporters ranked 'below the salt.'

Of course, Scott had no doubt about their ability to do their basic work which was to report faithfully other men's words. This was virtually all that they had been asked, or allowed, to do in the 1868 campaign. Through more than three months of the election meetings – for this must have been one of the most protracted election campaigns in history – the *Guardian* reporters recorded speech after speech of daunting similarity. Frequently for an evening meeting they worked in 'rings' of three or four reporters, each man taking his turn to report for a short period while the others got on with their transcription so that the complete text of the speech was available in longhand a few minutes after the speaker sat down. If necessary, a special train was engaged to bring the report back to Manchester. In this way it was possible for the *Guardian* to give five and a half columns, over 9,000 words, of what Mr Gladstone had said at Warrington the previous night at a meeting which did not start until 7.30. Three days later similar arrangements were made for Mr Gladstone's meeting at Liverpool.[10] Reports of evening meetings on this scale were considerable printing as well as journalistic achievements since every word had to be set by hand. The telegraph, still in private hands, was used for distant evening meetings – *Guardian* reporters went as far afield as Edinburgh, Birmingham and King's Lynn.

There is no trace in the 1868 reports of what the reporters thought, felt or saw. They only heard. They were trained to be self-effacing men, rigidly impersonal and impartial in their work. The only slight exception to this rule is the faintly personal note that crept into the account of nomination day at Manchester:

'. . . although, while reporting the speeches, we were unable to see which side began the affray, and each party charged the other with being the aggressors, by far the largest number of stones and cinders were thrown from the Tory crowd, probably because they had the greatest amount of material to hand from the ground of the unpaved part of the square . . . Many persons were struck on the head, and the faces of several were covered with blood; others were knocked down as the combatants rushed from side to side; some stones fell among the gentlemen on the hustings, and several of the reporters were struck . . .' (17 November 1868)

In 1874, a snap election with a campaign almost as short as 1868 had been long, Scott allowed the reporters more scope to describe and interpret what they saw. Of course there were the same verbatim reports, but there were also what we should now call sketches and commentary. One Monday the whole of two facing pages – fourteen columns containing well over 22,000 words – was devoted to speeches by Gladstone at Woolwich, Disraeli at Aylesbury and Bright at Birmingham. In Birmingham 2,000 members of the central and ward election committees filled the time before Bright arrived by singing the 'Hallelujah Chorus' to celebrate his unopposed return. They reminded John Cash of the 'perfect adequacy to all conceivable needs of the Prussian military system.' The London office covered the other two meetings. One story told how Disraeli's descent, disguised as a country squire, on the farmer's 'Ordinary' at Aylesbury brought so many visitors from London that the farmers were almost crowded out of their own dining-room. The other dealt with the open-air meeting at the gates of Woolwich Arsenal to which Gladstone came with his wife and daughter in an open carriage pulled by his supporters. The crowd was enthusiastic, but not unanimous. For half an hour eggs, rotten apples, oranges and pellets of mud were thrown, and windows were broken in the 'dramshop' which served as a Tory committee room. Through it all 'Mr Gladstone had gone on, with scarcely a momentary hesitation, dealing boldly and cheerfully with point after point of Mr Liardet's circular and Mr Disraeli's already demolished address.'[11]

The party leaders' speeches, of course, had to be covered by any newspaper that wanted to keep its readers. The journalist's skill lay in selecting other contests which were worth special attention. They were especially numerous in an election which the Liberals lost largely because of their own bitter feuds over Mr Forster's Education Act. The left wing, but not the *Guardian*, regarded the Act as a surrender to the Church and in many places Liberal fought Liberal as well as Conservative. The *Guardian*'s seven reporters could not be everywhere even with the help of the London office. Its Radical rival, the *Examiner*, was in the same difficulty. They seem to have arranged to help each other out over the key contests of Forster at Bradford and Kay Shuttleworth at Accrington.*

Everyone was interested in the consequences of the Liberal split over religious education. The *Guardian* was also specially interested in what happened to the handful of manual workers who were standing for election. Two seemed to have a good chance. Both constituencies polled the same day. Spencer found it difficult to make up his mind which to choose. He first marked C. W. Graham to go to Stafford but then crossed it out and substituted Wigan, adding as a note 'especially Pickard', the miners' agent. The Conservatives won both seats and Pickard, 'labour candidate' as the *Guardian* described him with a small 'l', beat one of the official Liberal candidates who was bottom of the poll. Graham saw no 'acts which, considering the general character of the crowds, could be considered violent; but there were many playful kickings and pushings which citizens of other boroughs might have considered objectionable.' But the eve of the poll had been marred, he wrote, by the kicking to death of Andrew Young, a horse tenter at a colliery, for which five Irishmen were in custody. Graham certainly did his best and gave a good analysis of the cross-voting, but Spencer had guessed wrong. The same *Guardian* leader, which had to regret that Mr Gladstone would only be the junior member for Greenwich, went on to say: 'The Liberal success at Stafford will be the talk of the clubs. Mr MacDonald is the first working-class candidate who has been returned to the House of Commons; and if no worse choice is ever made by the trade unions, the country will have but scant reason to complain.' This is a significant change in tone from its comment during the 1868 election: 'It is a saying of accepted truth that the man who pleads his own cause in a court of law has a fool for his client. Is it very different with the working man in the House of Commons?'[12]

The *Guardian* had not been happy about Gladstone's sudden dissolution after a date had been fixed for the reassembly of parliament. It also distrusted his half promise to abolish the income tax: 'We can only say that we believe and tremble – more, it must really be owned, than we admire.' But it felt that there was still much good work to be done by the Liberal government as well as a remarkable record of reforms achieved.[13] As late as 31 January it believed that Gladstone would have a considerable majority. Three days later the *Guardian* reported despondency in the Reform Club, but comforted itself that 'if at the sacrifice of a few seats Mr Gladstone can produce more co-

* This at least is the probable explanation of these entries in the Reporters' Diary: January 28 Bradford (Forster) EX; January 30 Accrington (Shuttleworth) joint tel. EX J.T. (John Turner); February 2 Bradford (Forster) joint tel. J.T.

hesion among his followers, he will have accomplished no small portion of his own object.' Another two days and South-East Lancashire Liberals finally made up their mind to adopt one left-wing and one right-wing candidate for the two seats. They chose the radical Peter Rylands and Edward Taylor. Rylands had just been defeated at Warrington which he had narrowly won in 1868; Taylor was standing for the first (and only) time, and with evident reluctance. In its leading article the *Guardian* modestly explained: 'Of Mr Taylor we must speak with more reserve. His relations to this journal are well known in this district and, perhaps, we cannot do better than refer our readers to his address.'[14] Did Scott feel slightly embarrassed as he read there that 'the proposed abolition of the income tax cannot fail to prove a great blessing to large numbers of the middle class. and it is satisfactory to know that such relief will be accompanied by other remissions which benefit those who are exempt from the burdens of direct taxation'?*

Rylands and Taylor fought well, always appearing together and skilfully avoiding attempts to drive a wedge between them. Alexander Ireland, the publisher of the rival *Examiner*, sat on the joint Liberal election committee. But the battle had been lost before it began. Their Free Trade Hall meeting took place the day after the Liberals had lost two of the three Manchester seats. The *Guardian* gave four columns to its report, but in its leader it had to concede that Disraeli would have a working majority in the new parliament. Understandably there was a nostalgic note in the Liberal speeches at the Free Trade Hall which looked back again and again to the good old days. Edward Taylor devoted his peroration to the scene at Lancaster Assizes in 1819 when his father, John Edward Taylor, was acquitted of criminal libel, thanks to one juror's obstinacy in a good cause. 'Who did they think that man was?' the *Guardian* report concludes. 'It was the father of his (Mr Taylor's) colleague in this contest. (Loud cheers.) Was it a wonder that he asked, if he pleaded with all supporters of his, to give their votes to Mr Rylands as they would give them to himself? (Loud applause.)' They did. Only nine votes separated Rylands and Taylor at the declaration, but the Conservative candidates were some 1,500 votes ahead. The next week *Guardian* readers were able to turn their attention from politics to coursing at Aintree, and enjoy very full reports of the Waterloo Cup.[15]

---

* M.G. 5 February 1874. The South-East Lancashire division contained much of what is now Manchester as well as many neighbouring townships.

CHAPTER FOURTEEN

Matters of Taste

I

'HE is a somewhat dour little dissenter and his heart is not in his work.'
So Scott wrote during his first year on the *Guardian* about G. V. Marsh,
the chief reporter.* He was complaining about a theatre notice which
Marsh had written and which Scott felt was so bad that he himself
must write a second notice to put things right. This unguarded sentence
in a family letter tells a good deal both about Scott and about his plans
for the *Guardian*. The pejorative use of 'dissenter' comes rather oddly
from the man who only five years before at Oxford 'had contrived to
tell Jacobson to-day that I was an extreme dissenter. But both Scott
and his father were theologically rather than socially dissenters. As
early as 1838 the first John Edward Taylor had complained that C. P.
Scott's father was 'leaving the Dissenters' because he was leaving
London for Bath. The answer he got was curt: 'I hardly know whether
I rightly apprehend the sense in which you use the expression. If you
think I shall associate less with them that is hardly possible . . . we visit
only the Miss Martineaus.'[1] Scott's dissent had little in common with
the self-contained world of Lancashire and Cheshire nonconformity to
which Marsh belonged.

Years later another chief reporter of the '*Guardian*,' its first hisorian,
Haslam Mills, reconstructed this vanished world. In a series of sentitive,
nostalgic essays in the *Guardian* he evoked the social life of his youth
in chapel-going Ashton-under-Lyne in the 1880s where The Chsurch
was generally tolerant of the circus, but the Chapel decided, with few
dissentients, that there was no place for circuses in its ethical scheme.'
'In those old days such was the niceness of our nose for these things,
there was an ethical distinction between the theatre at our own doors
to which we did not go and the one in Manchester to which we

---

* 'an anti-vaccinationist, an anti-tobacconist, a teetaller, a vegetarian, a strong
Radical, and of course, a Nonconformist, he was not intolerant even of cranks . . .
But oh, what a martinet.' (T. S. Townend in the *Manchester Guardian House Journal*
January 1921.)

travelled by the 6.19; and as for the music-hall, it was rather emphatically a place which we had not been inside.'[2]

Mills collected some of these essays into a book with a title, *Grey Pastures*, chosen to match the sober, puritan, nonconformist colour that predominated in North-west England when Scott came to Manchester. Many of its leading merchants and shopkeepers and cotton operatives were devoted to good works both at home and in foreign missions, The works really were good works, and their supporters really were devoted. They were men with a mission; but, as such men are apt to be, a little humourless in their impassioned advocacy, and a little blind to other values. One of their most needed missions was 'temperance.' Drunkenness was a major social problem in Victorian England; for many individuals, no doubt, 'total abstinence', 'taking the pledge' or 'wearing the blue ribbon' was the only salvation for family life. Edward Taylor felt this strongly; Scott agreed with him, but not strongly enough for Taylor's liking. At any rate, Taylor's letters to Scott repeatedly recur to the theme that the *Guardian* was not firm enough on this issue.

What, in fact, the *Guardian* was doing was letting a little light and air into the rather stuffy, over-solemn atmosphere of the temperance meeting. In 1882, for instance, when Francis Murphy came to Manchester from America and collected 6,730 pledges in ten days, the *Guardian* described his meetings in the same kind of manner in which three-quarters of a century later it set the scene for Billy Graham:

'Francis Murphy . . . has the power which "converted prize-fighters" and the rest of that dismal fraternity have of speaking from personal experience. At the same time he is not only transparently honest, but has a very considerable command of eloquence, which has been trained and studied more carefully than would at first sight appear, and flavours his utterance with a rollicking Irish humour which is often irresistible. He seems perfectly at home on the platform, laughs at his own jokes, caresses his moustache when he thinks he has said a telling thing, slouches up and down to show how the drunkard slouches home on Saturday night, and appears to say everything as if it had just occurred to him for the first time, and as if he had never said it before . . .' (27 February 1882)

A similar eye for detail that is significant because it is incongruous appears in occasional flashes in the London Letter of those days, the ancestor of the present Miscellany. F. W. Farrar is remembered to-day largely because he wrote that immensely sentimental school story, *Eric, or Little by Little*. But in his lifetime he was greatly respected as a leading liberal churchman as well as a distinguished public school headmaster. He was a Fellow of the Royal Society; his *Essay on the*

Origin of Language attracted the attention of Darwin; and his *Life of Christ* ran through twelve editions in 1874, the year of its publication. Two years later his first sermon as a Canon of Westminster was, therefore, something of an event. The *Guardian*'s London Letter demurely noted that 'The large congregation was supplied with what is surely a novelty to regular churchgoers – highly perfumed programmes.'[3]

In slightly edged words like these, and still more by the quality of the attention that it gave to the arts, the *Guardian* helped to change the mental climate of Manchester. It was through the *Guardian*, as Scott first made it, that Haslam Mills graduated from his upbringing among men like his dour little dissenting predecessor, G. V. Marsh, to the enlightened emancipation of Edwardian Manchester. He, and many others like him, accomplished this spiritual pilgrimage without losing their conviction that life was serious as well as amusing. They grew out of Little Bethel, but they did not foul the nest in which they had been brought up.

2

Within a short time Scott brought a new quality to the regular dramatic criticism in the paper. The interaction between the plays in the Manchester theatres and the comments on them by *Guardian* critics enlivened many minds. The great days both of the Manchester theatre and of the *Guardian*'s dramatic criticism still lay ahead; but already in 1876 a young man catching the 6.19 from Ashton might not only have seen Henry Irving as Hamlet but compared his own impressions with those of the *Guardian* critic* who carefully weighed Irving's 'striking merits' against his 'no less striking defects.'

'In his conception Mr Irving takes Hamlet's self-confession for absolute truth and makes him not merely a weak and irresolute man, faltering beneath a terrible duty, but reduces him to the level of absolute contempt . . . Again, though Hamlet no doubt is fundamentally a poor creature he is also the glass of fashion and the mould of form. His weakness is unsuspected by those around him, unsuspected by himself probably until it is put to the test. Mr Irving forces it on us from the earliest moment.' (6 September 1876)

Such dramatic criticism was a new thing in the *Guardian*. It represents Scott's determination to bring to the cultural life of Manchester the disciplined, thorough examination which, true to his Oxford train-

---

* Probably A. G. Symonds, secretary of the Manchester Reform Club and a first cousin of John Addington Symonds, the historian of the Italian Renaissance. A letter of W. T. Arnold's, written in 1879, says, 'This part of the work used to be done by a certain A. G. Symonds', and goes on to identify him.

ing, he felt any work of art deserved. Only the best was to be good enough. This was to apply alike to the play, the actors and the critics. It was similarly to apply to music and to literature. The high seriousness with which politics and business had always been taken in the *Guardian* was to be extended to the arts. This was not to be primarily a matter of more space in the paper, but of better quality in the discrimination and the writing.

Music, perhaps, was the first of the arts to be fully developed in Manchester. It did not divide the otherworldly from the worldly as the theatre did, and it found a firm basis in the German community. The two great festivals of 1828 and 1836 had been linked by regular series of concerts on a smaller scale. But the history of Manchester as a permanent international musical centre in its own right really begins in 1848 with the coming to Manchester of Charles Hallé, a young man of 29, a Rhinelander who since 1836 had been domiciled in Paris where he had become a friend of Chopin and Berlioz. He came to Manchester to play the solo part in the 'Emperor' concerto and, according to the *Guardian*, 'fully justified all that we ventured to say of him the other day upon hearsay.' Hallé, on the other hand, had been disenchanted: 'The orchestra, oh! the orchestra . . . I seriously thought of packing up and leaving Manchester so that I might not have to endure a second of these wretched performances.'[4] But he was persuaded to stay, and he successfully carried through the revolution he had been invited to lead.

The Hallé Orchestra itself was established on a permanent basis as a result of the Art Treasures Exhibition of 1857. Ten years later George Freemantle became the *Guardian*'s music critic. He served the paper for over a quarter of a century, dying only shortly before Hallé. The interplay between conductor and critic over so many years was important both for Manchester music and for the *Manchester Guardian*. Without the paper's help Hallé could hardly have built up the large steady audience which a symphony orchestra needs. But Manchester music gained more than the pulling power of publicity. It gained a public that was informed, prepared, aware. When the 'St Matthew Passion' was sung in Manchester in 1873 – it was only the fourth or fifth English performance – the audience was no doubt better in its power of appreciation as well as in numbers because of the long introductory article in the *Guardian* on the morning of the concert.[5] Hallé, too, gained from the regular opportunity of hearing how his work struck a perceptive and sympathetic listener. On its side the *Guardian* gained the possibility of becoming an all-round paper reflecting every side of artistic life. A newspaper reflects; it does not provide. A city, or a country, without music can only have musically mute newspapers.

Much of the *Guardian*'s artistic reputation rests upon its publication in a city that has had its own symphony orchestra for well over a century. Opera was a visitor; orchestral music was a resident.

But in another sense music in the 1870s was a resident alien. Little English music was performed; as far as was realised there was little English music worth performing. Hallé set his standards high. On the other hand, there were works by foreign composers waiting for a first performance in England. Some had waited a long time. In 1868 Hallé gave the first English performance of the Mozart Serenade in B flat for wind instruments and in the following year that of Beethoven's Leonora No. 1. In 1879 and 1880 came two first English performances of works by Berlioz – the Symphonie Fantastique and Faust. The *Guardian*, for its part, did not confine itself to noticing works performed in Manchester. In 1876 it published two long articles on the first Bayreuth Festival which was opened with a complete cycle of the 'Ring,'[6] and in 1882 it gave full notices to each night of the 'Ring's' first English performance in London.[7]

There were, however, people who felt that there was undue neglect of British music in Manchester, and this found expression in a number of letters to the *Guardian* in 1875. George Freemantle wrote privately to Arthur Sullivan. His proposal can only be inferred from Sullivan's reply which suggests that he was being sounded about conducting in Manchester. 'Hallé is an old and esteemed friend of mine,' Sullivan wrote, 'and I could not, of course, do anything or take any steps that would in the least degree imply that I was working in the matter unknown to him. All that I can say is that if a change is made, and the thing thrown open to everyone, I would (under certain satisfactory conditions) take my chance with the rest.'[8] But there, wisely, the matter rested.

3

Manchester's appetite for visiting art exhibitions was insatiable; and so, the *Guardian* believed, was its appetite for reading about them. In 1857 over a million and a quarter people had visited the Art Treasures Exhibition. Even more would have come, a reader thought, if the railways had been more awake to their opportunity. Only one excursion, he complained, was run from Nottingham, and that left at the inconvenient hour of 6.45 a.m. and did not arrive until noon.[9] But, even so, the Manchester attendance does not compare badly with the six million who went to the Great Exhibition in London in 1851. For weeks the *Guardian* was filled with elaborate accounts of the pictures, gallery by gallery. These were republished in pamphlet form. The articles on the British Gallery alone made a substantial pamphlet of 120 pages which was sold for 6d. The *Guardian*, however, over-estimated the market and about 4,000 copies of the series of handbooks were sold to John Heywood, the wholesalers, at a cheap rate. But this did not deter Edward Taylor from covering on the same gigantic scale other art exhibitions in other towns. In 1868, for instance, the *Guardian* published seventeen long articles on the Leeds exhibition. G. T. Robinson, the *Guardian*'s war correspondent in Metz, could not complain of being short of space in his more usual role of art critic.

Very early in Scott's editorship Robinson seems to have been demanding a monopoly of art criticism. Taylor told Scott that this could not be allowed[10] and, as it happened, the first senior appointment to the staff made during Scott's editorship was of a man especially well qualified in this field. Scott was still unfamiliar with the world of London journalism from which Richard Whiteing came. Moreover, Whiteing had a quite different background to that of most of the men whom Scott personally chose for his staff. It may well be that Whiteing was as much Taylor's last editorial appointment as Scott's first.

Whiteing is remembered to-day only for his immensely successful novel of social criticism, *No. 5 John St*, which deals with the London of the Diamond Jubilee. But a burning concern for the under-dog was apparent in Whiteing's work throughout his life – something which he owed in part to having sat under F. D. Maurice, the Christian Socialist, at the Working Men's College. He first made his name by a series of articles in the radical *Evening Star* in which he commented on London's currently fashionable exploration of the slums by reversing the process and allowing an imaginary costermonger to report on Belgravia. This brought him a place on the *Morning Star*, Cobden's newspaper, under Justin McCarthy. From there he moved to Paris as European corres-pondent for the *New York World*, covering such events as the Alabama arbitration in Geneva and a revolution in Spain. But there was another side to Whiteing. He had served an apprenticeship as an engraver of seals and attended art schools at night. He had worked in Paris under the Second Empire as the £2 a week secretary of an international work-ing men's art exhibition, and he was thoroughly at home in the world of painters and dealers.

What did Whiteing do on the *Guardian*? Art criticism, no doubt, but what else? It seems likely that some of the social investigations described in the last chapter were his. Scott's recollection years later that Whiteing was 'the best, shortest and (word omitted) descriptive writer we have ever had'[11] suggests that he may have been the man who observed on May Day at Knutsford in 1873 that 'Mr Barnacle, the vicar . . . tries to choose, not the prettiest, but the best girl of the year, taking the ordinary school standards for his test. That the queen of this year happens to be very pretty is really not her fault . . .' The following month one of the reporters, John Turner, went to Wigan to cover the visit of the Prince of Wales. But did he do the sketch as well as the speeches? Such an occasion demands length; but there is really nothing to say. John Turner or Richard Whiteing – one does not know which – said it well, noticing the strange slatternly look of the Wigan house roofs, 'as if they had been subjected to three earthquakes and a bombardment,' but more or less hidden for the day by charitable red cloth – new and fresh, not tired and worn like London street decorations which do duty time after time. Young reporters of 1873 may have tried to write like Richard Whiteing just as a later generation sighed after C. E. Montague's style. 'School of Whiteing' is perhaps the safest attribution for the old lady of Wigan smoking her clay pipe:

'It is not wicked to smoke a clay pipe, but it is odd. The oddness is increased when the pipe is not only of clay, but of white clay, and not only of white clay, but in length nearly a yard of the same. Assuredly, one of the funniest of old ladies; and it is to be hoped that she not only saw, but was seen by her Prince and his laughter-loving wife . . .' (4 June 1873)

Whiteing was the sort of man who was happy only in capitals. He returned to Paris in 1875. It was probably inevitable: Manchester and Salford were, he admitted, in size big enough for anything, but they were 'still only varieties of the same thing', while London (or Paris) was every city. But he did not stay long enough in Manchester to discover how cosmopolitan it really was. It needed, perhaps, someone like Haslam Mills coming from an outlying cotton town to recognise in Manchester an infinitely varied capital with its 'Strangeways, where Saturday is quite universally the first day in the week . . . and Kersal, where conversation is largely carried on in modern Greek and where Venizélos might easily be staying for the weekend without any of the rest of us being any the wiser.'[12] He might have added its large Armenian colony and, before the First World War, its great German community – so firmly based that a boys' outfitter, 'Andrew Macbeth und Söhne', for the occasion, thought it worthwhile to publish an advertisement in the *Guardian* written wholly in German.[13]

But that was in November 1876, and by then Richard Whiteing had been back in Paris for more than a year. He had liked the *Guardian* as much as he disliked Manchester, and he continued to write for it as an occasional contributor from Paris. His was an engaging if undisciplined mind, and his habits of business seem to have been similar. In 1878 we find Buxton, the *Guardian*'s business manager, writing to him in Paris to enquire why a cheque sent the previous year had not been presented and suggesting as if, from old experience, that he had 'stowed it away somewhere and quite forgotten its existence.'[14] Whiteing was back in London in the eighties and worked regularly for the *Guardian* in London on a small salary or retainer until he joined the *Daily News* in 1887. He kept up his friendship with Scott and remained an occasional contributor until 1920, retaining to the end that affection for the *Guardian* which is common to many who have been, even if only briefly, on its staff. Looking back in 1915 on the newspapers of the seventies, he felt that the *Guardian* was 'then, as now, among the best, local only in its place of origin, metropolitan and more in its vision, and in its championship of all the great causes, win or lose.

> *S'il gagne bataille*
> *Aura mes amours.*
> *Qu'il gagne, ou qu'il perd*
> *Les aura toujours.*

Perhaps the nymph was a prophetess with such a paper in her mind.'[15]

When he looked back after forty years to the Manchester he had known, it was the lavish, misguided picture-buying of its merchants which he most vividly – and perhaps a little fancifully – recalled.

'The Manchester man who had just done well on 'Change took his favourite picture dealer's on the way home to repeat the stroke. His business, in the one place, was to know all about coming cargoes, and in the other, about coming men . . . You bought at a stiff price to stimulate the sense of luck in the purchase, and four figures was the almost inevitable rule. The idea was that you had better make haste about it, or they would soon be five. In that expectation many invested in pictures as they might have invested in diamonds and put them on the same footing as money, land or houses in their wills. This went on until heirs began to realize, with sore disappointment in lieu of the expected portion . . . It was all too foolish and so unnecessary. The John Edward Taylor sale showed what a good investment good art might be, when the investor was also his own connoisseur.'[16]

It is safe to say that the *Guardian*'s intense and continuous concern for art owes more to Edward Taylor than to Scott. As long as Taylor was alive the quality of the judgment which the paper brought to the work of living or dead masters was ensured. He wanted and secured good technical criticism, not just that anecdotage which was easy when every picture told a story. Thus a half-column notice on the leader page of Lady Butler's 'Scotland for Ever' was concerned much more with the composition and the painting of the picture than with the story of the charge at Waterloo which was its subject.[17] It may not have been a great, though it was certainly a popular, picture; but the notice was true criticism of the painting. This Taylor insisted on; what Scott added was an equal insistence that all *Guardian* critics, whatever they wrote about – plays, painting, poetry or music – should write well. They usually did, as in the notice of the William Blake exhibition in 1876.

'. . . There is a copy of the large folio edition of the "Night Thoughts" with every page bordered with some wild and mysterious vision, drawn by the hand of Blake, representing what he saw implied in the poet's sombre lines . . . a wonderful instance of Blake's rapidity and of his inexhaustible variety. Variety, indeed, he had *ipso facto*; he lived, he would seem to say, among a crowd of spirits differing from one another as much as mortals do . . . The hidden things of the universe were not hidden from his unearthly eye; he honestly believed that he *saw* angels and demons, and he drew them as he saw them.' (22 April, 1876)

4

Scott attended to the notices of art exhibitions, theatres and concerts as a good editor should. He knew that they were vital to the kind of paper he wanted the *Guardian* to be. He took care that they had sufficient prominence and that they were in good hands; and then he sensibly left them to those hands. Indeed, W. P. Crozier, who served under Scott for many years before becoming editor, believed that Scott had long given up reading the music notices and that they would only have infuriated him if he had. But books were another matter. No man whom Oxford had marked so indelibly for her own could possibly take only a professional interest in seeing that the reviewing was well done. And besides, while an art critic or a music critic is writing about somebody else's medium, a reviewer is writing about his own. Not for nothing did Scott's son-in-law and lieutenant, C. E. Montague, call one of his books *A Writer's Notes on His Trade*. At first Scott was his own principal reviewer and, to the end, he always insisted on seeing each night the list of books going out and the reviewers to whom they were being sent. This he would read carefully and, on occasion, amend.

Scott started with the asset of one remarkable reviewer. George Saintsbury had been for a short time on the staff of the Manchester Grammar School to which he had gone in 1866. This led to his 'long and close connection with the *Manchester Guardian*, for which he wrote the great bulk of the literary reviews until his retirement from journalism.' When he died, a *Guardian* leader (one might guess it was by Allan Monkhouse) remarked:

'No sitting on fences for Saintsbury. He knew what he liked and he never had the least hesitation in letting others know it too . . . In the world of literature he saw no fences – or at least none on which he or anybody else need attempt to sit. Whatever else Saintsbury's . . . readers (took) from his books, they would at least take away this: the conviction that in the kingdom of letters there are many mansions, and that most of them were habitable.'[18]

The appeal of theatre, concert and exhibition notices is largely confined to those who can hear or see what is written about. One has to be in the right place at the right time. But books can be read anywhere. First-class reviewing attracted readers in London, in Oxford and Cambridge and the country as even the best notices of Manchester concerts and exhibitions could not. The prominence that Scott gave to book reviews and their much better quality under his editorship helped to spread the *Guardian*'s influence outside its immediate surroundings.

Perhaps there is nothing very surprising in devoting a column and a half to a review of Jowett's translation of Plato, or even in a young man's confident verdict on it: 'We may unhesitatingly predict that it is destined to take a high place among the English classics.'[19] But new authors are a different matter. How are they to get reviews? And, from the other side, how is a raw literary editor to know which untried authors are worth reviewing? Introductions are useful. They can secure reviews, but they ought not to guarantee good reviews. A reviewer ought to make up his own mind, even at the risk of being wrong. Just before Easter 1872, Scott received a copy of *Erewhon*. The book was anonymous, but it came with a note of introduction from Robert Bridges, who had been at Corpus with Scott, and a letter signed S. Butler. *Erewhon* irritated the reviewer so that, though he appreciated the writer's skill, he failed to recognise that Butler had written a really remarkable book:

'. . . Greatly as we dissent from our author's view of moral philosophy, his opinions are such as have the support of the metaphysical school now predominant in England, and the manner of presentation is certainly very ingenious and the details worked out with much skill and liveliness . . . We need not enlarge on a chapter in which infant baptism is elaborately attacked, or go into the account of the colleges of unreason where the hypothetical language is taught, and professorships of inconsistency and unreason exist. This last is a skit on the Oxford course with its combination of scholarship and philosophy. Altogether the satire strikes us as not particularly happy or original . . . the author of Erewhon is a very clever and original person; but we cannot on the whole think his work successful.' (24 April, 1872)

Nearly fifty years later the *Guardian* made handsome amends to Butler's memory when the biography by Henry Festing Jones came in for review. The literary editor remembered that Bernard Shaw had described Butler as 'in his own department the greatest English writer of the latter half of the nineteenth century.' He asked Shaw to review the biography. His reply was prompt: no daily paper could afford the space the book deserved. Scott took the bait. Shaw's review filled two-thirds of a page.*

Eighteen-seventy-three brought the first volume of poems by Robert Bridges for review. His good wine at least needed no bush to commend it to the *Guardian*:

'We have heard a certain wine much praised by competent judges . . . on which a pleasing coincidence has bestowed the euphoniously peculiar name of Chateau d'Yquem. The summer which it makes in the veins is short and passing, as it is a wine for sipping not for deep potations; to the port drinkers of the Establishment it is a foolishness; nor is it fitted for the multitude which empties flagons of Gladstone claret for no better reason than that it is athirst. Yet a glass of this wine lingers pleasantly on the experienced palate; and when a man owns flagons a summons to his table is not likely to fall on deaf ears. Mr Bridges will excuse the triviality of the comparison; but the gentle pleasure which his little volume of poems has given us irresistibly suggested it . . .' (6 February, 1873)

Was this review the work of George Saintsbury, the future author of *Notes on a Cellar Book*, then still in his twenties?

Some idea of the range of reviews may be gathered from a few of the titles in the 1876 files. A single batch of novels included *Dead Men's Shoes* by the author of *Lady Audley's Secret, My Young Alcides* by Charlotte Mary Yonge, and *The Manchester Man* by Mrs J. Linnaeus Banks. It was natural that Trevelyan's *Life of Macaulay* should have had a long notice: and that Leslie Stephen's *English Thought in the* 18*th Century* should receive an enthusiastic and discerning review. A Liberal newspaper might even have felt bound to notice *Homeric Syncretism* since the author was Mr Gladstone, but Jebb's *Attic Orators* surely discloses the special interests of the editor and his wife.[20]

---

*'I have ferociously shown up Butler as being ten times worse than his father and grandfather, the moral being that the country parsonage, the public school, the university and the Church produce even more disastrous results when their human products are geniuses than when they are blockheads.'
Shaw-Scott 24 October 1919. The review appeared on 1 November.

5

The literary side of the paper was further developed after Scott's marriage and in consequence of it. Mrs Scott became a regular reviewer of novels and appears to have acted as something like an unofficial literary adviser. This book is a history of the *Guardian* and not a biography of the Scott family. But Rachel Cook, whom Scott married in 1874, may almost be regarded as a member of the staff. In the office the legend grew up that she wrote leaders, but this was only because her husband used to dictate to her so that some of the leaders were in her handwriting.* 'I can remember so clearly,' her daughter wrote, 'him walking up and down the room, dictating, pausing sometimes to think out the next bit, and asking her when he went on to read out the last sentence, she meanwhile sitting very quietly, not making any suggestion or breaking his train of thought, but sometimes continuing writing at a letter of her own if the pause were rather long.'[21] In the evening, a family friend recalled, husband and wife would sometimes go together to the office. 'When anything special was on and Mrs Scott was well enough, both went down about six o'clock, taking with them a can of milk, eggs, rolls and butter, so that they could have a meal down there. Many a time it was two o'clock in the morning when they returned.'[22]

George Eliot considered that Rachel Cook was the most beautiful woman she had ever seen. But, more to the point, she was also one of the original seven undergraduates of what was to become Girton College, but which was then at Hitchin, an even more discreet distance from Cambridge. In 1872 she was placed in the second class of the Classical Tripos and her paper on Aristotle was considered better than Butcher's, the famous translator of the *Odyssey*, who was a candidate at the same examination. It may have been almost as important that she was the daughter of a Scottish professor. Neither she nor her husband had been brought up in London. They had not felt the gravitational pull by which the capital seems to hold nearly all who are once caught up in it.

Scott's marriage reinforced the influence of the old universities and kept him free from the social pull of London life. The friends they made in Manchester and the men he chose to be his colleagues shared this outlook and this detachment. The sun of Oxford shone directly on Manchester, not deflected from London. And the culture which Scott had got at Oxford was also to be found in abundance at Owens College, now the University of Manchester.

*Before he became an M.P. Scott wrote frequently. Taylor warned him against the strain of a daily leader: 'Very strong and wiry men say it is too much.' Taylor-Scott 29 July 1884. See also p.373

Scott's first mistake on the paper, made in his first week, was caused by his failure to recognise this. He 'stirred up a hornet's nest' (the phrase is Taylor's) by ignoring Owens and suggesting in a leader that Manchester merchants would do well to send their sons to Oxford to read a little science even if they were not going to take a degree. But the Principal was easily appeased and Scott soon made many lasting friends among the staff. And where Scott made friends, the *Guardian* was apt to find contributors. There was, for instance, A. W. Ward himself, who was later to become Vice-Chancellor first of Manchester and then of Cambridge University and to edit the *Cambridge Modern History*. Long after he left Manchester he continued to review books for the *Guardian* and to advise Scott about staff appointments, though he had to give up dramatic criticism. James Bryce was another life-long friend and collaborator. His main influence on the paper, perhaps, was in the help he gave over Near Eastern affairs. His passionate concern for Armenia sprang from his journey in Caucasia in 1876; that winter the *Guardian* published a long and authoritative series of articles on the Armenians.[23]

Owens College in its youth and the *Guardian* in its middle age recognised each other as powerful allies and acted accordingly. 'I was astounded one day to hear that Dr Adolphus Ward, Principal of Owens College, had been to my lodgings to call upon me,' J. B. Atkins wrote about his life in Manchester a few years later. 'Professor Oliver Elton . . . came soon afterwards. These attentions were little expected by an obscure member of the *Manchester Guardian* staff, even though the alliance was strong, and such civilities were inspired by the institution, not by the individual.'[24]

But Oxford does figure portentously large in the *Guardian* of those days. One cannot read far without finding either the Boat Race, with the result cautiously kept in doubt until the last line of the report, or even the university bicycle races, or the opening of Keble College Chapel (taking a whole half-page), or a column and a quarter on the 'Indian Civil Service and the Universities.' Oxford appears again in serial form in 1884 with J. M. Cape's *Recollections of the Oxford Movement*. A whole column of 'their' paper devoted to a nostalgic picture of Newman at the University Church must have shocked many of the *Guardian*'s nonconformist readers. Would they have been appeased if they could have seen the writer's rather pathetic note to Scott, a young man but an old friend, bidding him 'when you write, please write large and black as my sight is bad'?[25]

That same year the *Guardian* carried two long articles on Mrs Opie, an almost entirely forgotten Regency novelist, based on old family letters. The contributor recalls how in 1814 her mother and Mrs Opie tipped a waiter a guinea to let them into the hotel where the Emperor Alexander, 'that demi-god of beauty and heroism', was staying, and how they stroked his coat sleeves while more forward young ladies kissed his hand:

'How childish it seems! Such things are never done now; we are far above such folly. It cannot be in these days that a racquet used by royalty was handed round in a select company assembled in the rooms of a learned college don and devoutly kissed.' (3 July, 1884)

Here is an authentic liberal voice, but it is gayer than that which came from the chapels in the mill towns. To many a reader of the *Examiner* it must have seemed that the *Guardian* was becoming not so much light as frivolous in its treatment of serious themes. And, once again, we are back in Oxford. The contributor was Mrs William Sidgwick whose husband had been tutor at Merton. This time the connection was not established through Scott, though he gladly took it up and Mrs Sidgwick became a regular reviewer. The information that Mrs Sidgwick had material she wanted to use came from Mrs Gaskell's daughters who still lived in the house where *Mary Barton* and *North and South* had been written. There they kept open house for generations of *Guardian* men. One of them was once asked whether 'it would look' – here they hesitated – 'at all "unbecoming", or "just a shade too unconventional" for two maiden ladies to provide cigars for the men after dinner.'[26]

This is, of course, pastiche Cranford; but by this time 'Cranford,' and all Mrs Gaskell's books, were as firmly included in *Guardian* literary country as Knutsford was in its circulation area. It had not always been so. 'Mary Barton,' though 'beautifully written', was severely trounced when it came out because of the lessons it taught the working classes. Since then the *Guardian* had learned its own lesson in literary criticism. 'But what does it teach? People always ask that in England about any work of imagination . . . To have that clear and enlarged comic vision, and share it, may not be to teach, but it is to impart a faculty for happy learning.'[27] These words, in fact, occur in a leading article of 1910 on the centenary of Mrs Gaskell's birth. But they might have been written almost any time after Scott became editor. That is one measure of what the *Guardian* owed to Scott, and Scott to Oxford.

CHAPTER FIFTEEN

Balkan Adventures

I

ALMOST by accident, and again through Scott's Oxford connections, the *Guardian* stumbled on a distinctive, and often, indeed, a unique viewpoint from which to survey the troubled Balkans of the 1870s and 1880s. It had no share in reporting at first hand those Bulgarian atrocities which brought Mr Gladstone from his retirement to demand the expulsion of the Turks 'bag and baggage' from that province. It relied on the London papers, notably the *Daily News*, for its information from Bulgaria. But in Bosnia and Herzegovina, where similar problems arose, it had its own independent source which other papers lacked. Here it led British opinion. This is how it came about.

Scott's uncle, Joseph Prestwich, had been by occupation a wine merchant, but he had gradually built up a national reputation as a geologist. One day on his way to give expert evidence in a law suit over water rights, he met in the train a paper manufacturer, John Evans, who also had established a firm reputation as a geologist and who had been called to give evidence on the opposite side. The two men struck up a deep and lasting friendship. In 1874 Joseph Prestwich, although a non-graduate, was appointed to the first professorship of geology at Oxford. Later that year, in December, his friend's son, Arthur Evans, the future discoverer of Cnossos, took a first class in the new Oxford School of Modern History. He set out almost at once to travel through Bosnia and Herzegovina and rapidly became an ardent lover of the South Slavs. He loved the people, the land and the openings it provided for archaeological and historical work. He hated the Turks, though not the Bosnian Moslems who were Slavs; and he was already on the way to hating the Austrians. He decided to make his home in Dalmatia at Ragusa, which was just inside Austrian territory. His parents were wealthy and he had a reasonable allowance, but he was glad to earn a little extra. More important was his need to find some paper in which he could make known the sufferings of the Slavs with whom he increasingly identified himself. Prestwich introduced the young man to Scott. His own book, and several articles in the *Guardian* in 1876 from occasional contributors, had made it clear that there was plenty of news to be got which Englishmen ought to know.* Evans set out for Ragusa† in January 1877 with £100 to cover telegraph expenses and a commission to act as the regular *Guardian* correspondent. But the young man was in one way a surprising appointment for the *Guardian* even of those days. 'I don't choose to be told by every barbarian I meet that he is a man and a brother,' he had written in his book. 'I believe in the existence of inferior races, and would like to see them exterminated ... but ... a man must be either blind or a diplomatist not to perceive that in the Slavonic provinces of Turkey the choice ultimately lies between despotism and a democracy almost socialistic . . .'[1] At 26 Evans may have been something of a snob, but he was certainly something of a prophet.

In fact, as Dr Joan Evans wrote in her biography of her half-brother, his 'letters . . . altogether exceeded Mr Scott's expectations; they were lively, well written and well documented, and infused with a dramatic sense that he had hardly expected from the myopic archaeologist, looking like an undergraduate, whom his uncle had produced for his inspection. He wrote warmly to his correspondent to thank him for his "admirable" letters and to ask for more and more; he sent marked copies of the papers containing them to eminent members of Parliament'[2] and thereby let a little wholesome air into a complacent and indignant corner of the British Consular Service. Evans telegraphed to the *Guardian* news of a series of atrocities, and then set off alone to investigate what had actually happened in one remote mountain village called Ochievo where eight people had been murdered and between twenty and twenty-five women raped. This outrage was a typical, not an isolated occurrence.

Against everybody's advice Evans crossed from the friendly area occupied by the insurgents into Turkish-held country. Nobody would go with him. It was still winter and there was a raging torrent to cross. There was no bridge and the swollen river was too deep to ford. He half stripped, left his revolver behind, plunged into the ice-cold river and swam across. He was soon lost in a wilderness of rocks and stunted pine-woods, but was found before long by a refugee from Ochievo. Together they made their way to the deserted village:

---

* One or two have the same vivid qualities as Evans's work, e.g. the brisk account of the Turkish soldiers who 'extemporised a game of football with a couple of heads they had managed to secure,' kicking them up to where the writer sat. (M.G. 17 April 1876 but referring to events of November 1875)

† Now known as Dubrovnik.

C. P. Scott in middle age

W. T. Arnold after his retirement. He was principal
leader writer when the *Guardian* turned Left

A letter from Lloyd George in 1911 with Scott's endorsement on the envelope. The incident is described in Chapter 25

A Radical leader. C.P.S. pen in hand, a pad of copy paper in front of him. There is no telephone in sight, and no typewriter

'A more hideous scene of havoc I have never seen . . . Two homesteads alone remained unburnt . . . but even these were partially wrecked and entirely gutted. What made the havoc even more melancholy was its two-fold character. There were first the blackened foundations of the homesteads burnt the other day with the fresh smell of fire upon them; and side by side with these the debris of the former village burnt by the Turks on the 24th of July last year. To discover the little hoards of money which the rayah families might possess, the pillagers had in many cases grubbed up the earth floor of the huts, and in one I saw the actual hole from which the hoard of the most well-to-do family – amounting, so my guide declared, to £8 in paper money, but this was probably an exaggeration – had been grubbed up by the Bashi-Bazouks. We . . . were surveying (the ruins) of the lower village from a height above, when my Bosnian guide, with the quick instinct of a savage, sank down on hands and knees behind a rock, and pointing to a partially wooded mountainside beyond, whispered to me "Turski! Turski!" . . . We pursued the same path which the fugitive villagers had taken . . . I found here plenty of traces of the stampede . . . on a thorn bush part of a woman's clothing, and the remains of a family chest thrown down in the hurry of flight, but rifled now of its contents whatever they may have been. I also picked up some Turkish cartridges . . . and, nearing the river, the hoofmarks of the pursuing Bashi-Bazouks.'*

Evans went on to record his interviews with the survivors whom he sought out in the many different places in insurgent territory or over the Austrian border in which they had taken refuge. He then went on to visit Kulen Vakup, the Moslem town whose people had had the chief hand in the atrocities. There, too, he found refugees – Moslems, this time, who had fled from the Christian insurgents and had had their villages burnt, though 'as far as I could learn without any other circumstances of atrocity.' The troops were turned out and presented arms as Evans rode into the town on a beautiful Arab charger which had been brought for his use. There he found a letter written in antique Cyrillic since the Bosnian Moslems knew neither Osmanli nor Arabic and addressed on the outside to ' "The Emperor of England" and to myself, and in the interior to the Queen of England and again to your correspondent under a Bosnianised version of his name . . . The Czar of England in the eyes of all true Vakuperanis is . . . no one else than His Most Gracious Majesty the Sultan – though with infinite politeness they admit the co-existence of our Queen!'

'I had interviews with, or rather granted audiences to the Begs and the

---

* Rayahs were Christian peasants who held their land by customary tenure from their feudal Moslem lords, the Begs; Bashi-Bazouks were Turkish irregular mercenaries. (21 April 1877)

Mahomedan merchants to my full contentment and heard from their own lips their grievances, their hopes and fears and their view on things in general . . . "You are impoverished and ruined by the flight of the rayah. Why not hold out your hand to him and welcome his return?" "They can return to-morrow," they replied with one accord, "and we should be only too glad to take them back, – but on the old footing." "But do not think," said old Mahomed Bey Kulenovich, who was one of the chief speakers and by no means the worst of the Begs – "do not think that their lot will be the same. Yes, we will receive them back; we will not harm them or their wives or their children; but their lot will never be as favourable as before." And this he said with determined emphasis. "Will you take more from them," I asked, "if they return?" "No," was the short reply; "we will not take more, but their lot will be worse." "Property is property," remarked another sententiously.'

It was a remarkably thorough and careful investigation that Evans had made. As the *Guardian* said in its leading article: 'By dint of energy, resource and courage, and something more than the usual athletic qualities of Englishmen, he has come safely out of a difficult and dangerous enterprise and has been able to give evidence which even official incredulity can scarcely traverse as to the facts which he had previously reported.'[3] Official incredulity had been very firm in its denials. W. R. Holmes, the consul at Sarajevo, reported that there was no truth whatever in the assertion that there had been an increase of murders and outrages. He quoted extracts from Evans's messages to the *Guardian* 'just to show how incorrectly what passes in Bosnia is represented by Slavophiles who, from their vicinity and facility of correspondence, ought to be better informed, if they desired to be so.' He explained that he believed the outrages committed by Christians had been 'as hideous as those committed by the Mussulmans but which, as the Turks . . . have thought it more dignified to revenge than to complain, had had no chroniclers.' He quoted the Vienna correspondent of the *Times* to prove that 'the so-called insurrectionary movement is but brigandage on a large scale.' He promised the Foreign Secretary that he would urge the Turkish governor 'to take steps at once, if possible, to sweep those bands of brigands out of Bosnia.'

Time and again Liberal MPs raised the matter in the Commons – on 9 March, 10 April, 25 April, 12 May and 10 July. Mr Forster enquired if the consul had been asked to report on the particular outrages which Evans had detailed. The reply was that he had not been asked and that the right honourable gentleman should remember that the cost of telegraphing was very heavy. But at length the Foreign Office and the consul were goaded into activity. The vice-consul was sent to investigate. His report substantially confirmed the accuracy of what Evans had written – but Mr Holmes got his knighthood just the same.[4]

On his return to England Evans revised and published his *Guardian* messages under the title Illyrian Letters. In the preface he argued that the ultimate reconstitution of the Habsburg monarchy on a South Slav basis was the only way he could see by which Russia could be kept out of the Adriatic. Meanwhile in his reluctant opinion Austria ought in everybody's interests to incorporate Bosnia. That was, in fact, the solution to which the Congress of Berlin came.

In the summer Evans married Margaret Freeman, the daughter of E. A. Freeman, the Oxford historian, and returned to Ragusa, dividing his time between archaeological work, local politics and *Guardian* correspondence. This went on until March 1882, when he was arrested by the Austrian authorities and held in prison for nearly seven weeks before being deported.

It had not taken either Evans or his beloved South Slavs long to decide that the Austro–Hungarian régime was only a slight improvement on that of the Turks. Evans told the *Guardian* what was happening. As early as May 1880 he was warned by a friendly Austrian officer to keep off politics in a letter written with English words in Greek capital letters and purporting to be an exact copy of an ancient inscription found at Olympia. Evans did not take the hint and continued to supply the *Guardian* with news, but for a time the trouble blew over. As unrest developed into open insurrection, Evans found means of smuggling his messages by 'express messenger to Udine' in Italy, whence they were telegraphed to Manchester. Once he amused himself by testing the Austrian censorship by telegraphing from Ragusa an English translation of a paragraph from the official Austrian Military Gazette which the post office promptly refused.[5]

He reported desertions from the Slav regiments of the Austrian army, gave details of the deployment of the Austrian military and naval forces and recorded in his last message to the *Guardian* before his arrest his interview with Herzegovinian rebel chiefs 'in a rocky stronghold on the Herzegovinian border which I forbear further to localise.'[6] Dr Joan Evans recited with a dry comment the charges against her half-brother – that he was ' "ostile agli interessi Austriaci", that he was in relations with insurgents and other suspected persons and gave them money, that he had freely expressed his opinions in public without any regard to the present abnormal conditions, or to the maintenance of public safety, and that his letters to the *Manchester Guardian* were bitterly anti-Austrian. It was a very fair statement of fact.'[7]

This was by no means the end of Evans's connection with the

Balkans or with the *Guardian* in connection with South Slav affairs. The next year he toured Greece, Turkey and Bulgaria with his wife. He was arrested at Salonica for being out after dark, innocently this time, without a lantern, and again in the Bulgarian frontier town of Bela Palanka where he was kept in custody all day until he could produce his passport which he eventually found in his pocket late in the afternoon. In Sofia they ran into an involved political crisis which kept Evans busy telegraphing to the *Guardian* once he had crossed the Rumanian frontier. The complexities of this Bulgarian crisis are suggested by his wife's entry in her diary: 'The Prince practically a prisoner in his own Palace, treated, as he himself said, "like a servant" by the Russian special envoy, unable to go to the camp for fear of meeting the (Russian) Minister who refused to accept his dismissal, with apparently no alternative but that of abdication before him, but to whom abdication means bankruptcy as according to common report he is deeply in debt, is (oh, what an involved sentence) well "nuts" to "our own correspondent".'[8]

In later years Evans continued to act at intervals for the *Guardian*. He was in the Balkans in 1890 and had his papers confiscated by the Turks, but luckily managed to substitute unobserved a blank diary for the one in current use. In 1898 he was in Crete where he denounced the British commandant as 'an assistant Pasha' in messages to the *Guardian* which he reprinted for private circulation.[9] Throughout the First World War and the peace-making that followed it he was a constant contributor to the paper, arguing the South Slav cause first against Austria–Hungary and then against Italy. Some of his later articles of this period and a leader written on them were republished in a French translation in Paris in 1919.[10]

2

It is time to return to the Balkans of 1876–78. If *Guardian* readers had had to depend only on what Evans saw they would have had a very limited and oblique vision. His was correspondence in depth, not only of contemporary detail but in its communication of the underlying history. But Evans reported what was happening on only one frontier of Turkey, though an important one because it was where three empires met. It so happened that the *Guardian* had a correspondent at Constantinople who was well qualified to give a counter-balancing picture of events as seen by a friendly observer in the capital. No man could have been more unlike and yet more like Evans than H. F. Woods. He was a British naval officer 'of good yeoman stock', as he used to say.

But in his first ship, which he joined in 1858, he was a shipmate of the Duke of Edinburgh, Queen Victoria's second son, and the two became firm friends. Woods grew familiar with courts as well as with ships. In 1867 he was stationed at Constantinople as second-in-command of a dispatch vessel provided for the British ambassador. He served as the British representative on the International Commission on the Bosphorus which provided lightships for its safe navigation. In 1869 he transferred to the Turkish naval service to undertake the training of naval cadets. He remained in the Ottoman navy for the rest of his active life. On the title page of *Spunyarn*, his autobiography, he described himself as 'Sir Henry F. Woods, KCVO, Lt RN; late Admiral and Pasha in the Imperial Ottoman Naval Service; Grand Cordon of the Medijeh and Osmanieh; Knight Commander of the Saxe–Coburg Order; Aide-de-Camp for some years to the late Sultan, Abdul Hamid'[11] – a highly improbable description for a *Guardian* correspondent.

Indeed, although there is much in *Spunyarn* about Woods's relations with the English press, there is no reference in it to the *Guardian*. But there is no doubt about the connection. There survives one isolated volume of the manager's business letter book covering the period from July 1878 to November 1879. This records regular monthly payments to Woods for his contributions and his expenses, addressed in the early letters to Capt H. F. Woods, RN, and later to Capt H. F. Woods, IOM (presumably Imperial Ottoman Marine). There is nothing to show either when his connection with the *Guardian* started or when it stopped. He was probably working for the *Guardian* from the summer of 1876 onwards – there are fifty columns of messages from 'our Constantinople correspondent' in the last five months of that year. He certainly continued with the paper, as the letter book shows, after the Congress of Berlin, but his connection had probably come to an end well before 1889 or E. A. Freeman, Arthur Evans's father-in-law, would hardly have been allowed to demand in the paper the clearing out of all 'foreign intruders' from 'those lands that are still unhappily marked Turkey on the map . . . Such are "His Imperial Majesty", with whom Woods Pasha dines. Such are the whole "Ottoman Government," "the Sublime Porte" and all its pashas, beys, agas and everything of the kind, Woods Pasha among them.' By this time Woods and the *Guardian* had taken quite irreconcilable positions about Armenia. A pamphlet Woods wrote in 1890 made his position clear by the praise he gave Abdul Hamid, 'whose solicitude for the welfare of all his subjects alike, whether Mahomedan, Christian or Jew, is shown by the generous manner in which substantial aid is speedily given . . .'[12]

Woods wrote for the *Guardian* long, detailed descriptions of events

in the Turkish empire as they looked to one who hoped for a regenera-
tion of the country by a liberalisation of its government. He was
strongly anti-Russian and favoured what he called a 'Stratfordian'*
policy – 'good advice not only tendered to the Sultan but its acceptance
pressed upon him.' Woods wanted more direct British interference in
the internal affairs of Turkey and believed that, for instance, many
Turkish liberals were ready to accept British advisers in key ministries.
After all, the Turkish fleet was commanded by a British officer, and
Woods himself was in Turkish service. The key to the situation was in
his view unilateral, independent British action coupled with a guarantee
against Russia.

Woods knew that reform was necessary and, Turcophil though he
was, he admitted that there were atrocities in Bulgaria:

'Dark rumours have been coming for some time past but it was difficult to
ascertain the truth as all letters arriving by Turkish post were opened by
the authorities before delivery. Within the last week, however, one or two
travellers who have made their way through the country under escort relate
the most revolting tales of the treatment of women and children. One instance of the kind – which appears to have been well authenticated as an
account of it even appeared in a local paper – is that of the burning alive of
some seventy young girls. This sort of work however has not been quite
confined to the Mussulmans, for the half-savage people from the upper
Balkans, who form the principal portion of the insurgents, have been equally
ready to wreak their vengeance upon all of Mahometan faith, without distinction of age or sex . . . the employment of these Bashi-bazouks has done
more harm to the Ottoman cause than a rebel victory. Instead of going to
attack the insurgents in their strongholds in the mountains, they have
swept down upon the Bulgarian villages in the more open places like a
flight of locusts, destroying all before them. Fire and sword have been carried
through the country, and many villages have been destroyed the inhabitants
of which had never thought of joining in the revolt and had previously
given up their arms to the authorities. If this sort of thing were to continue
foreign interference must be expected.' (29 June 1876)

But more frequently Woods's messages move adroitly through the
maze of palace intrigues. The new reign opened with the murder of
two of the principal ministers, a 'sad affair which has cast for a time
quite a gloom over the place', though opinion was divided 'as to
whether the loss of Hussein Avri at this juncture is a loss to the country
or otherwise.'[13] This was followed by the unsuccessful plot to carry off
the deposed and insane Sultan Murad, a plot which in Woods's opinion

* Lord Stratford de Redcliffe, 'The Great Elchi', had been ambassador at
Constantinople for 22 of the 48 years between 1810 and 1858.

was likely to have been encouraged, if not originated, by Russia. 'It is said that Mr Stravridis, the ex-*employé* of the British Embassy, one of the chief characters in the plot, had been seen a great deal of late in the company of the first interpreter of the Russian Embassy and that the design of the conspirators was to get ex-Sultan Murad away to Odessa,' where the pretender to the Turkish throne would give the Czar 'a very strong card.'[14]

From the beginning of the reign Woods approved of Abdul Hamid. He praised his constant activity in visiting departments of state, inspecting the defences and altogether setting out to prove that Lord Salisbury, our special ambassador, was not the only active man in Constantinople. At first Woods seems to have had some hesitation about the Sultan's power to command. But by the autumn of 1877 he was satisfied: 'I had not seen the Sultan very closely since the day when he rode in state through the streets of Stamboul to be girded with the Sword of Othman, and I certainly then thought Abdul Hamid but a poor representative of majesty . . . But yesterday I must say that the Padishah appeared at home both on horseback in the streets, acknowledging the salutes of his people, and in receiving the official world in the imperial palace . . . When he moved forward at the end to salute his ministers on retiring, it was with the firm step of one conscious of the power to command.'[15]

The military campaigns of 1876–78 were reported for the *Guardian* by special correspondents with the rival armies – men of quality whose names one would like to know.* Naturally during this period Woods himself wrote a good deal about Turkey's defences. He had a concealed purpose to fulfil. Woods Bey, as he was then called, put his loyalty to his adopted country before his duty to his own country's newspapers. He used them for counter-intelligence.

'I took advantage of the correspondents thirsting for news to send draughts for the enemy to swallow through the columns of the big London dailies. I gave them lots of information about minefields where none had been placed, and accounts of large and formidable torpedoes which never existed. There was a good deal of "faking" about the whole business, but then I always took care to explode one torpedo wherever I was supposed to be placing a large number, and I never failed to give notice to certain special friends amongst them, so that they might witness the spectacle.'[16]

* The *New York Herald* took the *Guardian* service during the campaign of 1877. Its London correspondent wrote on October 11, when the arrangement was brought to an end, 'Mr. Bennett . . . desires me to thank you for the opportunity of being in alliance with the *Guardian* and to express his entire satisfaction with your despatches.'

One wonders whether an incident which he himself reported to the *Guardian* fell into this fake category:

'To-day His Majesty . . . proceeded to the Princes' Islands in the Sea of Marmora to witness the explosion of a large torpedo which had been placed opposite the Naval College . . . The torpedo, which was a cylindrical iron case containing some 650 lbs of large-grain powder, exploded with great effect, completely destroying a large hulk which had been placed above it.' (20 December 1876)

Certainly foreign observers carefully watched the news stories from Constantinople. Once, for instance, the Russians fired a Whitehead torpedo which was recovered unexploded by the Turks at Batoum and sent back to Woods. This he recorded in the *Times*, and also in the *Guardian*, perhaps in other papers as well. It brought post-haste to Constantinople a representative of the Whitehead Co. with orders to purchase the torpedo unopened no matter what it cost. But the Turks had already dismantled it and learnt its secret. On the strength of this they made a highly profitable arrangement for the cheap supply of Whitehead torpedoes.

According to Woods Bey's account he worked mainly by feeding material to English newspaper correspondents. But after the end of the war he was in Batoum, a Moslem district which was due to be ceded to Russia. The story was over as far as the journalists were concerned. They had gone to other assignments. Woods decided to fill their place. 'I did a journalistic feat,' he recorded, 'in writing and dispatching simultaneously articles which were published in all the great London dailies, including the organ of Mr Gladstone. Although these letters from "An Occasional Correspondent", or "Our Own" as the editors chose to head them, differed somewhat in their wording, the text of the exhortation was always the same: "Do not let Batoum go to Russia".'[17] Certainly his article in the *Guardian* of 17 June 1878 made a powerful moral case against annexation.

One would like to know what Scott thought of the stories that Woods sent. There is, perhaps, a faint suggestion that he may not have liked all that he received, though he was happy to go on employing Woods. One letter from the business manager runs, 'Mr Scott is travelling in Italy and will be away three or four weeks more – no doubt he will agree that articles held over for pressure of space be charged at full rate.'[18] Somehow 'pressure of space' does not ring true when one looks at the *Guardian* of 1878, but there is no knowing whether the articles were 'spiked' because of Woods Bey's politics or because of some suspicion that the news was 'doctored.' It is, however,

almost unthinkable that in this latter case the *Guardian* would have gone
on employing Woods. A third possible explanation is that, since the
articles were sent by post and averaged ten days in transit, they were
frequently overtaken by later news sent in outline by telegraph. This
would be plausible but for the fact that in 1878 one is frequently
conscious that this is just what was not done – one reads the news
first in telegraphed summary and then, days later, in detail when the
mail arrived.

3

Back in Manchester there were news and views from a great variety of
sources to be carefully weighed. There were first of all the *Guardian*'s
special sources – Evans in Ragusa; Woods in Constantinople; von
Kohl of the *Neue Freie Presse* in Vienna whose telegrams were models
of brevity and news sense; Professor Vanbéry in Buda-Pesth, a Turkish
apologist; and the war correspondents with the principal belligerent
armies. There were Reuter's telegrams and the reports of the London
papers' special correspondents, of which the *Daily News* and the *Times*
were the most useful. There were the European newspapers to be read –
the *Levant Times*, the *Phare du Bosphore*, the *St Petersburg Herald* as well
as six German and Austrian and at least two French papers.[19] There
were the speeches of Liberal and Conservative politicians to consider,
and neither party was altogether of one mind. And there was
the private information available to the great business houses of
cosmopolitan Manchester to take into account.

Overseas correspondents were allowed a wide latitude to express
their own opinions, but ultimately the paper had to take up its own
position and expound its views so that its readers might be brought,
if possible, to the editor's standpoint – that was the function of the
leading article, always regarded by Scott as the most important part of
the paper, almost the reason for its being. The two men most concerned
with this crystallisation and expression of *Guardian* opinion were Scott
and H. M. Acton, the senior leader writer, who joined the paper in
1848, the year of revolution. He had served under Garnett, when the
paper was firmly for Palmerston, 'the most English minister', and
Palmerston was still a hero to Acton. 'Lord Palmerston', Mr Disraeli
was reminded, 'would never have compromised his country and himself by attempting, even for such an object as the "integrity" of Turkey,
to minimise the infamies of Bulgaria.'[20] The paper took up in general
almost a cross-bench position in these years. Its touchstones were two.
The first was a straightforward hatred of oppression from whatever
quarter it sprang, and the *Guardian* went thoroughly enough into the

details of Eastern European politics to see that nobody had clean hands. Obviously not the Turks:

'A Government which can permit, and not only permit but reward the wholesale murder of peaceful subjects is not a Government which can be tolerated in Europe, or at least is not a Government which can be permitted to govern without restraint.' (8 August 1876)

But the Christians were not much better. Serbians persecuted Jews and Orthodox Russians persecuted Roman Catholics:

'First of all, Jews are forbidden to deal in nearly everything except money, and then it is made a charge against them that they avail themselves of the only opening that is left.' (5 October 1876)
'The Roman Catholic inhabitants of a village were assembled; were beaten to soften their hearts, and then driven through a half-frozen river to remove the stains of heterodoxy. For fear of mistakes it may be observed that this did not happen in Bulgaria, though it did happen the year before last . . . It certainly would not have occurred to anyone without His Imperial Majesty's assistance to identify the Cossacks and the whip with the ineffable goodness of God.' (17 March 1876)

The *Guardian*'s second touchstone was 'a sense of the possible.' A country should do what it could, but it could not do everything. It could, for instance, do more than Mr Disraeli would – 'Nothing would do,' he said, 'but the *status quo*; but it is precisely the *status quo* which will not do.' It ought not to attempt as much as Mr Gladstone wanted: 'It is not impossible to condemn the enormities of the Turks as strenuously as Mr Gladstone himself and at the same time to condemn Mr Gladstone's resolutions' which, would have drawn us into the Russo-Turkish war. Two days later, 'By withdrawing some (he) has saved the others from the discredit of doubtful company. They remain innocent but inoperative.'[21] That was the rub. Britain had sometimes to see the innocent suffer. It might be Negroes on Dahomey or Moslems in Batoum:

'The role of universal redeemer of wrongs is one, however, which England cannot undertake to sustain.' (4 July 1876)
'We entirely reject for our part the doctrine that a Power which abstains from making a *casus belli* of every act of injustice in every part of the world becomes an accomplice in spoliation.' (19 June 1878)

CHAPTER SIXTEEN

Arnold and the Leap of Faith

I

'MATHEMATICAL certainty is not attainable in politics, and in every great question there comes a moment when one has to take a jump. One is bound to make the jump as short as possible . . . But the necessity of taking it cannot be altogether obviated.' Thus, sadly, in the Home Rule crisis, the *Guardian* said farewell to Mr Goschen as a Liberal leader, whose 'splendid talents' were to be lost to the party because he lacked 'that one grain of faith which is necessary to make a great innovating politician.'[1] What Mr Goschen lacked, the *Guardian* found; and on the same occasion.

Mr Goschen was far from alone in refusing the jump. 'What has come to the Dukes?' one *Guardian* leader began, and went on to say that no respect for the great traditions which they represented could induce the mass of the Liberal Party 'to approach the Irish question in the spirit of the Duke of Westminster or Mr Gladstone in the spirit of the Duke of Bedford.' The great Whig aristocrats were indeed in full and natural flight from the Liberal Party, and nothing would hold them. Most sadly mourned by the *Guardian* was Lord Hartington for whose conversion the *Guardian* leader writer still vainly hoped – the Nationalists 'ask for an ell and he offers an inch, but the inch may grow into an ell.' But the *Guardian* sketch writer who listened to Lord Salisbury and Lord Hartington speaking from the same public platform saw more clearly what had happened: if Mr Gladstone had been present, he thought, 'his Homeric studies would probably have suggested the celebrated reconciliation scene in the Iliad when Agamemnon, king of men, and Achilles, swift of foot, declared before the assembled Greeks that henceforth their wrath should cease.'[2] So Troy fell; and the Liberal Party was out of office with one brief interval for twenty years.

It was understandable that the right-wing members of the Liberal Party should secede to the Tories; what passed belief was that Joseph Chamberlain, the most prominent of the radical leaders, should join their pilgrimage. In humble, chapel-going homes, where classical allusions would be lost but biblical simile sprang to mind, Joseph

Chamberlain's defection was mourned as David mourned Absalom. When Chamberlain quarrelled with Gladstone over Home Rule in 1886, 'it was in many houses as though there had been a divorce between the two heads of the family.' This was how Haslam Mills remembered the way in which that great reversal of roles afflicted homes in Ashton-under-Lyne where the Bible was read every day and the *Manchester Guardian* every weekday until it 'was carefully put into a kitchen drawer on Saturday night and in the length and breadth of Sunday never dared to show its face.'[3]

Most of the past history of the *Guardian* suggested that, like its hero, Lord Hartington, it would refuse the jump. It had, indeed, never ceased to be a Liberal newspaper; but after the first two or three years its liberalism had been with moderation. Scott had not altered this, although he had made many changes. In the first seven years of his control the paper had reached a new level of achievement. It was not only better than it had been in the journalistically dreary 'sixties, but better than it had ever been. Its editorial policy, however, had not changed: it was still to the right of the party, to the right, indeed, of much of its own special reporting. This last point may well explain why it was that in the crisis of 1886 the *Guardian* stood firm. It did not so much follow Mr Gladstone as scout ahead of him, preparing its readers, and itself, for the decision which could only come from Hawarden. It was not 'inspired' by Gladstone or any other Liberal leader. It did not follow anybody's brief; it briefed itself and its readers. For several years it had been carrying out independent, painstaking enquiries in Ireland so that its readers knew what the condition of that country really was. The readers were free to accept or to reject the conclusions the paper drew, but all the evidence was put before them. The thoroughness of these investigations makes them still worth reading by anybody who wants to know how Ireland came to be what it is.

How did the *Guardian*'s final conversion to Home Rule come about? In the end inevitably by a leap of faith – but 'one is bound to make the jump as short as possible.' This narrowing of the gap is what Scott had been unconsciously doing in the first half of the eighties so that, when the time came, the *Guardian* found itself taking the jump in its stride while the radical *Examiner* hesitated and, journalistically, was lost. In the fortieth year of his age, and in the fifteenth of his editorship, Scott the near-Whig became Scott the radical. After more than sixty years on the right wing of the Liberal Party, the *Guardian* returned to its original position on the left. The change was dramatic, but it ought not to have been unexpected.

2

The origin of the change may be placed in 1879. In the spring of that year Scott paid a visit to Oxford to look for a recruit to the editorial staff. The paper had an occasional contributor there in Humphry Ward. At his house Scott was introduced to W. T. Arnold, Mrs Ward's younger brother, then aged 26. Arnold had nearly everything to commend him to the Liberal editor. Scott needed a man of real academic distinction, of wide cultural interests, knowledgeable about politics and liberal in outlook. Arnold was all those things. He was, to begin with, a member of one of the most distinguished middle-class Liberal families. His grandfather was Thomas Arnold – Arnold of Rugby. His uncle, Matthew Arnold, was then at the height of his fame. Another uncle by marriage was W. E. Forster, the Liberal Cabinet Minister who had piloted the most famous of Education Acts through the Commons. A. W. Ward was his cousin. His father had been professor of English at Newman's Catholic University in Ireland. Admittedly, this Thomas Arnold had become a Roman Catholic but Willy was a Protestant.

What Arnold had done was, of course, more important to his prospective employer than who he was. His record was already impressive. He had been head of the school at Rugby and had taken – to his own disappointment – a good second class in both Mods' and Greats at Oxford. He had edited part of Keats's 'Hyperion' for the Clarendon Press and won the Arnold Essay Prize with a study of 'Provincial Administration in the Roman Empire.' This was already certain of its place as a standard work on its subject – one of the few prize essays worthy to rank with Bryce's 'Holy Roman Empire' which had won the same prize fifteen years before. That dour old man, Mark Pattison, commended its author's 'exactitude' and 'extent' of reading, qualities which Scott was ancient historian enough to judge for himself. These marks of scholarship were important; so, too, was the imaginative but realistic mind which appreciated a long past situation in terms which suggested the writer's ability to come to grips with the administrative problems of his own day. Twenty-five years later, as Arnold lay dying, he was told that a senior member of the Indian Civil Service had been reading the 'Provincial Administration' and found that it threw light on his own frontier problems. That greatly pleased Arnold. No doubt it was this quality of contemporary relevance that indicated to Scott that Arnold's scholarship had in it the making of a journalist.

By the autumn of 1879 Arnold was settled in Manchester. It was easy to predict that he would be happy on the paper, less certain that he and his wife would find Manchester congenial. They did; and it was with affection that Arnold used to speak of 'T' Owd Smoky.' Besides the companionship of the *Guardian* office and of Owens College there was stimulating society to be found at the Brasenose Club where Manchester's artists, musicians and intellectuals met. Among the older members were men like H. M. Acton and his intimate friend Edwin Waugh, 'the Lancashire Burns,' once a journeyman printer, whose songs were sung in almost every Lancashire home. Arnold's contemporaries included Spenser Wilkinson, soon to be his colleague on the *Guardian*, and Richard Pankhurst, a brilliant lawyer, who might be better remembered if he had not also been Mrs Pankhurst's husband.

A letter from Arnold to his mother gives what are virtually his first impressions of life on the *Guardian*:

'I can't tell at all yet about staying here. The dramatic criticism has now been put entirely into my hands, and I have two stalls for every new performance . . . This looks more or less as if Scott wanted to make a permanent thing of it. But I can't the least tell. He says nothing about it, and still less of course do I. All I know is that I like the work very much, and strange to say like Manchester or at all events the Manchesterians as also does H (his wife) . . . At present the work is nothing very severe. I turn up at the office about 10.30, talk to Couper,* digest the *Times* and put anything in hand that has to be done. Write in the afternoon, get away about 5 or 6. After that there is nothing unless perhaps a theatre – after a performance at which I go straight off to the press, clamber up endless flights of stairs to the composing room, ensconce myself in a small den reserved for my use, where is a deal table, writing materials, and a flaring gas jet, and straightway indite something or other about the performance. This has to be ready not much later than 11.30. They go to press (crossed out and "have papers printed" substituted) about 12.30. It is not, of course, an altogether satisfactory arrangement that all leaders should be written in the afternoon and if I stay Scott will put me on to writing late on later telegrams.'[4]

This reform in the leader-writing arrangements was soon made, and Arnold settled down to a life in which he devoted the mornings to Roman history and the afternoons and evenings to the office – usually for six days a week in the course of which he wrote three or four long leaders, theatre notices, reviews and a number of short leaders.

* At this time home news editor: 'Many newspapers have one recognised utility man – a sort of "little poker that does most of the work" . . . in an emergency he could write a leading article that was quite up to the standard of the paper', especially on religious and educational matters. (T. S. Townend in The *Manchester Guardian House Journal*, January 1921.)

Then, as now, Manchester was a good place to get out of and within easy reach of places good to get to. Arnold was half a Northerner by adoption long before he joined the *Guardian*. Fox How, his grandfather's house at Grasmere, had been a holiday home for him ever since he came back from Australia at the age of 5. Now each Saturday he and his wife and the dogs took the train from Manchester: it might be to walk over Kinder Scout in winter snow, and to watch delightedly, as his sister put it, 'for the first frenzy with which a town dog resumes possession of the open earth.' Arnold had a sapper's eye for the structure of the landscape and a poacher's for the lie of the land; and he could communicate in words the excitement with which he saw. This love of the country overflowed into the pages of the *Guardian*. It belongs as much to Arnold's public as to his private life. Throughout the 1880s the *Guardian* gave its country-loving readers abundant pleasure. In one year alone (1882) it provided them with long series of articles on 'Rare Birds of Lancashire,' the 'Past Fauna of Lancashire and Cheshire,' and 'Our Northern Birds of Prey.' A shorter series followed the River Irwell downstream from its source, and single articles discussed 'The Sea Birds of Walney Island' and 'A Westmorland Haunt of Sea Birds.' So it was each year. Some of this writing was probably Arnold's own; more was due to his influence and stimulation.*

3

Arnold's country tastes served *Guardian* readers well in the most serious political and human problem of the day. The failure of the Irish potato crop of 1879 made men fear the famine of 1847 would come again. Scott sent Arnold to investigate. In previous emergencies the paper had just relied on the Irish papers and on local correspondents. John Harland, it is true, had travelled in Ireland in 1852 and written twelve articles, but they were pure holiday features. Later, in 1873, John Turner, one of the abler *Guardian* reporters, had been sent over to cover the Galway election petition, but this was just a straightforward reporting job. Arnold's mission, then, was a new departure. Its success made it a precedent. In future the *Guardian* from time to time sent over trusted men to use their eyes, their ears and their minds so that the editor, and his readers, might be properly informed. It is one of the oddities of *Guardian* history that Scott, who was to be so

* Not all the nature articles were North Country. Richard Jefferies was a valued contributor, and when he was desperately ill and poor between 1886 and 1888 Scott was generous both of time and money in helping him.

closely concerned with Irish affairs, rarely went to see for himself what was happening only a few hours away from Manchester.

Arnold spent two winter months slowly travelling the country from Skibbereen in the south round to Donegal. He sent the paper thirteen long reports of what he found; perhaps 35,000 words in all. They abound in detailed description which gives life and particularity to a problem, but the details are there not to make a good story or to extort charity but to provoke thought. What fundamentally was wrong?

Arnold's method was to work through the parish priests, the Protestant rectors and the agents of improving landlords. He would sit through the meeting of a Board of Guardians or attend a local relief committee. He went visiting with a priest in Macroom, a small township in County Kerry:

'We visited together many of these – cottages shall I call them, or rather dens of typhus, which a humane man would be sorry a dog should live in. These wretched hovels are often no more than twelve feet square, and in them sometimes live three people, sometimes six, sometimes a man and his wife and six or seven children. There are no sanitary arrangements at all in these poorer lanes, and the stench at the door was sometimes unspeakable. Crouching down and entering the room we saw one dismal scene of misery after another. Now it was an awful sight of a poor stricken woman, her face half eaten away by scrofula, tossing feverishly on a wretched pallet under a few filthy rags; now a strong man sitting idly by the turf fire with his wife, ready for any work there was to be had, but unable to earn a penny for the last six weeks; now a poor old woman lying on an apology for a bed, her face yellow and sunken with illness and semi-starvation, who burst forth into a shrill torrent of Irish when the priest appeared, struggling against the weakness which choked her breath, and determined to give him the full tale of her misery and poverty. For such dens as these the rents average tenpence or a shilling a week.' (31 January 1880)

Of course better houses were needed, but time and again Arnold comes back to the point that they would be of no use if they were let at more than £2. 10. 0 or £3 a year.

Arnold realised the need for assisted emigration and argued for it. He used his eye for country to bring home the truth of over-population in a way that would strike *Guardian* readers.

'The road from Killybegs to Glencolumbkille is the wildest I have ever seen, rising and falling over wide expanses of moorland and barren fell, only diversified by the trenches of ice-covered water here and there, where the peat has been cut for fuel, and occasionally by mountain tarns – not the true tarn, "round as the red eye of an eagle owl," hemmed in by black rock-walls on every side but one, but a shallow indefinable expanse of water straggling uncomfortably hither and thither, and looking melancholy enough as the grey clouds fly overhead, and the pitiless rain whips the face and blots out the distance. Through the mist finer mountain slopes are faintly seen to the left, and the wayfarer knows that at their bases the Atlantic, "the hoarse old mother," is incessantly moaning. Such a district could hardly be prosperous if burdened with a dense population, and the population is as dense as it can possibly be . . . Let anyone who knows the Lake district well imagine Honister Pass dotted from end to end with cabins, each with its bit of tillage and pasture struggling up the mountain side; let him imagine Dunmail Rise the site of a considerable village, and see the blue peat smoke rising beside Grisedale Tarn, and he will form some idea of the unlikely spots into which the Irish cabin makes its way. Such a population cannot but be poor.' (27 February 1880)

Relief was a hateful necessity not only in Arnold's eyes but in the parish priest of Dingle's – 'he speaks with the bitterest shame and indignation of the demoralisation of his people caused by the system of pauper doles. It makes liars and hypocrites of them . . . The starving must, of course, be fed, and the naked clothed; but what all right-minded men ask for is employment for the poor people.'[5] Arnold returns again and again to the need for work – land drainage, better roads, more railways, and short-term efforts to provide really good seed potatoes – Arnold noted that where Champion potatoes had been planted the crop had not failed. He praised the work of good landlords like Lord Kenmore whose wages bill for relief work on roads and drainage schemes had risen to £360 a week. He wished there were more, but by the end of his tour he had come firmly to the conclusion that it was no good trusting to good landlords and local initiative even with loans from the Irish Board of Works behind them.

'If all landlords had capital and understood the business of "improvement", and were unembarrassed pecuniarily, and were resident, and were well disposed, we might trust to the landlords. As things are, reliance simply on the agency of the landlords would make Ireland a series of bright spots, happy islands of comfort and prosperity, surrounded by dark seas of misery and gloom . . . Sooner or later, – such is the conviction of all persons with whom I have conversed – the government will find itself obliged to come forward.' (27 February 1880)

The *Guardian* had taken its first step towards the point where it would be faced with the leap of faith. From the time of this journey there is quite a different 'feel' to the *Guardian*'s writings about Ireland. It writes about neighbours, not strangers.

4

Arnold came back from Ireland to find the country in the middle of a general election. Disraeli, the Conservative Prime Minister, had dissolved on the issue of 'No Home Rule for Ireland' which the Liberals to a man prudently refused to take up – 'as for Home Rule,' the *Guardian* remarked, 'everybody knows that there is not a single English or Scotch Liberal member who has declared himself favourable to it.'[6] This was good enough to win the election for the Liberals, but it was short-sighted enough to hide from them, including Scott, Arnold and the *Guardian*, the realities of the Irish situation. They knew that a fresh Land Purchase Act was needed; they pinned their faith to it. But evictions and agrarian crime continued to rise together.

Throughout this period Arnold was, under Scott, responsible for the *Guardian*'s Irish policy. He was well placed to do this. His father lived in Dublin and paid regular visits to Manchester on his way to and from Oxford. His uncle, W. E. Forster, became Chief Secretary for Ireland in the Gladstone government. He had his own recent experience with which to interpret the reports which the paper's local correspondents in Dublin and Cork were now plentifully supplying. These men were, of course, journalists on the staff of Irish newspapers who supplemented the supply of general news through the Press Association and other agencies. A little later we know that the Dublin correspondence of the *Guardian* was provided from the *Freeman's Journal* office and it is likely that this arrangement was already in force. Similarly the Cork correspondence almost certainly came from the *Cork Examiner* office. In the 1880s these local Irish correspondents provided the paper with a reliable service. They gave the news in considerable detail but without comment. They did not attempt to colour it.

Occasionally the *Guardian* sent a reporter from Manchester. In 1882 David Paton, 'dark, dapper and sartorially so correct that he might have given hints to King Edward,'[7] paid three visits – in connection with the Phoenix Park murders, for the Irish exhibition which inevitably included a major Nationalist demonstration, and for the Dublin police strike. But on two of these occasions he was not sent until the news story was past its peak so that on the whole he added little to what the Dublin correspondent had already sent.* A full Irish news service, such as only a staff man could have provided, would have given the editor, and his readers, that guarantee of impartial investigation which

* The Phoenix Park murders took place on the afternoon of Saturday; Paton was not sent over until Sunday; his first story appeared on Tuesday.

could never quite be attached to an Irish journalist's stories when they went beyond straight reporting. Paton's investigation of the shocking affray at Ballina, an unplanned by-product of his first Dublin visit, need not then have stood alone. The trouble started, as such things do, as a petty Saturday night incident, but developed into a serious matter when a police officer, offended by the crowd's disobedience, ordered his men to fire with fatal results. Paton did a remarkably thorough piece of fact-finding which confirmed Arnold's suspicion that the system of military magistrates would not do.[8] More probing of this kind below the surface of Irish administration would have been a public service and a journalistic investment, but only a resident correspondent could have undertaken it.

'It may be that Mr Forster will prove to have been right.' So Arnold wrote the day his uncle resigned because the Government released the leaders of the Land League as a result of the 'Kilmainham Treaty.' It was no doubt an open question, but Arnold made it clear that he thought Forster had been wrong. Five days later the new Chief Secretary, Lord Frederick Cavendish, and the Under-Secretary were murdered in Phoenix Park. Most of England was convinced that Forster had been proved right; the *Guardian* still thought him wrong. 'On no conceivable grounds is there any reason to suppose that . . . any of the leaders of the Land League have had part or lot in this matter . . . This is the Fenian protest against what it believes to be the Land League capitulation.'[9] The universal horror of the Irish leaders gave grounds for Arnold's optimistic belief. He went to Chatsworth to report the funeral of that 'loyal friend and gallant gentleman, and zealous well-doer who was in all the vigour of life and health but five short days ago . . . Qui nunquam recte fecit ut facere videretur, sed quia aliter facere non poterat.' He came back to Manchester to write in the leading article that evening, 'If Ireland is inclined to turn over a new leaf, at least a fair chance should be given her. Let her be administered like any other civilised country and then perhaps she will be less apt to incur the reproach of barbarism.'[10]

So the *Guardian* carried its Irish policy another step farther. It turned its attention seriously to the problem of crime in Ireland. The only special problem was agrarian crime, and that was linked with the need for agrarian reform, on which the *Guardian* already had its policy. The experience of 1882 made the connection clear to those who would bother to study it – that year nearly 10,500 families were evicted and there were some 2,500 agrarian crimes. 'The whole face of Irish society must be changed before we can hope for permanent reform.' But meanwhile detected crime must not go unpunished. Local juries were too frightened or too hostile to convict even on the clearest evidence. The cure for that, the *Guardian* believed, was a simple change in the procedure for arranging trials. There was no need to deny the right to trial by jury which, as Lord Lansdowne said in a Lords debate, formed 'the connecting link between the dry technicality of the law and the people of the country.'[11] But at this juncture Mr Gladstone hesitated. He produced a new Crimes Bill. The secret societies had not miscalculated. The murders in Phoenix Park had achieved their end.

The *Guardian* continued to advocate conciliation. It was not a popular policy in the country, and it seems doubtful how united the staff of the paper was. Agrarian crimes continued, and one particularly brutal outrage at Mallaghadrumna, where an informer's whole family were savagely murdered, made it more than ever difficult to keep the calm temper without which conciliation would be impossible. The day the news arrived the *Guardian* 'pitied the feelings of all honest Irishmen, members of a race that once justly prided itself on chivalry', but took some comfort in the fact that the use of special jurors and the transfer of trials out of the disturbed areas was beginning to have effect. Two days later more revolting details of the outrage were available. There was no further leader comment, but the writer of the news summary, who was accustomed to comment on as well as to condense the news, wrote a paragraph that surely shows a divided state of mind in the office. 'The account of the murders', he wrote, 'will inspire greater horror and disgust than anything which has happened in the dominions of the Queen since the Sepoy mutiny. Greater loss of life has followed a foray of savages in the far West, but nothing more irredeemably hideous was ever committed by Apache or Comanche.'[12] The news summary was often more violent in its expression than any other part of the paper, and on stylistic grounds one is inclined to assign it to one of the old guard trained in the ferocious habits of the old journalism – possibly to Acton, but probably to Couper, 'the sub-editor', or what would now be called deputy editor. It seems likely that neither Scott nor Arnold saw this particular bitter paragraph either in copy or in proof. Not only was it written on a Sunday night in the holiday month of August, but there was sufficient hard news from Egypt that night to take people's attention off Ireland.

5

There was nothing of the dilatoriness which marked the *Guardian*'s handling of Irish news in the arrangements it had made for reporting the new Egyptian war. While the increasingly grave news from Alexandria was still being given in the *Guardian* under the sober single column headline 'The Egyptian Difficulty', its special war correspondent, Capt Fitzgerald, had already been appointed.* When fighting began the news was presented in a way quite novel to the decorous *Guardian*. The story of the bombardment of Alexandria was given six headlines, while on the 1st of August no less than nine were used to introduce the main news story.†

From the beginning of July Fitzgerald was telegraphing several messages a day, the last was sometimes dispatched as late as 10.50 p.m. and yet found a place in the next morning's *Guardian*. For the later stages of the campaign a second correspondent, Le Mesurier, was added. They confined themselves to hard news. For picturesque detail and emotional colour the *Guardian* relied on the London papers, especially the *Daily News*. Fitzgerald was enterprising. He managed, for instance, to interview Arabi Pasha in his palace late one evening. Thirty-six hours later Fitzgerald was on a British warship watching the bombardment of Alexandria. Once he found himself on a wild goose chase, misled by steps which Wolseley had taken to deceive Arabi. He and Cameron of the *Standard* had gone to Aboukir, where a landing was expected, in a specially chartered steamer arranged by Lord Charles Beresford. But Wolseley was, in fact, engaged on his switch from the Mediterranean to the Red Sea.[13] More serious was the *Guardian*'s failure to have its own news story of Wolseley's crowning victory at Tel-el-Kebir. But here the paper was the innocent victim of Fitzgerald's enterprise. His telegram was the first news of the battle to reach Alexandria and it was sent by the Military Governor to the War Office for the information of the Government instead of to the *Guardian*.

But this, of course, only came out later when an inquest was held on the fate of the missing telegram. That night Spenser Wilkinson, working in Manchester, had to make do with Wolseley's official communiqué. To all appearance he made a mess of it. The *Guardian* placed the Highland Brigade to the north of a canal when all the other papers put it on the south. It is easy to imagine the young man's misery. He had been taken on by Scott on a short-term arrangement specially

---

* Fitzgerald was not a member of the *Guardian*'s permanent staff. It was the habit to appoint freelance war correspondents on temporary contracts for the duration of hostilities to serve a paper or syndicate of papers. It was not until 1897 that the *Guardian* sent a staff man as a war correspondent when J. B. Atkins covered the Greco-Turkish war.

† These were: Egypt [M. de Lesseps's Plots. [The Cairo Mission. [Sentence on a Turkish Spy. [British Midshipman Decoyed. [Arab Denunciation of Ourabi. [A Tale of Horrors. [The Indian Contingent. [Important Russian Action.

to handle the Egyptian news at the Manchester end. Now he had made the kind of blunder which the journalist who commits it remembers long after others have forgotten. Spenser Wilkinson had to live with it for a fortnight before one of the London war correspondents complained that his paper had altered his message and put the Highland Brigade on the south side of the canal. Then the truth came out. The explanation was simple. The official telegram contained no punctuation. It was a question of where a full stop should be inserted. Wilkinson got it right; the other sub-editors got it wrong. Wilkinson got it right, he thought, because his work as an equity barrister using unpunctuated documents had taught him how to punctuate.[14]

Wilkinson's supposed howler was the more glaring because it was boldly marked on a map. This was the first war for which the *Guardian* provided maps of the scene of the fighting – the beginning of a long tradition of excellence in this field. Spenser Wilkinson had to foresee well in advance what maps he would be likely to need. This was because there was about a week's delay from the time he handed a map over to the wood-engraver to the time that a metal block had been made and was ready to be printed. Wilkinson prepared eighteen maps. There was one for every engagement of any consequence and every shift of interest, and at the end of the campaign there was only one map left over. He drew on many sources – Admiralty charts, War Office staff maps, Turkish military maps and maps which a Royal Engineer officer drew for Fitzgerald as well as on the ordinary published atlases. He found a way to keep his pre-fabricated blocks up to date. When news came of the Battle of Tel-el-Kebir he marked the position of the various units on a proof, had holes drilled in the block to correspond, and identifying letters inserted in type to which he provided a key in the legend. This was how the Highland Brigade's position came to be so clearly marked.

There was no denying Wilkinson had done well. He already knew enough about the art of war to form shrewder judgments than many more experienced men on other papers. When London newspapers criticised the delays imposed by Wolseley's decision to shift his base from Alexandria to Ismailia, Wilkinson defended him on logistic grounds. This was long remembered to his and the paper's credit by such good judges as Sir Frederick Maurice who later wrote in the *Fortnightly Review*: 'The most valuable support that was given to the general during all that trying time was not publicly given by any minister or any statesman, but by the very able military critic of the *Manchester Guardian*. There are newspaper correspondents and newspaper writers who understand war.'[15]

6

Wilkinson understood war and did not lack pugnacity. He had had to
fight hard to make his way on to the *Guardian* staff. On the face of it,
he was well qualified. He had taken his London BA from Owens
College and gone on to Oxford with a classical scholarship to read
Mods and Greats. He was a practising barrister in Manchester and a
sound Liberal in politics. He was fluent in German and French; had
brought back the military training game of Kriegspiel from Germany
and founded the Oxford University Kriegspiel Club. He was a founder
of the Manchester Tactical Society, an enthusiastic Volunteer officer,
and he had become an occasional contributor to the *Guardian* on military
matters in 1881. He had now done brilliantly in his handling of the
Egyptian campaign and had determined to make his career in journalism and on the *Guardian*. He told Scott. Scott was not impressed, but
agreed to give him a six-months' trial, purely on space rates. The six
months stretched to eight, and Wilkinson tackled Scott again. He was
offered a job at a figure which Wilkinson thought too low. He said so,
and Scott increased it by £100. So Wilkinson fought his way on to the
paper, but his relations with Scott were never easy and often difficult.

This did not prevent Scott making good use of Wilkinson's talents.
Under Arnold's sympathetic but ruthless guidance he added skill as a
leader writer to his military knowledge. Not the least of Arnold's
contributions to the paper was the help he gave young recruits in
mastering this specialised form of writing. Both Wilkinson and, later,
C. E. Montague picked out this quality in Arnold. And Arnold himself
was conscious of its necessity, 'It really seems,' he would say, 'as if
every Greats man needed a year in a newspaper office to unlearn his
journalese.'[16] Wilkinson's main contribution to the *Guardian*, however,
in his early years was in special reporting. When an international conference met in Berlin in 1884 to decide the fate of Central Africa, and
especially of the Congo basin, Wilkinson was sent as the *Guardian*'s
special correspondent. He turned luck to solid advantage. By chance
he spent eight hours in the train to Berlin alone with Ludwig Bamberger, the German Liberal Party leader. Wilkinson did not recognise
him; they discussed the Congo question and Wilkinson told him that
the speeches about it in the Reichstag which he most admired were Dr
Bamberger's. They became close friends. In Berlin Wilkinson had the
next hotel room but one to H. M. Stanley and quickly contrived that
they should breakfast together each day. Mr J. A. Crowe, one of the
British diplomatic team, became a friend on the strength of a common

interest in painting and used to brief Wilkinson on what had happened at the closed sessions. Three years later Wilkinson married his daughter. Another important contact was Mr Goldie Taubman (later Sir George Goldie), the founder of the British Niger Company, who wrote to Scott, 'I can honestly congratulate you on your choice of a representative at Berlin. Mr Wilkinson's amiable qualities make him an admirable correspondent as he gets information which would be refused to others.'[17]

Wilkinson's most important sources were Stanley and Colonel Strauch. To Stanley he owed the exclusive news of his proposal to establish free trade not only in the Congo basin but round Lake Nyassa and the Great Lakes as well. He struck up a friendship with Colonel Strauch at a dinner at which the two of them discussed nothing but Napoleon's campaigns of 1814. From Strauch Wilkinson learned, not for publication, that the Congo International Association, of which Strauch was president, was really a private enterprise of the King of the Belgians. From him, too, he obtained for publication a map showing the exact boundaries which the various Powers were claiming in the Lower Congo. This he posted to Manchester on a Monday, but the *Guardian* held it up to Saturday, thus allowing the *Times* to get in first to Wilkinson's lasting fury. From Strauch, too, there came through his secretary the text of the treaty by which the United Kingdom recognised the Congo Free State, which first appeared exclusively in the *Guardian*.*

Wilkinson came back from Germany at Christmas 1884 to find that H. M. Acton was retiring on pension. Acton had found himself increasingly out of sympathy with the more radical line that the *Guardian* had begun to take. Scott, having found in Arnold the man he wanted as chief leader-writer, was anxious to put him officially in that position. Moreover, he had taken Wilkinson on the staff and at a bigger salary than he had planned. Taylor and Scott agreed in the summer that the time had come when Acton must go, but Acton was apparently not told of their decision until October. 'I pointed out to him that it had become necessary to recruit the staff with young men, that it was further necessary to bring them on and to throw the more important work of the staff upon them, and that in consequence his own position had become very much of a sinecure,' so Scott reported to Taylor.[18]

---

* Wilkinson tells the story of this and the delayed map at length in his autobiography, *Thirty-five Years*, pp. 68-73. His anger with Scott seems at least partly to be accounted for by the fact that in the affair of the map he was himself partially responsible for the success of the *Times* by playing politics with Strauch as well as news-getting for the *Guardian*.

7

Gladstone's second government was by this time tottering to its fall. Even Arnold, who was a firm supporter of Gladstone in everything else, admitted that 'the Egyptian muddle almost made me a Tory.'[19] By June 1885 Mr Gladstone was out and Lord Salisbury in. Meanwhile the Irish problem had been growing even worse. Some men in both English parties were beginning to think that some form of Home Rule might have to be conceded, and the *Guardian* took the third step towards the leap of faith – a recognition that Ireland was a nation and must be treated as one. There was room for argument about the exact political consequences. Certainly neither Scott nor Arnold envisaged a nation state. The *Guardian*'s Irish campaign started at the very beginning of 1886 when the Conservative government was still in office though it had been defeated in the general election. It began with two series of signed articles. The fact that they were signed meant that the editor was not committed. The standing of the signatories guaranteed attention. Arthur Evans's father-in-law, E. A. Freeman, the Regius Professor of History at Oxford, wrote six articles on 'Why Ireland Asks for Home Rule.' He followed the history of Ireland through the ages, sharply pointing one and the same moral in each article:

' "What are we to do in Ireland?" So wrote a really eminent member of the House of Commons to me a few days back. The form of the question itself almost supplies the answer. A great deal of meaning lurks in that little word "we." It is in short the root of the matter . . .' (4 January 1886)
'The Irish do not wish that "we" should do things for them; they had rather do things for themselves. In this they are like the rest of mankind . . .' (19 January 1886)
'If we will not have Home Rule, we must have the opposite of Home Rule. The fiction of the United Kingdom cannot go on. Ireland must either be free or it must be more thoroughly conquered than ever before . . .' (23 January 1886)

The second series of articles was by J. O'Connor Power, a Rochdale-born Irishman who had been one of the ablest of the Parnellite MPs.* He analysed closely the governmental system in Ireland and showed that the key positions of power were regularly in the hands of Englishmen. His articles discussed the grievances of Roman Catholic majorities in some of the Ulster counties. He looked across the Atlantic and con-

---

* 'The Brains of Obstruction' was the title 'Vanity Fair' gave to Spy's cartoon (25 December 1886.)

cluded that 'the influence of Irish America on our domestic politics is at the present moment one of the great dangers'.

At the end of January the Conservative government was defeated in the House and Gladstone returned to power. Scott had it in mind to follow Freeman's and O'Connor Power's articles with a third by John Bright.[20] Bright, however, refused, 'for to tell you the truth I am sorely puzzled and have no well-defined idea of what can be done or ought to be attempted.'[21] When the crisis came a month later Bright sided with Chamberlain against Gladstone.

The next step in Scott's Irish campaign was investigation of the economic and social situation in Ireland by Spenser Wilkinson. It was clear that Arnold could not now be spared for long absences from the office. It was equally clear after Wilkinson's success in Berlin that he was the man to send. He was in Ireland during February and March. Wilkinson mixed more politics with his survey than Arnold had done four years before. The times made that essential, and perhaps it accorded better with his nature. He spent much time with such Nationalist leaders as John Dillon and Tim Healy. He fell ill and Michael Davitt came and nursed him. He even persuaded Davitt to give him a sealed letter which would have introduced him to the Moonlighters had not Scott recalled him at the critical moment. But Wilkinson did not neglect the close study of actual farming and living conditions in Ireland. In this respect his work was as careful and as detailed as Arnold's had been. Because he had seen for himself and set out the evidence fairly, his conclusions carried conviction.

The most important was contained in the last but one of his articles:

'From recent conversations with Nationalists I think their party would admit in principle the policy of a measure for restoring order in the disturbed districts of Kerry. They think it reasonable that such a measure should be twofold – dealing, that is, at the same time with outrages and with evictions . . .' (17 March 1886)

It was perhaps this suggestion which caused John Morley, the new Chief Secretary, to ask that the anonymous writer of the *Guardian* articles should come to see him in Whitehall on his return.*

Wilkinson concentrated in his articles on the first two steps in the *Guardian*'s Irish policy – land reform and crime. He left the third, the political consequence of Irish nationalism, to Scott and Arnold. This was not a matter for fact-finding but decision-making. The steps by which the *Guardian* approached the final leap of faith were these:

* Later in the year Wilkinson's articles were published in book form under his own name with the sadly optimistic title of *The Eve of Home Rule*.

'What we have to do now . . . is to take the Irish leaders into consultation, to treat them not as rebels in disguise but as sensible and honest men who have the good of their country at heart.' (30 January 1886)

'Unless we are going to give pretty much what the Irish want, there is no sense in giving anything.' (19 March 1886)

'The demand for Home Rule has to be frankly refused or frankly granted, and the only way to govern Ireland with the consent of the majority of the Irish people is to do the latter.' (29 March 1886)

It was at this point that Goschen and the Dukes and Joseph Chamberlain found they lacked 'that one grain of faith.' Not only was the Liberal Party shattered, but the country was driven at last, through bitter experience, to discover the truth of the *Guardian*'s warning, that 'The consequence of denying a settlement now would be to compel one later on, under circumstances much less favourable and certainly much less honourable to ourselves.'[22]

CHAPTER SEVENTEEN

Edward Taylor and his Partners

I

Who had decided that the *Guardian* should support Home Rule? It was the most important political decision that Liberal newspapers had to make in the nineteenth century, comparable in its difficulty and in its consequences only to the Conservative choice between Free Trade and Protection forty years before. When the decision had to be made Scott had been a partner in Taylor, Garnett & Co. for twelve years, but he was not even a part-owner. The copyright and the whole business belonged entirely to his cousin, Edward Taylor. The Articles of Partnership were for a period of five years at a time and, on occasion, were even allowed to lapse by oversight. The strength of Scott's position did not depend on his contractual rights but on the complete trust felt in him by Taylor, now a frail man who seemed much older than his 56 years. This trust sprang not only from family feeling but from a common political viewpoint. In 1886, however, the old land-marks suddenly disappeared. Did the editor or the proprietor decide the path the *Guardian* took through the unfamiliar country? Did Scott acquiesce in Taylor's decision, or Taylor accept Scott's lead? Or did they merely happen to think alike?

Scott, of course, was tied to Manchester which Taylor had left twenty years before. Taylor usually spent the winter in France, either in Paris or on the Riviera, but at the time of the Home Rule crisis he was in London and could easily have come to Manchester or sum-moned Scott to London. Yet there is no record of the two meeting to talk things over, although they certainly discussed the situation fully by letter. Some of Taylor's but none of Scott's letters have survived. Three of them help to make the relation between the editor and the proprietor clear. The first[1] was written while Gladstone was busy forming his Cabinet. It passes on political gossip about Ireland which Taylor had gathered from such Liberal politicians of the second rank as A. J. Mundella and George Otto Trevelyan. The fact that some of the gossip was true and some unreliable does not now matter: what is significant is that although Taylor was a keen politician and moving in influential circles, he did not attempt to suggest to his editor what line his own paper ought to take. The second letter was written during the anxious period between the introduction of the Home Rule Bill and its second reading. Without waiting for Taylor's opinion, Scott committed the *Guardian* to the view that, though the objective was good, the bill was bad and would need extensive recasting. Taylor wrote:

'I fancy you may like to hear from me in this critical time and to know how far I concur with you in the line you are taking in the *Guardian* . . . I think the best hope is for a coalition of the strongest, most moderate men of both parties for the definite object of settling the Irish difficulty . . . I wish I could have talked with you on all these questions and I have had half a thought in these last two days of just running down for a few hours to talk to you about them. Meantime I should just add that on the whole and in their main bearings I have entirely approved the arguments you have used . . .'[2]

Here there is a tentative suggestion of a new political line, but there is no request to Scott to follow it in the *Guardian*. In fact, the paper did not take it up. Nor did Taylor return to the idea of a coalition but, as the year went on, he moved steadily to the left. He had made up his mind that he would vote for the second reading if he were an MP. By the end of May he mentions how reluctantly he had declined an invitation to stand as a Gladstonian Liberal for South Buckinghamshire: 'Oh! for ten years of strength and youth to contend in so good a cause.'* Taylor's progress can be traced in his letters to Scott. They follow after and endorse the leading articles in which, unprompted by his proprietor, Scott himself took the paper step by step to the radical side. Taylor summed up his feelings in a New Year letter in words which Scott must have treasured:

'You have raised the paper to a position it never won before and put its praise in the mouths of all true Liberals. I am constantly told that the *Guardian* is the one only journal throughout England which has been equal to the occasion and I hear it spoken of always in terms of the highest respect. I cannot listen to such praise unmoved and I do not think I ought to allow my feelings to remain unuttered.'

If Taylor had reason to congratulate himself on having so great an editor – the familiar adjective is beginning to be appropriate – Scott was fortunate to serve a proprietor who was content to trust and not to interfere.

Two factors combined to give Scott the editorial freedom without

---

* Taylor's country house, The Coppins, Iver, was in the constituency. (Taylor–Scott 31 May 1886.)

which the *Guardian* could never have become the paper we know. The first was the poor health from which both Mr and Mrs Taylor suffered. This, as we have seen, led them to spend a great part of each year abroad. There was no international telephone system and no possibility of close day-to-day control of editorial policy. In the rapidly moving crisis over the Parnell divorce case and the consequent split in the Nationalist Party, for instance, Taylor was grateful for a succession of long news telegrams from Manchester: 'you cannot form an idea of the wearing impatience one feels to be exiled here and quite out of reach of news less than thirty hours old,' he wrote from Mentone.[3] Day-to-day directives on policy from the proprietor were plainly impossible.

The second factor was Taylor's knowledge that, with three exceptions, he could sit back and count on reading in the morning's *Guardian* the things he wanted written. Two were matters on which Scott, if left a free hand, would write or sanction leaders which did not reflect Taylor's views. Taylor did not insist that his paper should say what he believed. He was content if it refrained from contradicting him. On these points policy directives were accordingly given. He writes to Scott on the Female Suffrage Bill of 1892, 'your article . . . was adroitly done and your display of the cloven foot most discreetly managed; still it was quite visible. I must ask you *not* to advocate this measure whilst I live. The restriction cannot last very long.' He was less absolute about proportional representation, but still he made his wishes clear enough: 'Do not you ride that proportional representation hobby too far. You know I have not much affection for the principle.'[4] The directives were clear, but experience showed that they had to be repeated.

On 'temperance' and the licensed trade Scott and Taylor did not hold contradictory opinions, but differed seriously in the relative importance which they attached to these matters. This is the only recurring issue on which Taylor constantly issued positive orders about the line to be taken. They were not very effective. 'I am sorry you failed to deal with the licensing matter I sent to you . . . I do not think the *M.G.* does its full duty', Taylor wrote in September 1890. 'Could you not find a clever fanatic and let him keep all temperance and licensing matters alive?' A month later he was disturbed about the firm itself: 'the demons of drink and dissipation seem to have invaded the place and corrupted the men all round.'[5] Moral issues in the narrow sense excited a more belligerent puritanism in Taylor than in Scott. He thought, for instance, that the *Guardian* might have been more severe than it was with Parnell over the Kitty O'Shea affair, and he was insistent that the Prince of Wales must not be spared in the Tranby Croft baccarat scandal. Taylor asked Scott to comment on it, with 'a very firm hand' and in 'a very resolute tone.' A few days later Taylor noted with regret that Scott had not answered this part of his letter and rubbed in again the need to deal severely with 'the revelations that we get of the Prince's unworthy conduct.'[6] But these orders and embargoes add up to only a small encroachment on the freedom which Taylor allowed Scott.

2

Taylor was able to exercise a more effective control over the management of the firm because business decisions rarely had to be taken from hour to hour. He had two main correspondents in Manchester during this period – his brother-in-law, Peter Allen, who was in general charge of the business side of Taylor, Garnett & Co., and J. H. Buxton, his principal assistant. Peter Allen was 56 when Scott joined the *Guardian* and had already been twenty years with the firm. He lived to be 77, but for ten years before his death he was gradually withdrawing from active business, leaving more and more to his deputy and spending as much time as he could in his country home at Beaumaris in Anglesey. Only a very few of Peter Allen's letters of this period survive so that it is difficult to say with confidence how he regarded the various critical business decisions that had to be made. His views, however, may usually be inferred from what Taylor told Scott. Buxton had been with the firm for a good many years before he became a partner in 1884. The relative importance of the three Manchester partners is indicated by the terms of the new partnership. The existing arrangements gave Peter Allen £2,800 a year, Scott £1,800 and Buxton £600. The new arrangements were designed to yield Allen and Scott £2,500 each and Buxton £1,000. To make this possible Taylor reduced his share of the profits from seven-tenths to eighteen-thirtieths, which would have been equivalent to a cut of £800. In fact, however, the paper's prosperity enabled all the partners to draw bigger sums than these.

By the end of the 1870s Taylor had decided to build entirely new offices and works facing Cross Street, Manchester. He arranged a competition limited to six invited Manchester architects whose plans had to be submitted by midnight on Saturday, 14 June 1879. On the 13th Buxton wrote anxiously to enquire whether Taylor would agree to Oldham, the night watchman, 'who is very reliable', receiving any entries that arrived after office hours. Two days later he reported, 'Oldham tells me that the last was brought and delivered just inside the door as the chimes of the twelfth hour began, but before the hour began to strike.' On the following Friday Taylor, accompanied by Mr

Barry,* paid one of his rare visits to Manchester. They came to inspect the plans. They found prepared for them in their private sitting-room in the Queen's Hotel 'a dinner of soup, boiled salmon and a dish of nice cutlets with asparagus' which Buxton had ordered for them that morning. The six architects had already each received his honorarium. They were warned that they would have to wait several weeks for the result of the competition. The *Guardian* had to wait several years for its new building.

It spent the interval in temporary premises off Blackfriars Street, Salford, with the usual crop of inconveniences. How were telegrams, for instance, to be delivered promptly enough to prevent rival papers, whose offices were much nearer the central telegraph office, securing an advantage? Taylor was prepared to use modern methods where there was economic advantage. Plans were made for a pneumatic tube to deliver telegrams direct from the Post Office to Blackfriars. On the 18th of May the Post Office were requested to go ahead with the installation; on the 23rd the *Guardian* was printed for the last time in its old building; on the 11th June the plumber was advised that the idea of the pneumatic tube had been reluctantly abandoned 'owing princi-pally to the action of the Corporation.' Planning permission – in this instance for the necessary street works – could be as difficult to obtain in 1879 as it is to-day.

The decision to rebuild was connected with technical improvements in the printing industry. For twenty years the *Guardian* had been printed on Hoe rotary presses made in America. These printed from stereo-plates instead of directly from the type-formes, thus adding another department to the mechanical side of the firm. But they greatly increased the speed of production since it was possible to print simul-taneously from two or more stereo-plates made from the same type-forme. The *Guardian*'s Hoe presses, however, were still fed with individual sheets of paper. Two of them at least were 'eight-feeders', that is to say that at eight different stations sheets of newsprint were fed into the press. Taylor now decided to introduce roll or web presses, printing not from individual sheets but from a continuous roll of newsprint from which the machine finally delivered papers folded ready for distribution. Two of the old folding machines were sold to the *Wigan Observer*. There were economies in manpower. Buxton gave instructions that 'whatever hands remain that you and Mr Braithwaite can dispense with should receive the usual week's notice.'

The machines chosen were three Victory presses made by the

---

* Probably E. M. Barry (1830–1880) who reconstructed Covent Garden Opera House and built extensions to the National Gallery.

The Firs, Fallowfield, the house three miles from the office which Scott rented from 1882 until his death

'There he goes, the silly old—, and not a line written about him' Attributed to George Wainwright in charge of obituary files. (Scott continued to bicycle to and from the office until he was over 80.)

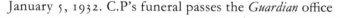

> Mr Scott
> You are a dirty
> fenian and
> a camp follower
> of the irish party
> a radical of no
> importance you
> know as much about
> politics as a pig knows about
> a white shirt. to hell with
> you and you shadows.

> Traitor Scott.
> I cannot under-
> stand why a creature
> like you is allowed
> to encumber the earth,
> nor to produce such a
> vile rag as your Kaiser
> subsidised paper.
> You have made the name
> "Manchester" stink in the
> nostrils of all loyal
> people, with your peace
> at any price principles,
> sympathy for the Hun,
> care for the C-O, love
> for the dastardly assassin
> the Irishman and
> brief for the Yankee.

Two typical anonymous letters. The first was written in 1899; the second in 1916

January 5, 1932. C.P's funeral passes the *Guardian* office

Liverpool firm which had supplied the first Mark I model to the *Glasgow Star* nine years before. With this experience behind them the makers ought to have been able to produce machines free from teething troubles. They did not. They had to be told that Taylor, Garnett & Co. did 'not feel disposed to make any further payments on account of them until we are satisfied.' Three weeks later one press jammed and was out of production for the whole night; another worked 'with such extreme difficulty as to throw the publication late by nearly five hours' – a serious matter for a newspaper. It was another two months before they were working satisfactorily and, even so, Peter Allen was unwilling to sanction further payments for the time being. Meanwhile a fourth web rotary press had been ordered from Hoe & Co. It was then more than two months overdue when the manager's letter book stops. These were, however, only teething troubles. Eight years later Buxton told a business enquirer that the firm's eleven Victory machines 'work admirably – none better . . . I should regard (them) as incomparably superior to all others, in every sense.'[7] He went on to urge his correspondent to add the one thing necessary to achieve perfection – to fit his Victory machines with the special stop press box which had been developed by the firm's 'practical men' and for which Taylor, Garnett & Co. held a patent. By this time Buxton and Taylor, who kept a lively interest in the technical side of newspaper production, were experimenting with machines to replace the old method of setting type by hand which was virtually unchanged from the beginning of printing. The change-over is described in Chapter Twenty-one.

All the ordinary commercial business of the firm also fell to Buxton to supervise. The Paris correspondent, for instance, had to be assisted to prepare his accounts in an intelligible form and to learn what a 'float' was. 'Dear Mr Gallighan,' Buxton wrote, '. . . if you are right there need be no feeling of annoyance. *I* do not experience annoyance because I know the exact state of things can be ascertained . . .' A few days later, when Gallighan had had time to digest Buxton's statement of his accounts for the last six years, he was invited to come over, if he could not understand it, with all his books and papers at the firm's expense 'so that we may thoroughly investigate the accounts together.'[8] The long-suffering, bantering tone used by the 'counting house'* to the unbusinesslike journalist has a familiar and not unpleasant ring.

Long before Buxton became a partner he was in regular weekly correspondence with Taylor, who wanted to keep a very close eye on the progress of the *Evening News* and its weekly publication the *Weekly*

* This Dickensian phrase was in common use in the *Guardian* until after the Second World War.

Post. Buxton sent him weekly statements of the circulation day by day and the total advertising revenue for the week. He does not seem to have supplied similar information for the *Guardian*, although there are occasional mentions of the month's 'remittances' to the two papers which show the *Guardian* receiving about four times as much as the *Evening News*. Probably the *Evening News* figures needed more constant watching than the *Guardian*'s because of greater fluctuations. The *Guardian*'s average daily sale was at this time between thirty and forty thousand copies. In the first nine months of 1879 the average daily sale of the *Evening News* ranged from 48,800 in a bad week to 77,900 in a good.

All sorts of miscellaneous matters were personally attended to by Buxton. He arranged for the Post Office to keep a special fortnight's check on the delivery in London of Taylor's copy of the *Guardian* which had been arriving late. Going through the *Guardian*'s old records one is impressed with the confidence with which writers relied on the prompt delivery of letters. On the other hand, the new-fangled telephone – still in private hands – was not yet dependable. Scott had one installed in his room but complained of defects and Buxton wrote to ask the company to 'investigate and explain to him what has gone wrong.'[9] Perhaps it was these early experiences which made Scott into an incurably reluctant user of the telephone and a confirmed letter-writer.

3

While the *Manchester Guardian* was in exile in Salford a fierce newspaper war broke out in the North-west. Manchester was accustomed to three morning papers, costing a penny each, and two evening each costing a half-penny. The three mornings were the *Courier*, which was Conservative, the *Guardian* and the *Examiner*, which was still to the left of the *Guardian*. The two evening papers were the *Evening News*, which belonged to Taylor and Peter Allen, and the *Evening Mail*, which was published by Sowler of the *Courier*. In the summer of 1882 a new morning Conservative paper was launched – the *North Times* which sold at a penny. This merely further sub-divided the opposition to the *Guardian*, which was impregnable in its position as the leading medium for advertisements. But as interest grew in the war news from Egypt the proprietors of the *North Times* saw a chance to establish a half-penny morning paper. On Monday, 11 September there appeared the first number of *The Latest News*.

Taylor was in Wiesbaden and Scott had just started his holiday.

William Evans, the mainstay of the *Evening News*, was critically ill. The first report to reach Taylor came from Peter Allen; it was followed at once by a telegram from Scott. Taylor's first reaction was that the obvious thing was to bring out the *Evening News* in the morning (its first edition was published at 1.45 p.m.), but on reflection he thought there were two objections to this. The *Evening News* would stake its whole existence on its success as a morning paper. This carried a double risk: failure would kill it; success might harm the *Guardian*. A completely new and separate half-penny morning would be, he thought, a better proposition. So he wrote in his first letter to Scott that critical Monday. Later in the day he wrote again asking Scott to go carefully into the possibilities of a separate half-penny morning paper and to produce a rough estimate of its cost. He did not suppose that his idea would be welcomed by Peter Allen and the *Evening News* people, but 'I think the same paper will not succeed both in the morning and the evening.' By Wednesday Taylor had seen the first issue of *The Latest News* and thought little of it: 'They have made the paper so large – larger than the *Evening News* – that I do not think they can make it pay without advertisements,' which they would not get.

Taylor was quite right in thinking that Peter Allen would not agree with him. On Thursday afternoon he received a telegram from Allen saying that he was sanctioning the temporary publication of a morning edition of the *Evening News* and that the *Evening Mail* was taking a similar course. Scott also sent a telegram to Taylor some time on Friday directing his attention to the publication of the *Morning News* on Thursday. Taylor then did a little research and discovered that Allen's Thursday telegram had only been sent off after the first issue of the *Morning News* was already out. 'I was sharply stung when I learned these facts,' he wrote to Scott, 'and I cannot throw off the painful reflection they occasion. Had I written yesterday to Mr Allen I could only have done so in stinging words. To-day calmness has succeeded to some extent to the outbursts of anger and I have tried to write a letter to Mr Allen which whilst sufficiently resolute and remonstrative should be couched in temperate language. I send you a copy.'[10] – which unfortunately has not survived.

But the absentee proprietor could not, or at any rate did not, override Peter Allen's forestalling action. The *Morning News* and the *Morning Mail* continued to appear until the end of the year. The *North Times* and *The Latest News* had by then been dead a fortnight and it was possible to revert to the comfortable *status quo*. The danger to the *Guardian* and its Manchester contemporaries from a half-penny morning paper was postponed, and Taylor, Garnett & Co. continued to flourish. The income tax returns for 1886, 1887 and 1888, calculated on the three years' average basis, showed a steady rise from £14,406 to £15,316 and then to £17,318.

4

The newspaper war of 1882 was followed by a very serious illness for Taylor. This brought out into the open the changed relations between the two senior partners. For a time Taylor was too ill to write and it was left to his wife to correspond with Scott. Her letters are pathetic. She had asked her husband if he would like to see Scott. 'His reply was "if Charlie comes without Mr Allen – Mr Allen would behave badly to Charlie, as he would be jealous and show temper. I would not dare to see Charlie alone".' She complains of the tone of Peter Allen's letters to her: 'a very rude and vulgar production of a vulgar mind' was her description of one letter.[11] Taylor's thoughts naturally turned to the future of the *Guardian*. He wanted Scott to know what his will contained so that he could be assured that his plans would be carried out. He jotted down the facts for his wife and she sent them to Scott. Taylor's note read:

'As far as I can recall the figures of my will, I have left the *Guardian* to be offered equally to Peter Allen and C. P. Scott at £40,000 . . . That would be either £20,000 (or it might be £25,000) for Charles's half. I have also nominated him to succeed to the *Evening News*.

I desire to know that these terms would be acceptable to him in order that I may rest satisfied that he will continue to edit the paper and, what I especially and fervently wish, to maintain its high character unimpaired. He must be prepared to take firm ground and be able to assert his rights. He will always justify my fullest confidence I know.'[12]

Scott took a week to think the offer over. When he replied he made it clear that he did not believe in divided control of a newspaper and that the particular form of division which Taylor had in mind could only lead to 'a period of painful and prolonged conflict.' 'In regard to almost every important principle in the conduct and development of the paper . . . we have differed and shall continue to differ hopelessly, and there are I must say in addition features in Mr Allen's character . . . which would make me in the last degree reluctant to be placed in a position where it might be my duty, with limited powers to resist the personal claims and interests of himself and his children.' Scott went on to say that, if the *Guardian* were to come to him, he hoped that it would be to his sole control. He was grateful for the offer of the

Evening News, but he would gladly surrender any claim to it.[13] It was then, of course, a much less important and profitable paper than the *Guardian*. Taylor cannot have been surprised by Scott's reaction since he felt the same dissatisfaction with Allen.

In these circumstances Taylor turned increasingly to Buxton, and it seems probable that from 1884 onwards Peter Allen dropped steadily into the background. There was much to please Taylor in Buxton's work. He saved the paper, for instance, £1,400 one year on ink alone in spite of larger papers and increased circulation. His letters set out the business fortunes of the firm so clearly that Taylor knew just how things were. He analysed the expenditure of the various departments and suggested where more needed to be spent, especially on the circulation side, and where economies could be made on the editorial side. Taylor was sure that Scott would be grateful for these suggestions – Scott's replies do not survive – and that he would cut down the amount spent on outside contributors. Too many of the leading articles, for instance, especially the 'shorts', were written outside the office on space rates and the reviewing, Taylor thought, was getting rather too heavy.[14]

But from an early stage there were also difficulties. At first they seemed to centre round Peter Allen's desire to provide his sons with a secure future in Taylor, Garnett & Co. and its two subsidiaries, Wm. Evans & Co., which published the *Evening News*, and Taylor, Garnett, Evans & Co. which undertook general printing from the Salford works where the *Guardian* had had its temporary home. There was also from 1884 to 1891 a London subsidiary, Allen, Scott & Co., which ran a general printing business and held the contract for printing *Tit-Bits*. At first Taylor was inclined to think that Buxton needed all the support that he could be given against Allen. Although Taylor felt morally bound to Peter Allen, he did not feel under any similar obligation to his sons. Indeed, Taylor had at this time on the whole a rather poor opinion of his nephews, the eldest of whom, Russell Allen, was only 24 when Buxton was admitted to the partnership. He was to change his opinion later – partly, no doubt, because they proved their worth,* and partly, perhaps, because it became clear that Buxton's fears were to some extent paranoid. In 1888 Buxton had a very severe nervous breakdown. He could not be persuaded to take the long holiday in America which Taylor thought would cure him, but continued to work – and apparently with effect for the firm continued to prosper. But his mental condition rapidly deteriorated. According to Taylor he suffered from 'manifest delusions' and was 'partially insane.' Instead of

* Russell Allen ran the *Evening News*, Edward Allen took over Taylor, Garnett, Evans & Co. C. P. Allen and A. A. Allen both became Liberal MPs.

defending Buxton against Peter Allen's sons, Taylor now found it necessary to protect the eldest, Russell Allen, against Buxton.[15]

The situation was complicated by the fact that Buxton, too, had a son. And, like Peter Allen, Buxton thought Taylor, Garnett & Co. was a suitable place for a boy. Harry Buxton had travelled on his own in the United States and Canada when he was 17. In 1886, at the age of 20, he started a business venture on his own, *The Halfpenny Novelette*, which was printed for him by his father's firm. His father devoted what might be thought an undue amount of time and influence to pushing his son's venture on Taylor, Garnett & Co's advertisers and correspondents. The *Novelette* may have been 'always of high tone and strictly proper in every sense', but it seems doubtful whether the father should have lifted advertisements for it from the *Guardian* and then pressed the advertisers to follow up this free publicity by taking space in the new paper. Unfortunately there is no trace of what J. W. Riggs, the *Guardian*'s New York correspondent, thought when he received with his monthly cheque an invitation to himself or one of his 'enterprising sons' to publish an American edition and share in 'the gigantic fortune to be reaped at no distant period.'[16]

Whether or not Harry Buxton was employed by Taylor, Garnett & Co. in 1886 is not clear. Taylor was uncertain about it, and we have no means of finding out. It is, however, certain that Taylor started by being prejudiced against 'young Harry Buxton' and, when the young man tried to join the *Guardian* in 1890, Taylor repeatedly warned Scott against taking on 'a young man who at the time when he should have been settling down to hard work . . . preferred to spend the best years of his life in a vagrant and bohemian existence.'[17] However, a few months later he was made manager of Allen, Scott & Co, though refused the partnership in Taylor, Garnett & Co. which his father tried to get him. Taylor was at first highly delighted with his work, then dissatisfied and finally placated. The sale of Allen, Scott & Co, a firm which seems to have been mismanaged from the start, brought heavy loss to all the partners. Taylor always looked on it as a general printing venture. Scott clearly had hopes, which Taylor discouraged, of using it to provide the *Guardian* with a London outlet.* Both were disappointed. The odd thing is that the only serious damage from the chaotic business management and crazy family bickering of the 1880s was the loss of this London subsidiary.

* 'Your views of a London newspaper are far above me. I have sometimes thought that the London scheme might lead to a connection with some such project. But that we should do it – No! – That must be for younger, bolder and stronger men than I am.' Taylor–Scott 31 March 1884.

5

In Manchester all went well. The great newspaper feature of the years 1888–1894 was the protracted death of the *Manchester Examiner*. It never recovered from its hesitation during the Home Rule crisis of 1886. It lost its radical readers to the *Guardian* and could not get them back when it declared for Gladstone. In 1888 it was clearly in financial danger. Liberal leaders tried to persuade Taylor to buy it to save it from Chamberlain's Liberal-Unionists or from extinction. But Taylor was cautious. He was unwilling to pay more than he thought the *Examiner* was worth – and that was very little. He was sorry for Alexander Ireland, the ageing manager, and Henry Dunckley, the editor, and wished that they could get the benefit from any sale but, since they would not, that was as far as he let sentiment go. On the business side he felt that the *Guardian* gained from having two rivals instead of one. He argued that, if the *Courier* were left alone, it would automatically attract all the advertisers who wanted a second medium. In this way it would strengthen its advertising revenue and could afford more vigorous competition.

In 1889 the *Examiner* was sold to the Unionists. Taylor continued, rightly as it turned out, to discount the effect that this would have on the Liberal Party and the *Guardian*. He delighted in the story that the new editor from London prudently bought a return ticket for his journey to Manchester. The old editor merely crossed the narrow passage that separated the offices of the *Examiner* from the *Guardian*. He brought with him 'The Letters of Verax' in which for a dozen years he had each week 'roamed over all the field of politics and touched frequently on those questions of political theology which were always burning while England was still ruled by its Nonconformist chapels.' 'If you saw it in a "Letter of Verax" it was so.'[18] This was the tradition which Haslam Mills, the first historian of the *Guardian*, inherited from his father who was music critic of the *Examiner*. He recalled that the Letters were even more read in the West Riding than in Lancashire. Certainly when they were transferred to the *Guardian* most of the remaining good-will of the *Examiner* came with them. The paper itself languished for five more years, changing hands again in 1891. Its proprietors toyed with the idea of a third Manchester evening paper but abandoned it. Finally they tried the desperate solution of reducing the price to a half-penny. Taylor was right in holding Buxton off from the repeated offers to sell for he was much too eager a purchaser. In the end Taylor secured the *Examiner* building without having to buy the paper. The back half of the *Guardian*'s Cross Street office occupied the site.

The idea of securing Dunckley's services seems to have started with Scott. Taylor saw both the advantages and disadvantages and urged Scott to make a provisional arrangement for one year. He feared that the famous old editor of thirty-four years' standing would find it difficult to work under his rival who had been an editor for only half that time. He believed that Peter Allen would not welcome anybody who came from the *Examiner* – indeed, both Allen and Taylor were convinced that the *Examiner*'s competition had been anything but fair in the old days. He urged Scott to make sure that his own staff, especially Arnold, were told of the proposal in advance. In this he showed that he realised one of Scott's marked weaknesses. He showed his awareness of another when he wrote that, since Dunckley's proposed salary (£600) was low, 'it would have been a graceful consideration to have given the holiday without deferring the commencement of the salary.'[19] Scott might well have lost Dunckley who toyed with the idea of syndicating his 'Letters of Verax.' It was six weeks after the letter just quoted before Taylor could write, 'I am very pleased to hear that you have made something like a regular engagement with Dunckley . . . if you will *pay him well* . . . you may hear nothing more of the Syndicate. He is rather an indolent man. I take it the arrangement of a syndicate would give him a lot of trouble . . . and if we only make up an income for him he will probably refrain from applying elsewhere.'[20] Taylor was right.

The appearance in the *Guardian* of the 13th July 1889 of the first of the new series of 'Letters of Verax' was a landmark in the paper's history.* Scott, with Arnold's help, had already converted the semi-Whig *Guardian* into a radical newspaper; Dunckley's appearance in its columns made the fact plain for all the Nonconformist world to see. There was to be no more competition from the Left.

* The series continued until 1896. The last article appeared on June 30, the day after Dunckley's sudden death.

BOOK FOUR

The Testing 1895-1907

*

CHAPTER EIGHTEEN

One Eye on Westminster

IN 1878 W. S. Gilbert poked fun at W. H. Smith, the newsagent turned
First Lord of the Admiralty, who

> '. . . always voted at his party's call
> So now he is the ruler of the Queen's Navee.'

He might not have bothered to-day; but in 1878 the House of Commons
counted for more than it now does, its individual members had more
freedom and responsibility, their votes were not automatic, and their
speeches were read. Eighteen-seventy-eight was not only the year of
Pinafore but of the Select Committee on Parliamentary Reporting which
led in 1881 to the provincial papers being admitted to the Press
Gallery on the same terms as the London papers.* The long fight had
been worth winning. The men voters who provided the bulk of newspaper readers were eager for parliamentary news. When elections were
often won or lost by a hundred votes each voter could feel that his
might be decisive.† It was worth keeping his eye on his MP and on the
parliamentary struggle. The *Guardian*, like the other great regional
newspapers, made this easy through the long and often verbatim
reports by its own staff men and through the closely reasoned leading
articles which almost day by day commented on the business of the
House. To its readers, and they included a growing number of MPs
of all parties, these leaders were almost as much a part of a full-dress
parliamentary debate as the speeches themselves. It was natural, then,
that Scott should think of standing for parliament.

It was also reasonable. After a dozen years as editor Scott had made
for himself the kind of reputation which political bosses look for in
candidates. He had become a representative Manchester man, and he
had something to say which even Londoners were beginning to listen
to with respect. He had not only a local and a national position but
sufficient financial backing. No doubt Scott for his part considered that

---

* The black market operated before 1878 by the London papers with the con-
nivance of the Serjeant-at-Arms was described on pp. 148-150.

† Scott fought four parliamentary elections. In two a turnover of less than sixty
votes would have altered the result. The largest majority was 677.

the paper would gain in reputation if its editor were a member of parliament. There is no suggestion that he thought of giving up his editorship if he were elected. Indeed, in those days when members of parliament were unpaid he could not have afforded to do so. Nor was there any compelling reason why he should resign provided he made appropriate arrangements to cover his necessarily long absences.

Scott approached the question with characteristic caution. He had first to make sure of Taylor's support. In 1884 he mentioned to Taylor how his outside work was increasing, presumably to see what the reaction would be. 'Yes! I see your public work does increase!' Taylor wrote. 'You will see that this is not carried too far, will you not?'[1] Scott made no reference to his parliamentary ambitions at this time, but they were already there. Two years later in the excitement of the Home Rule crisis Taylor's attitude changed. It was he who suggested that Scott might become a candidate in the approaching general election. 'Are you disposed to try your strength and fortune?' he wrote on 31 May. But a fortnight later he expressed some misgiving about the consequences. 'I feel very much as you do,' he wrote, 'respecting the effects on the paper which your adoption of a parliamentary career would have; they would be mixed, there would be obvious advantages; drawbacks would be considerable and I think, on the whole, the paper must suffer somewhat. Still those drawbacks and disadvantages might perhaps, by some contrivance, be greatly mitigated and almost annulled.'[2] Taylor went on to tell Scott that as far as their business relations were concerned, he was quite free to decide as his conscience and judgment indicated. In the event Taylor gave Scott full support both in his unsuccessful attempts to win N.E. Manchester in 1886 and 1892 and in his successful campaigns in Leigh in 1895 and 1900.

There was no doubt that the presence of the editor of the *Guardian* in the House of Commons and his absence from the office in Manchester would inevitably alter the working of the paper. There was bound to be both greater freedom and more responsibility for the senior members of the staff. Would the proprietor and the editor realise this and recognise it in their pay and status? Taylor did. It was reasonable to assume that Scott would. The prospect of seeing their editor in the Commons had then its attractions for Scott's lieutenants. Who would be the main beneficiary?

Arnold was, in fact, the principal leader writer, in Scott's opinion the most responsible position under him, but Acton was still nominally Arnold's senior. Scott might have been content to leave it like this for a few years – Acton was 57 – but Arnold as well as Scott had his career to consider. He was seriously tempted to resign when in June

1884 he was approached by Benjamin Jowett, then at the height of his national reputation as scholar and academic statesman, to return to Oxford as secretary of the University Press. He told Scott about the offer and asked him about his position on the paper. Scott consulted Peter Allen whose advice was to let Arnold go, though he admitted he was out of touch with the editorial side of the paper and may not have known of Scott's parliamentary ambitions. Both Scott and Arnold consulted Mrs Humphry Ward, Arnold's sister, through whom Arnold had come to the paper five years before and through whom Jowett had now made his first approach. She wrote to her brother in an undated letter:

'Mr Scott has just been here and we have been talking about you and Oxford. What a good fellow he is! Evidently he wants to keep you but he feels the responsibility of dissuading you. *We* feel now that it is a doubtful matter and one that nobody but yourself can really form an opinion on. But we thought you might like to hear some of the things Mr Scott said, though very likely he has said them all to you already. Humphry spoke of the possibility of his (Scott's) own going into Parliament. "Possible" he said "but not certain or near. However he may be sure that whatever there is going in the office he will have the best chance for it. Mr Taylor likes him and thinks well of him." He says that in the natural course of things you must soon be the chief person on the staff and that he means you to see more of the business of the paper. All this sounds to us as much as Mr Scott *can* say – probably. It is evident that he likes and values you greatly.

'At the same time Oxford is a great opening in its own line – not to be lightly said No to, certainly, and I believe you would like the place and society better than you think now. Uncle Matt (Matthew Arnold) is wavering and sees the advantages of Manchester more clearly. Has anything been said of a *share* in the paper. Certainly I think that Mr Scott will do his best by you.'

It had become not only a question of who would be the chief beneficiary from C.P.'s political ambitions, but who would be the victim. As soon as Scott heard of Jowett's approach to Arnold he got in touch with Taylor. The partners agreed in July that Acton should go, and so anxious were they to make the change that they agreed to give him a pension – an extravagance which rankled for the next twenty-two years. But Scott seems not to have told Acton until October when, as he reported to Taylor, 'I pointed out to him that it had become necessary to recruit the staff with young men, that it was further necessary to bring them on and to throw the more important work of the staff upon them, and that in consequence his own position had become very much of a sinecure.'[3]

Acton's enforced retirement marked the end of an era. He was the last of the journalists who had served on the *Guardian* when it was still a bi-weekly paper. Garnett had appointed him when he was 21 and he had retained much of Garnett's outlook on life which meant he had less and less in common with the way Scott was shaping the paper both in politics (Acton was more of a Whig than a Liberal let alone a Radical) or in the arts. Acton's great outside interest was the theatre. Among his close friends had been his contemporaries Charles Mathews and Charles Calvert, who managed the Theatre Royal in Manchester for many years, and among younger actors Henry Irving, who was one of Calvert's company in Manchester from 1860 to 1865. The prologues in verse which Acton wrote for special theatrical occasions and a romantic burlesque which was produced at the Theatre Royal show him as clearly as do his leaders to be in spirit a mid-Victorian.

By getting rid of Acton, Scott had made room for Arnold at the top, though probably without making him any firm promises for the future. At any rate, Arnold decided to stay, and continued to improve his position on the paper though he had to ask for everything he got. Two years later, in 1886, when Scott was about to stand for N.E. Manchester, Arnold secured an increase in his salary to £1,000 a year with Taylor's full agreement. Arnold had to wait nine years before he got any more. Once again the occasion was a general election. This time Scott fought Leigh instead of N.E. Manchester. Leigh was a constituency with a large number of miners and, in view of the paper's strong support of their cause in the great lock-out of 1893, it was almost certain that Scott would win even in that year of Liberal disasters. It really was necessary to see that there were adequate arrangements for the conduct of the paper after the election. Taylor fully realised this.

As early as January 1895, when the annual salary review was in progress, Taylor had on his own initiative made two additions to the list submitted by Scott. One was to C. E. Montague, then a young leader writer; the other was to the almost equally young manager, Dibblee, who was given more money specifically on the ground that when Scott was in parliament the manager's responsibility would be much greater.[4] There had been another omission in Scott's list – Arnold. Just before Easter Arnold submitted a memorandum asking for £1,200 rising to £1,500 by 1899. In a long letter from Paris written on Easter Day, Taylor made three points on Arnold's application. They are by implication criticisms of Scott. 'I am very sorry he was not voluntarily put up to £1,200 before now . . . to attract and secure men of the calibre we require we shall have to pay these high salaries . . . you would be wise to have a full and frank and a foreseeing conversation with him . . . he should fully understand what will be his exact position when you go into the House. I fancy you rather underrate the changes which that event will entail. But they must be well thought out and provided for, and I should much like myself to have a full discussion of the matter with you.' It was apparently more than a month before Scott had the suggested talk with Arnold. After it took place Taylor was relieved to hear that Arnold was content with the increase in his salary. He hoped (but was obviously not sure) that Scott had also discussed with Arnold 'the Editorial arrangements to provide for the time of your absence.'[5] Scott could be both obstinate and evasive. He disliked any formal delegation of power. He probably succeeded in avoiding it on this occasion.

The kind of provision for his absence which Scott himself recognised as necessary was of a different kind. Beyond handing over a certain number of administrative jobs which he normally undertook himself, it was limited to making sure that all the leader-writers were not only men of ability but men on whom he could depend to think his own thoughts without his being there to guide them. He would need to feel confident that when he opened his paper in London he would read only what he would himself have approved. This involved both a positive and a negative side. He had to make sure that he had sufficient of the right men – so he appointed C. E. Montague in 1890 and L. T. Hobhouse in 1896.

He had also to ensure that he had no wrong men, that is to say, no men who might write leading articles with which he would disagree. It was for this reason that Wilkinson 'had to go'* in 1892. There were other temperamental difficulties but the main reason was undoubtedly the fact that Wilkinson did not share all Scott's views. In 1890 Scott had refused Wilkinson an increase in salary because his work showed a lack 'of a real hold of Liberal principles which has been very disquieting. The consequent uncertainty in which I have been as to how you might handle new or difficult questions has further limited your usefulness to us.'[6] Or, as Wilkinson put it two years later in a letter to Scott, 'You admit the quality and honesty of my work and my industry, and declare that the reasons which make you wish to part with me are not faults for which I am to blame. You admit in short that I can no more help thinking as I think than you can help thinking as you think.'[7] Fortunately for the paper Scott had found Wilkinson's limited usefulness tolerable for ten troubled years. During that time Scott never paid him more than £650 a year, though, rather oddly, when he gave him twelve months' notice he put up his salary to £750 and then under

* Scott's expression for getting rid of a man.

pressure backdated half of the increase to the previous January. For that small salary he had secured a man who, in addition to leader-writing and dramatic criticism, had done distinguished work in Ireland and as a diplomatic correspondent, and who had made the *Guardian* beyond much question the best informed paper on military matters and an influential mouthpiece for the army reformers. *The Brain of an Army*, a study of the German General Staff, was written during Wilkinson's later years in Manchester and was, as the Dictionary of National Biography later said, 'immensely influential.' Taylor was clearly right in telling Scott, 'He will be missed more than you suppose, but he is a man difficult to work with I should say.' Four years later Taylor was still commenting sadly on things which since Wilkinson's going had been left undone by the *Guardian*.[8]

If Scott had been willing to introduce some of Taylor's 'contrivances' it should have been possible to arrange Wilkinson's work in such a way that the paper continued to benefit from his gifts without the risk of being committed to policies of which Scott disapproved. But this, as far as hindsight allows one to see, would have involved two changes which Scott was unwilling to make and which would indeed have altered his whole style of editing the paper. He would have had to appoint a general all-purposes deputy with full powers to act in Manchester during the long months of the session when he himself would be away in London. That was the first change and the one which Taylor presumably had in mind when he pressed Scott to have his 'foreseeing' talk with Arnold.

The second change would have been the introduction of specifically defined responsibilities for each of his leader-writers. Certain leader-writers acquired a customary right to deal with particular subjects, but this was never formally acknowledged. From 1884 to 1892, when Scott was trying to get into parliament, it was generally recognised that Arnold would write any leaders that were needed about Ireland and that Wilkinson would deal with military and colonial affairs. But anybody might be called on to write about what was normally another man's speciality, and everybody had frequently to write trivially but presentably on subjects about which they knew little and cared less. And any leader-writer was liable to see for the first time in the paper a special article on one of his own subjects about which he had never been consulted. There were no formal conferences, no written directives, only generally accepted conventions established by a special fifth sense or derived from some *obiter dictum* of the editor to a member of the staff and passed on by him to his colleagues. A good *Guardian* man was expected to develop such an instinct for the paper's line that he would know without being told what the line should be even on an issue that had arisen that night for the first time. On subjects which were important, but in which Scott was not himself deeply interested, a leader-writer was required to bring to the paper the thorough and dependable knowledge which Scott lacked, and on the strength of this to express the opinions which Scott would have arrived at had he mastered the evidence. The trouble in this case was that it was precisely on these subjects that Scott was most open to the influence of the party leaders. When he himself was personally concerned about an issue he would never accept the party line simply because it was the party line. Where he lacked personal interest he was more amenable to official Liberal Party opinion and less to that of his own leader-writers, especially if they were relatively junior or, like Wilkinson, temperamentally unsympathetic.

This entirely personal system had grown up and worked well in a situation where the editor and his staff met daily. Scott's normal practice – and this remained unchanged until his death, apart from the ten years when he was in parliament – was to come down to the office in the early evening and there to discuss separately with the individual leader-writers their suggestions for the five or six leaders which the paper would carry next day. Sometimes, of course, the Long or first leader virtually fixed itself. More often its selection remained an open question until Scott had heard what each member of the staff had to suggest. Then Scott would often go home or out to dinner and the man responsible for the Long would sit down to write the three paragraphs which provided as fixed a pattern for the first leader as the octet and sestet for a sonnet. Two or two and a half hours later he would have completed his twelve to fifteen hundred words* – a hard task which could only be satisfactorily completed by a man who was already a master of the subject he was writing about, a quick thinker with the gift of concentration and the acquired knack of seeing an argument readily in three stages to correspond with the traditional three paragraphs. The other members of the staff would then settle down to write one or more short leaders (not all of which might be used that night), to attend to obituaries, write reviews or theatre notices, prepare outside contributions for publication, or get on with the time-consuming job of keeping up-to-date in their special subjects. Arnold, for instance, and Wilkinson both read large numbers of foreign papers and periodicals.

* Between the two world wars the length was more often one thousand to eleven hundred words. In 1968 the average length of the first leader was between five and six hundred words and the formal division into three paragraphs has been abandoned.

Arnold's room was remarkable for its vast collection of pigeon-holes which provided him with a home for his meticulous collection of cuttings. If the editor was spending the evening in the office and 'taking leaders' he would see and pass the Long in manuscript paragraph by paragraph. If he was working at home or was out to dinner he would not see it until the night messenger brought it out to his house in proof.

Scott clearly wanted to continue while he was in parliament this system under which he trusted all his editorial staff completely, but would entrust nothing absolutely to any of them. On this basis he was wise to get rid of men whose thoughts were so much at a tangent to his own as Acton's and Wilkinson's. They could only work effectively for the *Guardian* if the editor, or somebody with editorial power, were daily present to hold them to the paper's line.

However firmly Scott might resist the idea of a deputy with full powers, it was necessary for somebody to decide what subjects should be written about each night. This selection could never be automatic in the nature of things. It was also necessary to decide who should write on the various subjects selected for the night. This could not be automatic on the *Guardian* in view of the refusal to allocate definite departmental responsibilities. Scott could not avoid putting somebody in charge in this limited sense. Here further difficulties arose.

The position in the office in 1895, when Scott got into parliament, was different from the position in 1886 when he fought his first election. In 1886 Arnold was strong and with boundless energy. In 1895 he was, though nobody suspected it, on the eve of a serious illness. All that Scott and Taylor knew was that some of the spring had gone out of his work. He was not, they agreed, quite as good as he had been. The situation in the office in 1895 had changed too in another way. In 1886 Arnold had been the rising young man on whom the sun shone and for whom Acton had had to make way. But in 1895 a new star had risen in the *Guardian* firmament. C. E. Montague had been five years on the paper. Would history repeat itself? Taylor and Scott agreed that Montague was writing better than Arnold now was and the young men of the paper felt the same – 'the staff desired to go to school to Montague, not to Arnold, although it was a bad night for them when they tried to imitate Montague' was how J. B. Atkins, a new recruit in 1896, put it.[9] But Taylor's letters make it clear that he thought Scott was a little ungenerous in his forgetfulness of Arnold's past services, and a little blinded by Montague's brilliance to Arnold's present worth. 'Has not Arnold rather suffered from comparison . . . ?' Taylor wrote. 'I think when we look at the matter all round, we must still say Arnold is an excellent man for us . . . I certainly hope we shall never for a moment lose sight of his splendid handling of the Irish question . . . If St Loe Strachey, whom I know, be worth £1,500 a year to the *Spectator*, certainly Arnold ought to be worth as much to us.'[10]

And so, when Scott took his seat in the House of Commons, Arnold took charge of the paper as he had done before when Scott was away. One thing is certain. There was no jealousy on Montague's part. He was first the disciple, then the devoted friend, always the warm admirer of W. T. Arnold. The last thing he wanted to do was to supersede him. But fate determined otherwise. History repeated itself, though not in precisely the manner of 1884. By the summer of 1896 Arnold was desperately ill and had to give up work. He struggled back to the office for a few days in 1897; but in 1898 he had to give up altogether. For him, as for Acton, the partners provided a pension – it was unavoidable, they realised, but a sad precedent not to be repeated. Younger men must be warned to save. Arnold did not live to draw his pension long. He died in 1904.

Montague now regularly took charge in Scott's absence, but again only in the customary *Guardian* way by special arrangement and not as of right. Nothing must be taken for granted. As late as 1899, when Scott had been nearly five years in parliament, he could go off to London and only at the last moment, after the leader-writers had gone home, remember to leave a note telling one of his key men the arrangements he had made for his absence. Other members of the staff had nothing in writing, but were left to discover for themselves what was to happen. 'I think I forgot to tell you,' Scott wrote on this occasion to L. T. Hobhouse, 'I had arranged with Couper about the two points we spoke of – Montague will be responsible for the leader when he is on duty and you when he is not. Montague will also open and deal with my letters – Couper entirely approves of both arrangements – had them in mind, indeed, he says before as desirable.'* It is not surprising that the refusal to confer overall responsibility or to define departmental or subject authority was one, though not the chief of the factors which a little later led to the loss of Hobhouse, the man whom Scott most trusted and admired of all who ever worked for him. In a long letter Hobhouse wrote:

'If one is as much responsible for the policy of a paper as I have been on certain matters I think one ought to have a recognised consultative voice

* Scott–Hobhouse 5 February, 1899. This secretiveness was a vice of which Scott never broke himself. Years later, in 1926, the first intimation to W. P. Crozier, then assistant editor, that E. T. Scott would be in charge during his father's absence was a similar belated note, which Crozier not unnaturally resented.

in deciding what subjects should be treated in leaders and also whether the occasional articles and contributions that come to hand bearing on one's subject should be used. On such points I have hitherto felt that I can only request and suggest and I have sometimes felt considerably hampered by the rejection of my suggestions. I am not speaking of times when you are here . . . What I want to feel is that my view has a *right* to be considered and *on my own subject* ought, unless definite reason is assigned to me for the contrary, to be taken.'[11]

Taylor certainly felt after 1895 that his misgivings were being justified by events. In 1896, at the moment of Arnold's breakdown, Mrs Scott was taken ill. Her doctor thought she should go abroad and Scott asked Taylor's leave to go with her. Taylor's reply was, as usual, considerate but forthright. 'Of course, in a matter of health I could not possibly stand in the way; but with the long absences which you are for various reasons called on to make, I do feel that the question of something like a fixed arrangement should be come to. This I must say frankly. But it is a matter to discuss when we meet, if that ever happens, not by letter.'[12] Scott's response was characteristic. He evaded the main issue, but proposed a convalescence in Britain instead of Italy. Taylor was not hoodwinked – 'when you are at Tenby you might as well for the purposes of Editorship be at Como' – and he repeated that it was not Scott's absences but his failure to plan adequately for them to which he objected.[13] Two years later Taylor was more specific in his complaints and threatened to give the manager more control of editorial expenditure 'as a corollary to your frequent and necessary absence.'[14]

The following year there was another similar but more bitter clash between editor and proprietor. Mrs Scott's renewed ill-health involved an autumn abroad to be closely followed by a winter and spring in London for the parliamentary session. Taylor returned to the attack, once again demanding a large measure of editorial reorganisation. Scott's reply was once again unsatisfactory. In a second letter[15] Taylor once again reluctantly waived the matter:

'I do not know that much good can come of my attempting to discuss by letter the subject of providing for the proper exercise of Editorial functions during your absence. You know that I have more than once spoken to you of it. I suppose you do not see things as I do. To me, it seems that the administrative work of an Editor is not the most important and that the daily inspiration, direction and control which an Editor ought to exercise . . . are his highest and most valuable work.'

It is unlikely that Taylor was deceived by Scott's answer in which he looked forward to a discussion and remarked that his earnest desire was to do 'exactly what is best for the office and most in accordance with your own judgment.'[16]

At Christmas time that year Taylor wrote from the Riviera in reply to a letter from Scott who was in Rome. Scott had outlined various new arrangements which seemed sensible to Taylor as far as they went, but he left the central issue untouched. Taylor wrote: 'The Editorial organisation is, I fear, so far as suggestion, direction and initiative go, non-existent for two-thirds of the year. It is a very real defect, but, as you will not see it, I suppose we shall muddle along and suffer the natural results . . . it is a sore trouble to me to feel that . . . for want of proper direction . . . the concern is not in a fit condition to meet a strenuous competition.'[17] A draft of Scott's reply survives. It is heavy with alterations. But there are no erasures in the sentences that read: 'I am absolutely in your hands and my seat will be resigned on the day that you wish it. That, however, is a rather grave matter and I shall wait to see you before taking any decided step.'[18] The sacrifice was not demanded. Scott had not lost Taylor's confidence. Throughout the whole of this period Taylor's letters contain far more appreciation of Scott's work than they do of criticism. If Taylor had not admired and supported Scott's editorship, he would certainly have terminated it on this issue about which he felt so strongly. But, because he had no intention of getting rid of Scott, he was helpless in the face of Scott's obstinacy. It looks as if both men realised this.

How much did the paper suffer from having an absentee editor? Were the defects which Taylor saw persisting throughout the 1890s matters which Scott would have put right if he had not been concerned with his parliamentary career? Were the paper's strong points, developed during the first period of Scott's editorship, weakened during this middle passage? Or were both the defects and the virtues of the *Guardian* so much a reflection of Scott's masterful personality that both were present all the time, whether Scott was physically present in the office or not, and that neither was materially affected by his frequent absences in this period? The answers to these questions may become clearer in the subsequent chapters. Meanwhile there is perhaps a clue in the fact that it is from this time on that it seems more natural to write of the *Manchester Guardian* or the *M.G.* than simply of the *Guardian*. There was, of course, no change in title. Throughout the whole of its history recorded in this book the private office note-paper was headed 'The Guardian Office, Manchester,' and the title over the leading article read 'The Guardian, Manchester,' with the date. From the beginning, on the other hand, the masthead on the front page was 'The Manchester Guardian,' and that was the heading on the common note-paper for

general use by members of the staff. As long as the paper was largely
confined in its influence to Manchester, it was unnecessary to use the
prefix, and this was commonly ignored. But as it began to be read and
quoted far afield it had to be distinguished from the numerous other
Guardians. Neither expression ever dropped out of use, but from
1886 onwards 'the *M.G.*' was an expression well known wherever
newspapers were printed.

CHAPTER NINETEEN

Before the Bombardment

I

'If an English Rip van Winkle had gone to sleep five or six years ago and were awakened to-day, he would surely be conscious of a very surprising change. He would have gone to sleep in a country steeped in profound peace, filled with ideas of social reform, of educational progress, of humanitarian zeal.' If he were to wake up now – the year was 1900 – the *Guardian* believed that he would find that the things that merely make men's lives happier and brighter had paled before the excitement of a fight; and that things were now tolerated which would have been regarded as morally impossible six years before. 'But perhaps nothing would surprise him so much as that these things pass almost without protest . . . Looking at these facts, our Rip van Winkle might contend that it is the world and not he himself that has been asleep.'[1]

This English Rip van Winkle must have been a *Guardian* reader since his first question on waking would have been 'whether we had settled the Irish problem, how the Labour movement had developed, how far we had carried the reform of the liquor trade, what we had done for education, for the housing of the poor, for the abatement of pauperism, for the reform of an antiquated prison system.' These were the *Guardian*'s main concerns in the 1890s. One or two of them will serve not only to show the kind of newspaper the M.G. had become but also to introduce the men who were then working for it and who stood by it in the bad time ahead, intent that there should be at least one voice to protest against the things that would not have been tolerated half a dozen years before. In the nineties there was a new generation of *Guardian* men; most of them were to serve the paper in one way or another well into the twentieth century. There were no deserters even in the darkest days when to be a *Guardian* man was to be labelled an enemy of one's country, a 'pro-Boer.' The staff was indeed a remarkable group of highly talented, strongly marked individualists; men of whom any paper could be proud, serving the only paper which at that time could command their full allegiance. Of course there was at times between them some of that friction which is bred by temperamental differences in a small, closely-knit, competitive society. Of course they did not think that on the M.G. everything was for the best in the best of all possible newspapers. But they were where they wanted to be. By others they were either envied or hated. No wonder they stood together, 'inspirited, as though the gale were blowing down some nasty yet quite manageable "chimney" in a rock.'

2

These words occur in Oliver Elton's memoir of C. E. Montague.[2] Montague was on any reckoning the first of the new wave of *Guardian* editorial appointments; first in the time of his appointment, first in the estimation of his colleagues and first in the glamour that his reputation with young men and women brought the paper throughout the first half of this century. If, when men spoke of the *Manchester Guardian*, they thought first of C. P. Scott, hard on his heels would follow C. E. Montague. Twenty years after Scott's undergraduate essay had caught Taylor's attention, two trivial happenings settled Montague's future. The Master of Balliol, Benjamin Jowett, told Montague – 'You must write for the newspapers', Scott read in the *Oxford Magazine* 'How Thucydides went to the Trials.' A few reviews for the *Guardian* written in the autumn of 1889 after Montague had finished with 'Schools' (he took a First in Honour Moderations, but a Second in Greats), a month's trial 'on the Corridor'* in February, and his appointment was confirmed. He was 23 when he came to Manchester; he spent thirty-five of the remaining thirty-eight years of his life on the staff of the *Guardian*.

A knowledge of Montague's parentage and upbringing is a clue to several aspects of his work and his life on the *Guardian*. Both his father and mother were Irish; both by their own action were cut off from virtually all fellowship with their countrymen without acquiring more than a stranger's, a reluctant stranger's, footing in England. Montague's father was a Roman Catholic priest who at the age of 43 married an Irishwoman of 32 and settled in London. Montague's father never went back to Ireland; the four sons were brought up at home and taught by their father – in C.E.M's† case until he went to the City of London

---

* This was the term long used on the *Guardian* to indicate the status of the leader-writers, whose five rooms opened on to a corridor at the head of which was the editor's room where C. P. Scott worked at his desk under an engraving of Charles James Fox.

† Christian names were seldom or never used in the office but some people were regularly known in talk by their initials – C.P. (C. P. Scott) and C.E.M. are examples. They are here used sparingly to give contemporary colour.

School at the age of 10. They had no relatives to visit, and their parents made virtually no English friends. Their strong Irish Nationalism made them still regard England as the enemy and the English as oppressors, while the long training and the segregated life of a Roman Catholic priest had set up barriers to easy social contacts which the father did not overcome. The isolation of the family was increased by the fact that the elder Montague never took up any profession in England and therefore was without business friends and acquaint-ances.

This background explains the *Guardian* tradition of Montague as the proud, immensely reserved man to whom the relaxed social life which is one of the pleasures of journalism was painful and, indeed, impossible. Many people thought that he would not unbend, but the truth was that he could not. With his family and a very few close friends at home or in the mountains which he loved it was a different story. But in the office his aloofness deepened the division between 'the Corridor', where the initiates of 'the higher journalism' wrote and thought (the unfortunate phrase comes from Hobhouse), and the rest of the office. The underlying social discontent may unwittingly have been the creation of these two men – C.E.M. out of too great self-consciousness, and C.P. out of a lack of awareness of other men's feelings. 'I should have liked once to have spoken to him', said T. W. Evans, for very many years the manager of the *Manchester Evening News*, after almost a lifetime of passing Scott on the stairs.

Each night Arnold, Spenser Wilkinson and Montague used to walk home together from the office to their homes on the south side of the city. As they walked, they talked; and in 1890 Ireland must surely have been the most frequently discussed topic.

Harold Frederic, the London correspondent of the *New York Times*, had been covering for the *M.G.* the Commission hearing the case of the *Times* against Parnell. He had told how the judges joined heartily in the laughter during the forger Pigott's cross-examination, while the two leading counsel for the *Times* (one of them the Attorney-General) 'sat forlorn . . . huddled together as if for warmth, like two moulting birds on a deserted bough in a snowstorm.' Taylor was delighted with Frederic's treatment of Pigott's flight from justice:

'The sweet credulity which has been extended to Mr Pigott . . . had taken it for granted that of course he would turn up in court this morning . . . The blank surprise which fell upon the assemblage when it was found he had bolted was almost comical to behold. The Commissioners had been seated perhaps three minutes . . . when Sir James Hannen asked gently, "Well, where is the witness?" The Attorney General, who had been gazing meditatively at the floor, started at the enquiry, and rose to explain that he did not know. His tone was full of surprise that anybody should suppose that he knew anything about so trivial a matter.' (27 February 1889)

Six weeks later came Sir Charles Russell's speech for Parnell:

'Through the splendid lines . . . the ear followed him with rapt anxiety, for it seemed that at every word the voice must choke itself in tears. It fell into a sob when he uttered the words about "the land of my birth," and after rising to its highest pitch and thrilling power when with a magnificent gesture he pointed to the *Times* people as the real accused in the case, it fairly sank beyond hearing in his last touching lines . . . As the last quavering sound fell upon the air he sank to his seat and covered his face in deep agitation . . . Sir Charles sat silent with downcast eyes and flushed face, panting still with the stress of his emotions, when the Commissioners rose. Then it was that Mr Parnell whispered his earnest thanks and congratulations. Close upon these came a pencilled note from Sir James Hannen – "A great speech, worthy of a great occasion" . . .'

It is tempting to assume that Frederic was also the special correspondent who spent much of August and September 1889 in Ireland assessing the 'Plan of Campaign.' Frederic had for some time been contributing regular articles and occasional leaders to the *Guardian*, and he kept up his connection in the 1890s. He was noted for his Nationalist sympathies and this series is plainly the work of a highly skilful journalist. But the identification is no more than possible. Typical touches are the characterisation of the people of Louth as 'a singularly mild, timid and lotus-eating race,' and the acid comment on the court which tried William O'Brien at Clonakilty – 'These things the magistrates might have considered, but a special train, ordered beforehand, was waiting to take Mr O'Brien to prison, and – well, they did their "duty".'

In 1890 the O'Shea divorce case threw both the Irish Nationalists and the English Liberals into disarray. On the night of the verdict, the M.G. thought that the Irish would stand by Parnell and declared that, as far as England was concerned, 'We fail to see that, judged by the ordinary standards which govern our estimate of public men, Mr Parnell must be drummed out of public life.'[3] The *Guardian*'s Irish correspondent, J. F. Taylor,* at first formed a similar impression. On the 19th he telegraphed (for almost the only time in fourteen years):

* J. F. Taylor was not related to the proprietor of the *Manchester Guardian*. He is also to be distinguished from the paper's 'Dublin correspondent', a professional journalist probably on the *Freeman's Journal*, whose job was to provide news, not views.

'The great Napoleon used to say of himself that he was no Capuchin, and it is only too sorrowfully clear that Mr Parnell may well say so too. But Napoleon was not the heart but the head of France, and Mr Parnell is similarly the head of Ireland . . . let us judge Mr Parnell by his public conduct, in justice not to him but to Ireland . . .'

J. F. Taylor continued to fear, and of course rightly, what would happen to the Irish cause 'if the real fight began again, and if instead of Moltke we had only dashing captains of Uhlans to direct our warfare.'[4] But it soon became clear that both the M.G. and J. F. Taylor had underestimated on the one hand the strength of the Liberal Party's nonconformist conscience and, on the other, the determination of Mr Parnell not to retire. Soon the paper and its Irish correspondent realised that Parnell must go if Home Rule was to be saved – 'it is . . . for no other reason whatever, that we earnestly desire that the personal sacrifice now called for may be made' was the conclusion of the leading article ten days after the verdict.

At this point Scott made an unusual decision for him. He sent Arnold, his principal leader-writer, to London to watch the intricate manœuvrings of the Irish members in Committee Room 15 of the House of Commons. At the same time he sent Montague, his newest recruit, to Dublin. Why he should have selected the untried Montague instead of Spenser Wilkinson, who knew the Irish political scene at first hand, is not clear. But why Scott was not content to rely solely on J. F. Taylor is clear enough, and not at all to Taylor's discredit. Taylor was not a professional journalist and had other things to do than gather news. He had been recommended to Scott by Mrs Alice Stopford Green, the historian J. R. Green's widow, and since 1888 had contributed a regular political commentary under the heading 'The Position in Ireland.' He was what would now be called a columnist, though an anonymous one. Scott gave him a free hand. As a result he had to defend his correspondent from bitter complaints by Morley when he was Chief Secretary for Ireland. Scott, of course, was right – Taylor's job was not to support the Liberal administration, but to express an independent Irish view. For a similar reason Scott was right in 1890 to send his own man to represent the paper – Taylor's work was part of Montague's evidence.

Presumably J. F. Taylor must have been one of Montague's first contacts. One wishes greatly that he had left some account of his meeting with this remarkable man – anyone who figures several times in 'Ulysses' and in all three sections of Yeats's 'Autobiographies' is clearly worth recalling. Yeats described in a rather patronising way Taylor's 'coarse red hair, his badly rolled, shabby umbrella.' He gave a quick sketch of his career – 'born in some country town, the son of a little watchmaker, he had been a shop assistant, put himself to college and the bar, learned to speak at temperance meetings and Young Ireland Societies and was now a Queen's Counsel famous for his defence of country criminals, whose cases had seemed hopeless – Taylor's boys, their neighbours called them or they called themselves.' But what both Yeats and Joyce found remarkable was Taylor's oratory before an undergraduate audience. A student magazine reported one such occasion, picturing 'Dreamy Jimmy (Joyce) and J. F. Byrne, standing on a window-sill, looking as if they could say things unutterable'; the silliness of 'private business' during which 'even the *Irish Times* reporter contented himself with a blank notebook and a sarcastic smile'; but then the speeches: 'we began with an orator, a poet followed, in Mr Taylor we found a prophet. It has been said that he is the only true descendant of Grattan and Flood at the Irish Bar. He certainly showed it this evening.'[5]

At a similar meeting there was a debate on the Irish language:

'Taylor had come there you must know, from a sick bed. That he had prepared his speech I do not believe for there was not even one shorthand writer in the hall. His dark lean face had a growth of shaggy beard around it. He wore a loose neckcloth and altogether he looked (though he was not) a dingy man . . .'

Both Yeats and Joyce recalled almost exactly the words with which Taylor had pictured the youthful Moses bidding his people resist the temptation to become Egyptianised. Joyce, indeed, not only reported the speech but made a recording of his version. Had Moses fallen in with the Ascendancy, 'he would never have spoken with the Eternal amid lightnings on Sinai's mountain-top nor even have come down with the light of inspiration shining in his countenance nor bearing in his arms the tables of the law, graven in the language of the outlaw.' It was these words that Yeats heard one man murmur to another a dozen years after they were spoken 'as I might some Elizabethan lyric that is in my very bones.'[6]

The same passionate concern for the Irish language sometimes crept into Taylor's work for the *Guardian*:

'But the gentlemen to whom a smile won in a country house in England by a poetic story invented to defame their countrymen is bliss indeed . . . without knowledge decry the language of the ancient people and discourage its study . . . Three hundred years have passed over Trinity College, and it can boast that no one can lay to its charge that it ever gave the least encouragement to anyone who wished to know how the ancient people of this country lived and thought. I am wrong: a chair of Irish was established in Trinity for the express purpose of teaching modern Irish to Protestant missionaries bent on the evangelising of the unenlightened Papists. Surely sweetness and light could go no further . . .' (10 March 1899)

There can have been few more difficult assignments for an entirely inexperienced journalist than Montague's. But from the beginning Scott was delighted: 'You have been doing extremely good work for us the last few days and have had the field all to yourself. Now there will be a mob of specials, no doubt, and the Associations (the news agencies) are taking up the running.' Taylor was equally pleased. He thought, and the messages bear him out, that Montague's work 'gave evidence of patient and well-directed investigation,' and again, 'Nothing that reaches me in any other paper is at all equal to it.'[7] The following year Montague went to Ireland to cover the Carlow by-election, almost the last incident in what J. F. Taylor called Parnell's 'coming forth from Elba, to be soon followed by Waterloo.'[8] The interval between Montague's two visits had shown how hopeless Parnell's struggle had become. He was 'freely insulted now by scores of peasants who seemed six months ago to feel that gratitude required them to be no worse than sullen . . . On the railways nobody marks him, and very few will leave the hay to hear him speak.' It was a situation to grip Montague's imagination. He noted in Parnell's speaking 'the scrupulous care and searching after verbal clearness and exactness,' which he too valued and achieved. With regret, but with rueful admiration, he observed how:

'With a few sentences of confusing rhetoric he persuades a group of sensible men that he has still a right to present himself as an undismissed party leader. And then he talks such excellent sense to them about land reform as makes them forget that his own position is indefensible and that his present campaign is damaging the prospect of every reform for which he asks support.'

Years later Montague recalled the fascination that Parnell had exercised over him: 'He was a strange, romantic beggar in all the little I saw of him in 1890 – enormously more so than anyone else that I have ever met.'[9]

The Carlow by-election was Montague's last visit to Ireland, but it was only the beginning of his long and influential connection with Irish politics. After Arnold's illness in 1896 he wrote more on Ireland than anyone else. Ireland became 'one of his subjects,' though it was also very much one of C.P.'s. It remains an enigma why with his unmixed Irish blood and his Irish political sympathies he never went back to the land which would have made him especially welcome. It is strange, too, how naturally English in feeling his approach to the Irish question always was. His line of thought was to decide what we, as Englishmen, ought to do to put our country's record straight. Montague was an intensely patriotic man, but an English not an Irish patriot. Anything else, of course, would have been inappropriate in the *Manchester Guardian*, but there seems to be no element of role-playing in his standpoint.

Ireland, of course, was only one of Montague's subjects. He wrote on art, on books, on plays and probably was responsible for more foreign leaders than anyone else at this period. It was indeed one of his leaders on the Venezuelan crisis of 1895 that brought Edward Taylor a compliment from Mr Gladstone himself when he sat next to him one night at dinner. At the time of the crisis Gladstone had been at Hawarden. He first read of President Cleveland's manifesto in the *Guardian*: 'I read the leading article upon it which appeared to me excellent – so good, indeed, that I cannot think, in the London papers or elsewhere, any better could have appeared.' Taylor told Gladstone that the writer was a young man 'not much more than 26.' 'Tell him from me,' Gladstone replied, 'a man of 86, that I hope he may live another sixty years of happiness and usefulness.'[10]

It was indeed a decade when everything went Montague's way. His salary rose rapidly. He began with £300 a year – £50 more than the customary starting salary; in 1893 it was increased to £600; in 1896 he got £800 (and according to Edward Taylor was worth at least £1,000); in 1897, £900; and in 1898 he reached £1,000, the four-figure salary which was long regarded as the hall-mark of business success. But 1898 was a memorable year for Montague in much more lasting and important ways. His marriage to Scott's daughter, Madeline, was one that brought him immense personal happiness; but our concern is with its public aspect. It was the last of the great *Guardian* dynastic marriages. To the Taylors, the Scotts and the Allens, there were now added the Montagues. There are no more Taylors. It is nearly fifty years since Allens were connected with the paper. But there are still Scotts and Montagues.

3

Second in Rip van Winkle's *Guardian* catalogue of questions came the progress of the Labour movement. Here the man mainly concerned was L. T. Hobhouse, the last to join of the new wave of the *Guardian* men of the nineties. He was brought on to the paper when it became clear that Arnold was unlikely ever to return, but it is to Arnold's days of full vigour that we must go for the beginning of the *Guardian*'s continuous concern with the Labour movement. Hobhouse, like Montague, was an inheritor of established tradition.

The *Guardian*'s leader-writing on the strike for 'the docker's tanner' in 1889 fell to W. T. Arnold. The dispute was over the difference between 5d and 6d an hour. But it was also about the need for trade unionism. Since the early days of Scott's editorship the *Guardian* had periodically devoted time, space and skill to industrial struggles,* but it had not committed itself to consistent editorial support for organised labour, or rather for the policy of getting all labour organised in trade unions. From 1889 the M.G. made collective bargaining part of its own policy, though, of course, it did not support every action of every union. It argued that 'the lowest priced labour is not always the cheapest,'[11] as the dock employers seemed to believe. It pleaded for the de-casualisation of dock labour, although in those days that ugly modern word had not been invented:

'There is nothing in the way of employment which a steady, capable workman dreads so much as irregular and uncertain occupation. The consequence is that by their present system the dock companies get an inferior class of labour . . . but if the labourers or the majority of them were permanently employed as are the porters and other workmen on the railways, they would require less superintendence, and might with economy be paid better wages than are now given to casual labourers.'[12]

The *Guardian* defended the strikers against the charge of running a 'socialistic' agitation: 'The cohesion of the men . . . is a triumph for the principle of trade combination, which is a very different thing.' It wanted 'the creation of extensive and powerful unions in East London,' and it hoped that provision by the unions 'of out-of-work benefits' would prevent negotiated wage rates being undercut by the willingness of the unemployed to accept work in desperation on the employers' lowest terms.[13] The leading articles were cast in this prudent argumentative fashion to convince, if possible, thoughtful employers – and employers formed a fair, and probably a high, proportion of *Guardian* readers.

From the London office there came careful news stories about the vacillating prospects of a settlement, and descriptive stories which did justice to the picturesque propaganda of the strikers with their great marches through the City of London. Lancashire people could read how John Burns told the strikers that he knew 'what it was to travel on a penn'orth of gingerbread and a sour apple – which was the largest

* See pp 169-172.

and cheapest meal they could get, "as it swelled after it got down".'
They learned about the pickets at the East India Docks at half-past
five on a wet morning, 'their faces turned towards the doors with an
expression resembling that of a cat watching a mouse-hole.' They could
follow the scene on Tower Hill when the Coldstream Guards relieved
the Grenadiers at the Tower, and John Burns, hat in hand, called for
cheers for each company as it passed – 'the pick of the manhood of the
English working classes' who 'when they had served their six years
with the colours would be fighting at the docks for bread.'[14] We do
not know for certain how the London reporting was done, but much
of it was probably by Vaughan Nash who was to spend twelve years
in journalism divided between the *Daily Chronicle* and the *Daily News*
before becoming private secretary to two successive Prime Ministers,
Campbell Bannerman and Asquith.*

The dock strike was a London matter about which Manchester
people could take a progressive line without affecting their own
pockets. A more severe test of the M.G.'s good intentions came with
the Manchester gas strike later that autumn. Basically, the issue was
the same – the struggle to organise the general labourers and to secure
recognition from the employers – in this case the borough councils of
Manchester and Salford. The *Guardian*'s handling of this local situation
is curious. It provided a first-class presentation of the men's case and
gave it prominence. But this was not the work of its own reporters,
though there was both the skill and the sympathy available for the
purpose. It is impossible to say whether this was due to caution on
Scott's part or to lack of initiative by John Cash, the chief reporter,
who was inclined to see his whole duty in reporting speeches rather
than in seeking news. At any rate, the exposure of the employers' sharp
practice was left to John Oakley, the Dean of Manchester, a valued
contributor to the paper on other subjects under the pen name of
Vicesimus. He dealt with the gas workers' strike under his own name
in the form of Letters to the Editor several columns long. He visited
John Burns and Will Thorne at the Union headquarters; he invited the
local leaders to the Deanery and there, with two other clergymen, he
carefully took down a long statement of their case. Questioning brought
out the shabby story of the employers' dealings with the men. All this
he told, largely in their own words, on the main news page of the
Guardian. The next day he added his comment.

* In 1890 he contributed 72 London Letter paragraphs on the docks and other
labour matters. The records for 1889 are lost, but the *Guardian* reports closely
resemble the pamphlet which he and Llewellyn Smith wrote that year, The Story
of the Dockers' Strike: Told by Two East Londoners (Fisher Unwin 1899).

'If I speak of "taking advantage" it is because I can literally find no other words to describe the policy of the Gas Committees of the two boroughs when it became clear to them that they were dealing with an ignorant, un-organised and impecunious union, led by ignorant and simple men . . . My point is that the men met all this with the courage and clear consciences, and the openness and frankness of gentlemen. No doubt they showed cards which they might more prudently have concealed. But if the masters have got the tricks, the men perhaps have won by honours.'

Two days later the *Guardian* broke its own editorial silence in a short leader commending the appeal fund in terms which left no doubt where its sympathies lay. 'Even Mr Howorth (the chairman of the Salford Gas Committee) will, we should gather, moderate his wrath so far as to consent to this. Mediation was, in his opinion, a crime; it is a relief to find that charity is not equally an offence.' Next year John Oakley died, and the *Guardian* picked out for praise his breadth of sympathy and the absolute directness and fearlessness which marked him out from all lesser men. 'Where others would hesitate or study the impression that they made, he went straight to the mark with an almost audacious unconcern.'[15]

In 1893 there was a great mining dispute. Trade was bad and the employers in the Lancashire, Yorkshire and Midland mining districts tried to enforce what with incredible stupidity they called a 25 per cent reduction in wages, but which was really 18 per cent net. This time the bulk of the leader-writing was undertaken by Montague because Arnold was busy with Ireland and Mr Gladstone's second Home Rule Bill. The arguments of 1889 are further developed and there are additional perceptive touches. To those who opposed as 'tinkering' any settlement on the basis of a smaller reduction in wages than the owners demanded: 'tinkering means compromise, and compromise is the essential principle of almost every just settlement of an industrial dispute,' witness the famous Brooklands Agreement which had recently brought peace in the cotton trade. On why the owners offered arbitra-tion and the miners rejected it: 'It is supposed that the owners are only required to state their profits correctly, not that they are bound also to prove that they have obtained the best returns possible. It is also supposed that the rate of wages ought never absolutely to extinguish the owner's profit. Now the Miners' Federation . . . want a different body of rules . . . The difference between them is not a thing that can be split, and almost all arbitration is a splitting of differences.'[16]

The *Guardian*'s leader-writing on the miners' dispute was much better than its news service, which was worse than it had been on the Welsh strike of 1873. It was strangely lethargic in reporting the tragedy at Featherstone in Yorkshire where the troops were ordered to fire and three miners were killed. The news that the Riot Act had been read reached the M.G. late on Thursday and was given in Friday's paper. On Saturday there was a half-column story from the agencies, including the news of the three deaths. Only on Sunday was a reporter, R. C. Spencer, sent.* It is difficult to see why something like sixty hours were wasted. He did a good fact-finding job with sufficient imaginative insight to enable the *Guardian*'s middle-class readers to see and feel what had been happening: the police who had been sent away to Doncaster races, and the military who were called in; the 'regulations' which insisted on live ammunition when the magistrates wanted blank; Wakefield looking like a beleaguered town garrisoned with troops and police from all over England; the fraternisation between soldiers and miners, especially where men had foreign service to gossip about; the greater hostility in the villages; and the women who urged the men on with a kind of feminine savagery made more eager by hunger.[17] Soon Spencer became a specialist in labour matters. He has a fair claim to be considered the *Guardian*'s first Labour correspondent, though the title was not used until well after his time.

The early campaigns of the 'new unionism' had been watched with passionate interest by a young don, L. T. Hobhouse, 'a tall, queer, energetic figure striding through Oxford, dressed in homespun with a red tie.'[18] His father was an Anglican parson in Cornwall and a Conservative; the son was a firm radical and, if possible (so his friend Oliver Elton thought) an even firmer agnostic. He had been head of the school at Marlborough, had gone up to Corpus Christi,† Scott's old college, taken Firsts in both Honour Mods and Greats and been elected to a prize fellowship at Merton in 1887. He had spent as long as he could at Toynbee Hall in the autumn of 1889 and saw the dock strike from that privileged position: 'I think that the mere fact that the men have won is so good. It seems to me like a turning-point in the history of Labour.' Back in Oxford he divided his time between his own academic work, taking pupils – Barbara Bradby, for instance, who married J. L. Hammond – and holding trade union recruiting meetings in Oxfordshire villages. In 1893 he brought out his first book – *The Labour Movement*. Three years later he finished his first major philosophic work, *The Theory of Knowledge*, which was quite as much out of step with the

* He had been appointed in 1889 on the strength of a series of nature articles on the Isle of Wight (M.G. 7 July, 20 August, 19 September 1889, and 22 January 1920) and news stories on the naval manœuvres (M.G. 3, 5 August 1889).

† To-day the name would probably be shortened to Corpus, but an MS note by Scott forbade the appearance of this and other similar vulgarisms in his paper.

Oxford of the nineties as were his politics. Its poor reception in the university made him ready to leave Corpus Christi, where he had been a fellow since 1894. His social and political interests made him anxious to move out of a city that was then an economic backwater. Oxford was still effectively without Cowley.

At this point Scott told Arthur Sidgwick that he was looking for a recruit. Sidgwick sounded Hobhouse and sent his reply on to Manchester. It indicates where Hobhouse's interests lay as well as his ignorance of what the life of a journalist involved. He would, he said, like to contribute 'articles of a somewhat solid and useful character.' 'If, e.g. the contents of a Blue book had to be presented in readable form I would like to undertake it. Such a thing for instance as the movements of wages shown in the Labour Dept's report seems to want summarising in some place accessible to the vulgar.'[19] But he stipulated that whatever he did must not interfere with his own studies. In view of the fact that Arnold's breakdown was then attributed at least partly to overwork, and that Mrs Scott thought he had had no business to give up his mornings to Roman history, it is a little surprising that Scott was prepared to consider Hobhouse on these terms.

But from the first Scott trusted Hobhouse completely, valued him as a friend, and looked up to him as a man and a thinker. Most of Scott's appointments in the eighties and nineties were of men who were beginners in life. The M.G. 'Corridor' became, as it were, a graduate school for public affairs – and a very good one too. But perhaps the editor never quite realised that those who had so much to learn when they started did, in fact, grow up. Hobhouse entered on a different footing. He was 33 when he was appointed. He had found his feet without Scott's assistance; and he stood where Scott stood. There was almost nothing that Scott would have refused him. But he did insist on Hobhouse settling in Manchester. He came for a month at Easter and worked in Arnold's room. In the winter, when Scott was in London for the session, he went higher: 'I occupy your chair at the office and feel as if I was Editor and Lord of all Creation,' he wrote to Scott.[20] '. . . Couper solemnly charged me not to make your room as untidy as I made Arnold's, so I am doing my best.' Of course, this arrangement was only during Scott's absence, but that it existed at all is significant. 'I have a picture of him in my mind,' wrote C.P. after his death, 'sitting with his eyes about three inches from the table – for he never wore spectacles – and pen coursing rapidly and continuously over the paper. Then, in less than half the time that most men would take, his tall figure would stalk into my room and deliver the goods.'[21]

Hobhouse at once found himself deeply engaged with a dispute

in the engineering trade. He was responsible for most of the leader-
writing, and in R. C. Spencer he had a colleague who kept him excellently informed of all the cross-currents among employers, trade
unionists, non-union men and the Board of Trade, which after long
delays tried to arrange a compromise. During the whole of the second
half of 1897 and well into 1898 Spencer was employed almost full-time
on the engineering dispute, with what amounted to a roving commission to go and get the news. This he did, and the contrast in the
Guardian's news coverage between the miners' dispute of 1893 and the
engineers' in 1897 is marked.

The correspondence columns contain many critical letters, but also
more than might have been expected from enlightened employers who
did not share the old-fashioned views of the *Times*. Reading the files,
one is struck by the *Guardian*'s clear realisation of the danger to collective bargaining because able-bodied men feared unemployment and
old men feared the sack. Hobhouse saw how important the friendly
society benefits provided by craft unions were as a safeguard for
effective collective bargaining. The *Guardian*'s next move was a brisk
campaign for Old Age Pensions, a first instalment of the Welfare State
which in time effectively altered the conditions under which collective
bargaining took place.

4

Somewhere about Christmas 1895 C. E. Montague was sent on a
recruiting mission to Cambridge. He called on J. B. Atkins, a young
man of 24, in his rooms at Pembroke. 'He was like a diplomat paying
an official visit, dressed in a tail coat and tall hat, and he addressed me
as though I deserved ceremonious treatment. Although he was only
30 years old his hair was white; his manner was diffident, but his speech
was precise, practised, economical. We both seemed to be sitting on
the edge of our chairs.'[22] Mr Scott, Montague explained, was looking
for a new leader-writer. Atkins and Montague agreed after a little talk
that Scott must look elsewhere. But before Montague left he hinted
that there might be another opening on the paper. Some months later
there was. By June Atkins was installed in Manchester to write, as he
put it, about 'sport, literature and oddments' – three of his major
interests in life. Politics was out.

It is refreshing to turn from the steady round of Oxford men with
Firsts in Mods and Greats to a Cambridge man who was nearly a
rowing Blue and got a Third in the Theological Tripos. Atkins was a
new type of *Guardian* man. Among his predecessors he came closer,

perhaps, in spirit to Richard Whiteing than anyone else, different though their politics came to be. Both men revelled in the particular, the apparently trivial accident, the significantly odd. They were more at home with human beings than with humanitarian principles, with people than with propositions, with descriptive journalism than with leader-writing. Atkins's parents were both Irish Protestants – his father from County Cork, his mother from the North. This Irish heritage was intensely real to him – 'I never go back to Ireland without feeling that I am going home,' he wrote in later life, '. . . we Anglo-Irish feel confident enough of our position to sing the old Irish "rebel" songs with more gusto than I ever heard them sung – if I heard them sung at all – by rebels.'[23] It was, in fact, this Anglo-Irish heritage, this other Irish nationalism, which stood between Atkins and *Guardian* leader-writing.

His father had been a ship's captain in the days of sail and then an Elder Brother of Trinity House, determined to educate his large family since he could not leave them money. Atkins was sent to Marlborough; and then, without entering the sixth form, he went up a year early to Cambridge in order to save money. He spent a year at his college mission in the East End to decide whether he wanted to be a writer or a parson, a year tutoring Sir Charles Dilke's son for Little Go* and a year bear-leading him round the Empire. He went back to his old college to help with coaching its rowing men – a word which covers two activities – and there he was when Montague visited him.

In Manchester Atkins lodged in the same house as Montague, walked home with him every night the two miles from the office, and longed in vain 'to get at my faults during that early morning walk. If only Montague could have brought himself to lecture me, or rag me, or kick me, I should have been pleased. I suppose that his shyness – or was it courtesy? – was insurmountable.' On the other hand, when parliament was not sitting, Scott himself took great pains to show Atkins just what he wanted. He personally went through with Atkins the proof of some of his articles, pausing to alter a phrase here or a word there and explaining why he did so. ' "Reliable" was at that time a barred word – you only rely *upon* a thing or a person,' he explained, 'so the adjective ought to be "reliable upon" – but that won't do. Why not "trustworthy"? It says all you want.'[24] Atkins learnt his stylistic lessons quickly – he had a natural passion for words and rhythm and was emerging from a prolonged bout of Stevenson idolatry. He learnt another lesson – the help which the individual constructive suggestion can give. He adopted it as his own policy when he became the first

* The Cambridge University entrance examination.

real London editor of the paper and handed it on to his successors. But that is a later story.

After two months Taylor told Scott that he fully approved of the proposal to use Atkins on cricket and special sports reporting. A year later he made a suggestion, which was not carried out, that somebody should be sent to investigate the behaviour of the Chartered Company in Bechuanaland and Rhodesia. 'Atkins, I doubt not, would do it well. He is very capable. I have just been reading his account of the Cesarewitch which is instinct with life and character.'[25] This is surely an odd qualification for a delicate piece of social investigation, but in fact Taylor had a little more to go on: Atkins had not long returned from covering the Thirty Days' War between Greece and Turkey. Instead of Rhodesia he was sent to cover the Spanish–American war where Taylor thought 'he did excellently in Cuba and at very small cost.'[26]

Soon Atkins was writing Saturday articles. They were a recent innovation which was being developed by Scott with Taylor's warm support. The Saturday issue was not only still considerably bigger than any other day's because of the heavy advertising but, also for the same reason, it had a considerably bigger sale. Taylor saw that, if the M.G. could get distinctive and attractive Saturday features, some of these occasional purchasers might become regular readers. A series of 'Saturday articles' was therefore an important assignment for a young man. It became intimidating when his job was to follow G. W. E. Russell.

Taylor thought that his first series on 'Bye-Ways of Manchester Life' 'promising', though a poor substitute for Russell. Another series a year later on 'Stray Humanity' was distinctly better. Here Atkins dealt with problems of poverty, crime or race relations, for example, by means of anecdotes of the strange characters he met in Manchester. Two years later he returned more directly to the study of one particular social problem in a series on the slums of Manchester and Salford.

In the spring of 1899 Atkins was sent, apparently at Taylor's suggestion, to London to write the parliamentary sketch, which he did to Taylor's entire satisfaction. 'The only doubt I have is that when one sends one's good men up to London they have a way of not coming back,'[27] was Taylor's comment born of experience; but when Atkins finally settled in London it was at his paper's own request.

5

Nicknames and the like were not common on the M.G., but Herbert Sidebotham was always 'Sider' and to everyone alike. Even C.P.

thought of him in this way, and long after he had left the staff began a letter to him: 'My dear Sider – how naturally one drops into the address!'[28]

Sidebotham's father was an insurance agent and, the son thought, probably not a very effective one, a gentle man lacking aggression, a devout Congregationalist. Sidebotham went to Manchester Grammar School, and from the opposite side of the street James Agate watched and was scared of the older boy 'with a dome of a head too big for his short, squat body, more books under his arm than anybody else could have tucked, and . . . an odd gait which suggested two things – the nod of Lord Burleigh, for sapience marked the child, and the rhythmic bobbing of a horse's head.[29] At the Grammar School he was a member of a remarkable generation, a little junior to Lord Hewart, senior to Ernest Barker, and the same year as Sir John Bradbury whose signature appeared on the first pound notes. He went up to Balliol with a classical scholarship two years after Montague went down. At Oxford he won almost everything that could be won – Firsts in both Mods and Greats, the two Gaisford prizes for Greek prose and verse, and he was 'proxime' for the Ireland scholarship.

Sidebotham might have been thought a natural choice for the M.G., but in fact he had to fight desperately hard for a job. Like Atkins, he was visited by Montague at the university and encouraged to apply. He had an interview with Scott and thought he had been promised a trial. Scott thought he had turned him down. Sidebotham waited two months and then wrote to ask when his trial would start. Scott told him that there was no opening. Sidebotham protested and was promised a little reviewing. He then called in Oxford allies. A friendly don wrote to the *Guardian* manager who passed the letter on to Scott. 'He is a man of such ability that I should strongly advise his being taken; however injudicious he may be at the start, depend upon it he will come out all right.'[30] Scott yielded, but all through his time on the M.G. Sidebotham's relations with Scott were coloured on both sides by this beginning.

Like all new recruits, Sidebotham had to try his hand at many miscellaneous jobs, including the writing of light, humorous leading articles. One brought him an additional £50 in salary 'to encourage his wit', for Taylor told Scott that 'the only amusing bit of writing I have seen in the paper for many long days was Sidebotham's little article on the Westminster play.'* A few months later, however, another of his light leaders led to a libel action, the nightmare from

---

* Taylor-Scott 28 December 1896. The reference is to the topical epilogue which traditionally ends the Latin play performed at Westminster School.

which every journalist recurrently suffers. Mr Maskelyne was a conjuror. He was also an astute business man who saw profit in Victoria's Diamond Jubilee. He acquired the use of a site overlooking the processional route. He undertook to pull down an existing building and, after the Jubilee, to replace it with a new stone-fronted one. His profit would lie in providing a stand with 1,500 seats to let at a minimum of 15 guineas each.

It did, perhaps, sound a little too good to be true. At any rate, Sidebotham wrote a leader about Mr Maskelyne, 'the magician of the Egyptian Hall, who can do a great many things and pretend to do a great many more' and of his 'Aladdin's Palace' – 'but it is unfortunate that the architect should be Mr Maskelyne who has so often seriously deceived the public.'[31] Maskelyne's solicitors demanded not only 'reparation' but the disclosure of the name of the writer. Taylor, very properly, gave explicit instructions that on no account was Sidebotham's name to be given. He heard from the manager that Scott did not propose to attend the court or even to be in London: 'It is very likely that if you were absent you might be challenged to go into the box and your absence strongly commented upon.'

The case went better than anybody could have expected. The Lord Chief Justice intervened almost before Edward Carson had finished his opening for the plaintiff. Had it not been Mr Maskelyne's business all his life to deceive the public? Carson tried laying stress on the word 'seriously', but got nowhere – 'Seriously deceive – he has deceived me,' said the judge. 'Is this really a libel? It really is a thing which ought not to be proceeded with . . .' The jury returned a verdict for the defendants without evidence being called. The *Times*, while insisting that the *Guardian* had poked its fun at the conjuror 'in a rather clumsy way' and in language that 'was certainly not well chosen,' hoped that the Lord Chief Justice's words would check 'the mischievous and growing abuse' of the law of libel as applied to public comment in the press.

But this was not the end of the matter. Maskelyne was furious. He wrote to the *Times* saying that the *Guardian* had first refused a courteous request for a correction and then had offered to settle for a handsome apology in court, paying substantial damages. Scott at once replied denying both Maskelyne's assertions. Taylor was afraid that Scott's letter would not be published, in which case he wanted it inserted as an advertisement in all the London papers – the opinion of the profession was what mattered. Maskelyne returned to the charge. It took a letter from Sir Edward Clarke, who had been the *Guardian*'s leading counsel, to establish beyond question that the *Guardian* had never been willing to compromise and that he himself had never offered any terms of settlement.[32]

Sidebotham must have wondered just how his prospects on the paper had been affected by this tiresome controversy. There was no need for worry. Taylor wrote on Christmas Day to Scott that 'Sidebotham, who has become very useful, and will be more so next year, in view of important military discussions, must be rather insufficiently paid at £250. It is small pay. Do you think he is quite contented? I should not like to lose him.'

Military questions soon became recognised as 'one of Sider's subjects.' There was a succession of little wars in the handling of which he first made his name. The protracted fighting on the North West Frontier of India and the slow, methodical advance down the Nile into the Sudan were two examples of work which occupied most of his time. By 1899 he was known as a very useful man in many fields: 'To my thinking,' wrote Taylor to Scott, 'he is very likely to become the strongest man we have.'[33]

Such were the principal members of the *Guardian* staff on the eve of the Boer War – a group of young men who could have excelled in many walks of life. Round them were a group of contributors on special subjects who also were men of real distinction in many fields. The paper had not suffered in any positive sense from the long absences of its editor. In many respects, department by department, it was indeed stronger than it had been before Scott went into parliament. But probably its resources were not fully used. This was certainly a recurrent theme in Taylor's letters to Scott; but it is right to close this chapter with his verdict on 1898, a verdict that in effect answers the questions with which the last chapter closed. 'I think, looking back, we may say the paper has made a distinct advance this year. You are entitled to much credit for guiding the paper wisely and for having collected about you and trained a staff which I believe to be second to none on the English press for high character and aims, for thoroughness and ability.'[34]

CHAPTER TWENTY

We Happy Few

I

WHAT happened between the Diamond Jubilee in 1897 and the end of the Boer War in 1902 nearly killed the *Guardian*. But what it did in those years, and what the London Liberal papers failed to do, made the *Guardian* the dominant expression of radical thinking among educated men and women. Once again, as in the days of Cobden, Bright and the Manchester School, the leadership of the intellectual Left came from the North West, only this time it was from the *Manchester Guardian*. Radicals in the South East had their London political weeklies, such as the *Speaker*, but only Manchester provided a morning paper which fully met their needs – or would have done if they could have obtained it more easily. What they were prepared to put up with in order to secure the M.G. shows how far the London Liberal dailies fell short. It was Scott's, and Taylor's constancy in those bad times that made men feel that in the M.G. they had a paper on which they could implicitly rely. Clearly this was a paper that could not be bought; one that would not trim its views to meet its financial interests. It was stamped with an editor's integrity, which is something like a writer's or an artist's, the kind of integrity that such men understand. For this great good they were prepared to put up with the *Guardian's* many deficiencies, some of which must be exposed in this and the following chapter.

The crucial year was 1899. It started with the grotesque affair of the Mahdi's head, in which a few bold, oddly assorted figures such as the aged Queen, an impetuous young soldier, Winston Churchill, and the middle-aged editor of the *Guardian* felt, and expressed their disgust at what the hero of the moment had done. After the battle of Omdurman Kitchener ordered the tomb of the Mahdi to be opened and his body to be thrown into the river. His head was cut off and sent back to the base en route for England. The Mahdi had been a charismatic leader of such authority that a strong case could have been made for destroying his tomb and the cult that surrounded it, had it not been for the gruesome episode of the severed head. This made the whole affair a mixture between a repulsive kind of souvenir head-hunting and a squalid revenge for our failure to save General Gordon sixteen years before. The Queen was furious at the indignity done to one who 'after all was a *man* of a *certain* importance.'[1] This, of course, was not publicly known at the time. Had it been, some of the abuse which fell on Scott's head might have been prevented.

The story of the Mahdi's head leaked out, questions were asked in the House, the official defence on the grounds of policy seemed thin and the *Guardian* and other papers of the Left made their own enquiries. A contingent of Royal Marine Artillery returned to Portsmouth. A *Guardian* man interviewed a group of NCOs who rather reluctantly described how the Mahdi's head had been cut off and put temporarily in a kerosene can where it was shown to curious officers. It was then put in a packing case for dispatch to England. 'The War Office, I should think, will know where that box is. I must say no more,' was one comment. Actually Lord Cromer at the base in Egypt had shown more delicacy and good sense. He had intercepted the packing case, but had not been able to stop the story. The more it was probed, the more callously wrong-headed did the action appear. The reporter learned that, whether by chance or tasteless design, the officer in charge of the RMA party ordered to rifle the tomb and dismember the body was General Gordon's nephew. ' "It was perhaps because of his name," as one of the men said, "but I believe that he did not himself fancy to do anything but his exact orders".' Certainly, revenge of this kind would not have appealed to 'the Christian general' any more than it did to Queen Victoria, to the *Guardian*, to the NCO's who did their duty, or to young Winston Churchill who was 'scandalised' – 'All the Tories thought it rather a lark. So here was I already out of step.'[2]

Behind the spectacular business of the Mahdi's head, which came to symbolise the barbarism of which a British general was capable, there was the more serious matter of the treatment of the enemy wounded during and after the battle. Were our native camp followers allowed freely to kill and plunder the enemy wounded? Were British soldiers themselves guilty of killing their wounded enemies? Were the surviving enemy wounded left untended on the battle-field for days after the easy victory?

The *Guardian's* war correspondent had been a young Bedford schoolmaster, Henry Cross, a former Oxford rowing Blue. 'Quiet, gentle, patient, brave, sincere . . . the type of an English gentleman' was how another, more professional correspondent described him.[3] He apparently paid his own expenses, as did some of the other correspondents, and was to receive a fixed sum for each article or 'letter' sent. His

The (Manchester) "Guardian" of the Mahdi.
(MR. C. P. SC-TT.)

A cartoon from *Punch* 1 March 1899

messages are straightforward descriptive reports of what he saw – completely unpolitical, the work of a man to whom the life of a military expedition was strange, exciting, attractive. There is certainly no bias in them against either the purpose of the campaign or its conduct. He was present at Omdurman, but went down with enteric fever immediately afterwards and died three days before his last article, a description of the battle, was received.* In it he had written:

'One of the chief features of this advance was the conduct of the black campfollowers, who hurried out in front of the lines and hastily looted the dead and the wounded. They took good care that the latter were soon numbered with the former. It was a shameful sight to see them shooting down the stricken dervishes at such close quarters that many of the bodies were set on fire, and the smell of burning flesh was added to the horrors of the battlefield ... (They) continued their grisly task throughout the day, stripping off the jibbehs, rifling the pockets, and gathering sheaves of spears and swords.

* Scott proposed to pay his estate £60, the stipulated sum for the work actually done. Taylor thought that £75 would be better. Taylor–Scott 10 October 1898.

Many a jibbeh and spear which will be exhibited in triumph after this campaign has been bought at the price of the life of a wounded man. In a few cases a revolver was necessary in self defence, but the wholesale slaughter that was carried on by the blacks was indefensible.' (24 September 1898)

This was a straightforward complaint about the failure of the commanders to control our African auxiliaries. It might have been the result of oversight or lack of foresight. The higher command is never so popular that those who attack it are automatically branded as un-

AN ATTACK ON THE GOVERNMENT'S SOUDAN POLICY.

(Mr. John Morley and Mr. C. P. Scott.)

A Little Job.

A cartoon by F. Carruthers Gould in the *Westminster Gazette* 1899

patriotic. But the two other complaints – that British soldiers had killed wounded men who asked for quarter, and that nothing had been done to look after the enemy wounded – were of a different order. Neither was put forward in Cross's last message. The first attacked the honour of British soldiers, an unpardonable crime. The second accused their commanders of gross inhumanity which was nearly as bad. If the *Guardian* endorsed either of these complaints, it would expose itself to the anger of the majority of its countrymen as it had never done before, not even over Ireland.

The matter was brought to a head by an article in the *Contemporar*

Review by E. N. Bennett, a don at Hertford College, Oxford. He had been an undergraduate there a year or so after Cross went up and, like Cross, he had been an amateur war correspondent during the Omdurman campaign. In his article he made all three complaints. He seems to have been naïvely unprepared for the result and was inclined to blame Scott with whom he seems to have discussed the matter before publishing his article. 'It will probably end in the loss to some extent of one's friends and one's prospects,' he wrote. 'How bitterly I regret that you did not give me some note of warning as to the way in which the public would take it.'[4]

The *Guardian*, of course, took the article seriously in another sense. During the next few months it gradually collected and published confirmatory evidence from a variety of sources. It reproduced from the *Daily Telegraph* both sides of the acrid controversy between Bennett and Balfour Burleigh, that paper's well-known war correspondent. It drew heavily on Charles Williams, who had followed the campaign for the *Daily Chronicle*. It quoted from local weekly papers in which returning soldiers had said their say or in which passages from letters home had been printed such as that in the *Middleton Guardian* in which a Lancashire soldier described how he had been ordered to bayonet everyone dead, or alive, as a necessary precaution.[5] There was Churchill's evidence from his own experience of the wounded left lying for days on the burning sands outside Omdurman without water, let alone medical aid. What was lacking in the *Guardian* was any attempt to employ the reporting staff in detailed and systematic enquiries among officers and men back from the war. Whether this was caused by John Cash's lack of drive or to lack of direction from above in the editor's absence is not clear. Its effect was obvious. The *Guardian* rested its case too much on quotation from others; too little on direct enquiry.

The newspaper campaign might have faded away and been forgotten had it not been for the Government's decision to give Kitchener a grant of £30,000. Scott decided that this must be resisted, and he made up his mind to fight not only on the Mahdi's head but on the graver issue of the treatment of the wounded. Sidebotham, who spent some part of the session devilling for Scott in London, saw Bennett who gave him his evidence. But Bennett was still upset by the storm his article had raised, and begged Scott not to quote him in the House. Scott wrote to E. E. Bowen, the Harrow school master, author of the best known of school songs 'Forty Years On.' He wrote also on military subjects, was a Liberal in politics and put Scott in touch with L. Oppenheim, one of his former pupils. Oppenheim was willing to call on Scott, but apparently, like Bennett, he did not want to be quoted. As the editor of the *Daily News* put it, 'Not being in the profession, he was at one time very outspoken. But he has many connections and I imagine would not at all like anything he said to be quoted.' Oppenheim may well have been the writer of the private letter from which Scott quoted in the debate in the House since, as he told Hobhouse, 'I'm afraid I have not been able to add anything material to the published evidence about Omdurman beyond the one letter which I have permission to read and to give the writer's name in confidence to a Minister.'[6]

The division showed how unpopular was the line that Scott and the *Guardian* had taken. The minority could only muster fifty-one votes and twenty of these were from Irish members. Less than a fifth of the Liberals in the House voted against the grant. Only two were privy counsellors – Sir Charles Dilke and John Morley, who was content to confine his case to the Mahdi's head.[7] Morley was already inclined to look on Scott, according to Hobhouse, 'as a hen on a duckling that takes to the water,' and he had made it clear that he hoped that the M.G. and Scott would not take up the matter of the Dervish wounded. Morley was reckoned the leader of the radical wing of the Liberal party. By rejecting Morley's counsel of prudence Scott now put himself and the M.G. on the far Left, beyond the pale as it must have seemed to many.

During the debate J. B. Atkins, who had just taken over the parliamentary sketch, noticed Kitchener in the gallery. Some thought his presence brave, others embarrassing. Atkins watched Kitchener's face with amusement – 'when he was praised, or when he was exculpated by a clever point he smiled with a satisfaction that made one discount all the attributions to him of immobility.'[8] But Atkins did not mention that young Lt Churchill was also in the Gallery and found himself sympathising not with Kitchener but with C. P. Scott. That autumn Churchill published *The River War*. In it he wrote,

'I must personally record that there was a very general impression that the fewer the prisoners, the greater would be the satisfaction of the commander. The sentiment that the British soldier is incapable of brutality, is one which never fails to win the meed of popular applause; but there is in fact a considerable proportion of cruel men in every army . . . The unmeasured terms in which the Dervishes had been described in the newspapers, and the idea which had been laboriously circulated, of "avenging Gordon" had inflamed their passions, and had led them to believe that it was quite correct to regard their enemy as vermin – unfit to live. The result was that there were many wounded Dervishes killed.'[9]

Neither Churchill nor Scott lacked prudence or courage. Neither suffered in the end because sometimes they allowed prudence to give place to courage.

2

Side by side with the affair of the Mahdi's head there was a peace crusade which had its origin in the Tsar's appeal for international action to prevent wars. Montague backed this with a fervent leading article and the paper followed it up by quite disproportionate coverage of the national campaign in which 'fierce-looking, fuzzy-headed' W. T. Stead[10] made what was inevitably more or less the same speech at least twenty-five times in eight weeks; and Arthur Hawkes laboured to make it appear somewhat different in the M.G. on twenty-five separate occasions. Stead had made his name with his flamboyant articles on the white slave traffic in the *Pall Mall Gazette*, 'that disgrace to us all,' as Taylor called it to Scott. 'The spirit of the writer was thoroughly bad, mean and degraded. He revelled in the filth he was compounding.'* Now Stead was editing the *Review of Reviews* and bringing to the cause of peace the same vulgarisation that he had brought to that of purity, but this time with the *Guardian*'s approval. There is no reason to doubt his sincerity on either occasion; every reason to regret his taste.

At Birmingham, on 20 January 'Mr Stead began with a prayer, the utterance of which quivered and left its dew upon the cheek. Avowedly he spoke under an overwhelming sense of responsibility; . . . now with the right hand uplifted, now leaning forward and meeting the gaze of his auditors as though he would hustle them out to compel men to enlist in the army which is to fight for an end of fighting.' At Leeds, ten days later Stead 'began by reading "the first psalm in the Crusade Psalter", Kipling's Recessional.' Poor Hawkes continued to do his best through a wearying tour which took him from St Austell to Newcastle, from Plymouth to Carlisle. By Southport on 10 March he had clearly had enough. 'The temper of the meeting was admirable, and the audience

---

* Taylor–Scott 15 August, 1885. The *Guardian*'s attitude to sex and crime in this period is interesting. The trial of Mrs Maybrick in 1889 was reported on a gigantic scale which clearly pleased readers to judge by the columns of Letters to the Editor which followed the verdict, but which distressed Taylor and also, oddly enough, Scott. On the other hand, the trial of Oscar Wilde was unreported to Taylor's mixed regret and pride: 'Imagine that no paper in England had done other than as the *Guardian* did . . . where would have been one half the punishment of the guilty and where the warning to others, which – between ourselves – is sadly needed I fear?' (Taylor–Scott 9 April 1895.)

failed not to appreciate any point made with average clearness. The Worshipful Mayor spoke like the uncompromising friend of international concord that he is. It must be admitted, however, that he had nothing new to say on the subject. The first succeeding speaker was the Rev John Chater, Congregationalist. A little homily on "All's well that ends well" came before the main things he wanted to say. Of that saying one's personal opinion may be put aside in favour of the description the next orator gave to it – eloquent and brilliant.' The M.G., too, perhaps had had enough. Other men covered the closing stages of the campaign. But Stead, like Lord Beaverbrook on a later occasion,* seems to have been too good a journalist to mind having his meetings guyed provided it were well done. Hawkes left the *Guardian* at the end of October. Where he went next does not appear, but he was working for Stead in 1903.

The Peace Crusade had been designed to mobilise public opinion behind the International Conference at The Hague. There the *Guardian* was represented by Stead himself. The cost of the operation was considerable. Stead's fee for the two months the Conference lasted was £300 and the cost of telegrams £370. He provided good reliable news but of a kind that is by its nature unrewarding to quote after the event. The same may be said of Sidebotham's closely argued leaders on the law of blockade and the rights of neutral shipping. The only lasting outcome of the Conference was the establishment of the Permanent Court of International Justice. It is a useful, if limited, institution. Its limitation was immediately underlined by its complete powerlessness to do anything about the Boer War.

3

By itself the peace campaign would have done the *Guardian*'s reputation little harm. Its more conservative readers would have put it down as just one of the expected and pardonable sentimentalities of the Left. But served on the same plate as the Mahdi's head, it was more damaging. The *Guardian* seemed to be not only woolly but wicked. It did not mind fouling its own nest. This conviction was reinforced by Scott's next move. Attention turned to South Africa. War did not start until well into October 1899, but from the beginning of April the *Guardian* devoted a great deal of space to exposing what it regarded as the shady attempt of Cecil Rhodes and his financial friends to engineer an

* When he engaged Howard Spring for the *Evening Standard* on the strength of his sketch in the M.G. of Beaverbrook as 'the pedlar of dreams' during the 1931 lection campaign.

official war to carry out what Dr Jameson had failed to do by private war.

The *Guardian* returned again and again to Britain's absolute promise to respect the Transvaal's complete independence as far as her internal affairs were concerned. One typical example was the leader on 2 May. The first paragraph warned the public that 'they may wake up any morning now to the announcement of a new Jameson raid, with Sir Alfred Milner and Mr Chamberlain riding this time as troopers of Mr Rhodes.'* The second paragraph dealt with those who relied on our alleged 'suzerainty' to justify our right to interfere. In their view, 'a treaty which expressly precludes us from interfering in any way with the Transvaal's domestic affairs authorises us implicitly to interfere with them just when we like, where we like, and as much as we like.' The third paragraph developed the M.G.'s characteristic vision of patriotism. 'The destruction of the Transvaal's independence would give a little more money to a few very rich men, it would make a few more posts in which Englishmen could show fine administrative qualities, and it would blot out from the mass of red on the map of South Africa a spot of brown. But that spot, so long as it remains, is such a monument to British good faith and self-respect as we may never be able to raise again. Nothing stands between it and annihilation but the desire of Englishmen to keep a promise which they can break at any moment they like.'

In July Scott asked J. A. Hobson to go to South Africa for a fee of £100 a month plus expenses. The choice of correspondent was significant. Hobson's appearance suggested a don rather than a journalist. Frank Swinnerton remembered him as 'erect, emaciated . . . and considered economically unorthodox. That does not matter very much, it may be; for so clear an intellect shines from his remote, noble head that I for one would allow him to think originally along his own lines until, if need be, he reached absolute topsy-turvydom.'† In 1899 Hobson was already forty-one and had made his reputation five years before with his 'Evolution of Modern Capitalism.' It was to find out what modern capitalists were up to in South Africa that Hobson was now sent. Before he left he contributed a series of five articles on 'The Transvaal Problem.' Seventy years later one is struck by Hobson's objective look at the situation. The Outlander‡ case is fairly stated,

* Sir Alfred Milner was 'our man in Capetown'; Mr Chamberlain was Colonial Secretary.

† 'Swinnerton', p. 292. Like Hobson, Swinnerton was for many years a regular *Guardian* contributor.

‡ This translation of the more frequently used Uitlander was characteristic of Scott's love of 'plain words.'

but the conclusions drawn are on balance favourable to the Transvaal
on most issues, Before the series was completed Hobson was on his
way to South Africa. He hoped to send a sixth article from Madeira
'unless the weather should knock me out,' which apparently it did since
no sixth article appeared.[11]

Throughout August, September and early October Hobson sent
from South Africa occasional telegrams, some of them lengthy, and
mailed articles which carried further his analysis of the economic factors
and included a survey of opinion among the Cape Dutch and in the
Orange Free State as well as in the Transvaal. His articles, which were
republished in a book form with additional material from the *Speaker*,
have lasting importance for their first-hand examination of economic
imperialism as a factor making for war. His interviews with Olive
Schreiner, whose *Story of a South African Farm* was already a classic,
and with Presidents Kruger and Steyn, enabled English readers to
judge for themselves the standpoint of those South Africans whose
views were deliberately kept hidden from British readers as far as
money could do this.* The greater part of the South African press had
fallen into Rhodes's hands and some part of the London press as well.
The channel was very narrow through which news from South Africa
hostile to the Outlander lobby could reach England. Even if the M.G.
had been wrong in its facts and its diagnosis, it would have served
public interest in asserting the freedom of the press – not from official
'doctoring' or, as yet, from censorship, but from the power of great
capitalists. 'The mischief of it is that though nine plain men out of ten
feel rightly when they see plainly, it is the hardest thing in the world to
make them see plainly when it is the interest of a very strong and rich
party that they should not see at all.'[12]

When war broke out Hobson returned to England and Atkins
went out as war correspondent – his third campaign in three years. A
little later he was followed by Filson Young, a man of only 24, on his
first full-time newspaper job. His father was a Presbyterian minister in
Manchester, an Irishman and a remote connection of the Scotts and
Taylors. Filson and his elder brother Tom both went to Manchester
Grammar School and both went straight into business. Money was
probably tight. Certainly neither boy lacked ability or literary interests.

* *The War in South Africa: Its Causes and Effects* (Nisbet) 1900. 'I suppose there
is no man in England who understands anything about South Africa or South
African affairs except my friend J. A. Hobson – and I don't know that he understands anything of the lay of things *now* – though he understood wonderfully when
he was here four years ago.' Olive Schreiner to Mrs Francis Smith 12 July 1904
quoted in *The Letters of Olive Schreiner*.

Tom Young had started working for the M.G. part-time in 1896, providing Ship Canal news. By 1899 he was fully employed but Filson had only just begun to do occasional descriptive articles in his spare time. After a rather shaky start in South Africa during which his brother had to mediate between an irate editor and an equally irate correspondent – a little more money spent on explanatory cables would probably have avoided the trouble – Filson produced some excellent work.

Both Atkins and Young were under orders to send only very short news telegrams. Their more important work followed by mail three or four weeks later. The first impression, therefore, is disappointing. The *Guardian* man was present at the scene of action, but he sent a terribly meagre account and the bulk of the story had to be taken from other papers which spent more on telegrams. Thus, all that Atkins reported by cable of the disaster to the armoured train at Estcourt made only thirty-six lines in the paper, heavily 'leaded' to make it appear of respectable length. The reference to Winston Churchill merely said that he 'exposed himself heroically in getting volunteers for the work . . . Mr Churchill was last seen advancing with a rifle among the Dublin Fusiliers. He is believed to have surrendered himself to cover the retreat of the others.' The *Daily Telegraph*'s story, which was given underneath, was much fuller.

Readers had to wait three and a half weeks to read Atkins's full version, three columns long, which he wrote on the same day as his short cable. Then indeed they could read how Atkins and L. S. Amery,* the chief correspondent for the *Times*, had hurried off on foot towards the sound of the firing:

'We found twelve men . . . who had escaped from the disaster, and gradually we pieced the story together. We heard how Mr Churchill had walked round and round the wreckage while the bullets were spitting against the iron walls and had called for volunteers to free the engine; how he had said "keep cool, men," and again, "This will be interesting for my paper" (the *Morning Post*), and again how, when the engine-driver was grazed on the head and was about to escape he had jumped in to help him and had said, "No man is hit twice in the same day".'[13]

---

* Amery was, Atkins recalls in his autobiography, already a *Guardian* legend. Two years before he had telegraphed to Scott for an interview, arrived in the office at midnight and left a few minutes later with a cheque for £100 and a roving commission in the Balkans, where he assaulted a Turkish Chief of Police. 'I had an unopened umbrella in hand which, somehow, broke in two on his head while he collapsed in the mud.' The British Embassy protected him; the *Guardian* recalled him; the *Times* appointed him. L. S. Amery: My Political Life (Hutchinson 1952), Vol. I, pp. 72, 81–83.

A similar contrast is provided by Filson Young's two messages on the relief of Mafeking. His original telegram was padded out by 'leading' and large type to make nearly three-quarters of a column, but the description of the final scene was confined to 'I had the honour of being the first correspondent to enter Mafeking, having ridden on with the advance guard under Col Peakman, and with him Major Hon Maurice Gifford and Capt Smith. We received a warm welcome from Col Baden-Powell at 3.30 a.m.' In the full version, written the same day but only published three and a half weeks later, this became:

'We left the squadron and the five of us went on, this time at a gallop, over trenches, past breast works, redoubts and little forts until we pulled up at the doors of the HQ mess. Ah! the narrative is helpless here. No art could describe the hand-shaking, the welcome and the smiles on the faces of those tired-looking men; how they looked with rapt faces at us commonplace people from the outer world as though we were angels, how we all tried to speak at once, and only succeeded in gazing at each other. One man tried to speak; then he swore; then he buried his face in his hands and sobbed. We all gulped at nothing, until someone brought in cocoa and we gulped that instead; and then the Colonel came in, and one could only gaze at him, and search on his jolly face for the trace of seven months' anxiety and strain... we lay down and were immediately asleep – in Mafeking.'[14]

In this way the delays caused by strict economy deprived the *Guardian* of some of the advantage of having two correspondents of its own in the field. There were, however, exceptions. A combination of a short news flash at the expensive ordinary cable rate with a longer, slower cable at press rates enabled Atkins to give a report of the confused and bitter fighting at the Tugela which the *Guardian* manager considered to be 'by all odds the most complete account received' by any newspaper.[15]

Young came back to England after the relief of Mafeking and Atkins followed a month later. Both made books from their articles. Atkins's book, 'The Relief of Ladysmith,' had been published less than two months after the event while he was still in South Africa. Instant book-making is not altogether new. Spenser Wilkinson, who was at this time on the *Morning Post*, reviewed the book in the *Guardian*. No papers were farther apart in their politics than the *Morning Post* and the *Guardian*; but, whatever Wilkinson's differences with his old paper, he did not mistake its caustic criticism for lack of patriotism. In the prevailing temper of April 1900, with Pretoria still uncaptured and Mafeking likely to fall, it was generous of him to sign a friendly review in the *Guardian*.

5

Public opinion, inflamed by the Jingo press (and that was nearly the whole press) and infuriated by Boer resistance and British defeats, had turned its hatred on the M.G. and all those who thought with it. What people found impossible to understand was the paper's view that, while we must seek to win 'this tainted war,' we must not seek to profit from it. To take what was not ours would not be made moral by the fact that we had won a victory. The war was only a month old when events left it the only great morning newspaper which continued to oppose the political war aims of the Government. There were two penny Liberal mornings in London – the *Daily News* and the *Daily Chronicle*. The *News* under E. T. Cook had long supported Milner as honourably as the M.G. had opposed him. The *Chronicle* had taken the same line as the *Guardian*. But in November its proprietor suddenly ordered the editor, H. W. Massingham, to change the paper's policy. Its readers were deprived of the only London morning paper of standing which expressed their views. It is no disparagement to the *Morning Leader*, a small half-penny radical paper, to say that it did not carry the same weight as the *Chronicle*. The senior *Chronicle* men were left with the choice between resigning or following the new line. Their position was different from that of journalists who join a paper knowing that it does not express their views but who do an honest professional job by it. They had joined the *Chronicle* because it stood for what they stood for. Now that it was compelled to say what they did not think and to suppress what they believed to be true, they felt that they must go. But where?

H. W. Nevinson, who was later to undertake many important commissions for the *Guardian*, came back from the siege of Ladysmith to the *Daily Chronicle* office to find that 'the old staff, almost without exception, had resigned and were scattered, some taking shelter, like Massingham himself, on the *Manchester Guardian*, which stood as the City of Refuge for the honourable journalist in flight from the children of wrath . . . but the City of Refuge was crowded up, and there was no other place from which to make the voice of reason heard.'[16] Massingham himself spent a year in the *Guardian*'s London Office, looking after the London Letter, which as always in those years needed improvement, and writing the parliamentary sketch which prevented his giving sufficient time to the former job. Harold Spender came to Manchester for a time as a leader-writer, living with L. T. Hobhouse who with characteristic generosity had offered to be content with half his salary to make room for a displaced *Chronicle* man, an offer which Scott of course did not take up. Spender did not like Manchester; and the Misses Gaskell, as he records, did not take to him. He stayed only a short time. He had a roving commission to cover the khaki election of 1900 for the M.G. He visited Caernarvon where 'is collected all that there is of Jingoism in North Wales. Struggling against a strong radical sentiment, here in the meeting of the tides, – two religions, two languages, two races, two political creeds, – always fighting, always arguing, living in the midst of his people, talking their language, joining in all their movements, thus Mr Lloyd George has hitherto held his own.' He met John Burns in Battersea Park 'riding towards me on his bicycle, the handlebars decked with a bunch of blue and white ribbons; alert, robust, radiant with confident strength. He greeted me with a gay smile, and, riding side by side, we left the crowds of his too urgent followers and glided into a quieter street. With that quick gift of intimacy he answered my unspoken question. "We're going to win," he said.' Good journalism, perhaps – but a shade too openly egotistical for Scott's *Guardian*. Taylor was anxious to keep Spender when he became restless after a long tour in Canada, but Spender left. Taylor thought that this was because he was not offered enough money to stay, which was probably true; but Scott could, and did, pay well when he really wanted to keep a man – Montague or Hobhouse, for example.[17]

A third *Chronicle* man who came to the *Guardian* for a time was Vaughan Nash. He undertook one specific commission for the paper and did it superlatively well. His articles on the famine in India, reprinted as *The Great Famine*, achieved the difficult task of combining compassion, readability and analysis of the economic causes and consequences of different administrative policies. The Viceroy, Lord Curzon, gave Nash full facilities to study the situation, telling Scott that the *Guardian* was, he thought, 'the first great English newspaper to do so.'[18] This purely non-party, humanitarian investigation no doubt helped to keep some friends for the *Guardian* among those who most strongly disliked its African policies. It would be wrong to think that this was why it was undertaken.

The revolution in the *Daily Chronicle* office was followed just over a year later by a take-over of the *Daily News*. The paper was bought by George Cadbury and others. Their object was to provide London again with a paper that should 'apply Liberal doctrine to South African affairs as fully as to every other part of the Empire' as the *Guardian* London Letter put it in announcing the purchase.[19] E. T. Cook was faced with a decision as serious as that which had confronted Massingham. Neither was dismissed. Both were ordered to conform. Neither did. Cook joined the *Chronicle* as chief leader writer. Massingham, Spender and Vaughan Nash, confirmed Londoners to a man, moved to the *Daily News*. Theoretically, the score was even. But each revolution left a sour taste. The *Guardian* gained not only because of its consistency but because of its resistance to pressure. It had proved that it could be counted on even when times were bad.

For the City of Refuge had been under siege. Just before his death in 1967 H. O. Rouse* recalled how as an apprentice in the composing room in 1900 he used to bring a large parcel of sandwiches with him to work. Several times he was challenged by the police who had been put on to guard the building and had his parcel searched to see if it contained a bomb. A sharp drop in sales was obvious and somebody at the rival *Manchester Courier* got a brass band to march round the *Guardian* office playing The Dead March in 'Saul.' The relief of Mafeking, signalled to the waiting crowds in the street by the hoisting of the Union Jack on the *Guardian* roof, ended the fear of violence. As the technical staff entered the building with a bravado whistle on their lips they felt that they too had stood a siege and won a victory. C.P. went on his way unmoved. 'To any elements of personal danger he was by a happy constitution indifferent,' Hobhouse wrote, 'and he took little more note of police protection than of the violent and sometimes filthy letters from unnamed patriots which I have seen him open at the breakfast table or have heard him mention in a jest.'[20]

But the relief of Mafeking and the fall of Pretoria did not end the war. The Boers introduced commando raids. The British replied by farm-burning. This was followed by the introduction of concentration camps since there had to be somewhere for the displaced families to be sent. Commando raids into Cape Colony were followed by martial law. During the first half of the war the *Guardian* attacks had been mainly directed against our war aims and our administrative blunders. During the second half they were turned against our methods of making war. This was an even more unpopular line and, though the wave of physical violence had passed, circulation dropped still further. By the end of the war the M.G. had lost nearly one-seventh of its readers, though even so its sale was still greater than that of the *Times* (41,900 to 36,700). But then the *Times* cost threepence to the *Guardian's* penny.

---

* Rouse joined the paper in 1900 and served it for over fifty years, becoming head of the composing room. His father was chief reader.

5

During the second half of the war the *Guardian* was without a staff man in South Africa. The official communiqués and dispatches, the news agencies and the special reports of the London papers were all given an almost Kremlinological analysis by Sidebotham who by a careful scrutiny of casualty lists and similar data was able to elucidate a good deal that the authorities wished to hide. What he confessed himself unable to decide was whether the mystification was practised in Whitehall or at GHQ. Although the M.G. had no war correspondent of its own after July 1900, it gave its readers at least as informed a view of what was happening as any other paper. Foreign observers, like General Kuropatkin, are said to have been so impressed by Sidebotham's work on South Africa that they took the M.G. during the Russo-Japanese war to see what he had to say about their situation.

One of the principal anxieties was the attitude of the Cape Dutch. Much, possibly all, depended on their loyalty. The British Government distrusted them, and tried to enforce loyalty. The *Guardian* thought this was the wrong way to go about things. It believed in their original loyalty, but thought that we were making them disloyal. Facts were obviously more important than opinions, and here the *Guardian* profited from the newspaper revolution in the *Chronicle* office. Its correspondent in Cape Town had been Albert Cartwright, the editor of the *South African News*, the only English language Liberal paper in the colony. He was not content to serve Massingham's successor, got in touch with Hobson and arranged to take over the *Guardian* correspondence from the beginning of 1900 at a salary of £200 a year. Cartwright, who had been brought up in Manchester and who was known to Scott (had he once served on the *Guardian?*), had himself been the victim of a newspaper revolution. He had been the editor of the *Diamond Fields Advertiser* at Kimberley when it had been a Liberal paper, and lost his job when in 1898 it was purchased in the Rhodes interest.[21] His reports on the way in which martial law was administered in Cape Colony were important because they were detailed and factual. They were widely quoted in the European press as Taylor observed. It may indeed be that Taylor's support for Scott's lonely stand against British war aims and methods was strengthened by the fact that he lived so much abroad that he could see how his paper's international reputation gained as much as its national reputation suffered from the line it followed.

Cartwright's correspondence came to an abrupt end in 1901. He was arrested at the beginning of February, charged with seditious libel, and sentenced in April to a year's imprisonment. This was clearly designed to silence an awkward opponent. The article for which Cartwright was convicted was copied from the London *New Age*. In the United Kingdom it had been printed also in the Dublin *Freeman's Journal*, the London *Times* and other papers (but not in the M.G. because it took the form of an anonymous letter). In South Africa it appeared also in a paper published in Port Elizabeth. Of all five editors only Cartwright was prosecuted. The *Guardian* strongly supported 'one of the few quite truthful and public-spirited journalists in what Mr Winston Churchill pardonably called "that land of lies." '22 It returned time and again to his defence. It drew attention to his treatment in prison, where he was reported to have been deprived of his wife's visits because he had been found reading the M.G. – 'could lawlessness and insubordination go further?'23 A year later it protested against the police supervision and confinement to South Africa which followed his release, thus depriving him of the opportunity to earn his living. But, for some reason, the *Guardian* never referred to its own connection with Cartwright.

During Cartwright's imprisonment a young member of his staff, C. F. L. Leipoldt, took over the *Guardian* work. He had already helped to investigate the working of martial law up country. Taylor was 'much astounded to find that he is little more than a boy,' and considered that he was 'certainly a wonderful correspondent for his age' – he was 21 when he did his first work for the *Guardian*. The particular messages which drew Taylor's praise were his accounts of the police raids on the *South African News* office, the carpeting of the managing director by the military governor, who made it terribly plain that 'the functions of a newspaper neither owned nor controlled by Mr Cecil Rhodes have for the moment disappeared,'24 and the decision of the company to suspend publication. The *South African News* had survived its editor's arrest by only six months.

Leipoldt's first published work had been a prize essay in the *Boy's Own Paper*. His contributions to the *Cape Times* brought him an invitation to meet the editor, who was surprised to welcome a boy in knickerbockers. Leipoldt was indeed a wonderful boy who became a remarkable man – journalist, children's specialist, poet in two languages, and pioneer of Afrikaans as a literary language. When the *South African News* stopped publication Leipoldt came to England and, as he later reminded Scott, 'I find that I owe you thanks for your interference on my behalf at that time.'25 In England he set to work to qualify as a doctor and eventually became the editor of a medical periodical. He continued to do occasional work for the *Guardian*, sometimes on South

African affairs, sometimes on medical matters. During the controversy over the National Health Insurance bill in 1911 he contributed articles from a doctor's standpoint. The next year he returned to South Africa where at different times he worked on *Die Volkstem* and practised as a pediatrician in Cape Town. He remained an occasional contributor to the M.G.

After Leipoldt's departure the M.G. was almost as completely cut off from reliable news sources inside South Africa as if the whole of the country had been occupied by the enemy instead of being mainly in British hands. Indeed the situation was worse. The M.G. was not only without news of its own, but the honesty of the news it had been giving from South Africa for the last five or six years had come under heavy attack. The *Guardian* had been able to give remarkably accurate accounts of the Jameson Raid and what brought it about. These were published with the by-line 'From a South African correspondent.' He was F. R. Statham – poet, composer, minister of an Independent chapel in Edinburgh, editor of a Natal paper on the recommendation of Benjamin Jowett, convict, and placeman of the Transvaal Government: an undoubted curiosity amongst nineteenth-century Englishmen. By the autumn of 1896 the *Guardian* had begun to suspect prejudice in Statham's work and made less and less use of it. But it was not until October, 1900 that it learned from evidence given in Johannesburg to the Transvaal Concessions Committee that from early in 1896 until the outbreak of war Statham had been getting a salary from the Netherlands South Africa Railway Co to act as what would now be called a PRO for the Transvaal Government. The *Daily Express* then dug out the story of how Statham had been sent to prison for embezzlement as a young man – he was now 57. Statham replied by writing *My Life's Record*[26] in which for the first time he made known his connection with the *Guardian*.

The *Daily Mail*[27] spread its review over two days, giving it great prominence under the heading 'How the pro-Boer Press was Hoodwinked.' Taylor considered it 'a malicious attack on R. F. Statham with incidental thrusts at the M.G.'[28] Stead defended Statham in the *Review of Reviews*:[29] 'The only misfortune was that Mr Statham did not frankly and openly avow that he was being retained by his Dutch friends . . . these arrangements only left him free to do that which he had been doing all his life to the best of his ability, and his own free will, without fee or reward . . . ever since the facts came out Mr Statham has been persecuted and shunned like a tainted sheep. It is very unjust and most patently absurd.' Montague's review in the *Guardian* was sympathetic about everything except Statham's action in hiding his retainer from the Transvaal Government. Even on that Montague agreed that Statham thought he had done nothing wrong:

'In concealing from the conductors of the English newspapers and magazines to which he contributed the nature of his relations with the Transvaal Government he was guilty of a grave offence against them and against the code of honour by which reputable journalism is governed. The whole body of the contributions (to the MG) from his pen that were published . . . after his acceptance of the "unofficial consulship" referred to was inconsiderable . . . But that does not palliate the acceptance of a double position which can be maintained only by unfair concealments. Of such an acceptance Mr Statham, an able man and a man of great knowledge of certain kinds, and one, too, who evidently makes out for himself a defence that he sincerely accepts in the court of his own conscience, cannot be acquitted.' (3 September 1901)

Statham sat down and wrote a vicious letter to the *Manchester Courier* on the plea that he 'was afraid that the *Manchester Guardian* would not allow him to reply.' He wrote:

'how is it that well up into 1899 I was constantly consulted by Mr Scott with regard to South African affairs? How is it that my advice was sought as to the selection of correspondents in South Africa? (Mr Merriman, I may say, was asked to act as a correspondent on my recommendation.) . . . And how is it that when, in 1899, Mr J. A. Hobson visited South Africa as the *Guardian's* correspondent, I was specially asked by Mr Scott to furnish him (Mr Hobson) with all possible introductions and informations? . . . If I had been guilty of the "grave offence" now alleged how is it that as late as January 1901, I was in correspondence with Mr Scott on terms as friendly as ever . . .?'[30]

Taylor's first reaction was that Statham's letter should be copied into the *Guardian*, but there was an obvious difficulty. Scott was in Pontresina. By the time he had seen the letter and commented on it – as was plainly necessary if the letter was to be republished – some time would have passed and there was a risk of merely reviving a dying story. The *Courier*, like the *Mail* the previous month, ran an offensive story for a second day but then let it die. The *Guardian* held its peace; but an unknown amount of damage had been done. Dibblee, the manager, thought it was considerable. He wrote to Taylor: 'our judgment as technical experts in news has always been as much acknowledged as our honesty. The latter is not doubted now even by our bitterest opponents but the former, I am sorry to say, is now discredited by S's shameless revelations and his direct attempts to identify us completely with himself . . . Observe how skilfully S throws his corrupt mantle over Hobson and Merriman and hints that their inspiration in South Africa was from sources provided by himself and tainted with his untrustworthiness.'[31] It was a long time before the M.G. heard the last of Statham. As late as December 1903 a Lancashire man, J. K. Bythway, circulated a privately printed pamphlet 'On Mr Statham's Articles . . .'

The Statham affair must have made the *Guardian*'s exposure of the concentration camps less convincing than it would otherwise have been to probably the majority of its readers. 'We must remember,' Dibblee told Scott, 'that out of about 150,000 daily readers some 60 or 70,000 are Conservatives and others are Liberals who are in favour of the war or at least less opposed to it than the *Guardian*.'[32] The Statham handicap was unfortunate since there seems little doubt that the M.G. was substantially right in its running controversy with the War Minister, the *Times* and other newspapers over the camps in which Boer women and children, made homeless by the policy of farm-burning, took refuge (according to the Government) or were confined (according to the paper). The first person to draw attention to what was happening was Emily Hobhouse, L. T. Hobhouse's sister. She had gone out to South Africa at the end of 1900 and came back six months later with a report full of practical recommendations. She returned to South Africa to work, was refused permission to land, transferred to a troop-ship under military guard and deported to England. For the rest of the war she provided the M.G. with a number of valuable articles based on letters from friends in South Africa.

Meanwhile the Government had taken fright at the outcry which her report had provoked and sent an official party of prominent women, several of them hand-picked for their staunch imperialism, to do again what had just been done. This took another eight months and confirmed what Emily Hobhouse had said. All this time the horrifying death rate had gone on mounting, and it became clear that Britain had blundered into a major crime against humanity. The *Guardian* devoted much skill to the dissection of the mortality figures and to the construction of a true basis of comparison with the death rates outside the camps. In this Hobhouse pretty certainly had the help of Dr F. S. Arnold, W. T. Arnold's brother, who was in practice in Manchester.* What the

---

* He had been the medical spokesman on a deputation, including L. T. Hobhouse, which visited the Lord Mayor of Manchester to press for action about conditions in the camps. During the later stages of the war he regularly read the Dutch newspapers and provided the M.G. with translations, mainly from the *Algemeen Handelsblad* and *Nieuwe Rotterdamsche Courant*, of important or graphic stories from the Boer side. He had learned Dutch especially in order to do this work.

figures meant was brought home in a leader on 16 December 1901.

'Take the population of greater Manchester roughly at a million. In a year, at the rate of camp mortality, there would be in this area 250,000 deaths. Every day there would be about 680 funerals. The deaths would outnumber the births by about nine to one, and everywhere in a few months there would be houses standing empty . . . True, reform is under consideration, but Lord Milner protests that he must not be flurried. His whole time is being absorbed "to the great detriment of other business." '

6

A present day reader or member of the *Guardian* staff can hardly leave the Boer War without asking what the paper had to say about the majority of the population who, then as now, were neither of English nor of Dutch ancestry. The record is clear. The M.G.'s fundamental objection to Rhodes and the Outlanders was based on the exploitation of native labour in the mines. Neither Boer farmer nor English (or German-Jewish) capitalist* behaved as they should to Africans, but at this time the oppression of the capitalist was more onerous and dangerous than that of the farmer. In a passage which hardly seems dated after seventy years the *Guardian* wrote of an article in the *Bulawayo Chronicle*: 'It would be very sad if Rhodesia decided to rebel because the mother country refused to enslave some of its black subjects for the sake of increased dividends for some of its white subjects, but the British Empire might survive even that shock.'33

It is one thing to protect natives; it is another to give them equal rights. Here, too, the *Guardian* was not lacking in foresight. In a leader reviewing 'The Natives of South Africa,' the report of a private committee of enquiry, the *Guardian* wrote:

' "The Commonwealth of the future in South Africa ought to include the mass of the native and coloured people, and legislation should lead to this result . . ." That is the real crux of the matter. The overwhelming majority of the white oligarchy, British and Dutch, who rule South Africa, politically and industrially, have no intention of genuinely recognising and realising this claim. We welcome in this volume the first serious attempt to impress upon the British Government and the British people the supreme duty of securing this claim of the Kaffirs to form part of the Commonwealth".'
(27 April 1901)

---

* Hobson falls into uncharacteristic anti-Semitism in his discussion of the Rand magnates. See *The War in South Africa*, pp. 191–193, and Hobson's letter to Scott, 2 September 1899: 'The bulk of Uitlanders excepting the actual miners I believe to be Jews . . . Many of them are the veriest scum of Europe.'

CHAPTER TWENTY-ONE

The New Manager and the New
Reading Public

I

ANYBODY could see that Buxton had to go. He had been, indeed he still seemed to be in many ways a good manager. But he had become increasingly unbalanced. As early as 1884 he had shown unbridled jealousy of Peter Allen's sons. In 1888 he had a severe nervous breakdown. The following year there was what Taylor described as 'another outbreak of Buxton's hallucinations.' By 1890 Buxton was complaining to Taylor about Scott in the same sort of terms that he had formerly used about the Allens. Taylor made up his mind that Buxton was 'partially insane'[1] and that a mental specialist ought to be consulted. Whether modern psychiatry could have cured Buxton cannot be known, but the course the partners chose – a long holiday abroad – could only aggravate the situation since Buxton was bound to suspect he was being got rid of. In June Taylor made up his mind that an assistant must be found who could be trained up to succeed Buxton. But it was not until midsummer 1892 that Buxton finally left the firm.

Even this did not end Taylor's troubles with his old employee and partner. In 1895 the doctors reported that Buxton was likely to become violent. Two years later Taylor had to call the police to eject Buxton from his home. Buxton still wanted to be restored to his old position but, Taylor told Scott, 'you might as well talk of restoring the Saxon heptarchy.'* The dispute, which developed into a legal action, dragged on for another three years.

The search for a new manager must rank as one of the curiosities of newspaper history. It was no doubt inevitable, since Taylor was not prepared to sack Buxton straight out, that the man appointed must be young and relatively inexperienced. He had to be willing to come in

---

* Taylor–Scott 28 December 1897. Over sixty of Taylor's letters to Scott deal with the problem of Buxton's mental health. The firm was very long-suffering.

as an assistant and, in Taylor's words, he had to be 'fairly acceptable' to Buxton. Beyond this Taylor favoured Cambridge and Scotland as recruiting areas – 'depend upon it the mathematical and arithmetical turn of mind offers the best basis for our needs.'[2] Scott, as always, turned instinctively to Oxford and to literary and philosophical interests. The first favoured candidate was H. B. Smith of Wadham with a First in Maths Mods and in Greats – but he preferred to go to Sutton Valence as a schoolmaster. He passed on the news that the *Guardian* was looking for a 'Sub-business manager' to Gordon Hewart, the future Lord Chief Justice, then in his last year as an undergraduate, who made the first of several unsuccessful attempts to join the paper. He did excellent work as an outside contributor, but he never got on the staff.

Meanwhile Scott was negotiating with two other candidates. One was still an undergraduate and would have had to leave the university without taking his degree. The other was Michael Sadler who was at that time a young don at Christ Church, Oxford. His lack of obvious qualifications almost seemed a recommendation to Scott: 'we prefer a man – provided he is the right sort of man – who has had no previous training in another newspaper office.' Scott held out the prospect of a partnership, 'rather sooner than later,' and assured Sadler that the income of a partner was large – 'Larger than the biggest school-master's.'[3] So Sadler wrote in a pencilled note to his wife after he had been to Manchester for an interview. This was in July. It was November before Sadler made another visit to Manchester to tell Scott just why he could not take the job. He felt that he could not give up the university extension work to which he was devoted. It was a right decision. Sadler had before him a singularly distinguished and useful career in education. Scott lost the manager he wanted, but he gained a consistent friend for the paper who was always ready to help with contributions or 'briefing' on educational matters. Sadler, of course, having turned the offer down, had his own candidate for the post – a relation of his wife's, a young history don at Oriel. He had not had 'any direct business experience but he managed his own affairs as an undergraduate, though in a position of some difficulty, with great economy and good sense.'[4] It proved an insufficient recommendation.

At this point Scott thought of giving the job to Montague, who was still a very raw recruit to the paper. Taylor approved, but asked 'Is he methodical in his work? and has he any aptitude for accounts?' Presumably Montague was approached; and presumably he declined. Prudently, and to the paper's double advantage. The next serious candidate was Taylor's. He heard that J. A. Spender, the 31-year-old editor and business manager of the *Eastern Morning News* at Hull, was looking for another job. Mrs Taylor heard from Spender's fiancée that he had turned a loss of £1,500 a year into a profit of 3 per cent for which his uncle, the owner, paid him a salary of £250. As soon as the paper became solvent it was sold and Spender's prospects disappeared. It was felt that his uncle had behaved badly – 'not surprising; he does not know what good faith is' was Taylor's comment on a man he had known well in business. Unfortunately, though Spender hoped his experience in management would be useful, his inclination was 'all towards literary work.' He moved to London and became editor of the *Westminster Gazette*, nicknamed 'the sea-green incorruptible' from the colour of its paper and the nature of its politics, which were to other evening papers what the M.G. was to the mornings.[5]

Nearly a year had passed and the *Guardian* was no nearer getting a suitable assistant manager. The need was urgent. A man was found who, like Sadler, was very much the kind of man that Scott liked to appoint to the editorial staff and who, he clearly thought, must therefore be suitable for management. There does not seem to be any rational basis for this opinion, but in this instance Scott's instinct was reasonably sound. G. Binney Dibblee had just turned 24 and had recently been elected a Fellow of All Souls. He had a talk with Montague and applied for the job. He quickly proved himself a thoughtful, if too sanguine manager. His small book on *The Newspaper* in the Home University Library is a good description of this side of newspaper work at the turn of the century. What Scott did not perhaps appreciate was that the kind of man he wanted for manager, the kind of man with whom he felt he could work, was not likely to be content to remain purely manager. Almost inevitably he would want to influence editorial policy. It would have been so with Sadler or Montague. It was so with Dibblee.

Dibblee's apprenticeship was short. All he got was eight months in the office with Buxton, from whom 'he must be protected' as Taylor put it, followed by two or three months at the *Scotsman* where Scott had trained twenty years before. He took over the managership in the summer of 1892. Next year he went to the United States as part of his training and to represent the paper at the Chicago World Fair. He postponed his return by a week because, as he told Scott, 'while I was staying on my way through Canada with my aunt, I met a cousin there whom I want to make my wife.'[6] Nothing came of it. Back in Manchester he wanted to marry the editor's daughter but, as Scott recalled in his old age, 'I definitely refused him Madie's hand for she was only 19 when he made her an offer – a very beautiful girl and he was not unattractive.'[7] Two years later Madeline Scott married Montague; Dibblee also married. With an old man's hindsight Scott traced a connection between these events and those described in the next chapter.

2

During the greater part of his managership Dibblee tried to help the *Guardian* break out of its natural but confined circulation area in East Lancashire. The first foray was across the border into Wales. North Wales was to some extent a No Man's Land for morning newspapers. It was inaccessible to daily papers published in South Wales; it was too sparsely populated to support a great regional paper of its own. It depended largely on the Liverpool papers whose Welsh sales Dibblee put at about 4,500 in winter and perhaps double in summer. Readers were mainly concentrated, like the population, along the coastal strip. Many had Liverpool connections. In the geography of retirement, of the 'stockbroker belt' or its equivalent, and of holidays the alliance between Manchester and the Lake District was paralleled by that between Liverpool and North Wales.

But in the hills behind the coastal resorts, Welsh Wales with its roots in the chapels had an intense cultural life of its own. This North Wales would never really be satisfied with an English newspaper, but Dibblee thought the M.G. had a chance to establish itself there on a profitable basis. North Wales was predominantly Liberal. It wanted disestablishment of the Church which, as in Ireland, was the church of a minority. Lloyd George, the young radical member for Caernarvon, first elected in 1890, described himself in Dod's *Parliamentary Companion* as a 'Welsh Nationalist.' The politics of the M.G. would fit a majority of Welsh voters. The high literacy of the Welsh countryside promised a fair proportion of M.G. readers. Dibblee suggested a special Welsh edition of the M.G., as Welsh as it could be made, designed to catch the national feelings of the day. Scott concurred. Taylor agreed without enthusiasm that the M.G. should produce what Dibblee claimed would be the first localised edition of a daily paper published on this side of the Atlantic.

Dibblee's original budget provided for three columns of specially Welsh matter a day but on occasion it rose to a whole page. To begin with there were not only Welsh news items and features from the Principality itself, but also regular Welsh features from London. The Welsh edition had its own Lobby notes in addition to those in the normal English editions. It is in this connection that Lloyd George's name first appears in the history of the *Guardian*. In 1893 he contributed

140 paragraphs to the paper, earning £57. 12. 0. Some may have been contributions to the London Letter, but most were pretty certainly Welsh Lobby notes. News from Wales itself was cheap enough. Dibblee's budget allowed only one pound a column and, though this was no doubt exceeded for special features such as a column from Thomas Darlington on 'The Linguistic Condition of Wales' or two columns on 'The Present Position of Welsh Disestablishment' by Sir G. Osborne Morgan, MP, other featured items probably cost no more than the special sub-editor's salary of £3 a week. Under this heading would fall the long-winded replies to the questionnaire distributed by the M.G. to the Welsh clergy of the Church of England asking their views on Disestablishment and Disendowment.[8] On the whole it seems probable that Dibblee's budget seriously underestimated the cost of the Welsh edition if only because it contained nothing for expenses in the London office.

Even on Dibblee's figures the Welsh edition required a circulation of 8,000 a day to justify itself, compared with an existing sale of 600. He hoped ultimately for 10,000, nearly twice the total sale of English morning papers in North Wales in 1892.* To reach either figure would involve not only capturing readers from the Liverpool papers, but breaking new ground. How difficult this would be can be seen from the fact that the M.G. could not get to Llandudno before nine or Holyhead until ten. Mid-Wales deliveries were even later: Barmouth and Portmadoc about eleven and Aberystwyth in the afternoon. A remunerative circulation in the face of these almost impossibly late delivery times was almost impossible. Readers were sought among the Welsh colonies in Manchester and Liverpool. Any Manchester newsagent would supply the Welsh edition on request; four Liverpool newsagents undertook to have it on sale. The new edition quickly reached a sale of 2,000, but there it remained for some time. The first year's working showed a loss of £562. By 1894 the loss was down to £76 and in 1896 for the first time it made a small profit. But in 1898 Taylor doubted if it had been worth doing, and in 1900 whether it had ever paid. He may well have been right.[9]

There was another, and in some ways a more promising, no man's land in the Potteries. In its industrial interests it was neither Birmingham nor Manchester. It lacked a good morning paper of its own. It was accessible and populous. It was certainly worth while to push the sales of the *Guardian* in the Potteries; it was doubtful whether a localised edition was justified. Dibblee argued enthusiastically for it. Scott appears to have acquiesced. Taylor demurred. The project was dropped.

* Dibblee's estimated 5,400 probably excluded newspapers sent by post.

That was in 1898. Two years later Dibblee returned to the attack. He had succeeded in increasing the sales by two and a half times, but they were still only about 800 a day. This time Taylor reluctantly agreed on the understanding that the affair was to be on a much less ambitious scale than the Welsh edition and that no more journalists would be needed.

At the same time Dibblee took steps to increase *Guardian* sales in the North and in Yorkshire. In 1900 two special newspaper trains left Manchester for the North, one running to Wigan where it made a connection for Scotland and the Lake District, the other to Leeds with connections to Bradford and Halifax. By 1901 the *Guardian* reached the principal Yorkshire towns by 4.15 a.m. There was, of course, no question of localised editions for these areas which had their own regional papers. The sale of the M.G. was confined to business men who needed to follow Manchester's business and to keen Liberal politicians for whom there was no substitute.

There was one other major attempt at this time to extend the sale of the M.G. into new territory. It was not one which Dibblee favoured. During the short interregnum between the defection of the *Daily Chronicle* and the capture of the *Daily News*, when London Liberals opposed to the Boer War had no satisfactory morning paper, Taylor and Scott decided that something must be done. The M.G. had long been on sale at selected newsagents in the City and at certain bookstalls on the Inner Circle, but that was all. Now a bicycle delivery was introduced. Of course it could only serve the inner residential core of London. Wimbledon and Richmond, for instance, could still only be reached by post. Of course, as Dibblee gloomily pointed out, 'some days when the train runs late it will be ten-thirty before the paper is delivered.' He complained of the cost of the necessary advertising and forecast that the new subscribers would be found at the end of the year 'to have cost about £5 apiece.'[10] Neither Taylor nor Scott thought the bicycle delivery would pay. They regarded it mainly in the light of a public service and partly as a useful, if expensive, piece of prestige circulation. It was both. The service long continued in a small way. In 1928 there were four Bicycle Delivery Boys, employees of London evening papers, putting in a little extra time on their own. Gradually they motorised themselves – they were responsible for their own transport – and had extended their radius to six or seven miles by the outbreak of the 1939 war. But, if the events of 1899–1902 enlarged the *Guardian*'s slight access to London, they curtailed its availability in the universities. For some time newsagents in both Oxford and Cambridge had supplied the M.G. In 1900 W. H. Smith ceased to sell it in Cambridge, though whether for business or political reasons there is no knowing. It remained on sale in Oxford.[11]

3

Taylor's general objection to localised editions and to circulation campaigns outside the paper's natural area was that they diverted attention from strengthening the paper's hold on its main base. Perhaps one should say the firm's hold rather than the paper's since the struggle that lay ahead in the newspaper industry was for the custom of the new readers whom the Education Act of 1870 had produced. These new readers were also new voters. They were canvassed as eagerly by politicians as by newspaper proprietors. Taylor was both. He wanted their support, but knew that the *Guardian* would not suit them. It devoted a third of its space to detailed financial and commercial news. It reviewed all new books of importance in almost every branch of university study – the names of a third of its strictly anonymous reviewers of the early nineties appear in the 'Dictionary of National Biography.' It devoted two columns a week to erudite articles on farm management, and had regular features on hunting, shooting and fishing by a son of the Earl of Perth. Such a paper would hardly appeal to the manual workers of Hulme. Even the exclusion of polo – 'I think polo is too much of a luxury for the public or us to indulge in,'[12] as Dibblee reminded Scott – would hardly be sufficient to turn a quality paper into a popular one. Almost the only thing that the *Guardian* shared with the coveted new readers was a common political outlook. And in Lancashire even this could not be taken for granted. The industrial North-West was the home of the Conservative working man. Political opinion there did not divide as closely along class lines as in many other parts of England.

The marginal nature of Lancashire constituencies made the provision of a good Liberal working-class press even more important. Already in the later 'eighties, when the *Manchester Examiner* was tottering to its fall, Taylor had shown interest in securing its popular weekly edition, the *Weekly Times*. Nothing came of it then, but no sooner was the Welsh edition of the *Guardian* launched in 1893 than plans were prepared for a new popular family weekly to be published by Taylor, Garnett & Co, which would expound a robust Radicalism. There was considerable discussion about a suitable editor. Law of *The Scotsman* advised Taylor 'to pick out a smart junior reporter; whereby I suppose he meant . . . a man who would be fresh and in full sympathy with the taste of the class which a Weekly must now appeal to, the working man, the clerk and the small shopkeeper.'[13] R. C. Spencer was chosen and, though he was replaced after six months, he had been brought into close contact with its principal regular political contributor, Tom Mann. This must have been useful when Spencer became virtually Labour correspondent of the M.G. soon afterwards.

A name for the paper was as elusive as a good editor. Taylor on the whole favoured 'Northern Light.' In the end the choice fell on 'The New Weekly' but not before other suggestions such as 'Voice', 'View' or 'Lamp' had been canvassed. 'These,' Taylor considered, 'could only be redeemed by tacking your name on to them thus, "Scott's Voice, View or Lamp" '[14] – an unfortunate combination since anything which could truly be called 'Scott's Voice' would hardly be popular, while only what was popular would pay. The *New Weekly* was first published in January 1894. It never paid. At the end of April 1895 a special balance sheet showed an accumulated loss of £8,960. When the paper closed down in May it had lost altogether £10,314. 0. 2. The blame must be shared between the editorial and managerial sides. It was no doubt bad luck that an illustration in the first number should have been printed upside down, but it was not this that caused Harold Frederic to tell Scott that it suffered from 'an utter lack of physical beauty.'[15] The chief blame may fairly be considered Dibblee's. Not only did he persist, despite Taylor's opposition, in trying to force a way into the London market, but he assumed the role of 'managing editor' (it was not clear whether he was granted the title for which he asked) with supervision of editorial as well as managerial affairs.

4

Technically the firm was well placed to produce for the expected mass market. It had kept well up with technological progress and had sometimes shown the way. During Buxton's managership, for instance, Mark Smith and Braithwaite of the firm's engineering staff had solved a puzzle which had long perplexed evening papers. Up to the minute news, especially of racing results, was very important for their sales. News arrived in a continuous flow, but only three separate editions were printed. It would be a great advantage if late news could somehow be inserted during the actual printing of an edition. There were at least thirteen patents, and no doubt innumerable other experiments, before Mark Smith found a practicable way of allowing short news items set in movable type to be placed in a 'box' and inserted in a reserved place on a page during the actual process of production. This 1884 'stop press' patent saved one and a half minutes; an 1888 improvement saved another five or six seconds – both worth-while economies in evening paper work. How worth-while was shown not only by its widespread adoption under licence by evening papers in other towns, but by the successful application of the *Manchester Evening Chronicle* in 1898 for a compulsory licence under the Patent Act. This was followed by an attempt to break the firm's patent made by R. C. Annand of North Shields. He won his case in 1899, but lost an appeal.

During his first six years as manager Dibblee had supervised a revolution in the production of the *Guardian* and the *Evening News*. The steps then taken were necessary in the interests of the existing papers. They also put the firm in a position where it could undertake the printing of a new morning paper. In 1894 the firm bought the *Manchester Examiner* building which was immediately behind the *Guardian*'s office in Cross Street. In Cross Street the plant was almost entirely renewed. Buxton had been devoted to Victory presses; Dibblee found them unsatisfactory and went over to the rival Hoe machines whose output was much higher. Two triple-web presses were brought into use at the beginning of 1896 and another five were ordered in March. The total cost of the new presses was nearly £28,000.

Each Hoe machine could print 24,000 copies of the *Guardian* or 48,000 of the *Evening News* in an hour. They were needed to meet the increasing circulation of the evening paper; they were also used to increase the size of the morning paper.

In 1891, the year before the re-equipment started, Dibblee estimated that the *Guardian* print averaged about 45,000 a day; the *Evening News* about 152,000, and though the *Guardian* had more pages than the *Evening News*, there was still a built-in surplus printing capacity on the morning paper side. Technically, Taylor, Garnett and Co were, or could very soon be, in a position to produce a half-penny morning paper.

In 1887 the *Guardian* had been set by hand just as it had been in 1821. Plainly there was scope for radical new inventions. The first composing machine that really worked had been patented by Robert Hattersley, a Manchester engineer, in 1857. It seems to have been tried in the *Guardian* office in 1861, but it was not adopted. Other North Country newspapers, however, introduced Hattersley machines, starting with the *Eastern Morning News* in Hull in 1866. The *Manchester Courier* bought some as late as 1891. By that time the *Guardian* was experimenting with the American Thorne machines some of which were ordered in 1887. Each machine needed a crew of three – the keyboard operator, the 'justifier' (who saw to the regular spacing of words and lines), and the 'man behind', usually an unskilled boy, who attended to the distributing machine which replaced the type after use. The Thornes reduced the cost of type-setting by about a third according to Dibblee's calculations. But they were not completely satisfactory partly because of labour troubles but more because of mechanical deficiencies.

An effective solution on the mechanical side was found in the linotype designed by the American Ottmar Mergenthaler in 1886 and introduced into the *New York Tribune* in the same year. The linotype was quickly taken up by North country English papers, starting with the *Newcastle Chronicle* in 1889. Early in Dibblee's managership it was decided to try linotypes side by side with the firm's Thornes. Two were hired in 1893 for £100 each per year. Two years later the decision was made to turn over completely to linotypes. If Dibblee happened to open his predecessor's letter book he might have read with wry regret how in 1889 the firm had refused an offer of founder's shares in the Linotype Corporation.[16]

At the close of the long process of re-equipment Dibblee had a special valuation of the plant made for insurance purposes. It was estimated to be worth £71,000. Three-quarters of a century before the first John Edward Taylor had borrowed £1,000 to start the paper.

The introduction of linotype machines had solved the technical problem of mechanised type-setting, but it left outstanding the problem of redundancy. The compositors were naturally anxious. So was Taylor on their behalf, and it was only reluctantly that he agreed to the change. There was a certain amount of labour agitation against the firm, much of which was either misinformed or unscrupulous. The *Labour Leader*, for instance, reported that the *Guardian* compositors had been told that 'on account of the improvements in machinery' it would be necessary to reduce the present staff by half. 'The workpeople were dumbfounded at receiving this intimation as they had been assured by one of the proprietors, after his return as MP at the late election, that no introduction of machinery would affect the present hands.'[17] It was perhaps principally due to Taylor that serious trouble was avoided. He insisted on generous severance pay and considered that Dibblee's proposed scale was too low. When Scott said farewell at Christmas 1895 to the displaced hand compositors there were in fact only four or six men out of the seventy-two employed in October who had to go.[18] The expansion in the size of the *Guardian* planned for 1896 enabled the remainder of the threatened men to be absorbed.

The progressive mechanisation of the *Guardian* was in fact carried through with much less labour trouble than might have been expected. The *Guardian* staff got a share in the benefits. The last word may be left to the compositors during the khaki election of 1900:

At a special Chapel Meeting . . . the following resolution was unanimously adopted: – 'As statements are being made . . . that the firm with which he (Mr Scott) is connected did not pay the standard rate of wages and had otherwise dealt unfairly with some of their employees, the members of the *Manchester Guardian* Composing Room give the most unqualified contradiction to the statements which are entirely without foundation. The custom of the firm on the retirement of any of the old hands has always been to substantially superannuate them. At no period in the existence of the firm have any but the most generous conditions existed in the treatment of their employees, who have always enjoyed advantages and privileges beyond the requirements of the Manchester Typographical Society, of which we are members. Amongst them may be included the unsolicited concession of a 48 hour week.'

5

In 1896 Alfred Harmsworth successfully launched the *Daily Mail* from the platform of the *Evening News*, a derelict paper which he had bought two years before and rapidly made the best selling London evening paper. Harmsworth was 30 when he started the *Mail* with a sale of 177,000. By 1898 it was selling 400,000. No newspaper proprietor was ever better entitled to talk of 'his' paper.

The *Guardian*'s North Western territory was still insulated by distance, but Taylor, Scott and Dibblee knew that their immunity from half-penny competition would not last. Either from London or in Manchester, or both, the threat would develop. The worse-off *Guardian* readers – clerks and shop-keepers, for instance, and others on the fringe of the middle-class – would quickly transfer to the *Daily Mail* if it came to Manchester and justified its claim to be 'a penny paper for one half-penny.' The gain to the *Mail* would be marginal – to succeed it needed readers Taylor never knew – but the loss would be serious to the penny paper for a penny.

Edward Hulton might well do in Manchester what Harmsworth had done in London. Indeed at first his seemed the more immediate and serious threat. In the 1860s Ned Hulton had been the compositor who set up the type for the contents bills for the *Guardian*.* He had also studied the sporting news that came into the office. On the basis of his

* Until the 1939 war all newspapers printed contents bills and distributed them to newsagents and street sellers. A *Guardian* legend maintains that one day, when its rivals announced 'Fall of the Government' or some similar national catastrophe according to taste, the M.G. bill read 'More About the Boll Weevil' (a cotton pest).

studies he had started a pirate sheet of his own, the *Prophetic Bell* or *Sporting Tissues*. The firm got rid of him. Five days after Scott joined the *Guardian* Hulton started the *Sporting Chronicle*, the original paper in the large group which became first Hulton Newspapers, and then Allied Newspapers. They were published from Withy Grove, off Corporation Street, a few hundred yards from the *Guardian* office in Cross Street. Four years later Hulton added *The Athletic News*, and in 1885 *The Sunday Chronicle*.

Hulton prospered because he could pick men as well as horses. Nunquam, Dangle, Hubert and The Bounder – the columnists of the *Sunday Chronicle* – were men of whom any paper could be proud. Dangle was A. M. Thompson, the theatre critic and part-author of such successful plays as 'The Arcadians' and 'The Rebel Maid.' He had been a school-boy at a Paris lycée during the Commune and was one of the mainstays of *The Clarion*, the socialist weekly founded in 1891. So, too, was Nunquam, Robert Blatchford, ex-regular soldier and in 1893 the author of a best selling *Utopia* which W. T. Stead thought worthy to be 'The People's Plato.' It got a cool review in the M.G. but brought Blatchford an invitation to meet C.P. who wrote 'I have been reading "Merrie England" and (*pace* the reviewers) find a great deal in it.'[19] Was he considering Blatchford as a possible recruit for the projected *New Weekly*? Hubert was the Hubert Bland who contributed the final essay to *Fabian Essays* which Bernard Shaw edited in 1889. The Bounder, E. F. Fay, was a passionate admirer of Laurence Sterne and brought a good deal of his favourite's manner into his London Letter with its endearing title of 'Babble from Babylon.'

Hulton had the experience and had the men to start a half-penny morning paper in the North with a good hope of success. If he did it would present an economic and a political threat to Taylor. Hulton was not a politically-minded man; but men without defined politics tend to be conservative, and Hulton's newspapers, in spite of the men who wrote them, in the end came down on the Right if only because the M.G. and the *Manchester Evening News* did not. In 1897 Hulton's son, later Sir Edward Hulton, was largely responsible for launching the Manchester *Evening Chronicle* which for over fifty years competed on equal terms with the *Evening News* in everything except advertising. Economics, in the sense of idle printing capacity, and ambition made it probable that the *Evening Chronicle* would soon have a morning counterpart, and that it would be a half-penny paper.

From 1896 to 1900 Taylor's and Dibblee's letters contain numerous references to the double threat from Hulton and Harmsworth and how it should be met. At first Taylor and Dibblee thought of running a half-penny paper of their own. Scott's views can only be inferred from what the others said. In 1896 Dibblee raised the issue with Scott in a way which assumed that Taylor, Garnett and Co would bring out its own half-penny morning. He suggested two possible editors from among the *Guardian* staff.* Both were excellent journalists; both were typical *Guardian* men. Neither, therefore, almost by definition ought to have been considered. Taylor was nearer the mark when, later in the year he told Dibblee that what was needed would be more like a morning edition of the *Evening News* than an emasculated M.G.[20] At this time, to Taylor's surprise, Scott was hanging back – the reason may very well have been that he had little sympathy for any paper after the style of the *Evening News*. He found its connection with the firm an embarrassment when his friends at the university complained to him about its crudities.

At the end of 1897 Dibblee produced an estimate for the cost of a half-penny paper. He based it on a print of 36,000 and a sale of 30,000 a day – about three-fifths of what the *Guardian* was selling. Dibblee allowed less than £6,000 a year for all editorial expenses in Manchester and London including £500 for the rent of a private wire between the two offices. He proposed to pay the editor only £600 and to give him only two sub-editors and three reporters, averaging £250 and £233 a year respectively. It was a hopeless budget on which to fight the *Daily Mail* should it come to Manchester. How could an unfledged paper run on a shoe string compete with one which sent G. W. Steevens 'With Kitchener to Khartoum?' Steevens had covered the story so brilliantly in popular form that the book made from his articles ran through twenty-two editions in two years. How too could a half-penny morning from Cross Street stand against the implied threat from Edward Hulton with his brilliant *Sunday Chronicle* team? But as time went on Scott seems to have come round to Dibblee's views about the desirability and the practicability of starting a popular morning since in 1898 Taylor, who had changed his views, wrote sadly to him, 'I cannot say that I like what you say of a half-penny morning. It is all very well for you young people. I am far too old for such adventures.'[21] Taylor, Garnett and Co did not embark on a new morning paper.

Just over a year later both threats materialised. Hulton published

---

* (Dibblee–Scott 19 June 1896.) James Drysdale served the *Guardian* from 1889, when he joined as a reporter, to 1924, when he died in the press gallery of the House of Commons. There was a gap in his service from 1898 to 1902. F. S. Attenborough was appointed in 1893 as sub-editor for the *New Weekly*. When that failed he became a *Guardian* reporter for a short time and then a sub-editor. He was chief sub-editor from 1904 to 1939.

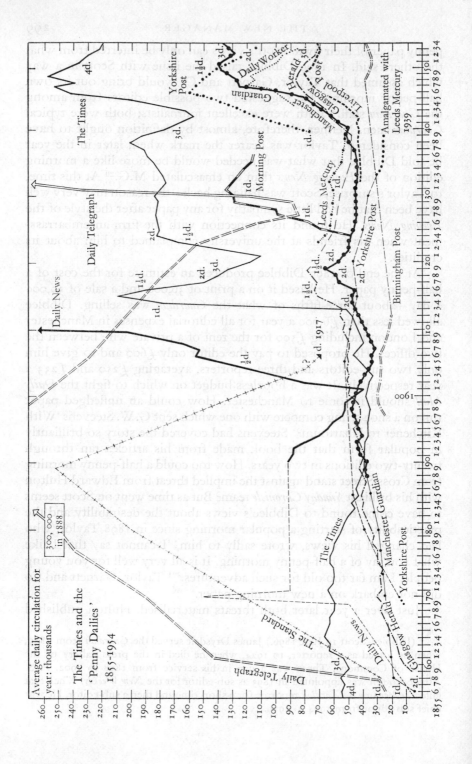

Average daily circulation for year: thousands

The Times and the 'Penny Dailies' 1855–1954

the first issue of the *Daily Dispatch* on 5 February 1900. It went on eventually to reach a circulation of half a million. Two days earlier Harmsworth had published the first northern edition of the *Daily Mail*. For some time the way had been prepared by the use of a special train to bring the London edition of the *Mail* into Manchester in time for delivery in the city itself. The *Guardian* suffered. At Christmas 1899 Dibblee wrote to Scott, who was in Rome, a letter full of schadenfreude mixed with whistling to keep his courage up:

'The *Daily Mail* competition is not terrifying at all, in fact I like the interest which the rivalry throws into business, but I have all along said that it was an opponent not to be despised. On certain limited lines it is most efficient. I had a curious proof last week of the harm it has done to our circulation . . . Twice during the past week the DM train has been late and immediately demands came into us from the newsagents with the comment that they can sell a great many more *Guardians* when the *Mails* do not arrive. You see for some people we are already become the second paper . . .

'. . . When you left England the *Daily Mail* had just begun to come to Manchester, now at your return they are probably selling about twice the number we do in the limited area which they can reach. Within a couple of months their local paper will be in full swing and they will soon cover all the ground, and more, than we can do, but I hardly expect them to do us any more harm . . .'

By 1900, of course, all idea of a half-penny morning companion to the *Guardian* had been given up. The paper was fighting for its survival. For the first time the year's working showed a loss. Meanwhile the *Daily Mail* and the *Daily Dispatch* were busily enlisting the new newspaper readers of the North. To the extent to which they took their politics from their newspapers (but that was not perhaps very far) they would become Conservative Voters, though neither paper was a tied party organ. The *Dispatch*, for instance, was highly critical of the Taff Vale judgment. The Radicals had lost their opportunity. The *Guardian*, which had been more consistently and intelligently devoted to popular education than to any other reforming cause, had to see the generation that had profited from its efforts turn to papers of a very different character. It was sad.

But perhaps it was also fortunate. The record profits of 1895 and 1896 (£23,000 and £24,000) might well have tempted Taylor, Garnett and Co to take a step which would probably have failed. A rapidly ageing proprietor and a frequently absent editor unwilling to delegate authority were not fit rivals for the Hultons and the Harmsworths. There is nothing to show that Dibblee thought boldly enough or had the imagination that was needed. If only, one is tempted to say; if only

the *Sunday Chronicle* writers had been based on Cross Street instead of
Withy Grove and Taylor had been twenty years younger, the North
might have had the popular paper it deserved. As it was, it was well
that the cobbler stuck to his last. The *Guardian* had its own job to do.
If Taylor, Garnett and Co had launched a half-penny morning in 1897
there might well have been no *Guardian* by the end of 1900.

CHAPTER TWENTY-TWO

The War of the Taylor Succession

I

'To run and edit what poor dear old Russel (of the Scotsman) called a "kept paper" would be absolutely intolerable, but when it comes to be run by a lot of depraved plutocrats it would be infernal.' This was Taylor's comment when Dibblee was offered the editorship of the Johannesburg *Star* in 1898. Scott eventually persuaded Dibblee to turn it down and Taylor remarked: 'I hope . . . he will forget the glamour of £3,000 a year amidst the El Dorado of South Africa and settle down to steady but honourable work in the gloom of Manchester.'* This was the end of a brief crisis in the management of the *Guardian* which, if it had been resolved as Taylor originally wanted, would probably have given a very different turn to the troubled history of the paper in the five years after the Boer War. The episode of the South African offer, part of Rhodes's plan to monopolise the flow of news, sets the scene for the struggle for the control of the *Guardian* which Scott all but lost in the year of the Liberal party's greatest political triumph.

The whole line of the *Guardian*'s colonial policy – its opposition to the Chartered Company in Rhodesia and its detestation of the Jameson Raid and all that followed – was offensive to its manager. And Dibblee, as might have been foreseen when he was appointed, was not a manager who was content to keep his political views and his business life in separate compartments. No doubt he made his views freely known on his periodical visits to All Souls. By the third week in December 1898 negotiations with South Africa were sufficiently far advanced for him to tell Taylor about an unspecified but attractive offer which had come to him through Sir William Anson, the Warden, and which was 'more congenial to a man who has had an exceptional education than the purely business career in which I now find myself.'[1] He asked when he

---

* Taylor–Scott 2 and 4 January 1899. According to Hobson ('The War in South Africa', p. 208) the editorship was turned down by three journalists in London before it was accepted by W. F. Moneypenny of the *Times* who was promised editorial freedom but felt bound to resign in 1903 because he opposed indentured Chinese labour.

could be released if he decided to accept it. Taylor was outraged. It was difficult to see why he took it so hardly since at this stage Dibblee had given him absolutely no indication of what or where the new job was. True, Dibblee owed his training entirely to Taylor, Garnett and Co, but he had already given them six years' service. On the face of it the six months' notice he suggested seems reasonable. There must have been some deeper reason for Taylor's extreme displeasure. Perhaps he had heard a rumour about the nature of the job. At any rate he felt left out of Dibblee's confidence: 'I have always been on pleasant terms with him,' he told Scott, 'and yet there has always been something cold and distant in my relations with him.' Taylor thought that Dibblee had better be taken at his word, or rather at his hint and be allowed, or perhaps forced, to go. He had thought so when he received Dibblee's first letter. When Scott interceded, Taylor held to his opinion: 'You take a very charitable view of the position which I cannot quite fall in with. I should never feel myself to be on the same footing as before and I shall never again feel any confidence.'[2] But when Dibblee turned down the offer, Taylor agreed that he should stay – 'at this season one must always conquer one's enmity and ill will' – and told Scott to bind him by a five year agreement.[3]

So it came about that Dibblee remained manager of the M.G. throughout the whole of the Boer War, committed to a declining paper with whose views he was out of sympathy. He could feel none of the elation and pride with which Scott, Montague and Hobhouse faced the storm. It might have been better for the M.G. and better for Dibblee's reputation if he had left in 1899. But it was not until February 1902 that he told Scott that he could have his resignation whenever he liked and asked him to pass this information on to Taylor. Nothing happened then, but six weeks later Dibblee himself resigned. What he wrote to Taylor is not known, but in his covering letter to Scott he said 'I should like you to see that I have endeavoured fairly and straight-forwardly to present a difficult matter.' Scott agreed that he had, but added 'I think though that your disagreement is less with me personally than with the paper – a much bigger thing.' 'It rather knocked me over,' Taylor admitted, but after a night's rest he decided: 'We shall lose a man of rather remarkable business ability, who has desired to serve us honestly and loyally; but, as you indicate, if we can get a man of less business capacity (sic) the deficiency may be made up to us if there be real sympathy with the aims of the paper by the stimulus of enthusiasm and common purpose.'[4]

It had been well it had been done quickly, but Dibblee showed no desire to go until it suited his convenience. May 1903 was suggested

The Reporters in 1916.

Back row: J. V. Radcliffe, J. J. Sullivan, George Bigwood, Walter Meakin, William Longden, Ben Leech

Front row: George Leach, W. Haslam Mills, W. A. Shovelton, H. Lockett Haslam Mills was the author of the centenary history; Leach, Radcliff and Meakin reported the Easter Rising in Dublin

On the left is the back of the 1886 building with the carts lined up ready for the delivery of the *Manchester Evening News*. On the right is what had been the Manchester Examiner office which now belonged to the *Guardian* and was connected with it by the bridge

In 1929 the
Examiner
building was
replaced by the
extension
shown in this
picture by
L. S. Lowry

Cleaners and Porters

Back Row: Mrs. Aimson, Mrs. Grosvenor, Mrs. Howe, Mrs. Etchells, Mrs. Morris, Messrs. J. Strogen, S. Shufflebotham, S. Berry.

Front Row: Mrs. Waterton, Mrs. Fitchett, Mr. F. Johnson, Mrs. Mitchell, Mr. F. Horner.

The Centenary. The first and last pages of an album presented to C. P. Scott

Directors

Back Row: Messrs. E. T. Scott, C. E. Montague, J. J. O'Neill, W. P. Crozier, J. Bone.

Front Row: Messrs. J. R. Scott, C. P. Scott, L. T. Hobhouse.

by Scott and unenthusiastically accepted by Dibblee 'if you want a definite understanding.' 'I had never conceived,' he explained, 'of my obligations to you as terminating at a definite date. I had rather thought that friendly ties would lead me to hold myself at your disposal indefinitely.'[5] Reasons can usually be found why a change-over is inconvenient at a particular moment. Some new project is pretty sure to be in hand which would be better seen through by the man who planned it – in this case it was the introduction of display advertising, the treatment of a block of space in a newspaper more as if it were a picture or a poster than a column of news. Delicate negotiations with advertising agents were involved. New rates had to be fixed. Questions of taste arose. Who was to settle the total appearance of each page and of the paper as a whole? It was obviously a convenience to Taylor to deal with Dibblee whom he knew and who understood the problem. Dibblee found an ally for his policy of procrastination.

He moved to London, which he wanted to do; he continued to exercise a general control over managerial policy. Taylor, who had vainly objected to an absentee editor, seems to have welcomed an absentee manager. It is not surprising that recovery from the paper's hard times was long delayed. Advertising revenue did indeed rise steadily each year from the bottom of the slump in 1902. By 1907 it was up by 20 per cent and had passed the 1898 figure. But the drop in circulation continued and by 1907, the worst year, the average daily net sale was 27 per cent lower than it had been in 1898.

Dibblee's continued involvement was guaranteed by the steps Scott had taken to fill his place. Naturally he made enquiries in all kinds of directions. He wrote, for instance, to his old friend Adolphus Ward who was now Master of Peterhouse, Cambridge. Ward took advice and sent Scott a dozen names of men worth considering. Some were college bursars. One was a mathematician employed by a railway company but 'probably has not a specially high literary faculty.' Was Scott still hankering for a manager who could write as well as any leader-writer? It looks so from Ward's rather surprising first choice: Lowes Dickinson, in later years a frequent contributor to the *Guardian*, who 'is thought to have good business capabilities.'[6] The youngest man suggested was D. H. Macgregor, later well-known as an economist, who had only taken his degree in 1901.

2

In the end none of these was chosen for Scott brought in his second son, John, who like Macgregor had graduated in 1901. He had taken a First in the Mechanical Sciences Tripos from Trinity. In the summer of 1902 he returned from a year at the Massachusetts Institute of Technology to join, as he hoped, a Manchester engineering firm. But on the last Sunday in July John Scott went to London to see Taylor. He joined the staff of Taylor, Garnett and Co on the first of August and was paid £104 for the rest of the year's work. He was just 23.

Dibblee had been only a year older when he was appointed. But at that time the paper was prosperous and it had been possible to give him a period of training on the *Scotsman* and a business trip to America before he settled down to the work of management. John Scott was pitch-forked – the job was certainly not of his seeking – into the office at a time of financial crisis and strained personal relations.* A considerable overlap was necessary before he could possibly be fit to take over responsibility. In fact Dibblee continued in Manchester as manager until the end of March 1903 when he moved to London. The paper was published over his name for another two and a quarter years. During this period there was a lamentable contradiction between Dibblee's official and actual position. Officially he was manager; in practice he was a part-time consultant busy about his own business affairs from his own office in Bouverie Street. John Scott was in executive control in Manchester, a rather lonely young man in an office where seniority counted. The head of the counting house was T. R. Dain who was just completing fifty years of service. But the division of responsibilities was not as simple as this. Dibblee was in fact virtually John Scott's commanding officer – the man who had access to the proprietor, the man whom John had to satisfy if he was to keep his job or obtain the position for which his father had destined him.

The interregnum was protracted beyond reason because John Scott failed to satisfy Taylor. To succeed in the position in which he found himself he would have needed not only energy and ability but comsummate tact. He had not inherited his father's sure touch in humouring the great. He lacked, too, if one may judge from later days, that appreciation of orderly record keeping for its own sake which Dibblee possessed and Taylor valued. And he would not write letters – a disinclination which he never overcame. When he did write, he was terse. After he had been six weeks in the office Dibblee asked his father: 'By the way what kind of a letter does John write? His letters to me are curt and a little careless and perhaps he hardly realises the usefulness of the little formalities and circumlocutions of correspondence

---

* 'C. P. Scott did not train me for the job. I was trained as an engineer, which was my personal inclination, and pitchforked into this.' J. R. Scott—Wadsworth, probably 1946.

especially in transactions with half educated people.'[7] Or, he might have added – and it was a far more serious matter – with a powerful old man of an earlier generation. Clearly John was happier helping T. M. Young, now commercial editor, to get out the first annual engineering supplement. 'He is entitled to a very big share of any credit there is in the thing,' Young told Scott. 'He has worked like a Trojan: we both spent all day yesterday in the composing room seeing that the make-up was right and then he spent the whole night until seven this morning in the machine room.'[8] Dibblee was pleased, too, with John's success in organising special late editions giving the latest test scores from Australia in the stop press and beating the *Daily Dispatch* most mornings in this matter. In this John found more than purely technical interest. He was both a gifted and an enthusiastic player of games – just as concerned as the *Guardian*'s other readers to know the state of play.

Taylor could, and did, appreciate John's services on the production side, but he did not find it sufficient proof of his readiness to run the whole business. During January 1904 there was what may well have been a disastrous exchange of letters about John between Scott in Cannes, where he was looking after his wife who was seriously ill, and Taylor and Dibblee, both of whom were in London. Taylor made it plain to Scott that he was not yet prepared to have John as manager and that he resented the paucity of letters from him: 'As to my own position in the matter I must tell you frankly that I feel that without Dibblee I should know nothing of the affairs in the Managerial department of my paper.'[9] This letter crossed one from Scott of which a heavily corrected draft survives. But for once Scott's deft touch failed. Taylor replied: 'I am sorry that in my past life and my past conduct to you, of which you have had long experience, you find so little to give you confidence in my justice, honourable conduct or even kindness of disposition to those with whom I am in relations.'[10]

At this point John himself wrote to Taylor and made a better impression than his father had done. 'A very proper letter' was Taylor's comment to Scott. 'Dear John Scott,' Taylor's reply to John begins; it ends: 'I think you should not be in too great a hurry to claim entire independence. Let that come about gradually. It is not possible to fix any definite term, but I see no reason why if you cultivate strict and careful business habits and keep ever in mind the traditions and policy of the paper this culmination should be long delayed.'[11] While John was waiting for Taylor's letter he wrote again to his father and shrewdly put his finger on what was probably the cause of the trouble.

'I had a long talk with Dibblee about the matter yesterday evening and I think he really means to act well but yet I cannot help feeling that he is partly responsible for Mr Taylor's present attitude towards me. Without any very definite intention and very likely with some truth he has I think given Mr Taylor the idea that I am quite inexperienced and flighty. Also he has fostered in Mr Taylor's mind an exaggerated notion of the effect of your absence and the idea that he (Dibblee) was the strong man at the helm.'[12]

John was sufficiently satisfied with Taylor's conditional promise that the 'culmination' should not be long delayed to write an appreciative and dutiful letter of thanks. Taylor was pleased: 'I have had a very agreeable letter from John,' he told Scott on January 17 1904. Not until the beginning of July 1905, however, did John become manager, and even then Dibblee did not disappear. Taylor had come to find him indispensable. By the end of March 1905 he had determined to take Dibblee into partnership. When John became manager he found that Dibblee, 'though not having any specific duties assigned to him,' was still to be 'available at all times for consultation and advice' to Taylor in return for a tenth share of the profits. The new manager and the new partner took office on the same day.

3

The new partnership did not last long. At the beginning of October Edward Taylor died. There followed the worst ten weeks that Scott was ever to know. The trouble came from the terms of Taylor's will which had been made in the summer of 1904. His nephews, the four sons of Peter Allen, were the residuary legatees. Three paragraphs in the will were of crucial importance. Paragraph 15 said 'before selling . . . my . . . copyright . . . and my . . . share and interest in the . . . business . . . to any other person . . . my trustees . . . shall offer to sell to Charles Prestwich Scott the whole of the . . . copyright . . . and my shares interest in the . . . business . . . at the price of £10,000.' Paragraph 16 went on to 'empower and recommend my trustees to offer for sale to Charles Prestwich Scott . . . the . . . offices and business premises . . . at such a price as my trustees shall think fit notwithstanding that such price may be less than might otherwise have been obtained therefor it being my wish and desire . . . that the same should be sold to him upon moderate and reasonable terms.' These two paragraphs amounted to a handsome legacy to Taylor's cousin and partner of thirty years' standing. It was indeed no more than Scott had been led to expect though the terms were more generous than he could have guessed.

Financially Taylor made no distinction in his will between his two papers – he put an arbitrary value of £10,000 on his sole ownership of the *Guardian* copyright and of £5,000 on his half-ownership of the *Evening News*. But, while his trustees were bound to offer the *Evening News* to Russell Allen, they had no need to offer the *Guardian* to Scott. The fatal paragraph, which applied only to the *Guardian*, was No 14. It empowered them either to sell or 'during such period as they shall think fit to carry on . . . the said business . . . with power to employ . . . any editor or manager . . . having regard to my earnest desire that the . . . newspaper shall be conducted in the future on the same lines and in the same spirit as heretofore . . .'

This paragraph reflects Taylor's anxieties about the way in which Scott was running the paper – not about the line it was taking, but about how it was being administered. Taylor remained satisfied with Scott's policy, and his letters during the last year of his life often expressed his appreciation of what was in the M.G. and of the new men who were writing in it. In his last letter to Scott, written only a fortnight before his death, Taylor summed up a number of appreciative comments with the remark: 'Altogether the paper has had a great deal of interesting matter in it lately.'[13] What continued to upset Taylor was the paper's viability. There were probably three main matters which worried him. First, certainly, was his concern about the largely absentee editor who refused to make arrangements for the long periods during which he had to be away. Secondly, there was probably a deep-seated fear of nepotism. This seems to have been a recurrent trait in Taylor's character. It may have been associated with the fact that his own marriage was childless. Twenty years before he had been accustomed to complain to Scott about Peter Allen's desire to push his sons forward. Later he was worried by Buxton's ambitions for his son. Now it was Scott's turn to be suspected. The critical year was no doubt 1902. In January Scott's eldest son, Laurence, joined the editorial staff and became a colleague of his brother-in-law, Montague. In July Scott suddenly put forward his second son as manager designate. Taylor was not likely to welcome this concentrated family party. In fact he found occasion to complain not only of John, as we have seen, but also of Laurence. Twice in the second part of 1904 he took serious exception to short leaders by Laurence which he regarded as in bad taste. In one instance – a light article on the harmless suggestion that men would look better in knee breeches for evening dress – Laurence's offence was made worse by the fact that the suggestion had come from his father. Both instances are later in date than the will, but these were probably not isolated examples. Dibblee and Charles Allen both spoke of Taylor's dissatisfaction with Scott's sons as a known thing.

The most reasonable explanation of paragraph 14 of the will seems to be that Taylor wanted his trustees to satisfy themselves that the *Guardian* was being competently run from a business-like point of view before they handed it over to Scott. The paper came first in Taylor's thoughts as it did in Scott's. The will was designed, if this was how Taylor's mind worked, to carry on his control beyond the grave. Things were to continue for a time as if he were still alive. His trustees were to exercise his powers. For what purpose? The clause in the will that empowered them to act as newspaper proprietors said that their object should be to carry on the *Guardian* 'on the same lines and in the same spirit as heretofore.' These words, written after the bitter experience of the Boer War, surely implied that fidelity to principle was to be put before profit. But it is the duty of executors and trustees to look after the material interests of those to whom the testator leaves his property. The residuary legatees were the descendants of Peter Allen, several of whom were minors at the time of Taylor's death. Their financial interests could only be reconciled with the high principles of paragraph 14 on the view that in the long run it was possible to make 'readable righteousness remunerative' as John Scott was to define his occupation many years later. In the short run it certainly had not been. And when it is most needed, it rarely is. The trustees, then, were confronted with a pretty conflict which it is difficult to believe that Taylor intended. Lawyers – and Taylor was proud of being a barrister – often make bad wills.

There were four trustees. Mrs Taylor had always been Scott's warm friend. She had never liked the Allens. She continued to hold these views during the struggle over the *Guardian*. Cecil Harcourt Smith was 'a cronie of Mr T. in art matters'[14] and a senior member of the British Museum staff. He knew nothing of newspapers and was included among the trustees presumably because of his expert knowledge of the value of Taylor's art collection. On Mrs Taylor's death in 1912 it was sold for £358,000.* Charles Allen, Peter Allen's second son, had been a noted Rugby footballer. He had played three times in winning Oxford sides against Cambridge and been capped twice for Wales, scoring its first try ever made against England. But that was twenty years before. Since then he had travelled in the Balkans, written a few articles for the *Guardian*, served for a time on the *Evening News*, won a Conservative seat for the Liberals in the khaki election of 1900. He had had to fight against his remote connection with the M.G. of which his opponents had made capital, accusing him of being its proprietor. It would

* The sale lasted twelve days and the *Times* placed it fourth in the order of sums realised up to that date. The M.G. reported that the amount originally paid by Taylor was less than a quarter of the sum realised.

have been to his financial interest to carry out paragraph 14 in the way least favourable to Scott; but, like his brother Arthur, a Liberal candidate in the forthcoming general election, he might be influenced by what the leaders of the party thought. Neither Arthur nor his two brothers, Russell of the *Evening News* and Edward of the general printing company (Taylor, Garnett, Evans & Co) were trustees. They were directly interested in securing control of the *Guardian* with which their business interests were closely linked. The fourth trustee was Dibblee. He had no financial rights under the will beyond the specific legacy left to all three men executors, but he had great expectations if his fellow-executors decided to carry on the paper themselves and made him manager or managing editor. He might, because of a tightly drawn codicil affecting the youngest of the Allen brothers, have reasonably looked forward to a profitable appointment which could have lasted for the rest of his working life as Scott explained when he consulted Sir Robert Reid, soon to be Lord Chancellor in Campbell Bannerman's new government.[15]

Both Scott and the trustees took legal advice. The lawyers on both sides agreed that the trustees could not sell the *Guardian* to the Allens or anybody else unless Scott had first been offered it for £10,000 and refused to buy it. They also agreed that Scott had no right to insist on a sale. Nor had he any right to continue as editor. The partnership, on which his position as editor depended, expired at the end of the year. The trustees could then re-appoint him, or they could appoint somebody else. They had an entirely free hand. Indeed one legal opinion was to the effect that Scott should be removed from his office as soon as possible since he might become a purchaser. If the trustees were to look after the financial interests of the Allens they had in practice only two courses open to them – to carry on the paper themselves with or without Scott as editor, or to sell it to him for as great a sum as they could count on making if they retained control. They could not agree among themselves since two of the trustees, Mrs Taylor and Cecil Smith, had Scott's interests at heart and were determined to do as much for him as the law allowed. The other two had not.

Scott reconciled himself to buying at an inflated price – he was an eager purchaser; half the trustees were unwilling sellers. But his offer was turned down in principle without a price being suggested. He steeled himself to working under the trustees which, as he understood it, would mean having Dibblee virtually in the position that Taylor used to occupy, the man who had to be satisfied. Scott wrote to Charles Allen to that effect on November 27. That evening Rachel Scott died. For thirty-one years she had shared all her husband's triumphs and anxieties in the conduct of the *Guardian* and for most of them she had played an active part in its literary pages.

'I have felt all this week,' Montague wrote to Hobhouse, 'as if I had never known – much as I thought of him before – one half of what there is to love and respect in him. You can't conceive how absolutely simple and controlled and unself-pitying he has been. You know how frightfully pathetic it is to see a small child, quite alone, trying to do the best with a great breakdown of something it has been absorbed in. It is like that, infinitely magnificent, to see him going about all the arrangements that have had to be made – just the same kind of circumstantial moral heroism, and unconsciousness of it.'[16]

A fortnight after his wife's death Scott had arranged to meet the trustees to discuss future arrangements. He did not go because shortly before the time fixed for the meeting he received the details of their plan. He was to be paid a salary of £2,000 as editor; but Dibblee was to be not only the virtual proprietor, as the only knowledgeable trustee, but also the actual executive manager in Manchester. John Scott was to be got rid of with £4,000 as compensation. The proposal was altogether unacceptable.

But from the moment of Scott's dramatic refusal Cecil Smith and Mrs Taylor began to gain in power among the trustees. Disagreement among them would have to be reported to the Court and a direction sought. This would not have suited Dibblee. It would be difficult to explain why he had insisted on becoming manager and refused a sale on advantageous terms. The *Guardian's* future in Manchester was not bright in 1905. Not only had profits been falling for three years after a short recovery at the end of the Boer War, but expenditure seemed bound to rise if the paper was to hold its own. The challenge in 1905 came not only from Manchester's two half-penny mornings, the *Daily Dispatch* and the *Daily Mail*, but from a rejuvenated *Courier*. This was a direct challenge in the quality paper field where the *Guardian* had been free from really serious competition for twenty years. At the end of 1904 Harmsworth had bought the *Courier* for £114,500. He had brought down Nicol Dunn from the *Morning Post* to edit it.* The situation was dangerous. Could the *Guardian* survive? Moreover Scott was known to be considering the possibility of founding a northern counterpart to the *Westminster Gazette*. This might hurt Russell Allen's *Evening News* as well as weakening the *Guardian* in its fight with the *Courier*. If radicals found an evening paper more to their liking than a

---

* Nicol Dunn had been editor of the *Morning Post* since 1895. He left the *Courier* to edit the Johannesburg *Star* in 1910. The *Courier* survived until 1916.

Dibblee-controlled *Guardian* they might well take Scott's paper in the evening because of its views and features and buy Harmsworth's *Courier* in the morning for its news. This was, no doubt, only a hypothetical danger, but it could not be left out of account. In this situation dare prudent trustees reject an attractive offer from the only authorised purchaser?

Moreover, if the trustees did not come to terms, though they might continue to run the *Guardian*, it would be the *Guardian* not only without Scott, but without many of his principal lieutenants. The M.G. had been a City of Refuge for exiled radical journalists when Massingham lost control of the *Daily Chronicle*. Now a new quality radical morning paper was just starting in London and was able to offer an asylum for at least some of those Manchester men who felt that it would be an intolerable dishonour to serve under Dibblee. Hobhouse had left the M.G. in 1902 in order to give more time to his philosophical work but partly also because of difficulties which arose through C.P.'s reluctance to appoint a deputy or to define responsibilities. Now he was back in journalism as the political editor of the new *Tribune*, financed by the rich Bolton business man Franklin Thomasson. Hobhouse, Montague and Scott worked in close alliance during the desperate ten weeks to ensure that, if Dibblee won, he would find that he had captured a ship without a crew, or at least without competent navigating officers.

The two principal members of the *Guardian* staff were Montague himself and Sidebotham. They were very differently placed. Montague put their relative positions clearly in one of his letters to Hobhouse:

'. . . though he (Sidebotham) would hate the change, it is, I think, possible that he might try to stay on, making terms for a long engagement, and resisting in detail the transformation of the paper. I feel I can't say anything that would help to make him resign with me, or refuse the editorship if it should by any chance be offered, but I was hugely glad to be able to tell him of your letter and let him feel that there might be work elsewhere. His position is specially difficult as he has lately moved to a better house, has done much furnishing and has incurred a small debt to befriend an acquaintance, so that he has no reserves. I am, comparatively, in clover, as my wife and I have nearly £300 a year between us and, with all our children quite young, we could easily stick it out in a cheap place in the country and save up anything I could make by odd jobs against the time when schools come on. If circumstances should make it possible for the *Tribune* to make Sidebotham an offer at the time when he has to decide here, it might, I think, be a tremendous gain all round – save him a damnable struggle to be honest, and give the *Tribune* a real first-rater – for the last two or three years he has acted as a sort of advising chief sub-editor and seems to me to have got the completest knowledge of the whole machinery of journalism of any man I know while still improving at his writing.'[17]

The *Tribune* offered Sidebotham £800, a third more than he was getting on the *Guardian*. He consulted Scott and, at his suggestion, put it to the trustees, who alone could decide. This was before they had made their terms known, while it was still likely that Scott would continue as editor under their direction. Dibblee promised Sidebotham his £800, and Sidebotham turned down the *Tribune* which had asked for his decision by the end of the month. No doubt Sidebotham used a favourable opportunity to get a salary out of the *Guardian* more nearly equal to his merits, but that did not imply (as Scott felt and resented) that he would have been willing to work for a different kind of *Guardian*. It is true that Sidebotham drew a legitimate distinction in his own mind between working for the M.G., which commanded his deep loyalty and affection, and working for Scott whom he admired, but well this side of idolatry. Montague, a more generous man than Scott, was more sympathetic to Sidebotham. Apparently the *Tribune* was still a possibility. On the eve of the crucial meeting which did not take place Montague wrote to Hobhouse: 'I fancy Sidebotham will resign here, if things go wrong. He was much cheered by his communications with you. You must certainly think first, if any opportunity arises, of securing him. I can stand a siege much longer.'[18]

Three days later Montague in despair formally applied for the post of dramatic critic of the *Tribune*, an application which he withdrew when hope revived. He did not know what Sidebotham had decided. 'Many thanks for your note,' he wrote. 'I went over at once to Sidebotham and put the advantages of joining the *Tribune* as strongly as I could. We were interrupted before he had said what he meant to do.'[19] Because of that interruption we too do not know what Sidebotham meant to do.

The trustees were probably quite as much in the dark about Sidebotham's intentions when they again invited Scott, in spite of his complete rejection of their plan, to meet them to discuss the position. On 13 December Scott explained to them some of the reasons for his refusal. Prudently he did not mention what he considered to be Dibblee's personal unworthiness for which Dibblee was grateful. Scott followed up this meeting with a formal offer either to carry on for an experimental year working for the trustees as he used to work for Taylor, but insisting on John as manager, or to purchase the copyright at an arbitrated price plus 20 per cent. On 15 December Scott heard that the trustees had turned down the idea of an experimental year. Three days later they agreed to negotiate for the sale of the *Guardian*. 'Heaven make Smith Chief Librarian of the British Museum,' wrote Montague to Hobhouse.[20] It did not; but, perhaps more appropriately, he became Director of the Victoria and Albert, and Surveyor of the King's Pictures.

4

The ten weeks of despairing crisis were followed by nineteen months of weary, miserable haggling. Nineteen hundred and six was a good year for advertising, a slightly better one for circulation and a much better one for profits thanks to the end of the Russo-Japanese War. But the cards were stacked against the Scotts. C.P. was determined to purchase. But every success that John had in management – and in 1906 he proved that Taylor's fears had been groundless – worsened his father's bargaining position. 'The paper is doing better; very well, you can afford to pay more' was an argument impossible to counter if the purchaser was determined to buy whatever the price.

But, quite apart from any moral considerations deriving from Scott's past services or Taylor's expressed wishes, there were solid economic arguments pointing to a low price. They were set out in a letter which J.S.R. Phillips, editor of the staunchly Conservative *Yorkshire Post*, wrote to Scott after the negotiations had been dragging on for five months:

'In the first place, you must insist upon the fact, that you have no security, and can have no security, for the continuance of the arrangement with the Evening paper. That paper might be transferred by the proprietor to offices of his own . . . Further, in the event of his death, his executors might think it right to sell the paper, or he himself, being a man of wealth, might sell the paper. In that case, it might either be transferred to Messrs Harmsworth (in which event the arrangement with you would certainly come to an end . . .) or you would be compelled to pay a very high price for the property in order that you might retain it in your premises to share the fixed charges.'

This was a real danger. Harmsworth had spare printing capacity in his northern offices of the *Daily Mail*. An evening paper would have been directly useful to him in his competition with the Hulton group, and indirectly, by weakening the M.G., would have strengthened the hand of his *Courier* in the quality field. If Scott was right in his belief that the Manchester-based Allens wanted to get hold of the *Guardian* there were obvious possibilities for mischief.

How seriously Scott and his legal advisers took their ambitions is evident from the scare which followed the conclusion of the negotiations over the price. The draft contract made no reference to the will. Scott's lawyers saw in this omission a loophole which might be used to dispute the validity of his title and permit Russell Allen to use his second option under the will to purchase the copyright for £10,000. Apparently the trustees would also, so the lawyers at first thought, be permitted to retain the purchase money. These fears were probably groundless, and there is no evidence that Russell Allen had any such idea. But by then relations were so bad that, as John Scott put it, it seemed 'rather a lot to stake on the chance that one of our friends would not have the astuteness or good luck to detect a possible flaw and the malignity to utilise it.'[21] In the end counsel decided that the practical risks were small and that, if an action were brought, there was a defence that would probably be sound.

Another point which Phillips urged was the fallacy of the argument put forward by Dibblee and the Allens about the profits missed through Scott's riding of hobby horses:

'I am told that your paper has been run "as a hobby" and not purely upon a commercial basis. If you had not devoted so much space and expenditure to special articles, you would have had instead to spend much more on other classes of news . . . But beyond this, whether the policy has been altogether wise from a commercial point of view – and the criticism to which I have referred is based upon the supposition that it has not – . . . it is certain that the reputation of the paper is built upon the policy pursued during many years, and that if this policy were reversed the loss of prestige would affect not merely the favour in which the paper is held by a very large and important class of readers but also advertisers . . . would regard it as a sign of failure . . .'

Phillips was emphatic in his opinion, which was presumably given with a view to being passed on to the trustees:

'These considerations go to my mind very strongly to shew that you ought not to be burdened with a large number of years' purchase, and that there ought not to be any allowance for that entirely hypothetical extra profit which, it is alleged, might have been made had the paper been run in a different manner and in different conditions.'[22]

How many years' purchase was the copyright really worth? Some idea of Taylor's views on this are fortunately available. At one time he was apparently quite often consulted by other newspaper owners on this kind of question. In 1895, going through old papers, he came across a copy of a letter he had written to James Law of the *Scotsman* who had asked his advice in 1868. In his letter Taylor referred to calculations he had made in 1854. At that time, when provincial papers were still bi-weekly, he put the proper price at three to five years' purchase based on the average profits of the past three years. In 1868 he considered that the same range held good and that the *Guardian* and the *Scotsman* were entitled to the higher multiplier because they were the principal papers of a region and drew more than half their revenue from advertisements – in his view an important criterion of stability. Circulation by comparison was expensive and fickle. In 1895 he thought that 'the values of both the *Scotsman* and the M.G. and indeed all similar newspapers have materially increased so that I should be more inclined to place the values of each at 7 years.'[23] But that was written towards the end of a golden age before the coming of the half-penny mornings and the invasion of the London papers. After 1900 he would certainly have fixed a lower figure, though the proportion of the *Guardian*'s revenue from advertisements never fell below 58 per cent and in 1905 and 1906 was over two-thirds. The following table gives a comparison of the value of the M.G. at different times on Taylor's method of calculation:

Estimated Value of M.G. Copyright at 3, 5 and 7 Years' Purchase

Year	3	5	7
1854	£32,300	£53,900	—
1868	£53,200	£88,700	—
1895	£55,000	£91,700	£128,400
1901	£7,800	£13,000	£18,200
1905	£12,200	£20,400	£28,500
1906	£16,500	£27,500	£38,500

In the light of these figures the £80,000 Scott had to pay for the copyright, equivalent to twenty years' purchase on the 1905 figures, was clearly extortionate. The rest of the bargaining was equally one-sided. Taylor had directed that his trustees should sell the premises and plant 'upon moderate and reasonable terms' and accept a price that might be 'less than might otherwise have been obtained.' But the trustees put forward a valuation for the printing presses which was double the value that Scott's valuers considered them worth. For the linotypes the trustees' valuation was half as much again as Scott's valuers put them at. The final agreed total for premises and plant was £100,000. Scott had to raise £240,000 to buy the paper, including the pay off of existing loans, but these included his own £37,000 of capital in Taylor, Garnett and Co. Finally on 17 July 1907 the last of the trustees signed and on 10 August Scott was able to tell his eldest son 'we have our first meeting of the new Company (John and I probably) on Tuesday to elect directors etc.'[24]

Scott's own fortune, which in 1906 stood at £48,000, formed the whole of the ordinary shares of the new company the Manchester Guardian, Ltd., apart from the qualifying shares of the other directors, who were all members of the immediate family. The rest of the capital was raised in four per cent preference shares. Now that his children were all of age they were able to release the £18,000 in their mother's marriage settlement trust and all this was put into preference shares. Scott's three sisters contributed £30,000 between them – two-thirds of it came from Mrs O'Neill with the remark, 'Perhaps my strongest motive was that Father would have wished it. I know that had the emergency come in his lifetime you would have had at once an offer of £50,000 or £80,000 as you might need it. It has always been my wish to use the money that came from him as though it were still his.'[25] No doubt Scott's two unmarried sisters, Kate and Isabella, would have endorsed Sarah O'Neill's view. Thus for the second time the *Guardian* was saved by Russell Scott, who had once held the copyright of the *Guardian* himself in trust for his two young Taylor nephews, and who had come to the help of Edward Taylor and Peter Allen in the financial crisis of 1858. The misfortunes that followed Edward Taylor's attempt to control his paper after his death were cured largely by Russell Scott's legacies. The most remarkable of the contributors to the preference shares, however, was certainly a fourth woman, Edward Taylor's widow and trustee, who showed conclusively what she felt about the situation by lending £20,000, almost the whole of her personal fortune. A large mortgage and an overdraft of £20,000 provided the rest of the necessary funds. This large sum of money was raised with comparative ease, but it involved a much heavier load of debt than the paper could safely carry. Scott never drew any dividend on his ordinary shares – the overriding need was to pay off debts and to build up reserves. Looking back, John Scott reckoned that the paper remained in danger until 1910 when the bank overdraft was paid off.

5

The first intense stage of the crisis over the Taylor succession can be fully reconstructed from Scott's side largely out of the letters that passed between Scott, Hobhouse and Montague. Unfortunately no comparable material is known to survive from the trustees' side. The middle part of the long war of nerves which occupied 1906 is much more obscure. There are only occasional letters to show what was happening. The last five months of the struggle are once again better known – for a sad reason. Scott's eldest son, Laurence, a young man of

30, an indefatigable mountaineer and a man of great strength, was taken seriously ill with tuberculosis contracted during his work in the slums of Ancoats where he was a devoted member of the university settlement. He was sent to a sanatorium in Aberdeenshire where the disease took its dreaded course of alternating hope and gloom. C.P. and John wrote regularly telling him how the negotiations were going – miserable enough news, often, for the invalid. But in the end C.P. was able to say, 'It is fine that the thing is done at last and I don't think one quite knows yet what it means or will feel like. For those who come after me, if not for me, it should mean a lot and one hopes that for many a long day there is an element of sanity and health kept alive for the nation.'[26]

At least, unlike his mother, Laurence had lived to see the paper saved for his father and for the public good. But his father's plans for Laurence to succeed him as editor were doomed. Next May Laurence died. Probably his father had long known that this must come. The surviving letters have a tenderness which is unusual in C.P. It is shown in the way they open – 'Dear Old Man' or 'Dearest L,' very different from his customary 'Dear John' or 'Dear Ted' to the younger boys. The obituary notice in the *Guardian* is unmistakably Montague's. It may well stand at the end of this chapter of sad and often sordid happenings to show what journalism would have lost if it had lost Scott's *Guardian* – and what the *Guardian* lost in Laurence Scott.

'. . . Like other writers of sensitive mental integrity and independence, who will say nothing by rote and adopt no ready-made method merely because it has answered in other hands, he had to fashion his own instrument of expression, and he threw himself into the task with the passionate absorption which alone makes it possible . . .

'. . . He had no trace of what sometimes passes for the philanthropic spirit, being quite unable to conceive of himself as a beneficent force to be directed upon objects qualified by poverty or want of education . . . He was of so perfect a kindness, simplicity, and humbleness of heart that many of his friends will feel that they owe to their comradeship with him their fullest knowledge of the meaning of those words.' (19 May 1908)

BOOK FIVE

The Power and the Glory
1907-1925

*

CHAPTER TWENTY-THREE

Manchester

I

'YESTERDAY was one of the most agreeable days I have ever spent in my life (I wish I was not too idle to write it all up). The fact is that *this* sort of thing is the real reward for having written a few decent books.' So Arnold Bennett closed an entry in his diary.[1] It is sad that he stopped there. The novelist who caught so exactly the feel of a draper's life or an hôtelier's would surely have given a masterly description of a journalist's. Indeed three months later, when the *Guardian* gave Montague's first novel, 'A Hind Let Loose', to Bennett for review, he wrote 'The important chapter . . . the one on which everything turns, is solely concerned with the concoction of newspaper articles – not as newspaper articles are dashed off in other men's novels but as they actually do get themselves done in real offices, phrase by phrase, with the phrases set down for the novel reader one after another.'[2] That certificate of authenticity was probably based not only on the internal evidence of the book itself but on a lively recollection of his day with the M.G. Fortunately Bennett had recorded in his Journal this impression of his hosts before sloth ended his entry – to take over the word he surprisingly used to describe one side of Montague.

'I was entertained to lunch (he wrote) by Haslam Mills and G. H. Mair. The second, Scotch, educated at Edinburgh, Glasgow, Grenoble and Paris. Evidently considered to be one of the stars of the future. Slight, delicate man with a face retreating at the bottom. Scotch accent. The renowned C. E. Montague was present; also A. N. Monkhouse. Montague, though a Londoner born and bred, looks the typical provincial – rather like an intelligent Sunday School superintendent; quite grey hair, low collar and queer necktie. A rather tight prim way of speaking; when he disagrees, or is not convinced, he is sometimes silent, with a slight working of the muscles of the face; probably due to sloth. They told me afterwards that he lived in a shell; but yesterday he came out and people were surprised. Monkhouse a large, grave man, slow speaking with an extraordinarily sedate charm.

The lunch was very agreeable indeed. Mills has a good manner, which he has conventionalised and hardened, of telling yarns. All the talk was "shop."

Lunch lasted till 4. I then went with Mills and Mair to the file-room of the *Guardian* . . . We came back to the Midland. A man called Agate (not quite on the staff) and another man joined us. Younger than the others but still very fine. Even the satellites on the *Guardian* have their precise notions about De Goncourt. We took tea till 6.15 . . . (then Bennett went on with his hosts to the Gaiety Theatre).

Then I went back to the *Guardian* office and was introduced by Mair to another series of *Guardian* men, and I stayed till 1 a.m. to see the first edition printed and dispatched.

Bennett was not entirely accurate in all his personal details. Mair's British universities were Aberdeen and Christ Church, Oxford with first class degrees in English and history. The reference to Glasgow probably belongs to the man 'younger than the others but very fine.' He is most likely to have been A. S. Wallace who had joined the staff the previous month and had just written his first important theatre notice on 'Il Trovatore.' Wallace ultimately succeeded Monkhouse as literary editor and Montague as dramatic critic.

2

'All the talk was "shop".' Politics must have formed part of it. Hosts and guests were all keen Radical politicians, and even the most un-politically-minded people were excited in December 1909. 'I had rather a dog's life,' Montague wrote to Francis Dodd a few days later,[3] 'with all the speeches there are to be read every night but it's good to have something worth trying for in politics. If we don't hammer the House of Lords this time, Liberals may pretty well put up the shutters and let the Labour men have a try . . . Anyhow I'm much too excited to mind anything else – I can't write any imperishable masterpieces in my mornings.' Day by day for two weeks on end Montague had been enjoying himself writing long leaders about the coming general election just as he had done four years before in the previous election when he had written the Long each night for three weeks. Then his main theme had been the threat of Protection. This time it was the defence of the Constitution against the revolutionaries in the House of Lords. The quality of these leaders may be tasted in a few phrases selected almost at random:

What more natural than that he (Lord Milner) should want to take from common Englishmen now a part of the power of self-government of which he tried to deprive the Cape Colonists . . . One cannot grudge the assailants of the common voter a partisan who has always been so positive and always so wrong. (25 November 1909)

ARTFUL ARTHUR, THE HARDY PLEDGER.

ARTFUL ARTHUR: JUST TILL SATURDAY, MR. BULL!

A cartoon about A. J. Balfour by K. R. Brady, a member of the *Guardian* staff, December 1910

'To-night the Lords are expected to commit that trespass in pursuit of power about which they have been talking for a week . . . Of course they talk of duty. Very few actions, good or bad, are suggested in our virtuous Western Europe except on grounds of duty . . . and some of the richest men in the country are calling it a sacred duty to dodge the super-tax because it will cause such misery in slums.' (30 November 1909)

'No one in the House of Lords itself has made so extravagant a claim in its name as Mr Balfour did . . . triennial Parliaments when Liberals are in, and septennial Parliaments when Conservatives are in.' (3 December 1909)

Bennett first thought of Montague as 'aristocratically fastidious' and then thought better: 'I have used the adjective "aristocratic." It is insufficient. "Scornful" is the epithet. A fine scorn, a noble scorn, but scorn!' True, Bennett was writing of 'A Hind Let Loose' but what he wrote fits as surely this series of leaders and the others that followed hard on it, sparked by 'the fierce fire of the ideal grand inquisitor.'

The Friday which Bennett spent with the *Guardian* men was the first day of the general election campaign. When the protracted lunch party at the Midland Hotel broke up, Montague went back to stand at his high desk, very likely with the office cat on his shoulders, and to write yet another leader. This time he drew on what overseas visitors had been saying about our slums and linked it with the line that Winston Churchill took that evening in the first speech of a memorable Lancashire tour. Churchill had dealt with the crying need for what we should call a welfare state. Montague recalled 'the colourless cheeks, the lightless eyes, the hopeless, defeated looks, the springless muscles, the arrested growth' which had 'haunted and filled with misgiving many men who had come here full of the natural affection of cadets of a family for its immemorial home and with the natural predisposition of such visitors to see all things as easily as possible.'

Meanwhile Haslam Mills had caught a train to Preston. A team (or ring, to use the technical term) of five of his fellow-reporters were there to take Churchill's speech verbatim. Mills had the task of providing the 'sketch' for the main news page. This meant presenting the high lights of the speech in such a way that the reader would want to read more – perhaps even all five columns of the full report. But Mills had also to make his work self-sufficient so that a man who read the sketch, and that alone, could still follow Churchill's argument. He had in addition – and this is where Mills excelled – to give those who were not there the sense of being present, of sharing in the excitement, of catching the human touches which remain in the memory, of responding as the great audience responded. There was then no television

ALGY IN WONDERLAND.

(With all the necessary acknowledgments.)

(The Peers are taking the platform in their own cause, as Lord Curzon suggested.)

The Algy and the Ancestor Were walking hand in hand; They wept like anything to see The voters in the land. If they were only cleared away, They said, " It would be grand."	"Oh, voters, will you walk with us," The Algy did beseech, "A pleasant walk, a pleasant talk, Upon the Tariff beach!" But unearned increment was not Referred to in his speech.

A cartoon and verse by Stanley Houghton, one of the *Guardian* dramatic critics, December 1910

camera to switch attention from 'the tremendous cheers of an audience which filled every recess of the great hall' to 'the last whispered reassurance from the young wife who sat by Churchill's side', no BBC commentator to point out that Sir John Gorst who took the chair had been Randolph Churchill's comrade in the campaign for Tory democracy which began when Winston 'was in the nursery and had failed while he was still at school.' In those days the unseen audience were readers, not viewers. They came fresh next morning to what Mills had to tell them in the M.G. about the feel of the meeting, not stale as we are now when we open the papers after the night before's live, but momentary and truncated television. Mills had a more influential job than the sketch writer of to-day but also in this respect an easier one.

He gave his readers a depth in his reporting which few of his contemporaries achieved. This was most marked when his mind and the speaker's naturally marched together. Mills might have been made to report Churchill. 'We learned much history,' Mr Churchill said, 'when we were at school. The great thing is to recognise history when it happens before our eyes, to pick out what is significant and abiding from the ordinary ebb and flow of party affairs.' This reminded Mills of Burke's ridicule 'of "the retrospective wisdom and the historical patriotism" of some of his contemporaries who, "while playing the part of Tories" in the events of the eighteenth century, were excellent Whigs in the issues of the seventeenth.'[4] Very likely Mills was the only man in the hall to whom this thought occurred; but he made it part of the awareness of that much larger audience who followed the speech in the M.G. A good sketch writer, like Mills, can be to the speaker something of what an accompanist is to the singer.

Was this aside about Burke carefully thought out in advance or a genuine impromptu reflection? T. P. O'Connor thought Churchill's Lancashire speeches were all in type in a newspaper office, presumably the M.G., before they were delivered. He said so in the *Daily Chronicle*. He was wrong. 'They were never fully written out at all, were never in type beforehand and indeed attained their final shape only at the moment of delivery . . . The speeches as they appeared in the press were based on the verbatim shorthand notes made by reporters who were present, and on no other source.'[5]

One may feel reasonably sure that much of the political 'shop' talked that day at the Midland was at a less rarefied level. Elections are about power. 'Who will win?' is the question every one tries to answer. The hosts at the lunch party were not only journalists but keen party politicians. Their editor, C.P. Scott, was at this time president of the Manchester Liberal Federation, an active political boss, closely concerned with party headquarters as well as with Cabinet Ministers. The secretary of the Federation was E. W. Record who had been their colleague as a reporter on the *Guardian* until 1908. There were seventy-six seats in the four North-Western counties – more than Scotland had, two and a half times as many as Wales. Relatively few were safe seats for either party. Polling was still spread over several days. The constituencies which voted on the first day could influence the rest. Manchester was among them. North-West Manchester was regarded, perhaps wrongly, as especially important because it contained the business centre of the city. It was normally Conservative. But Churchill had won it in 1906 only to lose it at a by-election in 1908.* How did this happen? Need it happen again?

It would be surprising if the talk had not turned in that direction.

* He had been appointed President of the Board of Trade and in those days this involved the new Minister in submitting himself for re-election.

Somebody probably quoted the articles in the previous day's paper by the *Guardian*'s two regular religious columnists. One might have expected Alpha, the Free Churchman, to denounce the Lords' veto and couple it with the brewers and so he did. But Quartus was a different matter. Of course, as Canon E. L. Hicks,* he was a regular writer of Letters to the Editor on political subjects. But normally as Quartus he refrained from politics. This time, however, his anger had overflowed:

'Every organisation of Churchmen in certain dioceses is being drilled and engineered for the Tory party. Churchmen are instructed to vote only "for the Church and her schools"; all else is to be forgotten. Such voters are not the men who flock to meetings, or excite themselves about politics. But, when the polling day comes, the Tory motor picks them up to a man. What is being done more or less by the Church of England authorities is being done with yet more of organised pressure by our Roman Catholic neighbours. Even Irish nationalism, if the clerics can have their way, must bend to the needs of the Church; the Irish must not be green, but black. This is the way in which North-West Manchester was won for reaction . . .'

But this time the electors were not dragooned. The seat was recaptured by the Liberals.

There was another tricky side to the election which may well have come up for discussion. What effect would the militant suffragettes have? How should the M.G. deal with their protest demonstrations? It was a problem that arose on this first day of the campaign. At Preston the authorities had taken full precautions. The streets round the hall had been barricaded. A visitor from London brought a message written on brown paper and wrapped round a stone which read 'To Winston Churchill, thrown through the window of the Public Hall to remind you of your broken pledges to suffragists at Manchester and Dundee.' She had in fact thrown it through the Post Office window instead since all the windows of the Public Hall had been boarded up. She was, of course, arrested as she intended to be, and so were three other women. All this was duly reported in the *Guardian* – facts are sacred, as Scott said, and not to be suppressed. It was even given on the main news page, but tucked away in a discreet quarter column at the foot of the page, and Haslam Mills left it severely alone. The *Guardian* was, after all, a political paper. It passionately wanted votes for women. It believed that Mrs Pankhurst's followers might make it impossible to get them.

* Bishop of Lincoln 1910–1919.

3

But probably still more of the talk was about books and plays. The lunch party for Bennett was a gathering of writers. Montague was, after all, the M.G.'s chief dramatic critic. It was a sign of the depth of the political crisis that for two weeks he had not been to a theatre although there had been six notices to write leaving out of account the Carl Rosa season at the Theatre Royal, which was the responsibility of the music critics, and the music halls, which were done by the reporters.

All but one of the men who had written these notices were there at lunch. The missing critic was Stanley Houghton, the dramatist, who had been to a farce which suggested to him that 'American plays are made like American machines, with standard parts, so that you could slip a scene . . . from one play to another without anyone being the wiser.' Allan Monkhouse had seen the Abbey Theatre Players from Dublin in 'The Playboy of the Western World', that 'wonderful, engrossing comedy, which passes naturally and easily from the dunghill to the stars.' Mair too had seen the Abbey Players and written enthusiastically about Sarah Allgood and Maire O'Neill, 'ladies whose beauty of presence would condemn them in London to the dreary round of doing *jeune première* with dresses by "Maison N'Importe" and all the rest of it' but who here 'were playing mother and daughter alternately in two pieces in the same evening, and in each case portraying wrinkled old age or Irish girlhood with a delicacy and sureness of touch and an incorrigible sincerity that never fails in its confident appeal to the emotions which they seek to touch.'*

Mair had indeed had an exciting week. He had also been to the Gaiety to see Ben Jonson's 'Every Man in his Humour', the play which Bennett attended that evening. Mair evidently thought it a poor play, brilliantly acted: 'Comedy of manners, like Molière's,' he remarked, 'remains salient and biting to the end of time . . . "Comedy of Mannerism" will hardly last the eight or nine years which the grave-diggers told Hamlet to be the limit of mortality.' No doubt Mills would not have given a longer life to the impersonation of Harry Lauder by Miss Clarice Mayne, but he had not been ashamed to enjoy her turn at the Hippodrome perhaps as much as he had enjoyed writing about it. On the other hand Agate, who had seen the Abbey Players the previous

---

* 'Riders to the Sea' (Synge) and 'Cross Roads' (Lennox Robinson). Sarah Allgood and Maire O'Neill were sisters. Maire O'Neill's first husband, J. M. Synge, had died in 1909. She married G. H. Mair in 1911. They became engaged in Agate's Derbyshire cottage. (Agate 'Ego', p. 88.)

week, had not enjoyed the farce to which he had been sent where the audience 'laughed with all the gusto we as a nation reserve for our worst jokes.' But no doubt he took pleasure in saying how much better a French farce would have been since one could be sure that a French author's wit would 'illumine' whereas English writers were only practical jokers whose stock types were not 'real people doing insane things in a preposterously comic self-revelatory way.'

Some at least of the 'shop' talked at lunch was bound to be about French plays and French books. Politeness to a guest would have indicated it since Bennett's passion for France always obtruded itself. Gilbert Cannan in his review of 'The Old Wives' Tale' in the *Guardian* thought that the second half was spoilt by 'too many of those errors of taste which seem to be bred out of the influence of the French novel on the Nonconformist mind.'* Several of the hosts might have fallen under the same censure. Sardou would creep without shame or blame into a notice by Montague of 'Hippolytus' in Gilbert Murray's translation. Mills, as a friend remembered, had blown 'into the cathedral atmosphere of Cross Street like a combination of D'Artagnan and Villon.' Mair was steeped in French literature. Agate has described his own and Montague's feelings in a beautiful pastiche of the kind of note he would get from Montague when Bernhardt or Coquelin visited Manchester.

'He would explain that nobody had ever written or could ever write quite so understandingly about the French theatre as yourself, but that since his own French was in danger of becoming rusty, would you do him the charity of accepting the seats for "Are you a Mason?" which, he understood, was a topping little farce? And on the following morning there would appear over the well-known initials such a spate of erudition concerning Molière, couched in such torrential wit, that you went hot all over at the double thought of the halting article you would have written, and of Montague reading it.'[6]

There was, of course, much trash to be seen in Manchester theatres besides many decent plays which have not withstood time's winnowing. But a regular theatre-goer before the 1914 war could have seen most of Shakespeare, Shaw, Ibsen, Yeats and Synge besides regular seasons of German and French classics if he could follow them in their own language. He could have seen plays of quality by Lancashire writers, many of them associated with the *Guardian*. Janet Achurch was at one theatre, Miss Horniman at another. She had moved in 1907 from Dub-

---

* M.G. 11 November 1908. Cannan may, perhaps best be remembered as the translator of Romain Rolland's 'Jean Christophe.'

lin, where she had assisted and helped to finance the Irish Players, to Manchester, where she gave England its first repertory theatre. At the Gaiety she gathered round her a company which included Sybil Thorndike and Lewis Casson, Basil Dean and Esmé Percy. Naturally the M.G. men and the Gaiety people were friends but friendship was not allowed to temper the critics' judgment. Not everyone believed this. 'The office much as usual,' wrote Montague to Dodd. 'All our dramatic critics except me are writing one act plays for Miss Horniman or Janet Achurch, which makes a generous public perceive that they and me alike are a bad, log-rolling lot.'[7]

Scott himself was not closely concerned with the theatre but he was brought in as arbitrator to settle the tiresome dispute which arose between Yeats and Lady Gregory on the one side and Miss Horniman on the other about the withdrawal of her subsidy from the Abbey Theatre. It was arranged by Mair, a comparatively junior member of the M.G. staff, who, as Frank Swinnerton said, 'had more fingers in more pies than anybody else' he ever knew.[8] Characteristic of all parties was the outcome. Scott found for the Abbey. Miss Horniman promptly sent a cheque for the amount awarded. Yeats and Lady Gregory refused to accept it unless Miss Horniman would say that she had been wrong. Miss Horniman would not. Scott was pleased that the dispute had brought him into contact with Yeats and Lady Gregory.[9]

The reading and reviewing of books is, of course, virtually independent of locality. *Guardian* reviewers lived all over England; there were *Guardian* readers in London and most university towns. But the work, of course, centred in Manchester. When a member of the staff wrote a book Scott himself usually chose the reviewer. He must have selected Bennett to review Montague's book; he certainly arranged with him to review Monkhouse's *Dying Fires* in 1912 and negotiated the price. Bennett pointed out that he had agreed not to write for London papers at less than £26. 5. o per column but added: 'The *Manchester Guardian* is not a London paper, nor should I ever regard my contributions to it as a purely commercial transaction. I shall be perfectly content with whatever payment you think proper to make.' He got eight guineas for a column and a quarter. He worked from proof sheets and then, in a compliment which must have pleased the author, he asked Scott for the review copy 'as the book is one I should like to keep.'* Monkhouse never allowed himself to be called

---

* Bennett–Scott 21 October and 4 November 1912. Bennett kept his manuscript of this review. James Agate bought it at the sale of Bennett's papers in 1936. Agate: 'Ego' 2, p. 397.

literary editor – 'there's no sich a person' he told Swinnerton, and Scott would have approved his modesty. But that in practice is what he was, writing the weekly Saturday column on Books and Bookmen and arranging for the reviews which then appeared every day.

Manchester remained as much the home of good music as it ever had been. During those two December weeks of 1909 there had, of course, been two Hallé concerts conducted by Richter; Paderewski had played at the Free Trade Hall and there had been a Wagner promenade concert. All of those had been the subject of notices by Sammy Langford – nobody ever thought of him as anything else – who had succeeded Ernest Newman as the principal music critic.

'In appearance Langford was a mixture of Socrates' Mussorgsky (as depicted by Repin) and Brahms. He was small and podgy, with shaggy whiskers and a dome of forehead. He waddled over the earth, seldom lifting the soles of his boots from the ground . . . I never heard him make a commonplace remark . . . His writings on music, though the most penetrating and, as prose, the richest in the language, reveal only the half of him. Conversation expressed the full man, and he never ceased and never talked for effect, or at you; he merely gave audibility to his thoughts during a polite recognition that you were present . . . C. P. Scott could never understand Langford's complex of intellectual austerity and physical unbuttonedness. He belonged to no class – upper, middle or lower. He was philosopher and poet and peasant. He despised the moral and didactic point of view from which Scott and his school tended to look at life and learning. He said of Montague's writings that they would be all the better for a "spade or two of dung out of my garden".'*

The *Guardian*'s second music critic was Montague's friend, Ferruccio Bonavia, born an Austrian subject in Trieste and for ten years a violinist in the Hallé under Richter. His Italian accent remained with him throughout his life, but 'he wrote English with style and sensibility, and when it came to string playing of any kind he was a critic without a peer.'[10] Like Langford, Bonavia had had a full fortnight – several friendly notices of the Carl Rosa Opera company and then a very special occasion: the first performance by the Brodsky Quartet of Grieg's posthumous quartet in its entirety with a newly discovered movement. Grieg had stayed with Brodsky on his last visit to Manchester. He had promised to write a work for his quartet. This composition was almost certainly the result.

Painting, too, got its share of Montague's attention and of the

---

* Neville Cardus: *Autobiography*, pp. 205–207. Langford's father was a market-gardener – hence the reference to 'peasant.' Sidebotham had been responsible for Langford's appointment.

Guardian's. Francis Dodd had left Manchester in 1904, but he kept up a lively correspondence with Montague. Laurence Scott had been the *Guardian*'s art critic in Manchester (as Laurence Housman was in London) until his final illness. Then there came a short time when Montague had to take it on himself. His sense of artistic integrity was outraged and he begged Dodd to find him a successor. In 1908 B. D. Taylor was appointed – a man whose taste welcomed the new men but whose style reassured the old: 'You'll have seen Taylor's pamphlet? Ain't he a good one at it? He has the momentous staid manner that tells a town councillor's heart that this is no wildcat artist but a Reliable Man.'[11]

One incident in 'A Hind Let Loose' is directly traceable to Montague's reluctant art criticism. Compare these accounts which Montague gave of his visit to an art exhibition in the Free Trade Hall:

'Mr Tom Mostyn's large painting of "Christ in the Wilderness" . . . is exhibited very skilfully with a view to a certain kind of effect. It is seen in an almost darkened room with a strong and unevenly distributed artificial light cast obliquely downward on the face of the Christ . . . so that the picture comes at you as if out of a proscenium . . . He stands like an actor under the limelight.' (14 March 1907) (unsigned)

'I have been damning my immortal soul several times by going *vice* LPS and "criticising" pictures . . . It's an awful business. I've gone into a dark room with a T. Mostyn "Christ" in it, where a commissionaire was kept just inside the door to look at my hat till I took it off. I said in print I didn't like seeing pictures in a cellar, and some one wrote to say I'd scoffed at what them as knew considered as one of the sacredest of sacred pictures.' (to Francis Dodd 31 March 1907)

'I am getting bowed with shame at going about impersonating LPS and doing the patter, sometimes about things that are no more to me than shut books (done up in brown paper too) like T. Mostyn's justly God-forsaken "Christ".' (to Francis Dodd 13 June 1907)

'You know what a hit was made last spring by Mr Tom May's Biblical triptych, "Gadarene Demoniacs", shown in New Bond Street in a room devotionally dark, with the dealer's men breaking its message to you in awed whispers and staring if you kept your hat on – a piece reverent in its perception of Gospel truth, yet fully abreast, of the van of serious study of insanity . . . Well, that picture . . . was actually conceived in the Wigwam smoking room, in talk with Hutton, a young alienist much liked in the club, and Curtin, then manager of the Theatre Royal, who had long thought that more might be done with limelight to give a haunting quality to the painted eye.' ('A Hind Let Loose' 1910 (pp. 160, 161)

But, if Montague was unhappy about writing publicly on pictures, he was delighted to support in leaders those who tried to give Manchester better pictures to look at and better conditions in which to see them. At the time of Arnold Bennett's visit all was going well and the Art Gallery Committee could be praised instead of slated. 'If they stick to it,' he wrote to Dodd,[12] 'they'll really get Manchester to be a place that counts in its dealings with pics as it is in music and (at last) the theatre, and not a mere second-rate Liverpool.'

4

'It was the late Samuel Pope, QC, – if one's facts are right – who exclaimed before the Parliamentary Committee on the Ship Canal: "Millions! In Manchester they talk as if millions were threepenny bits".' So Monkhouse once started a theatre notice.[13] Monkhouse, and Agate for that matter, would have spent that Friday morning on 'Change before they joined Arnold Bennett at the Midland. Agate was a partner in a cotton manufacturing business, earning his £2,000 or £3,000 a year, but working also, for enjoyment but very little money, on as many evenings a week as the *Guardian* would send him to the theatre. Monkhouse had been a yarn agent before he joined the *Guardian* staff at the end of 1902 at a salary of £500. He was to divide his time between commercial and literary work. This was not the beginning of his association with the paper. For half a dozen years he had been reviewing books and writing articles on golf. Now his cotton reports supported his literary work just as the cotton trade made it possible (though not inevitable) for Manchester to be a great artistic centre.

Edwardian Manchester was still in an economic sense something like a city state. One might almost claim that to its merchants Great Britain was only 'a geographical expression.' Their ties with New Orleans or Alexandria; with Constantinople, Hamburg, Calcutta and Shanghai were in many respects closer than with Birmingham or Newcastle. Just as Lombard Street was the financial centre of the world, so a still growing proportion of mankind were clothed from the stately warehouses that lined Portland Street in Manchester. The cotton trade was something in which London had virtually no part except as the principal purchaser for the home trade – ordinary people were just beginning to buy their clothes ready-made and retailers were changing over from piece-goods to made-up shirts. But in 1913 the home trade took only an eighth of Lancashire's production. Seven-eighths went overseas. No other industry approached cotton's export record. Its value was two and a half times as great as that of the nearest rival – iron and steel. Textiles as a whole accounted for half the United Kingdom's exports; cotton for a third. No wonder that the Manchester Consular Association comprised representatives of thirty-six different states.

The raw cotton business was centred in Liverpool. Its reporting was a specialised matter for which the *Guardian* relied on a Liverpool agency. But the rest of the innumerable bargains which marked the cotton trade were struck just across the road from the *Guardian* in the Royal Exchange whose great hall, nearly 4,500 square yards in area, was already by 1906 too small for the men who came to do business there. Decision-making in the cotton trade was widely distributed. There were nearly 9,000 members of the Exchange; all of them – it is safe to assume – readers of the *Guardian*. Between them they must have been getting on for a fifth of its readers. Each needed the other. City reporters, alone among journalists, provide news on which men buy and sell, make a profit or incur a loss. Markets of all kinds are sounding boards for rumours; city journalism at its best is a corrective to the wilder flights of fancy. The *Guardian*'s commercial staff had to be judicious and incorruptible. Monkhouse was – and he had a gentle, allusive humour which sometimes escaped into his market reports. One wonders what some of his business readers made of his comment on men who believed that cotton prices would go still higher: 'Like Ajax, who went so far as to defy the lightning, they are prepared to defy genial sunshine, cooling showers and good growing weather generally.'[14]

Day by day he made his way from group to group, moving freely among the bleachers, carriers, chemical manufacturers, mill furnishers, accountants, tanners, timber merchants, stockbrokers and even wine merchants who frequented the Exchange in addition to the spinners, manufacturers, exporters and their agents for whom it primarily existed. As Monkhouse recorded dealings, he observed life. He noticed that 'as it was often clearly to the advantage of the buyer that he should receive immediate delivery, he did not object to water (in the cloth) in moderation, but art soon began to run a little ahead of nature.' But the fault was self-correcting: too much water made it difficult to obtain a repeat order. In an industry where there were so many independent sources of supply, sharp practice tended to defeat itself. The Manchester trade indeed depended largely on the observance of certain honourable conventions. 'These points of honour', Monkhouse noticed, 'may seem to be arbitrarily selected, but they are an important part of the scheme . . . large transactions are commonly completed without witnesses, though before the contract or memorandum of sale passes the fluctuations of the market may have made the bargain, to one side or the other,

In its first few years the *Guardian* very occasionally printed maps, plans or even news pictures like this one in 1823. Illustrated advertisements were common—several are reproduced at the ends of chapters

The block of this drawing of construction work on the Manchester Ship Canal was made by Allen, Scott and Co., the firm's London subsidiary whose fortunes are described in Chapter 17. They regularly did this work for the paper

Illustrations were not used again until the 1880s. Drawings were then introduced to accompany feature articles such as this on the turning of Thirlmere into a reservoir to increase Manchester's water supply. The artist was Alfred Rimmer, a regular contributor

Hedley Fitton was a regular contributor of illustrations to the *Guardian* at this time. Trafford Park has now long been a major industrial estate

Gladstone's Golden Wedding was celebrated by a full length feature, including a poem of twenty-seven verses as well as these pictures of young Mr. Gladstone, Hawarden Castle and church

THE QUEEN, PRINCE ALBERT, AND PET DOGS.

Cecil Aldin's drawing formed part of the ambitious supplement
provided on Queen Victoria's death

In 1906 Jack B. Yeats contributed a series of drawings of Manchester
life. This one shows the old Slip Inn

a very bad one.' The bargain would be observed, but perhaps none too quickly. A manufacturer might find it difficult when prices rose to obtain prompt delivery of yarn he had bought at a low rate since, as Monkhouse put it, 'some spinners have a curious, indefensible preference for delivering their high-priced orders.' But he recorded, too, how rare litigation was: 'Lancashire traders generally have only vague notions of the bearing of law upon their transactions, and a wholesome dread of the experience that would lead to better knowledge.' This salt, which gave distinction to Monkhouse's trade notes in the *Guardian*, overflowed into the account of the cotton trade which he wrote for the eleventh edition of the 'Encyclopedia Britannica' on which this description is largely based.

5

Monkhouse ranked from the start as a senior member of the staff – he was 44 when he joined – but he worked under Montague in literary and dramatic matters and under a much younger man, T. M. Young, in commercial. Young, who had been dealing with Ship Canal matters for several years, reviewing books and writing a fair number of short leaders, became commercial editor at the same time that Monkhouse undertook the cotton reports. Nobody, of course, could fill such a position as Young now occupied without a very thorough grounding in cotton. That had been provided in 1902 by a prolonged tour in the United States to study its rapidly growing cotton manufacturing industry. What he saw he turned into twenty-five descriptive and analytical articles – the longest series the M.G. ever devoted to a single topic. They were republished as a book which became a standard work of reference and was translated into French, Spanish and Japanese. Only three years before this Young had written to Scott: 'I need not say, then, how shocked and disappointed I am to receive from you a letter which, in spite of its kindly and considerate wording, I can only construe as a notice of discharge. Is that its meaning?'[15] It was not. It only meant that Scott saw no reason to pay Young more. In 1898 'Mr Young's salary of £175 per annum covers everything.'[16] But in 1903 it was raised to £450. By 1906 it was £800. It never went any higher.

Right at the beginning of his commercial editorship Young had had a difficult issue to tackle, one which illustrates almost as clearly as the workings of the cotton trade the overwhelming desire of Lancashire business men to run their own affairs without outside interference. In the early winter of 1903 ugly stories had begun to circulate about a take-over of one of Manchester's two leading banks. London bankers were becoming more and more interested in country business where at that time bigger profits could apparently be earned. In mid-November the *Guardian* carried a story which, without actually naming the banks, warned the business community of danger. A strong hint was given which, one would have thought, would have identified the London bank, but one of the London financial papers in a follow-up a few days later guessed wrong. The other papers were silent. A fortnight later the *Guardian* itself named Lloyd's and the District. By that time the arrangements had virtually been concluded. Only staff pension rights remained to be settled. No other paper seemed really interested although the merger was to be between the largest London and the largest country bank. The new Lloyd's would have been by far the largest joint stock bank. The *Courier* carried a short story on the same day as the *Guardian*, but it was so thin that it was almost certainly lifted from an early edition of the M.G. After that it let the matter drop. The *Daily Dispatch* had nothing until next day when it ran a full-length story that was hardly even a re-write of the *Guardian's*, so closely did it follow it with some unacknowledged borrowings from Young's earlier November story. It was forty-eight hours before the *Times* carried the news and then only in a very cursory form.

But the *Guardian's* correspondence columns showed how excited Manchester business men had been. For a week the paper carried a series of letters which were remarkable in two ways. They were overwhelmingly opposed to the amalgamation; and all but one of the writers used pseudonyms. These two things were probably connected. The most common argument used by the writers was the fear that interloping bankers from London and Birmingham, who knew nothing of the particular customs of Manchester trade, would be let into the secrets of their business and decide what credit they could be given. The intensity of the reaction was entirely spontaneous. It did not represent a campaign by the *Guardian*. Indeed Young made it clear that on balance he thought there was a good deal to be said for the amalgamation. But he had rightly judged that this was a news story which ought to be given although the two banks were anxious to keep it secret until every detail was settled. Manchester itself did the rest. On 9 December the two boards decided that they might be faced with something like a depositors' strike if they persisted. They withdrew their proposals. The District Bank directors were left to find what consolation they could in the fact that, as the *Guardian* leader put it, 'it must be recognised that the objections to them are of a kind that are entirely complimentary to the bank and its management.'[17]

6

Two points remain to make. The first is that in the history of the M.G. as a newspaper, rather than as a business, the new era begins in 1902 after the Boer War, and not in 1907 after what we have called the War of the Taylor Succession. That was a private struggle behind closed doors which, had it gone otherwise, would have altered the whole course of the paper. But because Scott retained control the paper was able to go straight forward on the lines laid down in 1902.

The second point is the nature of the world which the *Guardian* served. One comes back again to the comparison with a city state – small enough to be a community; rich enough to afford more than a bare living; yet old enough to have outgrown the frontier brashness; with citizens sensitive enough to value and to create more things than material goods. The M.G. was able to be the paper it was because at this time Manchester was such a city. Its music, its theatres, its scholarship were supported financially by its world-wide trade and personally by many of its traders. It was this that distinguished Manchester from the purely industrial towns. This was why there could be a *Manchester Guardian*, but could not conceivably have been a Five Towns Guardian. Walter Greenwood tells a story about a young man he met at a Hallé concert during the 1914 war:

'Look' – he pulled the *Manchester Guardian* from his pocket: it was open at the theatre advertisements page. 'Quay St, Peter St, Oxford St.' The Free Trade Hall is in the centre of these contiguous streets. He began to tap the advertisement columns. 'Eight theatres in three streets, all number one dates – all on your door-step. I don't think you realise just what you've got.' The fire died from his eyes and was replaced by a hungry suppliance. 'What I'd give to live here. Once a month, that's the only time I can get away. Have to leave 15 minutes before the concert's end to catch the last train.'[18]

When in his autobiography James Agate looked back twenty years to the days before 1914, he remembered how 'in my time Manchester was a city of liberal culture, awareness and gaiety, which it owed almost entirely to the large infusion of German-Jewish brains and taste.'[19] This was, of course, to ignore the M.G. which had virtually no such infusion; but, though exaggerated, the point had substance. The German colony was large, influential, public-spirited and cultured. In 1911 about 450 people attended the dinner given in Manchester on the Kaiser's birthday; one of the several regular series of Manchester concerts was that given at the Schiller Anstalt, the German club of which Engels had once been president; the conductor of the Hallé was the great Richter, whose last season this was. He had been 'the premier musician in Vienna, the intimate friend and helper of Wagner, the instrument of his final triumph.'[20]

But the *Guardian* could not hope to be the paper of the majority of Manchester people; certainly not of the men with 'the colourless cheeks, the lightless eyes' who stirred Montague to compassion and to rage. Reporters, like Haslam Mills, would not fall into such an error. Leader-writers might. Perhaps the editor had. One of the firm's lino-type mechanics may have conveyed a needed warning when he wrote privately to C. P. Scott:

'I have gathered the impression that our editorial staff believe the *M. G.* to have much influence with the electors of Manchester. This, I think, is an illusion. Among cultured and earnest people, on the one hand, and mere commercial men on the other, the *M. G.* is undoubtedly a great force. But the majority of the electors belong to the working class, and working men do not read the *M. G.* Outside the little news-shops in working class districts one rarely – very rarely indeed – sees a *M. G.* contents bill, and a survey of the printed matter in the windows of these shops is productive of profound depression. The *Daily Mail* and *Dispatch* are bought largely by working men; the *Daily News and Leader* has a select body of Nonconformists and temperance subscribers, but not nearly so numerous as those of the other two papers. Probably it would surprise you to know how large a proportion of working people make the *Umpire* and other hardly less salacious publications their sole Sunday reading.'[21]

A sad commentary provoked by the eleven leaders in thirteen days devoted to the 1912 by-election in North-West Manchester which the Liberals had just lost.

CHAPTER TWENTY-FOUR

London

I

NINETEEN-TWELVE was a significant year for the *Manchester Guardian*. On New Year's Day James Bone became its London editor, though Scott true to his doctrine of the editor one and indivisible persisted in calling him London manager, a plain misnomer. At the time, however, it was not Bone's appointment but G. W. E. Russell's silver wedding to the paper (for so he described it) which received public attention. He told his own story in one of his usual Saturday articles.[1] His first contribution to the paper, a description of the Jubilee garden party at Buckingham Palace, was reprinted by its side and there was an attractive portrait sketch by Frank Emmanuel to complete the page. Better still, Bone gave up two of his precious London Letter paragraphs, the highest honour a friend could desire, to the intimate and fruitful 'collaboration', to use Russell's word, between this gifted and eccentric radical member of one of the great Whig families and the *Guardian*'s full-time London staff.

From 1887 to 1892 Russell had been a frequent contributor to the London Letter: virtually every social event of any importance was chronicled by him and many paragraphs recounted High Church doings in an informed and friendly way hardly to be expected from a nonconformist paper. Then for nearly ten years Russell had no connection with the London Letter. During Gladstone's last government, when Russell was in office, he gave up journalism altogether. He soon came back as the regular writer of Saturday articles, but even the offer of a salary failed to tempt him to take up the Letter in 1896. 'You asked if I would like a salary for writing a London Letter,' he reminded Scott, – 'and I said yes and so I should. As dear Mat Arnold used to say – "We all like money".' But the money offered cannot have been enough to overcome Russell's dislike of the 'incredible amount of suspicion and ill-will which hangs about London Letters and their writers.'[2]

It was not until Atkins, back from the Boer War, took charge of the London office that Russell resumed his 'collaboration' in producing paragraphs for the London Letter. Then there were no more comments from Taylor to Scott like these: 'tends to get deadly dull'; 'ponderous and long-winded'; 'the last thing it deals with is London, the principal topics being China, Central Africa and other outlandish places.'[3] Atkins gave the Letter shape, balance, form. There were probably not many more good paragraphs than there had been in the past – certainly not more than during Russell's earlier spell as a contributor – but they became more visible when the mediocre and the dull were weeded out. The whole thing became worth reading, and consequently got read. The introduction of crossheads at Sidebotham's suggestion ensured that the important news which the Letter sometimes contained would not be virtually overlooked as happened to the Chinese Government's announcement that it would prohibit the export of coolies to the Rand.

Russell and Atkins understood and liked each other. They established agreeable working arrangements. Atkins gave much of the credit for the success of the Letter to Russell: 'he gets us stuff that no other paper gets: it is unique,' he told Scott.[4] Sometimes Russell wrote his own paragraphs, more frequently he 'inspired' them by giving what he called 'tips' to Atkins and his two successors in the London editorship. These suggestions might be made in a pencilled note which must have needed skill to decipher since the sub-editors in Manchester had given up the attempt to deal with the copy for his Saturday articles and left the composing room to do their highly creditable best with it. There were also regular Tuesday morning sessions in Wilton Street during which 'one London editor of the *Manchester Guardian* after another learned with joy that half an hour in Mr Russell's company will make the waste places in Burke's Peerage to blossom like the rose, or will unlock in talk the doors of almost every notable old house in England.'

'If one had to make a guess at the thing he enjoys most,' continued this paragraph about the contributor of so many, 'one would be inclined to say that it was putting on the sonorous tones and the full-mouthed positiveness of his old chief, Mr Gladstone.* Then the listener discovers that Mr Russell has the great gift of being able to see the foibles and the ridiculous sides of people whom he likes and admires greatly . . . The debt of these successive editors to him would be wholly beyond payment were it not that each of them, fortunately, ministers in some degree to his sense of humour. Some of them have been known to experience the mildly uncomfortable feeling that however much they have filled their journalistic pockets from his treasure-house he has filled a pocket or two of his own from what he might call their innocence.'

* Russell had been Gladstone's private secretary as well as a junior minister in 1892. He was sadly disappointed not to be asked to write his official biography.

Russell had no doubt which of the three possible writers was responsible for this affectionate tribute. The example of 'innocence' quoted in the paragraph gave him the clue. He told Scott: 'You will readily guess who it was that, surveying my books with a lofty smile, said – "This isn't much of a library to look at; but somehow it always seems to contain what one wants." '5 Atkins had left the *Guardian* early in 1905 to become Paris correspondent of *The Standard* but was now back in London as assistant editor of *The Spectator*. He was fresh from writing Russell's obituary for the M.G. which fortunately was not needed until 1919.

Atkins's London editorship was important not only for its collaboration with Russell, but also for the partnership between his two juniors, Gretton and Bone, who were to be the next two London editors. They were close friends – Taylor compared them to Damon and Pythias – but markedly dissimilar in temperament. R. H. Gretton, an Oxford graduate, had been a sub-editor on *The Star*, the radical London evening paper, before Atkins enlisted him for the *Guardian*. Gretton's temperament – his strengths and weaknesses – appear clearly in letters from Russell to Scott:

'My collaboration with your two "Young Lions" has interested me much. If you care for my judgment on them, here it is. *Both are intelligent fellows*. G. has more interest in intellectual pursuits, and more knowledge. *A*. has more talent for writing, and a natural literary style. I liken him in this respect to E. Grey,* who has hardly ever opened a book, but uses by instinct the choicest diction. G. is far more diligent and plodding than *A*. but is much more timid; and has not *A*.'s remarkable quickness at the "up-take." I mean that, if I give *A*. a "tip", I am much more certain that he will make good use of it, and beat out the gold very thin. This I take to be a high journalistic gift. On the other hand, if I wanted a thing hunted up, or proved from records, I should entrust the task to G.' (11 September 1904)

'*A*. often has brilliant ideas, but so wonderfully little knowledge – except about athletics.' (16 September 1904)

'What I have said will sufficiently indicate my desire to continue in the service of the *M.G*. – to do a little more for it, and to get a little more. This is plain speaking, more in the style of Jack Atkins than of Gretton or Meredith.' (7 March 1911)

After this it is difficult to see why in 1905 Scott chose Gretton to succeed Atkins. It may be that Scott was in one of the moods in which he was 'off' Russell. 'Why do you and I always fall out after a little amity?' Russell once sadly enquired. 'We begin nobly – as in 1887 – and soon the little rift appears, and gradually it widens to a rupture. This is

* Grey is, of course, Sir Edward Grey, Foreign Secretary from 1906.

tragic. Must it be?'[6] Scott, however, may merely have underestimated the tenacity which news-getting demands. His own career had made him more familiar with leader-writers and sub-editors than with reporters – his London editor needed to be something of all three.

Bone was thirty when he joined the paper in 1902. No one who ever worked with him had the smallest doubt that he was great as a journalist and as a man – a gay man whose zest for life never evaporated throughout his ninety years; a man of great friendliness and curiosity, boundless energy, staunch loyalty, as clannish about the paper he served as about his own remarkable family, whose doings the M.G. never forgot to mention. Two of his brothers, Muirhead the artist and David the Commodore of the Anchor Line, were knighted and James himself was made a Companion of Honour. Their father worked on the *North British Daily Mail* in Glasgow and so did James after a spell as a clerk in a shipping office. He stayed with that paper till it stopped publication in 1901. For a year he worked as a free lance, writing descriptive reports for the *Glasgow Herald*, shipping notes for the *Daily Record* and art criticism for the *Evening Times*. He had also written the text for *The Spirit of Glasgow*, the first of four books in which he collaborated with his brother Muirhead. Bone was already a journalist with a keen sense of news, skill in securing it and – which is more surprising in a man who left school at 14 – an artistry in presenting it in words which never lacked feeling and rarely fell into sentimentality. In one of the letters which passed before his appointment he remarked that he had not yet had experience in sub-editing. But he soon proved himself a master at making good copy brilliant and humdrum work readable. Many young men discovered by watching the apparently simple changes that Bone made in their copy how much better it might have been – and saw how to make it so next time.

It was clear by 1901 that James Bone had a great career in journalism in front of him. The only doubt was where it would take him. Fortunately for the *Guardian* A. N. Monkhouse happened to visit Glasgow, happened to stay with the parents of his friend Francis Dodd, the painter, and happened at their house to meet Bone. They liked each other and Monkhouse spoke to Montague about Bone. Scott took a long time to make up his mind but eventually gave Bone a trial in 1902 and a definite appointment in 1903. He was then offered either £250 a year subject to three months' notice or £280 a year for a two-year contract. Scott already knew he had got a man he must keep.

Something of the freshness of Bone's early days in Fleet Street when he was learning to love every corner and aspect of London can be found in this glimpse of an industry that was young when he was young.

'It seems to me that the denizens of Flicker Alley (as they call this passage) will have something characteristic that marks them off from ordinary men. Possibly the endless film they look at affects the eye nerves or teaches the mind to think of the eye as something to switch off and on – a glance, a calculation, another look, a "glad eye", another calculation and so on. They flicker. Their conversation flickers too, mainly in rapid Yankee slang jerked at a hard pace, a well-known figure there creating the illusion best with an inimitable stutter. They rush about all over Europe and America, these quick, handy, cheery people . . . You see no old men. The "father of the trade" looks about forty. With them antiquity was last week, and posterity is coming round to look at their films to-morrow.' (*M.G.* 17 November 1911)

Or, watch Bone desperately trying to come to terms with the Post-Impressionists and recording a reluctant failure:

'*Cézanne's* portrait of a man with a blue tie certainly has a strange hint of life and character, but the face is twisted in its planes like a face in a concave mirror . . . In the landscapes each seems to express one hard and surly fact, the twist of a road, the yellowness of a house, and so on, but in none does the idea seem to dictate a noble and beautiful manner of statement.'

Van Gogh's 'sunflowers have the rankness of sunflowers, and his iris the hardness and strength of form and colour of a certain iris. They are painted with a fierce, arid skill which seems to rob the iris of its floweriness. In one way the identity of the iris is heightened, and the admirers of Van Gogh prove their point. But the flower, all the same, has been wronged.'

Gauguin 'presents a more attractive problem. He has lived in Africa and Tahiti. The wildness of his subject-matter makes a harmony with his methods which the others miss. He has a strong decorative quality, and many of his pictures flaunt like flags.'

'In the end one was unable to line up with the minority of the elect and testify to the existence of masters among the Post-Impressionists . . . This opinion will be shared by the great majority who hate any new form of art, good or bad; but that cannot be helped. As the old Scots judge Lord Young said when he heard that at last a decision of his had been upheld by the House of Lords, "It may be right for a' that".' (*M.G.* 11 November 1910)

Montague had surer insight. He saw the exhibition a week or so later and told Francis Dodd: 'From what James Bone and Yeats and others had said, I expected more buffooneries, but I thought some of the P.I.s had a good lot to say for themselves.' He was delighted to find that Dodd agreed with him for 'the door has to be everlastingly kept open by violence for anyone to enter in when he has got a really new thing to say in any art.'[7]

Bone, for all his devotion to the *Manchester Guardian*, was in many ways conservative. He was certainly a romantic. He had a romantic affection not only for the M.G. but for all newspaper work. There is something of Kipling's MacAndrew in this review of an old journalist's indifferent autobiography:

'Of the strangeness, the uncanniness of newspaper life, of the unknown voice speaking through print in the night and the tens of thousands listening to it in the morning, of the harlequin mingling of public and private in a life with its own laws and lights, throbbing and moving, and occasionally sparking, like a cinematograph screen – of the effect, in short, of newspaper life on the imagination Mr Catling gives us only one glimpse.' (7 February 1911)

As Bone looked back in approaching old age to the world which he first reported it was to the beginnings rather than the ending of things that he turned. His eye had been fixed on the present – as any journalist's must be – but it was the present that presaged the future even more than the present that recalled the past which delighted him. Talking to Fleet Street friends who entertained him in 1946 he said:

'I was the first British pressman not to fly in a plane. I mean a pressman in an aeroplane that didn't rise. It was Cody's plane at Aldershot. My colleague George Mair, dead many years ago, a gifted soul, made the first flight by a pressman in a plane in England. The *M.G.* was one of the few papers then that took Cody seriously. Cody offered a second trip and I went down. The machine was a primitive biplane. Cody had long hair and a cowboy hat. I remember his patter and how he tested the air with a handkerchief. He got in and I got in, sitting on open seats, and his assistants set the engine going – but rise she wouldn't although they all tried for an hour or so. Perhaps it was as well. The plane was tied together with what looked like gingerbeer wire . . . He was a plucky pioneer was Cody.'

2

Nineteen-eleven was the last year of Gretton's London editorship. It was also a year when much happened in London. The two were connected. Two critical incidents, memorable in themselves, will serve to illustrate the problems confronting the *Guardian*'s London editor and the resources on which he could draw.

The year started with the siege of Sidney Street. 'Peter the Painter' and a fellow criminal had been traced to a house in this East End slum. They were armed. The police failed to catch them unawares; shooting began and fighting continued from 7 a.m. until 1.30 p.m. Two platoons of Scots Guards were brought into action and a detachment of Horse Artillery was sent for though the guns did not fire. For the last hour and a half the fighting was watched by the Home Secretary. 'At the further end of the block from us,' one M.G. reporter wrote, 'a group of officers sheltered. Now and then we saw someone in a tall hat and heavy coat come daringly out and take a look at the house. This was Mr Winston Churchill. "He's a cool one," some one said. But this was nothing to the risk he ran a little later on in the day. He seemed to be commanding all the operations.' Churchill's personal intervention caused criticism at the time but ensured the passage of an essentially trivial episode into English historical folk-lore. With its own unpersonalised sense of news the *Guardian* gave Churchill only those two or three lines towards the end of the story below a modest side-head: 'The Home Secretary.' The siege itself got lavish treatment. The whole of the main news page was given over to it; so were the first two London Letter paragraphs and the first leading article, while on the back page there was a long interview with the general Secretary of the International Anarchists' Association who spoke of Russian *agents provocateurs* and not unnaturally denied the strong rumour that Peter the Painter was an Anarchist.

The sub-editors in Manchester made fair use of the agency messages but the bulk of the very heavy reporting fell to the *Guardian*'s own men. It is impossible now to distinguish individual contributions but Gretton could probably only call on three others in addition to himself – a thin number to cover so startling a news story as well as the rest of the day's events. Bone we have already met. He had been joined on the London staff by Francis Perrot – another 14-year-old school leaver – who had moved to London from Manchester late in 1909. He owed his job on the M.G. to J. L. Paton, the famous head master, who had met him on a climbing holiday with the Co-operative Holidays Association, and wrote of him as 'the only man I know, not a classic, who reads Chapman's Homer with real pleasure.' That was in 1901 when Perrot was just 22, on the *Sheffield Independent*, earning £95 a year.[8] During his Manchester years a fellow *Guardian* reporter, an Edinburgh man who shared a Derbyshire cottage with him, recalled how he 'radiated confidence, egotism, literature, art, music, scorn, high spirits, friendship, impatience, blunt candour . . . He had no tolerance for absence of mind in the other and starker sense, and as his standard was high his presence was bracing and wholesome – like the East Wind of Edinburgh. But you see only strong men in Edinburgh because the weaklings have been killed off; and some good men did not survive the Perrot climate.' Perrot, Bone said, 'was a great reporter. He was, of course, other things too – a critic, a political commentator, a poet. But in these fields he was one of many; as a reporter of what he saw and heard he was of the very few.' 'How excellent, how increasingly excellent is Perrot,' C.P.S. once said to another *Guardian* man.[9]

The Sidney Street battle took place in the parliamentary recess so that Gretton probably also had available James Drysdale, the elder brother of the man who had shared a cottage with Perrot. He too had been a *Guardian* reporter in Manchester in his time, had gone to the *Liverpool Daily Post* in London and had refused repeated attempts to lure him back to Manchester as chief reporter. Like Perrot he knew that his inclination and his strength lay with descriptive and not administrative work. Since 1902 he had been responsible for the parliamentary sketch which was one of the highlights of each day's *Guardian* during the session. Between them these four men – with help from the Hon R. H. Drummond on 'automatic pistols' (he still contributed regular articles to the M.G. on shooting, fishing and hunting) – provided a succession of vivid stories: 'The sightseers fingered with pleasure the bullet-holes in the window of a shop opposite the alley; it was something definite,' Perrot noticed. They kept it up unflaggingly for several days while the public interest lasted. But somehow one feels that Churchill's intervention was worth more attention than the *Guardian* gave it. Other papers thought so too.

3

On Thursday 4 May Lloyd George introduced his National Insurance bill, 'the draft, imperfect it may be in details but singularly bold and drastic in outline, of the greatest measure in our time both of public health and of social justice.' That was how the *Guardian* leader described it on the Friday morning. It might have added that here at last was the means of giving effect to many reforms which the paper had long advocated. But for the M.G. this great occasion was something of an unhappy non-event. There was, of course, nothing wrong in its presentation of the scene in parliament itself or of the summary of the bill's provisions. Later, in the fierce controversies that arose over recalcitrant doctors and duchesses who would not stick stamps, the *Guardian* was at the top of its form in argument, explanation and suggestions for finding a way round the difficulties. But immediately before and immediately after that Thursday the *Guardian* did much less well than it should. On the Wednesday, A. P. Nicholson* the exceedingly skilful Lobby correspondent of the *Times* had written an advance story, clearly based on a sight of the bill or at least on an authoritative briefing on its contents, in which he hinted, for instance, that there might eventually be a tie-up between insurance provision and the non-contributory Old Age Pensions which had already been introduced.

* Nicholson was a Unionist Free-trader.

The *Guardian* had nothing of this; nor, in fact, did it give any preliminary information about one of the most important occasions of the session. Saturday was worse. In the *Morning Leader* Harold Spender (who had once briefly been a *Guardian* man) published a long interview with Lloyd George about how his scheme would work. Whether ordinary readers noticed that other papers had stories which the M.G. missed is doubtful, but the professionals – politicians and journalists – certainly observed that the M.G. was left outside on the very kind of issue on which it might have been expected to be on the inside. What Scott thought is not directly known, but may be inferred from a surviving letter from Gretton written on the following Tuesday:

'I am in a great difficulty when you look, as you naturally do, for advance information of such things as the Insurance Bill. I am afraid that I cannot get any right of entrance, so to speak, to Ministers, unless you would be good enough some time when you are in town to take me to see them. I *have* tried to see Lloyd George on several occasions, and tried, of course, when you first wrote of the Insurance Bill. But whenever I have asked for an appointment I have received no reply *at all*, and to go without an appointment is hopeless; one only sees a junior secretary (possibly indeed only the hall-porter which happened to me once) and gets nothing. Spender and Wilson* are both personally known to George, but his view of the *M.G.*, which is also the view of other Ministers, is that if we want any information you will come and see them yourself. The Chief Whip said this to me once when I spoke to him on some matter.'

This was not the kind of letter to placate Scott. One is reminded of Russell's adjective 'timid', a fatal defect in a political correspondent. Moreover, as Scott knew, Gretton had virtually cut himself off from Russell and thus lost one of the paper's valuable 'special sources.' It happened in this way. In 1910 Gretton had married a woman whose first marriage had been dissolved. Russell disapproved of all divorce, but took the view that he could continue collaboration with Gretton if he had not himself been a party in the case. He asked Scott, who very properly referred him to Gretton; he asked his friend the President of the Divorce Division; he was so far satisfied that he agreed to continue collaboration. But Gretton not unnaturally, but to the paper's loss, appears to have let the connection drop as two letters from Russell to Scott show:

'This Session seems to promise opportunities in which I can be useful . . . but G has only been to see me twice (I think) since his return.' (18 February 1911)

* Wilson was the parliamentary correspondent of the *Daily News*.

'R. H. G. never came here very regularly, now he does not come at all. I suppose he feels – poor fellow – that he has done a foolish thing, and is shy about it.' (7 March 1911)

In June Scott decided, to use his habitual words, that 'Gretton had to go.' Bone quixotically intervened, without Gretton's knowledge, to ask for a reprieve:

'. . . 'Everyone has remarked about his description of the lying-in-state of King Edward and of the Abbey ceremony (the Coronation) last week . . . But working under him every day for many years one saw how he did everything better – in sub-editing and fudging blue-books and in planning and organising for a big event, and in his grip over the telegraphic as well as the office staff . . . Five years ago the *Daily Mail* people attempted to get him to join their staff, but he, of course, refused at once.

Now when Gretton has been awakened to the supreme importance of exclusive news and sees things (as I have reason to believe he does) with rather different eyes I would venture to suggest, if the matter were left open to the end of the year for reconsideration, things would not take their present course.'[10]

But Scott had made up his mind. No doubt he reflected that what Gretton had not acquired in six years in charge of the London office was hardly likely to be mastered in six months. Bone was put in charge of everything but the Lobby work, for which G. H. Mair, a man superbly sure of himself, was brought up from Manchester because, as Scott reminded Bone, 'You have no great political knowledge or interest.'[11] It was true. When Bone retired from the London editorship, he remarked that he had only been in the House of Commons three or four times in his life. The regular Tuesday sessions with Russell were resumed and kept up by Mair until the outbreak of the war. The London office settled down to thirty-three years of remarkably fruitful comradeship under James Bone.

4

There were things in London which Scott and nobody else could do. He could do them partly because of his long comradeship with Ministers when they had sat together in the House in lonely isolation, a minority within a minority; and partly because he was editor and owner of the *Manchester Guardian*, the only surviving 'quality' radical daily and the dominant newspaper in the North-west. From 1910 onwards Scott kept interview notes, usually written in the train on his way back to Manchester, of many of his discussions with Ministers. They talked freely to him off the record, often in sulphurous terms about one another; and in turn Scott argued with them. If they did not always read the M.G.'s leading articles (they usually did), they heard them over breakfast, a meal which could on occasion stretch from nine to noon.

Many of these discussions turned on foreign politics, the subject of the next chapter. Many were principally concerned with the suffrage question. This was one of the very few subjects on which Scott himself wrote the leaders – perhaps because in Taylor's day it was forbidden ground; perhaps because it had been one of his wife's great interests. What happened between 26 October and 24 November, 1911 will serve to illustrate Scott's activities in and about Whitehall and to show what value the paper got from them.

During the morning of 26 October Scott was at 12 Downing Street, talking to the Chief Whip, when Lloyd George came in and carried him off to lunch. Lloyd George was toying with a new way out of the mess into which the suffrage question had got the Cabinet and, more especially, himself. The Government were preparing a manhood suffrage bill. He was thinking of proposing, and backing, an 'adulthood' amendment which would give women votes on the same terms as men. If this was carried, well and good. Asquith, although opposed to votes to women, had promised to give full facilities for the decision of the House of Commons to be carried out. This promise had been made when the Conciliation Bill was introduced, a bi-party proposal, which would have given votes to some women but on a qualification that in Lloyd George's view meant that most of them would be Tories. For this reason, he had been a bitter opponent of the bill. Now he was prepared to drop his opposition to it, but only if his own 'adulthood' amendment was tried first. Would Scott take soundings of the various suffrage groups and report back?

For the next few days Scott was busily engaged on this. H. N. Brailsford, the secretary of the Conciliation Committee, was an old *Guardian* man; Mrs H. M. Swanwick, the editor of *Common Cause*, the non-militants' journal, was a *Guardian* reviewer and an intimate friend of Scott's – one of the very few of his correspondents with whom he was on Christian name terms; Mrs Pankhurst, the militant leader, was an old Manchester friend whom he had visited in prison, but she was in the United States. Evelyn Sharp, H. W. Nevinson's wife, was another militant. She was one of the most regular contributors of stories to the 'Back Page.'

No one was better placed than Scott to act as a go-between. He could be, and was, discretion itself. In fact from the paper's point of view he was too discreet. By 8 November it was known that the reform bill would be drafted in such a way as to allow the 'adulthood' amendment. This, of course, was duly reported in the *Guardian*, but not a word appeared about Lloyd George's offer to accept the Conciliation Bill as an ultimate fall-back. It was another ten days before Scott used this information incidentally at the tail end of a leader. He was writing about the Prime Minister's explicit promise to a deputation from the Suffrage societies of government help if they could win a majority on a free vote:

'Yet this is the moment ... chosen by one great suffrage society ... to employ every engine of a misguided fanaticism in order to wreck, if it be in their power, the fair prospects of their own cause. It would be a subject for pity if it were not for anger, and perhaps it is a subject for both ... Moreover the Conciliation Bill would have met with the uncompromising hostility of Mr Lloyd George – a very formidable obstacle – whereas it is known that if the wider amendments had failed he would no longer feel justified in offering the same opposition to the narrower one.' (18 November 1911)

That day half the London Letter was given up to the deputation in addition to a report occupying three-quarters of a page. But there was no mention of Lloyd George's change of front except in the leader.

Four days later active militancy revived. Two hundred and twenty-three arrests were made in the course of an attempted raid on the House of Commons. The atmosphere of those days of 'violence' – violence only in a strangely diluted form – recalls more clearly the 'non-violent' student demonstrations of our times than anything in between. Compared with much of the industrial unrest of those pre-war years, the most militant Suffragettes were moderates. So were the police. So was the *Guardian*.

On 21 November it used a team of three reporters – Perrot, whose copy was unsigned; G. H. Mair, who was allowed to initial his; and H. W. Nevinson, whose name was printed above his column. Perrot and Mair moved about among the crowd outside Caxton Hall, the militants' headquarters, and in Whitehall. Nevinson was first stationed inside the hall and then watched the police cordon outside open and shut to let the demonstrators through in groups of ten. All three agreed that the police 'used the greatest forbearance.' All agreed that the crowd of onlookers were sympathetic whereas in 1910 they had been hostile. Nevinson (Shrewsbury and Christ Church) attributed this to the wisdom of the militants in holding the demonstration at night 'when decent working people could be present' whereas 'on Black Friday it was held in the afternoon, and the crowd consisted of the idle and respectable classes.' Perrot noticed that the crowd in Parliament Square was so thick that the demonstrators had to make great efforts to squirm their way through to get at the police. Mair reported how a young girl near him told the crowd, 'I suppose you know why we are doing this, you men. All the laws in the past have been men's laws'; and how 'everybody listened and nobody jeered' so that he thought 'the London crowd is beginning to do what crowds so rarely do. It is beginning to understand and respect an idea.' But then 'a mounted police orderly came galloping down Whitehall. His hurry explained itself at the Strand where policemen were gathering, and many windows in a bank, a post office and a café yawned jaggedly on the passers-by.' Only one demonstrator ever got near the doors of the House – a woman whom Perrot saw calmly ride through the lines on a tricycle. The last word may go to the friendly policeman with whom Perrot started his story: 'There was a policeman outside Caxton Hall last night who told us that just a year ago he was at Tonypandy.* "a year ago to the day," he said, "and a bright, cold night, like this, but there was blood flowing then. This job'll be child's play to it".'

Back in Manchester Scott wrote a leader with more sting than usual about the demonstrators who 'made their protest in riot and window-breaking against what they denounce as the insult of a proposal to enfranchise about seven millions of their sex. Their courage and devotion (was) worthy of a better cause and saner leadership.' The paper received a vast number of letters, a selection of which filled the correspondence columns for several weeks. To each letter Scott added an editorial foot-note or made comment in a leader. Thus, Emily Wilding Davison, who was killed in 1913 when she threw herself in front of the King's horse in the Derby, wrote 'No undeserving cause could succeed by violence. The success of violence is the test of the righteousness of the cause.' Scott's foot-note read: 'The really ludicrous position is that Mr Lloyd George is fighting to enfranchise seven million women and the militants are smashing unoffending people's windows and breaking up benevolent societies' meetings in a desperate effort to prevent him. To compare that with any great popular uprising of the past is too absurd a plea to require confutation.' Scott evidently enjoyed being the reasonable man, fighting a war for sanity on two fronts. It is just possible, however, that had he made something in the news columns of Lloyd George's concession over the Conciliation Bill before positions hardened, there might have been less cause to fight the militants. Was there a moment when a little less secret diplomacy and a little open publicity might have helped? Probably not if, as

* When troops were sent to South Wales to deal with a strike.

Brailsford told Scott early in the negotiations, 'Christabel Pankhurst envisaged the whole suffrage movement in its present phase as a gigantic duel between herself and L.G. whom she designed to destroy.'[12] But publicity would have done no harm – and some good to the *Guardian*. One sees what Gretton meant.

5

At the beginning of January 1914 Lloyd George went on a holiday trip to Algeria with T. P. O'Connor and Sir Charles Henry. O'Connor was the Nationalist MP for the Scotland Division of Liverpool, a journalist and an old friend of Scott's. Sir Charles Henry, another Liberal MP, was a very rich man and part-owner of the *Westminster Gazette*. Lloyd George was back in London on the 14th and Scott had breakfast with him next day. Most of their talk was about the Navy Estimates and the impending crisis; but, as Scott's interview note, written in the train that evening, records, 'Incidentally L.G. asked if we would be prepared to consider a proposal to start a London edition of the M.G.; he knew some person or persons who would put down £100,000. I said we were bound to consider the matter if a serious proposal were made and I could ask our business manager to come up with me next day.'[13]

Accordingly next day John Scott and his father went up to London and met Lloyd George and Sir Charles Henry at the Treasury towards the end of the afternoon. Scott's note written two days later, records what happened:

'Sir Charles Henry prepared to raise £250,000 for the purpose of establishing a penny morning London paper on lines of *M. G.* and as part of same organization. Desired also to bring in *Westminster Gazette* of which he is part proprietor. Prepared to buy *M. G.* and amalgamate it. Told him out of the question. Only arrangement we could consider was a London edition of the *M. G.* with all purely local matter and advertisements left out. He objected to name; suggested "London and Manchester" or "Manchester and London Guardian"* with small type for the London and Manchester alternatively in the two places. Said we would consider proposal but in any case must have complete control. All special matter to be common and cost shared by the two issues. Trial period to be five years. J. estimated £60,000 as cost of machinery and installation, thought £200,000 should suffice to cover loss on trial period. Further communication with more detailed scheme to be made

---

* The obvious solution of dropping the place name was not possible as long as the Church newspaper, *The Guardian*, existed. The M.G. used to print its list of church appointments with acknowledgment to *The Guardian* (London).

direct to Sir Charles Henry. Declined to take any responsibility for *Westminster* beyond printing it.'[14]

Scott took the proposal very seriously and although nothing came of it, negotiations were still going on at the end of the month. He consulted Hobhouse who had become a director of the Manchester Guardian, Ltd in 1912, the first non-family member of the board. On Sunday 25 January Scott had lunch with Lloyd George at Walton Heath and asked him about Henry. The reply he got was not altogether satisfactory, as he told Hobhouse:

'He is a very rich man, lazily interested in the America copper syndicate and along with Mond is one of the people responsible for the *Westminster* which he would have liked us to take over. He is a Jew and probably the other people acting with him in the matter would also, some of them, be Jews . . . Henry's politics, I gather, were rather of the *Westminster* type, but George says he is coming on and would give no trouble. Still one would prefer people of a different kidney. He might be all right about general politics, but what about Labour?'[15]

A London edition could not be financed by Scott himself. Outside capital would have to be brought in. Hobhouse had already approached Sir John Brunner, one of the most advanced Radical MPs. 'I see no objection at all,' Scott told Hobhouse in the same letter, 'to your going on with the informal negotiations with Brunner, but on the contrary considerable advantage. If the Henry scheme goes forward I should greatly prefer to have a portion of the capital held by a tried Liberal, thoroughly in sympathy with the *Guardian's* politics. Indeed I only wish it could all be in such hands.' It seems strange that with such reservations in his mind Scott continued the negotiation, but he sent Hobhouse a copy of a letter he had just written apparently making definite proposals. There the matter seems to have ended. It was just as well. Before the suggested five year trial was up, Lloyd George had held the notorious 'coupon election.' Sir Charles Henry duly received his.

The idea was not quite forgotten. In 1916 Lloyd George and Churchill raised it again with Scott at breakfast:

'They discussed the old theme of bringing (the M.G.) out in London. "What would it cost?" asked Ll.G. I said £20,000 a year. "That's not much," was the the rejoinder. All the same it is.' Scott added a footnote: 'The local name must be preserved – would be English analogue of great German provincial papers, such as the *Frankfurter Zeitung*.'[16]

CHAPTER TWENTY-FIVE

Ubique

I

In the early days of the Russo-Japanese War Bernard Pares, a 37-year-old scholar who was to become Britain's foremost Russian authority, was planning one of those regular visits to Russia which he had started in 1898. He wanted to write in an English liberal newspaper about what he saw. He got friends to approach Scott who agreed to take a series of articles. They were good. Scott wanted more. Pares's reply was not very helpful. He would have liked to do the work himself, but on Trafalgar Day, Russian warships on their way to the Far East fired on English trawlers fishing on the Dogger Bank. They had mistaken them for Japanese torpedo boats. War with Russia seemed possible. Pares decided to stay in England. Moreover the account he sent of the English journalists in St Petersburg was not encouraging. Pares had given the *Guardian* a good and unsolicited start in interpreting the Russian situation, but no more. Years later, during the Second World War, he was to repeat this service, but for the present Scott was left without a suitable correspondent.

It was probably by the same post that brought this disappointing letter from Pares that Scott heard from an unknown young journalist living in Paris. He had first written a month before but without result. This second approach came at a fortunate moment. Scott could not have found a better man, though in fact the 'finding' was not by his seeking. Nor, in 1904, could Harold Williams have found a more suitable employer. He became the *Guardian's* first regular resident staff correspondent in a foreign capital.[1]

Harold Williams was then in his thirties and had been working on the *Times* for a little over a year, covering such news as could be got from the Russian liberal exiles who had made their first headquarters in Stuttgart. In 1904 the exiles had moved on to Paris and Williams had gone with them, but the *Times* had not renewed his contract. It was not surprising. After a fortnight's trial in Berlin in 1901 he had confessed, 'I enjoyed the work so far as it was merely journalism, but I felt a sort of oppression at the thought of being attached in any way to the *Times*. I respect the ability with which the *Times* is managed, the high standard of its English, and the completeness of its organisation, but really I have little sympathy with the *Times* conception of life.'[2] He was much nearer to the M.G. and so were the sources on which he knew he could rely: 'a correspondent for a Liberal English journal would meet in Russian Liberal circles with a welcome that would be accorded to the correspondent of no Conservative paper, however eminent.'[3] For the next three and a half years Williams represented the *Guardian* in St Petersburg at first on a small salary of £300 a year, and then from the summer of 1906 on space. This change was made at his own request – and no doubt to Scott's pleasure – on the ground that Russia was no longer so prominently in the news. In 1908 he joined the *Morning Post*. His wife made this comment on the change: 'As the correspondent of the *Manchester Guardian* in Russia, he did not merely describe the struggle for liberation, he was inspired by it. The *Morning Post* expected more formal telegrams, and wanted information chiefly about Russian foreign policy.'[4]

Williams was so singular a man – and in his singularity so typical a *Guardian* man – that he requires description. He was the son of a Methodist minister in New Zealand and himself followed his father's career for a short time. But above all he was a passionate linguist – he knew Latin, Greek, Hebrew, French, German, Maori and Italian by the time he was 11. While still at school he compiled a grammar of one native language and published a vocabulary for another. He took his doctorate at Munich with a thesis, 'Grammatische Skizze der Ilocano Sprache mit Berücksichtigung ihrer Beziehungen zu den anderen Sprachen der Malayo – Polynesichen Familie.' He read grammars for relaxation as others read detective stories.

Williams was also a passionate Tolstoyan. He had come to Europe determined to seek out his spiritual master. It was one of the first expeditions he allowed himself from St Petersburg. Tolstoy gave him an interview which filled two and a half columns in the *Guardian* of 9 February 1905. Williams came to it straight from the scenes of Bloody Sunday and from an interview in the Putilov works with Father Gapon whom he already half suspected of being an *agent provocateur*. With his mind stored full of his first encounter with violence, Williams was a little disappointed in his old pacifist hero. Tolstoy, unbelievably, seemed somehow irrelevant. 'It is in the stormy life of the cities that the battle of Russian freedom is now being fought out, and not, as one would like to believe, in the happy, peaceful haven of Yasnaia Poliana.'

Williams covered, usually as an eye-witness, all the great events of 1905 and 1906 which took place in St Petersburg or Moscow. He was present when the police arrested 300 members of the first Petersburg Soviet. He attended that clandestine conference of journalists whose meeting place was changed from day to day to deceive the police – at the close of each session members were given sealed envelopes containing the place for the next meeting. He and Dillon of the *Daily Telegraph* were the only two outsiders admitted to the second congress of Zemstvos (county councils) which forced the Tsar to agree to an elected Duma. They worked closely together and, when Dillon was ill, Williams stood in for him. A letter from Williams to Scott illustrates the pitfalls that await an inexperienced foreign correspondent in his dealings with his own and other papers:

'A few days afterwards Dr Dillon told me he had received a telegram asking him to return to London at once on important business. He asked me to take over his *Daily Telegraph* work again . . . though he said that he would probably be away only for a few days he threw out hints that he might possibly be detained by sickness for a very long time, perhaps even months but to these hints I attached no importance. It was only after the wireless telegrams from the *Kaiser Wilhelm* began to appear in the *Telegraph* that I began to suspect that Dr Dillon had gone to America, and it was only when the long despatches, obviously in his style, appeared from New Hampshire that I became finally convinced that he was with the Russian envoys (to the conference that ended the Russo-Japanese war) . . . I should be very much obliged if you could spare time to write me your opinion on the affair . . . I would gladly do Dr Dillon's work for six months if he continued ill for so long but I strongly object to the *Daily Telegraph*'s exploiting me and through me the *Guardian*.'[5]

Unfortunately Scott's reply does not survive.

Williams was regular in his attendance at the first Duma in which the Cadets, his wife's party, had a great majority – the party which, it was said, had 'one good man and he was a woman.' Mrs Williams could not, as a woman, be elected to the Duma, but she belonged to the Cadets' parliamentary caucus so that the *Guardian* was fully informed of everything that happened. This was not the only way she helped her husband and his paper. When Williams was in Moscow and postal and telegraph connections with the capital were cut, he was able to persuade a friendly railway guard to take his message to St Petersburg and deliver it to his wife who sent it on to Manchester.

But Williams was not confined to St Petersburg and Moscow. In the spring of 1905 he was in Poland, a revolutionary country, he decided, but unlikely to start a rising though it would enthusiastically join in. He noted the contrast between Russian and Polish Jewry, and described his contacts with the Polish Socialists and their underground paper

Robotnik, 'the only illegal journal that has succeeded in maintaining its existence for ten years.' He went south to Kiev and on to Odessa to investigate the mutiny on the battleship *Potemkin*, northwards to Helsinki, and eastwards to Stettin for the visit by the British fleet. He came back to Manchester for consultations with Scott.

There were really no differences of approach to iron out. The new foreign correspondent and his paper saw things in the same light. Compare, for instance, the news and leader columns on the assassination of the Grand Duke Sergius. Williams telegraphed:

'With him falls the chief pillar of reaction in Russia. As Governor-General of Moscow his name was a by-word for oppression. He was a bitter anti-Semite. He expelled 20,000 Jews from Moscow. He harassed the professors and the students. He repressed all liberal initiative . . . The news of his death will cause even more relief to those whom he persecuted than did that of M Plevhe . . .'

The paper commented:

'The murder is the people's answer to the murder of their fellows in St Petersburg . . . after what has happened surprise or even deep indignation would be affectation. Whether any provocation is sufficient to justify such horrible reprisals is a very debatable moral question, but if assassinations could be justified on moral grounds it would be in the case of the Grand Duke Sergius.' (18 November 1905)

The foreign news editing of the *Guardian* at this time was in Herbert Sidebotham's hands and most of the foreign leader-writing. Some of the Russian leaders were, however, written by H. N. Brailsford, who, like Williams, was the son of a Methodist minister. His father had rather unkindly sent him to Glasgow University 'in a knickerbocker suit, a tam o' shanter and a patent collar of his own invention.' There he had been taught by Gilbert Murray, who presented him with a revolver when he went off to fight for the Greeks.[6] He was one of Brailsford's sponsors to the *Guardian*. Brailsford had represented the M.G. in Crete and Macedonia, and for a short time in Paris during one of the critical phases of the Dreyfus case. He was deeply committed to the Russian reformers and in 1905 rashly lent his passport to an exile who wanted to return to St Petersburg under an alias. His misuse of a British passport was discovered by the Russian police when the borrower was blown up by what was thought to be his own bomb. Brailsford was prosecuted and while the case against him was *sub judice* he had to leave the paper. Scott, however, sympathised with him and lent him £100 to help with his defence. The court fined him but believed him when he said that he thought that the Russian was a peaceful reformer. Brailsford then returned to the *Guardian* and during the last quarter of 1905 wrote a third of the paper's long leaders. He left to go on the ill-fated *Tribune* but kept a close connection with Scott over women's suffrage and Balkan politics.

One corner of the Russian empire had a particular interest for the M.G. Finland was a country with a highly developed way of life. It was a country where, unlike England, women had the vote. But its executive government was entirely under Russian control and its liberal institutions existed only on sufferance. Once again fortune – and the fact that the *Guardian* was the sort of paper that radical young men wanted to write for – enabled Scott with no trouble to himself to secure a correspondent with initiative and distinction. Scott's old friend A. W. Ward was now Master of Peterhouse and always willing to put ambitious young Cambridge men in touch with Scott. In 1906 he did this for John Dover Wilson, who was going as Lektor in English to the University of Helsingfors (Helsinki). The immediate consequence was that the *Guardian* was the first paper to get the news that Father Gapon, who had turned police spy, had been secretly executed by his revolutionary comrades. Gapon had unwisely tried to enlist one of his associates as an informer.

'On Tuesday 10 April, therefore, he was invited by his former friend to a villa in the country. Here a conversation took place, overheard by four labourers of the Revolutionary party, who were concealed in the next room. Gapon was told that he would be exposed, and the fact that he was a spy would be published. "I should deny it," Gapon replied; "no one would be-lieve it." "I must call witnesses," said the other. Gapon laughed. "What witnesses can you call?" The door was flung open and the wretched man was confronted by four men whom he realised with terror were not only witnesses but judges and executioners as well. The men, infuriated to madness by what they had overheard, made short work of the business and soon the former Savonarola of Russia was dangling from the ceiling of the sitting-room of the villa, where he probably remains to this moment.' (23 April 1906)

This was Dover Wilson's first contribution to the *Guardian*. Three weeks later he gave further details and made a correction: 'I said that Gapon was hanged from the ceiling, but it now appears that he was fastened to a large hook in one of the walls. The point is not very material, but as my account has met with a fierce and absolutely un-warranted denial I should like to feel that every detail is absolutely exact.'* There surely speaks the future discoverer of 'What Happens in

---

*M.G. 14 May 1906. David Soskice (see p. 404), the *Tribune's* St. Petersburg correspondent, had denounced it as 'a cock and bull story of some irresponsible

Hamlet.' The Contributors' Ledger records the normal payment of two guineas for these two articles, which made about a column in all. An amendment shows 'ten guineas – per CPS.'

Whether this was done on Scott's initiative or whether Dover Wilson protested, as well he might, does not appear. The rate of pay rankled until the day of his death, but with the courtesy of an older generation he decided to make no comment on it in his autobiography.

For three years Dover Wilson continued to send the *Guardian* messages which were much more than the rehash of local papers which is all that many part-time correspondents provide. He made contact with members of all the Finnish parties. In a time of serious unrest, when students play a leading political role, the position of a Lektor, not quite a don nor quite a student, may give its holder unusual opportunities of finding out what is afoot. When the time came for Dover Wilson to return to England he handed over his work to his successor as Lektor, A. R. Reade, whom he commended to Scott as a man who had not only won the Newdigate but 'furthermore is a sound radical.' Thus right up to 1914 readers of the M.G. were constantly reminded how little freedom there was and how precariously it was held even in the most enlightened and emancipated part of the Russian empire: 'In the Russian Empire,' as Dover Wilson had put it, 'to-morrow is a ravenous beast that swallows down to-day and all its hard-won victories.'[7]

2

'Dear Mair (If an old Professor may presume to address so a Leader of public opinion) . . . For the *Guardian* I should be quite ready to send letters – signed – I am now so obnoxious to the Foreign Office that I cannot be worse, hence I may write openly. I must of course be free to say what I think . . .'[8] The writer was Mair's old professor at Aberdeen, Sir William Ramsay, 'the foremost authority of his day,' to quote the 'Dictionary of National Biography', 'on the topography, antiquities and history of Asia Minor.' The offer was too good to be missed. Ramsay came to Manchester to see Scott before setting off once more for Anatolia. He arranged to write regular articles – there were eighteen in 1910 and twelve in 1911 – and kept up a lively private correspondence with Scott which lasted until shortly before Scott's death. They shared many prejudices which they freely expressed to one another:

---

journalist.' Wilson's source had been Konni Zilliacus, the father of the Labour M.P. (J. Dover Wilson: 'Milestones on the Dover Road', Faber 1969, pp. 54-56)

'The more one is able to see of the working of our diplomacy the more crooked and less enlightened it seems . . . I don't believe that we get the best men for the diplomatic service, or that the mind of one in ten of them is open to what can be called Liberal foreign policy.' (Scott to Ramsay 24 April 1910)

'Two things are certain (1) the English Ambassador does not care a — what happens to any English enterprise, so long as he can get his shooting and his golf, and avoid being pestered wtih Turks or business. (2) The German Ambassador is watchful, active, always on the outlook to be hospitable to the Turks, and as full of experience and knowledge as the English one is ignorant of facts and men.' (Ramsay–Scott 6 May 1910)

'A friend of mine who was a contemporary with Grey at Winchester and Oxford told me long ago that Grey never opened a book of any kind all the time he was at Oxford, until he was sent down by Jowett, for making his rooms at Balliol a gambling hell . . . utter ignorance of the foreigner is not the best equipment for a Foreign Secretary.' (Ramsay-Scott 17 October 1925)

'Thanks for your interesting letter which throws a somewhat lurid light on Grey's early days. I saw a great deal of him in the time before the war and his mind seemed to me essentially wooden. Is that the meaning of a blockhead? He isn't that, but I could never trace a spark of imagination in him.' (Scott–Ramsay 19 October 1925)

The same forthrightness of style and sentiment marked Ramsay's work for the paper:

'It would be comic if it were not mournful to see a Government of free-thinkers stimulating fanaticism, making regulations to require the outward show of piety, and flogging Moslems who had not strictly observed the Ramazan fast.' (15 June 1911)

'Holy men and dignitaries of the faith put the tiniest pinch of salt into their *raki* or cognac; this transforms it into vinegar and makes it lawful. Ordinary Turks take it straight. I have already mentioned the new habit of staring at ladies.' (7 July 1911)

'Formerly, in cases of crime the gendarmes did not desire to arrest the criminal; they arrested innocent persons in order to be paid to let them go free again. That simple plan is no longer practised to any serious extent in these parts.' (7 July 1911)

Ramsay had already spent thirty years in archaeological work in Asia Minor. He knew officials of every rank – an archaeologist had to be a diplomat if he was to get his work done – and peasants, shop-keepers, Turks, Syrians, Greeks, and Armenians. He loved the 'fundamental soberness and self-control of the Turkish nature,' he hated the corruption and the tyranny of its government. Like Arthur Evans, he used the *Guardian* to put forward what was best for the peoples of the land in which he worked. He was not really concerned with Britain's interests, with the balances of alliances, with international politics, though he could hardly avoid discussing them. He was concerned with the welfare of the Turks and their subject peoples, with Turkey's internal politics: its 'foolish policy in Albania and insane policy in the Yemen.' Welfare demanded economic development which in turn involved foreign capital and concessions. Here, and here only, he came into conflict with Scott's policy in the M.G., and only on one issue.

Ramsay sent Scott an article which he refused because it approved of the Italian conquest of Tripoli as 'the sole hope for the present' though 'possibly the future may disclose some other hope.' 'Italy', he said in his covering letter to Scott, 'has in an ugly way taken a necessary step.' Ramsay like Gladstone had concluded that 'the Turk must go, bag and baggage, and be confined to the one country where they can constitute *nearly* a half of the population, i.e. Asia Minor' and that 'the only way . . . is war.' Scott was prepared to accept the 'bag and baggage' theory for the Christian populations provided it did not involve them in greater evils or risk their future independence. He feared Russian and Austrian imperialism. He thought the 'bag and baggage' case weaker for the Moslem subject races and had not realised, as Ramsay had, how deeply 'the Arabs hate and despise the Turk and have always done so.' Would not the Christian domination of Italy be worse? Scott asked.[9] Ramsay's article was given as a Letter to the Editor under a pseudonym.

3

Scott's notes of his interviews with the great are not a complete series.* They refer only to talks in or about London and to talks for the most part with Cabinet Ministers and not even to all of these – certainly as far as the years before 1914 are concerned. It is probably significant, however, that though they refer only incidentally to Turkey, references to Persia are frequent. Turkey was not going to involve us in a war, Persia might. Both Scott and the Liberal Government realised this. Cabinet Ministers were happy that the *Guardian* should say what it

* See Professor Trevor Wilson: *The Political Diaries of C. P. Scott* (Collins 1970). Except where indicated by the suffix MS, quotations from the interviews are from this edition.

thought to be right about Turkey. It was important that the *Guardian* should be persuaded to say what they thought to be right about Persia. And Scott returned the compliment. Somehow or other he must persuade the Government – and that meant Grey who was 'wooden though not a blockhead' – to do what a Liberal Government ought to do.

The editor who thought our diplomacy 'more crooked and less enlightened' the closer he looked at it was not likely to follow a Foreign Office brief without enquiry. The closer he enquired about Persia the less satisfied he became. His main informant was, characteristically, a university don – E. G. Browne, professor of Arabic at Cambridge and the greatest Persian scholar of his age. 'I do not know how Browne's reputation in Persia fares to-day,' J. B. Atkins wrote in 1947, 'but when I used to meet Persians who visited him at Cambridge they emulated in their regard for him, the reverence and affection with which the Greeks speak of Byron.' Ever since the Russo-Turkish War of 1877, when he was a boy of 15, Browne had been filled with a strong affection for Islam and with so deeply ingrained a suspicion of Russia that he used to complain that his Christian name Granville recalled Gladstone's foreign Secretary.[10] Browne was inspired by a passionate love for Persia. His contributions to the M.G. – sometimes as articles, sometimes as Letters to the Editor – were directed to exposing Russian intrigues and excesses not primarily because they were a danger to British interests, but because they were robbery and exploitation of the weak by the strong: 'Let no one imagine or pretend that the triumph . . . will be a victory of Christianity over Islam; it will be a victory of materialism over those who, even if they err, do for the most part truly believe in God and His justice and the transcendent importance of spiritual over material things.'[11] But, of course, British interests were involved. The Foreign Office clearly put the maintenance of the Triple Entente first and was unwilling to harass Russia; but the India Office was concerned not to offend Moslems; while Manchester's merchant community wanted freedom of trade. 'No matter from what point they start,' the *Guardian* remarked, 'all independent minds arrive at the same conclusions. Lord Curzon with his ripe experience, and Mr Dillon with his instinctive resentment of injustice, Professor Browne with the enthusiasm of learning and Manchester commercial houses with their plain blunt demand that our Foreign Office should not work against their interests even if it will do nothing to further them – all hold views about Persia that may differ in details, but in substance bear the closest resemblance.'* This was tantamount to denying independent minds to

* M.G. 24 November 1911. Curzon had just made a markedly pro-Persian

the Foreign Office and Sir Edward Grey, and this in fact was the
conclusion to which Scott had come.

4

One Thursday in July 1911 Scott went to breakfast with the Lord
Chancellor, his old friend Bob Reid, now Lord Loreburn. They spent
the whole morning in talk. The conversation turned to the danger of
war with Germany over Morocco. 'Do you know Asquith well?' asked
Loreburn. 'He is very friendly and ready to see me,' Scott replied. 'Then
I advise you to go and see him at once, but don't tell him I have said
anything to you.' 'Is it urgent or will next week do?' 'Better this week
than next; better to-day than to-morrow.' Scott did his best. Vaughan
Nash, Asquith's private secretary, an old *Guardian* contributor, tried
to get Scott an appointment, but it seemed that Asquith was hopelessly
committed until Tuesday. Scott went back to Manchester. No hint of
the gravity of the situation appeared in the *Guardian*, but Scott wrote
privately to Asquith. He wrote not as editor of the *Guardian* but 'as
officially responsible for the Liberal organisation in Manchester':

'That we should go to war in order to prevent Germany from acquiring a
naval station on the West African coast has, I believe, not occurred to most
Liberals as even a possibility, but what I have no doubt of is that if such a
thing were to happen it would pulverise the party. There is no feeling among
Liberals here against Germany – it is generally recognised that her policy of
the open-door in Morocco has been of material service to us – and that there
would be any deadly dangers to our interests in her acquiring a West African
port would be wholly disbelieved. I can imagine no more foolish war and
none more fatal alike to party and to national interests than one with
Germany on this matter . . .' (20 July 1911)

Next day, Friday, Lloyd George spoke at the bankers' dinner at
the Mansion House. The very first sentences of Perrot's sketch report
in the *Guardian* made the danger clear: 'People came away from the
Mansion House to-night . . . asking one another almost uneasily what
did it all mean. For, instead of the harmless non-party discourse on
national finance usual on these set occasions, they had heard a few
sentences read, not, as is the Chancellor's invariable habit, spoken,
and dealing not with finance at all, but with dangers that may threaten
international peace. The speech had all the air of a Cabinet pronounce-

---

speech to which the M.G. gave a column and a half report compared with 'a bare
and inadequate summary in the *Times*, 30 lines or so in the *Morning Post*, a bare and
empty reference in the *Standard*.' M.G. 17 November 1911.

ment.' The nearest approach to comment in the paper was provided by the few incidental remarks in Perrot's sketch:

'We all listened in tense silence to the statement that "Britain must at all hazards maintain her place and prestige among the Great Powers," a commonplace truly, but not uttered by a commonplace man in a commonplace office, and to the words "if . . . Britain be treated where her interests were vitally affected as if she were of no account in the Cabinet of nations, then I say emphatically that peace at such a price would be a humiliation intolerable to a great country like ours." The merchants cheered, but they had not time to consider what they were cheering exactly . . . But the phrase that set the guests talking most was this: "I feel sure nothing will happen between now and next year" . . . We all proceeded to find for ourselves a rich crop of significant meaning in the words "between now and next year".' (22 July 1911)

Why was there no leading article to accompany the report? It was a subject on which Scott felt strongly and on which Sidebotham was well prepared to write. He had indeed been doing so steadily and persuasively ever since the French sent troops to Fez, and Germany the 'Panther' to Agadir. The reason for the *Guardian*'s silence was that Asquith, Lloyd George and the Chief Whip had realised that Scott disagreed with what the Chancellor of the Exchequer was going to say, and that his disagreement would be damaging. Two messages reached Scott late on Friday afternoon through the London Office of the *Guardian*. The first, which invited Scott to breakfast with Lloyd George next day, said:

'The Chancellor of the Exchequer asks you not to write anything about the German business without seeing him. This is *urgently* requested as a personal matter . . . He and the Master of Elibank (the Chief Whip) feel it of the utmost importance that nothing should be written without you seeing him. The Chancellor asks me to send him a message to the bankers' dinner giving him your reply.'

The second was from Asquith:

'Further message from the Master of Elibank. Your letter has only just been received by the PM tho' it appears to have been sent yesterday. The PM is most anxious that you should not misapprehend the situation, and hopes very much that you will be able to come up to town when he would see you after your breakfast with the Chancellor.'

Scott accepted the invitation and returned to London. In the evening on his way back to Manchester he made notes of his day's work. He had seen Lloyd George, Churchill, the Chief Whip and the Prime

Minister – the first three together, the last alone. He had also had further talk with Lloyd George by himself:

'They were all civil and apologetic for bringing me up. Churchill said to Ll. G. that I ought to be kept constantly informed over all important matters. Ll. G. said that was just what he tried to do and rather reproached me for not coming to him sooner now. Ll. G. rather laid it on about the *M. G.* – it would smash party if we and Government were at odds. *M. G.* he had found much more considered in Germany than any other Liberal paper and if we let Government down in international controversy it would be inferred that they had no sufficient backing in the country . . .'

The Government's anxiety about the M.G. was understandable. The Cabinet, as Loreburn had put it to Scott on Thursday, was predominantly a Liberal League (i.e. a Liberal Imperialist) government. It could count on this issue on the support of the Conservative press, but its standing with its own papers, and with the radical voters who read them, was less certain. On Saturday morning only the *Daily Chronicle* had commented. Under Donald's editorship it was especially close to Lloyd George and could be relied on. 'A Word in Season' was the title of its leading article. The *Morning Leader* had given only a cursory report of the speech which indeed only just got on to the front page with much less space than the heat wave. The *Daily News* had no leading article and provided studiously non-committal 'heads' to its news story. By Monday, however, it was safely behind the Government – 'when Mr Lloyd George spoke on Friday he spoke for the nation.' The *Morning Leader* began to take a different and more pacific line. But these were all London newspapers. Though the *Daily News* had printed a northern edition in Manchester since 1909 its accent was still pure Cockney. The future of the Government at an election depended on the marginal seats in the North. The *Guardian* mattered.

On Monday the *Guardian* continued to take a line of its own. It thought that Lloyd George's wording had been loose and pointed out that he had made no attempt to define our 'vital interests' which, the M.G. agreed, had to be defended. 'We certainly cannot accept the account of them given in the English Opposition papers. The *Observer*, for example, writes, "We must stand with France at any cost against unreasonable demands, no matter of what nature"; and evidently quite sincerely regards that as Mr Lloyd George's meaning too. We should put the matter much lower, and so, we are inclined to think, would our French friends.'[12] There was a risk in encouraging France in a policy which would have more serious results for her than for us.

This article appeared on the day that Grey saw the German ambassador and 'received a communication . . . so stiff that the Fleet might be attacked at any moment.'[13] Scott received a message inviting him to breakfast with Grey the next day and travelled up to London for the third time in a week. He spent an hour and a half with Grey on Tuesday after which he saw the Chief Whip who was anxious to know what impression Grey had made on him. Scott's notes, written as usual in the train on his way home, show that Grey admitted that he had got little satisfaction from the German ambassador. But Grey had not mentioned that he had received a protest about Lloyd George's speech, and he had entirely failed to convey to Scott any idea of how serious the situation had become. Wednesday's leader in the *Guardian* consequently began: 'Mr Asquith, Sir E. Grey, and Mr Lloyd George yesterday conferred on Morocco, and afterwards Sir E. Grey spoke with the King for an hour; but there is no reason for thinking that our diplomatic troubles have taken a turn for the worse. On the contrary . . .'[14]

Scott had been misled, not converted. The *Guardian* continued to urge a policy which ran contrary to that of the dominant group in the Cabinet but which probably reflected the majority opinion among Liberal voters. The debate went on from year to year. Two of Sidebotham's leading articles in the summer of 1912 put the M.G. view succinctly. The first dealt with the navy, the second with the army in relation to foreign policy:

'Simultaneous supremacy both in the Channel and the Mediterranean . . . would involve not a two-power standard but a three, four or even five power standard . . . It is unthinkable. That brings us to the second of Lord Crewe's* alternatives, that . . . we should form "definite agreements" of naval assistance with France, and possibly also with Russia. For our part we dislike and fear it even more than the first course. There is no such thing as a limited naval agreement. It would mean an alliance involving France in the risk of reprisals on land, and us in the moral obligation to support her. The third alternative . . . is that we should be content with a reasonable superiority. Against this course too Lord Crewe found objections to urge, as that it violated Mahan's dictum that the sea was all one. We are not impressed . . . If it be really true that the sea is all one, then the object to aim at is supremacy at the decisive point . . . a wise strategy has always refused to allow the fleet to be tied down to the defence of fixed positions. If the defence of Malta kept a considerable part of the fleet away from the decisive action we should be throwing away the substance for the shadow, for if we are superior in the decisive action all the rest will be added . . .' (3 July 1912)

* Secretary of State for India and Leader of the House of Lords.

The second leader was about a debate in which Leo Amery had spoken prophetically of things to come. In his sketch Drysdale explained that, according to Amery 'in the event of a war between Germany and France we should have to be prepared to send a military force to the aid of France sufficient to ensure a victory, and not share in a defeat . . . One gathered that the arrangements – except, of course, those of our own War Office – are all cut and dried. Eighty thousand German troops are to march on France through Belgium, and "it is on our Expeditionary force that the brunt of the attack will fall." "Oh, oh," murmured a peace-lover, stirring uneasily in his back-bench solitude. "Yes," insisted the prophet with withering scorn, "and yet we have not been asked for a single additional battalion".'

Half of Sidebotham's intensely realistic mind agreed with Amery:

'Sir Edward Grey has subscribed to the doctrine of the balance of power in Europe; we agree with Mr Amery that we cannot uphold that doctrine except with an army of Continental size . . . The only answer to Mr Amery's arguments is to repudiate the premises from which he begins . . . Not only is England an island, but all the Englands across the seas are also islands in the sense that they are all defensible by sea. . . The whole fabric of Imperial defence has been based on this insular as opposed to continental strategy . . . The project of alliance with France would (make us a Continental power) in Europe . . . our army . . . would have to be such as to insure France against Germany by land. Tried by such a standard our expeditionary force is . . . a sham, and our military reforms a mockery . . . With our present military resources . . . we are worthless as a military ally. We may act as provocative agents, but we cannot save our friends from the consequences . . .' (5 July 1912)

Looking back in later years Gretton once described Scott as 'a Bashi-bazouk of a pacifist.'[15] It was a widely held view, but quite wide of the mark. Two things made the M.G.'s criticism of the Government's foreign policy telling. One was that it argued from a clearly thought out defence policy of its own; the other that it pointed out that the Government policy depended on our aligning ourself with the most reactionary power in Europe. When Scott looked at Europe, he saw Russia, and he did not like what he saw.

But a different result could be reached by looking first in a different direction. Montague looked first at France, which he regarded as the heart of the European Liberal tradition, and at Germany which he saw through the eyes of his friend, W. T. Arnold. Arnold had inherited the mid-Victorian admiration for German scholarship and culture, but towards the end of his life he had become increasingly aware of the new, dominant chauvinism. In his last illness he read intensively the writings of German historians and soldiers. 'Uncle Matt never thought of this,' he would say. 'What is going to happen if this dreadful stuff is believed?'[16]

Of course, Montague was aware of Russian pogroms and Scott of German militarism. Each detested both alike, but the difference in starting point made a difference in their balance of judgment. Scott objected to any Entente which could be interpreted as an 'exclusive friendship.' His whole attitude was summarised in a Sidebotham leader:

'The Entente with France we know and prize; the Convention with Russia we accept as a possibly prudent corrective of past Tory follies; but the Triple Entente has no meaning or reality for us, and we owe no manner of allegiance to it. The natural Liberal development of European politics is towards a closer understanding between England, France and Germany, the only Entente of which it could with certainty be predicted that it would make for the peace and liberal progress of the world.' (6 January 1914)

Montague disagreed with Scott's line and had long dropped out of foreign leader-writing. He did not return to it until after the outbreak of war; and then, as he told Atkins, 'I never had to keep such a hold on myself. I could not allow myself in a single sentence to seem to say "I told you so".'[17] Scott might have said the same. In his view the outbreak of war confirmed, rather than invalidated what the M.G. had long been saying. It was in these circumstances that Sidebotham enjoyed his period of greatest influence on the paper. He brought to foreign policy a cool analytical appraisal of what was involved in different varieties of power politics.

5

One thing that was certainly involved was the fate of the Liberal social programme. 'Peace, retrenchment and reform' could clearly be seen to belong together. Inflated naval estimates meant an end to the attack on poverty. On this issue Lloyd George and Scott were agreed. Early in 1911, before the Agadir crisis and while McKenna was still First Lord, Lloyd George had fought the whole Board of Admiralty and achieved a compromise. Scott had breakfast with him on the morning before the show-down when he was still hesitating whether, if necessary, to carry his opposition to the point of resignation. Next morning Scott saw him again. Lloyd George was jubilant. Hard bargaining had ended at 10 p.m. with a promise of reductions. 'I think your journey is worth £4 million to the nation – and a half,' Lloyd George told Scott. Scott jotted it down at once on the back of an envelope and endorsed it 'his own words,' and this he copied into the interview notes he wrote in the train.*

The jubilation was short-lived. Churchill succeeded McKenna at the Admiralty and the big navy men became bigger navy men. On New Year's Day, 1914 Lloyd George opened a campaign for a reduction of armaments in an interview which he gave to Robert Donald. The improved political relations with Germany, he said, gave naval disarmament its best chance for twenty years – and anyway Germany would have to turn her attention to her army in which she had not anything like a two-power standard. Lloyd George had made his claim. Would he follow it up?

When Scott went to breakfast at 11 Downing Street a fortnight later he found waiting for him on the table a letter from the Chief Whip. It read: 'Much will turn on the nature of the advice you give this morning. *Weigh your words.* I need not say more.' Four times in ten days Scott was to travel backwards and forwards between London and Manchester in an ultimately fruitless endeavour to persuade Lloyd George to have the courage of his convictions. Churchill was thought to be on the point of resigning and might well carry most of the Sea Lords with him. Scott thought his bluff should be called. He urged Lloyd George to make a stand 'even to the point of resignation,' and repeated in a letter written in the train a week later, 'I feel it in my bones that the fight has got to be now or never – and that in spite of adverse conditions. And it doesn't seem such a difficult fight. I can't quite imagine the PM dissolving because he won't accept the pre-Churchill standard of preparedness to which for years he was a party, and that is the key of the situation.' In the event, of course, neither Churchill nor Lloyd George resigned. Scott and his radical friends were powerless. By 6 February, after a talk with Reginald McKenna, Scott noted 'Ll.G. has given up the fight. He is now Churchill's man.'

In the five critical weeks after New Year's Day the M.G. devoted seven long leaders to the forthcoming naval estimates. But not once in the last three of those weeks, during the acute Cabinet crisis with which Scott himself was closely occupied, did the paper refer in any way to it except to deny with gentle irony the stories that filled the Conservative papers with comparative truth. Was this perhaps a case where comment was free but fact taboo?

* The complete interview is given in Trevor Wilson pp. 39-41. The envelope is reproduced facing p. 193.

CHAPTER TWENTY-SIX

Making War

I

AT the end of July 1914 Scott paid the last of three visits that year to Germany. He went on each occasion to consult an eye specialist who was finally able to reassure him that, though he had permanently lost the sight of his right eye, there was no tumour and no risk to his left eye. He was back in London on Monday the 27th and saw Lloyd George and Dillon. The crisis both in Ireland and in Europe was worse, but Lloyd George told him that he saw no risk of the Government becoming involved in a European war 'in the first instance.' The news from Ireland, therefore, seemed the more immediately alarming. In Dublin men had been killed when the police with almost unbelievable stupidity fired on Nationalist gun-runners – an ominous contrast to the way in which Unionist gun-runners had been allowed to land their cargoes without interference. Scott wrote a leader for Tuesday's paper which he called 'Black Sunday in Ireland.'

Back in Manchester Scott found troubles of his own. There was an uncomfortable letter from Montague. The letter has disappeared but in it he apparently offered Scott his resignation. Scott must have refused it in alarm for on the Friday Montague wrote again explaining that he had only been 'afraid that, out of regard to me and because of all the personal ties, it might seem possible for me to keep, in form, my old position on the paper after it had ceased to be a reality.' 'What still perplexed me when I wrote was the question whether I had already to face such a permanent change of conditions as would not allow me to go on.'[1] Scott replied the same day telling Montague that his loss would have been 'an irreparable calamity,' that his capacities were 'almost unique in journalism' and that the paper wanted 'every bit of them.' 'The matters in which we might in some degree have differed (why shouldn't we differ within limits?) are almost lost to sight in far greater and more pressing issues as to which we are wholly at one.'

What lay behind Montague's unease? There was, of course, the different way in which the two men looked at the European situation but this was not new. Sidebotham had long been the principal foreign leader-writer. What was relatively new was the return of L. T. Hob-house to the paper as a most favoured contributor. During his five years on the staff at the time of the Boer War there had been some slight friction between him and Montague.* Hobhouse had acted as an unofficial additional political correspondent during the constitutional crisis of 1910, and in 1912 he had become a director of the Manchester Guardian, Ltd – the first outside the family. There was no doubt that Scott trusted Hobhouse as he never trusted any other member of his staff: they liked each other and they approached problems in the same way. Scott was always happy to leave the control of policy to Hobhouse during holiday periods. Although Hobhouse never returned to the staff he became a steady contributor of leading articles – forty-seven, for instance, in 1913.

There was another threat, less immediate but quite as serious, to Montague's position. Ted Scott, the youngest of C.P.'s children, had joined the paper early in 1913 from the *Daily News*, where he (unlike that former *Guardian* man R. C. K. Ensor) had 'survived the massacre caused . . . by the coming amalgamation with the *Morning Leader*.'[2] Ted was now thirty, an economics graduate, whose main con-tribution at first was in this technical field which was certainly not Montague's. He took over much of the work done by T. M. Young who left the paper in the autumn to become Deputy Public Trustee – a nice tribute to the *Guardian*'s reputation for commercial integrity. But did Young see in Ted's coming his own eventual eclipse? Did Mon-tague? Before long he recognised that Ted had become his father's 'nearest assistant in a lot of things.'[3]

Even more important, however, was the change that had come over C.P.'s habits as editor. In the first seven months of 1914 he had written the principal leader forty-seven times compared with thirty-seven 'long leaders' in the whole of the previous three years, and with the earlier peak of twenty-three in 1910 during the constitutional crisis. Moreover most of Scott's writing was now about Ireland. In the pre-vious ten and a half months he had written about it seventy-one times. Ireland had been Montague's subject, and Montague, though he always wrote as an Englishman, never forgot that he was an Irishman. Nevin-son recorded how in France he 'never entered into a dispute, except once, when one of us insulted Ireland. Then indeed his blue eyes glared a deeper blue, and he seemed to tear the wretched victim to pieces and spread him on the floor.'[4] Scott was right to take over at the moment when serious horse-dealing over Ulster must begin. Striking a bargain over something that he cared desperately about was not in Montague's

* See p. 243-4.

nature. It was in Scott's. It was C.P. who was Dillon's intimate friend, who visited Ireland (how regularly we do not know), who talked Irish business with Geoffrey Dawson of the *Times* and J. L. Garvin of the then Tory *Observer*, who had contacts with the *Round Table* group and with moderate Ulster men.* If there were to be private discussions and kites to be flown in public it was right that the same man should do both. It was not that C.P. and his son-in-law, the editor and the principal leader-writer, differed as to ends. They probably disagreed over means. They certainly wrote very differently on delicate subjects. Montague was always forthright, caring above all for integrity. Scott was persuasive. It was persuasion that was now needed. But the cumulative effect of this and the other changes since 1912 was inevitably to leave Montague with a much smaller outlet for his strong political feelings. He was increasingly confined to literary and dramatic work. He felt cramped, and perhaps a little unwanted.

Whatever the reason, there was a dramatic change in the office arrangements as soon as the war started. C.P. virtually withdrew from leader-writing until the end of the year. He wrote a few not very important 'shorts' and only four Longs. Why did he give up? Perhaps he had only just realised how isolated Montague had felt and was anxious to prove that the paper still needed him. Perhaps he himself was tired out. He had had a year of great physical and nervous strain complicated by acute anxiety about his health. He needed four months' fallow. Looking back towards the end of this period he told Hobhouse: 'I think it stupid of me to have held off from writing so long. I don't quite know why I did it, but at first it seemed impossible to write honestly at all without raising questions which we had decided to leave alone, and then there was what seemed the impossibility of getting any harmony of feeling between what I could write and what Montague had written and was writing . . . You are the only person who quite understands about these things and cares.'[5]

During these early weeks of war Scott exchanged letters with old friends like Bryce, Loreburn and Morley in which they grieved over the way in which we had drifted, unnecessarily as they still thought, into a position in which there was no honourable escape from war. But they agreed, and Scott made it plain to E. D. Morel, who was busy

* 'It is possible that I may be in Dublin (which I like to visit occasionally). Scott-T. M. Healy 9 March 1910. Geoffrey Dawson was in 1910 still Geoffrey Robinson, but it is less confusing to use his later name. The Round Table group's most prominent member was Lionel Curtis. The most important Ulster contact was Alec Wilson of Harland and Wolff's, 'a Protestant of high local standing . . . rich, well educated, broad-minded, tolerant', as Roger Casement described him in a letter of recommendation to Scott in 1912.

setting up the Union of Democratic Control, that 'post-mortems' must be postponed. The proper task for the present was to fight the war vigorously and to plan the peace boldly. 'We've all got to help to put the thing through – you and I and all who hate the war quite as much as the rest. Success will bring great dangers but failure incomparably greater.'[6] Once Scott broke his public silence to support the *Morning Post*'s rather surprising plea that we should renounce any territorial ambitions. 'If we owe this to ourselves,' he wrote, 'we owe it also to those who are to-day our enemies, but who are not always to be our enemies, a great nation whose achievements in every sphere of human activity have made the world richer and whom the world can never spare.'[7]

It would indeed have been difficult to reconcile the feeling of this passage with Montague's fierce attack on Nietzsche in a leader on 'The Philosophy of Savagery.'

'The ideal life was to be a blaze of triumphant and arrogant egoism without fear and with complete indifference to reproach; it might mean crime, shame and disaster as most of us call them, but from these the right man was to draw wild and sombre delights akin to the thrills that a sensitive spectator obtains from the horrors of a grand storm or from the agonies of King Lear. In short, Nietzsche was a sentimentalist . . . It was the sentimentalism of the old lady in Smollett who spent her time writing poems that . . . (told) how she would like to
  "toss the sprawling infant on my spear
  What time the mother's cries salute mine ear."
The German campaign of barbarism in Belgium is simply Nietzsche's bookish dream of a conquering pitilessness put into action.' (13 October 1914)

It may well have been leaders like this which caused Emily Hobhouse to give up the *Guardian* because, thinking back to the Boer War, 'it is too painful to read it now by contrast and because any other does as well.' In this rather hysterical letter, dated Mars-mas Day and written from Cornwall, there is a passage which runs curiously close to a leader Scott had just written for Christmas. In her letter Emily Hobhouse wrote: 'To fight and kill you want hatred and violent passions – which are duly instilled by the speakers and press of the countries. But when the first effects of this have worn off and opposing soldiers have met in the field – and as prisoners of war – they begin to respect each other and find virtues in each other in contrast to the civilian war of hatred which goes on in the background.' Scott had written: 'There is no fury in the mind of the common soldier . . . What we see is, rather, a stoical endurance maintained by the spirit of military pride and duty and of patriotism, and coupled with this a great deal of good humour, and respect of and even a queer sense of comradeship with the soldier on the other side of the trenches who is enduring the same hardships and daring the same dangers with feelings and from motives largely similar to his own.'[8]

2

Twenty-third December, the day when Scott wrote this Christmas leader, was Montague's last night in the office. He had for some time been trying to get into the army. His first choice was the London 'Sportsmen's' battalion, but he was turned down because he was 47. Then he went to Newcastle where an Irish battalion was being raised. He failed again. Even as a young man his hair had been white. He guessed it went against him. 'We have all heard of men,' H. W. Nevinson later wrote, 'whose dark hair through fear has turned white in a single night, but Montague is the only man I know whose white hair in a single night turned dark through courage.'[9] It worked. Montague was accepted, and for four years he passed out of the *Guardian* story. He served in the ranks, rose to be a sergeant and was seriously wounded when acting as a bombing instructor. He spent the last part of the war as a press conducting officer escorting war correspondents and notables as near the front line as was safe, and often a little nearer.* He served, too, as a censor of other men's stories and at the end he confided to his diary: 'O that I might have had the chances the war correspondents have wasted of describing this war . . . a man might have written, piecemeal, a book that would be read for ever.'[10]

If only, one must add, the *Guardian* could have used him as its war correspondent – but that would not have satisfied Montague in 1914. C.P. reported to Hobhouse a conversation with his daughter. 'Madie says the vain quest (to join the army) is beginning to tell on him – I suggested that it was partly the sheer love of adventure which made him so keen – "No," she said, "he wants to kill a German!" Isn't it rum? I can easily imagine myself fighting, but to want to kill *any* German implies a wholesale reprobation which I could never rise to. But it seems to me to explain a lot – what a sifting thing is war.'[11] Mrs Montague may have been right or wrong in her reading of her husband's

* One of the visitors was H. G. Wells who thought Montague 'a radical bound, hide bound, in a conservative hide,' 'Galsworthyissimus.' 'We talked as we trudged along very happily of the technical merits of Laurence Sterne.' ('Experiment in Autobiography', pp. 682, 683.)

mind before he enlisted; she could not possibly have made the same judgment three years later. War is a sifting thing.

It was not only Montague who left. Before Easter Ted had gone. Montague wrote to Francis Dodd, 'I think Ted has had a miserable time over the weighing of obligations and counter-obligations, but it should feel like a lifted weight now.'[12] But not to his father, who shared the anxious worry of all parents until the bad day came three years later when the common load was suddenly increased by the news that Ted was missing. A month later Scott heard that he was a prisoner of war. 'We could hardly believe the good news at first,' he told Hobhouse, 'as it reached us in so unexpected a way by a rather uneducated note from a quite humble address in Moston. However we dashed off in a taxi and found it was all right. The thrifty Bosche (sic) has now adopted the plan of sending five addresses on a post-card to a sixth person to communicate with the other five.'[13]

There were other gaps in the staff. First to go was G. W. E. Russell who received on 6 August 'a remarkably curt note (one side of note-paper, I think) in which you terminated our engagement.' Russell, after twenty-seven years' work with the *Guardian*, was understandably hurt. Scott tried in later letters to soothe his feelings but with indifferent success: 'I can forgive, but I cannot help feeling' was Russell's final comment.[14] The sad episode illustrates one of Scott's weaknesses – his insensitivity to the feelings of others, an insensitivity which existed side by side with an acute sensitivity to the rights not only of Man but of men. No trouble was too great for him if he could prevent or correct an injustice.

The other great loss at the beginning of the war was G. H. Mair. By September he was employed on Government propaganda to neutrals and, though Scott asked him to continue as naval correspondent and to provide occasional political notes, it seems to have been one of those arrangements which just do not work. His place in the Lobby was taken by Harold Dore, a quizzical, lovable little man with unmanage-able pince-nez glasses and a consuming passion for English grammar. In Manchester R. C. Spencer, the chief reporter, was retired and went to cultivate his garden at Streatham from which he wrote regularly for the Country Diary throughout the war. Haslam Mills took his place.

The paper was smaller as a result of the war but that did not lighten the load on the staff. In fact the war greatly increased the burden of the editor and his colleagues on the Corridor. There was no decrease in the volume of leader-writing. One Long leader and five 'shorts' were still provided six nights a week. Scott and Hobhouse between them wrote nearly half the long leaders in 1916 and over half in 1918. In 1915 and 1917 they wrote well over a third. In 1918 Scott wrote nearly half himself and in the last two months well over half. On top of this must be put his visits to London to see Cabinet Ministers and other leading politicians. The surviving Interview Notes are not a full record of these journeyings but they account for seventy-one days in 1916 and 182 days in the four years.

Sidebotham's share in writing was even larger. There were frequent leading articles on military subjects from his pen. Twice a week, on Mondays and Fridays he wrote an appreciation of the military situation under the signature of 'A Student of War.' In addition he planned and edited the *Manchester Guardian History of the War* which appeared in fortnightly parts. He was by far the major contributor to it – his own share ran to half a million words in four years. This *History of the War* was not a simple republication of his Student of War articles, but a quite separate undertaking planned and written as a book. It was on the strength of Sidebotham's work that the M.G.'s reputation as a paper of sound military judgment was based. Albert Marshall, the economist, Sir George Otto Trevelyan, the historian, and Hilaire Belloc were among those who praised Sidebotham's work to Scott. So was Lloyd George who thought him 'much the best military critic' and told Hankey, the secretary of the War Cabinet, to cut out his articles.[15] Admiral Lord Fisher followed Sidebotham's work and praised it warmly when it agreed with his own views and was perhaps less rude than usual when it differed, e.g. 'I congratulate you on your article on Balfour and Coronel! QUITE ADMIRABLE!'; but 'It would be a great pleasure to see Mr Sidebotham *especially as he requires to be put right ! ! !* He don't at all understand the astounding facility of a Sea "coup de main"!!! We have no rivers to cross or mountains to climb!'[16] But this brings us into the middle of the oddest association which Scott ever formed.

3

'As I was going into Churchill's room Lord Fisher was coming out. Churchill introduced me and immediately he heard the name of the M.G. he became extremely cordial and begged me to come and see him which I promised to do.' So Scott wrote of their first chance meeting seven weeks before war broke out. Probably Scott did not at first realise what an undiscriminating lobbyist of the Press Fisher was and felt more flattered than he should. But, though he must soon have discovered this, the alliance continued and grew more intense. It was

Scott's only close acquaintance with a senior officer in either service and he had nothing against which to measure the vain, indiscreet and suspicious character of the man who bombarded him with letters and invitations. A regular officer might be a British Israelite[17] – it was a known risk – without his professional judgment being affected, but one would expect Scott to fight shy of the man who, hearing that Bonar Law thought he was mad, immediately sent Scott a copy of a letter in which he had written: 'NB. It's very interesting that the Saviour was voted "Mad" by his family, and they wanted to lock him up. For they said: "He is beside Himself!" But he never argued and went straight on and did the Biggest Thing on Earth.'[18] Whatever Scott may have thought of the good taste of such a passage, he was prepared to believe that Fisher might turn out to be the saviour of his country. He had, of course, no illusions about Fisher's political ineptness.

'He lives in an atmosphere of intrigue in which he does not appear to play a very skilful part. A very foolish thing he had done was to send for T. P. O'Connor in order to propound to him in all seriousness a wild idea which he had conceived of making Redmond Prime Minister, and a good deal of my time was taken up in seeing O'Connor and pressing on him by every means in my power the obligation of a deadly secrecy as to the revelations which Fisher had also unfortunately made to him as to the naval peril – a hard task for a born journalist.'[19]

But this too Scott was prepared to forgive the man who had twice been First Sea Lord, who had been responsible for the introduction of Dreadnoughts, and who undoubtedly had the drive, imagination and confidence which Scott felt was lacking in the direction of the war and especially of the anti-submarine campaign. He continued to insist on the paper taking his view when Sidebotham became sceptical: 'The leader was of course Sider's. I am sorry to say that under Hurd's influence he has become anti-Fisher (for no valid reason that I can discover) and the few words about Fisher were inserted by me.'[20]

Scott's association with Fisher has to be seen in the light of his general political activity during the war. He had never had a high regard for Asquith whereas, though he might and did disagree strongly on occasion with Lloyd George and Winston Churchill, he liked both. His disagreements with them before the war had been over matters which were irrelevant now that war had come. To be warlike – that was essentially his pre-war complaint – was now a virtue. He stood with them in the moves that brought about the first coalition under Asquith and the second under Lloyd George. He was active in helping Churchill to make his way back from his regiment in France, where he was not really needed, to the House of Commons where he was. He had very largely to take their military judgments, but on the home front – the muddled Derby scheme, the labour troubles in the engineering industry for instance – he could and did make his own enquiries. They were thorough. They were not encouraging. 'I have just finished a second reading of the *Guardian* special articles on the industrial troubles,' Walter Runciman wrote, 'and I presume to send you a strong word of commendation for publishing the articles at all and for selecting as your investigator a man who has powers of observation which take him well below as well as over the surface.'* Right to the end of the war Scott was conscious of the necessity of urging greater vigour on the Government. Lloyd George himself was all right – in this respect – but too many of the rest were not. Scott was outspoken in conversation and in letters, restrained and moderate in what he wrote in the *Guardian*. Yet he left no doubt that more energetic government was needed.

By energetic government the *Guardian* did not mean repressive government, though it recognised that the one increased the risk of the other, and it knew that in time of war repression is popular. It used ridicule, scorn and indignation to reduce these dangers. The action of the Penarth police in seizing Bishop Gore's 'Sermon on the Mount,' presumably as a dangerous pacifist tract, did not escape comment[21] and Artifex could always be relied on to act as an eminently readable spur to prick sluggish Christian consciences. Thus on atrocity stories he wrote: 'Christian people seem to have misinterpreted the apostolic assurance that "charity believeth all things" and to have forgotten the further assertion that "charity delighteth in the truth" . . . It seems to me that the present is an unrivalled opportunity, such as most of us have never had before, to practise a little Christianity. And it seems to me that most people are resolving, with an unanimity never seen before, not to avail themselves of it.'†

Never did the M.G. neglect the defence of ordinary men who found themselves in a minority. At the beginning of the war it defended aliens and people with German names who were persecuted in petty and sometimes in major ways by the mob. Later, though it had reluctantly accepted conscription as a necessity, it defended conscientious objectors when they were most unpopular and the tribunals most unfair. As

* Runciman-Scott 2 July 1917. The articles, by J. V. Radcliffe, a reporter who had been specialising in Labour matters for many years, appeared between 19 and 27 June.

† M.G. 3 December 1914. 'Artifex' was the pseudonym of Canon Peter Green, rector of the slum parish of St. Philip's Salford, probably the best known parish priest in the Church of England, who had succeeded 'Quartus' as the *Guardian's* Anglican contributor when Canon Hicks became Bishop of Lincoln.

Scott put it 'When the history of this war comes to be written perhaps the most discreditable thing about it, so far as this country is concerned, will be found in our treatment of the genuinely conscientious objectors.'[22] This was written after the armistice when conscientious objectors were still serving long sentences. Two months later he returned to the subject and remarked that 'even Mr Lloyd George, if he had five minutes to spare to consider what is really implied in his handling of men a little better than himself, might possibly relent in the extraordinary ardour with which he has gone about to "make their way hard," as he once expressed it.'[23] But the M.G. was not always nagging. When the Manchester Relief Fund agreed to assist the destitute wives and children of interned Germans and Austrians the *Guardian* remarked that 'A good rough working rule for wartime is that when the combatant sees a head he should hit it, and that when the non-combatant sees distress he should relieve it.'[24] It was on the whole the *Guardian's* own practice.

4

One evening in September 1914 Mrs Eckhard gave a party in Manchester for the supporters and staff of her School for Mothers, the voluntary fore-runner of official post-natal clinics. One of the doctors was Vera Weizmann and she brought her husband, Chaim, the future President of Israel, who in 1914 was in his own words 'not quite a professor' at Manchester. Among the guests was C. P. Scott. During the evening Weizmann was introduced to Scott, but did not catch his name. They fell into deep conversation which Scott ended by suggesting that they should continue it at the office the next day. 'What office?' Weizmann innocently asked. When he realised to whom he had been speaking he was worried lest he had said all the wrong things to the man whose acquaintance he had first vainly hoped to make soon after he first came to Manchester. But, though their meeting had been long delayed, and in the end came by chance, it happened just when time was ripening. Britain declared war on Turkey on 5 November. 'The war has made a good many things possible which were not possible before,' as Scott wrote to Weizmann. 'It is well there should be compensations.'[25]

In the first few weeks after Mrs Eckhard's party Scott and Weizmann had several long talks. Their nature, and their effect on Scott, can be gauged by extracts from two letters. The first in mid-November 1914 was from Weizmann to Scott: 'It is the first time in my life I have "spoken out" to a non-Jew all the intimate thoughts and desiderata, you scarcely realise what a world of good to me you did in allowing me to talk out freely. In this cold world we, "the fanatics", are solitary onlookers, more especially now. I shall never see the realisation of my dream – "the 100 per cent Jew", but perhaps my son will see it. You gave me courage and please please forgive my brutal frankness. If I would have spoken to a man I value less, I would have been very diplomatic.'[26]

The second letter was written by Scott two months later commissioning an article in which the Zionist aspirations were to be expounded. 'I have had several conversations with Dr Weizmann on the Jewish question and he has, I think, opened his whole mind to me. I found him extraordinarily interesting – a rare combination of the idealism and the severely practical which are the two essentials of statesmanship . . . What struck me in his view was first the perfectly clear conception of Jewish nationalism – an intense and burning sense of the Jew as Jew; just as strong, perhaps more so, as that of the German as German or the Englishman as Englishman – and, secondly, arising out of that, necessary for its satisfaction and development, his demand for a country, a homeland, which for him, and for anyone sharing his view of Jewish nationality, could only be the ancient home of his race. To you, no doubt, these views are familiar, elementary perhaps, but they are not to most people and were not to me.'*

The strangeness to Scott of the Zionist dream is surprising. In 1913 and 1914 the *Guardian* had carried long descriptive articles about the Jewish agricultural settlements in Palestine. Each Zionist Congress from 1905 onwards had been covered for the paper by Israel Cohen, the Manchester-born London journalist, who carried on this work for the paper until 1946. There was only one break in this series – the Congress of 1907, and that was because the paper then sent Weizmann himself and Harry Sacher, a member of its editorial staff. (The entry in the contributors' ledger under Weizmann is endorsed 'rewritten by Mr Sacher.')

An even stronger reason for surprise at Scott's ignorance of Jewish nationalism is that two of the senior members of the Corridor, though Gentiles, had long been keen Zionists. Sidebotham's Zionism had the distinctive slant of the military critic who saw the Suez Canal as an imperial artery and realised that a canal could not be both an artery and a frontier. Palestine in Jewish hands as a British Dominion would be a defence for the Empire. 'Empire' was not then to liberals a dirty word but, at its best, a promise of fair-dealing.

---

* Scott-Sacher 16 January 1915. The article by Sacher, though written, was never published, since before it was printed a similar article by the same hand had appeared in the *Daily News*.

W. P. Crozier, the other Gentile Zionist, was eight years Sidebotham's junior on the paper. He was a near neighbour and a close friend – Sidebotham was 'Uncle Sider' to the Crozier children. He shared his interest in military affairs and had established his reputation in the office by his sub-editing of the news of the Russo-Japanese War. He had succeeded Sidebotham as news editor at the end of 1912. Like Sidebotham, Crozier was a Manchester man who had been at Manchester Grammar School and taken a first in Greats at Oxford. Perhaps even more than Sidebotham Crozier was wholly committed to the welfare of the paper; a reserved man, devoted to his family, but with few friends outside it. He was the son of an overstrict Methodist minister. The father's non-conformist conscience persisted so strongly in the son that it had impelled him into a scholarly and reluctant agnosticism. Crozier kept up not only his classical but his biblical reading and he found in Zionism a secular but profound fulfilment of his strongly scriptural imagination.

Sidebotham and Crozier owed their Zionism principally to the slightly younger Harry Sacher. Twice fate took a curious hand, fortunate for Zionism, in the affairs of Sacher and the *Guardian*. In 1904 Harry Sacher had just taken a First in history at Oxford but had failed to secure election at All Souls – not very surprisingly for in those days the college was hardly likely to welcome a clever young Jew from the East End who was both a socialist and a Zionist. But Dibblee, who was a member of the college, had been so impressed by the quality of Sacher's work that he suggested to Scott that here was a possible recruit for the paper. A year later, of course, a recommendation from Dibblee would have been fatal, but by the time the 1905 crisis broke Sacher was safely installed in Cross Street. He had already met Chaim Weizmann; and, when Weizmann brought his wife to Manchester, it was Sacher who met them at the station and took them in a cab to their new home. Naturally Sacher brought Weizmann and his *Guardian* friends together. But, although a young recruit in his early twenties might interest a friendly senior member of the *Guardian* staff like Sidebotham in his enthusiasms, he could not approach the remote and rather terrifying editor in the same way. One kept one's distance from C.P. Scott. So it was that Weizmann and Scott had to wait nine years to meet each other, and that Scott was then perhaps a little surprised to find that he had already on his staff men who were deep in the counsels of the Zionist movement.

Sacher had left the *Guardian* in 1909 for the *Daily News*. In June 1915 the Russians carried out mass deportations of Jews from Lithuania and the British Foreign Office acquiesced. Sacher wrote an angry leader in protest. But Russia was England's ally and Sacher was told on 9 June that the proprietors were so displeased at what he had written that he must leave next day. He wrote to Scott and at once began to do occasional work in the *Guardian*'s London office, and by August he was back on the staff in Manchester.

The line-up for the two years' campaign which led to the Balfour Declaration was complete. In Manchester there were Sidebotham and Sacher in the *Guardian* office and two young business men, Simon Marks and Israel Sieff, in close and often daily association with them. Weizmann had just moved to London to work on the application of his acetone process in the manufacture of explosives for the British Government. There he was near his close collaborators, Leon Simon and Leonard Stein, and in often uneasy contact with Nahum Sokolow, his senior in the Zionist hierarchy. Scott, 'the old man in Manchester' of Weizmann's letters, was indeed at 69 old enough to be the father of Weizmann and his friends. Sidebotham and Weizmann were in their early forties; Sacher and Crozier in their thirties; Sieff and Marks in their twenties. It was a young man's movement.

Scott's part in the campaign began when he put Weizmann in contact with Lloyd George in December 1914. The first interview was favourable, but well begun was nothing like half done. Lloyd George 'attends to telegrams, he does not to letters' as Scott told Weizmann in advising him how to get an interview.[27] Time after time, Scott himself contrived to help forward Weizmann's case by talking to Ministers or writing to them. Sometimes he was concerned with the necessary facilities for Weizmann's scientific work – 'I was surprised and disappointed to find so small (as he appeared to me) a man in so great a position,' was how Scott summed up his impression of the obstructive Secretary of the Admiralty.[28] He fought equally strenuously to get Weizmann paid for the work he had done. He badgered Lloyd George, Reginald McKenna, A. J. Balfour and Edward Carson about this. Nothing was too much trouble. Scott felt that Weizmann had performed a notable service for the country; and he felt that his personal honour was at stake in having advised Weizmann to trust implicitly in the honour of the British Government.

Scott was equally insistent in his efforts to get Weizmann a hearing on the Palestine question and to recommend his views to those members of the Cabinet with whom he was in closest touch. Above all, he constantly put the Zionist case before Lloyd George with whom, after he became Prime Minister, the final decision rested. Balfour, of course, was sympathetic but, in Scott's view, too much in the hands of his permanent civil servants to take bold decisions. Scott early suspected that a bargain had been made with the French which would effectively block Zionist plans, but the enquiries he made of Lord Milner and others convinced him that there was only a provisional agreement which could be set aside. In the early part of 1917 he used all his influence to persuade Weizmann not to go out to Egypt as he wanted to do, until the Government had committed itself to a declaration of policy in favour of a British Palestine with a view to the establishment there of the Jewish National Home. Scott was convinced that out of sight would be out of mind; that success for Weizmann depended about equally on patience and importunity. It was wise advice. Scott himself acted on it on Weizmann's behalf.

At last on 20 June 1917 Weizmann was able to write to Scott: 'Together with Lord Rothschild I saw Mr Balfour yesterday and Mr Balfour promised to give us a document in which the British Government would express its sympathy with the Zionist movement and its intention to support the creation of a Jewish national home in Palestine.' The same day he wrote to Sacher asking him to draft a form of words which the declaration might take. Between this first draft and Balfour's famous letter of 5 November to Lord Rothschild there were many difficult negotiations. The final text, apart from the substitution of 'Jewish people' for 'Jewish race', followed a formula suggested by Lord Milner and revised by Leo Amery who in the days of his service with the *Guardian* in Macedonia had distinguished himself by breaking his umbrella on the head of a Turkish chief of police. In his leader on the day of publication Scott wrote: 'We speak of Palestine as a country, but it is not a country; it is at present little more than a small district of the vast Ottoman tyranny. But it will be a country; it will be the country of the Jews.'[29]

It is curious how relatively scanty was the attention given to Palestine and Zionism in the *Guardian* between 1914 and 1917 in view of the active part that the editor and his staff were playing behind the scenes. One or two leaders, one or two 'Saturday articles', an odd reference in a military leader or 'A Student of War' article – it is a meagre tally from three years' newspapers. But it reflects Scott's shrewd tactical judgment. Lloyd George had to be convinced – that was quickly done. He had to be reminded and fed with arguments. This was best done by personal interviews, not by a press campaign which could only embarrass the Government in its tricky relations with France. After the Balfour Declaration, not before, was the time for the *Guardian* itself to take up the cause.

But before there could be a Declaration there was need for public propaganda of a more specialised kind than would be appropriate in a general newspaper. The Jewish community in England was divided in its views on Zionism. The opponents had to be won over. Then, men with a particular interest in the security of the British Empire and its communications had to be convinced that these could best be served in association with the Zionist cause. The two tasks were distinct but overlapped. Both were undertaken by the monthly *Palestine*, the organ of the British Palestine Committee, whose headquarters were in Manchester and whose direction was effectively in the control of Sidebotham, Sacher, Sieff and Marks. Sidebotham and Sacher were almost entirely responsible for the editing of *Palestine* which in its short life from early 1917 to 1920 had a small but influential readership. It had no official connection whatever with the *Guardian* though, contrary to his usual practice, Scott had agreed to give his name as a supporter to the British Palestine Committee,[30] and *Palestine* expressed views with which he was in general agreement. It faithfully represented Weizmann's outlook, but this did not prevent some stormy passages when it said aloud what Weizmann thought should only be whispered. It was often too independent to please the Zionist Organisation which wanted to impose a preliminary censorship in return for the promise of a subsidy of £500. 'Under no circumstances,' Sacher told Weizmann, 'would our common dignity suffer us to accept a subsidy to which such terms were attached.' Anyone reading now the papers and the correspondence of those days before the Balfour Declaration must be struck, as Scott was struck, by one argument freely used by Weizmann and his friends, not least in the *Guardian*. It is the role which they saw for 'the Jews of Judaea' as a bridge between the cultures of the West and the Middle East, a repetition in our times of the part played by Jews in the Moslem civilisation of medieval Spain. In the light of all that has happened and is happening this hope seems so remote and vain that one is tempted to wonder whether it was ever seriously entertained. Was it perhaps, just an argument to win converts? Or was it an integral part of the Zionist hope? In 1967 one of the few survivors of the 'Manchester Group' gave this answer. 'No,' he said, 'it was not just an argument. We often spoke of it among ourselves.'

5

When Padraic Colum sailed for America soon after the outbreak of war a rich period of Irish reporting ended for the *Guardian*. Nineteenth century investigations of Irish conditions for the paper had usually been written by Englishmen and marked by painstaking analysis and deep compassion. Comparable series at the beginning of the twentieth century were written and illustrated by Irishmen and were in fact off-shoots of the Irish literary revival. Twice J. B. Yeats went on a tour of the West of Ireland for the *Guardian,* visiting many of the places which W. T. Arnold and Spenser Wilkinson had studied a generation before. The sketches he made formed a composite whole with prose impressions written by J. B. Synge on the first occasion in 1905, and by Padraic Colum on the second in 1909.

Colum was then still in his twenties, not much older than he was when A. E. first knew 'an enchanting boy who rushed up to meet you, his overcoat unbuttoned, the pockets of it stuffed with railway waybills and handbills all scribbled over in the intervals of work in the railway offices, and began to read you his latest masterpiece – the great play in which the thud of hoofs continued from first curtain to last – till he suddenly discovered that he had the wrong waybills and was really reading from his great epic on St Brendan the Navigator.'[31] Colum was one of the founders of the National Theatre. His first contribution to the *M.G.* was a notice of Synge's 'The Well of the Saints' in 1905. He continued to notice plays at the Abbey until he sailed for America. Then he sent back a farewell back-pager in which he describes how:

'An Irishman who watches the dances (of the emigrants) or listens to the music might think himself beside a wet hedgerow under a moon just like the one above. The music that they bring with them was once the marching tunes of fighting clans, changed in a century of defeat into the music of jigs and reels. So changed, the music lives on, holding the people together: –
Ye have the Pyrrhic dance as yet –
Where is the Pyrrhic phalanx gone? (19 October 1914.)

This echo of Byron was a little unfair on Colum's fellow-country-men regarded as soldiers. They had long provided a disproportionate share of the British Army and in the first months of the war recruiting in Ireland was brisk. But if Colum was thinking of the Irish as soldiers in a national Irish army the quotation was doubly apt – the Irish in their nationalist struggles had on the whole fought shy of fighting but, like Byron's Greeks at the time he was writing Don Juan, they were about to start.

On Good Friday morning, 21 April 1916 Sir Roger Casement had landed in Kerry from a German submarine. He had been arrested and brought to London. That was the main news in the paper on Tuesday the 25th. But at the same time the office heard of a rising in Dublin on Bank Holiday – whether it was a rebellion or a riot was still obscure.

Early in the morning at five o'clock a soldier returning from Dublin called at the *Guardian* office and gave an account of the beginning of the outbreak 'which, however, it was not possible for us to publish in advance of an official announcement' as the paper put it when it finally gave his story on Saturday the 27th. On the Tuesday evening Scott, in his leader for Wednesday's paper, described the outbreak as 'a disagreeable incident' and thought that to call it a rebellion 'even in the most modified sense' was 'too great a compliment.' But he thought it serious enough to send two reporters, George Leach and J. V. Radcliffe, to investigate, and that was something the *Guardian* rarely did for a straight news story. On Saturday Walter Meakin was added. Radcliffe was a smallish man with a small black moustache, a teetotaller and non-smoker, a strict parent, a man who kept the Sabbath. Walter Meakin had come from the *Yorkshire Observer*, that famous nursery of M.G. men, in 1912. Like Radcliffe he was already something of a specialist in Labour affairs. He was later to become well-known as the author of *The New Industrial Revolution* and labour correspondent of the *Daily News*. Howard Spring recalled him as 'a spectacled thin man with a small straggly moustache, a family man much given to gardening, with a great gift of earnestness.'[32] Nobody would have said that of George Leach. He was one of ten children of an Irish mother and a schoolmaster who became clerk to the Rochdale Board of Guardians. Nevertheless, on his father's early death, Leach had to leave school at the age of ten. He learned his trade, and got his education, first of all on the *Rochdale Star*, a paper of such political inconstancy that it was taunted by the *Rochdale Observer*, Leach's second paper, with the old jingle, 'Twinkle, twinkle, little star; How we wonder what you are.' From there he went to the *Yorkshire Observer*, and then for ten years to the parliamentary reporting staff of the *Guardian* in London before he settled in Manchester as a reporter in 1910. By that time he was not quite 30, had been called to the bar, become standing counsel to the National Union of Journalists, been chairman of the Gallery Committee and a member of the council of the Newspaper Press Fund.

The impression Leach left on Haslam Mills at their first meeting was 'of something tough and resisting in his nature, not one of the pale and feathery people who blow so much about Fleet St. . . . for one thing he was passionately provincial.' Mills thought 'he recalled in many ways some of the great lawyers, especially the eighteenth-century Lord Chancellors, whose lives he was fond of reading. He had the same love of company and late hours and the same power of forging his way through a question until he came out at the other side . . . With just another handful of the second-rate qualities – a little more application, a little more pliability and veneer, and so on – he would have made upon the world at large the impression which he made upon his friends.'[33]

The only things that Radcliffe, Meakin and Leach really had in common were their great skill as reporters and their experience in getting Irish news. Radcliffe, for instance, had been in Ulster when the Covenant was signed in 1912. The major stories, unsigned on this occasion, had been written by H. W. Nevinson, who followed 'King' Carson from meeting to meeting and pilloried his semi-royal behaviour with a fervour that equalled any Orangeman's but in the opposite cause. The more sober, analytical messages were Radcliffe's. He investigated carefully the amount of discrimination in work, and probed the extent to which there was concealed dissatisfaction with the Orange drums among steady Protestant bankers and shopkeepers and parsons.

George Leach for his part was in Ireland when the 'Curragh mutiny' took place in 1914. Characteristically, one of the first things he had done was to seek out Larkin, who was generally supposed to be in England, to get his views. They were simple: 'The officers in Ireland have proved absolutely what I've been saying is right. They've shown what a hollow thing all their talk about a soldier's duty is. It has only to be the case of calling on them to oppose their own class and they resign.' A private soldier to whom he talked next day took the same view: 'It is all a class and political business, and that is what most of us think about it . . . What would have happened to us if we had done the same thing?' He went on to describe the formal welcome given by a detachment of the 16th Lancers to General Gough and Colonel MacEwen on their triumphant return from London.*

How the three men divided the work in 1916 cannot now be determined but it seems that Leach was the first to reach Dublin late on Wednesday. He had gone to Holyhead but the mail boat was not running. However he got a passage to Greenore on the Ulster border and then by train to Drogheda and on in a hired car to the suburbs:

Walking into Dublin from Drumcondra I found the central portion of the city in the possession of the rebels. At the Parnell Monument at the end of Sackville St bullets were whistling down from the Post Office, the principal

* Scott took up Leach's point: 'Is the British army to be a national army or the private army of a class and a party?' Unhappily one of the disaffected officers in the 16th Lancers was the eldest son of Russell Allen, the proprietor of the *Manchester Evening News*, who took the *Guardian*'s strong comments ill. Scott explained that they were not intended in a personal sense, but the incident revived unhappy memories of the 1905–1907 struggle for the *Guardian*. M.G. 24, 25 March 1914

but not the only seat of the insurrection, and a Sinn Fein sentry ordered me to put up my hands. On submission he was obliging enough, after borrowing a cigarette, to conduct me to the back door of the Gresham Hotel, where after a long parley behind barricaded doors, they gave me shelter.

But the sub-editors in Manchester still had to make do with official hand-outs and agency messages often based on returning travellers' tales.

'It had been a fairly simple thing to enter Dublin on the Wednesday but it was plainly going to be far from simple to get out (on Sunday). When leaving Dublin by the Kingston road it was considered desirable "for safety's sake" – whether for someone else's safety or my own was not clear – to pass me from one sentry to another (though they were only a few yards distant) under armed escort. The last escort gave me this advice. "When I leave you," he said, "go across that open stretch and the bridge like blazes," and he followed up the exhortation with a lusty "Go." I went – for sixty yards perhaps – and then "Halt" came from a rather startled sentry ambushed in the stone angle beyond the bridge. It would have been awkward to have continued that sprint any further . . .'

It took altogether eleven hours from the Gresham Hotel to Kingstown* whence the first *Guardian* story from inside Dublin was sent in time for Monday's paper. Next day Leach and his colleagues filled the whole main news page and half another with graphic connected narrative. The last instalment was telegraphed from Holyhead when the mail boat got in at 1.30 a.m.

That page and a half gives something of the feel of Dublin in those days. There was, for instance, the feeling of isolation—these were the last days before broadcasting.

I found myself not more eager for news than those I met. They were hungering and thirsting for information of events outside Dublin. Was the situation in Manchester and Glasgow infinitely worse than in Dublin? Were reinforcing armies of Sinn Feiners on the march through Ireland to the capital? Had 20,000 Germans landed in Kerry? The city had had no news for three days, and it was information to a Nationalist member of parliament that Sir Roger Casement had been taken prisoner.

There was the misguided gallantry of the rebels – many of them young boys between 15 and 18 years of age; some of them women:

I was told by a priest who was admitted to the building (the Post Office) it contained some 600 men and a score or so of young women who proposed to cook and nurse. The priest heard the confessions of many of the men who told him they were going to die for Ireland. He counselled the young women

* Now Dun Laoghaire.

to leave, but they replied that they were determined to stop and die with the men – a spirit too good for so bad a cause.

The unpreparedness of the authorities was already clear:

The plans had been carefully and elaborately made, they were carried out with exact method and discipline. Audacity and secrecy combined to give them success. The surprise was complete. The Government was wholly unprepared, and just by walking into the Post Office the rebels partly prevented the Government's communicating with the forces that should have been under its command . . . The Lord Lieutenant was about to leave for Belfast. The officers of the regiments at the Curragh were at the races.

The people, too, were taken by surprise:

The city has grown accustomed to seeing the different contingents on parade. They have met periodically for drill and have practised manoeuvres in the Dublin mountains. It was not in itself a particularly noteworthy fact that a parade should be called for Easter Monday and the populace watched the Volunteers start off from Stephen's Green without any misgivings.

The twilight deeds of Monday night stand in contrast to the clean fighting that followed:

The spirit of revolution was abroad, and the ignorant and the depraved interpreted it in their own way. The authority of law and order had been driven from the streets and lawlessness came in free and uncurbed. The rebels . . . were waiting for their usurpation to be challenged . . . While it was preparing there was an interval of uncontrolled and reckless looting. Not only were small and portable things taken away but heavy and cumbrous articles, even bed-steads were carried away. Eye-witnesses have told me of the passing to and fro of many men and women burdened with loads of loot and of the diamond rings they saw on the fingers of frowsy and bedraggled women.

Already knowledgeable assessment was possible:

Pearse is a well-known Irish barrister and orator, and he was the general leader of the Sinn Fein movement, while Connolly was the Dublin leader. He was the brain which really directed the Larkin strike three years ago and his keenness of intellect and organising ability would have carried him to great success if they had been employed only in lawful Labour movements.

By Monday afternoon, a week after the outbreak, peace had been re-established; great crowds had come out to see the damage and 'a curiously reassuring sign of the re-establishment of order was the appearance of the police in the streets in full force. Up to Sunday afternoon no policeman had been seen for six days.'

In Manchester meanwhile the editor was writing almost nightly, and with growing agony, about the Rising and its disastrous aftermath. At first he was mainly anxious to safeguard the good name of the Nationalist party – 'it is against them that this futile movement is primarily directed.' As late as Friday in Easter week he drew hope from the speeches of Carson and Redmond in the House of Commons, 'the most hopeful augury of the good that may yet arise out of this almost intolerable evil.' By 4 May the first executions became known: 'it is a fate which they invoked and of which they would probably not complain. Is that not enough as an example and a warning?' On the 9th 'the Dublin military executions are becoming an atrocity.' Next day he added 'every life taken now . . . is a new source of danger . . . to the relations between the British and the Irish; and the word Irish means not only the people of Ireland, but the millions of Irish in America' – a point which Sidebotham had made in his Student of War article eleven days before.

When the Prime Minister went to Ireland to take stock of the situation, Connolly and MacDermott were still alive but under sentence of death. 'By the unwritten law of such cases they are to be nursed back to life before they can be put out of it. By a similar law of mercy their lives ought then to be spared.' But it was not to be. Scott contrasted the missed opportunity with the doom that he saw advancing:

The execution of Mr Connolly and Mr MacDermott has been carried out as a tribute to that sense of symmetry which stands in place of justice in times of rebellion and repression. Would the bones of any of the men previously executed have cried out had these two been spared? . . . The revolt, which seemed for an hour to threaten the whole fabric which statesmen had been patiently building up, in reality revealed the solidity of the new structure. But good-will was to be subject to a more dangerous assault . . . What effect the executions have actually had, how much is now irretrievable, how much may still be saved, we cannot tell. (13 May 1916)

6

Scott began the war by fearing the worst for the paper and made drastic economies. He and other senior members of the staff accepted temporary cuts in their salaries. But in fact what happened was by no means unfavourable. Advertising kept up, circulation went up, profits increased. By Easter 1918 the salary cuts were ended and arrears made good. Shortage of newsprint forced the firm to reduce the size of the paper and in the end the price had to go up from one penny to 2d. – at first only on Saturdays, but before long for the whole week.

In October 1916 Scott's seventieth birthday was celebrated at a dinner given him by his colleagues on the paper. It brought him, of course, many warm tributes from men at the top of every profession. Two letters, however, from relatively unknown men are perhaps better worth quoting here. His old tutor at Corpus, J. W. Oddie, wrote to him on 8 November in a remarkably firm hand telling him how each day he walked to the railway station at St Leonards to collect his M.G. at 6 p.m. from the bookstall – but that sometimes, alas, W. H. Smith had forgotten to send it down and sometimes it arrived with a richly fishy smell which he thought inappropriate for so upright a paper. The next day Colonel J. H. Rivett-Carnac, ADC to the King (so a rubber stamp on the note paper proclaimed) wrote from Vevey: 'I see the *Guardian* occasionally and admit that I am impressed with its fairness and steadiness in this crisis.' Rivett-Carnac had been Indian correspondent for the M.G. forty years before and, as he reminded Scott, had used the money he received for his articles to pay for the education of Sir Charles Townsend of Kut, the son of a friend,

Scott's sister Isabella, the family historian, was determined to add the seventieth birthday letters, cuttings and speeches to her collection. C.P. sent her a selection and with them a letter in which he reflected on how the paper stood.

'I was astonished and rather overwhelmed by the kindness and appreciation shown, but if I have at all deserved it in the past I mean to do a lot more on the same line before I have done.

'The MG has held its own wonderfully on the material side during the whole period of the war and is one of the few papers in England, I expect, which is not losing money. Since almost all the ½d papers raised their price to 1d and the *Times* has gone to 2d we have picked up a lot of circulation and shall go on picking it up so long as we see our way to the necessary paper – this last a very doubtful point. However we shan't spring in price till we are compelled. It is better to spread the influence and widen the basis of the paper than to grasp at profits. If we do go up, it will be only because we are compelled to check circulation. We have taken no money out of the paper since we owned it, but have all been paid by salary – latterly considerably reduced! Our two Supplements – the American and the "Empire" one – have been great successes – particularly the last and have brought in money as well as reputation. As to the last it seems to grow in a sort of snowball fashion and I honestly think that in the formation of policy we now carry a good deal more weight than *The Times* – perhaps that isn't saying much!'[34]

CHAPTER TWENTY-SEVEN

Peacemaking

I

TED SCOTT was home by Christmas, 1918. He wrote three 'back-pagers' on his life as a prisoner of war and then went straight back to his normal work on the paper. Montague too had been demobilised and rejoined the paper on the same day.

And so the *Guardian* began a new chapter in its history in a world so disordered that it seems strange to talk of normal work. Life on a newspaper is never more itself than when life outside is most disturbed. It is then that journalists most easily feel that they are fulfilling the purpose to which all their work is directed. But the war had been so well controlled that it had been for newspapermen a time of frustration. The golden age of the war correspondents was past. The machinery of government had caught up with them. They had become in effect the generals' or the politicians' or, more reputably, the private soldiers' public relations men. News could now travel so swiftly that censorship had had to slow it down or suppress it – often to save lives, sometimes, journalists thought, to save reputations. Only, in a curious way, the official war artists had escaped, as Montague had noticed. 'What a cornucopious distributor of laurels is Buchan – quite unavoidably, no doubt, for I suppose you cannot say semi-officially "Quite a nice fellow, this, but came rather a cropper at – " or "Educated at Harrow; appointed to command a division 191 – ; Stellenbosched 191 – ." Your judgments,' he told Francis Dodd, 'can be much more frank, thanks to the purblindness of the great. One of your drawings really tells all about the necessity of one past change in a command, and another goes far to justify the new appointment.'[1]

But now over much of Europe events were over-running governments. Even in the United Kingdom this could not be ruled out. There was news to be got for the seeking, news which could now be published without asking leave. For a paper run on a shoe-string budget the *Guardian* managed well. In one way only can it be said with confidence that it would have managed better if 'peace' had come a year earlier.

There would not then have been the gap in its ranks caused by Sidebotham's departure.

Six months before Ted Scott returned, Sidebotham had left the *Guardian*. One day, as Lloyd George recalled, 'I happened to tell Lord Northcliffe that in my opinion the soundest and shrewdest appreciations of the war were those that appeared in the *Manchester Guardian*. The next thing I heard of Mr Sidebotham was that he was on the staff of *The Times*.'[2] Northcliffe got his way only because Scott resisted Sidebotham's desire to earn a little more and to feel a little better appreciated. The *Guardian* paid him £900; the *Times* suggested £1,500 but raised its offer to £1,750. Sidebotham used in later years to tell his family and friends that he would have stayed with the M.G. for another £200. At the time he even told John Scott that another £50 or £100 would have contented him, but he also brought out into the open his feeling that he was being passed over. 'His "grievance",' Scott told Hobhouse, 'is that he was refused a directorship and I am sorry to say that he was jealous – of you! I think he is very genuinely sorry to leave and probably with good reason, for he belongs to the soil here and will not easily make himself at home in the rather superior circle into which he will now be drawn.'* The last clause is betraying. If Sidebotham in spite of his brilliant Oxford career and polished scholarship† was regarded by Scott as not quite socially presentable (and this is what Scott's words suggest), it is easy to understand the mixture of smouldering resentment and honest, proud admiration with which some of his men who had not been to a university regarded their editor.

Sidebotham's loss was severely felt. The strategic implications of the wars in Russia, Turkey and Poland lacked his hand to bring them into the open. They were fully discussed on Wilsonian principles of self-determination while admirable maps elucidated the mixture of races in Eastern Europe. But readers who had grown accustomed to finding in the *Guardian* a balance between idealism and realism now had to do without Sidebotham's assessment of the probable in terms of the possible. For the last few months of the war Crozier took over Sidebotham's military work and finished the M.G. *History of the War*; but Crozier's work, though sound, lacked, as Scott said, Sidebotham's salt and, once the armistice was signed, administrative cares seem to have taken almost his whole time.

---

* Scott–Hobhouse 3 May 1918. Hobhouse was the first non-family director. Sidebotham got the empty title of 'political director', without a seat on the board, and an extra £100 a year; a consolation prize that did not console.

† As late as 1936 Sidebotham published for private circulation some of Shakespeare's sonnets in his own Latin verse translation.

Scott realised that he had made a mistake. He did not repeat it when in the autumn of 1919 Crozier was offered the editorship of the *Daily News*. Scott promptly made him a director and also brought James Bone on to the board lest he too should feel passed over. But Sidebotham could not be replaced. First as 'A Student of Politics' in the *Times* and then as 'Scrutator' in the *Sunday Times* and 'Candidus' in the *Daily Sketch* he became the best-known columnist of the inter-war period, but he too probably never found again quite the satisfaction in his work that he had enjoyed in the good company of his youth in Cross Street. When Scott finally gave up the editorship Sidebotham wrote to him and got an answer which is unique in tone among all Scott's letter-writing:

'My dear Sider – how naturally one drops into the old address! – thank you ever so much for your kind remembrance of me and of the good times we had together. I recall in particular the magnificent work you did during the war, but indeed this was only one of the ways in which you added so much to the reputation of the paper. May I say, even at this late day, that the greatest fault I am conscious of ever having committed in the conduct of the paper was in not holding on to you by main force when the critical moment came . . .'[3]

2

Twelve days before the Armistice Scott invited J. L. Hammond to cover the peace-making for the *Guardian* at a salary reckoned at the rate of £1,500 a year. He gave him this brief: 'The great issue will be the maintenance, broadly speaking, of the Wilson terms . . . and, above all, of the League of Nations as an integral and effective part of them.'[4]

This was Hammond's first considerable assignment for the M.G. Once before there had been talk of his joining it. When he was 27 he had applied for a job with the support of John Brunner, a left-wing Radical, who rather quaintly commended his secretary to Scott on the ground that he was 'a gentleman and the son of a gentleman – the latter to my mind a very important matter.'[5] Nothing came of it since Hammond took up the editorship of *The Speaker*, a new Radical weekly which in 1907 changed its editor to H. W. Massingham and its title to the *Nation*. The M.G. referred sympathetically to Hammond's work on *The Speaker* and to its unexpected ending. Hammond was grateful: 'it is a genuine consolation for many disappointments to be spoken of in such terms by almost the only paper whose praise or blame matters.'[6] There followed for Hammond a short period on the ill-fated *Tribune* and then a long spell as secretary to the Civil Service Commission. It stopped neither his journalism nor his serious historical work. He agreed 'with characteristic generosity of spirit,' as H. W. Nevinson put it, to serve the *Nation* under his successor. Nevinson has left us a picture of Hammond at the weekly lunches at the National Liberal Club when the *Nation*'s next issue was planned.

'Violent contradictions, personal insults, and missiles more material flew across the table, and even I more than once had seized the tablecloth with the wild intention of clinching an argument by dragging it off . . . At (Hobhouse's) side might be J. Lawrence Hammond, his pale and intellectual face almost hidden in the bush of dark hair and beard, until the war transformed him into a spruce officer in the Gunners, almost beyond the recognition of his earlier and more pacific friends. To us he brought, not only his unequalled knowledge of the workers in towns and villages a century ago, and not only his knowledge of eighteenth-century politics, and the character of all politicians from that date onwards, but the keenest insight into present situations and living personalities.'[7]

The *Guardian* had done well to secure an outstanding scholar-writer to represent it at the Peace Conference. By the end of November Hammond was in Paris where the lobbying had already begun. He had the help of his wife Barbara, whom years before Hobhouse had tried in vain to persuade Scott to employ as a personal assistant.* Until March he also had the assistance of Gilbert Murray's daughter Rosalind whose husband, A. J. Toynbee† was in the Middle Eastern section of the British Peace delegation. There were plenty of good easy contacts. 'You will get the best information from House and from Lippmann who I understand is to be his secretary at the Conference,' Scott assured him. 'I have been told that both House and the President regard the M.G. as the particular representative of the President's policy in this country and rely on its support.' James Bone told him that 'G. H. Mair is going over for the Foreign Office gang. I think he is to be a buffer State against the foreign powers. He will be at the Majestic. The American press men should be rather useful. I am asking the New York *Tribune* people to put their representative in Paris in touch

* 'My former pupil is a person of first rate ability, very clear head, sensible, and intellectually as well as morally trustworthy.' Hobhouse–Scott 14 May 1899.

† Toynbee himself became a *Guardian* war correspondent. 'When I was in the train – somewhere in Western Bulgaria – en route from Istanbul to London after having been observing the Greece-Turkish War in Anatolia as the *Manchester Guardian*'s special correspondent I . . . found myself jotting down, on half a sheet of notepaper, a dozen headings which turned out to be the subject of the principal divisions' of *A Study of History*. (Experiences: OUP 1969 p. 101.) Sixty-five messages from Toynbee appeared in the M.G. between 25 January and 4 October 1921.

with you.'[8] The Hammonds, too, of course, had their own circle of friends among politicians, and among the historians who were having a field day as guides through discordant claims.

Hammond started cheerfully: 'I think the friends of a Wilson peace may draw a reassuring inference from the general belief that the proceedings will not be protracted. If his principles were not in fact accepted, a long discussion would be inevitable.'[9] But even in this message he brought out some of the hazards: the denial to the Austrian Germans of the right of self-determination, however natural a reaction to fear, 'would be a challenge to the forces on which we rely.' With misplaced optimism he thought: 'Most Frenchmen recognise this and see also, as a very distinguished historian said to me, that nothing would help the cause of Imperialist reaction in Germany more effectually.' Before long Hammond began to measure the gulf between accepting Wilsonian principles and applying them. His story of the formal opening of the Conference ends with 'considerable surprise and indignation' at the exclusion of Armenia. 'It is difficult to understand why Haiti or Guatemala should be supposed to have a greater interest in the future of the world than the people whose wrongs have been for half a century one of the outstanding scandals of civilisation.'[10] In February his optimism revived: 'The first great battle for President Wilson's principles . . . had been won. It is no secret that Mr Lloyd George in an act of conspicuous courage and statesmanship has accepted a solution which will make the German colonies the wards of the League of Nations.'[11] A month later he was once more depressed. He expected that peace would be signed by mid-April but nobody could be sure whether it 'would be a blessing or a curse to mankind.'[12] When April came Hammond wrote that 'the Council must reach final decisions within a week if Peace is to win her desperate race with anarchy'; a week later, 'the answer still hangs in the balance. It is not yet certain there will be a peace on paper. It is still less certain that there will be a peace in fact.'[13] At the end of the month Hammond returned to England, sad and gloomy. The final stages of the treaty with Germany were covered by C. M. Lloyd who next year began his long career with the *New Statesman*.

This was the end of Hammond's connection with peace-making in Europe; but it was only a preliminary to a connection with the *Guardian* which was to last until his death thirty years later. His Paris messages strike one to-day as hardly vintage Hammond. He did not prove a great news-getter or news displayer – perhaps he hardly realised that the men who talked to him were no longer speaking to a civil servant whose lips were sealed but, as they well understood, to a journalist whose pen was presumably ready.* He was, perhaps, also too academic to take easily to the descriptive touches which Crozier, a sound *Guardian* news editor, wanted. President Wilson's landing at Brest, he reminded Hammond, had been covered by Perrot from the London Office; but nobody had attended to his arrival in Paris. Hammond's best conference articles were probably his interviews with men like Feisal (attended by T. E. Lawrence), Branting, Venizélos, Leon Bourgeois, Vandervelde and Painlevé. These had been suggested by Crozier who told him what he might offer for articles: 'Cachin, perhaps on Alsace, four or five guineas a column, Painlevé about six and Anatole France, if you can get him, about seven or eight.' Marcel Cachin wrote an excellent leader page article on 'the Entente and the Central Empires – a plea for Moderation,' the interview with Painlevé made a 'turn-over' on the main news page, but Anatole France could not be got. Crozier warned Hammond off 'too esoteric' foreigners; 'Jugo-Slavs and such like are really important, I know, but it is possible to feed the public up with them. A man stopped me here the other day to ask whether the Dodecanese, about whom (sic) we had been writing, was a people or a disease.'[14] His method – which did not differ from that of other *Guardian* men and indeed of reputable English journalists in general – was in marked contrast to the 'needling' political interviews which television has made familiar. Hammond's object was simply to enable the man he was interviewing to expound considered views in a coherent and readable fashion and to guide him to concentrate on the issues that were really important.

It is not Hammond's work so much as that of Haslam Mills which remains in the memory. Mills succeeded Mrs Toynbee as the second member of the team and was employed mainly on what were no doubt regarded as light-weight sidelines. But there is shrewd insight into many Englishmen's feelings in his account of a press tour of the American occupied zone in Coblenz: 'For the first time in my life I am walking roughshod over a townfull of human beings. That is a curious situation, and in time it begins to find one out . . . When a man looks at me across the tables in one of the cafés I have to turn away, and the only reason I can think of for this is because I have won and he has lost. I am afraid of him because he is helpless and cannot hurt me.' And there is sound observation in what he had to say about frontiers: 'The truth is Europe is not quite fast-dyed. One country spills over into another, and politics are in this respect rather like frontiers in time – like the frontier, for example, between youth and

* Unfortunately his private background letters have been lost.

middle age, which a man does not know he has passed until some time after he has crossed it.'[15] Or, he might have added, the frontier between the *Guardian* before and after Haslam Mills. He came back to Manchester at the end of March, but within a few months he had left the paper. On 23 August he 'marked the book,' that is he filled in the engagements in the Reporters' Diary, for the last time and ended with a flourish: 'W.H.M. finishes and leaves his best wishes to all in the room. W.H.M.' But as we shall see in the next chapter, he left more than his best wishes. He left a staff of reporters, largely of his own recruiting, who were to play a vital part in another of the *Guardian*'s attempts at peacemaking.

3

'The desperate race with anarchy' of which Hammond wrote from Paris, comes out in the headlines which the *Guardian* gave to a signed story on its main news page on 13 December – 'Moscow to Berlin; Revolution all the Way; Bolshevik Strength in Russia.' The writer was Philips Price, who had been in Russia for the *Guardian* since 1914. A week after the Armistice he set out from Moscow where 'all was quiet, the food problem was much less acute. The Bolshevik Government, stronger than ever before, is engaged in creating a Red Army of over a million men. The Menshevik and the small bourgeois parties have published a declaration calling on workers all over the world to rally to the support of the Russian Revolution against the Imperialism attacking it.' At Smolensk Price saw trainloads of Russian prisoners pouring in from Germany. At Obscha he found the Red Army busily occupying parts of White Russia evacuated by the Germans. 'Everywhere,' he noted, 'Soviets of workers and peasants are being formed. The landowners and propertied classes are fleeing to the Ukraine.'

At the first frontier post, forty miles east of Minsk, the Russians handed Philips Price over to the German Soldiers' Soviet. 'I found the German soldiers mostly backward Bavarian peasants, who allowed the officers still much power, and even elected them to the Soviet . . . (but) The nearer I approached the German frontier, the more revolutionary I found the German Soldiers' Soviets. At Eytkunen I was passed through the German Customs which was run by common soldiers only. During the journey through East Prussia soldiers boarded the train, turned the officers out of the compartments, and made them stand in the corridors.' Philips Price finally reached Berlin, at that moment a thoroughly revolutionary city where anything might happen, after a journey lasting six days.

This was the first message from Philips Price to reach the *Guardian* for five months. Many had been sent; some may have miscarried; others had been intercepted by the Allied censorship. So, when this message from Berlin was received, Crozier took it as a sign that the M.G.'s continued protests about the censorship were beginning to take effect.[16] He was almost certainly mistaken. Only a fortnight earlier Harold Dore, the *Guardian*'s Lobby Correspondent, had been called to the Press Bureau and shown a Moscow message from Philips Price which was almost identical in tone and to a considerable extent in words with the opening paragraphs of this Berlin story. He was told that it was 'a piece of Bolshevist propaganda which it was undesirable to circulate in this country.' All the *Guardian* got of this 1,200 word radio message was Dore's rapidly noted summary sent to Scott purely for information.[17]

Other Government departments had their eyes on Philips Price. A week after his first Berlin message had appeared Basil Thomson, head of the CID at New Scotland Yard, wrote to Scott on another matter but added that he supposed Scott had seen some recent pamphlets by Philips Price. The letter took four days to reach Manchester. On Christmas Eve Scott wired that he had not seen the pamphlets: would Thomson send them on? The pace of Governments is slow and it was not until 13 January that they were posted. By this time four more messages had been received from Berlin and published. They were followed by two others which Scott decided to spike. He telegraphed to Philips Price to send no more messages and wrote to him to explain that 'it doesn't do for you, as our correspondent, to be carrying on Bolshevik propaganda. That might be right or wrong, but we ought not to be in any way mixed up in it, as I see we are in a pamphlet ('The Truth about the Allied Intervention in Russia'), of which a copy has been sent to me, where you are described as our correspondent in Russia.'* The language of the pamphlet was certainly inflammatory. It did not, however, call for mutiny by the troops in the field but for political action by the workers at home. Neither Scott's telegram nor his letter reached Philips Price and it was not until this book was being written that he received a copy of the letter.

The Philips Price affair smouldered on. The Government stated in the House of Commons that he had been editing a Bolshevik paper, *The Call*, which had incited the British troops in Murmansk to revolt. The Soviet Foreign Minister broadcast 'to the whole world' a denial that Philips Price had any connection whatever with *The Call*. In the autumn stories were published that he was a prisoner in Murmansk. A correspondent wrote to the *Guardian* to say that, on the contrary, he

* Scott–Philips Price 18 January 1919.

had been spending the last few weeks in the Tyrol on his honeymoon and there was no reason whatever to suppose that he had been anywhere near Russia.[18] In fact he had become the Berlin correspondent of the *Daily Herald*. From time to time the affair was revived by papers like the *Morning Post*, partly to attack Philips Price, partly no doubt to discredit the *Guardian*. Scott remained highly sensitive. In 1924 an advertisement for the *Labour Monthly*, a highbrow left wing paper, described Philips Price as '*Manchester Guardian* correspondent in Russia 1914–1918.' Scott wrote indignantly saying that this was an 'exceedingly misleading description.' It may be thought that the *Labour Monthly* had the better of a lengthy exchange of letters. 'I can think of no possible translation of "correspondant particulier" other than "own correspondent",' wrote A. E. Reade.[19] Nor, apparently could Scott. He did not reply.

<h1 style="text-align:center">4</h1>

It was at lunch at The Firs, Scott's home in a Manchester suburb, that Philips Price had received his credentials as 'le correspondant particulier en Russie du *Manchester Guardian*.' His great-grandfather, Robert Philips, was one of the eleven men who put up the money to start the *Manchester Guardian*. Now, in November 1914, neither the old editor nor the young Liberal candidate for Gloucester – Scott was 68, Philips Price 29 – was able to believe that the war had mysteriously liberalised the Tsardom. Philips Price had travelled extensively in Caucasia and written almost as extensively about his travels in the *Guardian*. Scott sent him out once more to see what he could of 'the track of the war in Poland and across the Caucasus' as he put it in a letter of introduction to Harold Williams who was once again briefly acting as the M.G. representative in Petrograd.

When the Tsar abdicated Philips Price was with the Russian Army in the Caucasus, the only British correspondent on that front. He was sent for to the palace in Tiflis to hear the Grand Duke Nicholas, the Tsar's cousin, make a statement:

'He clearly had not slept for several nights. His eyes were red and his cheeks pale. His voice was thin and we had difficulty in hearing him. "I want to tell you," he said, "that what happened in Russia in the last twenty-four hours is final and cannot be reversed. I would regard anyone who tries to do so as an enemy of our Fatherland." '[20]

'The revolution is a wonderful and glorious event,' Scott wrote to Hobhouse five days afterwards. 'I've telegraphed the salutation of the

M.G. Editor and staff to the President of the Duma. I gathered from a Russian of some distinction whom I met in London that this sort of expression of sympathy would be welcome.' Four days later he returned to the same theme: 'Don't you feel the Russian revolution rather stirring in your bones and making the growing invasion of personal liberty here more intolerable? The coldness with which this tremendous movement of political and spiritual emancipation was received by a great portion of our press and society . . . seems to show how far we have drifted from the tradition of liberty. I feel that perhaps we ourselves have not fought hard enough against the real persecution of the conscientious objector.'[21]

If this is how the old man in Manchester felt, it is not surprising that the young radical in Tiflis was overjoyed. He made his way to Moscow – not yet the capital – and there he had a shock. What sort of a revolution was it to be? What were the war aims of the new government? Philips Price heard that the Foreign Minister, Miliukoff, was about to leave Moscow for Petrograd. He went to the railway station where Miliukoff gave him an interview in the train.

'I asked him if the fall of the Tsar's Government meant a change in the foreign policy of Russia over Constantinople and the Straits . . . Miliukoff replied to me at once . . . "Russia must . . . insist on the right to close the Straits to foreign warships and this is not possible unless she possesses and fortifies them." I was so astonished at the bluntness of the Foreign Minister's statement to me that I sat dumb for a while in the carriage and had to be reminded that I had better get off the train as it was just going to start. I hurriedly thanked M. Miliukoff and rushed off to the telegraphic office which, though it was nearly midnight, was still open for press telegrams.' (26 April 1917)

The interview was at once telegraphed back to Russia. It served not only to warn English and French radicals that the Cadet leaders of the revolution were still imperialists, but to widen the gap between the parties represented in the Russian Provisional Government.

These important internal differences were reflected in the *Guardian* in a curious way. Scott was not satisfied to rely on a solitary correspondent in Russia whose last address had been at Tiflis 1,500 miles from the capital. At the beginning of April he arranged with Michael Farbman, then the London correspondent of a Petrograd newspaper, to go out to Russia. 'My first impressions of the new Russia surpass my most sanguine expectations,' he telegraphed from Petrograd.

Farbman was a 'peace without annexations or indemnities' man. One of his first actions was to secure an interview with Kerensky, at that time Minister of Justice. 'It was his duty, he said, delicate though the matter was, to contradict M. Miliukoff's statements, which did not represent the attitude of the Russian Government.'* This denial was, of course, as welcome to Philips Price as it was to Farbman and to Scott, but the tone of the message was so antagonistic that one can only conclude that Farbman thought that Philips Price agreed with Miliukoff.

This misunderstanding seems likely enough since the *Guardian's* Russian news service from 1916 to 1919 was conducted in a fog.† Farbman spent the month of May in Petrograd. Philips Price and he met, but apparently neither realised that the other was sending messages to the *Guardian*. In June Farbman was succeeded by David Soskice, the son of a Russian socialist emigré who had settled in England.‡ This was the first that Price had heard of another *Guardian* man in Russia. Soskice was not, apparently, to replace Price but to supplement him. It was left to the two men to work out some arrangement on their own without any indication of Scott's wishes and without any notification at any time directly from Scott to Philips Price. They agreed that Soskice, who soon became one of Kerensky's secretaries, should cover the Provisional Government's activities and that Price should see what was happening outside the capital. During the autumn Philips Price travelled on the Volga and in Central Russia sending the M.G. vivid accounts of how the revolution was affecting ordinary people in provincial towns and villages.

He was back in Petrograd when Kerensky was overthrown. And so it came about that at the critical moment one of the M.G. correspondents was inside the Winter Palace with Kerensky, the other outside with Lenin at the Smolny Institute. David Soskice wrote a graphic account of the events of that night which appeared in the M.G. when he got back to England. Philips Price's message was one of the many which miscarried. He gave his version in the *Guardian* fifty years later.[22]

* M.G. 1 and 5 May 1917. Farbman, who was 37, had been a publisher in Russia before the war and had written a *History of the Architecture of the Italian Renaissance*, which no doubt commended him to James Bone, whose proudest distinction was to be an honorary FRIBA. After the war Farbman founded the Europa Year Book series. Farbman was again in Russia for the M.G. in 1920 and 1921.

† Partly of its own making – it published the interview with the Grand Duke Nicholas twice over at a week's interval (in a truncated form in some editions). It rebuked Philips Price for telegraphing accounts of the fall of Erzerum because, since he was the only British correspondent there, the news would keep!

‡ In 1908 Soskice had asked Scott for credentials as M.G. correspondent. 'My object is largely to secure for myself a legal standing. I was safe so long as the *Tribune* existed – you know perhaps that I was the *Tribune's* St Petersburg correspondent – but should now be exposed to arrest and imprisonment. (Soskice-Scott 19 February 1908.)

The two accounts, though complementary, are not easily, or completely, reconcilable.

Philips Price remained in Russia. On November 23 he heard that the Soviet Government was going to publish the text of the secret treaties made between England, France and Russia after the outbreak of war. He was given the documents by which the Allies had agreed to divide great parts of Europe and Asia. *Izvestia* published the full text on 24 and 25 November. The *Guardian* carried exhaustive summaries on 27, 28 and 29 November. In this it was alone among English newspapers though the *Times* and some other papers gave a few discreet, short extracts. It was the full disclosure in the M.G., together with Colonel House's failure to secure an agreed statement of liberal peace aims from the European Allies, that led directly to the issue of President Wilson's Fourteen Points as a corrective on 8 January 1918.[23]

By this time an armistice between Germany and Russia had been signed. 'How cynical and hypocritical are the Allied Imperialists who seem ready to agree to a compromise and an annexationist's peace at the expense of Russia. What else did Lloyd George mean when he said Russia should make her own terms with Germany?' So Philips Price reported Trotsky. Hobhouse in a *Guardian* leader took up the point: 'Instead of giving such aid and sympathy as is due to the struggle, courageous and unexpected as it is, which the Revolutionary Government of Russia is making to resist the forcible annexation of the provinces in German occupation, our Prime Minister has announced in advance that it is of necessity hopeless and has moreover announced this with no obvious appearance of regret . . . Is it wonderful that this attitude of cold aloofness, this lofty passing by on the other side, should receive in Russia a much more sinister interpretation?'[24] But there was no help for the Soviet leaders. They had to sign the Carthaginian peace. The war with Germany was over. Undeclared war by the Allies followed.

This was a time of intense suffering for Philips Price. Famine was severe. 'I had lost one and a half stone in weight in three weeks,' he wrote. 'When I walked up to the Smolny to attend a meeting of the Soviets from my flat I had to sit down every hundred yards on a doorstep because I was so weak. I remember about this time having a bath and was so shocked at my physical state of skin and bones that in my weakness I burst into tears.'[25] He might have left Russia; he decided to stick it out, convinced that he was witnessing a decisive moment in the world's history. He found comfort and companionship with Arthur Ransome, then the *Daily News* correspondent who largely shared his views. Almost inevitably he took sides. The choice was between fighting the revolution or identifying with it. There was no doubt which his choice would be.

Meanwhile in England Farbman, 'always the calm and precise expositor and student of affairs,' urged on Scott the importance of appointing a neutrally-minded correspondent in Russia: 'There was nobody of any use except Ransome of the *Daily News* and he had gone over too completely to the Bolshevik side. A detached observer was needed.'[26] But he went on to urge recognition of the Bolshevik Government. David Soskice, too, was back in England and met Scott on several occasions. He was in favour of intervention against the Soviets. He urged it on Scott. So did Kerensky whom Scott met on the night Kerensky addressed the Labour Party Conference. So did Philip Kerr and so did the Prime Minister. They failed to move Scott. He thought intervention – taking sides in the civil war – morally wrong and politically self-defeating. He said so in the *Guardian*. He was far from identifying himself or his paper with the Soviet view point, as Philips Price had done, but when it came to what Britain should do he and his correspondent were in general agreement.

5

Philips Price had gone but Russian news was still needed. At first the *Guardian* had no single settled contributor. A textile engineer back from Petrograd wrote two leader page articles lamenting the deserted pastrycooks' shops and the fact that only soldiers and workers could afford to buy from jewellers. An anonymous correspondent contributed a column on the Revival of Religion: 'the churches, empty a year ago, are to-day filled; in Petrograd hungry citizens drag themselves into church corners to hear the majestic singing of the male choirs and there to die; peasants, complains the *Pravda*, swear oaths to kill all children of Bolshevik-enforced civil marriages as offspring of Antichrist.' Aylmer Maude, the translator of Tolstoy, sent a series of messages from the Archangel front full of hope that the Bolshevik regime would be overthrown. John Rickman, a doctor who had been serving with a Quaker relief agency since 1916, wrote five articles on the situation in Siberia. As an introductory note put it: 'He travelled across Siberia with the Czechs during their slow advance, and was able to watch the political events as they might have been seen by newspaper correspondents had they been there, and at the same time, because of his peasant pronunciation of Russian and familiarity with the Russian people, to catch the drift of undercurrents which are less visible from the view point of those whose dealings led them into high quarters.'[27]

In the spring of 1919 Scott sent out a well-qualified man to work specially for the *Guardian*. This was W. T. Goode, a man of 60 whose career had been primarily in the training of elementary school teachers – he had been principal of two colleges. He was a gifted linguist and the founder of the Anglo-Finnish society – Finnish was one of his languages. In the spring and summer of 1918 he had contributed articles on the Finnish situation from Stockholm. He now went to Esthonia which was at war with Soviet Russia but whose independence was equally menaced by the White Russian forces supported by the Allies. Throughout May and June he sent regular messages from Reval. Then he set out for Moscow with a Finn and a Dane who were on a Red Cross errand. On the last stage of the journey to Moscow they were arrested, held in custody for nine or ten days and then sent back because, so Goode thought, their Finnish leader had insisted on making statements which did not tally with their documentation. Goode's second effort succeeded. He spent a month in Moscow. Its highlight was an interview with Lenin who repeated his willingness to accept the terms for recognition which he had earlier given to America's unofficial envoy, William Bullitt.

This interview took place in August; it was not published until late October.[28] The reason reflects the difficulties which a liberal newspaper correspondent met. Early in September Goode reached Reval after a journey which for difficulty and danger was unique in his experience – and he had already made five hazardous crossings of the no man's land between the Esthonian and Russian lines, walking several miles each time with a pack weighing sixty pounds and carrying a white flag. His account of his journeys is more stimulating than the set-pieces of political and social enquiry which he wrote when he got to Moscow. Chance meetings near the front line showed how fluid the situation still was when the Soviet regime was not yet an irresistible tyranny. Goode described a company headquarters where the men crowded the room till it was suffocating and 'the officer suddenly appealed to them as tavaristche (comrades) and cleared the room, but he had to repeat the operation later on for all the men were as inquisitive as calves.' He was detained in Ostrov but only in a widow's house where he had the luxury of sleeping in a real bed instead of a third class railway compartment, and where, although there were two armed guards, one of them spent the evening cheerfully with Goode in the garden. Most of the Communists he met were desperately anxious to hear what the outside world thought of them, and vastly amused at what they heard – this was the time when stories of the nationalisation of women were widespread. Even his interview with Lenin seems to belong to an earlier, less effectively entrenched world. The questions were not submitted in advance: 'I had spoken of (them) to only one man, the commissary who accompanied me, and he became very depressed, and gave it as his opinion that Lenin would not answer them. To his unfeigned astonishment the questions were answered promptly, simply and decisively and when the interview was ended my companion naïvely expressed his wonderment.'

But on his third day back in Reval, Goode was arrested by the Esthonians at the request of the British Mission. Using a pocket-mirror as an improvised heliograph, Goode attracted the attention of a passerby to whom he dropped a letter addressed to an American journalist in Reval. Goode was released that evening and went to the British Consulate to protest. There he was offered as 'an act of courtesy' a passage to Helsingfors in a British destroyer. He accepted the offer only to find that he had been shanghaied. He was taken not to Helsingfors but to Björkö at Admiral Cowan's orders.

'I asked him . . . in what capacity I was present, whether as his guest or as his prisoner. He seemed a little disconcerted, but remarked that he had wished to see me, to which I replied that I had received no invitation but had been carried off on the open sea. He then said I was certainly his guest, on which we sat down and conversed. He asked me many questions, some of which I answered, others I declined to answer. At the close of the interview I was removed . . . to the light cruiser Danae on which I remained until I landed at Sheerness on Monday 29 September. During the whole of the period of three weeks during which I was detained I was not allowed once to set foot on shore . . . I was . . . refused any communication with the shore at Reval, Helsingfors or Copenhagen.' (13 October 1919)

Before embarking on the destroyer, Goode had taken all his papers to the Esthonian Foreign Ministry and had them officially sealed. The seal was broken and the *Times* correspondent in Helsingfors received some indication of what was in the packet for he transmitted a badly garbled account to his paper. On 13 September, while Goode was detained on the Danae, the *Times* printed what the *Guardian* rightly described as 'a wholly unwarranted attack' on him. On his return to England Goode went straight to Manchester. From there Scott wrote to Lord Curzon, the Foreign Secretary, to 'ask for an explanation of this extraordinary and to all appearance wholly unjustifiable treatment of a British subject' for which he felt that 'an apology and even reparation is due to Mr Goode.'[29] Meanwhile Goode had written to the *Times*:

'Your correspondent is pleased, absurdly enough, to describe me as a "thorough-paced Bolshevik agent." I am not an agent for anybody, but a newspaper correspondent with his proper work to do. I am stated by your correspondent to have brought back proposals for peace. I brought back no proposals for peace. I am stated to have intended to agitate in Finland, and to have been expected by the Red agents. I have not the slightest intention of agitating in Finland nor did I ever say I would. I did not say that Red agents were expecting me nor do I believe it. In fact I do not know any Red agents. I have no "intimate friend" who could have said, as alleged by your correspondent, that I was prepared to create a Red Revolution in England because it is something which I have never said, and so ludicrously untrue that it is not worth refuting. As for my being the sole conduit for Bolshevik communication with England, I must wholly repudiate any such pretension . . .'[30]

While Goode was still missing in Russia – two radio messages from Moscow were intercepted and only reached the M.G. 'from a reliable source in Helsingfors' after his return – Scott was already busily arranging for his successor. This time his choice fell on Arthur Ransome who had been a boy at Rugby with Ted Scott. Ransome had come back earlier in the year from his assignment in Russia with the *Daily News*. He went back to Moscow at the end of November and spent the greater part of the next four years there. It was the beginning of a dozen years of varied work for the paper in many corners of the world.

MR. ARTHUR RANSOME TAKES ADVANTAGE OF THIS YEAR'S EXTRA DAY TO VISIT MANCHESTER.

6

Scott liked to think that he had a 'special relationship' with President Wilson. In a sense this was true. Through Colonel House he heard on several occasions how much the President relied on the *Guardian*'s whole-hearted support for his policies. Scott on his side hoped that Wilson might give that leadership towards a just peace which it was now clear would not come from Lloyd George: – 'means well but is . . . squeezable . . . Lloyd George doesn't know (it is an intellectual defect) what principle means.'[31]

In August Scott paid a special visit to London to see Captain Walter Lippmann, as he then was, 'formerly one of the "Editors" of the *New Republic* (how Scott hated the plural!), now on special service as representative of the American War Office.' They had a long talk in which Scott made clear both his admiration for the President and his regret that 'the power of America was underestimated and her influence insufficiently exerted.' Asked to give examples, Scott mentioned intervention in Russia and 'the peace offers of the Emperor Karl, so insultingly and stupidly turned down by Clemenceau.' Towards the end of the interview Scott asked how he could get into 'effective contact' with the President's mind. Lippmann said he was quite sure that Colonel House would give all possible assistance and that he followed the M.G. closely, having someone in London who regularly sent him cuttings. 'But,' Lippmann added, 'for this purpose it was necessary that we should be represented in America. For this purpose it would be much best that we should send someone from this country.'*

It seems extraordinary that the M.G. should not have had a man in America, but after Rollo Ogden gave up the New York correspondence in 1909 there had been no satisfactory permanent arrangement. During the war the paper had relied largely on S. K. Ratcliffe, for fifty years a leading English Radical journalist and then London correspondent of the *New Republic*. He had covered the 1916 presidential election for the *Guardian*. Almost as remarkable as the absence of a regular correspondent is the kind of representation which Scott now began urgently to consider. He seems to have wanted an ambassador rather than a working journalist, a correspondent who would have access to the White House and would be able privately to brief Scott on Wilson's views rather than somebody who would provide the paper with a

---

* Interview Notes 17 August 1918 (MS). It was for sending the M.G. news of this Austrian initiative that Robert Dell had been expelled from France three months before.

regular news service or commentary. He may even have envisaged somebody who would represent his views to the President and Colonel House in the same way that he himself talked confidentially to British Cabinet Ministers with a freedom which he did not use in his leaders.

Scott's first choice was apparently A. E. Zimmern, who at that time was working in the Foreign Office. Zimmern was willing and Scott went to see his chief, Sir William Tyrrell whom he found 'a most shrewd, humorous and sprightly person' but also a possessive one. Zimmern could not be spared. Scott immediately approached Gilbert Murray who was 'a good deal interested but wished to be assured that he would be persona grata to the President.' Scott accordingly sent a cable to Colonel House to find out. 'I do not believe a better selection could be made,' was the reply. 'I believe it will be serviceable to both countries to have a man like Mr Murray here to interpret the one to the other.' But this, too, fell through. Scott thought next of Arnold Toynbee, Gilbert Murray's son-in-law, but he too was not available. So Scott turned once more to Tyrrell but, though 'very friendly and chatty,' he had no fresh name to suggest as a suitable American correspondent. It was more than two months since Lippmann had pointed out the need. No appointment had been made. No appointment of the kind envisaged ever was made.[32]

It is characteristic of Scott that the three men whom we know he approached for this important mission were all Oxford men, all 'Greats' men, and all dons – but then, of course, President Wilson was himself a professor.

The climax of the 'special relationship' was reached when Wilson came to England at the end of 1918. He reached Manchester on 29 December and invited Scott to come round to see him. They spent an hour alone together. What they said to one another was strictly private, but the fact of their meeting was news. From America S. K. Ratcliffe wrote to Crozier: 'Wilson in Manchester must have been great. I'd give something to hear the "gup" in the Corridor. The sending for C.P. made a sensation over this Continent. All good Americans who understand rejoiced. Some others gasped. The Boston Transcript, which looks the best and is the very worst (because it belongs to Boston) paper in the Eastern States simply foamed at the mouth.'[33] This is what it said:

'In the meantime, the Americans who are at present domiciled in Great Britain must be receiving a decidedly painful impression from the attempt which that recognised organ of British pacifism, the Manchester Guardian, is making to force the Wilson Fourteen Points, in their most pacifist interpretation, upon our French Allies . . . In spite of the intimacy of the President with the Manchester pacifist paper – its editor being the only unofficial person whom he has summoned to an interview since he arrived in Europe – the French Premier is depending on Mr Lloyd George and his associates, . . . instead of upon the *Manchester Guardian*, for the definition of England's position.'

By this time Scott had abandoned his search for an Englishman to send to America. Immediately after the President's visit he asked Lippmann, who was giving up his job with the American peace delegation, if he would act as the M.G. correspondent in New York. Lippmann, who was 30, remained the M.G. correspondent in America until the end of 1923 with several breaks during which sometimes S. K. Ratcliffe and sometimes Lewis Gannett* took over. Scott had no reason to regret his choice: 'Your work,' he told Lippmann, 'has given it (the M.G.) distinction such as attaches to the work of no other American correspondent.'[34] This judgment is underlined by the frequency with which points made by Lippmann are taken up for comment in leading articles.

The role which the *Guardian*'s correspondent had to play was radically different when Lippmann took over from what had been planned when he and Scott first discussed it in the summer of 1918. Then it had been to support the President's policy, 'the only great and disinterested influence at work in the war,'[35] by securing understanding for it. In 1919 the correspondent's job was to explain why this influence was waning. Lippmann shared the blame between Europe and the President. First, Europe's share:

Men may differ as to whether France should have the Sarre or Britain the bulk of the German colonies, but they agree vaguely that it is not a very inspiring business one way or the other. I report this because it is fundamental to future relations. For if it is true, as so many Englishmen have been saying in recent months, that a cardinal object of British policy is the perfecting of the understanding with America, then candour makes it necessary to remark that too much has been done to defeat that object. (28 June 1919)

Then Wilson's own character. Lippmann told Scott that the United States was suffering from a dangerous centralisation of responsibility. 'The President will not delegate, and his heads of departments will not make a move of any importance without consulting him.'[36] This weakness developed until, when Wilson was taken ill, Lippmann

---

* Gannett was born in 1891 and was on the staff of the American *Nation* from 1919 to 1928, when he joined the New York *Herald Tribune*. From 1930 to 1956 he wrote for it a weekly column, 'Books and Things.'

reported that his temporary abandonment of the struggle would help rather than hurt his cause:

'Six months ago by inviting Senators Lodge, Borah and Johnson to Paris he might have had a treaty that would have been accepted without much opposition . . . But never in all his career has Mr Wilson played so lone a hand. Mr Lansing (the Secretary of State) has virtually abstained from any effort to help the treaty. The other members of the Cabinet drift along, each in his own department, with little more than a newspaper knowledge of events. Almost all Liberals practically without exception are isolated from him.' (30 September 1919)

And so America withdrew into her shell, leaving Britain to play for another quarter of a century the role of a greater Power than in the ultimate reckoning she could be. Her change in relative status was concealed by America's abstention.

7

One unpleasant thing had become clear. It was that the picture Americans had of Europe – and to most of them Britain was simply part of Europe – was far from flattering. What was reported back to America was the jostling for place among the politicians and the jingo roar of the great mass of newspapers. The voice of liberal England went unheard. Scott's leaders – intolerable thought – were not reproduced in American papers, though the Central News had arranged to cable Sidebotham's 'Student of War' articles in full. Occasionally there would come back an echo of thanks for some leader on Ireland reprinted probably in the newspaper of an ethnic minority. Thus from Denver there came a letter in 1916 to say that 'Everyone here has read with great interest the splendid stand you have taken about the terrible murders by the Radical Government of the poor misguided Irishmen.'[37] But far more characteristic was the pessimistic view taken by Oswald Garrison Villard of the New York *Nation* who told Scott how few were the quotations in American newspapers from the English liberal press – little from the *Manchester Guardian*, nothing from the London *Nation*.[38]

Scott now took a step which provided a way round this conspiracy of silence as he would have thought it. In the summer of 1919 the first number of the *Manchester Guardian Weekly* was published. There is no record of the discussions which must have preceded this new venture and, on the business side, much was left to chance. The then circulation manager of the M.G. was on his honeymoon when the weekly was started and it was left to a new, junior employee* to improvise arrangements on his own initiative. The only guidance he got was the negative one that the weekly was intended for overseas readers and that circulation was not to be sought at home (though it was not declined) lest the daily should be harmed.

There was soon no doubt that the new venture was justified. After two months a progress report was given in the firm's house magazine: 'There is scarcely a corner of the civilised world to which it is not being posted regularly. As might had been expected its largest sale outside these islands is in the United States.' Other daily papers, such as the *Times* and the *Scotsman*, then had weekly editions for overseas. It is probably true to say that they appealed primarily to readers who felt themselves cut off from home. From the beginning much of the overseas circulation of the *Manchester Guardian Weekly* was among people to whom England had never been home. What its readers had in common was not a community of blood but a community of political faith. It may be for this reason that the weekly has outlived its competitors and is now in its second half century.

The first number is dated 4 July – Independence Day – and contained the news of the signing of the Treaty of Versailles. Prominent among the 'Notes of the Week' was a summary of the manifesto, or rather disclaimer, which General Smuts had issued as a rider to his signature:

'His justification for the terms of the treaty is, not that they are good, but that they bring to an end the state of suspense which has brought as much ruin to Europe as the four years of war. The treaty he regards as being no more than "the liquidation of the war situation of the world".'

This was also Scott's view. Both Scott and Smuts lived to see that the Treaty of Versailles was not even that.

* W. J. Lascelles, later himself circulation manager and a director.

CHAPTER TWENTY-EIGHT

The Crest of the Wave

I

'WHAT'S Mr Wadsworth been doing to-day?' George Leach's daughter used to ask her father. One day the question was answered before it could be put. 'You'll never guess what Wadsworth did to-day,' Leach announced as he opened the door. 'When I got to the office there he was sitting in *my* chair, with his feet on *my* desk, reading *my* paper.' One side of that many-sided little man had more than a touch of Arnold Bennett's Card. It may well have been especially prominent when he was young. Another story tells how, while others would linger painstakingly over the music hall notices in which they celebrated Little Tich or Marie Lloyd, Wadsworth would briskly finish what he was writing and then tease his colleagues with the annoying offer, 'Want any quotations?' But others who knew Wadsworth in those days, colleagues on the M.G. and contacts in Ireland, remember him as a shy young man. The two traits are not inconsistent.

It was at the end of June 1917 that A. P. Wadsworth came to the *Manchester Guardian* from the *Rochdale Observer*. Both place names are significant. Regarded as a candidate for the Corridor, Wadsworth in 1917 would not have been considered. He had not got a first-class degree; he had not been to Oxford or Cambridge; he had not been to any university; he had not even, like T. M. Young, been on the classical side of Manchester Grammar School. He had been to Rochdale Higher Grade Elementary School and left at the age of 14. But in 1921 he moved from the Reporters' Room to the Corridor and in 1944 he became editor. Like Jeremiah Garnett and John Harland, Wadsworth belonged to the intellectually self-made men of the North, the often forgotten counterpart of the financially self-made men whom polite London Society ridiculed in tiresomely snobbish jokes. 'Intellectually self-made' is, of course, true only in the sense that he came up the hard way. Wadsworth was a born historian, and no man could have had a better teacher than R. H. Tawney. In 1907 Tawney, then aged 27, became the tutor of the first university tutorial class, a landmark in adult education. Among the members was Wadsworth who was too young to be in-

cluded in the register as a 'grant-earning student.' It was the beginning
of a life-long friendship, which was important not only to Wadsworth
personally but to the M.G. On many matters, but especially on education, Tawney became a frequent contributor and an important
influence on the policy of the paper.

Wadsworth's unofficial higher education was not confined to
economics and history. Among the cuttings of his own early work
there are a few notices of plays which he had seen in his early twenties.
They include Montague on 'The Importance of Being Earnest' and
'Elektra'; Monkhouse on 'The Playboy of the Western World'; and
Mair on 'The Critic' and 'Man and Superman.' Between them Miss
Horniman, Janet Achurch and the *Guardian* critics could provide a
young man with a course in English literature which few universities
could surpass.

Wadsworth had been thoroughly trained as a reporter. Not only
was his shorthand good, but his inborn curiosity had been sharpened
to a professional watchfulness for even the most commonplace happening which might yield news. On the *Rochdale Observer* a reporter
was expected to notice when the blinds were down in any house he
passed on his way to work and to arrive at the office knowing who it
was that had died. Such minutiae were not for *Guardian* reporters, but
Wadsworth was using the same developed faculty when he noticed who
made up a group at the bar during the TUC or Labour Party Conference and who, unexpectedly, was not there. He would draw his own
conclusions, unobtrusively follow them up and next morning *Guardian*
readers would get the benefit of his observation, never suspecting its
humble beginnings in Rochdale. In his approach to news Wadsworth
resembled Leach, another Rochdale man, rather than Haslam Mills.

Between them Mills and Leach had recruited a remarkable staff of
'intellectually self-made men.' In 1915 A. V. Cookman and Howard
Spring came, but both joined the army almost at once and did not
return until 1919. Cookman came from the *Salisbury Journal*, a weekly
paper. He eventually became the *Times* dramatic critic. Spring, who
had started as a messenger on the *South Wales Daily News*, came from
the *Yorkshire Observer*; 'Don't write as if you're writing for the *Yorkshire Observer*,' was the editor's opening advice to Spring. 'Write as if
you're writing for the M.G.'* When a vacancy for a *Guardian* reporter
was advertised Spring applied. George Leach wrote to him: 'All of us

* The editor was A. M. Drysdale, *M.G.* reporter from 1899 to 1905 when he
went to the *Tribune*. Scott got him the editorship of the *Yorkshire Observer*. He
returned to the *M.G.* as parliamentary sketch writer, succeeding his brother in 1924.

who have ever met you are glad to know that there is a great likelihood of having you as a colleague on the M.G. We could wish for nothing better. We have always had a nice comfortable crew on board, and, with something like 200 applications, allowing for the usual percentage, there was always a risk of getting a bounder unawares.' He warned Spring that he would have to stay overnight because no appointment could be made without the 'laying on of hands' by the editor who in those days did not come down to the office until 8 p.m.[1] Spring went to the *Evening Standard* when he left the *Guardian*. Before long he settled in Cornwall to write the novels by which he is best remembered.

Nineteen-seventeen brought Cardus as well as Wadsworth. Cardus had been office boy; insurance clerk; cricket 'pro' at Shrewsbury School; headmaster's secretary; and music critic of the Northern edition of the *Daily Citizen*[2] at a penny a line, paying his own admission because concert givers did not consider the *Citizen* worth free tickets. But his heart's desire always took him to the *Guardian*. 'It must have been round about 1908,' Cardus recalls of the time when he was 18, 'that I often performed a ritual known only to myself. I would go and stand, fairly late on Monday nights, on the pavement at the corner of Cross Street and Market Street, opposite the *Manchester Guardian* building. I would look at the lighted windows and imagine that behind any one of them Montague was at work on a dramatic notice; that Agate was adding a finishing touch; that Samuel Langford, greatest of all writers on music, was meditating on Brahms over his desk.'[3] Now, nine years later, the door opened for him almost accidentally. He was out of work because he was a medical reject who might yet be called up. He applied for a job in the M.G. counting house. Scott read the cuttings which he sent with his letter and offered him employment as his personal 'semi-secretary.' It did not work. Cardus was again unemployed. Suddenly six weeks later Scott suggested that he might like to be a reporter and told him to go and see Haslam Mills. Cardus has worked up his interview with the elegant Chief Reporter into a conversation piece which Mills would have appreciated. ' "What," Mills asked, "are your expectations about or *in re* salary?" I told him I had no expectations at all. "Good," he remarked, "that provides us with a reasonably broad basis for negotiation. The emoluments which accrue on the *Manchester Guardian* are not large. Would you, could you, consider the idea of 30/– weekly, which is Mr Scott's tentative and preliminary proposal – plus 10/– for expenses, also payable weekly"? I accepted unconditionally.'[4] First as 'Cricketer' and then as music critic Cardus found work to his heart's content on the *Guardian* and an appreciation among *Guardian* readers which he would probably never have found elsewhere.

He has had his periods away on other papers; he has had his disagreements and grievances; but a homing instinct has brought him back. Cardus and Wadsworth were as dissimilar as any Cavalier and Roundhead, but each was a typical *Guardian* man; between them they represented a good two-thirds of the paper's special ethos.

Next to join was Matthew Anderson, a Scot who had insisted on leaving school when he found that the family idea was to make him a Presbyterian minister. His first newspaper job earned him 5/– a week. He came to the M.G. from the *Scotsman* in 1918 – one of the few reporters to be taken on by Scott and not by Mills, He was always rather a lone wolf in the Room. Two recruits in 1919 were Harry Boardman, whose father was a silk hand-loom weaver, and Charles Green, who had once been an engineering student at Leeds University. He had left without taking a degree. The only thing at which he had really worked hard was shorthand for his mind was set on becoming a reporter. Before the war Green had been on the *Yorkshire Observer*, Boardman on the *Manchester Courier*. While he was in the army Boardman had contributed a few 'back-pagers' to the M.G. When other men grumbled at C.P., Boardman would recall his kindness in writing to encourage his unknown young contributor. There was only one graduate among these new reporters. H. D. Nichols had read science at Manchester University.

Nineteen-twenty brought Frank Appleby and Donald Boyd. Appleby, like Spring and Green, had been on the *Yorkshire Observer*. He came with a reputation for political interests, but he was not considered (nor would he have wished to be considered) one of the 'writers.' This was then a current M.G. word which indicated a cleavage of ambition and of social life between two groups of M.G. reporters. Donald Boyd, who came from the *Daily Mail*, was emphatically a 'writer.' His father had started him off as a junior reporter on the *Wharfedale Observer* paying a premium of £20. He next moved to the *Leeds Mercury* at half a guinea a week with the promise of a whole guinea after a year.

All except Wadsworth and Cardus had served in the army. All were men who nowadays would have gone to a university. It is doubtful whether they would have been better educated. But, of course, they owed their intellectual life to the survival of the fittest. Many set out on journalism with high hopes; few reached the M.G. whose Reporters' Room, as Mills told Cardus on the day he joined, was 'not as reporters' rooms elsewhere,' but 'as a place for young writers (he did not call me a young journalist, oh dear no: "a young writer") was less a newspaper office than an Academy almost in an Athenian sense.'[5]

The Reporters' Room by Birger Lundquist

It is doubtful whether this war and post-war wave of *Guardian* reporters were better men than their predecessors. The fitful impressions one gets of earlier generations suggests that now forgotten men like David Paton and J. E. McInnes formed as interesting a company. What is certain, however, is that the new men had a unique opportunity. They took it. From Ireland Hammond wrote to his wife 'I think the real strength of the M.G. is in their reporters.'[6]

2

In Ireland their job was always exacting and sometimes hazardous, but they believed it was in a good cause. From the beginning of 1919 the *Guardian* had usually one, sometimes two and occasionally three staff reporters in Ireland. Nobody was sent who did not wish to go – a recognition that the job was dangerous. Not all who wanted to go were sent – a recognition that the job was not easy. They were young men. Even George Leach was only 42. Most of the others were under 30.

George Leach covered the period from the 1918 election to the start of 'the troubles' largely on his own. It was he, for instance, who reported how, 'by one of those coincidences which only happen in Ireland,' the Sinn Fein MP's walked into the Mansion House for the first meeting of Dail Eireann just as an official victory luncheon for the Dublin Fusiliers ended with 'God Save the King.'

'The Speaker called the roll of the Irish members with full solemnity. Sir Edward Carson, Colonel Craig and all the other Ulstermen were duly summoned without the suggestion of a laugh, and one of the three clerks at the table answered "Absent" with equal gravity. More usually it was an exclamation of "Imprisoned" . . . All the questions propounded were carried unanimously without being put. They included a declaration of Ireland's full independence . . . Their face value may easily be cheapened, but looking at the Assembly to-day, and recognising most of the gallery as men who pay the income tax, that would be dangerous. "An Dail Eireann", as one has seen it to-day, may be inarticulate but it has said a good deal.' (22 January 1919)

The same day Irish Volunteers killed two members of the RIC who were guarding a cartload of explosives in County Tipperary. 'The troubles' had begun.

A year later Leach developed pneumonia in Dublin and died there. He had made such a name for himself and the M.G. in Ireland that there were crowds to see his body taken home for burial. After his death the bulk of the reporting in 1920 was done by Wadsworth and Boardman. In 1921 and 1922 the major share fell to Boyd and Cookman. Spring covered the debates on the treaty in the Dail. Anderson was mainly in Ulster after the treaty. Green, Nichols and Appleby all spent several months in Ireland.

In Dublin the link with the *Freeman's Journal* was close. Its two leader-writers – Robert Donovan and J. W. Good – were in succession correspondents for the M.G. Donovan, a Catholic, was professor of English literature at the National University. Good, a Belfast-born man, held, according to Boyd who became a close friend, that 'one of the properest occupations of men is "to settle in an easy chair and read that moderate man, Voltaire". ' Much of the English press was bitterly hostile to Sinn Fein, but the *Guardian* was not so isolated in its position as it had been during the Boer War. Spring, for instance, formed a close working alliance with Hugh Martin of the *Daily News*, which took roughly the same line. Boyd worked mainly with Donald Spend-love who was once denounced by a Belfast paper as 'the Sinn Fein correspondent of the Press Association.' Their work involved close contacts with the spokesmen for the rival forces in what one side regarded as an international war and the other as the suppression of crime.

Contacts with Sinn Fein were easy. Mrs Green's house was a much used centre. She was the widow of J. R. Green, the historian, and had long had a hand in the *Guardian*'s Irish arrangements. Back in Parnell's time, for instance, she had recommended J. F. Taylor to Scott as Irish correspondent. Frank Gallagher and Erskine Childers were freely accessible to reporters though wanted in vain by the police. With both of them the M.G. men established easy relations which developed into respect and friendship. Boyd recalls Gallagher going round with leaflets tucked into the top of his socks or sitting in the kitchen of an eighteenth-century house singing 'Dark Rosaleen' over a mug of cocoa; and Erskine Childers handing over papers in Dame Street in the centre of Dublin in the face of the police.

Boyd remembers too how, when he used to visit Patrick Mac-Gilligan, another Sinn Fein Minister, 'I thought I should make myself small and enter through the letter box, but the door opened in the usual way and inside, as likely as not, there would be several senior officers of the IRA.' He recalls too, walks over the hills to see Desmond Fitzgerald, whose only protection seemed to be some rough looking young men who looked in to see if Boyd was a welcome visitor.

News from the Government side came from Dublin Castle where Basil Clarke headed a team of able young journalists. Relations here might have been difficult in view of the paper's political line. But with Clarke in charge they were not. He had, after all, once been a reporter on the M.G.,* a connection which he valued and took pains to maintain. The *Guardian* men felt that he did a difficult and distasteful job honourably and well. But outside Dublin the M.G. reporters had their moments of difficulty with the British authorities. There was for instance, the occasion when Boyd and the editor of the *Connacht Tribune* were sent for by a British colonel who gave them a token horse-whipping, striding round and round cracking his hunting crop.

On the whole there was remarkably little interference with press messages. Once, during the Civil War that followed the treaty, a censorship was suddenly imposed. Green tried to telephone the news to Manchester but was promptly cut off. A private wire, however, addressed to 'Attenborough, 3 Cross St Manchester' got through and the message, 'Should like to tell you more but unable,' was correctly

---

* He left in 1910 for the *Daily Mail*. Oral tradition has it that C.P. was shown one of his early signed articles in the *Mail*. After peering over it, he looked up and said, 'A very lucky escape, Mr Mills.' But Crozier thought otherwise. Asked to provide Scott with a brief for a testimonial, he wrote: 'He is about the only man I know who set out deliberately from nothing to become a good descriptive writer and succeeded out and out. At the start he bought an English composition book and practised incessantly.' (7 October 1916)

interpreted. (Attenborough was the chief sub-editor and the *Guardian*'s address was 3 Cross St). At other times telegraphic communication was interrupted and it became necessary to cross nightly by mail boat to Holyhead, telephone or wire the copy from there and return to Dublin in time for the next day's work – journeys which Spring remembered all his life because, though a keen small boat sailor, he was always sick on the Irish Sea.

But such incidents are commonplaces of journalism. What was not commonplace were the events the *Guardian* men had to report. Ten days in the second half of November 1920 may serve as an example. On Wednesday the 17th Wadsworth paid a visit to Tipperary. That night he sent off a full, painstaking account of what happened in the town during the 48 hours when it was cut off from the outside world and pretty thoroughly ravaged. When he got back to Dublin his next job was to defend his earlier report of atrocities in Galway which the Chief Secretary had contradicted. The Chief Secretary's views, Wadsworth concluded, were tenable only if one believed that the people of Galway had 'a fraternal love of self-mutilation to prove a case against the police.'

Meanwhile on Thursday the Chief Secretary was telling the House of Commons about plans to poison British troops with typhoid and to give their cavalry horses glanders. The more details he gave, the more improbable members found the story. Finally, according to Drysdale's parliamentary sketch, the House 'burst into a resounding and disconcerting peal of laughter' as the amateurish instructions on how 'to pour out microbes' blossomed into benevolence and ended 'with the pious benediction, faintly recalling the Christmas mood of Tiny Tim, "God bless you all".' From Ireland Green reported that the story was received there 'with incredulity.' He gave verbatim on Friday the Dublin Castle account, which he plainly doubted, of the midnight search of Professor Michael Hayes's house. The plans were said to have been discovered in the room of an unknown man who fled in his night shirt and escaped the pursuing soldiers by jumping a ten foot wall. In the afternoon Green managed to see the Sinn Fein leader, Arthur Griffith, who naturally dismissed the typhoid story as a ridiculous lie. Forty-five years later the little room concealed by a false wall at the back of the ground floor of a shop where Griffith was writing at a narrow table was still vivid in Green's memory.

Wadsworth's Friday message about the Galway reprisals had ended with the ominous news that there had been burning and beatings at a number of small farms in County Leitrim, showing that 'the police terror is still going on vigorously and that more districts are being opened up.' He set out for Longford and made a long round of visits following the trail of the Auxiliaries as they had followed the track of suspected Sinn Fein irregulars. The Auxiliaries' route could be traced by such scrawls on the walls as 'Down Sinn Fein,' 'Why Shield Murderers?' 'Up Black and Tans,' and 'God Save the King.' 'But,' Wadsworth went on, 'the work of their passage is more apparent in terrorised women and children, in men beaten and flogged, and in looted shops and burned cottages.' He visited, for instance, the farm of John Owens at Augharan which had been raided about two or three o'clock in the morning. The two elder boys were out; but the younger ones were at home.

'Between the two rooms of the house is a half-wall which does not quite reach to the roof. Over this was flung a halter and John Francis Owens, a lad of 16 years, was made to stand on a chair and the halter put round his neck. The chair was kicked away and the boy left half-strangled . . . The boy of 14 was tied in the same way, but fell in a faint in a tub of pigwash when the chair was removed . . .'

The elder boy had been beaten with the buckle end of a Volunteer belt found in the house, which was then set on fire. 'When I visited the house yesterday nothing was standing of the cottage or barn but the outside walls. All the crops had been reduced to ashes.' So Wadsworth ended his description of this particular visit. Everywhere he heard similar stories and saw similar destruction. 'One of the wretched things,' Boyd could never forget, 'was that the Auxiliaries were men like ourselves, who had just come out of the war . . . They weren't strangers; they were ourselves askew.'

Wadsworth's story from Longford was unexpectedly banished to an inside page in Monday's paper. It had to make way for Green's single-handed account of Black Sunday in Dublin. It was Black Sunday whichever way you looked at it. The IRA conducted a precisely timed military operation in the early hours of the morning. English officers concerned in intelligence and court-martial work were shot in their hotels and quarters and many of their papers destroyed. In the afternoon there was a large crowd at the Gaelic Football match at Croke Park, Dublin. Auxiliaries descended on it, opened fire and killed ten people outright and injured another sixty-five. That night the curfew was extended, railway travel stopped, cars ordered off the road – even doctors were forced to walk – while roving Auxiliaries fired shots down the main streets and the whole city was in a state of terror.

On Monday the *Guardian* reporters found that the official government story of what happened at Croke Park did not cover the facts.

Wednesday's paper contained the story of the mysterious killing of three prisoners in the guard room in Dublin Castle. There were no survivors to contest the official story that they were trying to escape. This was followed by the news that, in spite of protests, the enquiry into the Croke Park affair would be held in private. A week after Bloody Sunday Cardinal Logue, while denouncing the murder of the British officers, also condemned the Croke Park shootings. This 'may sound a little uncalled for to English people misled by a series of half-true white-washing accounts issued from Dublin Castle, (but it) none the less expresses the sentiments of Irishmen, even of moderates like Mr Stephen Gwynn.' It was sufficiently clear that it expressed also the sentiments of the *Guardian* reporters.

The diary of these ten days is typical of what they were doing month by month. Its importance is that it is typical. No reader of the M.G. could fail to be aware of what was happening in Ireland 'where no man exposes himself needlessly when a military lorry passes by' as the paper's own inquest on the Croke Park tragedy put it. Neither Sinn Fein ambushes nor British reprisals were exceptional events; they were everyday occurrences. The *Guardian* gathered all it could, and printed all that it collected. The Government, on the other hand, regularly suppressed or distorted half the facts – the atrocities committed by its own servants – while giving great prominence to the murdered police-men. It became the prisoner of its own propaganda and could only be freed to make peace if English people were told the truth. This truth-telling was the M.G.'s most important contribution to the peace-making. At first British people, including M.G. readers and not only the numer-ous Conservatives among them, did not want to know what was happening in Ireland. The correspondence columns contained many sceptical letters. But when they realised what was being done, they were certain it must stop.

3

This involved recognising not only that Ireland was a nation, but that it was already a nation state. The most important thing about the agree-ment that established the Irish Free State was that it was a treaty. Treaties are made between States. Readers of the *Guardian* had been able to follow the way in which the Sinn Fein shadow government gradually took on substance. They knew that the alternative to Dublin Castle's violent but ineffective attempt to maintain its authority was not anarchy but the recognition *de jure* of what was already in many parts of Ireland the *de facto* government.

Their preparation had started with George Leach's account of the first session of Dail Eireann. It had been carried on when Ivor Brown was sent out in the spring of 1920 to see whether Lloyd George's Government of Ireland Bill could be made acceptable. At first Brown over-estimated the strength of Irish Labour and its differences from Sinn Fein. He gave, for instance, too much weight to a trade union official who was 'as keen that the Irish nation should become a Worker's Republic as that it should become a republic at all.' 'What impresses me,' Brown wrote in a characteristic passage, 'is the way in which economic issues are beginning to supersede political issues in a country where every man is a politician.' It was not until he reached Galway that he began to realise the strength of Sinn Fein. He attended an illegal Land Court and saw how it inspired respect for 'some sort of positive law built up on the foundation of natural or divine law' to replace the total rejection of English law. He decided that these courts 'create no disorder; they prevent much.' 'The police have been driven into the towns, and even there they do practically no police duty as their main task is to look after themselves.'[7]

The first stage towards the peace conference was to make a truce. This took effect on 11 July 1921. During it Boyd was able to do a good deal to build up for M.G. readers a picture of the working of Sinn Fein. He visited Land Courts which had come into the open after a period underground. He interviewed the Republican Chief of Police, which was now quite a distinct body from the I R A. He attended army training exercises which were inspected by the Republican Chief of Staff. He described carefully the working of the Dail. A thoughtful reader could have no doubt when the conference opened on 11 October that it was one between governments.

C.P. had kept away from Lloyd George for over a year. He had tried reasoning with him, but the time came when he felt that Lloyd George was behaving not only with conspicuous stupidity, as he had done when he wrecked the Irish Convention by the threat of conscription, but also wickedly. Once the truce was made Scott felt that he could go to see the Prime Minister when Lloyd George wrote inviting him. No journalist, not even Scott, lightly surrenders a warm and intimate association with the Prime Minister of the day. He was glad to take it up again. Probably his influence was increased by his toughness during the past year. In the final stage of the negotiations with Sinn Fein he was in constant touch with Lloyd George and on several occasions acted as an intermediary with the Irish delegation.

The rise of Sinn Fein had entirely altered C.P.'s position in Irish affairs. Up to 1918 Scott had been exceptionally well informed from the inside about Irish opinion through his close association with John Dillon, his dearest friend among working politicians as Hobhouse was among political theorists. Now Dillon and his party counted for nothing and, though Scott never let this old friendship drop, he knew that it was now politically valueless. There was no one to take Dillon's place. Scott exchanged letters with Lord Justice O'Connor; he consulted Alec Wilson, the 'Ulster Imperialist' of the M.G. articles. Sir Horace Plunkett and A. E. wrote articles for him. These men thought as he did, but they all knew only too well that they were far from the centre of power.

In Ireland Sinn Fein was now clearly at that centre. Scott had no easy informal relations with its leaders. Before his meeting with President Wilson he had received a deputation from the Sinn Fein executive about the possibility of a hearing for Ireland at the Versailles Conference, but he does not seem to have had any other personal contact until he met De Valera immediately after the truce and before he and Lloyd George had made things up. His note of the interview shows how different De Valera's standpoint was from the M.G.'s:

'I remarked that I fancied he had a little quarrel with me for something in the M.G., and he replied with alacrity that he had and at once launched forth. Some time ago he had written a letter to his mother commending the M.G. as a broad-minded paper and friendly to Ireland. It was a private letter but somehow it got into the press and had gone all over the States. "So now you would like to recall it?" "Yes, I certainly would . . ." It appeared that his grievance was that we had denounced some of the Sinn Fein murders as on a par with the murders committed by the agents of the Government. I said we discriminated between acts which were really acts of war done in the open and assassinations of individuals like the Dublin murders which we certainly did utterly condemn. But he would hear of no such distinction.'

They went on to discuss Lloyd George's Caernarvon speech, which had 'almost completely estranged' Scott from Lloyd George. 'What (De Valera) objected to was the strong assertion of the right to coerce Ireland, not the means taken for doing it. "I don't think much about that," ' he said.[8] It was the means which outraged Scott.

Scott's talk with De Valera came about through 'shy, serious, witty, learned and kindly' J. M. Denvir, a sub-editor in the London Office of the M.G. who unobtrusively provided much valuable Irish news. James Bone chose Denvir as an example of the 'quietly extraordinary men' who somehow unexpectedly arrive in Fleet Street. In *London Echoing*, Bone recalled how in his boyhood Denvir had smuggled into Ireland in a fish basket illegal papers printed by his father in Liverpool, and how his father had hidden American Fenians who had come over to give a hand with outrages in England.[9]

Later, during the peace negotiations, Scott, acting as an intermediary for Lloyd George, saw Michael Collins. He obviously liked Collins better than De Valera:

'The telephone rang at intervals when he sprang upon it fiercely as an enemy and yelled a challenge that might have split the instrument. Then (Desmond) Fitzgerald would appear and he relapsed into gloomy silence until the interruption was over. In spite of these mannerisms I found him a straightforward and quite agreeable savage . . . In the course of the conversation I had occasion to refer to something in the M.G. which I supposed he did not see. Yes, he had seen it and "some damned bad leaders" in it. He was no doubt referring to our denunciation of the Sinn Fein murders as strictly parallel to the murders by the Black and Tans. Naturally that came home rather to him . . .'[10]

Scott and Collins met again during the last stages of the negotiation. Whatever the 'straightforward and agreeable savage,' may have thought of Scott's leaders, he thought well enough of the M.G. to write a leader page article for which he refused payment. It appeared on the day the terms of the treaty were published. His theme was 'Ireland as the Pivot of a League of Nations' in which he foresaw something like the association between the nations of the old Commonwealth as it developed after the Statute of Westminster.

Neither Denvir nor these very occasional meetings with Sinn Fein Ministers could take the place of Scott's old intimacy with the Nationalist leaders. There was need for somebody to play the role of lobby correspondent with Sinn Fein, somebody who could safely be talked to 'off the record' and brief the editor privately about the shape of Sinn Fein thinking. Most of the M.G. reporters in Ireland could have done this but, as far as is known, Scott never asked them for this help.

But if Scott failed to pick his reporters' brains, he respected their consciences. He never attempted to influence what they wrote. He would have regarded it as immoral to 'brief' them. At one stage Scott fell into the dangerous view that, if reprisals there must be, it would be better that they should be controlled and official than inflicted by 'the soldiery – the police in fact are soldiers, armed and acting as such – let loose, without direction and without restraint, on the population for all the world like Bashi-bazouks.'* Later a controlled,

* M.G. 23 November 1920. Compare the *Times* leader on 29 September: 'If we accept the evidence of Sinn Fein, the new constabulary out vie the Bashi-Bazouks.' Earlier, on September 14, it had written of a 'Saturnalia of reprisals.' Under Northcliffe the editorial policy of the *Times* was a good deal closer to that of the M.G. on Ireland than on most controversial issues.

official reprisal was made. C.P. sent Green to find out what the Irish thought about it, giving him no indication at all about what he wanted him to write. 'I reported in my message,' Green recalls, "As for the reprisal itself, it is the universal opinion here that it was cruel and unjust". 'That was printed just as I had written it. He was an editor of complete integrity.' And, perhaps because he was just that, he had a staff of complete integrity.

The *Guardian's* news of the negotiations came partly from Harold Dore, the lobby correspondent, and partly from J. L. Hammond ('Politicus' for the occasion), who gave up the whole of the autumn to the paper. Nineteen-twenty-one was an almost entirely Irish year for Hammond. It had opened with two long special supplements to the *Nation* – 'A Tragedy of Errors' in January followed by 'The Terror in Action' in April – with many other contributions in between. He had been principal leader-writer in Manchester during C.P.'s summer holiday and had 'done excellently for us' in his Irish leaders – seven Longs in twelve days.[11] He paid two visits to Ireland – in February and just before the Conference opened. What he saw and heard there appeared as outcrops in what he wrote on the negotiations. Sometimes horror prevailed – that Black Hole of Calcutta, for instance: a coal cellar in which seven prisoners were kept for several weeks with only an open grating for light and straw for a bed.[12] Sometimes it was hope. Hope even in the blackest times and, in the end, hope triumphant so that on the day the treaty was signed, he wrote 'In Ireland almost alone men hope' – a reflection on the Europe left by Versailles and of the euphoria brought about by what he took to be the end of an old, bad story.

It was, of course, hope partially unfounded and totally premature. The *Guardian* reporters were to be busy in the South for a long time with the bitter civil war between the two wings of Sinn Fein. In the North they are still busy.

Matthew Anderson went to Ireland in May 1922 expecting to make his headquarters in Dublin. The day he arrived a Unionist member of the Northern Parliament was murdered by gunmen in Belfast. Anderson moved to the North. Ominously the hotel manager insisted on his having an attic bedroom with access to the roof for safety's sake: the M.G. was not well liked in Belfast as it was in Dublin. He found he was persistently shadowed by armed plain clothes men whom he found it difficult to shake off. But when the Press was being carefully shepherded behind the British lines in the disputed territory near Enniskillen Anderson managed to cross the border the cattle drover way and see what was going to happen from the Free State side. 'The battle of

Belleek,' he wrote, 'began to-day at 12.47 with Commandant McGowan of the IRA and your correspondent as the innocent targets of the military forces.' The battle was in fact very little like the operation described in the official communiqué, but it was highly unpleasant for the ex-Scots Guards M.G. reporter, the IRA officer and the five irregulars who were all the men in and about the old Castle on Free State soil.

Back in Belfast there were stories that had to be written about burnt houses and factories, shot men and women, and fleeing refugees. Belfast, as he put it, cast a long shadow. He was thinking primarily of its extension throughout the province and beyond, but he was well aware too of its projection into the future.

Very little undoctored news was coming out of Belfast because most of the outside papers had decided that the treaty meant the end of major Irish stories. This gave added importance to Anderson's work. The *Chicago Daily News* and the *Daily News* were taking the M.G. service. Anderson grew used to seeing angry Orangemen in public libraries reading the *Daily News* and swearing to get the man who wrote those stories. At the same time he could read in the *Belfast Telegraph* about the 'outstanding falsehood' and 'all the clotted nonsense contained in the notorious falsification of facts' of which he was guilty.[13] It was small satisfaction that the blame was laid on the *Daily News* and not the *Manchester Guardian* which escaped unnoticed. Anderson did not. It became known that some of his family had come from Ulster so that he was 'a personal traitor.' In fact the Irish branch had gone back to Scotland because one of them had married a Roman Catholic and found life intolerable in Protestant Ireland.

4

Wadsworth started his fourth and last tour of duty in Ireland on 8 May 1921. In the Reporters' Diary for that day his initials are enclosed in brackets. The brackets are there because at the beginning of the year he had been promoted from the Room to the Corridor and was no longer under the orders of the Chief Reporter. One can still almost catch the sound – it was sometimes compared to a whinny – of the mocking laughter with which Wadsworth must surely have greeted the ludicrous idea of brackets as a status symbol. But one can sense, too, the underlying, hidden pleasure at the reality which they conveyed. The way towards that promotion had begun to open for Wadsworth on New Year's Day, 1919 when J. V. Radcliffe left the *Guardian* for the

Times. Radcliffe had been the regular second string to George Leach in Ireland, and had also for a good many years specialised in trade union and labour matters. Radcliffe's departure and Leach's death had left the way clear for Wadsworth to make a striking reputation in Ireland; but even before that he had established himself as the obvious man to cover a strike or to undertake a complicated piece of social or economic investigation.

Nineteen-nineteen was a year of painful readjustment in industry and social policy. This made it a year of opportunity for Wadsworth. It opened with great strikes on the Clyde and in Belfast, strikes which were directed by the new militant shop stewards against absentee trade union headquarters as well as against employers. George Leach covered the strike in Belfast, Wadsworth in Glasgow where the disturbances were far more serious and the army had to be called in. When the strike was over he was concerned with long investigations into miners' housing and into unemployment as well as into import restrictions, which involved careful documentation trade by trade. He covered the major police strike in Liverpool in August, working there for the first time with Boardman who had only joined the paper the week before.

Radcliffe's departure had cleared Wadsworth's way. Ted Scott's return meant that it led on to the Corridor. The Labour movement had never been one of 'C.P.'s subjects,' though he was generally sympathetic to it. He knew that it was going to be more important after the war. Early in 1918 he urged Hobhouse to make and keep contact with Arthur Henderson on behalf of the paper.[14] Twelve months later he tried to persuade J. L. Hammond to join the permanent staff 'especially in regard to Labour questions now becoming of such capital importance.' But Hammond was not to be persuaded in spite of the offer of 'a handy motor car,' £1,000 a year, and the promise to build him a 'rather modest' house and a 'first-class movable shelter.'*

At this stage Scott gave up the search for a new man to write specifically on Labour questions and turned instead to his younger son, Ted, who had taken up work again on the paper three weeks before the offer to Hammond. He wrote his first leader on trade unions, a 'two-par' on 'The Epidemic of Unrest,' on 30 January. Two days later came his first post-war long leader – on 'The Strikes' in Belfast and on the Clyde. From this time on he played an increasingly important part in expressing the policy of the paper. In 1919 he wrote the Long on an average once a week. In 1920 he was responsible for nearly a quarter of the Longs during the nine months he spent in leader-writing. In

* Barbara Hammond's health compelled an open-air life.

1921 his average rose to roughly two Longs a week. Before he enlisted it had only been about one a month. It is time to become better acquainted with him.

When Ted Scott came back from the war he was 35, married, with three children and settled in Manchester not far from his father's home. He was C.P.'s youngest son and, perhaps for that reason, had found his parents remarkably 'permissive' for the turn of the century. When he decided that Oxford was not for him and went down without taking a degree his father acquiesced. C.P. again raised no objection when three years later Ted left the LSE a few months before his finals in order to become private secretary to Sidney Olivier who was going out as governor of Jamaica. To those who met C.P. as the stern and sometimes quick-tempered disciplinarian in the office – he had been known to throw books across the room in a momentary rage – this parental indulgence must have seemed surprising. But it was prudent. Ted Scott was not a playboy. He continued to work at economics and took a London external degree. He shared his father's idealism as well as inheriting perhaps more than a fair share of the family's good looks, which he bore with a more winning and less formidable expression than his father's. As a student at the LSE, he had gone to live with J. A. Hobson. He was one of a succession of 'economic youths' as the family called these lodgers who helped to pay the household bills. Hobson's 18-year-old daughter, Mabel, had one look at him and decided that this one was for her. They were married when Ted was 23. It was not quite such an inturned M.G. marriage as might be thought from Hobson's decisive part in shaping the paper's policy on the eve of the Boer War. The Hobsons had gone to live at Limpsfield and, though they received the M.G. every day – but presumably the next day – it often went unopened into the waste paper basket. Their ability to live without the *Guardian*, though it was perhaps eccentric in so left-thinking a family, may well have struck Ted Scott as refreshing. It certainly helped his wife to put up with what she sometimes found the trying experience of being 'daughter-in-law to the *Manchester Guardian*.'

The immediate post-war years not only saw a great increase in Ted Scott's leader-writing but a considerable diversification in the subjects he wrote about. His early experience had been in the City offices of London newspapers. When war broke out he was commercial editor of the *Guardian*. He had been concerned mainly with markets, duties, taxes: impersonal subjects. He continued after the war to deal with them as far as they came into leader-writing. Before long he was to add the intolerable complexities of inflation and reparations. But an analysis of his work during the first three post-war years shows that well over a third of his writing was on labour relations and unemployment – subjects which certainly needed the discipline of quantitative thinking, but needed quite as much an imaginative grasp of what the workers wanted and a warm regard for them as men. His leaders often fall far short of endorsing what the trade unions claimed, but they always show a sympathy with men who might well have been gunners in his battery a year before. His views about Cabinet Ministers, company directors and trade union bosses often resemble a front line soldier's opinion of the staff.

His leaders show that his thinking on industrial relations was in the Arnold-Montague-Hobhouse tradition:

'It is tolerably clear that the existing trade union organisation does not satisfy a large class, especially of unskilled workers. Whether it should be remodelled on the basis of the workshop, instead of occupation, is a matter for the workers themselves to decide.' (1 February 1919)

'If for any reason the right to strike is withdrawn (from the police) it should be recognised as the deprivation of what is normally the most jealously guarded and most socially valuable means of progress.' (5 August 1919)

'The readiness of the present Government on all occasions to yield to pressure ... is a clear proof to (the working men) not only that direct action is exerted by the employing and capitalist classes but that such methods offer him too the quickest and surest means of attaining his desires.' (1 September 1919) But direct action is 'an extreme assertion of class selfishness and the complete denial of democratic government.' (11 September 1919)

'To all appearances strikes are still largely a question of hours, wages, and the material needs of life. That expression of discontent is apt to be misleading; it does not fully express the mind of the worker: it is almost an anachronism. The spirit of the men who fought for their country or toiled in the shops at home is not one of pure material greed' . . . (24 September 1919)

'Self-government in politics was a growth of centuries, and self-government in industry may come as slowly. But one can hardly doubt that it will come, and resistance to it may be futile' (23 June 1921)

'What could be more wantonly extravagant than to have cotton workers, woollen workers, bootmakers, miners and house-builders all out of work and all desperately in need of the products of each other's labour? Those, if one came to the matter fresh, one would say were the economics of a madhouse. Just because it has always happened, so most people see nothing odd in it, and will complacently label the proposals of the Labour party as extravagant nonsense.' (23 September 1921)

Edward Taylor Scott, editor from 1929 to 1932. The drawing is by
Francis Dodd R.A.

A Difference of Opinion. Montague had altered a review by Monkhouse of W. E. Henley's last volume of poems. The incident is described in Chapter 29

Merithouse C.U. Disley
Nov 26/1901

Dear Mr Scott,

I hope you won't think me very arrogant for complaining of an alteration of a review that I sent in. It was on Henley's poems and appeared to-day. The last sentence is absolutely different from what I wrote or meant to convey and though it may be just I didn't want to say it especially if, as I suspect, Henley is a dying man. I have often came to be grateful for the correction of my mistakes but I cling to the idea which you as editor can't admit, perhaps, that these reviews are done by individuals. Please don't think that I regard my work as sacred. I have grave doubts about my competence for reviewing

My dear Scott   Nov. 28

This was my doing. I am asking the country house for the copy, that you may see the original words for which I substituted the underlined ones. Their substance, as I remember it, was "whom" (or "whose attitude on such matters") "Mr Henley probably regards as contemptible. I did not like, even in the B. of W., to mention such a standpoint as Henley's without marking our aversion to it. Some of his verses on the Boers war struck me as going nearly as far in degradation as Swinburne's "whelps & dams" sonnet about the concentration camps. They beat Kipling.

Yours affectionately

C. E. Montague

I am keeping back the Dooley. The W. G. has not had it.

C. E. Montague, from a charcoal drawing

W. P. Crozier, Editor 1932–1944

The last horses and delivery carts from a photograph taken in 1952

When Ted Scott wrote these leaders he usually had Wadsworth's copy in front of him. Together they explored not only these national issues but curious local developments which in the end came to little or nothing, but which illustrate how fluid society was immediately after the war before the great depression settled on England. There was, for instance, the strange affair of the Wigan borough council's desire to issue its own currency notes which Wadsworth investigated on the spot and Ted Scott dismissed in leaders.

More promising was the Building Guild, a Manchester-based co-operative of producers, founded by S. G. Hobson. In 1919 and 1920 Wadsworth was in frequent contact with Hobson who had been Socialist candidate for Rochdale in 1905 when Wadsworth was just leaving school. Hobson had now come to Manchester in charge of Ministry of Labour affairs, but he never forgot that he was a Guild Socialist. The Building Guild built houses for Manchester Corporation under the Addison Act with sufficient success to incur the hostility of Sir Alfred Mond, Dr Addison's successor. It had a number of other successes in several parts of the country and became quite a big business. Richard Coppock, the building trade union leader and a principal sponsor of the Guild, later wrote, 'We owe a great deal of our early success to the help given by the *Manchester Guardian* in their impartial expressions on the objects of the Guild. The other papers, seeing the interest that the *Manchester Guardian* was taking in the venture, also gave us considerable showing in their columns.'[15] Certainly Ted Scott was intrigued, attracted, but not finally convinced by the experiment. That may be why Hobson wrote in his autobiography that 'E. T. Scott . . . studied at the London School of Economics. I think it narrowed his vision; but he was intensely interested in the Building Guild, even coming to some of our private meetings.'[16] In fact his vision was wide enough to welcome the Guild conception, but acute enough to notice defects in its management which he thought must share the blame for its failure with Sir Alfred Mond.

There grew up a close regard between Ted Scott and Wadsworth which soon developed into friendship. They were interested in the same things from very different angles – economist and historian; Radical employer with Labour sympathies and socialist employee with a streak of temperamental Labour conservatism; leader-writer and reporter. Things might well have remained on this footing but for the intervention of David Mitrany.

Mitrany, who was in his early thirties, had been born in Bucharest and studied before the war at the Sorbonne and the Kolonial Institut at Hamburg. There he had seen an advertisement for Toynbee Hall.

He came to England and enrolled at the London School of Economics. He was already an authority on peasant movements in Eastern Europe when Hobhouse recommended him to Scott to assist Hammond at the Peace Conference. Rosalind Toynbee had already been appointed so Mitrany came to Manchester for four years, serving mainly as personal assistant to C.P.S. for foreign affairs, which meant reading the foreign papers for him, drawing his attention to significant happenings and preparing full briefs. This was a time when C.P. was his own main foreign leader-writer. Mitrany had an especial gift for friendship with young children and was soon a welcome guest at Ted Scott's house. Wadsworth, too, rapidly became a friend. Most men would have thought several times before making a suggestion to C.P. about his staff, and then decided to say nothing. Mitrany had no such inhibition. One morning C.P. was talking to him about G. D. H. Cole, then acting as Labour correspondent for the M.G. in London. Scott was apt to classify Labour men pretty sharply into good and bad – he was more tolerant of his fellow Liberals. Thus, Tawney was good; the Webbs were bad. Now Cole was bad and 'would have to go,' but there was nobody to replace him. At this point Mitrany intervened and suggested that Scott had the right man on his own staff among the reporters. It had not occurred to Scott to look there. When he did, he was convinced. Wadsworth was brought on to the Corridor in January 1921. The arrangement with Cole was allowed to run down. It virtually ceased when Wadsworth returned from Ireland in June, 1921 and was formally closed at the end of August. E.T.S. and Wadsworth were thrown even more closely together. Their working alliance, which was also a friendship, was one of the closest in the *Guardian* history.

5

In 1921 the *Manchester Guardian* had its hundredth birthday, Scott his seventy-fifth and his fiftieth anniversary as editor. When other men would have been thinking of retiring he was carrying out new ventures. The year before he had launched the *Manchester Guardian Commercial*, a regular weekly economic review which for the whole of the inter-war period provided what many judged to be the best survey of trade and industry from a business man's point of view. It fell to his son to see to the actual launching of the new paper – that is why he wrote no leaders for three months in 1920 – but nothing happened on the *Guardian* except with C.P.'s active participation.

The part C.P.S. played in arranging about J. M. Keynes's work for the *Guardian* illustrates this. It might more naturally at his age have been left to his son who was a trained economist. But it was C.P.S. who undertook all the correspondence about the numerous articles Keynes wrote in 1921, who tried to persuade him to cover the Washington Disarmament Conference for the M.G., and who a few days before his seventy-fifth birthday went to Cambridge to persuade Keynes to undertake a series of Supplements to the *Commercial* on 'Reconstruction in Europe.' A day or so after their talk Keynes wrote to say that he liked the idea, thought he could make a good job of it, but was not prepared for his name to appear in a way that implied responsibility unless he could 'really exercise pretty detailed supervision over the writers.'[17] This, of course, is what Scott wanted and he approved the suggested themes for the twelve numbers. Much of the detailed preparation fell to Wadsworth.

Keynes's biographer, Sir Roy Harrod, describes these 'great' Supplements which at that time were the main vehicle for the expression of Keynes's views. They included, for instance, the first full account of the theory which he later summarised in 'A Tract on Monetary Reform.'

'The Supplements . . . contained expert information upon the whole field of economics. These were also published in French and German. Authors from many countries were brought into service and there were more foreign contributors than British. Keynes certainly laboured hard to attract authoritative writers, and I confess to finding fascination in the galaxy which appears in the list.'[18]

For its centenary the *Guardian* produced a special number, distinguished above its other special numbers because it included a long survey by Haslam Mills which was later republished with the title, 'The Manchester Guardian – A Century of History' – a jewel of English prose cut in the most fastidious *Guardian* manner. The number was introduced by a short signed article by C.P.S. – possibly his only signed contribution to the paper. It contains his best remembered words in which he described the function of a newspaper:

Its primary office is the gathering of news. At the peril of its soul it must see that the supply is not tainted. Comment is free, but facts are sacred . . . The voice of opponents no less than of friends has a right to be heard. Comment also is justly subject to a self-imposed restraint. It is well to be frank; it is even better to be fair.

There was, of course, a public dinner. Lord Robert Cecil* proposed the health of the *Manchester Guardian* and its editor. This was supported by, among others, two former members of the staff – Sir John Simon

* Later Viscount Cecil of Cherwood.

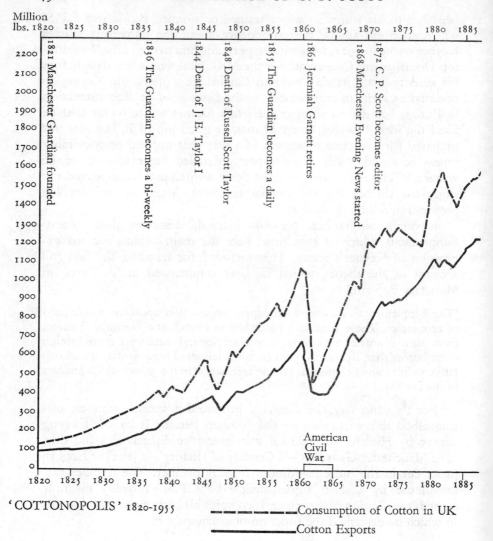

'COTTONOPOLIS' 1820-1955

Million
lbs.

Consumption of Cotton in UK

Cotton Exports

1821 Manchester Guardian founded

1836 The Guardian becomes a bi-weekly

1844 Death of J. E. Taylor I

1848 Death of Russell Scott Taylor

1855 The Guardian becomes a daily

1861 Jeremiah Garnett retires

1868 Manchester Evening News started

1872 C. P. Scott becomes editor

American
Civil
War

and John Masefield who spoke of his time on the paper as 'a most romantic delight.' Only a few days before the dinner Sir Gordon Hewart, never quite a member of the staff, had sounded C.P., presumably on Lloyd George's behalf, about the possibility of his receiving the C.H.[19] He refused the honour, but his pleasure in a message from the King stands out in the leader he wrote about it:

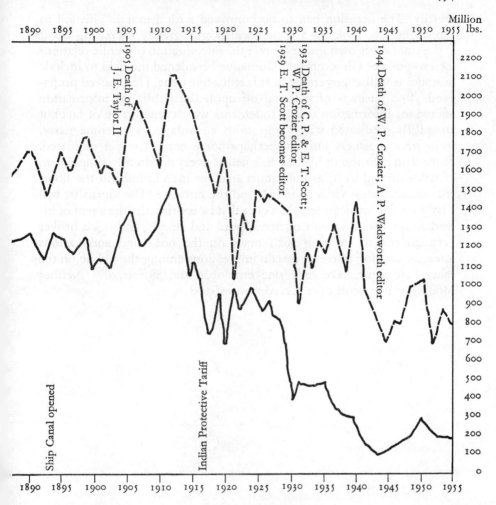

Million
lbs.

(Exports comprised cloth and yarn. Before 1860 cloth accounted
for between 55 and 68 per cent; afterwards for more; between
1900 and 1919 for 85 per cent.)

'For the person to whom it was addressed it is a greater honour than any
other which it was in his power to bestow . . . The King is no novice in the
affairs of the press . . . If, therefore, he praises, he does not praise without
knowledge. If he desired to confer an honour, he has done it in full measure.'
(5 May 1921)

But it would not have been like Scott's *Guardian* simply to sit back
and enjoy hearing all men speak well of it, and then to say thanks

prettily. The occasion had to be improved with a moral. This fell to Montague. He took up a theme which was greatly exercising Scott at the time as his own leaders show: the introduction of public relations men to puff the Government. Montague broadened the field to include business as well as government. It is still a live issue. He attacked propaganda 'the business of palming off upon the public, as information offered for information's sake, statements which seem to be of fact but are subtly medicated with suggestions advantageous to some party, some great business interest, perhaps some enterprise yet unfloated. More than ever the public has to smell at every apparently simple item of news offered to it, as mice must smell at each crumb on the floor, lest some tasteless virus be in it.' And the remedy? 'The journalist will have to feel more definitely than ever that he is primarily the agent of his readers for the collection of news, pure and simple, and not a broker between readers desiring such news on the one hand and various interests desiring to create certain impressions among the public on the other. He must have only [one] employer and not two.'[20] Neither Montague nor Scott ever served two masters.

CHAPTER TWENTY-NINE

Ichabod

I

IT is not difficult, looking back, to see that the tide had turned for good against Lancashire's particular 'treasure by foreign trade' before George V opened the Royal Exchange extension in October 1921 or the *M.G.* kept its centenary in May. If a date is needed, one that will serve is that Friday in March 1917 when a crowded emergency meeting of members of 'Change passed by a majority of between 4,000 and 5,500 to 10 a resolution of protest against the Indian Government's introduction of an import duty on Lancashire cotton goods.[1]

For a time the post-war famine for manufactured goods hid the consequences of what had happened. Lancashire had never had it so good or Lancashire business men behaved so ill. Spinners' profits had risen from a half-penny per lb in 1912 to eighteen pence in the first quarter of 1920; weavers' from 5d per piece to 5/–. 'At the fever's height four cotton men diced all their leisure for many days at £5 a throw; three others ran a motor race at over a mile a minute from Blackpool to an East Lancashire town for a triple stake of £1,500; a party of youths boasted that they had spent a fortnight's holiday in London at £50 a day each, outside living expenses.'[2]

It fell to Wadsworth to investigate what was happening. It was the peculiarity of the cotton industry that it was almost entirely financed by local money put up by men working in the trade. This took the form largely of loan money at 4 or 5 per cent out of which the mills were normally built and equipped, and partly of shares which were on an average only half paid up. In one instance quoted by Wadsworth only 10/–, of which half was a bonus issue, had been paid up out of a nominal £5 on which dividends of 40 per cent were paid. In the summer of 1919 there was a rush of reflotations:

'The public is tumbling over itself to find outlets in industry for its capital . . . It is to meet this spirit that the speculator has entered the industry, and without increasing its production by a single pound of yarn manages by refloating companies to increase the capital invested by anything from three to four times the old figure . . . The greatly increased capital is issued to the public, and at a premium into the bargain. The increased capitalisation has thus become not a paper affair, but an inflation for which cash is paid.

'The speculator's view of the matter is simple. The cotton trade seems good for another three or four years of abnormal profits. Production has decreased with the reduction of hours. No new mills can be built to inflict competition, and the world's demand will be such that foreign competition will not be felt . . . What will happen when the cotton trade passes through its next cycle of bad trade is another thing, which does not trouble those who long before will have been sharp enough to unload their shares . . .' (3 September 1919)

No doubt Wadsworth's articles saved some prudent readers from burning their fingers, but they did nothing to check the extravagances of the boom. There was still more than half a year to go before the first sign of recession. But when the depression came, it was deep and rapid. The margin between the spot price of raw cotton in Liverpool and the selling price of yarn in Manchester – the figure on which spinners had to work – fell from 43.32d in April 1920 to 14.17d in December. A year later it was 8.11d; by December, 1922 only 6.19d. Five years later, after a short and small recovery, it stood at 5.72d. Between 1921 and 1928 Lancashire lost 38 per cent of her pre-war export trade in cotton piece goods.[3]

At first the collapse was mistaken for just one more necessary correction in the customary course of the trade cycle. The very folly of the speculators of 1919 and 1920 seemed a sufficient explanation for misfortunes of 1921 and 1922. Good times and bad had alternated so long in the cotton trade that men were slow to see that there were to be no more good times. The *Guardian* saw no farther than others. This was understandable, but one would have thought the signs would have been clear to read by late 1922. But in September the paper was still on the whole cautiously reassuring: 'A slow but progressive decline in the demand for foreign textiles is probable, and perhaps inevitable. But no fanaticism, whether that of the crude Swadeshi movement or that of the latest and most "scientific" tariff, can suddenly wrest from Lancashire her economic preponderance in the Indian markets. At the worst she will be given time to find other outlets for her goods.'* Four years later the production of Indian cotton mills was nearly double what it had been before the war and not far short of the total volume of Lancashire exports to India in those happy days. There was no looking back.

Nor were other outlets for Lancashire's goods to be found. Cotton itself was soon to go out of favour. The name artificial silk is as old as 1855, but it was not until 1892 that the discovery of viscose made the production of rayon or artificial silk a commercial possibility. In 1910 the total world production was only some 8,000 metric tons; by 1924 it was 63,000. Three years later nylon was discovered by Du Pont's in the United States and ten years later nylon stockings began to come on the market. These new man-made fibres were products of the chemical industry in which giant companies predominate.*† The fibres might be made in the North-west – some of them are – but the industry was not domiciled there as cotton was, financing itself and snapping its fingers at London. The ultimate decisions were no longer made by a multitude of men on 'Change in Manchester but by a few men in London board rooms. The decay of cotton did not necessarily mean less employment in Lancashire or less money earned and spent there, but real power had gone elsewhere. Manchester had long been a great engineering centre. It became a greater one, but only one of many. There had been no other comparable cotton centre in the world. The business community in Manchester still needed business news, but it was increasingly the general news of the commercial world centred in London and decreasingly the special business news of its own city-state which the *Guardian* alone gave in full.

The *Manchester Guardian* had grown from a small provincial weekly to a newspaper with a world-wide reputation side by side with the expansion of the Lancashire cotton industry. Could it survive the industry's contraction? This anxiety haunted the Scotts and those who wished the paper well throughout the later part of the twenties and all through the thirties.

2

The Liberal party was disintegrating even more rapidly than the cotton industry. It was never to recover from the feuds between the followers of Asquith and Lloyd George. Most Liberals managed to stick to one or the other; Scott contrived to fall out with both in turn and sometimes both together.

Scott was fascinated by Lloyd George as a man, distrusted his lack of principle, admired his dynamic leadership and, I think, believed that, when ambition allowed, he was most truly himself in his radical phases.

---

* M.G. 26 September 1922. The reference to the Swadeshi movement is to Gandhi's campaign to replace imported textiles by home-spun Kadar cloth. His spinning wheel is the symbol chosen for the Indian flag.

† The M.G. did not neglect the post-war growth of the chemical industry. H. D. Nichols, later news editor, made his name as a reporter by a thorough investigation of the situation.

Typical of Scott's attitude are these unguarded expressions from letters to L. T. Hobhouse:

'I am lunching with Ll. G. Each time I say it shall be the last and then I go again to liberate my mind, with scant effect I fear.' (3 March 1918)

'Luckily G. is quite as ready to cast aside what is bad as what is good, and he has now left the General Election far behind.' (27 January 1919)

'What was so splendid about Courtney was his unshakable stand for principle . . . Could any contrast be greater than that between his whole mentality and that of Lloyd George, which seems to have infected our whole policies?' (31 October 1919)

Nor was Scott less outspoken in what he wrote on occasion in the M.G.:

'Could any conceivable Labour Government have made blunders so gross?' (over Russia) (5 January 1920)

'Is it then true that in winning the war Mr Lloyd George has lost himself?' (16 March 1920)

'A Government does not exist in order to commit outrages.' (15 October 1920)

But, in spite of much hard-hitting, Scott and Lloyd George understood and liked each other. This made it possible for them to get back to friendly terms even after disagreements so deep and outspoken, both in public and in private, as that over the Black and Tans. 'You and I have been so hopelessly at variance of late over Irish affairs that I was afraid it would be difficult for us to meet without coming to blows. But now that the atmosphere is more serene . . .' This might well have been written by Scott to Lloyd George; actually it comes from a letter of Lloyd George's.[4]

But it could not possibly have occurred in any correspondence between Asquith and Scott. Almost the only thing they had in common was their belief in an independent Liberal party. Their disagreements went back to the Boer War and beyond, were almost continuous, and were marked by personal dislike, certainly on Scott's side, probably on Asquith's. Scott expressed himself freely to Hobhouse:

'Really Asquith gets worse as he gets older and it is time he were dead and buried – politically!' (23 April 1915)

'What a nasty trick Asquith is playing us on the compulsion issue . . . He certainly is a champion in the arts of chicane.' (30 December 1915)

'Gilbert Murray believes in Asquith . . . and I don't, and rejoice to see the Liberal party leaders on the way to be purged by a little adversity. Shall we ever want to see them back in power again?' (27 May 1917)

Nevertheless in 1922 the M.G. was supporting Asquith against the Coalition. At the end of May the Conservative *Spectator* remarked: 'How oddly our statesmen sometimes behave – certainly not like ordinary people.' A ferocious letter from Asquith had appeared in the *Guardian* of 24 May. It contained only a quotation from a leader by Scott in the previous day's paper, and the words 'This is a falsehood.' Lloyd George had raised the question of a military guarantee by Britain to France. The M.G. was totally opposed. In January Asquith had spoken against 'entangling engagements,' but Grey had seemed well disposed to them. At the Liberal conference four months later a letter from Grey was read and Asquith spoke on foreign policy. Both stressed the need for Anglo-French friendship; neither referred to the guarantee question. Scott thought they should have done so. 'Are we, or are we not, to enter into a direct and exclusive agreement with France for the military defence of her territory? On this it might be supposed that Liberal leaders of a great Liberal assembly would have something to say. But in effect they have said nothing.' These were the words that Asquith declared a falsehood. Scott's footnote remarked: 'It is as grave a charge as he could make . . . Mr Asquith supplies no reason. It remains for him either to do so or, as we understand the duty of public men, to offer an apology for his attack.'

Scott's intention was to leave the next move to Asquith. Unfortunately, in Scott's opinion, James Bone asked Asquith for an interview.[5] Asquith agreed and, having agreed, what he said had to be published. It was not very helpful except to politicians on the sidelines. There was not a word of apology. Asquith again quoted the *Guardian* passage and repeated 'that is absolutely untrue and I think that the simplest way is to refer you to the speech I made . . . on 19 January.' 'Will it be believed,' Scott asked in a leader that night, 'that in the same article to which Mr Asquith has taken such violent exception we actually quoted the words which he now recalls, and said that here "there spoke in him the true voice of Liberalism"? Unfortunately it did not speak again with like clarity at Blackpool where clarity was most needed . . .'[6] In a kindly note in the *Nation* H. W. Massingham remarked 'Mr Asquith's laconic epistle stands out in my remembrance as an almost solitary appearance in the letter columns of a Liberal newspaper. If I were Mr Scott I should preserve it with the commemorative label "very rare, if not unique".'[7]

There were two curious postscripts to this passage of arms. In July Scott heard that Vivian Phillips, Asquith's Secretary, had been telling various people, including Clifford Sharp, the editor of the *New Statesman*, that the M.G. had suppressed two or three vital words in the Asquith interview – a charge quite as serious as Asquith's original 'falsehood.' Scott had taken unusual precautions over the interview. The final copy had been passed by Asquith himself with only one addition in his own handwriting. This duly appeared in the *Guardian*. The amended 'copy' had fortunately been preserved by Harold Dore, the *Guardian*'s lobby correspondent, but in spite of this documentary proof, Vivian Phillips refused to apologise.

The second postscript was a natural consequence. In 1923 the Athenaeum was preparing to celebrate its centenary. It proposed to elect a number of distinguished men. Scott's name was put up and his sponsor asked Asquith if he would act as proposer. He agreed. This caused Scott to write to his friend about Asquith: 'At the moment we are, so to speak, not on speaking terms . . . If by proposing me at the Athenaeum he means indirectly to make reparation I ought not to refuse to accept it. But what I could not accept is that he should suppose that the approach came from me.' Scott was reassured when he was told that Asquith could have had no such idea in his head, and he accepted Asquith's action as a sign that he wanted to restore friendly relations. He even wrote to Asquith a letter of not very warm thanks:

'It was very kind of you to accede to Mr Chisholm's request to take Bryce's place as my proposer at the Athenaeum. In his case no more than in yours had I the least idea in advance of such a friendly service . . . I am none the less grateful to you for your assistance.'[8]

The rows between Liberal leaders killed their party. The suspicion and distrust between Liberal and Labour leaders prevented the voters who supported them from getting their way. Between 1915 and 1945 there were only two Governments of the Left and between them they held office for only three years out of the thirty. During this period there were seven general elections at which roughly every other voter, sometimes slightly more, sometimes slightly less, was either Liberal or Labour. The M.G. did what it could do to heal these self-inflicted wounds of the Left, but without the slightest effect. Many journalists and public men talk very differently in public and private. That was never Scott's way. Compare the leader he wrote on 31 May 1924 with his letter to Hobhouse on 19 November:

'The bulk of each party are good democrats who differ from each other in principle no more than the various brands of Liberals and Radicals have always differed. When will they recognise that fact and act upon it?' (M.G. 31 May)

'Between Liberalism as I feel and understand it and moderate Labour there is next to nothing to choose. It is only through the accident of the war and what has come after it that they have ever been divided.' (to L. T. Hobhouse 19 November)

But nothing Scott could say made any lasting impression on the leaders of the three parties (two Liberal, one Labour). Scott remained a Radical member of the Liberal party, but he was ready to welcome Ramsay MacDonald with what now seems excessive warmth:

'A terrible Labour leader this. Something also of a philosopher. He happens to hold perhaps the greatest position at present existing in the world, so may we not be approaching, by a very unexpected road, to the Platonic ideal where the philosopher is king?'[9]

K. R. BRADY'S IMPRESSION OF ELECTION NIGHT OUTSIDE THE "M.G." OFFICES.

From the *Manchester Guardian House Journal*, December 1923

No doubt in writing thus Scott hoped to allay the bitter hostility to the Liberals which MacDonald had expressed to him – 'Mr Lloyd George's campaign in its gross demagogic vulgarity has also increased both the number and the value of the reasons why we should have nothing whatever to do with his party' on which, however, MacDonald would have to rely to keep his Government in office.[10] But, though there may have been policy in what Scott wrote, there was not hypocrisy. He was as forthright in praise of MacDonald in a private letter to Hobhouse – 'What a fine speech MacDonald made at Geneva – wise, far-seeing, and courageous. I wish we had a man in our party who could have done the like.'[11]

MacDonald's dislike of Liberals, or at least of Liberal leaders, was, however, beyond Scott's power to charm away. He had eventually to admit defeat – 'The Prime Minister, who can be so sweet to the foreigner from whom he differs most widely, has nothing but un-concealed dislike and exaggerated suspicion for those who in this country stand nearest to him in politics.'[12] There was no denying that the parties of the Left were led by the Three Incompatibilities. The electoral system, which Scott had done his best to change, necessarily put the parties into cut-throat competition; their leaders saw to it that they made the worst of this bad job. The *Guardian* at this time made compulsive reading for politicians, but it was written by frustrated men and read by frustrated voters.

3

Political frustration and economic depression taken together and taken neat make deadly reading. It was W. P. Crozier's job to produce a balanced newspaper in which liveliness might break through. He had been news editor, a new title for the M.G., since 1912; but it was only after Sidebotham's departure and the end of the war that he had begun to be in a position effectively to plan the contents of the paper as a whole, outside the leader columns. There were certain other things he had to take for granted. James Bone had a charter to do what he liked in London. His experts, Dore in the Lobby and Drysdale in the Gallery, had a remarkably free hand. This was a relic of the days before the war when Scott had given Mair an independent command. Bone put all his tireless zest into seeing to the other things that made life worth living in London. The result was a balance which Crozier would neither have wanted nor been allowed to disturb. In the same way neither he nor even Scott would have dreamed of controlling or interfering with Montague's general supervision of the whole literary and artistic side of the paper.

Another fixed point was the daily Miscellany column. It was different in purpose and temper from its successor with the same title. Its earliest editors had been John Masefield and Oliver Madox Hueffer. Between the wars it was run by Gordon Phillips, a grave, thoughtful man who as Lucio contributed polished light verse on topical subjects. Many members of the staff and innumerable readers earned modest half-crowns for short paragraphs arising out of the day's news, often involving the revival of old memories or the provision of curious modern parallels. Gordon Phillips gave Miscellany a unity which its name belied. Half the enjoyment of contributing was to decide what would catch G.P.'s fancy. One had to learn to know one's Lucio just as the successful crossword solver must enter into the clue writers' mind. The commercial pages too, were a world apart.

The rest was Crozier's province. The overall impression the *Guardian* made on its general readers, apart from the Gentlemen and Players of politics, came from his controlling hand. Of course, this was only so because the kind of paper he provided was the kind of paper Scott wanted. It was not, however, a matter of Crozier obediently following Scott's orders (though, of course, he would have done so) but of their both wanting by and large the same things. There are two ways of producing a newspaper – providing something with deliberate skill to a recipe for readers quite unlike oneself and providing a newspaper for like-minded people. The M.G. had always been the latter kind of paper. Scott spent his leisure bicycling in the Lake District with Mrs Lejeune,[13] sculling on Ullswater or playing tennis 'with a tricky underhand service.' Montague and John Scott were climbers; Monkhouse played, and wrote on golf; Arthur Ransome fished; Ted Scott sailed small boats (as, of course, did Ransome); John Scott was an early and informed motorist; and Crozier, though closely dogged by ill health, took an intense interest in all forms of sport. These men expected that *Guardian* readers would share this catholic range of tastes and would not only wish to read about them but expect to get keen pleasure from the quality of the writing. And so, in the course of the twenties, there was Neville Cardus as 'Cricketer' at full length every summer; Arthur Ransome's 'By Rod and Line': F. S. Smythe on the conquest of Kamet or Bertram Phillips on Travels in Arabia to name only a few series. The Northern Motorist became a regular weekly feature.

In May 1922 a daily Women's Page was introduced with a promise of particular attention to practical matters concerned with 'domestic economy, labour-saving, dress, household prices, and the care of children.' But on the second day it carried an article which fell under none of these heads – 'The Hospital Almoner: A Career for Educated Women.' Scott would certainly not have tolerated a page based on the assumption that woman's place was in the kitchen. The decision to make a daily feature of the kind of articles which had long been appearing sporadically was no doubt made at one of the morning conferences at The Firs at which major policy matters were discussed. Probably the suggestion came from Crozier and pretty certainly it was he who suggested that Miss Linford, his former secretary, should edit it. Looking back forty years later Madeline Linford recalled:

'It was for those days a very bold venture . . . There must have been many grave discussions and much misgiving before the directors, headed by C. P. Scott (whose feminism was idealistic rather than practical) decided to sanction it. Of this I heard nothing. I was just told that it would start on such and such a date that it would consist of three columns on six days a week . . . My briefing was lucid and firm. The page must be readable, varied and aimed always at the intelligent woman . . . There must be no concessions to popular jargon . . . Words like "perambulator" were to be given all their syllables and none of the terms loved by fashion writers – "chic," "modish," "ensemble" – could be allowed.' (11 September 1963)

The Women's Page quickly made good its claim to its place in the paper. It used established *Guardian* women writers whose names were well-known to readers, such as Evelyn Sharp and Mrs H. M. Swanwick and it introduced new young writers. Among them were Winifred Holtby and Vera Brittain. Ambrose Heath's Good Food headline was first provided for him by Madeline Linford.

Five months earlier another regular feature had been introduced, this time almost certainly on C.P.'s initiative. 'The Week on the Screen' appeared regularly above the initials C.A.L. until July 1928 when Caroline Lejeune transferred to the *Observer*, although J. L. Garvin had told her husband only a short time before to 'Go back to C. P. Scott and tell him from me that there will be no film column in the *Observer* as long as I am editor of the paper.' Thus, while the *Observer* started its serious film criticism only with the coming of the 'talkies,' the *Guardian* goes back to the best days of the silent films. Scott was right when he wrote in a farewell latter to Caroline Lejeune:

'I take some credit to myself for having instantly realised that you would be an incomparable person to handle that new and difficult subject and to raise it to its due level as an art. You have really fulfilled my expectation and among writers for the kinema have achieved an easy supremacy.'[14]

The initial 'k' is characteristic. Originally the *Guardian*, like everybody else, used the spelling cinema as it does to-day. This, however, probably merely meant that C.P. himself was not interested and had not noticed what was being written in an obscure part of his paper. As soon as he did, he insisted on the 'k' because that was how the Greeks would have spelled it. Caroline Lejeune, still in her student years, deserves credit not only for persuading Scott to give her a chance as film critic, but of persuading him that this was something that a paper which took the arts seriously ought to have. Two or three times a week Scott would bicycle round and call in for tea with Mrs Lejeune on his way to the office. It was on one of these occasions that her young daughter suggested a film column. 'He thanked me gravely for the suggestion and said he would consider it, adding the momentous words, "But I think that would have to be done from the London End".'[15] It was.

Scott and Crozier were quick also to see the importance of radio.

Each step that led to the formation of the British Broadcasting Company and then of the Corporation was given prominence in the M.G. as news and received careful comment. Sometimes this was of a kind that reads oddly to-day such as the comment that 'any approach to monopoly in broadcasting would be most objectionable.' Three days later the M.G. comforted itself with the reflection that 'the cost of equipping an efficient wireless station, not to mention the fees which eminent people may expect to receive for talking, singing and preaching in it, is considerable and brings no return. Profits can only be made on the sale of the receiving apparatus . . . (but) Any mechanically-minded person can make a simple receiving set for a pound or two.'[16]

Soon after eminent people began to talk, sing or preach over the air the M.G. began to provide radio criticism of their performances. From 1929 to 1934 Mrs Kathleen Hamilton wrote regular critical notes. In 1931 Crozier's daughter Mary made her first appearance as a radio critic. Scott and Crozier saw that here was a new and important way in which men would inform and amuse themselves, and one which deserved the paper's careful attention. They had no more cause to be jealous of the BBC than of theatres or concerts. For a good many years to come radio and newspapers were not in direct competition. People still on the whole first read the news rather than heard it, and the shadow of advertising by television was not yet visible. But perhaps they ought to have seen that radio could not annihilate time and distance without making Lancashire less apart and on its own.

Between the wars many Cross Street men moved to the B.B.C. and played a considerable part in its formative years. Kenneth Adam and R. T. Clark developed its home and foreign news services, E. R. Thompson became its first lobby correspondent. Donald Boyd and Robert Kemp were closely concerned with talks and feature programmes. A little later W. J. Haley became Director-General while the chairman of the Governors in his time was E. D. Simon, John Scott's friend and for several years a director of the paper.

4

Of course, even on the M.G., the news editor's main pre-occupation was not with features but with news. What did Crozier regard as news? How was it best got? That was one way of looking at the problem. It could be put another way. The M.G. had an especially gifted body of reporters in Manchester. How could they best be employed?

Up to the middle of 1923 events dictated a policy of full and worth-while employment. As long as there was civil war in Ireland the *Guar-*

dian kept a man, or rather relays of men, in Dublin. Reporters in Manchester could count on their fair share of the important national news stories. Manchester had been their base; after 1923 it felt more like a city in which they were besieged. Ireland had ceased to provide a welcome and an outlet, and Wadsworth had taken with him to the Corridor the monopoly of the main Labour and industrial stories. Not until he became principal leader-writer in 1932 did the handling of these stories return to the Room. There was little except by-elections and such traditional engagements as the Grasmere Sports or the Tarporley Hunt steeplechases to take men out of Manchester. And Manchester was no longer a town of such distinctive importance in the world as it had been. Reporters wrote, elegantly, more and more about less and less.

Some of the away engagements positively helped to make what had 'always been a happy ship,' as George Leach put it in 1915, a ship with a discontented and nearly mutinous crew by 1924. Crozier was anxious to broaden the base of the M.G.'s appeal. He probably did not want to attract readers of a new kind so much as to give greater satisfaction to the kind of people who were typical *Guardian* readers. Their business interests, their politics, their recreations, their literary and musical tastes were all admirably met, but something was missing. Men read detective stories; they are interested in crime. In this *Guardian* readers were like other men. And so was Crozier. He began to provide for this. When J. L. Hammond left Paris in 1919 his work was taken over by William Ryall who later became well known as William Bolitho of the *New York World*. Ryall interleaved his serious political reporting with vivid and intriguing accounts of crime in France of which 'The Paris Bluebeard' was the first example.[17] When Landru was tried, Ryall's stories appeared, usually on the main news page, day after day. No doubt the business men who complained to Crozier of the M.G.'s interest in the Dodecanese were gratified by the attention it gave to the continental underworld.

The same formula began to be applied to home news. Crozier found in Matthew Anderson a reporter whose work he liked and whom he began to send out frequently on crime stories. It started with Crozier noticing a paragraph about an epidemic of bicycle thefts in Liverpool. He sent Anderson there and he got an amusing story of thieves from all over Lancashire coming to Liverpool, stealing bicycles and exporting them to Dublin or Belfast. Anderson then began to be sent to cover some of the sensational murder trials that were frequent soon after the war. In the winter of 1922, for instance, he put in thirty-two days on the Armstrong case in its various stages, sometimes with

Green to do the straight report while he concentrated on a dramatic sketch. What he wrote was given a prominent position on the main news page.

Two years later there was an abrupt end to the *Guardian*'s foray into crime reporting. Patrick Mahon was suspected of murdering a Manchester girl in a bungalow near Eastbourne. Before an arrest was made most of the London papers, including the *Times*, had sent their own men down to Eastbourne and were carrying detailed stories of the investigation. Crozier sent Anderson down and told him to get all he could. Wisely Anderson insisted on written instructions. It is apparent that his heart was not in the job. His first story which, like several that followed, was given prominence on the main news page, ended in what was almost a formal protest: 'One observes that in certain quarters that this affair, contrary to the dictates of justice, is referred to as a crime, and even as a murder. At this stage it is neither, but is simply a mystery.'[18] His story four days later led the Attorney General to apply for a writ of attachment for contempt of court against the M.G. because 'the interests of the prisoner were gravely and indeed terribly affected.'* When the case was heard leading counsel for the paper told the Court that the only references made in the M.G. to the case, apart from this one article, were short agency messages. In fact there had been three previous messages from Anderson, all of which were given considerable prominence. It was, perhaps, fortunate that the Lord Chief Justice, Scott's old contributor Gordon Hewart, had read the paper no more thoroughly than the editor himself. (Scott told Anderson that he had been quite unaware until he received the summons not only of the stories in the *Guardian* but even of the murder itself.) Otherwise the fine might have been more than £300.

This was not the first period when the M.G. had given its readers all they could possibly want of murder trials. The report of the trial of Madeline Smith in Edinburgh in 1857 had run to some 70,000 words. In 1889 the trial of Mrs Maybrick at Liverpool took about 120,000 words. This time there were fewer words to read, but a new dangerous slant had been introduced as the Lord Chief Justice pointed out. It was the private investigation of crime by newspapers acting on their own for the interest of their readers. This was common newspaper practice at the time but it had not been the *Guardian* way. The staff of the paper were united almost to a man in dislike of this new approach

* M.G. 20 May 1924. The *Evening Standard* and the *Daily Express* were also found guilty of contempt. The nature of the offence is indicated by the headlines to the fourth article, 'Discrepancies in Miss Kaye's Letters: Helped Mahon to Hide his Identity.'

to crime. Reporters, sub-editors and members of the Corridor, among whom Arthur Wallace was prominent, met to protest. There was in fact no need. After the Crumbles case crime was left so well alone that rumour had it that even a corpse had to bear the prefix 'alleged' before it could get into print in the *Guardian*. There may well, however, have been less happy consequences. It seems likely that the checking of initiative in one direction may have led to a general retreat into safe parochialism in the employment of reporters.

At any rate by 1925 the Reporters' Room was an unhappy place. A former member of the Corridor, David Mitrany, told Ted Scott how bad the feeling was. It had been made worse by the decision to change the Chief Reporter. Ted Scott's reply was framed so that Mitrany 'might be able, in some respects, to reassure' his informant.

'I am deeply grateful to you for your letter. It is getting increasingly difficult for me to keep in touch with the real feelings of people in the office. But what you tell me I already knew fairly well from a few other sources which remain open . . . The Room badly needed a head of energy, character and determination, which I believe X possesses. If that is so, it will recover its independence. It has been put clearly and firmly, both to X and Crozier, by the Editor that it must do so. That is not to say that either the Editor or news editor loses his right to say, broadly, what the character of the reporting should be. The policy, both as to popularising and Manchesterising the paper, may be and will be determined outside the Room. That is not dictatorship in any offensive sense. It is for the Editor, not for the Room, to say what is popularising and what is vulgarising.

. . . A strong and capable Chief Reporter should be capable of holding his own against W.P.C., but there is no earthly reason why there should be trouble between them any more than there is between him and F.S.A. (Attenborough, the Chief Sub-editor). I am perfectly certain that no news editor worth his salt would have found it possible to leave things to Y. But even if, which I do not admit for a moment, Crozier interfered too much, a strong and capable Chief Reporter could rely confidently on not being let down by the Editor, if he should find himself held too tightly in leading strings.'[19]

This letter is a clear and reasonable commentary on a difficult internal situation. It is, however, confined to personal relations and the chain of command. It does not touch the underlying cause of discontent – the ebb tide in Lancashire's fortunes which had left a gifted group of men stranded with work which was too trivial to be satisfying.

The policy of 'Manchesterisation' continued and reached its culmination in the introduction in 1928 of a Manchester Letter to balance and imitate Bone's London Letter. Crozier's policy might have been successful in the Manchester of 1910; after 1921 it was impracticable. A newspaper cannot create a lively society; it can only work on what is there.

5

Reporters, however good, were expendable. Others as good, could be found. But in the whole British Press there was only one Montague. And in May 1925 Montague resigned: 'too heavy a blow,' in C.P.'s words, 'for me to be able to realise at once all that it implies to the paper and to me.'[20] In 1914 Scott had talked Montague out of going – 'Don't let us write any more – I begin to think that letters altogether are a mistake – but discuss everything.'[21] This time Montague waited until Scott was on holiday and he himself about to go to the Lakes. His mind was made up. He set out fully in a letter the reasons why he felt he ought to go:

The work that falls on me on the paper has for a long time been growing more unimportant to it. In the writing of long leaders my share is smaller now than at any time since my first years in the office. Those that I write are, as a rule, on minor subjects and serve as a stop-gap on off days or in the absence of other leader writers.

Monkhouse's work on the books is so good that my supervision is almost a form. In the few cases where I revise a decision of his, the point has, as often as not, been noted by you too and so would in any case, be dealt with. My other "side line," dramatic criticism, has lost most of such use as it may have had for the paper, since scarcely any serious theatre exists here now.

I fear I may have been too slow in facing the natural consequences of these changes. It is not easy to admit to oneself that a happy period of one's life and work has come to a close, and I do not think I have ever had so difficult a letter to write as this one. But I see it is right that at any time when you may wish to put Ted in charge of the paper, he should not be embarrassed – as he must be, in spite of his great kindness – by having about him an older colleague whose *raison d'être* in the office has so much diminished. In any case it must be bad for the paper to employ a leader-writer at a high salary on work which no longer corresponds to it.

So I resign my place on the staff and on the directorate . . .

It is so much beyond me to thank you as I should wish for the constant kindness you have shown me during these 35 years, or to tell you how much happiness I have found in working under such a leader, that I must not try – I should only make my feeling seem less intense than it is and always will be.

Ever yours affectionately,

C. E. Montague.'*

* Montague-Scott 13 May 1925. Montague was persuaded to remain a director. He attended most of the monthly meetings and usually contributed a short leader before going home.

There were, then, two sides to Montague's decision just as there had always been two sides to his work for the paper. It was perfectly true that the cultural life of Manchester was not what it had been. Miss Horniman's Gaiety had barely survived the war and finally declined into a cinema in 1920. The repertory theatre which succeeded it was a poor affair by comparison. There were few post-war theatre notices signed C.E.M. because there were few plays worth seeing. Neither Scott nor Montague could do anything about that. Music, too, had suffered from the war. Hamilton Harty was not a Richter. Montague could stay away from the theatre, but Sammy Langford had to continue to go to the Hallé. He wrote what he thought, and on occasion Scott had to defend him against attacks from those who were now providing Manchester's music. The truth was that Manchester's cultural life was suffering not only from the general decline in Lancashire's fortunes but from the special loss occasioned by the dispersal of the Germany colony.

It was true, too, that there was little for Montague to do about book-reviewing. Monkhouse had been very seriously ill towards the end of the war and when he came back to the paper he gave up the cotton side of his work entirely and attended to nothing but the books. There was indeed no case for Montague's supervision. Obviously the two men would not always agree about the merits of a particular book or particular reviewer, but by and large they shared the same outlook. Both were determined to be fair at all costs and to avoid smartness and the snide remark. For a quarter of a century they had worked together. In all that time only one serious difference of opinion is recorded. It concerned W. E. Henley's poems written during the Boer War. Monkhouse had referred to 'Englishmen whose attitudes he (Henley) regarded as contemptible.' Montague had made it read 'Englishmen who feel that some of his utterances on particular points of national conduct have been almost despicable.' Monkhouse protested to Scott that, though the changed statement 'may be just, I didn't want to say it especially if, as I suspect, Henley is a dying man.' Montague's defence was: 'I did not like even in the Books of the Week to mention such a standpoint as Henley's without marking an aversion to it. Some of his verses on the Boer War struck me as going nearly as far in degradation as Swinburne's . . . They beat Kipling.'*

A far more characteristic emendation of Montague's was his courteous expansion, years later, of a reference to an author's 'breach

* M.G. 26 November 1901; Monkhouse-Scott 26 November; Montague-Scott 28 November 1901. A portion of these letters is reproduced between pp. 432 and 433.

of taste' to 'breach of his own good taste' – more characteristic, that is, except where Montague's severe politico-moral principles were at stake. Then no quarter was ever offered. It may have been this forthrightness which had, as he thought, condemned him since the war to 'minor subjects, stop-gaps on off days.' The qualitative judgment is ludicrous, but he was undeniably right in saying that he had been largely crowded out of the principal leaders. By tradition leading articles are unsigned but, as C.P. said, 'Montague could never succeed in being anonymous. Do what he might, to those who knew him everything he wrote bore his signature all over.'[22] Applying this stylistic test, it is possible to attribute with some confidence only twenty long leaders to him in 1919, a year when Ted Scott certainly wrote forty-eight; and forty-three in 1924 when Ted Scott wrote 105 and C.P., an old man of 78, did sixty-seven.

One is left wondering helplessly why Scott made so little use of a man who wrote so well. These phrases from 1919 and 1924 leaders show no decline in Montague's power:

1919   'an election . . . is always, in some measure, the submission of the case of the fanatic to the judgment of the sceptic.' (14 March)

'British soldiers . . . are coming home is such a state of scepticism about official politicians as has probably never before possessed any great mass of men in the world' . . . (5 April)

'The watchers of the electoral weather say, that "voters are tired of hearing about Ireland" – as the Tsar was probably tired of hearing about unrest in Russia.' (23 April)

'Men and women are learning, each with his own measure of bitterness, the element of disillusion that there is in nearly all success. You fight the good fight, and, lo! the prize itself has changed while you fought, and alloy has crept into the gold. You finish the long race, and only then you find that the "you" who has won it is not the same "you" who once had it to win.' (27 June)

1924   'Mr Churchill for the second time has – shall we say? – quitted a sinking ship, and for the second time the reward of his fine instinct has been not safety only, but high promotion.' (7 November)

'There is a strong feeling in this country that a promise is a promise, even when the person to whom it is made has not got a first-class army with which to make you keep your word.' (1 October) (on the failure to set up an Irish boundary commission.)

Was Scott worried by such plain speaking by somebody other than himself? Did he distrust the new dislike of politicians as such, not only of Conservatives but of Liberals, that Montague had picked up in

France? This distrust is found frequently in his post-war leaders and was there bold and plain in *Disenchantment*, published in 1922, which pictures Liberals as 'sombre and dry, all-round prohibitors, humanitarians but not humanists, people with democratic principles but not democratic sympathies, uncomradelike lovers of man, preaching the brotherhood of nations but not knowing how to speak without offence to a workman from their own village.'[23]

Hobhouse might not be a Liberal but he would never have written such words about them. He was indeed himself, in Montague's opinion, 'a man whom you couldn't imagine going to a football match.' Scott might admit that Hobhouse could sometimes be a very dull writer (so he once told Cardus), but he trusted his judgment and he loved the man. Who was to take charge when Scott took his much needed holiday in 1919? It was a test case. Scott wrote to Hobhouse: 'One plan would be for me to be away *at the same time* as C.E.M. Either you or I so far as I can see, must for the present be continuously in charge.'[24] The precedent was followed in later years. Either Hobhouse or, later, Hammond came to take charge of the leaders when C.P.S. was on holiday.

As Montague realised, the decision had in effect been taken that Ted Scott was to be the next editor. The son was preferred to the son-in-law; the younger to the older man. For Montague that carried certain consequences. 'I see it is right that . . . Ted . . . should not be embarrassed . . . by having about him an older colleague whose *raison d'être* in the office has so much diminished.' With anyone else but Montague one would say that this selfless attitude was too good to ring true. But it exactly expresses his horror of intruding on 'all the personal home rule of a friend, his whole mental and moral autonomy, (which) must be a thing to guard and respect like one's own.'*

And so Montague left Manchester for Burford in Oxfordshire and a house which Kit Kempster, master mason of Wren's St Paul, had built for himself. That unpretentious craft description must have pleased C.E.M. who called his last book *A Writer's Notes on His Trade*.

'Bless you for understanding all about it,' he wrote to Francis Dodd. 'Half the people I know are congratulating me on the assumption that I'm going to sit in the sun and do nothing – evening of life etc! I'm as fit as can be, but damnably in danger of getting to do my easy, pleasant, profitable work on the M.G. as a sort of luxurious habit instead of finding each bit of work a

* M.G. 21 December 1925. In saying good-bye to his colleagues, Montague was explaining his failure to help younger men with advice as much as he should have done.

desperate hazard that has to be struggled with till it's downed. So it was clearly a case for closing the chapter and starting in on a new one while we both have a good kick left in us.'[25]

But the new chapter was never finished. Three years later Montague was in Manchester on a visit. He was taken ill and developed pneumonia. As he lay at The Firs fighting for life he said to his wife 'Every breath is an adventure.' He died on 28 May 1928. He was 61. Ichabod. With Montague, a glory had departed.

PART THREE

The Guardians

Adeimantus: It's the Guardians' own fault, of course, for the city really belongs to them, but they don't seem to get any good out of it as others do who own land and build great houses . . . one might almost call them mercenaries on perpetual guard duty.

Socrates: It would not be in the least surprising if our Guardians were very happy indeed . . . (but) don't force us to give them the kind of happiness that will make them anything but Guardians.

Plato: Republic Book IV

*

BOOK SIX

'The Younger Scotts and Crozier'
1926-1944

*

CHAPTER THIRTY

Ted Scott's Dilemma

I

MONTAGUE'S self-chosen rustication cleared the way for Ted Scott to be recognised as heir apparent. This was not, however, well handled. In January 1926, C.P. developed a cold and stayed in bed. He sent Crozier a hurried business note of three or four lines in which the operative sentence ran 'I've asked Ted to take charge to-night.' This was underlined. It caused the same kind of offence that nearly thirty years before had come from a similar scribbled note to Hobhouse. Two days later C.P. wrote again to say 'I feel I ought to explain myself more fully. You see when I die or am put on the shelf, Ted will I hope succeed me as Editor and he ought to be preparing himself for that, perhaps not distant, event.' He went on almost to plead for Crozier's understanding and assistance. This, of course, was readily promised 'both in the interests of the paper and on personal grounds,' but Crozier allowed himself to say 'I may as well confess that the first announcement of it seemed to me a little abrupt.'[1]

It was not only abrupt; it was in practice premature. C.P. did not surrender power easily. Ted's work in the office hardly changed at all. Ever since the war he had handled all economic matters as far as leader-writing and business arrangements were concerned. He had conducted the correspondence with G.D.H. Cole about his work as Labour correspondent; he dealt with questions affecting Oscar Hobson's* position as City editor – the most distinguished the *Guardian* had had up to that time. He went on doing this kind of work, but there is no sign that C.P. handed anything more over to him. In particular E.T.S. took virtually no part in the external life of the *Guardian*. He was tied to the Manchester office and given little opportunity to play himself in as a public figure. Because of the large part that economic questions, especially reparations and war debts, played in international affairs E.T.S. had soon found himself the principal foreign as well as

---

* He was a nephew of J. A. Hobson and financial editor of the M.G. from 1920 to 1929, leaving to become editor of the *Financial News*.

the principal economic leader-writer. He was not a good linguist and what knowledge he had of European countries and statesmen was largely book knowledge. But as C.P.'s son or as editor-designate of the *Guardian* most doors would be open to him in the capitals of Europe. He ought to make himself known and learn something at first hand of the men he wrote about. It was something, too, that he wanted to do. But it was only accomplished by a ruse. In 1924 David Mitrany made a plan with Ted and Mabel Scott. During one of his visits to Manchester he said to C.P. that Ted ought to make a political tour of Europe, but that unfortunately Mabel would never agree. The old man's eyes flashed. Next morning he announced that Ted was to go to Europe for two months provided that David Mitrany would accompany him. The journey took place, but it was not repeated.

The process of handing over was, then, doomed to be difficult, As long as, and perhaps a little longer than, C.P. was capable of doing things himself, he preferred it that way. In the six years that followed Montague's retirement, the last six years of C.P.'s life, there were two major English political crises – the short, sharp General Strike of 1926 and the protracted in-fighting of 1931 over the substitution of a National Government for a Labour Government. Both involved desperately difficult choices for all those on the Left in English politics. Both were bound to be personal crises for the *Guardian*, and for its staff, as well as for the country. In both most of the leaders were written by Ted Scott. In 1926 the major decisions were taken by C.P.; in 1931 the whole burden fell on his son. Ted had become editor in 1929 though, as Mabel Scott recalled, it was at first an editorship under supervision – 'It's all right, I'm still keeping an eye on things' was the kind of re-assurance that C.P. gave his friends. It rankled just a little when reported back to the new editor and his wife.

2

Anyone who has sifted historical evidence will recognise the excitement with which one comes across an utterly incongruous document. Such was a letter to C.P. from Sir William Joynson Hicks dated 8 May 1926:

'I have just received your Bulletin of the 6th May and I thank you very much for your kindly reference to myself.

You and I at one time were rather serious opponents but in this case we both see that this strike, which is really an attack upon Constitutional and Parliamentary Government, must be met and fought.

I am trying throughout to be fair to those on the other side but still at the same time very firm in the protection of the rights of those who are willing to work.'

Thursday 6 May was the third day of the General Strike. Less than six months before L. S. Wailes, head of the composing room, had made the paper's steadfast support of trade unionism the theme of his speech at Montague's farewell dinner. What then had C.P. done to earn the gratitude of 'Jix,' the Home Secretary, who was almost a caricature of what a Right Wing Tory Home Secretary might be expected to be?

The answer seems to be that the M.G. had not been quite as bad from the Government point of view as might have been expected. It is surprising that at a time of acute crisis an overworked Home Secretary could find time to write such a letter. It is more surprising that he should have been thankful for so small a mercy. It is, perhaps, a measure of his anxiety that he was. What Ted Scott had written in his leader was this:

'Once a conflict of this kind has broken out the Government must use all its powers to maintain the major public services. The technical branches of the army and navy are available . . . There is no reason why, if necessary, they should not be used. Sir William Joynson Hicks has taken steps to use them for the supply of electricity and motor spirit and for railway transport. But some other regulations which he has introduced under the Emergency Powers Act are highly dangerous. The right to arrest without warrant is, in particular, one which, even in hands more cautious than those of the present Home Secretary, is far more likely to be abused than to serve the cause of order and justice . . . That the Government should prepare for the worst is not objectionable but to assume the worst before it has happened is provocation.' (Thursday 6 May 1926)

This leader is, perhaps, marginally more favourable than what had gone before, but the difference is not great and there is no repudiation, then or later, of the paper's earlier position. On the last day before the strike began the *Guardian* had argued:

The difference between 'considering' and 'accepting' is the difference upon which the nation is plunged into strife . . . By making 'acceptance' of wage reductions a condition of the continued subsidy the Government were, in effect, asking the miners to write a very large cheque in exchange for a piece of paper of whose negotiable value they had but the faintest idea . . .' (Monday 3 May 1926)

Next morning, the last on which a normal full paper could be printed, all four leaders (one was a 'two-par') were given up to the strike. The first was Ted Scott's.

'The T.U.C. in ordering over a million men immediately to stop work . . . is clearly acting contrary not only to our laws but to the democratic principle of government. If it were successful in this it would have established a powerful precedent for a policy which would at one time or another have to be repudiated, resisted, and, if necessary, fought. But the manner and occasion which the Government have chosen to enforce a principle sound in itself could hardly have been more unfortunate . . .' (Tuesday 4 May 1926)

This was followed by a 'two-par' leader called Industrial War Psychology, probably written by J. L. Hammond, who was working from the London Office as a full-time leader-writer throughout 1926:

' "It is war", the Labour members are reported to have said . . . Some people like the excitement of it all; they see themselves in command, giving rapid decisions that determine the destiny of nations (or at any rate unions), making history, or at any rate securing publicity. The familiar phenomenon recurs of Government supporters emerging from their customary, and probably deserved obscurity to direct "controls" as Commissioners, and strong silent business men sacrificing their leisure to serve on committees that sometimes lead to knighthoods . . . It excites . . . a temper in which people become "bitter-enders" against their better judgment. And it is uncalled for; because a strike, even a general strike, is not war. The essence of a strike, or lock-out, is not violence or force, but passive resistance . . . Society suffers inconvenience . . . but the terminology, and still more the psychology, of war is out of place. Industrial disputes are not war, but business.' (Tuesday 4 May 1926)

On Wednesday and the subsequent days the M.G. like most other newspapers, was reduced to short bulletins. Two editions were produced each day – a duplicated paper of three foolscap pages and a printed version with news and comment on one side only of a single sheet privately printed in Ardwick. There was an anxious discussion in the *Guardian* editorial chapel of the NUJ about what members ought to do. It ended when Arthur Wallace got up saying 'Well, I'm going to see that the paper gets out.' He was the owner of a roomy old Standard car in which throughout the strike he crossed the Pennines each night distributing the M.G. in Yorkshire. By the end of the week NUJ headquarters had agreed that its members could help in the production of makeshift papers. Posts and telegraphs were working normally and a full supply of news reached the M.G. and other papers. Appleby was sent to Glasgow, where there was a good deal of rioting, and Spring to Cardiff, the town of his childhood. But all that could be printed of their stories were the barest outlines. Still the fact that the *Guardian* was getting its news from its own trusted men was a guarantee of truth to its staff and its readers in a situation where rumour was

This cartoon of Harry Lauder by Henry Ospovat appeared in 1909.

LIFE'S LITTLE IRONIES.

'It happens that this paper was the first on this side of the world to publish a Low cartoon.' This is probably it. This cartoon on the postponement of an International Peace Conference appeared in the *Sydney Bulletin* on October 29, 1914, and was reprinted in the *Guardian* on January 4, 1915.

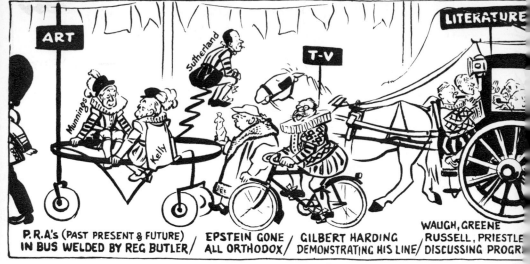

ART

LITERATURE

T·V

Sutherland

Munnings

Kelly

P.R.A's (PAST PRESENT & FUTURE) / EPSTEIN GONE / GILBERT HARDING / WAUGH, GREENE
IN BUS WELDED BY REG BUTLER / ALL ORTHODOX / DEMONSTRATING HIS LINE / RUSSELL, PRIESTLE
DISCUSSING PROGR

CULTURAL ADDITIO

GENTLEMEN, THE TOAST IS
JAMES BONE
THE LONDON PERAMBULATOR

"A FRESSHE, A FREE, A KINDLY MAN"

FLEET ST
LONDON
25TH JAN. 1946

"WILL YE NO COME BACK AGAIN ?"

DRAMA · MUSIC POETRY · CINEMA

LOW

| OLIVIER, GIELGUD & RICHARDSON SOLILOQUISING ON BRITISH DRAMA/ | BENJY BRITTEN SETTING T.S. ELIOT TO MUSIC FOR DONALD PEERS/ | RANK & KORDA LOST IN 4ᵗ D |

) THE PROCESSION

1953: Low's suggestion for an improved Coronation procession

Low's design for the menu given to James Bone. Bone and his brother Muirhead collaborated in books on London, Edinburgh and Glasgow of which '*The London Perambulator*' is the best known

This cartoon of Eden setting out for Suez and Kruschev for Budapest
appeared two days after Wadsworth's death

A. P. Wadsworth from a drawing by David Low

loud-voiced and more than usually inaccurate. And even the most abbreviated 'telegraphese' – reporters rarely telephoned in those days – could be made by a skilled hand to give something of the mood behind the deeds:

'Praise due to conduct of strikers and police (Spring wrote). Only occasional "bubblings over." Many unemployed finding work at last, particularly on trams, with guarantee of permanent employment. Pitiful to talk with strikers seeing jobs vanishing and yet maintaining half-doubtful loyalty to T.U.C. leaders. Here and there a few stealing back to work, and hundreds confess they had no idea T.U.C. could thus dispose of their fates. All T.A. (Typographical Association) men have returned to *South Wales News*.' (Monday 10 May 1926)

That was all there was room for in the *Bulletin*, but the essential news is there. Beyond doubt the decision to call out the men in the printing trades had been an act of crass stupidity. It silenced the Left, but allowed the Government through the BBC and its own propagandist *British Gazette* to swamp the country. In some towns newspapers were able to function normally. In Leeds the Conservative *Yorkshire Post* was able to print 110,000 copies on Wednesday and the *Leeds Mercury* 142,000. Five days later, according to a wistful paragraph in Bone's substitute London Letter, the *Yorkshire Post*'s circulation had reached 700,000. It was on sale from Carlisle and Newcastle to Manchester and in London where Plymouth and other papers were also being sold. The *Yorkshire Post*'s normal sale at that time was about 40,000. Meanwhile the two London Liberal papers, the *Daily News* and the *Daily Chronicle*, had been out of production for a week. The *British Worker*, the TUC's strike bulletin, gradually dwindled in size as the Government succeeded in stopping its supply of paper.

None of the *Guardian* leaders during the first week was written by C.P., but this was not because he was withdrawing from affairs. He was in fact extremely busy getting together in Manchester as many religious, social and business leaders as he could. A meeting with Hewlett Johnson, then Dean of Manchester, in the chair appealed to the Government 'to take the initiative in getting into touch with the TUC with a view to ending the general strike,' and to the TUC 'to call off the general strike and trust Parliament and the community to see that justice is done to the miners.' It is characteristic of C.P.'s tactics that no reference was made in the paper to the part that he or the M.G. had played in bringing the meeting about – pretty clearly because to have done so might have tarred a non-political meeting with a political brush. The good of the cause, then as always in C.P.'s mind, outweighed even the good of the paper.

But the TUC leaders had no doubt where the initiative came from. In July Ernest Bevin reported to his union committee:

'Purcell and I had been working together on the Organisation Committee to mobilise public opinion to force negotiations. Mr C. P. Scott, of the *Manchester Guardian*, had succeeded in calling a splendid meeting of the whole of the Lancashire business people. We knew he was going to do it . . . I went to the General Council and reported what was in our minds; our idea was to dispatch Purcell to Manchester the next day. He knows the place very well and the people in it. Our scheme never fructified because within a few hours negotiations were opened by the Negotiation Committee with Samuel, who had been brought back or came back from Italy.'*

Remembering the letter from Joynson Hicks, one wonders whether anything better could have been achieved if Purcell had gone to Manchester. It hardly seems likely since Herbert Samuel had been chairman of the commission whose report had preceded the miners' lock-out. But C.P. by 1926 had the strength of his almost emeritus position in public life and he was in a position to speak frankly to Churchill and to elicit the more generous side of his nature.

C.P. continued to work hard for what might be called a peace without annexations or indemnities. On Sunday and Monday nights he himself wrote two leaders – Towards Peace and The True Temper. In the first he asked, 'Why should not the King take a hand and call the parties – all of them – together? He could do no greater service to the people of his kingdom.' In the second he warmly endorsed the plea for a return to the *status quo* which had been made by the Archbishop of Canterbury and Free Church leaders and suppressed by Winston Churchill. It was, of course, 'in direct opposition to the policy of the (*British*) *Gazette* as directed by Mr Churchill. That is reason the more why it should have been published if the *Gazette* is not to be regarded as a partisan publication. Happily the Archbishop's sermon broadcasted on Sunday drives its lesson home. It is by this temper and this temper alone that the nation can be saved from immeasurable calamities.'²

On Thursday the M.G., still and for several days longer in skeleton form, was able to give its provisional summing up of the results of the strike which had been called off. A leader, probably by J. L. Hammond, was too optimistic:

'Will not the general strike cease to be counted henceforth as a possible or

* Quoted by Bullock: *The Life and Times of Ernest Bevin* (1960) I, p. 324. Purcell was a member of the General Council and knew the M.G. people well through his membership of the Manchester and Salford Trades Council.

legitimate weapon of industrial warfare? May not the very idea of treating industry as a theatre of warfare come to be regarded as barbaric? . . . But the lesson is not wholly one-sided. It has its warnings as much for the employers as the employed . . . They have a unique opportunity and immense power. Used vindictively it will be wasted. Used . . . with careful thought for the best means of developing the essential sense of partnership in industry, it may prove to be a boon and a turning point in our industrial history.' (14 May 1926)

Bone had two perceptive paragraphs in his truncated London Letter: 'It is only men too old to have been in the war,' he wrote, 'who now talk of "teaching the workmen the lesson they deserve" and "making them lick it," and all the ugly, futile old slogans of the stonehenges of the past. The volunteers went on driving 'buses, loading food and the rest of it, and the strikers went on trying to prevent them, but there was with most of them a sort of understanding that never existed before and they had a common trench language they never had before . . .'

But it was Wadsworth who most swiftly got to the heart of the matter. The short, stubbing sentences of his message from London opened the main news page:

'The general strike has been called off, but the aim for which it was declared is unaccomplished. Sir Herbert Samuel worked out with the General Council of the Trade Unions Congress* a basis of negotiations which the miners have rejected. The mining stoppage will go on, but the miners will no longer be able to count on the united support of the trade union movement. The effects on British labour will be profound. The history of 1921 has repeated itself. The support of the other trade unions has been withdrawn. The Government has committed itself to little or nothing. The mineowners are committed to nothing.'

But at least the miners were safe by the nature of the industry from the introduction of blacklegs. Wadsworth went on to chronicle the General Council's failure to extract from Baldwin any guarantee of reinstatement. Bevin had done his best. Of all the unions involved in the general strike his was the most exposed to that risk. 'Pitiful,' as Spring had reported, 'to talk with strikers seeing jobs vanishing and yet maintaining half-doubtful loyalty to TUC leaders.'

* sic: The M.G. under C.P.S. insisted on correcting the grammar of the Trades Union Congress.

3

C.P.S. retired from the editorship in July 1929 but remained Governing Director, kept his old room in the office, and liked to come down every evening in the old way. E.T.S. became editor. A few days after August Bank Holiday in 1931 he went away on holiday, leaving Crozier in charge. The political situation was tense and difficult but August, though a traditional time for wars to start, normally brought a lull in party politics. Ramsay MacDonald was in Lossiemouth. Baldwin had gone to Aix. With the 'glorious twelfth' only three days off politicians were deserting Westminster for the grouse moors. By the time parliament reassembled the Government would have produced a drastic economy programme.

Ted Scott had made clear in a number of leaders what he thought the Government should do. He went on his holiday feeling reasonably sure that his leader-writers would know what line he would want the paper to take on any likely developments. Severe economies were necessary, including a revision of unemployment benefit, but they should fall with equivalent weight on all sources of income. He argued in 1931, as he had argued during the coal disputes of 1926, that fixed interest charges incurred in a time of inflation must be trimmed to offset their increased value in a time of rapidly falling prices:

'The ascending curve of real wages is compared with the similar ascending curve of unemployment, and it is difficult not to see a causal connection between them. But a comparison of the curve of the real burden of the National Debt with the curve of unemployment would probably show as great a burden.' (25 June 1931)

His last Long leader had dealt with the political implications:

'it is plainly true that the situation cannot be tackled comprehensively and courageously by any Government whose measures, unpopular as they could inevitably be made to appear, were liable to exploitation by other parties. Is it entirely out of the question, even though a National or Coalition Government is as impossible as it is many ways undesirable, that a common basis could be found for dealing with an emergency so far beyond the normal range of party politics?' (5 August 1931)

Two short leaders further defined his position. In one, 'Keeping Labour In,' he attacked Lord Grey's view that Liberals had made too many concessions to the Labour Government.[3] In the other, 'The Strain on the Bank of England,' he suggested that private foreign investments should be registered 'with a view to their disposal to the Government, if need should arise, against the issue of Government stock.'[4]

Ted Scott left Manchester on 9 August; the Prime Minister broke off his holiday on 10 August and returned to Downing Street. He squared the leaders of the other two parties, but he failed to carry his own Cabinet with him. Ramsay MacDonald's Labour Government fell on the 24th and was at once replaced by Ramsay MacDonald's 'National' Government, a Conservative-Liberal Coalition with a few Labour Ministers. Ted Scott did not get back to Manchester until 27 August.

He found himself confronted with an internal crisis as well as a national emergency. There was an awkward and protracted discussion over lunch at his Withington home. Crozier was by far the senior man present. He had been a member of the staff for over a quarter of a century and a director for more than a dozen years. Next in standing was Wadsworth, the residuary beneficiary from Montague's resignation. After Hammond's emergency year as a London-based leader-writer, Kingsley Martin had been appointed in 1927 as a political leader-writer. He stayed three years, but neither he nor the Scotts were happy together. Both his politics and his writing proved unacceptable. The editorship of the *New Statesman* fortunately came vacant at the moment when Martin's arrangement with the M.G. finally proved unworkable. He was offered the appointment to the immediate satisfaction of the M.G. and the lasting advantage of the *New Statesman*. This left Wadsworth, a close friend of E.T.S., as the obvious choice for principal home leader-writer, especially as many members of the Labour Government were well-known to him from his ten years as a Labour correspondent. During Ted Scott's holiday all the leader-writing on the crisis had been done by Crozier and by Wadsworth who had been sending news and leaders from London.

There were also present at lunch two junior leader-writers, both of whom were to play an important role in *Guardian* history. Paddy Monkhouse resembled his father, A.N.M., in the craggy distinction of his features, though they were a trifle more rough-hewn. In spite of Rugby and Oxford, the OUDS and the Union, privileges denied to his father, he lacked as a young man A.N.M.'s gentle persuasiveness. His abrupt outspokenness had at first had more of the flavour of the Labour politics of the down-town ward in which he delighted than of the *Guardian* Corridor. He had been on the paper since 1927, but Ted Scott had at first found him difficult and would have got rid of him had not Hammond intervened. By 1931, however, E.T.S. had come to like him and to recognise his quality. His presence at this working lunch was a sign that his opinion had begun to count.

The other junior, Malcolm Muggeridge, had enjoyed as easy a start on the paper as Monkhouse's had been difficult. He had sent one or two freelance articles from Cairo to the M.G. Ted Scott asked Arthur Ransome, who was in Egypt on one of his foreign tours for the *Guardian*, to get in touch with Muggeridge. Ransome reported favourably, and felt no doubt that he had atoned for his own obstinate refusal to join the permanent staff. 'I am rather cross with him,' Ted Scott had written to Hammond, 'as I think he could have done it very well, and should have done; but he has some stupid notion of a personal career.'* Muggeridge was appointed. Ted Scott was delighted with the result. Egypt and India were important subjects. Muggeridge brought to them first-hand, if limited, knowledge and a freshness in writing which matched the innocence of his vision. A reader might feel that here was a man who could perceive that the King-Emperor wore no clothes. Or he might consider that Muggeridge was a wild and dangerous fanatic. Both views were held by faithful M.G. readers. Both were held by members of the staff. Both were represented at that awkward working lunch. What was one to make of passages such as these?

'The alliance of sacerdotalism, beastliness, prejudice, ignorance and inertia behind which (child marriage) is securely entrenched.' (30 May 1931)

'Does a boycott of cloth or a vile massacre at Cawnpore blind us to (the vitality of Indian nationalism) and make us think again in terms of conquered and conqueror? If so, there is nothing to do but to struggle on through a few more years towards inevitable disaster. The awakening of Asia is the essential fact of this age.' (4 June 1931)

'We simply cannot afford to allow Mr Winston Churchill to stage a new and improved version of the Black and Tan drama in India. No doubt it would be thrilling enough and the eyes of all the world would be upon it. But the cost is too great – in money, in blood, and in shame, – and even if we were less squeamish about investing in murder, massacre and demoralisation we should like a better guarantee than Mr Churchill's for the profits to be derived from his sanguinary speculations.' (29 July 1931)

'A certain magnanimity is required to support the proposals of another man. But magnanimity has always been the virtue of the Moslem, and the great soul in the insignificant-looking body is the distinguishing mark of the Mahatma.' (11 August 1931)

Ted Scott knew that he liked this kind of thing; Crozier that he did not. There was nothing in Muggeridge's work that exceeded the blend

* E. T. Scott–Hammond 6 March 1930. The 'stupid idea' was no doubt the writing of *Swallows and Amazons* (first published in 1930) and all the glorious children's books that followed.

of fierce indignation and passionate idealism with which Montague had been accustomed to fill the leader columns – but that had been twenty or thirty years before when Crozier was a young man. He may perhaps be pardoned in middle age for wondering glumly where this impetuous youth* would lead the editor and the paper.

Equally natural was the impatience of the younger guests at the lunch party with what Crozier had been writing:

'The National Government, formed for a specific purpose and for a limited time, should be warmly approved by a country which is, as a rule, suspicious of a Coalition . . . There is to-day an emergency of peace which is comparable with that of war.' (25 August 1931)

'Mr Snowden . . . will shortly be able to administer to the children of his own household those few plain words which many of his distinguished opponents have endured, and he will do it cheerfully. Mr Thomas will bring to the Government his vigorous buoyancy. That Thomas feeling should be good for any Government.' (26 August 1931)

It was, perhaps, this allusion to 'Bovril prevents that sinking feeling,' an advertisement then plastered on every hoarding, that most annoyed the younger men. To them Thomas was already a turncoat: to compare him with the man who rode the storm on a bottle of Bovril was more than an error of taste – it was to condone treachery. The root trouble in the *Guardian* Corridor was that it was itself an uneasy coalition of Liberals and Labour men. At this moment it was the Labour men on the *Guardian*, as in the country, who were most under stress and more than usually touchy.

What did Ted Scott think of the line the M.G. had taken in his absence? The situation with which Crozier had had to deal was unexpected and fell outside the guide lines which the pre-holiday leaders had provided. Two letters to Hammond, Ted Scott's closest political confidant, show the distress of his mind. The first was hurriedly dictated in the middle of the emergency.

'Dear Lawrence,
The general drift of politics seems to me terribly bad. I doubt if we shall ever get away again from the war of the classes. I begin to think there's more in the economic interpretation of history than I had supposed and shall probably end up as a doctrinaire Marxist, if I can ever understand what that means . . . I am afraid we may not be able to keep Muggeridge very long, and even P.J.M. (Monkhouse) may find it difficult to associate himself permanently with a paper that will remain bourgeois to the last. I wonder on which side of the barricade these clever young men will ultimately find themselves.'[5]

* Muggeridge was, in fact, 28, but he could have passed for less.

The crisis mouldered on. One September day Cecil Sprigge, the new City editor, went to a Treasury briefing about the need to save the pound. Sprigge was a dapper little Etonian with a most engaging smile above his invariable bow tie, who looked a little, but only a little, out of place in a role where, as he remembered thirty years later, 'City editors wore top hats and paid an almost ceremonious round of calls each afternoon upon leading city houses, sometimes even reaching Montagu Norman.'* After Warren Fisher had spoken Francis Williams of the *Daily Herald* and Sprigge questioned whether we either could or should remain on gold:

'On the rest of the serious men around the table it produced an effect of frozen horror like that portrayed by H. M. Bateman, depicting a guardsman dropping his rifle on parade. Sir Warren Fisher, Permanent Secretary to the Treasury and Head of the Civil Service, was particularly shaken. He found it impossible to remain seated. "To suggest we should leave the gold standard," he declared rising magisterially to his feet and pacing heavily backward and forwards across the room, "is an affront not only to the national honour but to the personal honour of every man and woman in the country." There was nothing for Sprigge and me to do but to slink away.'[6]

Within a week Britain had devalued. Sir Warren Fisher, of course, remained at the Treasury, Montagu Norman at the Bank of England and Ramsay MacDonald at 10 Downing St. He decided to hold a khaki election. The Conservatives in the National Government won an overwhelming victory. Ramsay MacDonald remained Prime Minister.

Soon afterwards Ted Scott wrote to Hammond a long, retrospective letter in his own hand:

'... There was a time – when I came back from my summer holidays – when I was really troubled both as to the line the paper should take and because it seemed that I had a team that was hopelessly divided. Crozier and A.P.W. had been writing the Longs on the one side and three junior members (including Paddy and Muggeridge) almost on the point of resigning on the other. And poor C.P.S. in a state of complete ignorance of what was going on. I have never told him and he couldn't really understand anyhow. Gradually, as you will have seen, I came more and more to a critical view of the pretensions of the National Government and got the team more or less together. Except for Crozier who, I fancy, takes a purely National view. I have never discussed policy with him and don't really regard him as of an M.G. way of thinking. Even now Wadsworth is much more inclined to take the National Government at its face value than I am.

* Sprigge-Hetherington 6 November 1959. He is more easily pictured as the M.G's Rome correspondent (see p. 504-599), but he was also a good City editor.

'. . . There is a lull in the storm now and so long as the Government behaves there will be no trouble. But it seems to me broadly that politics are getting into an ugly shape and that we shall be driven more and more to take an anti-property line. And that is fatal to a twopenny paper. I myself feel that I am getting more and more of a socialistic way of thinking (or rather feeling) but the more I look at the socialist party the less I like it . . .'[7]

'Gradually, as you will have seen . . . ' The progress of Ted Scott's disillusion can be traced in the leading articles he wrote that autumn. The first, probably written on the same day as the working lunch, echoes the last Long he wrote before his holiday.

28 Aug: 'The idea of party co-operation, and finally a national government, arose . . . from the knowledge that a financially sound policy would be liable to unscrupulous electoral attack. It is only too evident that all three sections of the Labour movement are now about to lend themselves to an attack of precisely this nature.'

22 Sept: 'The prospects of an ultimate rise in prices must increase the general doubts as to the social wisdom of a uniform reduction in unemployment benefit.'

2 Oct: 'It is not at all certain that the Labour party would not be quite as well equipped for a sound solution of the currency problem in so far as this depends on international action, as the present Government . . .'

6 Oct: 'This sham unity, this temporary and embarrassing alliance of tigers and sheep, is worth less than nothing. Taking as it does increasingly every day the form of an alliance against Labour, it is perhaps the greatest threat to national unity that we have.'

21 Oct: 'The last Budget deficit and the sudden discovery of an adverse balance of trade had about as much to do with the collapse of the pound as the murder of the Archduke of Austria had to do with the Great War.'

30 Oct: 'The public's fears were played upon more persistently and with even less regard to probability, or scrupulous regard for the whole truth than in 1924. A decisive verdict at the polls under such circumstances is evidence not of fitness for democratic government, but of fresh difficulties which must be surmounted before Democracy can be said to be safe.'

Thus in two months Ted Scott had taken the paper from a position where a continued drift to the Right might have been expected back to the empty place on the Left where it was needed. 'The effect on the paper has been mixed,' he told Hammond in the retrospective letter already quoted.

'A lot of letters of abuse, but almost as many of commendation recently. A lot of cancellation of orders – one agent cancelled a third, that was in a rich residential neighbourhood – Wilmslow, I think. Nevertheless as far as I yet know a rise in circulation. But a severe hit in advertising on top of everything else. Tonge had actually to withdraw the whole of his canvassing staff at one time – they were practically getting kicked downstairs. Boots withdrew the whole of their Christmas advertising and gave it extra to the *Daily Dispatch*. There have been other cases. But the resentment is dying down and some cancellations have been re-cancelled. It is quite different to the South African war in that . . .'*

Ted Scott had thought hard before he turned back to the Left. He was worried because Hammond did not go with him. They agreed to differ. Hammond admitted that 'it may well turn out that it has been a real benefit that so powerful a paper supported the Opposition when it was weak and attacked in the most unscrupulous way . . . Labour people are not specially good at gratitude or at taking advice but I hope and think that when advice has to be given then the M.G. will get the benefit of its line at the election. If so that will be a great public advantage.'[8] Ted Scott replied 'though I did have the most horrible misgivings during the early part of the election I am now taking a possibly cowardly and certainly Pharisaic satisfaction in thinking that at least I have not tried to assist this Government into office. It is so easy to forget what the only alternative Government would have been like, but I can still say that I would much rather have risked it.'[9]

4

The last letter in the Scott collection was dictated by C.P. to Hammond on 22 December 1931. He thanked Hammond for a Christmas present and added 'I am afraid that I am but a feeble help to my dear Ted in these days, but I think we pretty well agree about things . . . I am writing this from bed; being for the moment slightly disabled – nothing serious.' But ten days later in the early hours of New Year's Day, C.P. died. He had been failing for some years – his wonderfully clear and vigorous handwriting began to show occasional feebleness after 1926, his memory for things of the present became capricious, his attendance at the office something of an embarrassment. But he could still rise to

---

* E. T. Scott–Hammond 16 November 1931. C. W. Tonge was the advertising manager. Ted Scott would have enjoyed a letter from his nephew, Larry Montague, then an undergraduate at Balliol, to Crozier: 'You may be glad to know that we now take four copies in the J.C.R. compared with a single copy a year ago, chiefly as the result of the policy of the paper in the last nine months.' (7 May 1932)

an occasion and face a difficult decision. During the 1931 general election he wrote to encourage Ted in the unpopular line he was taking: 'I liked your leader much.'[10]

C.P. had resolutely declined the political honours offered him by Rosebery in 1895, by Lloyd George in 1921 and by Ramsay MacDonald in 1924 and 1929. He had gratefully accepted academic and civic honours. He had been greatly moved by George V's message on the centenary of the paper and his jubilee. His spirit would, perhaps, have been stirred even more profoundly could he have seen the dense, bare-headed crowds that packed the streets for his funeral on a cold January day. It might have been – indeed they made of it – a State occasion. The men of Manchester knew he loved their unlovely town. They recognised in the solitary figure that many of them had seen year after year bicycling down to the office in the early evening and back at midnight a man who was, as nobody else would ever be, their city's guardian.

There were, of course, tributes from all over the world. There is no need to reproduce them. A reader who has followed C.P.'s career through sixty years of journalism will have made up his own mind about him. It is now forty years on: his reputation is not yet *aere perennius*, but certainly more lasting than newsprint. He is remembered in many lands as, among editors, the one who most desired to form, but most disdained to manipulate public opinion. He cared greatly for the ends for which he fought – among them Irish freedom, votes for women, the Jewish National Home, and opposition to the Boer War, 'the best thing the M.G. has done in my time.'* But the means he used had to be as honourable as the ends. The means were, as they must always be in newspaper work, an end in themselves, and subject to the same strict scrutiny as other ends. They survive that test.

As soon as Ted became editor he had turned his attention to his father's obituary. He found already written a biographical sketch by Haslam Mills and an appreciation by Montague. C.E.M.'s is a fine, balanced tribute and right in its conclusion:

'Without any glamour of beauty or wit in writing or speech, without any skill in the study of his readers' prejudices, with unfashionable politics and a cold side for the strongest emotions of crowds, he pursued his own slowly chosen and frankly declared line in total indifference to what people might say about it or him. And yet the further he went the more influence did he gain over those to whom he made so few concessions: so strong is the instinctive feeling of many plain and sane minds – in England at any rate – that

* Scott–Lloyd George 8 April 1930 adding, 'We were together there.'

the friend who, in all friendliness and for no worldly motive, will withstand you to your face must be worth listening to.' (1 January 1932)

But Montague's judicious estimate seemed insufficient to Ted Scott who was perhaps over-anxious lest the paper might seem under the son to fall ungenerously short in praise of the father. 'Montague's (appreciation) seems to me not altogether happy and that is one of the things that has chiefly worried me,' he wrote to Hammond. 'It is very fine, for the most part, as you would expect and yet in spite of all the general impression seems to me cold.'[11] So Hobhouse was recruited to write a supplementary impression 'by a friend and colleague' – Montague's was given no by-line – and Hammond provided a lengthy political comment also unsigned.

C.P.'s daughter and his two sons quickly made up their minds to ask Hammond to write a biography to which Crozier contributed a chapter on Scott in the M.G. office. In spite of illness the manuscript was completed by the end of 1933 and the book appeared in 1934 soon after Spenser Wilkinson's autobiography with its critical references to his old editor.* Letters which passed between Hammond and Crozier make it clear that the book was written too soon, or at least that the authors felt too protective, to paint a wholly satisfactory picture of C.P. as editor. Thus Crozier told Hammond that after reading a draft, Attenborough, the chief sub-editor, 'addressed me (Crozier) for some time on the two texts: "You've let the old man down very lightly" and "He never cared a bit about news in his paper".' In a letter Crozier explained: 'It is not possible, of course, for me at this day to speak plainly of . . . his terrible habit of detaining stacks of "copy" all evening; the wretched sub-editors neither dared not to send it to him nor to go and get it away from him, so that the paper suffered – and this went on day after day and year after year.' In the biography this is reduced to one unobtrusive sentence: 'He kept "copy" late on his desk to the distraction of the sub-editors, and, apologising when at last he released it, did the same the next night.'[12]

In another letter, which has not been preserved, Crozier told Hammond of some personal shortcomings in C.P.'s dealings with men. Hammond's answer ran: 'I was always so indulgently treated by C.P. that I find it difficult to think of him in this different aspect but I suspect that if I had come under him when I was younger and less established I should have realised it quickly enough. I am inclined to enlarge that paragraph a little and to refer to Spenser Wilkinson's book. What do you think? At present I incline . . . to say that it represents

* See page 235-6, 239.

part but not the whole of the case. If C.P. was hard and exacting in some cases, he was generous in others.'[13] The book was not referred to. Later Hammond admitted that the deeper he got into C.P.'s biography the more doubts he began to have about him. On the other hand, starting from a worm's eye view, weaknesses which once bulked large in the present writer's sight have receded into a relatively minor place in the portrait of the whole man. Those weaknesses have not been concealed in this book.

5

Ted Scott did not move into his father's room. Some thought it a fit acknowledgment that the Old Man's place could not be filled. But at least the son at the age of 49 was now free to develop the paper in the way he wanted, knowing that he had already fought one difficult battle on his own. It had been a battle on two fronts – against the National Government in the paper and against National Government supporters in the office. He had established his personal position and made clear the standpoint which the paper would take. A new phase was beginning for the M.G.

He went for an April holiday in the Lakes with his eldest son, Richard, a boy of 15. The boat they were sailing on Windermere capsized in a sudden squall and Ted Scott was drowned on 22 April 1932. The news came first by telephone to Malcolm Muggeridge from the friends with whom Ted Scott was staying. He went straight in to Crozier and said simply 'Ted's dead.' There was, of course, no 'obit' in existence. It was a sign of Muggeridge's known personal standing with the editor that he was asked to write it. This was Muggeridge's last important work as a member of the M.G. staff. It marked the end of the era that never began.

CHAPTER THIRTY-ONE

John Scott's Problem

I

MOST of the people in this book were writers. John Scott was not. He positively disliked putting pen to paper. It was perhaps natural that the manager should not want to write in the paper, but J.R.S. carried this reluctance into business management. The series of admirable summaries of each year's working made by G. B. Dibblee stops short when he left. John Scott had far more important decisions to make than Dibblee ever had; but he made most of them in his head, leaving no record of his thinking. Some of the advice he got from outsiders remains, but that is all. Inside the office he encouraged people to talk to him rather than to write him memoranda. He demanded little in the way of documentation. Until well into the 1920s his only circulation records were weekly returns on slips of paper kept together by a metal clip. When the clip was full, he emptied it and began again.

Such a man must be difficult for a later generation to get to know. With John Scott there is an additional difficulty. He was quiet, a careful listener, intensely shy. His shyness made him abrupt, and this could easily be taken for rudeness as Russell Allen for one took it. On the other hand a boy of 16 who applied for a job as an M.G. reporter got a different impression when John Scott asked him to bring his father with him for an interview. 'I can still see J.R.S., nearly fifty years later, towering over the little schoolboy and the Russian Jew, a tailor's presser. I am still grateful for the courtesy and respect he showed my father, for the sensitivity toward my disappointment that I could not be hired there and then. He got me a job as a messenger with the sub-editors of the *Manchester Evening News*, telling me that I would learn the craft there.'[1] Joseph Frayman went on by way of copy-taking for the M.G. to a long and responsible career with the *New York Times*.

Most people thought John Scott cold. The trouble was rather that he found it difficult to show his feelings. Sir William Haley worked closely with him for many years. Haley had every reason to suppose that John Scott approved of him and appreciated his work. But he never said so. This was something that Haley had to infer. It would be idle to suppose that such a barrier, high in John Scott's lifetime, can be satisfactorily climbed twenty years after his death. The attempt must, however, be made because an understanding of the history of the *Guardian* in C.P.'s later years and in the troubled time after his death depends on it.

Fortunately John Scott just once provided a clue to his own personality. In 1946 Wadsworth edited a commemorative volume for the centenary of C. P.'s birth. Haley wrote an introduction to it which had much about John Scott. When John Scott saw it he sent Wadsworth the following note:

'The Haley 'intro' forces on me the uncongenial task of introspection. Why is it distasteful?

Chiefly, I think, because, although my many errors and omissions are probably much more present to my mind than to others, they are sufficently a matter of common knowledge to the initiated to raise smiles.

It is also rather like having a book on say Lancashire v Yorkshire matches at Old Trafford and writing the 'intro' around the groundsman. It is the star players who count and in whom the public are interested.

However I do feel that the basic financial policy of the papers is fundamentally important, that it should help for it to be understood by the public, and that publicity given to it makes it easier for succeeding generations to follow on the same lines. If therefore you honestly approve of it I am prepared to follow the policy of masterful non-interference in what is essentially an editorial matter.'

John Scott was tall, spare, physically gifted. As a boy he won the twelve mile cross-country run at Rugby; on his fiftieth birthday he ran the course again. He played tennis well, golf to a handicap of four and took great pleasure in climbing in the Lakes, a pleasure he shared with his elder brother Laurence, the son with literary and artistic gifts. John Scott's one identified contribution to the M.G. was a Letter to the Editor on a climbing accident in the Lakes, and among his wedding presents to his wife was a pair of climbing boots. He was a first-rate billiards player, and there were few games which he did not enjoy. One of his early jobs on the paper had been to organise special late cricket editions giving the close of play in the test matches in Australia – an assignment which must have been as satisfying to him as the production of the first annual Engineering Supplement.* For he was not only

* See p. 307.

an athlete but an engineer by training. He had taken a first in the Mechanical Sciences tripos at Cambridge and spent a year at the Massachusetts Institute of Technology.

An engineer must be an intelligent man; he need not necessarily be an intellectually curious one. John Scott was, although perhaps few members of the *Guardian* staff realised it. But James Bone remembered how when Einstein's theory of relativity was new 'John Scott seemed the only man of a rather learned circle who was able lucidly to expound it,' and Haley recalled that among the things J.R.S. savoured to the full were not only the cultivation of apples and his winter holiday in Switzerland but the latest book by Whitehead or Eddington. 'I have known no one who thought with greater economy of effort . . . He would allow neither his mind nor that of others to evade any dilemma,' was Haley's summing up.[2] Quick, logical thinking marked his work and his recreation. He had a sandwich lunch each day at the Manchester Reform Club and then settled down to a game of bridge, which he played well. He would not have enjoyed poker or been good at it.

John Scott was never content not to know when it was possible to find out. Two characteristic incidents illustrate this as well as throwing light on the working of the office. T. W. Evans, the manager of the *Evening News*, said when he retired that after fifty years in the office he would have liked once to have spoken to C.P.S. Somehow, although they frequently met on the stairs, this had never happened. When John Scott was told this some time later he claimed that it was quite impossible. But he went away and thought about it. He remembered that it was Russell Allen who had always attended the directors' meetings and decided that the story must be true. On another occasion he was asked why the directors' lunch at The Firs was held at an unusual time – and incidentally an inconvenient one for evening paper men, though that objection would have carried no weight. J.R.S. did not know, but he made enquiries and found out that it was because that was the time when the boys came home from school – or had done thirty years before.

In one way John Scott was more successful than the rest of the family in escaping from a dominant father. He was normally home before the others came down to the office. But in a deeper sense he remained his father's son. It was well for the paper that he did.

2

At the *Guardian*'s centenary dinner Lord Robert Cecil described C.P.'s work as 'making righteousness readable.' John Scott claimed at a

staff celebration that his was 'to make readable righteousness remunerative.' In 1921 he had reason to congratulate himself on the results of
the Manchester Guardian, Ltd. The paper had emerged from the war in
a strong financial position. The circulation, nearly 70,000 in 1919, was
higher than ever before – not far short of double what it had been at
the formation of the company in 1907. Advertising revenue was very
good. Profits had been rising, and in March 1920 the company decided
to capitalise £113,000 of its undistributed profits. The new ordinary
shares were allotted equally to C.P.'s two sons and to his son-in-law.
He himself took none. He was 74 and had at last to recognise, if not the
approach of death, the inevitability of death duties.

The *Guardian's* business recovery under John Scott had been
achieved in spite of the invasion of Lancashire by the *Daily News* which
started printing in Manchester in 1909, the second London paper to
come north. The *Daily News* had a special appeal to chapel folk, who
traditionally voted Liberal, and to elementary school teachers. It was,
therefore, in direct competition with the *Guardian* for readers and it
cost only half as much. Its northern edition must certainly have slowed
down the *Guardian's* recovery. In 1921 the Cadburys decided to economise by closing down the northern edition – mistakenly, as it turned
out, because it was in fact almost certainly paying its way. Of course
devoted readers could still obtain an inferior edition, and it was devoted
Daily News readers who were most akin to *Guardian* readers. Nevertheless from 1921 to 1928, when northern printing of the *Daily News* was
resumed, there was a marginal advantage to the M.G.

The war helped the *Guardian*; it killed the *Courier*. The last number
appeared on 28 January 1916. For ninety-one years it had been the
organ of Lancashire and Cheshire Conservatism with a circulation
that was especially strong in the country districts. Its death left the
Guardian as the only 'quality' morning newspaper published in Manchester. In itself this was, of course, to the paper's advantage, but it
was symptomatic of a general change in the newspaper industry which
was unfavourable to morning papers published outside London and
especially to the old 'quality' papers. The forty-two penny morning
papers published outside London in 1889 had been reduced to twenty-
seven by 1913. Some had died, others had become half-penny 'populars.' Of course there were special factors in the *Courier's* decline of
which the most important had been, first, its passing from Manchester
ownership to Lord Northcliffe and, second, Northcliffe's neglect of it
after he had bought the *Times*.

The death of the *Courier* was a warning as well as a benefit to the
Guardian. John Scott heeded the warning and saved the *Guardian*.

After the war advertisers began to switch a good deal of their custom from the provincial morning papers to the evenings. The change might be temporary or permanent. At first there was no knowing. John Scott decided that safety demanded the possession of one of each. This gave renewed importance to the relation of the M.G. to the *Manchester Evening News*.

3

From its birth in 1868 until 1905 the *Evening News* had been under the same ultimate control as the *Guardian*. After the War of the Taylor Succession it was a completely independent concern under Scott's cousin, Russell Allen, paying rent to the *Guardian* for its house room and sharing a joint printing account. The profits it made were entirely its own affair. There was no sentiment left to bind together the two related families and their newspapers – nothing but a marriage of convenience from which divorce was always possible. Indeed one of the most difficult issues in 1905–07 had been the possibility of the *Evening News* deciding to change partners and print on the *Daily Mail* plant. That threat might be renewed. The 1907 agreement would expire in 1927.

In 1919 Manchester had two evening papers, published within a quarter of a mile of one another. The *Manchester Evening Chronicle*, founded in 1897 as one of the Hulton group, appealed to much the same type of reader as the *News*. There was, therefore, much more fierce, direct competition between them than there could be between the *Chronicle*'s 'popular' morning partner, the *Daily Dispatch*, and the *Guardian* with its very different appeal. At times there had been a third evening paper in Manchester. As recently as the 1914 war the *Courier* management had revived the *Evening Mail*. What had been, could be again. If the *Evening News* moved elsewhere, the M.G. might have thought of starting a new evening paper as Scott had briefly done during the distracted days after Edward Taylor's death. This would have been to nobody's advantage. There was, therefore, the possibility of a reasonable bargain on strictly business terms between the Scotts and the Allens.

Russell Allen would be 60 in 1920. He was a good employer who took perhaps a deeper interest in his men as human beings than he did in what they produced. He had, of course, a real pride in his paper, but he was content to let its politics stray gently from his own – provided that they kept well to the right of C.P.'s views on Ireland and on votes for women. Both sides of the man come out in an obituary sketch which W. A. Balmforth, a former editor of the *Evening News*, wrote on the strength of his thirty-seven years' experience on the paper. 'I never knew Mr Allen harbour an unkindly thought or utter an unkind word. He was an ideal head. He could not see eye to eye with all that was written in the paper . . . but he never obtruded his own opinions on matters of public policy.'

There were some aspects of evening paper work which appealed strongly to Russell Allen. They were perhaps those most likely to endear him to many of his men. He was a frequent visitor to the stables and prided himself on the superiority of the *Evening News* team of Welsh cobs, which strode out naturally, over the *Chronicle* hackneys whose natural gait was more high-stepping. The beautifully groomed horses, drawing high two-wheeled carts, smartly painted in the livery of Cross Street or Withy Grove,* made indeed a splendid sight as they raced one another, threading in and out of the traffic in their determination to be first to deliver each new edition of their paper to the news-agents and street-sellers. 'First with the news' meant above all in evening paper work such things as being first with the half-time scores or the result of the 3.30. There was as yet no radio or television to compete with the evening papers as the main source of sporting news which, apart from test matches in Australia, all happened within their normal edition times.

The stop press 'box,' a Taylor, Garnett & Co invention in the days before the split, had been developed primarily for the *Manchester Evening News*.[3] This enabled late news to be inserted into an edition while it was being run off. Just as important was speed in news collection. Here the *Evening News* had its own pigeon post from local sporting events. In those days it gave a quicker and more reliable service than the telephone over reasonably short distances. The pigeons were of great interest to Russell Allen. There was a little wooden window which opened from his room into the manager's. When a result might be expected, the window would open and a voice would ask: 'Thos. W. E. Have the *Chronicle* sent up strags?' or some similar question. 'Thos. W. E.' was Allen's name for the nephew of William Evans who had been the principal agent in the founding of the *Evening News*.[4] 'Strags' was the local name for a decoy. Many attempts were made in devious ways to lure the *Evening News* pigeons away from their loft on the roof of the *Guardian* building. The episodes of this harmless rivalry made good telling in the Manchester Press Club and in the pubs where newspaper workers met.

Russell Allen would greatly miss these few sides of newspaper work

* Where the rival newspaper offices were.

which had something of a country flavour. But for the rest he would be glad to go. He had indeed had some thought of retiring even before 1914. In 1912 there had been preliminary negotiations with the Scotts which came to nothing.* Russell Allen himself much preferred country pursuits and country duties to newspaper work. His surviving son, Peter, had no desire to go into the family business. He was a notable show jumper and so was his sister Geraldine who won the Toronto Gold Cup. A nephew remembers Russell Allen driving over in a tandem on Sundays to see his father and announcing his arrival on a coach horn. The whole family in fact were country-bred: North Country, no doubt, but not the North Country of L. S. Lowry's landscapes or of the Armenian friends with whom John Scott played his regular rubbers of bridge.

Negotiations for the sale of the E.N. opened in 1919. They were not concluded until 1922 because of some difficulty in meeting the views of two of Russell Allen's brothers who had an interest in the *Evening News* profits. This 1922 agreement provided that when Russell Allen died or retired the M.G. would buy the *Evening News* for the sum of £108,000. Two years later another agreement, antedated to 30 September 1923, completed the sale to the Manchester Guardian and Evening News, Ltd, the new name of the company. It made interim arrangements for joint control to last until 1930. In 1927 Russell Allen died and a supplemental agreement with his executors in 1929 brought the interim period to an end.

C.P.S. was delighted with the conclusion of the sale. 'Six years hence,' he wrote to Hobhouse in 1924, 'we should after taking over the E.N. be making about £100,000 a year which seems fabulous. What should we do with it? Start a decent Liberal paper? That might mean competing against ourselves for the first place.' Then his usual caution intervened. 'But of course the basis of the edifice is precarious and would disappear if competition . . . should force us back to a penny M.G. and a half-penny E.N.'[5]

4

'To silence the press is to destroy an essential instrument of government. John is working hard at our particular problem and will have, I expect, something ready for us to consider before long.' So C.P. wrote to Hammond only nine days after the end of the General Strike.

* 'I had not quite realised how completely you desired to be released for responsibility in connection with the E.N. . . .' draft by J.R.S. of a reply for C.P.S. to send to Russell Allen 10 September 1912

What John was getting ready was the blue-print for a company union. A week later he explained it to the foremen of the two papers and 'was a good deal disappointed.'[6] There seem to have been three distinct reasons for his plan.

The least important was certainly management's natural desire to get on with its job unhampered by restrictions. Until recently the *Guardian* had been almost entirely free from labour disputes. There had been a one day strike by Manchester compositors in 1917 and a three week stoppage of all Liverpool and Manchester newspapers in 1920 during which the M.G. had produced a duplicated bulletin. John Scott had also been troubled by what he regarded as 'vexatious restrictions' on overtime and in the unreasonable limitation of apprentices.[7] But these were matters of minor friction and would certainly not have led to the establishment of a company union. They were, however, part of the background to John Scott's action.

The second reason for promoting a company union was a wish to move towards an organisation by which all who worked on the *Guardian* or the *Evening News* would be able to feel that they were constitutionally involved in what the papers were doing. Leaders written by Ted Scott in the early days after the war had expressed sympathy with aspirations of this kind; but the thought, like the desire, had been nebulous. Now, in the aftermath of the General Strike, there seemed to John Scott to be a possibility of doing something in his own firm by making it an island of industrial unionism but without necessarily severing its workers' connections with their own craft unions. After the doubts raised by his meeting with the foremen he took the highly unusual step for him of putting his ideas into writing and sending a circular to all employees. It is in some ways a naïve document, but it is patently sincere:

'. . . I want to say to you frankly that if you see nothing in the scheme beyond possible pecuniary benefit, you had better vote against it.

The last thing we want to do is to induce you, by immediate financial attractions alone, to give a reluctant assent . . .

We shall not run the papers on "What-can-I-get-out-of-it" lines, and the beginnings of co-partnership which this scheme opens to you can only be fruitful in our work and in our welfare if entered into in the same spirit.

If each side and each section is to be jealous of others, and is to have little or no thought beyond its own immediate advantage, we had far better leave things as they are. If, on the other hand, we can join forces as free men, and work in generous harmony, the proposals do offer a widening prospect of moral satisfaction, material welfare and service to our fellows, which the present system of antagonisms and divided loyalties can never evolve.

On this basis I should be as proud to serve with you as I am to serve the Company.'[8]

It was, however, the third reason for starting a company union which really counted. C.P. had been outraged by the inclusion of the newspapers in the General Strike. The situation was one in which independent opinion ought especially to be able to make itself heard. One side had controlled the radio and the *British Gazette* and abused its control. The other side had stopped the newspapers. C.P. believed that a direct appeal ought to be made to the King to become a peacemaker. He wrote a leader on it. But it could only be read by those few who were fortunate enough to get hold of one of the M.G.'s meagre strike bulletins. He felt that never again must the voice of the M.G. be silenced and said so. John Scott thought this over in his strictly logical way and decided that this could only be achieved by the formation of a company union. The effect, however, was to apply to ordinary industrial bargaining certain precautions designed to meet the quite exceptional circumstances in which the free expression of opinion had been denied. The TUC had clearly blundered in calling out newspaper workers in a dispute outside their industry at a time when the whole community needed their work. It was unlikely that the TUC would make the same mistake twice. But for the memory of the 1920 strike, C.P. might perhaps have been willing to trust to this. Possibly, too, John Scott's splendid power of quick decision operated adversely in this instance. He was perhaps committed to the plan before the consequences of 'going it alone' could become apparent.

There were two essential features of the M.G. and E.N. Society. One was that it was based on an industrial pattern instead of a craft one. The other was that its members gave up the right to strike and replaced it by conciliation procedure. In return they got considerable benefits in sick pay, pensions and other welfare provisions. The company guaranteed that hours and wages would never fall below trade union standards and later told the TUC that it was willing that officers of the craft unions should serve on arbitration panels. Nearly four-fifths of the company's employees voted for the scheme. Only the M.G. editorial and the E.N. composing room staffs had a majority against.

The printing trade unions and their members on other papers, however, were generally hostile. Although the plan allowed for members of the M.G. and E.N. Society to continue to belong to their own craft unions, they would be isolated from their fellow-members. They could not strike and the company would enter into no agreements except with its own union. Sir Henry Slesser and Arthur Henderson, junior, the two Labour barristers who had advised the company on the drafting of the scheme, found themselves in trouble with the TUC. W. M. Citrine brought down a deputation from the General Council which argued with C.P. and his two sons for three hours. Its report to the General Council stated that 'the putting in operation of the scheme would be interpreted as an act of hostility and would be resisted by the Trade Union Movement . . . The Company representatives dissented from this view, but admitted that the scheme was in itself a blow at the whole Trade Union Movement. They had appreciated that point when the scheme had been devised . . .'. C.P. asked that, when the matter was reported to Congress, its members should be told that he took strong exception to this passage 'which does not represent the view which we then expressed or at any time have entertained.'[9]

But this was the high water mark of hostility. The TUC itself was not bothered with the dispute. During the winter agreements were reached with all the various craft unions except the Typographical Association. Ramsay MacDonald, the leader of the Labour Party, tried to make peace between the M.G. and the T.A. 'I have seen some of the T.A. men,' he wrote to C.P., '. . . I found them very anxious to have some settlement and the way they talked about you and the grief that they had that there was a disagreement between you, was really very fine. They also confessed that they have provoked your son a good deal.'[10] John Scott went to London to see MacDonald, but nothing came of his mediation. Another attempt in 1936 also failed.

There is no doubt that John Scott and his father were both committed to the scheme. Ted Scott's position is more in doubt. Immediately after the visit of the TUC deputation the M.G. decided to publish the full details of the plan and an explanation of its purpose. The explanation was drawn up jointly by Hobhouse and E.T.S. and itself occupied two-and-a-half columns of the paper.[11] Ted Scott's close association with Wadsworth would have warned him of the probable trade union reactions. There is nothing left to show a dissenting attitude on his part in 1926, but it is probably significant that in writing to Hammond about C.P.'s obituary he said he thought there was no need to refer to the formation of the House Society as it was 95 per cent John's work.

From 1927 the M.G. and E.N. Society went peacefully on its way bringing real benefits to its members, but achieving nothing towards that general overhaul of trade union structure in the newspaper industry which had been one of John Scott's objectives. In the end the Society fell an indirect victim to Hitler. The severe raids made it necessary for newspapers to have emergency plans to use another plant in the event of a direct hit. No partner could be found for the M.G.

because of the continued hostility of the T.A. to the Society. It had to be wound up. The firm found the money to put its compositors in good standing with the TA.

5

C.P., as we have seen, had thought that the *Manchester Evening News* might be a springboard. It proved to be a safety net. The *Guardian* had survived the crisis in cotton with remarkably little damage; but in 1930, the year the purchase of the *Evening News* was completed, the M.G. ran into sudden, catastrophic trouble. So, of course, did Britiain and the world. But that was only part of the reason for the *Guardian*'s troubles. The terms of trade in the newspaper industry were turning against papers like the *Guardian*. The second inter-war decade was the great period of struggle between the 'popular' newspapers for the highest possible circulation. In the nineteen-thirties newspapers were sold, and readers bought. 'Some 50,000 canvassers were recruited and armed with a selection of merchandise ranging from cameras, fountain-pens, mangles and tea-kettles to silk stockings, flannel trousers and even gold wristlet watches. These they offered free to astonished housewives in return for an undertaking to become registered readers for two or three months.' Never was there such a boom in Dickens. The *News Chronicle*, the *Daily Mail* and the *Daily Express* lost £36,000 in disposing of 300,000 sets of the novelist's works. All the popular papers offered free insurance, and roughly three-quarters of their readers were registered.[12]

The newspaper war greatly increased the total number of subscribers. Each of the papers which took part in it gained many new readers. In 1920 only two papers, the *Daily Mail* and the *Daily Mirror*, had a sale of more than a million a day. By 1930 there were five. By 1937 two of the five, the *Daily Express* and the *Daily Herald*, were selling over two million. The five together sold over eight and a half million a day in 1937 compared with seven million in 1930. There were, of course, other factors besides free gifts and free insurance which increased their circulation. One of these which especially affected the *Guardian* was the growth in the number of papers published in Manchester. At the end of 1921 there were three morning papers, of which only the *Daily Mail* was a London paper. In 1930 there were six. Four of them were London papers. The *Mail* had been joined by the *Express*, the *Herald* and the *News Chronicle*. The last two shared a good deal of the M.G.'s political outlook and were to some extent rivals for the same readers. The *News Chronicle* had come back to Manchester in 1928 after a seven years' gap, the *Daily Herald* started there in 1930.

The 'quality' papers did not try to increase circulation by printing in more than one place. There were three London 'quality' papers in 1935 – the *Times*, the *Daily Telegraph* and the *Morning Post*, all of them Conservative in politics; all of them predominantly south country in their readership. Between them they reached nearly 14 per cent of the families in the South-East, but under 4 per cent of those in Lancashire and Cheshire and under 3 per cent in Cumberland and Westmorland.[13] The *Guardian* continued to enjoy a good deal of its natural protection by distance, as well as by the difference of its politics, from the competition of the London 'quality' papers.

All the 'quality' papers stood aside from the free gift campaigns which at times made the salesman – customer relation more important than that between journalist and reader. But neither the *Times* nor the *Guardian* could ignore its results. Both introduced cheap rate subscriptions for certain classes of readers – parsons, students and teachers, for instance. The *Guardian* added a rather different category – members of the Workers' Educational Association. These cheap rate subscribers were for the M.G. a new world which replaced the balance of the old. Up to the cotton crisis the paper had enjoyed a secure circulation among the thousands of small firms of which the industry was composed. Each firm almost automatically purchased a copy for each member of its staff who reached the level of a manager. As the number of mills fell, this part of the *Guardian's* circulation fell with it. But the paper's total sale remained constant, fluctuating between 45,000 and 50,000 until the Second World War. The old full-price business subscribers, many of them Free Trade Conservatives, were replaced by half-price subscribers who were attracted to the paper by its radical politics and its literary quality. In the nineteen-thirties those who read and those who wrote the *Guardian* became more like-minded than they had been for a long time.

But the cost to the paper was considerable. The cheap rate had been introduced in the nineteen-twenties. By 1930 nearly a quarter of the total sale was at this rate. It rose steadily and by 1936 was nearly two-fifths. The number of papers sold remained constant; the revenue from sales dropped sharply. This was one reason for the *Guardian* crisis which became acute just as the purchase of the *Evening News* was completed.

More important was the loss of advertising revenue. During the cotton boom the M.G. did very well. It reached a figure of about £300,000 a year for a time. When the boom ended it settled down between 1922 and 1930 to a steady average figure of £230,000. Then the world financial crisis hit England hard. Advertising fell by £40,000 in the twelve months to March 1931 and by a further £40,000 in the following year. This could not all be put down to the world's economic blizzard or the paper's unpopular politics. The effects of both would pass. More lasting, and therefore more damaging, was the diversion of display advertising to the 'popular' papers which could offer the mass audience needed for the marketing of mass-produced consumer goods. In 1937 the cost of display advertisements per column inch in the *Times* was £3; in the *Daily Express* it was £6. 10. 0. But the cost per thousand readers for the same space was 3¾d in the *Times* and not quite 2d in the *Express*. In the total daily amount of advertising the *Times* with an October average of 1,637 inches was only fifty inches ahead of the *Express*.[14] At the same time the corresponding rates for the M.G. were £1 per column inch, making 4½d per thousand readers. The average daily total for October was 736 inches.

The immediate 1930–31 crisis led to tremendous economies in the running of the paper, but cheese-paring and the partial national economic recovery were insufficient to keep the M.G. going as the 'quality' radical newspaper of world standing to which its readers were accustomed, and which the Scotts were alone interested in producing. Support from the *Evening News* was essential. But the *Evening News* itself was not immune from the newspaper wars. Between 1929 and 1932 there were bitterly fought struggles in Newcastle and Bristol between the Berrys and the Harmsworths. In both cities the Berrys owned morning and evening papers. The Harmsworths owned neither, but they started evening papers in both in 1929. In Manchester also the Berrys, who had taken over the Hulton papers in 1924, owned both a morning and an evening paper. The Harmsworths had a morning. There was great anxiety lest they should start an evening to keep it company. If this had happened John Scott's purchase of the *Evening News* might have proved a liability rather than an asset. All he could do to fight off the danger was to improve the *Evening News*.

John Scott consulted the senior members of the staff individually. W. J. Haley was the last to be called in. Sitting in John Scott's garden at Wilmslow he explained his views about what should be done. There was nothing in writing. Haley spoke freely. John Scott listened, only occasionally putting in a probing question. The gist of Haley's argument was that unified control was essential for evening paper work. One man must control news, distribution, advertising, the whole running of the paper. By the end of the interview John Scott had decided that this young man – Haley was not quite 30 – was the man he needed. Haley left Wilmslow knowing that he was to be managing editor with a seat on the board. John Scott had no cause to regret his decision. When Haley took over, the circulation of the *Evening News* was roughly 150,000 a day. It went up steadily each year. When he left to go to the BBC thirteen years later on his way to the *Times* it was over 200,000.

Some men might have resented the way in which the M.G. spent the profits of the *Evening News* and received the plaudits of the world. Jealousy would have been natural, but Haley was generous and sincere in his admiration for the M.G. His praise was worth having because it came from a man who wrote as well as any *Guardian* man. John Scott for his part recognised the *Guardian*'s debt when in the end he paid Haley more than he drew himself: 'After all, you make the money we spend.'

6

On the day of his death Ted Scott drove up to Windermere with his son Richard. On the way he talked to Richard about the tax problems caused to the M.G. by the death of C.P. 'I distinctly remember his saying that God knows what would happen to the paper if anything should happen to him or to his brother . . . the gist of what I remember is that it was very important that neither he nor J.R.S. should die before steps had been taken to deal with the situation.' So Richard Scott recalled in 1969 the events of 1932.[15]

The same day John Scott posted a letter to his brother which reached Windermere next morning and was returned unopened. In it he told Ted that he had seen their solicitor about their discussion on making new wills, and enclosed a draft letter to his old friend E. D. Simon asking him to become executor. 'Ted and I are making our wills,' the draft began, 'and an agreement in respect of the M.G. shares. The latter are rather a problem being highly taxable but of doubtful economic value. The agreement is that the survivor shall buy from the deceased's estate sufficient M.G. ordinary shares (at the price agreed by the revenue authorities) to pay the whole of the taxation upon the deceased's M.G. holding.' In his letter to Ted, John Scott glossed this agreement with the suggestion that the sooner the bulk of the ordinary shares were passed on to their children the safer for the M.G.: 'One does not like the idea of about one-third of the M.G. shares passing into the hands of persons outside the business but that seems to be almost inevitable unless we live to make proper disposition of the shares among the rising generation.'[16] The tax collector was in fact to prove a greater danger to the M.G. than were rival newspaper proprietors.

In 1914 C.P. had divided the bulk of his holding of ordinary shares between his sons and his son-in-law. His position as Governing Director sufficiently secured his control of the company and the paper. In the centenary year he made his will, leaving his two sons as joint (but not joint and several) Governing Directors for life. His ordinary shares passed to them. Each then held half the equity.* It was thus that the problem of shares of 'high taxable but doubtful economic value' arose. What value can you attach to shares on which no dividend has ever been paid or is ever intended to be paid? But the Inland Revenue wanted death duties. After C.P.'s death on New Year's Day the Revenue accepted a valuation at a quarter of their nominal worth. The great depression had come and, anyhow, C.P. was only a minority shareholder. In the Revenue's eyes, though in nobody else's, he could not help himself. But when Ted Scott died in April the Revenue took a different line. E.T.S. was not a minority shareholder. If necessary, the *Guardian* could have been killed or sold – the argument with the Revenue was not helped by the fact that Beaverbrook was only too anxious to buy – and the *Manchester Evening News* was a highly profitable property. Ted Scott was potentially a rich man and his estate had to be taxed on that basis. His brother honoured the uncompleted agreement and bought all his ordinary shares. But in fact neither brother was a rich man because both considered themselves under an over-riding obligation to run the *Guardian* 'on the same lines and in the same spirit as heretofore.' To the Inland Revenue this was not an obligation. It was a whim.

Ted Scott's death was serious: John's would have been a catastrophe had it occurred soon after Ted's because he now held all the ordinary shares. A way out had to be found. John Scott decided against his original idea of transferring shares to his sons and nephews. It was replaced by the idea of a Trust. Mr Gavin Simonds, the future Lord Chancellor, was consulted. 'It seems to me,' he said, 'that you are trying to do something very repugnant to the law of England. You are trying to divest yourself of a property right.' J.R.S. was, and Gavin Simonds assisted.

The Scott Trust was finally established on 10 June, 1936. All the ordinary shares were transferred to seven trustees – all of them closely connected with the paper. Three were members of the family – John Scott, his son Laurence and his nephew, Evelyn Montague. Crozier, Bone and Haley were all directors and working journalists on the *Guardian* or the *Evening News*. E. D. Simon was a director. By the Trust Deed John Scott bound himself never to receive any financial benefit

* Montague's shares had been transferred when he resigned.

from the *Guardian* or the *Evening News* except what he earned in salary or as a director – and that was only some £2,000 a year. But he kept the right to appoint and dismiss the trustees. In effect the Scott Trust in its original form was designed solely to restore the *status quo* before the intervention of the Inland Revenue.

When John Scott died Haley wrote: 'He regarded the papers as a trust. He could have been a rich man; he chose a Spartan existence. And when he made up his mind to divest himself of all beneficial interest in them he did so with as little display of emotion as if he had been solving an algebraical problem. Most men making so large a sacrifice would have exacted at least the price of an attitude.'[17] But John Scott had solved his problem. That was satisfaction enough.

CHAPTER THIRTY-TWO

Unexpected Eminence

I

C.P.'s will had established a dyarchy – two governing directors for life with joint and equal authority and no means of resolving a deadlock. Time had no chance to show whether this quaint arrangement would long have worked. Death soon restored the monarchy – still under the terms of C.P.'s will. The moment Ted died, John became sole governing director. His first job was to find a new editor. Inside the restricted circle of *Guardian* and ex-*Guardian* men there were four or five obvious 'possibles,' but hardly a 'probable' among them. Professionally, the most eligible would have been Herbert Sidebotham, who now had a unique position in London journalism, straddling the 'quality' and the 'popular' papers as Scrutator in the *Sunday Times* and Candidus in the *Daily Sketch*. He might not have been acceptable or available. Politically, the most obvious would have been J. L. Hammond who had just begun to write C.P. Scott's biography. But it was an accepted belief that his wife's health ruled out Manchester. Two other 'possibles' were James Bone, the London editor, and W. P. Crozier, the news editor in Manchester. But in 1932 it was as impossible to imagine Bone outside Fleet Street as Fleet Street without J.B. – and Bone was no politician, which was a strength to a perhaps over-political newspaper but would have been a weakness in its editor. Crozier was the man in possession, but only four months before Ted Scott had described him as 'not being of an M.G. way of thinking.' John Scott, of course, had not seen this letter, but he was certainly well aware of the storms in the Corridor.

Hammond came up for Ted Scott's funeral and stayed with E. D. Simon. He saw John Scott twice on the day of the funeral and lunched with him again in London on 2 May. Hammond's diary also mentions talks with Crozier and Wadsworth in Manchester and with Bone in London. John Scott had been, of course, beset by suggestions of suitable outsiders, but he had quickly decided to keep the editorship, if not in the family, at least in the office. Ted Scott had died on 22 April 1932. Crozier was formally appointed at a directors' meeting on 6 May.

A new situation had arisen. For twenty-five years the editorial side of the M.G. had taken undoubted precedence over the managerial, partly because the manager was the editor's son, and partly because the editor was also the owner. Now the manager had become the owner – the first time this had happened in the paper's history – and the new editor was not even a member of the family, only a salaried employee of the manager-proprietor. How would the editor's position be defined?

In *Guardian* tradition, and in family memory, Dibblee was the manager who interfered, the villain of the War of the Taylor Succession. His was an example to avoid. John Scott believed that a newspaper manager's duty was to make his paper as profitable as possible, and to refrain from taking part in editorial decisions. The first editorial decision John Scott made was when he appointed Crozier editor. He deliberately did not make another until, a dozen years later, death forced him to find a successor. It was not that he lacked interest – Crozier sent him copies of all important confidential memoranda to which occasionally J.R.S. would add a short, perceptive, but strictly non-directive comment. He kept out because he believed that the editor of the *Manchester Guardian*, just because it was the *Manchester Guardian*, must be as free editorially as if he were the proprietor.

John Scott not only abstained from interference himself but watched protectively to see that others did not infringe it. In the year of Crozier's appointment, he strengthened the Board by bringing E. D. Simon on to it. It was a convention of the paper that editorial matters were never discussed at Board meetings. But Simon was a keen politician and a devoted Manchester patriot as well as a great industrialist. As time went on he began increasingly to express at Board meetings his natural interest in the contents of the paper. He made no attempt to interfere with the paper's policy, but what he said was clearly an embarrassment to Crozier. Crozier remained silent, but his feelings were made plain by his heightened colour. John Scott and Haley noticed this and J.R.S. explained to Simon what the *Guardian* practice was. It made no difference. John Scott intervened. In 1938 Simon ceased to be a director.

2

Among the letters of congratulation which Crozier received was an excited but belated one from a man he had last seen thirty years before. Then, Crozier had been a schoolmaster – 'I liked the place little, and was thereby diverted into journalism'; and his correspondent, 'a grubby,

fairly intelligent little child, very unpopular, perhaps rather precocious.'
Now, Crozier was editor of what 'a widely scattered band . . . believe
to be the best paper in the world'; and his correspondent, Chief of the
Documents Division of the League of Nations. But the writer was also
a Hawthornden prize winner and had just finished putting his old
schoolmaster into a new novel. It was at this moment that he learned
accidentally – perhaps from Robert Dell, the *Guardian*'s Geneva correspondent who was a friend of his, – that the Crozier who had befriended
the small boy was the Crozier who now edited the *Guardian*.

When Crozier died, Geoffrey Dennis, by this time a major in the
Intelligence Corps, sent an appreciation which accidents of war delayed
until it was too late to publish. But what he wrote survives and still
conjures up the man, who in 1932 had become the *Guardian* editor:

'A good proportion of the boys was from the deep country, talked broad
Yorkshire, and used the second person singular and their fists as freely. This
shy and gentle recruit to the staff was palpably not in his element . . . The
bruisers tried their hand at a little baiting: I see now his face twitching as he
stood up to them, but he did stand up to them. His courage, and being a
champion footballer, pulled him through, and he got the upper hand . . . I
think I may have been the boy who knew him best, being so to speak his
opposite number among the boys as leading fish-out-of-water. He supported
me against the same gang that had tried conclusions with him, and when one
of them tore up the whole of my carefully prepared homework, he took me
with him one evening into an empty classroom and most immorally, and most
saintlily, dictated the whole of it afresh. We exchanged views – I was ten and
he I suppose twenty-three – on the general situation . . . His appearance was
faintly parsonic, high forehead with hair already receding a little, and a most
mild expression which his pince-nez enhanced. The expression became
curiously less mild when, the pince-nez removed, he charged with tremendous speed and indeed fury on the football field.'[1]

Crozier brought to his editorship an old-fashioned schoolmaster's
precision in the use of English. If he could not command good writing,
he could at least forbid bad and prescribe Plain Words. It seemed to
him a losing battle as a pessimistic memorandum to the chief sub-editor
shows: 'I reckon that in the last four years I have sent to you personally
not less than a hundred notes on "both – and" and "either – or" alone
(say one per fortnight) and not less than fifty (I think far more) on the
misuse of "otherwise." And roughly speaking, all wasted. Some
people say these things are unimportant. E.T.S. would certainly have
said so. But, unfortunately, I can't, and as long as I am, as the clergy
say, "spared," I shan't be able to take that view.' But, in spite of apparent total defeats – as by the sub-editor whom Crozier personally taught

Frank L. Emanuel was regularly employed as an illustrator,
his work often appeared several times a week

In 1908 the process department was set up and F. W. Doughty became
the first staff photographer. This is a characteristic example of his work

When the *Guardian* suggested to Max Beerbohm that he was wrong about the kind of man whom Labour would make Foreign Secretary he thought again and substituted the Etonian for the trade unionist

A Feverish Effort to Regain "Touch".

Max

Rapallo, Italy.
Boxing Day, 1921.

"When Labour Rules," or,
  What M. Cambon really foresaw, and why
M. Cambon left us.
  Secretary for Foreign Affairs (holding his first weekly reception): "Comme moi, Monsieur l'Ambassadeur, vous apercevez, sans doute, que la haute politique, le Quai D'Orsay, la rue Downing, et même ce qu'on appelle 'Labour', ne sont que d'illusions —et non pas des plus interessantes. Asseyez-vous. Causons des idées charmantes de votre illustre compatriote, Henri Bergson."

'Sartor's' faintly Beards-leyesque style was frequently found on the Women's Page

'with illustrations the use of "both–and" etc until he said he understood,'[2] the result of his persistent sniping was to keep slipshod writing within bounds which many papers envied.

In devoting so much attention to matters which to Ted Scott had seemed 'indifferent' Crozier was not merely indulging his own taste or practising his old sub-editor's trade. He was trying 'to carry on the paper in the same spirit as heretofore.' Primarily, of course, this was a political obligation, but Crozier saw it also as a stylistic duty. C.P. and Montague would have approved. C.P. had regularly cut from his own and other papers examples of faulty grammar; and, when it was the M.G. that was to blame, he had sent them on with a complaint. Sometimes there was an explanatory note. Thus, Montague once drafted for C.P. a reminder 'that "prior to" and "preparatory to" are adjectival clauses and should not be used as prepositions.' He went on to make a suggestion which eventually took form as the M.G. Style Book. Successive versions were produced by Crozier and Wadsworth.* Comparison shows many lost battles; a new version for the 1970s, perhaps overdue, would record many more. Montague's original suggestion was to include 'the few points in which sub-editors and reporters are apt to outrage the special hobbies of colleges, prelates etc. about their own nomenclature . . . Another branch might deal with forbidden things in French, like "Mdlle" for "Mlle", *morale* for *moral, raconteur* for *conteur* etc. I believe the *Times* keeps a regular Book of Leviticus on all these niceties, and the non-observance of one of them does somehow give an amateurish look to a whole stick-full of surrounding copy.'[3] To the end of his life W.P.C. would never tolerate *morale*.

'The best and most effective English for newspaper purposes . . . simple, direct, lucid, concise, short': that was Crozier's positive desire. It would be untrue to say that he based his style, or wished others to model theirs, on that of any other writer. But his reading was reflected in his writing. The Latin and Greek classics, and the Bible, were his daily companions. He recorded one fragment of conversation from a war-time lunch with Churchill. Churchill had used a Latin tag and added that this was something you could no longer do in the House. 'Sir Arthur Salter added "No, nor the Bible either!" I said "Why not," and he answered "Because scarcely any of them know it. It's not read." Salter added that he doubted whether anyone could be a great speaker in English who did not know his Bible.'[4] Crozier would have thought it improbable that such a man would be even a passable writer for the M.G.

When Crozier became editor he had to give up the serious study

* Crozier formed a committee to prepare his, but its members could not agree.

of the New Testament which he had been making for several years. But he retained his interest in Biblical scholarship, following the reviews even if he no longer had time to read the books. Thus in 1934 he asked Hammond to amplify his review of a book in the M.G. by telling him whether the author had seriously tackled 'the point that Jesus was clearly expecting the coming of the Kingdom at any moment ("like a thief in the dark").' 'I am immensely interested in this subject,' he continued, 'After many years of indifference I began to study the New Testament with a completely blank mind as to what I might discover, and I had ended, at the time when two years ago I had to stop the research, with some clear convictions.'[5] He had in fact hoped one day to write a Life of Jesus. That was not to be, but his slim *Letters of Pontius Pilate*, published in 1928, is a graceful and knowledgeable piece of historical fiction which had some success in England and, rather curiously, was translated into Finnish. It had some surprising readers, who drew some astonishing conclusions. A United States Marine wrote to Jonathan Cape, the publisher, in 1943 'to establish as a fact the statement "Tell that to the Marines" . . . My questions are: (1) Is this a precise translation of the letter? (2) Can we unquestionably establish this reference and the letter wherein it is contained? . . . it is thereupon my intention to add this fact to the recorded history of the United States Marines as maintained in our Headquarters, Washington, D.C.'[6] The passage which had caught his attention ran:

'My troops will enter Jerusalem in the dead of night. In the morning, when the Jews awake, go about their business, throng into the Temple, they will see the standards, with the images prominently displayed upon them, already established on the ramparts of the Antonia. They will storm the Antonia, you say? Tell that to the Marines.'[2]

Pontius Pilate did not get his honourable mention in Washington, D.C.; but the extract at least shows that close attention to the classics and the Bible need not make a man a pedantic or a pietistic writer.

3

John Scott had chosen his editor better than perhaps he knew. Crozier in place of C.P.S. in 1926 or E.T.S. in 1931 might have been a disaster. The M.G. might have forfeited for good the intellectual leadership of the Left and wandered, increasingly friendless, in the no man's land of internal Liberal Party politics, of 'lost causes, impossible beliefs and forsaken loyalties.' But by 1932 English internal politics mattered little – though they still seemed all important – except in their relation to a new, but as yet hardly perceived danger to mankind. A few days before Ted Scott's death Adolf Hitler had polled thirteen million votes in the German presidential election. Seven months later Hitler became Chancellor and the Nazi revolution had taken place.

No editor of an English newspaper was better placed than Crozier to appreciate what this meant for Germany, for Britain and for the world. The hour and the man were exactly matched. Crozier had been in charge of the M.G. foreign news ever since there had been a regular, continuous service from the paper's own men. He had built it up, and he continued throughout his editorship to give it his close personal supervision. He delegated nothing except the actual writing of leaders. His possessiveness was, of course, an old weakness. One of the reasons why David Mitrany left the paper soon after the First World War was Crozier's reluctance to pass on private letters from foreign correspondents. This was a persistent complaint of successive foreign leader-writers. Crozier's attitude was expressed in a letter to one of the foreign correspondents in 1933: 'I think, if you do not mind, it would be better if you sent such messages to me rather than to members of the staff. I pass on everything that I get in the way of information to the leader-writers. On the other hand if they get the information and then I dissent from something which they have written it is awkward if they quote some authority which I have not seen in support of their contention and against mine. I am sure you will understand the point.'[7] But a few months later he was telling Hammond 'if I can get a reliable foreign editor it would be the greatest relief to me and the paper that is conceivable. But how many years does it take to produce a foreign editor in these days of the authentic M.G. kind? The paper has been trying to find one since the end of the war and has never got anywhere near it.'[8] No doubt Crozier imagined that he wanted this relief. The truth is that he badly needed it; but he would have been extremely reluctant to surrender this particular part of his work. He was ready, indeed anxious, to maintain a voluminous correspondence with his foreign correspondents even if it killed him. It may well have contributed to the persistent ill-health of his later years – a perforated ulcer in 1936 and a serious heart condition in 1943.

Crozier's possessiveness was a vice; but in 1932 it was a vice suddenly turned virtuous. It had put him in a position where he was as well informed as any man in England about European affairs. Like other editors of 'quality' newspapers he had his own special sources, and he had the added advantage of knowing their strength and weakness from regular contact with them extending in every case but one over a long period of years. Most of these special sources were the

Guardian's own staff correspondents overseas. Before the war there had virtually been none, though there had been an irregular number of special contributors and what would now be called 'stringers.' Some of these had been young men with a career of high distinction in front of them such as Dudley Ward, who acted for the M.G. in Berlin in 1913 and 1914 and later held many important international appointments. The *Guardian* continued after the war to use this kind of service from minor capitals and the world's quieter spots, but in 1919 it began to build up its own regular group of full-time men for key places. They, like Crozier, were ready for the testing thirties.

4

The *Guardian* foreign correspondents between 1919 and 1939 knew each other well. All were men of some distinction. They had this common characteristic. They shared a belief in the unity of European culture and they tended to associate themselves closely, sometimes in love and sometimes in hate, with the country in which they were stationed. They interpreted what they saw in terms first of that country and secondly in terms of its impact on Europe as a whole. They were, of course, deeply concerned with Britain's role in Europe and with the effect on it of what happened in Paris or Berlin or Vienna as the case might be. But they were, perhaps, less concerned with diplomatic affairs than were some of the other English correspondents. Thus in 1933 they wrote rather less about the effect of Hitler's revolution on Germany's foreign policy and rather more about its effect on Germans than did the other correspondents. The difference is not great, but it is significant.

The key man in the M.G. group was J. G. Hamilton, short, sandy-haired, leaning towards one with hands stretched forward as if he were about to enter a Max Beerbohm cartoon. Hamilton had died three years before Crozier became editor, but the whole team in the Hitler period acknowledged him as in a sense their master. He was, too, of all the M.G. men the one whom Crozier knew best and trusted most. To some extent he was the guarantor of the others to Crozier. Hamilton had first joined the M.G. two years after Crozier and worked with him in the sub-editors' room. He came on Sidebotham's introduction and with the rather cautious support of the philosopher Samuel Alexander. 'I think his family is Irish,' he wrote, 'and he seemed to me to have both the aptitudes and the defects they often have.'[9] Alexander granted him intelligence but doubted his industry and his willingness to see a thing through. Had he not declined to read an honours course, given up the idea of studying for the ICS and gone to a 'College Apprentice-ship' with the Westinghouse Company? Scott no doubt saw advantages that Alexander missed in Hamilton's breadth of experience. He was not disappointed.

But in 1910 Hamilton told Scott in a letter full of blarney that he found the financial advantages of the foreign news editorship of the *Daily News* irresistible although 'the prospect of leaving the great newspaper, which adopted me and made me a journalist, and the little republic of men who have been so good to me is an exquisitely painful one.'[10] In 1919 Hamilton came back to the M.G. going first to Berlin where one of his early messages was a protest against the arrest by the German War Office of Philips Price, who was then working as the *Daily Herald* correspondent. He moved on to cover the Russo-Polish war, finding it easy to cross the lines of the two armies. His next job was a visit to Japan to arrange for a special M.G. Supplement. This was followed by a roving commission as 'European Correspondent' spent mainly in the South-East which lasted till the autumn of 1921. Then followed an unhappy spell with the *Daily Chronicle* during which H. W. Nevinson, who was covering the Washington Conference for the M.G., met him and later recalled how 'during the private discussions in which he delighted his forecast for our country was so gloomy that he would always begin with the ominous sentence, "England is doomed".'[11] Enemies of the *Guardian* would have said that a man who thought thus could only be happy with the M.G. – or, perhaps, but that would have been impossible for Hamilton, the *Morning Post*. At any rate Hamilton was back with the M.G. early in 1923. He became its Paris correspon-dent, succeeding Ryall who had gone to the *New York World* changing his name to William Bolitho. Hamilton's period in Paris covered both the invasion of the Ruhr and the Locarno interlude. He died in the spring of 1929 after a long period of illness.

Frederick Voigt was the central figure of the M.G.'s foreign team in the nineteen-thirties. Spectacles lent his face an air of enquiring innocence which seemed to be confirmed by the thin, straggling hair disclosing his high forehead. His remarkably deep voice was right for the profundity of his judgments. He felt and spoke with the passion of a Hebrew prophet, one of the writing prophets. But he was a prophet with a difference: no Puritan would have named the bed in his Berlin flat 'die Sündenwiese.' He really was at home in the exciting, intellec-tual and artistic life of the early Weimar republic, a frequenter of the Romanisches Café, an intimate friend of Georg Grosz. Quite as im-portant, however were his friendships with many manual workers and their families, rank and file members of the various socialist parties,

Physically, he was inept; and he liked to pretend that he was a frightened man – 'I have no liking for danger and am timid even about crossing streets when there is heavy traffic – like so many hatreds, my hatred of motor-cars arises from fear.'[12] This is preposterous. Voigt was a man of immense moral courage; foolhardy one would have said if there could be such a thing as excess of moral courage. And his physical courage matched his moral. His reporting of Nazi excesses in the bitter street struggles that preceded Hitler's triumph was not done at second hand.

Before Voigt was called up in 1916 he was already in contact with Harold Dore, the *Guardian* lobby correspondent and with Hamilton whom he had coached in German. When he was demobilised the first thing he did was to turn his letters and diaries into one of the earliest war books to which he gave the characteristically deprecating title of *Combed Out*.[13] The second thing he did was to persuade a willing Hamilton to get him a job on the M.G. He went out to Berlin in February 1920 and for a short time the two men worked together. 'Voigt is here,' Hamilton wrote, 'and I am drilling him into the duties of getting and sending news. After that, I am doubtful where to go. I am tempted to go to Budapest and then push on into Transylvania, where the Rumanians are practising their worst tricks. But then there is the Leipzig fair which, this year, will be of enormous importance. Please send me your ideas.'[14]

Soon Voigt was on his own. He was determined not to be tied to Berlin. He went wherever there was trouble. At the beginning of April he was in Essen where there was what amounted to civil war between the armed workers and units of the Baltic 'Free Corps', the ultra-reactionary force which after fighting in the Baltic States was taking a hand in German politics. Voigt was arrested and, as he described in the *Guardian*, maltreated by a Lt Linsemeyer. C.P. raised the affair in conversation with Lloyd George: 'He at once said there must be punishment, reparation and apology.' When Josiah Wedgwood asked a question in the House four days later, the Foreign Under-Secretary was able to say that Lord Kilmarnock had 'made a protest and demanded an apology and adequate punishment of the guilty parties. The German Government have expressed their regret direct to Mr Voigt at the Ministry for Foreign Affairs in Berlin.'[15] In the next twelve months Voigt paid long visits to Silesia, where the frontier between Germany and Poland was in dispute, and to Bavaria, where separatism was strong. On 1 March 1921 he was writing on 'Jew Baiting in Berlin.' He knew Germany in the days before its frontiers were settled or its form of government agreed, while it was a land in which public order was insecure and in which anything might happen. This long acquaintance gave his interpretation of what did happen between 1931 and 1939 a perspective and an insight which were unrivalled.

Robert Dell would have been delighted if C.P. could have persuaded Lloyd George to extract from the French Government on his behalf a quarter of the satisfaction that he got for Voigt. Dell was not demanding an apology; he was only asking to be allowed to return to the country from which he had been expelled at a month's notice in 1918. His deportation from Paris marked the end and also the climax of his first period of service with the *Guardian*. It had begun in a very small way, mainly with non-political contributions, in 1912. Gradually he began to contribute political messages which became frequent and increasingly polemical as the war came and gathered pace. It was during this period that H. W. Nevinson described him as 'a man of great knowledge, and possessing an extraordinary flair for information, upon which he based forecasts seldom fulfilled.'[16] It was not surprising that Dell was well informed. He had so much to give and gave it so delightfully that it would have been hard indeed if he had not received plentifully from others. He was at least as much at home in Paris of the Third Republic as Voigt in Weimar Germany, and he touched its life at as many different points. He was a former editor, though not for long, of both the *Connoisseur* and the *Burlington Magazine*. With this knowledge behind him he had run a Paris gallery in partnership with Philip Turner. Another side of Dell was represented by his interest in religion. He was the son of an Anglican parson and himself became a Roman Catholic, following the modernist movement and establishing friendships with its leaders, Tyrrell and Loisy. In later life he would have been called a free-thinker. Politically he was always to the Left. He was a Christian Socialist at one time and a pro-Boer in 1899. He had literary as well as political friends and, especially in France, many of his circle belonged to both worlds. Anatole France is one example – a bitter feature of Dell's deportation was the loss of a large collection of France's letters to him.*

Dell, like many *Guardian* men, was incapable of politic restraint. He would have translated *Magna est veritas et praevalebit* as 'Great is truth and it must be published', and he would probably have included his own comments in the truth. Late in 1916 C.P. had to pass on a hint to Dell that he was in some danger of expulsion: 'We have had a rather serious intimation concerning you from the representative in London of the French Press control. It appears that they regard certain communications of yours to the American press the *New Republic*,

* The collection was eventually recovered and is in the *Bibliothèque Nationale*.

I gather – as so injurious to the public interest that they are contemplating your expulsion from France.'[17] The danger passed and Dell remained busily at work in Paris until 20 May 1918. From Paris he sent a message about the Emperor Karl of Austria's peace feelers to France in the spring of the previous year. For this he was expelled. A month later Lloyd George told C.P. that Dell was quite right in reporting that he himself had been in favour of negotiation, and he denounced Clemenceau for his 'extreme folly' in relation to the letters.[18] C.P. passed the news on to Dell whose comment to his daughter was 'But he (Ll.G.) is an awful liar.'

When Dell was expelled from France he had gone to live with Hamilton, rent free though the two men barely knew each other before. They became firm friends. There was a chance of Dell going to Geneva for the M.G. in 1922 but he preferred to free-lance in Berlin. In 1924 he got permission to return to Paris where he worked once more as a free-lance. In both capitals the M.G. was already represented – by Voigt in Berlin and Hamilton in Paris. It was not until Hamilton's death in 1929 that Dell rejoined the *Guardian*. He then again became its Paris correspondent, but this time as a member of the staff. He was 64, but as young in spirit and impulsive in action as when he first worked for the paper. His trim figure, carefully brushed moustache, and silver-topped cane brought into the sombre decade something of the elegance of the Edwardian man about town, or rather the *boulevardier*.

M. W. Fodor in Vienna, one of Hamilton's discoveries, was a Central European whose eyes were turned downstream along the Danube and across the mountains to the Adriatic and the Aegean. His first assignment was the trial of Bela Kun and the Communist leaders in Budapest in 1920. After Hitler had occupied his beloved Vienna, he moved to Prague. Driven from there he sent his last stories to the M.G. from The Hague until once more the Nazis moved in. Somewhere in the later twenties Caroline Lejeune went visiting in Europe using her *Guardian* contacts to bring her in touch with artistic circles in Berlin; Rome, where Cecil Sprigge was enduring and exposing Mussolini, and Vienna. 'The kindest and most charming of all (the correspondents),' she found, 'was Herr Fodor, their man in Vienna, a passionate lover of his city and its ways, and nothing was too much trouble for him.'[19] Nothing was ever too much trouble for Fodor.

Fodor was the only one of the *Guardian* foreign staff correspondents whose native language was not English. The sub-editors, of course, removed the roughness of his style but could never give it the distinction his colleagues achieved. But he was thorough, well-informed, devoted – and desperately badly paid. A private letter to C. P. Scott, unimproved by sub-editing, shows Fodor at work better than his published messages. The occasion was two days of serious rioting in Vienna in 1927 provoked by the acquittal of Heimwehr men accused of political murders. Fodor's letter was in answer to one from C.P. praising him for his work. On the first day Fodor had been lucky or skilful in getting his message through:

Telephone calls to Berlin were limited to six minutes, but I used my connection and friendship and I found an official who, with his admiration for the M.G., promised me to keep the connection as long as possible. So I had 35 minutes on the phone and I wanted to give about a hundred words more. When, I however, completed the sentence 'Similar treatment was dealt out to the *Reichspost*' – the general strike was proclaimed . . .

The second day was less fortunate . . . I was unable to send a longer message and this was a question of money . . . by some mistake which never occurred before, I did not receive my salary cheque for May . . . just a fortnight ago I had such considerable private expenses on the birth of my son. So there was no cash at home. The banks closed early morning as soon as the news of riotings reached the city and the frightened bourgeoisie was afraid to part with his cash. Thus I was able to borrow only something like £25.

Early Sunday morning the 'specials' arrived from all over the world. The *New York Times* sent two men . . . The London *Times* sent its Berlin man and he had plenty of cash. When I reached Bratislava on Sunday at 3 p.m. by then telegrams for 17 hours were already piled up at the station. I wanted to telephone to Berlin – the phone was out of order. The *New York Times* had something like 5,000 words to send – *all dringend* – urgent. Ten words urgent in Bratislava would have cost £1 . . . As I had to pay my share for the auto, it was out of question to send it urgent. I had to use all my brains and persuasion. The ruthless correspondents of the *New York Times*, in addition, as I learned later from reliable sources, bribed the Bratislava officials with £500 ! ! ! ! to get their urgent message first. The London *Times* used bribery, too. I for obvious reasons could not do it. (This bribery case naturally only for your information.)

But I went and saw the director of the Bratislava Post and I told him he must remember what the M.G. had done for Czecho-Slovakia and try to get at least that one message which he did.

I hope, you will realise my difficulties on the second day. But for the first day we have beaten the entire serious press of the world.

Less need be said by way of introduction about two younger men who completed the team of full-time European correspondents in the nineteen-thirties. Charles Lambert was another of Hamilton's protégés. He worked as a sub-editor in Manchester for some years from 1924 and had had a brief spell in Berlin in 1929 and a similar one in Paris as Hamilton's assistant during his last illness. Alexander Werth's connection with the M.G. began when he took Dell's place between 1929 and 1931 at times when Dell was on holiday or in Geneva. Werth had been born in St Petersburg in 1901, taken a First at Glasgow University in 1922 and worked as a sub-editor on the *Glasgow Bulletin* until he went to Paris to represent the *Glasgow Herald* in 1929. From 1933 he was the *Guardian*'s Paris correspondent.

Such, then, were the men with whom Crozier was to work most closely through the first half of his editorship. They were not an easy team because they were men of strong personality, with different gifts, and different prescriptions for Europe's ills. But they shared the same values and the same conviction that in Hitler's Europe there was at least one necessary role for the M.G. to play. This held them together. In the past the M.G. had been served abroad by great scholars who were spare-time journalists. Now it was served by great journalists who were spare-time scholars. Their deep roots in European culture gave them a lively sense of what was being lost. C.P.S. had raised a good regional paper into one with a world-wide reputation. Under Crozier, these men – with one exception C.P.'s men – felt it their duty to use this reputation to serve Europe when it was covered by a darkness which many, even in England, took for light. What they accomplished in the thirties was something with which the Old Man would have been content.

CHAPTER THIRTY-THREE

Crozier's Duty

I

WHAT was Crozier's duty in face of Hitler's Germany? It was a question which he put to himself less in terms of journalism than of responsible citizenship. Part of the answer was clear; part very puzzling. He never had any doubt that it was his duty to tell the whole truth, so far as he could discover it, about what was happening inside Germany. This was a duty which he owed not less to his German than to his English readers. The *Guardian* had been Germany's consistent friend in the controversies of the twenties. This had led to a small German sale for the daily and a bigger one for the weekly. Both were read by men who had been influential in the Weimar republic and by students who might have hoped to be. It was important that, with the German Press muzzled, somebody should be able to tell them what was happening in their own country, and that the telling should be done by a paper which cared for them as much as it hated Hitler.

This was sound politics. It also made good journalistic sense, all the better because the editors of the other quality papers were at first reluctant to print all they knew and hesitated to meddle in the internal politics of a 'friendly Power.' The *Times* kept up this hesitation about intervention almost to the last to the damage of its own reputation and the enhancement of the *Guardian*'s. But the M.G. met initial difficulties of its own making when it was first confronted with Hitler as Chancellor.

There had been a reshuffle of the *Guardian*'s foreign correspondents. Robert Dell, for instance, had gone from Paris to Geneva. The last moves did not take place until January 1933. Voigt left Germany for Paris which he reached at the end of the month; Werth replaced him in Berlin on the 15th. There the aged Hindenburg, elected by the votes of the Socialists and moderates, was still president. The Nazis were in opposition. The Weimar republic was tottering, but it still survived. Werth expected to enjoy his work in Berlin: 'I find the *Guardian* here counts for more than any other English paper – which is different from France where the *Times* counts for more.'[1]

Three days later Hitler became Chancellor. The Nazi seizure of power had begun. 'I am certainly in for a tough time in Germany,' Werth wrote to Crozier. 'Much as I dislike Herr Hitler with his mad eyes, it's going to be enormously interesting as a news centre; unfortunately people like Hitler do not like a paper like the M.G. . . . Would you say that I should take full risks or only minimum risks? Curiously enough Ebbutt (the *Times* correspondent) showed me the article he wrote on Monday, and it was pretty violent; yet, at the London end, they cut out everything that was in the least likely to offend Hitler. In fact, it seems to me that the M.G. is the only paper in England that would tell the whole truth about this Hitler business – if it gets the chance. But will it?'* Crozier's advice was 'stick to the facts and avoid strong judgments. We, of course, may have to express the strong judgments and you may get put out for that, but I hope not.'[2] Meanwhile he should prepare private emergency methods of sending news from Germany to Voigt in Paris, keep his eyes open and report any instances of anti-Semitism.

So things stood until the Reichstag was set on fire on 27 February and the organised terror began. Crozier's *via media*, which Voigt and Werth had also thought the right way, proved at this point to be no thoroughfare. It led the *Guardian* to a position where it left undone things which it ought to have done and did a few things which it ought not to have done. But there was still health in it, and the deviation lasted only a few days or hours. A crucial day was Monday 13 March. Werth put forward the then common theory that Goering, the lieutenant, was a good deal more extreme than his master Hitler. He continued, under a sub-editor's unfortunate side-head 'Rumours of a Terror':

'There are rumours in Berlin about a sort of Nazi Cheka where terrible things are supposed to be happening, and while it is difficult to verify these stories, it is generally hoped that, whatever the Government may wish to do to its enemies, all reprisals of whatever nature should receive the necessary publicity. Without such publicity rumours about abductions, tortures and secret executions – which may be entirely untrue – are inevitable in the present state of nervous tension. That there is a great deal of illegality in the country may be seen from several cases reported in the press . . . Such acts are indeed being deplored by all law-abiding citizens – and no doubt by many Nazis, including Herr Hitler himself . . .'

Werth expected people to read between the lines, and with hindsight this is easy enough. But it was not easy in March 1933 for what was

* Werth–Crozier 2 February 1933. The Monday when Ebbutt's message was severely cut was the day when Hitler became Chancellor.

happening seemed unbelievable. Voigt wrote in agony from Paris to Crozier:

'In Monday's *Guardian* I read that the "rumours" about "abductions, tortures and secret executions" may be "quite untrue." What is the good of having a man in Berlin if he cannot establish the truth? Some individual outrages are mentioned, but there is no indication whatever that there is a Terror – a Terror is an organised thing, organised from top to bottom. It is systematic, and, while there are individual outrages too, it is a war and a particularly ferocious one, a war against everything the *Guardian* has ever stood for, a war against people who are now unarmed and helpless. It is not true that "many Nazis, including Herr Hitler" deplore it – they demand it and more of it, though they may think the form it takes now may make a bad impression abroad and should therefore be changed . . .'[3]

It is necessary to break off Voigt's letter and refer to another message which should have appeared in the *Guardian* on the same day as Werth's unfortunate story. Elizabeth Wiskemann has described[4] how she, Norman Ebbutt, Darsie Gillie of the *Morning Post* and Edgar Mowrer of the *Chicago Daily News* went out on the night of Friday, 10 March in response to an urgent call from a Jewish lawyer. What they discovered formed the basis of messages to the *Guardian* and three London papers. The 'copy' for Monday's *Guardian* survives, 'subbed' ready for publication, 'From a Special Correspondent, Prague.' It begins: 'The rumours of terrorism applied by Hitler's Storm Troops . . . are only too well confirmed as more detailed information becomes available from Germany. The special status granted to the Nazi Storm Troops by Captain Goering, which practically frees them from police control, has been used to established systematic persecution . . .' It goes on to give particulars of some of the atrocities committed in the Nazi headquarters in the Hedemannstrasse – the kind of story which it was difficult to credit in 1933, but with which the world has since become only too familiar.

Attached to the 'copy' is, however, a transcript of a snatch of telephone conversation between Werth and J. M. Denvir of the *Guardian's* London office:

Werth: As to that other matter, I don't think we should use it unless the others do. You know to what I'm referring?
Denvir: I do.
Werth: It would be silly and disturbing.

Bone rang up the three other papers and reported: '*Times* not using German message but may refer to some of it in leader in a day or two. They have already some matter quite as bad in their possession. *Post* not using. Think that correspondent is making "too big a fuss about nothing." *Herald* are using it. They have no correspondent now in Germany.' Accordingly the M.G. did not print it.

It is time to take up again Voigt's letter to Crozier:

'I would like to give you some indication of what is happening in Berlin . . . My information has come from friends who are in the thick of it all (one of them very daring, too daring in fact) and from the English correspondents (Ebbutt of the *Times* and Gillie of the *Morning Post**) by special messenger. They have deliberately left Werth out of it.'

Voigt went on to give particulars of the Terror and continued:

'Gillie has sent me a special message, begging me to do what I can to get something at least that tells the real story into the *Guardian* – the *Morning Post* will not speak up as he would wish it to . . .

It is not possible for Werth to write as a Berlin correspondent of the *Guardian* should be writing just now. How could he be expected to as a Jew? Even if he were to speak up, the argument – a dishonest one, but none the less deadly – against him would be: "He is a Jew . . ."

Besides, there is another thing. I doubt whether Ebbutt and Gillie are physically menaced (though that too is possible in Germany now). But every Jew who does not keep in the background is in danger of being beaten. I don't think it fair to expose Werth to this.

The fact remains that on the German news the *Guardian* is being beaten hollow by the *Times* and the *Telegraph* (not to speak of the French papers), whereas it should be the other way about.'

Was Werth a Jew? He recognised the anti-Semitism around him; but, like many another in 1933, he could not believe that he himself might be a victim. 'What seems to have complicated matters,' he wrote to Crozier, 'is Voigt's idea that my "looks" are against me. Honestly the idea strikes me as rather absurd; for I have never yet had the slightest difficulty on that account. As I already told you, my mother is English; there is some Jewish blood on my father's side – and not a high proportion at that. I don't think even the greatest race purists among the Nazis could make a big case out of that!'[5]

This was in fact Werth's last letter from Germany. Voigt had finished his agonised letter with an offer to return to Berlin. Crozier wired back 'Go Berlin immediately as arranged. Stop two or three days. Send nothing from Berlin but return to Paris. Withdraw Werth to Paris on our behalf on grounds of safety.'[6] Crozier's explanatory letter to Werth, which crossed with his letter of protest, ran:

'I have been uneasy about your safety all the time and should have been

* Gillie was to become a key man on the *Guardian* after the war.

still more uneasy about your safety if you had sent us more complete accounts of what has been going on; but as we gradually learned more and more about the Terror two things became clear – (1) that we must at all costs have a complete and unsparing account of the Terror . . . (2) that we must be perfectly free to do and write exactly what we like, and print what we like, in the paper without having constantly to fear the consequences to our Berlin correspondent. You have done all that you could, and I would not have (had) you do more, but the position has been that both the *Times* and the *Telegraph* have had a more adequate account of the Terror than we have had, and that we have kept certain things down in strength because we were not sure of the possible results to you.'[7]

Werth was not satisfied, and for some time there was friction between him and Voigt, but in the end he settled down as the *Guardian*'s Paris correspondent and served the paper there with increasing distinction until the fall of France.

2

As Voigt and Werth were struggling with Hitler's developing Terror, Malcolm Muggeridge was coming to recognise Stalin's rule for the Terror that it was. He had left the permanent staff of the M.G. soon after Ted Scott's death. He went to Russia in September 1932 with a commission to take Chamberlin's place, as far as the M.G. was concerned, during the latter's six months' leave of absence. W. H. Chamberlin, the author of several notable books about Soviet Russia, had been in Moscow for a good many years representing jointly the *Guardian* and the *Christian Science Monitor*. Muggeridge went out as an idealist in search of a faith, a devoted fellow-traveller. His disillusion was rapid and complete; his disgust was expressed in the M.G. in characteristically emotional words:

'A few numbers of Bezboghnik (the Atheist) are calculated to make the austerest Puritanism seem, by comparison, full of humanity and tolerance and the Wahabis overflowing with charity and neighbourliness . . . To say that there is no religious persecution in Russia is like saying that negroes have the vote in the United States. Both statements are technically true but actually false.' (18 February 1933)

On the day Hitler became Chancellor, Crozier approved a visit by Muggeridge to the Caucasus. On the day before the Reichstag fire Muggeridge posted articles describing his experiences in the famine area where, for instance, he had talked with a peasant who:

'looked round anxiously to see that no soldiers were about. "We have nothing, absolutely nothing. They have taken everything away," he said and hurried on. This is what I heard again and again and again. "We have nothing. They have taken everything away." They had nothing. It was also true that they had taken everything away. The Famine is an organised one.' (25 March 1933)

Crozier recognised that Muggeridge was 'always an interesting writer – a cardinal virtue in journalism.' He found the articles 'extraordinarily interesting and fascinating.' But, he went on, 'I am rather sorry that you did not restrict yourself to a plain matter-of-fact statement of what you saw. That is not because I disagree with any of your comment, but because I think it would have been the most effective way of presenting your case.'[8] Crozier sent the articles to Voigt for an opinion and published them at the end of March. They immediately followed a series on the Polish Terror in the Ukraine, recording Voigt's investigations there in January, and ran side by side with articles on the Nazi Terror which Voigt had written after his hurried return to Germany.

By this time, however, Muggeridge had finally lost his temper with the M.G. which he equated with 'the Kingsley-Martin-Bernard-Shaw-Sidney-and-Beatrice-Webb slop that frothed round that dark tyranny.'[9] In a broadcast talk in 1969 he recalled how 'I poured out my bitter disappointment in a satirical novel, 'Winter in Moscow.' The characters are all real people, many of them English, connected with the Soviet scene and easily recognisable by those in the know. Heaven knows what libel actions might have been brought.'* The final explosion as far as the M.G. was concerned was caused by the drastic cutting of the messages he sent about the arrest of some Metrovick engineers, including Allan Monkhouse, a cousin of the *Guardian* Monkhouses. Certainly, as published, the messages were jejune in the extreme. But if in their original form they were in the same vein as his letters to Crozier it is easy to believe that they were sent at 'a certain amount of personal risk.' It is also easy to imagine why Crozier, with his love of exactitude and strength by understatement, made the cuts of which Muggeridge complained in this letter:

'From the way you've cut my messages about this Metrovick affair, I realise that you don't want to know what is going on in Russia or to let your readers know. If it had been an oppressed minority, or subject people valiantly struggling to be free, that would have been another matter. Then any amount of outspokenness, any amount of honesty.'[10]

* 'Muggeridge Through the Microphone' (Collins 1969), p. 107. Muggeridge wrote another novel, dealing with his life in Manchester. The characters seemed equally identifiable. It was withdrawn before publication.

This, and there was a good deal more like it, reads like a letter to end all communication. Crozier could write a tart letter himself on occasion*; but, when Muggeridge wrote once again, he left the reply to E. J. Phillips, equable, erudite, keen chess-player, skilled student of racing form, and everybody's friend. Phillips was able to congratulate Muggeridge on being safe in Switzerland which he had reached by way of Berlin where he had found:

'the Nazis outside Jewish shops, and everyone with his story of murder and folly. In Russia the Jews have got all the shops, only there's nothing in them any more. They go on murdering and murdering because there's nothing else to do. It's silly to say the Brown Terror is worse than the Red Terror. They're both horrible. They're both Terrors. I watched the Nazis march along Unter den Linden and realised – of course, they're Consomols, the same people, the same faces. It's the same show.'[11]

3

Before Voigt left Berlin he called at the German Foreign Office so that neither Werth nor anybody else should be blamed for what he wrote. His reception was 'rather sour.' He could have saved himself the adverb if the official he met had seen the articles he wrote on his return to Paris, that civilised city where, he told Crozier, 'the only people in danger of being killed are the lovers of other people's mistresses.'[12] In the first of his articles on the March Terror Voigt pointed out:

'The Terror did not consist of sporadic excesses, . . . it was not a series of disorders, it was not mob rule, it was systematic and an integral part of the counter-revolutionary offensive. For the Terror as a whole the regime is responsible. Although it has ebbed, it has not ceased . . . A new Terrorist period is drawing on – the period of the legal Terror . . .' (25 March 1933)

Within a few days the M.G. was banned for the first time in Germany. Occasionally the ban was lifted but, since Crozier would not give up printing the truth, these were relatively brief interludes. Fortunately, readers of the M.G. *Weekly* were called into existence in the New World to redress the balance of the Old. Its sale in America increased

---

* e.g. to an old contributor: 'I have no intention of either printing or replying to offensive letters, particularly where the writer parades himself as an old friend of the paper. The practice of excusing rudeness on the ground of affection is, to a newspaper office, so old as to be tiresome.' (13 August 1936.) Or another in the same year: 'I have your letter of March 26. Neither I nor my predecessors have been accustomed to be corrected by a member of the staff.'

as refugees from Hitler took the habit with them. Some are still reading it half a lifetime later.

For six months the M.G. had no resident Berlin correspondent. In September Dell went temporarily from Geneva to cover the Reichstag Fire trial. He, apparently alone among foreign correspondents, was refused admission, but he provided a running commentary from Berlin. At the beginning of November it became necessary hastily to recall him. A woman friend of his, a German citizen, had been arrested by the Gestapo, closely questioned about him and about some other 'swine-hound who is slinging mud at Germany in the M.G.' She was first told that she would not be released until Dell had left the country, but was finally freed in the hope that she would go to Paris and spy on the refugees there – something very far from her mind.[13]

Crozier then sent Lambert to Berlin as resident correspondent with 'minimum risk' instructions. This was to be in addition to Voigt's special service. Poor though the *Guardian* was, and expensive as a duplicate service must be, Crozier decided that there were some economies that must not be made. It was his duty to tell his readers what Hitler was doing. The two services, Lambert's above-board and Voigt's underground, were kept rigorously distinct. In briefing Lambert on his way out to Berlin, Voigt explained that it would be better if he knew nothing more about Voigt's activities than he could read in the paper. It was a wise precaution.

A month after Dell's troubles Voigt told Crozier that the Gestapo had started a Paris branch and systematic espionage had begun. He was very anxious about his main channel for news – the French diplomatic bag. Various intermediaries took packets to the Berlin embassy for forwarding to Voigt but in another name. He feared, however, that suspicion would now be aroused and the Embassy watched. The only precaution he could suggest was that he should move regularly between London and Paris and try to give the impression that London was his headquarters.[14]

'I was rung up by the Quai d'Orsay yesterday morning. The French authorities have information of a Nazi raid which was to have been carried out with the purpose of seizing my documents, notes, and so on . . . I was advised to put all my documents in a safe place – they are now in the Quai d'Orsay, with my private correspondence, address book, and so on.

Three detectives have been detailed for my protection – one of them, armed with an automatic pistol of such a size that I'm sure it must come under the category of heavy armaments, sleeps in my room. The other two hang round and follow me about. They say that the affair must be serious because it hardly ever happens that three men are detailed – usually it is only one or two at the most (Benes when he was here had only one.) . . . The Dictatorship . . . is determined to silence the M.G. *at any cost*. There are just a few things (sic) they fear – Max Braun, the Socialist leader in the Saar, is one of those they fear and his assassination has just been attempted. In my case it was not myself, I am convinced, they were after, but my documents and, above all, my sources in Germany (which they would be able to deduce from my documents) – had these been seized there would have been hundreds of arrests as a result.'[15]

Voigt came to London for Christmas, accompanied as far as Calais by his bodyguard. He told Crozier that the Paris affair had turned out to be 'rather more serious than I at first thought.' He had imagined that the Nazis were hiring French burglars, but he had since learnt that 'apparently it was not to be a burglary but an assassination (like Professor Lessing's or like the one planned against Wels and Scheidemann and averted by the Czech police).' An agent of the Sûreté Génerale was detailed to live in Voigt's Villa Brune until his return.[16] The thought that he lived in a Brown House gave Voigt great pleasure.

Crozier brought Voigt back to London in the following summer to be the first diplomatic correspondent that the M.G. had ever had. He continued to run his underground German service. He remained constantly, and rightly, apprehensive about the safety of his sources and in particular for his principal agent Max Wolf, a Swiss citizen. In July 1935 Wolf guessed that the Gestapo were on his tracks and went to Switzerland. After an interval he returned to Germany, but before the end of the year he had to flee for good without even personal baggage for he had heard that a warrant was out for his arrest.[17] He came to London and worked as Voigt's assistant.

It was possible for Voigt in the early days of the Third Realm – to use his invariable, correct but idiosyncratic version of the Third Reich – to pay one or two short visits to Germany. He covered, too, the plebiscite in the Saar where the League High Commissioner thought him by far the best of the British correspondents. But thereafter he kept away – or rather was kept away by Crozier's prudence. In March 1936 he received an invitation to visit Germany. He wanted to go even though he would have had to avoid his friends and see only official Nazis. Crozier thought 'it would be madness' and told John Scott who quietly endorsed his note 'I certainly think there would be a considerable risk – bigger than we ought to take.' When Crozier wrote to Voigt, he pointed out:

'One has only to consider your stuff about the (concentration) camps, which is going in to-morrow. No one but yourself could have got that for the paper.

The S.S. know perfectly well that you are the author and, in general, are the most serious opponent of Nazi Germany in the English press, and, further, as you know yourself, they conspired against you in Paris. Besides, it isn't merely a question of getting rid of you by violence; they would have no trouble at all in trumping up a pretext for running you in, and neither we nor the Foreign Office would find it easy to get you out. Indeed, if I understand right, they would not need to trump up anything; under their laws, as soon as you set foot in Germany they could run you in for high treason committed many times over. No, it won't do.'[18]

4

How reliable was Voigt's German service? Its reputation was good with almost everyone except the Nazis. Sometimes the conservative opposition inside Germany found its reporting unbearable and said so in Letters to the Editor which Crozier was glad to publish – he was always anxious not to appear one-sided. Adam von Trott, for instance, protested about Voigt's survey at the beginning of 1934 of anti-Semitism during the first year of Nazi power. He regretted the letter at once: 'I have written a rather silly letter to the *Manchester Guardian* which I hope will not be published,' he told his mother. It was, and provoked a crushing retort from Voigt and a good deal of further correspondence in which von Trott took part. Here, as nearly always, Voigt's facts stood up to contemporary examination.[19] Only rarely have they been discredited by subsequent knowledge.

But reporting under a tyranny carries a high risk of error. The risk is increased when the reporting has to be done from outside its frontiers. And it is further increased when part of the opposition, as in Germany, comes from an anti-tyrant, as unscrupulous and as skilled in deception as the tyrant himself. Probability is often the reporter's only available test; *cui bono?* as much in his mind as in any detective's. It can mislead. It probably misled Voigt in his treatment of the Reichstag fire.

From the beginning he was clear that this could not have been the work of the Communist Party. He said so repeatedly in the paper. He was right. The Nazis insisted that it could not technically have been a one-man job. But whose work could it be, then, but the Nazis'? They had the motive. They were ready to exploit the occasion. It was improbable that their immediate, catastrophic response could have been suddenly improvised to make use of the chance opportunity provided by a foreign fanatic's solitary gesture. But, in the light of Fritz Tobias's investigation, that seems to have been what happened. If the Nazis were quick on the draw with terror, the Communists were almost as quick with forged documents such as the Oberfohren Memorandum. Voigt was the first to use it. He accepted it as a Nationalist document though, as he explained in the M.G., he did not necessarily believe all that was in it:

'It is a serious attempt by one in touch with the Nationalist members of the Cabinet to give a balanced account of these events. In spite of one or two minor inaccuracies, it shows considerable inside knowledge. While not authoritative in an absolute or final manner, it is at least a first and weighty contribution towards solving the riddle of that fire.' (26 April 1933)

Tobias found it 'surprising that the *Manchester Guardian* should have allowed itself to be taken in by the Memorandum.'[20] If Voigt could have known in April 1933 what is now known, it would indeed have been astonishing. But at the time, the Oberfohren Memorandum was plausible enough. There was nothing inherently improbable in the theory of Nazi guilt – later, when the Third Realm was falling, different groups of Nazis accused one another of responsibility for the fire. Indeed the theory of Van der Lubbe's unaided act and sole responsibility only became credible after the official Nazi case that it took several men to start the fire had been discredited.

How comprehensive was Voigt's German service? By and large the M.G. published all that could be discovered at the time about Hitler's Germany – as much as any other paper and more than most. In two directions especially it excelled. One was its reporting of the Christian opposition; the other, of the persecution of the Jews.

Voigt was quick to see the significance of the stand taken by the Confessional Church. It was not a political opposition as a Christian Socialist opposition might have been. It was not concerned with secular politics. Voigt's understanding of its nature comes out in a letter to Crozier over an article by Karl Barth.

I'm not sure whether I told you that Karl Barth sent me word through Wolf . . . that he would be glad to give a general statement of his view on the German religious conflict . . . He seems to me absolutely right when he indicated that the new German synthesis 'Christ and Hitler' (or 'Christianity and Nationalism') has developed organically from its predecessors 'Christianity and Reason' – 'Christianity and Civilisation' – 'Christianity and Socialism.' Many people in this country are in this stage (which has its variants, such as 'Christianity and Pacifism' or 'Christ and the League of Nations.') All these doctrines are equally false – 'Christ and Hitler' has, as Barth points out, been made into a doctrine and is being imposed by the State, so that the Church *must* fight, but it is not a bit falser than the other mixtures and I do not see any way out except Barth's 'Back to the Bible!'[21]

Voigt appreciated the fact that the Confessional theologians were 'great masters of German prose and to translate them into English is like translating Milton into German.' Hard though it was, this was a task he enjoyed and did well. The M.G. became a paper to which men could turn for news of this tough and unassimilable minority among the German people. It formed a considerable part of Lambert's work. All this, of course, was much to the liking of an editor whose spare time had been given to the *Letters of Pontius Pilate*. For Voigt himself it marks a transition. He recognised that a flaw in the men of the Weimar republic, whose life he had shared, had made them yield too easily to the new barbarism. He felt to some degree involved in their shame. But here he encountered German men and women whose hatred of iniquity (the phrase is Elizabeth Wiskemann's) was equal to his own; whose courage was as firm as the most devoted Communist's; but whose religion imposed a simple straightforwardness unknown to the Muenzenberg circle.* From the Sündenwiese Voigt caught a glimpse on the horizon of the Delectable Mountains half wrapped in cloud.

Crozier, the Gentile whose Zionism went back to a time before the Balfour Declaration, naturally saw to it that Hitler's persecution of the Jews, just because they were Jews or half-Jews, was fully reported in the news columns and denounced in the leaders. Recently Andrew Sharf has made an exhaustive study of the 'British Press and Jews under Nazi Rule.'[22] He found that the three 'quality papers' – the *Times* and the *Telegraph* in London and the *Manchester Guardian* – stood in a class apart. It was the special merit of the *Guardian* that it saw what was coming because it recognised it as a fundamental part of Nazi doctrine, and warned its readers in advance. As early as April 1932 – the fatal month of Ted Scott's death – it had printed a collection of anti-Semitic extracts from party writings. From that time on, and during the first two years of Nazi rule the M.G. gave more space to the Jewish question than any other paper.

In August, 1938 the SS paper, *Das Schwarze Korps*, wrote of 'the hard necessity of exterminating this Jewish underworld . . . the factual and final end of Jewry in Germany, its absolute annihilation.' The *Daily Telegraph*, the *Daily Herald* and the M.G. quoted these sinister words. They shocked but they could not surprise *Guardian* readers. Crozier had prepared them by seven years of faithful reporting to understand the 'still darker threats' to which he believed they pointed.

---

* 'I have long known both these persons (Otto Katz and Willi Muenzenberg) as being quite unscrupulous.' (Voigt–Crozier 24 August 1936.) It should be explained that the description of Voigt's state of mind at this time is only my personal interpretation.

5

'Would it be all right for you if when you rang me up you did not do
it till about 11 o'clock? . . . With this war crisis on top of my ordinary
work I am having very little rest, and not sleeping well either. When I
do sleep it happens to be more often than not in the last half of the
night or the early part of the morning, and your Geneva calls, interesting as they are, come a little early for me.'[23] For once Crozier did not
rebuke Dell for telephoning. It was clearly necessary. Italy had invaded
Abyssinia. Usually, however, long-distance telephone conversations
were too expensive for the impoverished M.G. Its men wrote letters.
We benefit, for we can still see the process by which the paper made
up its collective mind.

The real question, all the *Guardian* men agreed, was not 'Can Mussolini be stopped?' but that other question round the corner 'Can Hitler
be stopped?' They agreed, too, that the way Mussolini was treated
would largely determine this. A few weeks before the invasion Crozier
had written in a leader of 'a genuine "crisis", a turning point, not only
in Europe but even in world affairs . . . If the people of Abyssinia
go down by war . . . when the day comes, the League will not in the
great theatre of Europe . . . avert the threatened war.'[24] And in a letter
to Voigt: 'I think that if the League now fails we shall have to say
pretty frankly that it is only useful for discussion and consultation;
that the Covenant ought to be redrawn; and that all these alliances and
pacts are pretty much of the pre-war order. Also, we shall have to
defend ourselves more strongly and keep our end up.'[25]

Crozier himself had few illusions about a lasting peace in Europe.
Mary Crozier recalls how two years before, when the Nazis made their
spectacular bonfire of books, her father looked up from his paper and
said 'This means war.' She thinks he added within ten years. But any
chance of preventing it, however slight, must be taken. Foreign policy
must be judged by its effectiveness in preventing Hitler going to war
or of making sure that, if he did, he would lose. Perhaps, the *Guardian*
men thought, the order should be reversed. Only by making it plain
that a war fought would be a war lost could Hitler be stopped. The
Guardian's judgment of the situation was bound to be faulty unless it
could test the public statements of politicians by going behind them.
It was the job of the foreign staff to do just this. The *Guardian* men were
good news gatherers. But they could not keep their markedly different
opinions out of their news gathering and their news stories. Moreover
their relation to one another was as intricate as the relations of the men

about whom they wrote. It was a factor which Crozier had constantly to take into account.

To Dell's lucid and hard-riding mind, quickly made up, volatile and predetermined for the bold course, there was never any doubt what the British Government should do or the M.G. say. In his view, however, the Government rarely did its duty; the M.G. – well, more frequently. Dell was now more of a Leaguer than the League itself and much more so than the naturally cautious Crozier. Werth, on the whole, agreed with Dell. 'He is a very intelligent young man: he consults me,' so Dell in his vain but curiously unconceited way had once told his daughter. Voigt too, like Dell, had in his time been an embarrassment to his editor. In 1929 he had had a spell in Manchester as foreign leader-writer. Its end is made clear in one of Hammond's letters, 'It must be a relief not to have Voigt to think about, but you sound dreadfully short-handed.'[26] There had been so many subjects on which Voigt felt strongly and at right angles to the paper – the League, for instance, and the USA. There still were. 'I do not think there can be anything in Voigt's book in the way of disagreement with the M.G. that would come as a surprise to me. I had the most awful time with him over Italy, the League, Abyssinia, etc.'[27] Voigt was, for instance, though no pacifist, totally opposed to the sanctions provided for in the League Covenant. 'In my opinion the doctrine of sanctions is a false and dangerous doctrine,' he wrote to Crozier about this time. 'It *must* sooner or later bring us to the verge of disaster and it *must* make somebody let somebody else down if the disaster is to be avoided at the last moment.'[28]

But, if the League's condemnation of Italy was to mean anything, it had to be followed by action – that is to say, by sanctions. But what sanctions? And then, by what peace terms? The answers lay with England and France. They had been debating them for many months. So had Crozier, Dell, Werth, and Voigt. In both instances without reaching agreement, for:

A man convinced against his will

Is of the same opinion still.

What Crozier thought – and the editor's thoughts are decisive for his paper – may be read in leading articles and in letters to Voigt and Dell. On peace terms, an M.G. leader ran:

There are two world tides now meeting. There is the tide of acquisition; there are new peoples who are acquisitive as we ourselves and the French have been with such success . . . The other tide is one of withdrawal . . . it is flowing now in India and in Egypt, where, with various checks, the British power is gradually yielding its position . . . It is possible that . . . (Britain and

France) could still devise some transferences of territory . . . which would hold back Italy from Abyssinia . . . By involving the League as a direct mandatory to take over from them some of their 'trustee' and colonial tasks they might launch a movement that would ultimately restrain the hungry and discontented nations. (22 August 1935)

And in a letter to Voigt:

'I recognise the possibility that in order to get rid of the war and to keep the League together, it may be necessary for Abyssinia to lose more than she ought to. On the other hand, I should be extremely cautious about making concessions in that direction.'[29]

On sanctions Crozier wrote in a leader:

'Sir Samuel (Hoare) . . . left no doubt on one head: the Government contemplates nothing in the nature of military or naval sanctions . . . "as there will be no agreement for collective action of this kind . . . it is only dangerous and provocative to talk about it." The position is justified because economic sanctions . . . hold out the hope (which cannot be said of more drastic measures) of both shortening the duration of the war and limiting its area.' (22 October 1935)

And to Dell he wrote:

'I must say that to go in for naval sanctions by a process of dragging France in against her will seems to me to be a pretty rotten policy – I mean rotten in the sense of unsound. How in the world could one embark on naval action which might, and in my opinion would, mean war if France were dragged in against her will?'[30]

But by that time Britain was involved in a general election as well as in an international crisis. This gave the *Guardian* the chance of a 'scoop' which it did not take. Dell had been taken ill but was convalescing in Paris. There he had been given the text of an unpublished French note to Britain about sanctions. He sent Crozier a long news story with three verbatim quotes.

Crozier read it carefully and wrote Dell a letter explaining why he could not use Dell's 'enterprising extracts.'

'I cannot say that I like the choosing out of the three passages obviously designed for the purpose of embarrassing the British Government. I don't know how far the text of the Note, or of the surrounding passages, would have any effect on them, if it had any at all.'[31]

Dell was not easily defeated. Next time Werth tried his luck with a balanced summary. 'You will have seen Werth's message to-night about the matter,' Dell wrote the same evening. 'I left him to write it after a conversation between us and he showed it to me after it was written and made a few verbal alterations on my suggestion. The message seemed to me very good.'[32] So it did to Crozier. But although, like all newspaper men, he believed that political secrets exist to be discovered, he also believed, like all responsible editors, that there are some secrets that are better not told. This was one. He told Werth that it was 'a very good piece of work . . . and something of a scoop' and then explained:

There has obviously been a great deal of bad blood between the two Governments, and for that reason they have decided not to publish the Notes. I think they have been very wise, and to publish an account of the Notes now . . . would certainly assist to create the bad blood. I do not think we ought to do it unless we had some high purpose to serve by publication, and that we have not.[33]

Or had we? Dell certainly thought so: 'I frankly admit,' he told Crozier, 'that the quotations . . . were given to me chiefly for the purpose of helping the opposition in the Election campaign, but have we not the right to do that?' Werth took the same line: 'I can fully appreciate your point that it may be better, in the present international situation, not to rake it all up . . . Dell's point, of course, was that the verbatim passages in the Notes of 18 October would greatly damage the National Government – an opportunity not to be missed on the eve of the General Election.'[34] It was an opportunity that Crozier was determined to miss and did.

As soon as the election was over Crozier went to see Hoare. He noted that the only newspaper in the Secretary of State's waiting room was the *Morning Post*, but he found Hoare as broadminded as he remembered him to have been during previous talks at the India Office. His long note of the conversation ends 'Hoare made on me a strong impression of straightforwardness, sincerity and largeness of view.' He showed the note to John Scott who wrote on it 'It is particularly useful to know Hoare's mind. I have maintained high hopes of him ever since the India Act and everything you say confirms this. In view of Baldwin's age and known desire to get out of politics it is possible that the leadership may become vacant during this Parliament and it is important therefore to do all we can to strengthen Hoare vis-à-vis Neville.' This is probably the only political opinion by John Scott to be found in the files. It reads like a directive; it should probably be read rather as an endorsement. Whichever it was, it could have no effect. Crozier saw Hoare on 21 November. John Scott wrote his note on 25 November.

On 9 December the French papers carried the news of the Hoare-Laval Pact.

Crozier was on leave in London when the debate took place. The leader, however, certainly expressed his views – scorn for Baldwin who 'by earlier standards' would have found that 'his white sheet was assuming the shape and proportions of a shroud'; but sympathy for Hoare who, he thought, had made an error of judgment but had done nothing dishonourable. He should have reported to the League the risks involved in oil sanctions and an isolated position

'instead of precipitately offering to the aggressor . . . such a share of Abyssinia as bore no relation to the immediate moral and military situation.'

Harry Boardman, who had been one of the M.G. reporters in the Irish 'troubles', was now its Lobby correspondent. He struck an even friendlier note to Hoare:

Sir Samuel Hoare had a great personal success to-day; Mr Baldwin failed . . . A sick man . . . was bound to find an indulgent House. But his success to-day was only partially explained by the emotional appeal of his sad circumstances. He was able to offer the House a reasoned statement for his conduct . . . he managed to state it with a dignity, lucidity, and firmness that compelled admiration all round. Nevertheless, it is essential to make clear that Sir Samuel did not shake the great bulk of the Government supporters in their conviction that he blundered in accepting the Paris terms . . . As a speech it is the best that he has ever made, and so impressed were the members with its ability that to-night it is common to hear it said that Sir Samuel Hoare has to-day made himself the future leader of the Conservative party. (20 December 1935)

John Scott must have been pleased to read this echo of his views written, of course, by Boardman in complete ignorance of them. And Hoare surely found some slight consolation in the generosity of Boardman's words. It may well have been in his mind when years later, on Boardman's death, he wrote in a private letter to the editor that he was 'the best and most sensitive political correspondent whom I ever met; being very human he understood the hopes and fears of politicians.'

6

The main news story in the *Guardian*, and in most other papers, on 5 March 1935 was the White Paper on Defence; 'a melancholy, not to say a tragic document,' Boardman wrote, 'the first open confession by the British Government that they believe the collective peace system to have failed . . . and that consequently we must look to strengthening our own arms.' And Crozier called his Long leader that night 'Harvest of Dragon's Teeth.'

Any assessment of the *Guardian*'s record in the thirties involves a look at what it said about defence. Its position was bound to be tricky. Those of its readers who saw most clearly the menace of Hitler often saw least clearly the need for more arms to meet it. This was partly because the arms were asked for by a Conservative Prime Minister, and partly because they had been brought up to believe that armaments caused wars and disarmament brought peace. They had to be re-educated. Indeed the *Guardian* had to a considerable extent to re-educate itself. It learned quicker than many of its readers.

A good starting point is the spring of 1934, a year before Baldwin's admission. The following extracts illustrate its attitude year by year at the time the Defence Estimates were being discussed in March. The first comes from notes Crozier made for a lecture; the other two are from leaders:

1934   Germany, Crozier thought, 'did not desire or intend war at the present time' but hoped to become 'so strong that she could demand the redress of her grievances by diplomatic means, with the threat that if they are not redressed she will use other means.' The chance of disarmament was small, even limitation was doubtful unless Britain would give guarantees to other countries; competition in arms the most likely outcome. 'All the Powers except two are intent on peace, Russia as much as any. Is it not possible for all the peaceful Powers . . . to indicate their intention to stand together against any war makers?'

1935   'Of disarmament there can no longer be any question, while the re-armament of Germany up to a point that threatens to exceed equality makes any kind of limitation seem at present extremely improbable. But it does not follow that war is probable. Why? Because of the collective system.' (19 March 1935)

1936   'The only way to stop an aggressor is that the other countries should be as ready for war as he is. This is, as Mr Baldwin admits, "a horrible thing to have to say," for it means that the "free States in Europe" will have to arm to the level of the unfree. Had Mr Baldwin gone on to explain how these menaced "free States" were pooling their arms . . . the phrase "collective security" might have had some meaning . . . If our foreign policy were clearly defined, our defence policy would be formed in relation to it.' (11 March 1936)

These quotations reflect Crozier's mind, the mind of a peace-loving man, not a pacifist; a man who was prepared to accept the need for arms, but not to underwrite the demands of technical experts without examination. In a leader on the Navy Estimates of 1935 he asked 'What is this phrase "absolute requirements"? Must not requirements always be relative to the political and strategical situation?'[35] He had given much thought to the relativity of requirements. Defence indeed had been a life-long interest. As a boy at Manchester Grammar School he had been given Admiral Mahan's *Influence of Sea Power on History* as a prize for an essay on the same subject.* When Sidebotham left, he took over the 'Student of War' articles. He kept the paper's defence policy in his own hands, wrote most of the leaders on it and went to see successive Service Ministers from Eyres-Monsell onwards. Crozier played an important part in convincing men of the Left that in Hitler's Europe there was no safety without strength.

7

Voigt had spent the first half of August 1938 in Czechoslovakia. When he got back he wrote some remarkably objective articles in which he described what he saw and what he foresaw:

'Those who witnessed the collapse of the German Republic and now, with their own eyes, see what is happening in the "Sudetenland" will be impressed by the recurrence of the same familiar symptoms . . . the same trance-like condition (especially among the women) at meetings and demonstrations, the same disciplined defiance, the faces shining with the same hard purpose, the fists clenched with the same vengeful resolution . . . So close is the resemblance that the observer constantly forgets that this is not Germany at all and not the year 1932 . . . it is a preliminary engagement in the war . . . for the possession of the forest-clad mountains, blue grey and towering in the distance, where the Czech artillery is concealed, guarding the still so youthful Czechoslovak Republic – and much more.' (25 August 1938)

Voigt went on to describe the relentless intimidation to which the many Czech Germans who were not Nazis were exposed. In another article he described the Czech system of government: a freely elected, but not very powerful, parliament; a fair deal for the national minorities which were often represented in the government; and a bureaucratic oligarchy.

* This appears from Crozier's correspondence with Captain W. D. Puleston, USN, who was preparing a biography of Mahan. Mahan, he told Crozier, 'was a reader of the *Manchester Guardian* for many years. He was not a rich man and could not afford many magazines or papers, but he was interested in European affairs and I think that was the primary reason he selected your paper.' A secondary reason was its religious articles. (Puleston–Crozier 27 February 1937.)

If the machinery of government was not democratic, the spirit of the people was. 'Czechoslovakia,' he wrote, 'is a land of freedom and enlightenment. There are no concentration camps, there are no mock trials, there is no Czech Terror in the crude sense as there is a German, an Hungarian, a Polish and a Russian Terror. There is no persecution of the Jews or Christians, and no one is sentenced to death for political reasons.'[36] Throughout the crisis there were also well informed, moderately phrased messages from Fodor who, driven by the Nazis from Vienna, had moved to Prague as 'our Central European correspondent.' Readers of the M.G., at least, could not be included among those who, in Mr Chamberlain's words, found it 'incredible . . . that we should be digging trenches and trying on gas masks here because of a quarrel in a far away country between people of whom we know nothing.'

But by the time these 'ungenerous' words were spoken Fodor had been driven to cross another frontier. A week before he had sadly started his message with an emotional passage quite unlike his usual style:

'It is a terrible thing to witness the agony of two countries such as has been your correspondent's fate. Only a few months ago he saw the downfall of Austria, and now in these last days of gloom and desperation in Prague he is witnessing the dismemberment of Czecho – Slovakia. Everything seems to be over now, for under pressure Czecho – Slovakia was obliged at 5 o'clock this afternoon to accept the demands of France and England.' (26 September 1938)

There is still a shock of shame to be felt in reading England where one expects to find Germany. Four days later a message from Warsaw described his forty-eight hour journey into Poland across a closed frontier in company with British and American evacuees.

When Chamberlain flew to see Hitler at Berchtesgaden the *Guardian* leader-writer commented 'A man may always offer his own throat to be cut, but it would be indelicate of friends to make the offer for him.' When Chamberlain returned, Fodor described how men in Prague talked of Great Britain's 'third Abyssinia'; Voigt wrote of the 'surrender of the Western Powers' and their 'ultimatum with a short time limit' to Czechoslovakia; and Werth reported the words of the Czech Minister in Paris – 'Here you see the condemned man. He has been sentenced without being heard.' Next day the *Guardian* leader said 'it is important for our own future that we should be united in one thing, that we have accepted moral defeat which will have consequences beyond our present range of vision.'[37]

When Chamberlain came back from Godesberg bearing an even stiffer ultimatum from Hitler, Crozier wrote: 'It is true enough that the political system of other countries in itself is no affair of ours, but its consequences are . . . That is why a country so devoted to peace as ours, so slow to commit itself to military obligations, finds itself forced into saying with France that an attack by Hitler on Czechoslovakia will find them both at war.'[38]

There followed that extraordinary day in the Commons when Chamberlain rose to prepare the House for virtually certain war. Before the end of his speech he was handed a note inviting him to meet Hitler at Munich. The sketch was now being written by young Francis Boyd who had recently taken over from A. G. MacDonnell. He started his story in a way that reflected the country's strange mood; 'Members of the House of Commons got as near to-day to a sense of the peace of God which passeth all understanding as human beings are ever likely to do. It was a brief vision, but it was clear and will not be forgotten.' Boardman, by now an experienced Lobby man, found the scene 'the most remarkable that one Parliamentary journalist has ever seen at Westminster. The Commons standing on the benches and waving order-papers for Philip Snowden's Emergency Budget and his closing lines from Swinburne's great rhapsody of England's faith in her stars – that, the most memorable scene in the House of Commons for years, was nothing to this.' He described how the Tories cheered and cheered, how Grandi with his handsome Renaissance head led the diplomats in clapping, how the public gallery joined in, but, how, with few exceptions, the Opposition remained seated.

The *Guardian* also kept its distance. It could not help sharing the common thankfulness but it believed that most people would agree with the *New York Times* that Hitler had scored over the democracies of Europe the greatest diplomatic triumph of modern times: 'certainly the Czechs will hardly appreciate Mr Chamberlain's phrase that it is "peace with honour".'[39]

Throughout the crisis there was in the *Guardian* office professional as well as political anxiety. The news came in, as Crozier said, 'most awkwardly.' Night after night the main news page had to be made and re-made. Attenborough, the chief sub-editor, and his deputy, Hobbs, a wonderfully quick, concise and clear-headed worker, never did a better job. On several nights, too, there were three distinct and complete versions of the Long leader, the middle one never getting beyond proof. Three times the need for comment seemed to Crozier so great that, rightly or wrongly, he published two Long leaders end-on, dealing with the same subject in the same paper. The Czech crisis formed the topic for the Long every night from Berchtesgaden to Munich. Virtually all this writing seems to be by Crozier. One leader was by Hammond. It made a point which Crozier usually avoided but which Montague would have hammered home night after night. It was the curious hold which Hitler had over so many distinguished Englishmen. Hammond asked himself as an historian why in 1938 there was less fear of German hegemony among upper class Englishmen than there had been before the 1914 war. His answer was that

'The spectacle of a strong man imposing his will and giving order and unity to a whole people made such an impression on certain conservative elements in English society that he became something of a hero. Public men paid court to him, Ministers and ex-Ministers treated his Ambassador as a confidential friend, and the impression was spread abroad that his aspirations were not those of an ambitious and unscrupulous man but of a simple patriot.' (26 September 1938)

One domestic incident deserves to be recalled from the soiled and anxious days that lay between the Munich Settlement and Hitler's invasion of Poland. Somebody in the London Office, probably James Bone himself, had the idea of sending the editor a Christmas round robin of thanks for his leadership. It was signed by all the principal members of the staff. 'It gives us courage,' they wrote, 'that the *Manchester Guardian* is in the keeping of one in whom we have such trust . . . Our support for the course you have steered is as strong as our professional admiration and personal regard.' Some men would have had it framed. That would have been as much out of keeping with Crozier's character as was the round robin itself with normal newspaper habits. But it gave Crozier pleasure and he kept it.

CHAPTER THIRTY-FOUR

Fortune of War

I

IN the last dark days before Britain declared war one letter brought Crozier comfort. 'I have been thinking you will be losing your young men,' Hammond wrote. 'In that case it might be a convenience to you if I came to Manchester. As you know my physical powers are limited by my heart condition but I should be available for writing and for consultation and I should put myself, of course, entirely at your disposal. I have not taken any steps about Government work for I feel that my first duty is to the M.G.'[1] He was 67 and, as he said, in poor health. So was his wife. And they hated town life. In their carefully preserved diaries the entries merely record the price of provisions, the coming and going of guests and, as regularly and perhaps even more lovingly, of swallows and other birds. Not even C.P. had been able to persuade Hammond to come to Manchester for more than a few weeks' holiday duty. Now, at his own suggestion, he came and saw the six years' war through – the finest compliment he could have paid the paper and the best service he ever did it.

War, in fact, gave old men their chance. Or at least their second wind. Men who had retired from the paper came back. F. S. Attenborough, for instance, the chief sub-editor, had retired in January 1939 after forty-five years' service. He was 70, but he came hurrying back to work happily under his old deputy, C. H. Hobbs. Nothing would have kept him away. That is plain from a story which Crozier told at his farewell dinner. When summer time was first introduced the clock used to be put back on Sunday instead of Saturday night. That gave Attenborough a pleasure he never missed. At 2.00 a.m. he got up from his desk, put the hands of the clock back sixty minutes and worked the same hour twice over. Everything in his life was geared to getting the *Guardian* out, and he felt, though he did not expect, that those whose doings were to appear in it should have the same consideration that he had for its edition times. When the present Queen was born Crozier remarked to Attenborough, 'Well, I hear that the Duchess has had her baby and is doing well.' 'Yes,' said Attenborough with great bitterness, 'but she'd have done much better if she'd had it in time for the Welsh.' The mordant word-play is vintage Attenborough, but the sentiment is every good sub-editor's. Two years before this incident, for instance, an excited young messenger had run into the London office with the news that James Drysdale, the *Guardian*'s parliamentary sketch writer, had just died at his desk in the Gallery. 'Yes, yes,' testily replied Neville Smith, the London sub-editor, 'but where's his copy?' The last words Drysdale wrote were found to be, 'The House then rose.'

Other members of the staff were rapidly coming in 1939 to the age when men, however ruefully, think of retirement. Bone was 67 in that year, and John Scott and Crozier were 60. None retired;* two survived the war. Crozier had become news editor in 1912, Bone had been London editor since 1911 and John Scott manager since 1905. When war came in 1939, then, they had all been through it before in their present or somewhat similar responsible positions. That first time the three principal leader-writers had been C.P., Hobhouse and Sidebotham. Their ages in 1914 added up to 150 years. Between them they had been working for the paper for seventy-nine years. This time the three principal leader-writers were Crozier, Hammond and Wadsworth. Their combined ages in 1939 totalled 175 years. Between them they had worked for the paper over a period of seventy-eight years.

There was another kind of continuity besides length of service on the *Guardian*. The first of C.P.'s grandsons to join the paper was Evelyn Montague, C.E.M.'s eldest son, who joined the managerial side in 1928 a few months after his father's death. He had spent three years in Chile in the nitrates industry so that his appointment as company secretary the following year was not so rash a promotion as it might at first sound – not so preposterous, for instance, as the idea with which C.P. had for a short time toyed of diverting C.E.M. from leader-writing to management.† But Evelyn wanted to write, could write, and had something to write about which the paper needed. As a boy at Rugby, he had done well enough at classics to get a demyship at Magdalen and outstandingly well at athletics. At Oxford he won the cross-country and three mile events against Cambridge in two successive years, breaking the record for the latter in 1920, and in 1924 he was third in the steeplechase at the Paris Olympic Games. The M.G. had long prided itself on its sports reporting. A paper that had had A.N. Monkhouse writing on golf and which still regularly sent Neville

---

* John Scott became the Government's regional information officer. Haley became responsible for the management of both papers, but John Scott remained in Manchester and took part in all major policy discussions and decisions.

† See p. 288.

Cardus to cricket matches set an exacting standard. Evelyn Montague rapidly came up to it when he joined the editorial side in 1931 and took over the sports pages. 'No one could interpret so well as he,' the writer of his obituary remarked, 'the mechanism or the spirit of the "final spurt," and he put his knowledge into a style that was appropriate: pointed, concise, sinewy, and full of life.' It is not surprising that a later colleague recalls how he used to find him reading Tacitus in the office. In 1934 Montague moved to the London office as Bone's deputy. His brother, Larry, the second grandson to join C.P.'s paper, succeeded him in charge of the sports pages, but Evelyn kept up his writing on athletics and Rugby. Only rarely did his work take him across the border into the *Guardian*'s main concern of politics and then reluctantly – not because he lacked political interest but because he wished politics to keep its place and leave sport alone. When he urged that the Berlin Olympics of 1936 should be moved elsewhere or cancelled because German Jews were ostracised, he insisted that this was 'essentially an athletic and not a political opinion.' 'A lamentable amount of cant,' he wrote, 'has been talked about the Olympic Games, but behind it all there remains the root idea and sole justification of the Games – that they are an occasion when politics are forgotten . . . To any sensitive person who cherishes this notion it can only seem a disaster that the Games should be celebrated in a country where the whole atmosphere of sport is so entirely different.'[2]

J. L. Hodson, who worked with Evelyn Montague in France, found him 'not always an easy man to know; austere at times.'[3] That was in fact the common experience. Of all Montague's children, Evelyn was the one who most resembled his father. It was inevitable, then, that, when war broke out, he would find his way to the fighting although he was 39. Fortunately for the paper Crozier and Bone were more perceptive, and perhaps more approachable, than C.P. had been twenty-five years before. Evelyn Montague went out with the BEF as a war correspondent to France. 'I have never been as nervous since my wedding day as I am at this moment,' he wrote to Crozier on the eve of his departure. 'But I'll do my best. It is a grand chance and I'm deeply grateful.'[4]

But, of course, Hammond had been right. Crozier was 'losing his young men' and some of his middle aged. It is with the middle piece that we need here to be concerned. Early in the war Voigt was needed for what came later to be known as political warfare, leaving the way free for Lambert to take up the diplomatic correspondence after spending the war's first winter in Stockholm for the paper.

Cecil Sprigge left at once for Government service after ten totally unexpected years in the City Office – he had been recalled from Berlin in 1929 by telegram, went to Manchester to protest, but was told that for him it was the City or nothing. He was succeeded by his friend R. H. Fry, whom he had recruited as his assistant in 1938. Until that time Fry had been acting as a free-lance diplomatic correspondent for the *Yorkshire Post*. He was himself reluctant to lose the independence that a freelance has, but his wife saw the advantage of a secure staff job. It was, as it turned out, fortunate for him as well as for the paper. Fry held a Berlin degree in economics and commerce and was himself by origin a Central European. He spoke with a slight accent that was difficult to place until one knew that his English had been practised by reading Macaulay aloud to an Indian friend at Oxford. Like his predecessor, he was much more than a skilful technician of the money market. He was a man of wide culture in several fields and many countries, able to meet his business contacts over the whole range of their interests as man to man. Thus half reluctantly began a city editor-ship which was to last for more than a quarter of a century.

2

'We are facing the greatest crisis in our history with a Government weaker than any Government that has made war since Addington faced Napoleon.'[5] So Hammond wrote on the eve of the debate that brought the Chamberlain Government down. Week after week this long-sightedness of the historian helped those who read *Guardian* leaders to feel, like Napoleon's soldiers before the Pyramids, that twenty centuries of history looked down on them. At a time when we were almost alone in defending liberty there was special value in his constant reminder of our long descent through Fox and Burke and Chatham back to Cicero and Themistocles. History indeed was in many men's minds in 1940. Two days after Hammond had compared Chamberlain with Addington, Leo Amery rounded on the Prime Minister with Cromwell's bitter words to the Long Parliament: 'In the name of God, go.' But Boardman anxiously noted that 'Amery's philippic was delivered as usual to half-empty benches on his own side though there was a goodly muster of the Opposition to hear him.' But it was in fact the Opposition who decided the issue. All agreed that a National Government was necessary. Neither Liberals nor Labour would serve under Chamberlain. Churchill's government was formed just in time.

The day that Amery spoke, Evelyn Montague wrote of the empty war cemeteries, 'discreet preparation for the slaughter that has not yet happened.' The day on which Churchill formed his Government, Hitler invaded Belgium and Holland. On 14 May Boardman reported that the new Government had 'received a vote of confidence that was unanimous except for the opposition of Mr Maxton and Mr Campbell Stephen. These two parachutists, dropping from Cloud Cuckoo Land, insisted on dividing the House.' In the same paper Montague wrote of the German paratroops who 'variously disguised, have been dropped behind all the Allied fronts and have shown great courage and resource in their activities after landing.' His last message from Belgium was timed at 7.00 a.m. on 20 May and announced that 'this series of dispatches is likely to be brief and intermittent until the situation has settled down.' Two days later he and the other war correspondents were sent back to England. Another week and the main news story was his recapitulation of the last eighteen days with its sad close:

'Why was it not possible for the B.E.F. to cut its way southwards . . . and join the French? Why did the French not make a simultaneous attack from the South . . .? The answer is short and bitter. The French tried and failed; we did not even have the means at our command to make it worth trying. For such an attack in modern warfare, as all of us now know too late, two things are essential, armoured vehicles and the co-operation of low flying 'planes. We did not have enough 'planes . . . and we did not have nearly enough tanks.' (29 May 1940)

That was written on Tuesday. On Friday at Dover in the grey chill of dawn Evelyn Montague 'watched with incredulous joy the happening of a miracle . . . As the rising sun was turning the grey clouds to burnished copper the first destroyer of the day slid swiftly into the harbour . . . the soldiers on board shouted cheerful ribaldries to us who stood watching them with a mixture of pride and pity. They at any rate did not regard themselves as the central figures of tragic drama . . . Their eyes were red with weariness above dark bags of tired skin, but they were still soldiers and still in good heart.'[6]

3

It is difficult now, even for those who lived through them, to recall the tension and confusion of those days. Everybody had their own special problems to solve as well as their share in the national effort. For John Scott there were two special worries. Somehow or other the integrity of the *Guardian* must be preserved even if Hitler successfully invaded Britain. The paper itself, of course, would be suppressed. That went without saying. But, somehow or other, provision must be made for its rebirth. The Germans might seize the plant; they must not be able to seize the ownership. The legitimate governments of half the European States were in exile. Might there not be at least one legitimate newspaper in exile? John Scott took steps to change the membership of the Scott Trust* which held all the ordinary shares in the Manchester Guardian and Evening News, Ltd. Two new trustees were appointed whose most important qualification was that they did not live in England. One, F. A. Montague, a colonial civil servant, would maintain the tradition of the family ownership. The other, Paul Patterson, was the publisher of the *Baltimore Sun*, the great American newspaper whose London correspondent worked from the *Guardian's* office. Between the *Guardian* and the *Baltimore Sun* and their staffs there was more than a business connection. James Bone was the friend of every American journalist who visited London, but more especially of generations of *Sun* men. Paul Patterson's interest, then, might provide a base from which it would be possible to rebuild in a liberated England a new *Manchester Guardian*. There is something both quaint and rather touching in John Scott's careful concern for the niceties of copyright in a revolutionary situation. There is comedy in the fact that, having taken these legal precautions, he posted the precious Trust Deed to Paul Patterson in the United States in an ordinary envelope with a penny-halfpenny stamp.

The probability of invasion drove John Scott to make 'cloak and dagger plans' so alien to his character that they serve better than anything else to illustrate the desperate danger of those days. It was clear that he and Crozier,† the publisher and the editor of the *Manchester Guardian*, would be in danger if the Germans came. They at least would have to go 'on the run.' E. D. Simon promised to lend his boat for an escape though it was doubtful whether Crozier would be able to stand the exposure. Funds were a problem. John Scott consulted one of his Armenian friends with whom he daily played a rubber of bridge at the Reform Club. Through this friend a valuable emerald necklace was purchased and Haley went to Hatton Garden to collect it. There was no sense in depositing it in the bank since it would clearly be impossible to get it out if the emergency arose. Haley and John Scott took turns in carrying it on them. Once the risk of invasion receded

* See p. 492-3.

† Their names, and those of several other *Guardian* men, were included in the Gestapo Black List discovered at the end of the war. In the reticent manner of those days the *Guardian* published them merely in their proper alphabetical place without headline or editorial comment. *Guardian* men did not accept political honours. There was no need to make a song about this unwanted political one. M.G. 14, 15 September 1945.

the emeralds were sold back to the Hatton Garden dealer for the same sum which had been paid for them. Crozier, of course, knew of the escape plans but it is doubtful whether he knew how they were to be financed.

In any event he had other things to think about. The paper had to be got out and he had to decide what it was to say. It was, of course, pledged to Churchill who alone had 'the boldness, the imagination, the sense of social justice, the capacity to rouse the enthusiasm and devoted service that we need.'[8] When Wadsworth wrote these words, he spoke not only officially for the paper but personally for himself and his colleagues. Churchill had won them over as completely as he had the whole country. This had to be expressed, but at the same time the support the paper gave him could not be total and uncritical. What the M.G. had to say at this stage about the fighting forces was interesting and important at the time to its readers, but it could not by the nature of things be influential. What it had to say about the home front and the mobilisation of industry was both interesting and influential. The expression of the paper's policy here fell to Wadsworth. He was writing not only on subjects of which he was as nearly master as any man in Britain, but about Ministers, Ernest Bevin, Arthur Greenwood, and Herbert Morrison whom he knew and who knew him. He gave them the same whole-hearted but not uncritical support that he gave to Churchill:

7 *June:* (after praising Bevin's welfare, arbitration and training programme) 'if the country had been intelligently instead of slothfully led every step that the new Minister of Labour has taken in the last fortnight would have been taken six months ago.'

16 *August:* 'Mr Bevin has created something like a revolution, but, like all revolutions, it cannot stop. And the Minister of Labour must not take it amiss if he is pressed to act more boldly. No one understands better than he that he has to deal with a department that in some of its higher reaches has not been distinguished for energy or foresight.'

26 *August:* The Government 'has not given the impression that it has an economic plan for war that it is prepared to carry through, if necessary, with ruthlessness. It should be Mr Greenwood's business to supply this and to get it across.'

At this stage Wadsworth was inclined to put more trust in the energy and good sense of private citizens than in the wisdom of Ministers:

'The test the ordinary man applies is whether he himself is conscious that he has a particular part to play in what has become a 'people's war.' And when he sees around him jobs that, with his limited knowledge of defence, he conceives ought to be done, and when no one asks him to help to do them he feels frustrated and unsure.' (3 July 1940)

4

Promisi me non locuturum esse de demissioni mea.[9] 'I have promised that I will not talk about my resignation.' So Crozier wrote in his diary at the end of August, 1941, but he did not say to whom the promise was made – to John Scott, to himself, or to his wife? There was, as far as we know, no talk of resignation. Crozier soldiered on. But he was a tired man, often in physical pain, with frayed nerves, doing a continuously more exacting job with continuously diminishing resources. Readers of the paper can have had little idea of the mounting toll it took to get it out. The surviving pages of Crozier's diary,* however, enable one to look over his shoulder as he got back late from the office and jotted down in short, staccato phrases things that had happened during the day. The diary was neither comprehensive nor systematic. For example, he often noted who wrote the Long leader, but more frequently he did not. He mentioned most of the important interviews he had, but not what was said. Those notes he polished and kept elsewhere. The diary, then, was neither a business diary nor intended for publication. Nor was it, as far as one can judge, in intention an intimate diary. But in effect that is what it is. The formless jumble of entries, including a few snatches in Latin and Greek, chronicle the progress of his roses, the hunt for cigarettes for his wife and daughter, office rows, university business, the planning of a novel, illness, anxiety over the war, and the time spent in shelters. Their artlessness reveals the writer.

Key men left or broke down. 'Spent afternoon getting ready speech on E.J.P.' Crozier noted on 21 November 1940. E. J. Phillips was retiring at the age of 70 after forty years' service. He had been the first editor of the M.G. *Weekly*, had run for many years a chess feature, and at one time wrote preliminary articles on the big races in which he discreetly indicated what he thought would win. He did this so successfully that a London paper reprinted his selection as the 'M.G. tip' – which led to a deputation to C.P. and the end of this assignment.

---

* The diary was written on type-writing paper and kept in a loose-leaf folder. It starts on October 24, 1940 and continues until February 21, 1942. If there was more, it is lost. A similar diary covering a few isolated days in 1937 and 1938 survives.

> He was there when the Derby was started,
> And predicted the One, Two and Three,
> To the scandal of all the Free Churches –
> Which sounds like more moonshine to me.

So 'Lucio,' Gordon Phillips, had written for a dinner given in 1937 to his namesake on completing his fiftieth year in journalism.

E. J. Phillips's retirement hit Crozier in two ways. It deprived him of one of the few men on the paper to whom he could speak quite openly and without reserve, entirely as an equal. He became now more isolated than before. It also left him with too much of the burden of Letters to the Editor. There were, of course, always points that had to be put up to the editor for decision. The first entry in the diary records one such – a letter telling 'of growing protest among the part-time A.F.S. A suggestion that they should notify the public that on a particular night they will not answer the sirens! And the public will be told the date so that they may take extra precautions to put out fires, if any! I wrote rejecting letter and saying that any such threat would greatly harm their cause. Silly people!'[10]

The Letters were taken over by an inexperienced man. In consequence one Saturday Crozier spent 'from two to ten less Tea and Supper on Letters to Editor, initialling them, and memorandums etc. Read about twenty sent to me during the week by X! *Sunday* asked Garner to see all Letters that X wanted to send on to me and act as buffer.' Next week he found that there were thirteen columns of Letters in type – nearly a quarter of a war-time *Guardian*. He cancelled two columns straight away. Not only were there far too many Letters, but some might well be libellous – the cement manufacturers were already after Bishop Barnes, who had attacked them, and the papers, including the M.G., which had reported him. The Government had banned the *Daily Worker*, 'Much worried during the night and this morning about the *Daily Worker* letters. Think for future must make X send all letters in copy to R.G. – poor R.G.!'* This he did, and there are no more references in the diary to this subject.

Arthur Wallace's health, bad for years, finally gave way that winter. 'There's nothing for it,' he wrote to John Scott, in October, 'but to break the tie that has been the chief interest of my life for over thirty years.'[11] He recovered sufficiently to come back for a presentation the following May with speeches from John Scott and Bone as well as Crozier. Of these three men probably only Bone, a fellow Scot and a

---

* Diary 26 January; 3, 10 and 11 February 1941. R.G. was Garner, an experienced and remarkably level-headed sub-editor who became Night News Editor (a new post) later in the year.

fellow romantic, fully appreciated what Wallace had been to the paper. Wallace was a man of talent, able to turn his hand to almost any journalistic task and to produce acceptable work on time. He was allowed to become something like everybody's understudy on the Corridor with the result that, when he was young, he lacked the discipline of having to make himself expert in one field. He was at his best in the selection of 'back-pagers,' the literary sketches about a thousand words long which five days a week delighted readers and gave many writers their first chance. Later he inherited other jobs, doing them competently but without the flair of the men from whom he took over. Theatres came his way after Miss Horniman had gone, when Montague went. He took over the literary editorship when Monkhouse gave it up. He set himself to preserve their legacy when they would have set themselves to experiment.

But Arthur Wallace's real value to the paper lay in the office 'pub,' in the Press Club and at his home to which he was apt at all hours to take parties of apparently incongruous men who fitted happily together in his presence. His wife, a strict teetotaller herself, was always welcoming and must have known more about the personal relationships of *Guardian* men than any other woman. In Wallace's company one might meet the harpist from the Hallé, who as a boy had travelled with his father playing in villages where young men put a penny in the hat as payment for a dance. With him there might be an Irishman, an advertisement canvasser for the *Guardian*, who was the Labour MP for South Salford. Joe Toole would recall how as a boy, not daring to go home with his evening papers unsold, he got rid of them by shouting 'Horrible Murder in Salford' as he stood in a dark corner where purchasers could not see that there was no such news. In the party there might be the Lancashire tuberculosis officer, an old friend from Glasgow University, and, on his rare visits to Manchester, another contemporary, Walter Elliot, the Conservative Cabinet Minister. And, of course, there would be young men from the *Guardian*. Grumbling to or at Arthur was a useful safety valve since he was sufficiently senior to count as Establishment without being dangerous. More important, he was perhaps the main source of the vivifying oral tradition of the *Guardian*, told with affection and concealed pride, but spiced with the irreverence without which it would have been unacceptable. Crozier probably thought that Wallace led the young men astray. Perhaps he did, though each abetted the other. But in a more important sense he put them in the right way. Bone knew this. In London he did the same himself.

Gordon Phillips took over the theatres from Wallace and did them well, but he was in no state to take on additional work. Crozier noted 'G.P. very angry indeed' when he had to take over the pictures one night because of a muddle over days off. A little later there was a scathing paragraph in Miscellany about the suggestion that the pause before the nine o'clock news on the BBC should be observed as a time of prayer or recollection. Crozier felt that the tone of the paragraph was wrong and that the comment ran counter to editorial policy. This incident attracted three entries in the diary:

Sat. 28 June   G. P. Miscellany on Dedicated Minute.

Sun. 29 June   G. P. replies twice to my note of remonstrance.

Tues. 1 July   G. P. at Opera House. Heard from A.P.W. the history of his anger about the 'dedicated minute' on Friday night. Left at 11 p.m. to avoid too much conversation.

There was friction, too, between Gordon Phillips and Wadsworth who enjoyed being provocative. Next day's diary entry reads:

Wed. 2 July   Roses becoming a great sight.
G.P. very talkative about letter from Peter Green.
A.P.W., writing about petrol and horseracing, practically throws over G.P.'s short of some time ago on the subject of preserving the bloodstock market. I cannot find G.P.'s short and A.P.W. doesn't; at last got him to alter the stuff and I hope no one marks the inconsistency and writes in about it!
Still very hot.
We are promised lawn mower for to-morrow from the Stockport Distributing Company.

In fact Gordon Phillips had a slight nervous breakdown in 1942 and a more serious one in 1945.

Little personal problems cropped up with people at 'the London End.' Then Evelyn Montague and Crozier crossed swords over the raids on London:

Mon. 9 Dec.   (1940) E.A.M. disgruntled because I spiked pars (for London Letter) on last night's bombing of London. He said people are bored without a raid and glad to be bombed again. Also that the Germans after 48 hours lull, had done pretty poorly. ('not impressive')

Tues. 10 Dec.   E.A.M. now writes a letter to me protesting against me spiking his pars. He finds it 'mortifying and humiliating' that I should accept agency reports instead of his word.

Wed. 11 Dec.   Letter of apology from E.A.M. for his outburst.

Thur. 12 Dec. Wrote to E.A.M. in reply to his apology.

It would be silly to attach importance to such incidents. Things like this surely happen daily in almost any organisation. What is significant is the fact that Crozier bothered to note them in his diary. They get relatively more attention than such vital episodes for the paper as Bone's 1940 visit to the United States. He went out to attend the Democratic Convention at which the issue of Roosevelt's third term was to be decided. He travelled in the Yankee Clipper but was held up in the Azores and arrived too late. He was taken ill and had to undergo an operation. His return journey was even more unfortunate. This is how it was recorded in Crozier's diary:

Wed. 11 December. *Night* News from Cunard that JB is on the way back.

Sun. 15 December. *Night* Heard that JB might very probably be on the 'Western Prince,' torpedoed in the Atlantic 200 miles from Ireland. The (*Baltimore*) *Sun* had cabled to Kent to report developments in re the 'Western Prince,' 'especially regarding James.' Kent going to Glasgow to-night and so also Blyth (via Garner).

Mon. 16 December. *J. Bone* The shipping firm (Furness Withy) believes that all passengers are safe.* Ship not in by midnight. Blyth says Admiralty most helpful. J.R.S. and Haley enquiring for news.

Wed. 18 December. *Morning* 1 p.m. Turner† rang up – Bone safe in Glasgow.
Night 6 p.m. Bone rang up – sounds pretty well, but had had water down him a lot while in the boat. Post-operation – no damage. David Bone also spoke to me and said JB would be resting a bit. I wrote to JB and told him to rest.

Thur. 19 December. JB sent short message from Glasgow. Blyth reported to me that he thought JB was badly shaken . . .
Reading Gulliver, Psalms, Hosea and Thriller.

One would not gather from the Diary that Bone's 'short message' had filled two columns of the main news page. It was packed with detail, objective, rigidly controlled: 'Just before she plunged we heard two blasts on the whistle. "That's the old man's last words – Good-bye to you," said a sailor near me in lifeboat No 3.' Or this, 'About six hours had gone – it seemed like six months, – and then Mr Warburton, a passenger, said in a conversational tone, "Why, there is a ship; I can see it quite plain." He pointed without standing up.' Bone ended his

---

* In fact, six passengers and eleven crew were missing.
† Kent was the *Baltimore Sun*'s London correspondent; Donald Blyth was a *Guardian* reporter; Turner, Day News Editor.

story thus: 'The rescue ship did wonders in succouring the weaker and ill among us. It was blowing up heavily at night and there would have been little chance of the lifeboats riding it out in that sea. The line between wives and widows was a very close one that Saturday.'

This would have been good reporting in any conditions. Bone was 68 and recovering from an operation. When he got back to London, his beloved chambers in King's Bench Walk had been destroyed. In the spring he wrote of them in a leader page article. Its jewelled, fanciful prose is in strong contrast to the story of his shipwreck. A man may be sentimental over things and places; not over life and death.

In many ways the Temple seemed as close as an echo to the past. The tenant used to think of generations of tenants after him going up those old wooden stairs to those pleasant Chambers and tried to glimpse such ghosts of the future.

Not only the Temple's glories of church and hall have been ruined in the German's fury, but such curious, distinctive and irreplaceable caskets of traditional English life, dusty, perhaps, and lacking in some things; but who that has lived there can forget those sweet and mellow purlieus of the lawn? (29 May 1941)

It was no doubt the bombing which put the heaviest strain on newspaper men. The desperate need to meet edition times exacts a heavy toll on the nerves in the most favourable conditions. In that winter the impossible had to be made possible. Sometimes the trouble was in London;

Sunday night was a great Blitz on London – Fleet Street cut off from the Provinces; no communications with our London Office – Sunday, Monday or Tuesday – getting stuff via Y.P. and very badly.*

Sometimes it was in Manchester:

Sunday 22 Dec. – 1st day of the great Blitz on Manchester. The night's experiences. The scandal of the incendiaries elsewhere. Eleven incendiaries on our own roof – all put out . . . Home about 9 a.m.

Alerts were more frequent than bombs and as destructive of newspaper work. Crozier's entry for 20 October 1941 reads: 'Alert at 8.50. All clear about 12.20. M.G. down (in the cellars) for 164 minutes, much the worst of all!' But some of the 1940 entries show longer interruptions. It should be noted that the composing room was on the third floor of the building.

The air raids had a more lasting effect. They forced the firm to

* Diary Thursday 8 May to Tuesday 13 May: Y.P.: *Yorkshire Post.*

dissolve the M.G. and E.N. Society, formed after the General Strike.*
Alternative printing arrangements, necessary in case of bomb damage,
could not be made because of the opposition of the Typographical
Association:

'30 June 1941. G.P. Long account of the committee meeting of the Society.
Very bitter feeling, he says, about the action of the firm in giving them no
warning! Tried to explain to him why, after N.C. (*News Chronicle*) and D.M.
(*Daily Mail*) bombs, we *had* to move.'

More constant even than the alerts was the nervous pressure involved in the censorship. Crozier had no desire to beat the censorship
though, when he thought it foolish, he said so. The trouble was the
constant watchfulness it entailed. Two entries illustrate the problems
that arose:

Sunday 17 November 1940. 11.20 read Crowther (the scientific correspondent) on the Moon and Air Raids. Disliked Table of cloud covering for
Kew in 1937. London edition already printed off 5,500 copies – all cancelled.
Only 1st Edition had article. Caught London edition with new page and only
missed a few parcels.
Wednesday 15 January 1941. Censor stopped Duke of Kent in Manchester
matter at 8 p.m. Pictures now in the page. Said he did not know what the
M o I at Manchester had promised. (2 of them had said the stuff was all right
for Thursday's paper). D. *Herald* protested because its stuff had gone in early
editions. Censor rescinded his prohibition and the stuff went in – we took
emergency pictures off machine and restored normal page.

As the 'blitz' lessened the pressure on the staff grew less intense.
Entries in Crozier's diary like that for 26 November 1940 ('Unsatisfactory. Disliked the office and caught the 11.10 bus home. Dislike
of the office increasing') give place ten months later to 'Sunt meliora'
repeated the following day with the addition of 'Non morosus,' even
though this was followed by a question mark in brackets – 'things are
looking up. Not peevish.'[12]
There seem to have been two other reasons for the improvement.
The first was personal. Crozier had found an all-absorbing interest
not so much for his leisure as to distract his sleeplessness. The notes
of his general reading – Swift, Chaucer, Simonides, the Phaedo – are
replaced by notes of pruposeful reading with a view to writing a
successor to *The Letters of Pontius Pilate*. His first thought, noted in
August 1941, was for a series of Letters by one of the lesser known
people referred to in Paul's Epistles. This gradually changed to an
historical novel, with strong political interest, set in imperial Rome.

* See pp. 484-488. Diary 30 June 1941.

On 25 September he notes 'Inveni fabulam' – 'I have got the idea for a story.' There was now something to take his mind off the office. *The Fates are Laughing* was well named.[13]

The second reason was that things were looking brighter for the M.G. The paper ration was fixed as a proportion of the pre-war consumption. A paper could choose to print many copies with few pages or few copies with many pages. The London 'quality' papers, now reduced to two with the end of the *Morning Post* in 1937, chose the latter. 'J.R.S. said the London people are annoyed at the *Times* and '*Tel*' which were keeping up size *but* were spending the space not on the public but on advts!'[14] It is not clear how else they could compensate for their smaller sales. The *Guardian*, like the popular papers and the other regional quality papers, took the former course. It came down at this stage of the war to forty pages a week. The corresponding figure for March 1938 had been 120 pages. The drastic reduction in the size of each issue made possible a small increase in circulation thanks to other measures. At the beginning of the war the *Manchester Guardian Commercial* had stopped publication because John Scott expected that the war would kill its advertising – a mistaken forecast, but an economy which helped out the daily's ration of paper. Another economy was made by reducing the M.G. on Saturday to the same number of copies and pages as on the other days of the week. The Saturday issue had always had more pages and sold more copies. The editorial view was that the additional readers were attracted by the special Saturday articles and other features designed for week-end reading. The circulation department's view, which was probably right, was that the additional copies were sold to people who wanted to see the advertisements of scrap metal merchants and other similar trades which appeared only on that day.

In July 1941 Crozier noted with an exclamation mark that the sale was almost 58,000 – 2,000 better than at the same time in 1940. In September he rejoiced that it was over 60,000. This was 10,000 more than before the war. In fact the position was better than this 20 per cent increase suggested. Before the war about 40 per cent of the net sale had been at half price.* The cut rate was finally abolished in 1940. Virtually all the cut-price subscribers proved willing to pay the full price. There was even a waiting list of about 3,000 would-be purchasers. As many *Guardians* could be sold as could be printed. This was the common experience of all papers. But it was none the less encouraging for that. Crozier could begin to look forward with confidence.

Almost the last entry in his diary runs:

* See p. 489.

ἐλευθερία. ποσίς.   M.G.
βίβλιον.   Gradualness. san faery ann.
nihil irae.

The meaning is obscure, but it does not sound as if Crozier was down-hearted. The next entry begins: 'Telegram from PM asking whether I can lunch on Thursday. Replied No but shall be up Thursday and Friday of next week.'[15]

5

Crozier's telegram must have caught Churchill in a genial mood. The hint was taken and Crozier went to lunch the following week. He spent, as he usually did, two days in London staying overnight at the Cumberland – 'if it is there' he had once drily noted in his diary after inviting his son to meet him at the hotel. When he got back to Manchester he would take great trouble to write up his notes in polished form. They show Crozier in another light from the diary. Even allowing for the intimacy of the one and the professionalism of the other, it seems clear that in London Crozier became a different man. The petty cares of the Manchester office, exacerbated by the incurable staff shortage, seem to be forgotten as the reserved but tough provincial penetrated the great world. Superficially Crozier had little in common with Churchill:

He protested vigorously when I would have neither wine nor brandy and said he was sure they would do me good. Then he said pathetically 'Well, I work very hard and I think I am entitled to a little.'
When he found that I did not smoke either he looked at me hard and said 'Good God, man, you have got nothing you can give up.'[16]

But, like his Long leaders – which Churchill sometimes praised in Cabinet[17] – Crozier was neither stupid, impertinent nor over-awed. That probably was what Churchill liked about him. At any rate they went on seeing one another. There are records of sixteen talks between October 1939 – when they met for the first time – and October 1943. The discussion during and after lunch on that Friday in February ranged wide. It covered, for instance, the changes in the Government announced that morning (Cripps was there on his first day as a Cabinet Minister). Archibald Sinclair came in after lunch. 'PM (very solemnly): "Let me introduce you to the editor of the leading Liberal paper; no, the *only* Liberal paper; for who could apply that great name to a paper which, like the *News Chronicle*, is moved only by nervous hysteria?" They went on to discuss aeroplanes versus tanks in North Africa. But a snatch of conversation about the recent escape of the *Scharnhorst* and *Gneisenau* from Brest must typify the whole of that conversation and all the others. Churchill already knew, of course, what Crozier was thinking from a leader, 'Two Failures,' which had appeared in the M.G. on the Monday.* Everybody knew that the escape was coming, the leader argued, but did the Navy and Air Staffs believe that a Channel escape was impossible and that the Atlantic route would necessarily be chosen? Were the Navy patrols maintained? How was it that it took the RAF three hours of daylight to discover 'this large fleet with its strong air cover?' And how was it that apparently there was a gap of fifty-three minutes between the RAF discovering the German ships and the Admiralty being informed? But, characteristically, the criticism was given a positive and disarming twist in the final sentence:

One hopes that the Government will demand answers to such questions, both these and those about the defence of Malaya, for, at least, it is very necessary to discover those on the planning Staffs who foresaw what might be coming and were not taken by surprise.

Crozier's note of the lunch-time discussion runs thus:

PM: People talk as though these were the first German ships that ever got through the Straits in this war. Lots of them have got through – *hundreds* of them – they get through every week, and big ships too – 7,000 and 10,000 tons.

WPC: Merchantmen?

PM: Well, they get through – that's the point.

CRIPPS: What's puzzling is that these ships have been in such good form when we thought we had done them such a lot of damage.

PM: We did do them a lot of damage!

WPC: Not in the engine rooms if they could steam 20–30 knots on their own through the Straits?

WPC: Everybody's wondering about the point that there were only six Swordfish torpedo-carrying aircraft? It's all very small. We understand that torpedo-carrying aircraft are needed elsewhere and with the fleet and all that, and are still puzzled that there were so few to tackle these ships. If one may ask, have we developed this weapon busily . . .?

PM: Yes, but it's like everything else – there are so many demands everywhere for the weapon . . .

* M.G. 16 February 1942. The leader was written by Walter James, a brilliant young historian, who shared with Crozier, Wadsworth and Hammond the main leader-writing. He wrote at this time mainly on military subjects.

WPC: Well, are we multiplying this weapon?

PM: What we are after especially is to develop and increase *Carriers* for
         aircraft. That's the need. That's what we're after – Carriers –
         Carriers!

WPC: Well, another point. The Admiralty says that we are better off
         because the German ships are in German ports. Suppose that one
         of them, or one after another, or the whole lot sally out into the
         North Atlantic, or round by Iceland, to attack our convoys and
         hurry back again, how much better off are we if we don't catch
         them, or how about torpedo-carrying aircraft for catching them?

PM: Well, we have our dispositions. It will be like the pursuit of the
         Bismarck, and we sank her . . .

In the seven years before the formation of the Churchill government
Crozier noted talks with thirty-eight Front Bench politicians. In the
four years from 1940 to 1943 there were twice as many: seventy-six.*
He had only one interview each with Baldwin and Neville Chamberlain.
Of the Labour leaders he met only Arthur Henderson – but that was as
President of the Disarmament Conference – A. V. Alexander and
Herbert Morrison. He saw more of Churchill, Hore-Belisha (sixteen
times each) and Sinclair (twelve times) than of any other politicians.
The other main group of people whom Crozier went to London to
see were diplomats and leaders of foreign countries. He saw Vansittart
twenty times – more often than any of his other London contacts.
Dulanty, the Irish High Commissioner (13) and Bjorn Prytz, the Swedish
ambassador (12) came next. Raczynsky of Poland (7), Maisky of the
Soviet Union (6), Reventlow of Denmark (6) and Benes (5) were his
other main contacts. Sixty-two of these sixty-nine diplomatic interviews
took place in 1938 or later.

The second half of Crozier's editorship was marked by this much
more 'personal diplomacy.' In this way it resembles the middle period
of C.P.'s editorship, from 1910 to 1922, when he was frequently in
London for political talks. But there were important differences. C.P.
was seeing men whom he might have visited even if he had not been
editor of the *Manchester Guardian*, though no doubt they would have
been less glad to see him. Crozier made his contacts only because he was
editor and in that capacity. C.P. met friends; Crozier, business acquain-
tances. But there was one great similarity. Neither C.P. nor Crozier
used their interviews for news purposes. They treated them purely as
helping to form their own opinions which they would then express
in the leader columns. When Crozier got back to Manchester he at

* It is clear that at any rate in this later period either that some interviews were
not written up or that the notes have been lost.

once had a conference with Hammond about London opinion. Some at least of his interview notes he circulated to John Scott, and to his assistant editors, Gordon Phillips and Wadsworth.

C.P. sometimes used his interviews for log-rolling, as, notably, for Chaim Weizmann. Crozier, of course, would gladly have done the same for the Zionist cause, but he had not the personal position to make that possible. To Scott, Zionism had been one of many enthusiasms. It was Crozier's ruling concern. He was not given to sudden passions for small oppressed peoples – he knew only too well that they filled the paper and bored its readers. But Zionism was to him in quite a different category. Crozier's most regular correspondent and the man whose name appears most frequently in his interview notes was L. B. Namier who became professor of history at Manchester University in 1931. Between 1933 and 1938 Crozier noted twenty talks with him. When the war came and Namier moved to London, letters and memoranda – often several a week – took the place of talks. The *Guardian's* very accurate knowledge of what was happening in Eastern Europe owed a great deal to this briefing by Namier whose work for the Zionist organisation gave him a wide range of sources which his historian's skill helped him to evaluate. It would be possible to regard Namier as a PRO for the Jews engaged in cultivating the *Guardian*. It would be misleading. He and Crozier saw themselves as fellow workers in a cause. When Crozier took up in 1940 the refusal to allow the *Patria* to land its pathetic shipload of Jewish refugees in Palestine, Weizmann wrote to thank him for his 'inspired and inspiring article.' Crozier replied 'You need never thank me for anything that I am able to do in that cause. My heart is in it and so is my head, and I shall go on using both faithfully so long as I am here.'[18]

6

The *Guardian* was still a poor paper. Most of its war reporting had to be done through others. It took the *Times* service – that is to say it paid a fee for the right to use the reports of the *Times* special correspondents which appeared with the by-line at the top 'From Our Special Correspondent' and the words 'Times and Manchester Guardian Service' at the foot. The fact that this was possible illustrated how little the two papers competed – the *Times* hardly penetrated the *Guardian* heart-land and the *Guardian* sold only some 3,000 copies in and about London. Most of this reporting then belongs properly to the story of the *Times* rather than of the *Guardian*. But there were exceptions. When the British First Army took part in the Allied landing in North Africa

Evelyn Montague went with them. He stayed with them until the fall of Tunis, went through the conquest of Sicily with the Eighth Army and accompanied them into Italy. The same arrangement by which the *Guardian* used the *Times* service applied in reverse. '*Times* people say,' Bone wrote to Crozier, 'they've been asked by Major-General Wedderburn-Maxwell if they will print 10,000 copies of the article on "Foundation of Tunisian Victory" for distribution. He thinks it admirably gives facts not generally known and does justice in the right quarters. He is R A officer recently returned from Tunisia. The *Times* have published many reprints but never had a case before where the article wasn't their own stuff. Will we agree to reprinting and what about accreditation?'[19]

This favourable military opinion from the field was endorsed by the best known of military commentators, Captain B. H. Liddell Hart. Montague's reports from Tunisia, he wrote, were a source of information on which one could depend, not only for accuracy but for insight – very welcome to a commentator who had to 'probe for the truth in the half-truths of official information.' And Montague's companion from another paper, Alexander Clifford, wrote 'There is no doubt in my mind that Evelyn Montague was the most important war correspondent of this war.'[20]

To-day as one reads his longer articles summing up the lessons of the campaigns in which he took part it is possible to sense some of the quality which won his work this high praise. These sentences still live:

The degree of surprise achieved was remarkable . . . a detachment of the Derbyshire Yeomanry, roving round Bein Khalled, in the middle of the neck of the Cape Bon Peninsula, caught fourteen German officers enjoying a champagne supper. They reported that the supper was good but the champagne sweet. (18 May)

A soldier's education cannot be completed except by fighting. (19 May)

Now that all the excitement is over it must be repeated deliberately that the Italians scarcely fought at all. After a few days it was not thought worth while to mark their location on Montgomery's map. (25 August)

There never was a good infantryman yet who did not begin by dreading it (dive bombing) and end by treating it as a showy but over-rated form of attack which gave him the off-chance of crediting his personal account with an enemy aeroplane shot down. (26 August)

These parachutists were troops of the highest quality, experienced veterans of Crete and Russia, cool and skilful, Nazi zealots to a man. To fight against them was an education for any soldier. One must assume that Germany has given up hope of using these magnificent specialists any more in their proper attacking rôle if she was willing to sacrifice them as die-hard infantry. (27 August)

These campaigns were triumphs for British arms. No one reading Montague's reports would realise how tragic they were for him. While he was in North Africa news came that his wife was seriously ill. He was flown back only to arrive the day after her funeral. He returned to the army. Immediately after the landing in Italy the doctors ordered him home. Cyril Ray from the London Office went out as his replacement. When he arrived Montague was not to be found at Bari where he was supposed to be in bed. 'He turned up two days later and I had to help to lift him out of his jeep . . . There had been fighting at Foggia and he had refused to leave it unreported while his relief was on the way, though all his colleagues were eager to "cover" him and he could hardly walk.'[21] Like father, like son.

Ever since Hitler had invaded Russia the Left in England had clamoured for us to land in France and provide what propaganda called 'the Second Front,' ignoring the campaigns in Africa, Asia and Italy. No paper was more anxious than the M.G. to see France free – after the war a collection of Hammond's leaders was published, without his name, under the honest title 'Faith in France.'[22] But Crozier's cautious mind realised the immensity of the task and the folly of a premature attack. His conversations in Whitehall helped to keep the paper from taking what many might have thought its natural line.

At last in the spring of 1944 the time was ripe. The winter had been spent in preparation. The newspapers had their own little bit to do in getting ready. The M.G. had some difficulty. Evelyn Montague had eagerly looked forward ever since 1940 to going back to France with the BEF, but, like his uncle Laurence Scott before him, he was in a tuberculosis sanatorium in Aberdeenshire. To take his place Cyril Ray was brought back from Italy where his conduct at the attack on Ortona was to bring him a mention in dispatches.* He would have done the job admirably, but a sad misunderstanding caused him to leave the M.G., which he loved, and go to the B.B.C. at a most inconvenient moment for the paper. All was to do again with too little time to do it. The M.G.'s own suitable staff men were away in the Forces; so were most of the other men who would have been possible. Bone was sick

---

* 20 December 1943. See *London Gazette* 24 August 1944. The escorting officer's report recommending the "mention" said: 'The platoon commander and the sergeant were killed and the company commander asked for a volunteer to take a message ordering the platoon to withdraw. Mr. Ray immediately volunteered to carry out the task, which he achieved successfully, and brought the platoon to safety.'

and away from the office, though he came back sooner than he should. Crozier's heart had been giving trouble for some time and he had been ordered to take a day in bed each week as a precaution. No precaution could avail. His last short leader was published on 14 April 1944. He corrected the last page of typescript of 'The Fates are Laughing' on 15 April. He died the next day. D-Day was still seven weeks away. Soon after victory James Bone, talking to his colleagues, spoke of 'Crozier, the single-minded Roman who let nobody know his wounds but carried on so serenely and skilfully till Fate, who had nothing to laugh at there, struck him down.'

BOOK SEVEN

A. P. Wadsworth 1944-1956

*

CHAPTER THIRTY-FIVE

Silent Revolution

I

ONCE again John Scott had to choose an editor for the *Manchester Guardian*. He wasted no time. Crozier died on 16 April 1944. His successor was announced on 29 April. Never before had there been so few possible editors available among the *Guardian*'s own men. Two years earlier it would have been different. Evelyn Montague was in his early forties and had had a great width of experience – company secretary, sports editor, deputy London editor, parliamentary sketch writer and war correspondent. He was C.P.'s eldest grandson, and he had a different variety of his father's skill with words. But in 1943 he had been condemned by tuberculosis to a long, and possibly to a permanent, exile from the work he loved. Haley had been John Scott's right-hand man for more than a dozen years. His recent experience had been mainly managerial, but behind it lay editorial success and a books page in the *Manchester Evening News* which was thought worth reading by austere judges who would pass no other part of that paper's contents. But Haley had gone to the BBC in 1943 as editor-in-chief of its news services and was about to become its Director-General. A matter of months might, perhaps, have made Haley editor of the *Guardian* instead of the *Times* to which he went in 1952. But this is speculation. Ivor Brown had become editor of the *Observer* in 1942. Hammond and Bone were now in their seventies and both were sick men. Gordon Phillips, the senior assistant editor, was also ill. Outside the *Guardian* circle there were even in war time no doubt several possible candidates. John Scott made some tentative enquiries. But he turned back to his own men or rather, so it seems on looking back, to his own man. A. P. Wadsworth really chose himself. There was no serious competitor.

But Wadsworth also chose himself in another way. There was, so it soon appeared, no one who could have done half so well the particular job that was now needed. He was the man for 1944 just as surely as Crozier had been the man for 1932. In an odd way this was because his life had been more like that of the first generation of *Guardian* men, and especially Garnett and Harland, two of the first three partners. Garnett, Harland and Wadsworth had all learned their trade step by step from the bottom up. They had had to scramble for their education. They kept at it not for what it would get them but for what it gave them – self-taught men who never stopped learning. Garnett and Harland had lived in an industrial society that was fluid and open. From clogs to clogs in their time was still three generations. But this society had become less flexible by the time of Scott and his lieutenants. The Scotts and Montagues, Arnold, Crozier and Sidebotham had all received as good an education for an élite as any known in history. It gave them a profound sense of *noblesse oblige* – that was what their *Guardian* was about – but it had cut them off from much of the common experience of most Englishmen. Wadsworth, like that other Rochdale man George Leach, belonged to the other side of the great divide. His upbringing had not isolated him. His work as Labour correspondent had kept his ear to the ground. He sensed the loosening of social class that was coming out of Hitler's war. He noticed how the Forces had found a great reservoir of neglected, unsuspected talent. He knew that our economic survival demanded that we should continue to draw freely on it, and he believed that younger people would regard this economic imperative also as a moral imperative. That was what his *Guardian* had to be about. Indeed his own life typified it.

Haley would probably never have gone to the BBC if there had not been a successor in sight. It was quickly arranged that Laurence Scott should come to help his father. This was natural. It surprised no one. But it was not part of a long-term plan as many must have thought. It may, of course, always have been John Scott's hope that his eldest son would succeed him but, if so, he kept it to himself. He was determined not to be the dominant, perhaps domineering parent that C.P. had been. Laurence went to Rugby, his father's old school and one might almost say the traditional school for the upper *Guardian* circle.* He went on to Cambridge to his father's old college, Trinity. But, when it came to choosing a career, Laurence Scott was left strictly to himself – journalism and newspaper management were never mentioned to him. He chose to join the LNER as a traffic apprentice. But the railway age was passing. When Ted Scott died Laurence's father arranged for him to go as a trainee first to the *Financial News* and then to the *News Chronicle.*† After this Laurence Scott had expected to be

---

* e.g. W. T. Arnold, E. T. Scott, Arthur Ransome, P. J. Monkhouse, E. A. Montague, E. D. Simon, Darsie Gillie.

† In his 'introspective' note to Wadsworth in 1946 John Scott wrote: 'C. P. did

invited to join one of his father's papers, but John Scott made no move so his son got himself a job first as a sub-editor with the *Financial News* and then as personal assistant to the general manager of the *News Chronicle*. By 1937 John Scott felt that Laurence had done enough to justify bringing him into the company. But Laurence Scott wanted to be assured that there was a specific job for him to do. His father was a completely honest man. There was not, and he did not try to invent one. Laurence Scott remained with the *News Chronicle* group and became circulation manager of the *Star*.

Now there was not only a job but an emergency. He was willing to come. But it was not so easy to get him. He was serving in the RAF and, though Brendan Bracken, the Minister of Information, was anxious to secure his release, the Air Ministry was not helpful. Months passed. Crozier, who handled the application, realised that he should have stated the case more strongly.[1] Then the Air Minister, Sir Archibald Sinclair, wanted deferment for a journalist in his Scottish constituency. Deferment was Bracken's province. Laurence Scott came to Cross Street in 1944 at the age of 35.

The *Guardian* had a new editor, but the Corridor had an empty look. This was the result of the paper's policy of appointing young men who must be expected to go on after a few years to get more money or more experience. The immediate pre-war generation – as usual Oxford men with first-class degrees – had been a particularly strong one.* But Maurice Ashley had gone to the *Times* in 1937 and J. M. D. Pringle had accepted a job with the BBC in November 1939. E. C. Hodgkin had decided to go off on a protracted visit to India and China 'if there was no war.' But war there was, and both Pringle and Hodgkin had reserve liabilities which took them into the army. Their places could not be filled. Only Walter James remained. Crozier had asked him after Munich to write on Civil Defence. He thought this could best be done from inside. He joined the AFS on a part-time basis. At Easter, 1942 he became a full-time member of the National Fire Service in Manchester but with a rota of duties that allowed him to write a leader three or four

---

not train me for the job. I was trained as an engineer which was my personal inclination and pitchforked into this. One of the things for which I really think I can claim some credit is that, drawing wisdom from my own case, I did train Laurence very much better for it than C. P. trained me.'

* It might, perhaps, have been even stronger if Harold Wilson had accepted the trial which Crozier offered him in 1937 instead of accepting his advice to take a research scholarship and work with Beveridge – a course which led eventually to 10 Downing St.

times a week – mostly on military subjects, which he shared with Crozier. After Crozier's death the position became desperate. Gordon Phillips's condition was bad. Hammond worked at home and rarely came down to the office. Wadsworth had not taken a night off for a year. It was to be another four months before he could do so. There was nobody to leave in charge.

Among the congratulations that Wadsworth received on his appointment was one which had a lasting effect on the M.G. From London, where he was GSO2 (Training) at Combined Operations Headquarters, Pringle wrote: 'Ever since Crozier died a little group of renegades and exiles has been meeting here in London nearly every day to talk of that and other things and there was not one who did not hope that you would get it. It would have been a scandal if you hadn't.' But what mattered came later: 'I wish I were back! I think it only honest to say this in case you should be looking round for people after the war. The BBC have been very decent to me and still promise me a job; but of course I mean very little to them and they, to be honest, mean very little to me. It's rather like being engaged for five years to a woman and then wondering whether you really want to marry . . . I do not see how they could be broken-hearted if I never went there since I have never been.'[2]

Wadsworth got Pringle's letter on the first Monday of his editorship. By Tuesday evening Bone had asked Pringle whether he would come back at once if the army would release him. On the Friday Pringle dined with Bone and next day he wrote to Wadsworth: 'Perhaps you could also let me know roughly what job and what salary you propose to offer me. I have already made up my mind but it would naturally help me to know.' By return Wadsworth wrote 'I thought Bone would probably explain to you the idea of what you should do here. It was roughly that you should act as assistant editor and my deputy . . . I cannot give you a salary figure at the present moment, but I don't think you would have reason to be disappointed.' He added a postscript which it is to be hoped Pringle could read – Wadsworth's handwriting was perhaps the worst in the *Guardian*'s long tradition of illegibility – 'Don't say anything publicly about the Assistant Editor business yet for reasons you may guess.'[3] These letters are typical of much that was to mark Wadsworth's editorship. They show Bone's cautious reticence and Wadsworth's elusiveness as well as the kindness that he hid with his waspish tongue. His concern for Gordon Phillips's feelings was as genuine as his reluctance to tell him of the inevitable change in his position. Pringle's willingness to come without quite knowing what he was coming to shows he understood Wadsworth's preference for putting as little on paper as possible. Wadsworth liked to play his editing by ear. The *Guardian* men he liked best were those who caught the tune he hummed without his having to sing the words.

It took eleven weeks to secure Pringle's release. John Scott had no difficulty in getting Haley to agree to Pringle giving up his BBC commitment and Brendan Bracken tackled his old friend General Laycock, the Chief of Combined Operations, direct. But a replacement had to be found and trained and it was mid-July before Pringle came to Manchester. After he had been working in the office for a fortnight the War Office turned difficult, quite naturally objecting to Bracken's private deal with a subordinate formation. However things were eventually straightened out and by mid-August Wadsworth was able to write Bracken a final letter of thanks and breathe again. They had been three months of acute difficulty. Hammond had had a severe heart attack and was forced to give up work for some considerable time. It was quite impossible for Wadsworth and Pringle to meet during this period, but they wrote a good many letters to one another not only about the 'old boy' diplomacy needed to secure release, but on the future of the paper. Pringle was fertile in suggestions and the freedom of their letters shows how easily they took up the friendship where they had left it five years before. Wadsworth was old enough to be Pringle's father, but he never demanded from his juniors the deference which C.P. and Crozier had received and, no doubt, expected. If the young men liked him – but not all did – they gave him instead that admiration which in a happy team a competent performer or a rising young player delights to give to an acknowledged master. Who would want more?

Five days before Crozier's death Bone had been able to tell him that David Woodward had accepted the job of war correspondent with Montgomery's forces. Woodward had been on the foreign staff of the *News Chronicle* from 1936 until 1943, latterly as war correspondent in the Middle East. He knew the ropes. But Bone had read and disliked a book based on his messages because of the intrusive 'I' in the manner of popular, personalised journalism. He realised, of course, that Woodward might merely have been writing to order and Crozier decided that they had better try him. After a further talk Bone was relieved: 'He says he hates the first person singular and is anxious to study Montague's dispatches.'[4] The vacancy had been filled just in time. And well filled. Woodward was one of the three reporters who were landed in France from the air. His first story – the main news on 9 June – was headed by the editorial note 'He went by glider with a parachute unit. He was wounded, but not seriously, and is now in England.' The story he wrote was a first-class piece of descriptive writing. In some 1,800 words the first person singular only occurred four times. He did not get back to France until the end of July, but then he saw the campaign through to its final end.

But the British forces were now only 21 Army Group in Eisenhower's command. The interpretation of the whole struggle in the West had to come from his Supreme Headquarters which was, of course, at that time in London. Crozier died before the M.G. found anyone to be its military correspondent there. Bone was accredited but could not afford regularly to attend the twice daily conferences. He had a possible man in mind, but was not altogether satisfied. That was the position on the Friday night when Pringle dined with Bone. By Sunday Bone had heard with surprise that Wadsworth had 'someone in Manchester who was being groomed for a military correspondent.' His letter to Wadsworth suggests that he was not best pleased – he was always inclined to resist Manchester men being sent to London. 'If you wanted to supervise and counsel him wouldn't it be better,' he suggested, 'at any rate at first for you to have him in Manchester with the SCAEF reports from here in front of him?'[5] But that was not Wadsworth's idea at all. He had found the man he wanted and that was that. A fortnight before Crozier's death a letter had come from Captain J. R. L. Anderson, a pre-war Territorial serving in the Indian Army. He had contracted amoebic dysentery and been boarded out of the Army as medically unfit. He had been brought up in the West Indies, had spent three years in the *News Chronicle*'s Bristol office and eighteen months on a trade paper in Manchester. Wadsworth, as acting editor, took him on as a reporter. He liked the bustling enthusiasm and terrific drive of the moody young man with the gnarled face. He sent him to London as military correspondent when he had been only a month on the paper. A fortnight after D-Day Bone wrote to Wadsworth:

I must write to you about Anderson whose work in quality as well as in quantity is exactly what we have been lacking since the beginning of the war. Strange that it should come to us in this way . . . The only trouble is overzeal. He asked me yesterday whether we had anyone doing naval matters, as so much came up on that at SHAEF. Should he cover it? (He had about $2\frac{1}{2}$ columns in on Saturday.) Again, after a contortion or two in the chair, he asked could he do diplomatic subjects too? And the day before he said he had got himself accredited to the French for work in France where he would like to write on the settling down in the recovered country as it went on! Prodigious!'[6]

Anderson was to stay with the *Guardian* for the best part of a quarter of a century. He did not change. Military correspondent, Berlin correspondent, Labour correspondent, leader-writer, assistant editor, organiser and member of the Vinland expedition – prodigious! as Bone had said when it all started.

The present had been taken care of, but the future was threatening. How was the *Guardian* to manage in the post-war world which seemed so imminent in the euphoria of D-Day? The most pressing problem was its foreign service. This had largely disappeared. Pringle certainly, and Wadsworth probably, had decided that it would not be wise to bring Voigt back, even if he wanted to come, since his current views made him almost as unacceptable to the European Left as he still was to the Nazis. Werth was in Russia for the BBC. There had been a certain amount of friction with Crozier over his leaving the paper. Lambert had just given up the job of diplomatic correspondent and was off to the United States for the *Herald*. Dell was dead. There were many to give advice. Namier was still at hand. Mitrany was anxious to help. His friendship with Wadsworth was as close as his relations with Crozier had been cool. (Almost the first suggestion that Wadsworth made to Pringle was that he should get in touch with Mitrany.) But it was not advice but men who were needed. Crozier had already taken the first step. He had decided to put the diplomatic correspondence temporarily in commission between Max Wolf and Sylvia Sprigge. From 1929, when Cecil Sprigge left Rome for Berlin, Sylvia Saunders, as she then was, worked as a stringer for the M.G. in Rome until the financial crisis of 1931. Now she was to go back as a staff correspondent as soon as permission could be got, joining Cecil who would be there for Reuter. The double harness arrangement with Wolf concealed his inability to write English. Wadsworth soon realised that he would have to make a change.

The immediate problem was what to do about Paris. David Woodward covered the actual liberation admirably but, of course, the war swept him on. Anderson reached Paris at the end of September and for a time virtually doubled the rôles of military correspondent at SHAEF and French correspondent. But this, too, could only be temporary. Bone went to the BBC to see if their French service could suggest anybody. He put his question to Darsie Gillie who had been in charge since its beginning. 'Would I do?' he asked. Thus casually began more than twenty memorable years of work for the *Guardian*. He brought with him a long experience of Europe – Poland under Pilsudski, whose Memoirs he edited, Berlin, Paris and now of Europe in exile. He and some fourteen other Englishmen with about a hundred Frenchmen had staffed the BBC programme 'Les Français parlent aux Français.'

There he had worked closely with Jacques Duchesne, Michel de Saint Denis, Pierre Bourdon and Maurice Schumann. On 23 October 1944 he wrote about its end: 'Not all the members of the team were always in full agreement with De Gaulle's headquarters, and they may justly claim to have had a part in preventing the Gaullist movement from crystallising on too narrow lines.' A Paris correspondent for the *Guardian* in liberated Europe could have had no better preparation. A week later, still six months before VE-Day, he sent from Paris his first message as a member of the staff.

It was only half a year since Crozier's death. In that time there had been something like a silent revolution in the control of the paper which had passed, or was passing, from elderly men to men much younger. Wadsworth had already shown his hand. Laurence Scott had not, but he had come to certain conclusions.

2

'You can argue any way you like about the *Manchester Guardian*. Some people call it the greatest newspaper in the world. I have always called it the greatest viewspaper in the world. That is not a criticism of the *Manchester Guardian*, but that is exactly what the *Manchester Guardian* is. It is a paper that irritates one sometimes by the acuteness of its criticism. They know exactly where to hit and how to do it.' Brendan Bracken, Churchill's Minister of Information, was speaking to newspaper editors soon after Crozier's death. 'It is because Crozier stood always for allowing every side to state its case that I particularly mention him here to-day and say that his death is a sensible loss to our country.'

It was inevitable that readers of the *Guardian* with their highly developed political consciousness should judge the new editor by his views and by his sense of fair play. The first test came with the end of the war-time coalition and the general election of 1945. Between the Labour Party conference in May and polling day there were forty Long leaders. Eighteen dealt with the election. Fifteen were by Wadsworth. (The other three seem to be Hammond's.) For six and a half weeks Wadsworth wrote an election leader on three nights out of four since, in addition to these first leaders, he wrote a dozen supporting ones. Rollicking passages abound:

'So fantastic has the misuse of words become that we now find the *Daily Express* talking of "The National Socialists" (i.e. Labour) . . . Not only will the Labour people be "Communists," "Bolsheviks," "Socialists," but they will also be "Nazis." It is an odd world.' (7 June)

'The glass houses are many. Mr Churchill's alone rival Sir Joseph Paxton's in acreage.' (7 June)

'Why not a little healthy competition and free enterprise in electoral bribery? Let us remember: "There shall be in England seven half-penny loaves sold for a penny: the three-hooped pot shall have ten hoops; and I will make it a felony to drink small beer." Lord Beaverbrook's bright boys have still a little to learn in demagogy, but we need not despair; they have three weeks yet to go.' (12 June)

'Only someone with the matchless courage of the Prime Minister could describe the election campaign as "these piercing discussions into the roots of human society." ' (22 June)

It is clear that Wadsworth was enjoying himself. He was his own master now. There was no longer Crozier to restrain his pen (Crozier's diary records several tussles over its liveliness). He could let himself go with the same abandon that Montague had in 1909.* The two Beaverbrook passages are typical of several – Wadsworth's editorship was to be marked by a running duel with the *Evening Standard* and the *Daily Express* (enjoyable, one imagines, to both sides) which recalls Montague's protracted controversies with the *Morning Post*. The perceptible difference in tone is due partly to the lighter manner of the second half of the century and partly to a temperamental difference between the writers. Montague, who was not a 'clubable' man with his friends, could hardly be on familiar terms with his opponents. Wadsworth revelled in 'knowing where to hit and how to do it.' But at least against citizens of the Free World his foil was buttoned and he saw no reason why antagonists should not relax together.

But if Wadsworth enjoyed his electioneering he was serious about the issues. He blamed the Conservative machine for selfishly trying to capitalise the country's gratitude to Churchill, and, as the campaign progressed, he blamed Churchill himself for turning it into 'a personal plebiscite' – 'one wonders whether Mr Churchill's mind runs back to what Lord Randolph Churchill said of such a thing in a very famous election address . . . "a political expedient borrowed from the last and worst days of the Second Empire".'† He was indignant at eve-of-the-poll scaremongering. Churchill had claimed that, if Attlee won the election, he would have to take orders from Professor Harold Laski as chairman of the National Executive of the Labour Party. Wadsworth called his leader 'The Red Letter' in recollection of the Zinoviev Letter

* See pp. 324, 326.
† Lord Randolph Churchill's reference was to Gladstone's Midlothian campaign.

in the 1924 election. 'Our friends abroad,' he wrote, 'must be rubbing their eyes when they see their hero forgetting all about the Japanese War, all about tortured Europe, all about his Four-Year Plan, and exercising all his magnificent gifts on a trumpery exercise in political falsification. It is a pathetic descent.'[7] Papers were still small because of paper rationing. On the eve of the poll the *Daily Herald* had only four pages and the *News Chronicle* six. But the *Herald* reproduced the whole leader and the *News Chronicle* the first half.

In this leader, as in all but two of the series, Wadsworth had written for both parties of the Left, not distinguishing between Liberals and Labour. But it was, of course, a distinction he could not entirely avoid. The M.G. had been a Liberal paper from the beginning. For fifty years it had been on the radical left of the party, but it had never become Labour. It had gone as far in 1931 as to encourage Liberals to vote Labour in constituencies where the officially Liberal candidate was in Ted Scott's eye no true Liberal; but that was all. In seats where both Liberal and Labour candidates were sound Free Traders the *Guardian* advised voters to back the Liberals. It did the same in 1935. Wadsworth was the first editor of the *Guardian* who was not a member of the Liberal Party. His position was delicate.

He began a leader on 'The Nominations' with a sympathetic account of the revival of Liberalism indicated by the increased number of candidates – men and women who knew little, and cared little about the contested leadership of pre-war days, 'the shedding of time-servers and place hunters who had moved under the Conservative umbrella and the frustration that had followed defeat.' He recognised that these younger men found in the party something which better than the other parties satisfied their desire for bold reform combined with freedom and personal initiative. 'The Labour party can reflect,' he continues, 'that this revival of Liberalism is a sign of Labour's failure to exploit its opportunities, to broaden from a sectional into a national party.' But then he turned aside to consider the national danger threatened by an overwhelming Conservative majority. 'Mr Churchill fears that a small Conservative majority would mean weakness. On the contrary it is, short of Conservative defeat, the only tolerable thing that could happen.'[8] But he did not tell electors how their votes could secure either a 'tolerable' or the desirable result in constituencies where there were three candidates.

He never did. And, if he had, he would have told them wrong. For A.P., one of the shrewdest of political observers, made a serious misjudgment. He thought that Liberals might win many seats which Labour never could so that 'Liberal successes are an essential means of averting the great danger of an overwhelming Conservative majority like that of 1918, of 1922, of 1924, of 1931, of 1935.' He was convinced that 'the chances of Labour sweeping the country and obtaining a clear majority over all other parties are pretty remote,' but he believed that 'if the votes are cast wisely there is at least the chance of a Liberal-Labour majority, the most fruitful kind of Coalition in these times.'[9] With this end in view his last election leader tried to persuade floating voters to vote Labour in those constituencies, about half the total, where there was no Liberal candidate. He clearly thought they would be reluctant to do so. He gave no direct advice in triangular contests though he implied that the best way to get the Conservatives out would often be to vote Liberal. His misjudgment of Labour's chances enabled him to take a line which did not differ widely from what the *Guardian* had been saying for a good many years. Had he been a better prophet, he would have had a harder decision to make. But he must have been relieved to get this letter from Hammond soon after polling day but before the declaration: 'We went out to lunch with J.R.S. on Saturday and found him very enthusiastic over your Election leaders . . . You must have proved even to your own doubting self that you are *"capax imperii"*.'[10]

Newspapers often have to eat their words – rarely about what has happened, but frequently about what will happen. It is an unavoidable trade risk from which the *Guardian* was no more immune than any other paper. Fortunately public memory is short and most mistakes are soon forgotten. But Wadsworth must have been glad that in 1945 there was a gap of three weeks between polling and counting. 'Britain has undergone a silent revolution,' he wrote as the news of one Labour success after another came in.

'Few suspected it. Hardly a politician from one end of the country to another had ventured to forecast what happened at the polls. The people kept their secret. Yet, throughout the country, in country no less than in town they swung to the Left. And when they voted Left they meant it. They had no use for the middle-of-the-road Liberals; they voted Labour and they knew what they were voting for . . . We enter into a new political world, and though we (and the Labour leaders too) may shudder just a little at the thought of what is ahead, we enter it with confidence. Many bad things have been made an end of. It is the kind of Progressive opportunity that comes only once in every few generations – in 1832, in 1868, in 1885, in 1906.'

Wadsworth was both delighted and generous. 'The country,' he wrote, 'will part with Mr Churchill with many regrets. After all, he is the greatest Prime Minister we have known since Gladstone and the greatest national leader since Pitt. But he has been the symbol of an attitude of mind against which the world has turned.' It was harder to find the right words to describe the fate of the Liberal party. What he wrote was this:

'The submergence of the Liberal party is a disappointment . . . Its 300 candidates made a brave show, but it cannot be said that the electorate in general bestowed much encouragement on the idea of a revived Liberal party. Given Proportional Representation, the party would still have a future, but it is obvious that under the present system its hopes must be slender.' (27 July 1945)

Some older members of the staff who had always been Liberals naturally took the news more hardly than did Wadsworth who had never been one. In the London Office Bone read Wadsworth's leader as it came over the wire – the text was sent so that it could be distributed to other papers who might want to quote it. Bone wrote Wadsworth a letter – the only one in the whole long series which begins 'Dear Editor':

'I was much bewildered and distressed as the results came out to-day. Distressed because the party I had believed in since the Boer War, when politics first had a meaning for me, ended to-day.
Your leader opened new doors and as I thought and felt about it I found I could shake off much I thought mattered. But why I'm writing to you is that I'm proud that the M.G. produces such a leader at such a time. I'm glad I can feel its thrill.'*

The 1945 election ended the official link between the editor of the *Manchester Guardian* and the Liberal Party. It did not diminish the paper's liberalism. Nor did it lead to an official link with the Labour Party. Circumstances made the paper officially what it had long been in practice, an independent journal of the Left with 'the Radical temper that one likes to think is natural to her,' if one may apply to the paper words that its editor wrote that Thursday night about the country. The M.G. did not, of course, formally dissociate itself from the Liberal Party – that would have been bad business and bad politics. But it let certain connections drop. In 1947 the treasurer of the Manchester Liberal Federation wrote to Wadsworth about the tradition that the Editor of the *Manchester Guardian* should be a member of the Federation

* Bone–Wadsworth 26 July 1945. Bone's 'Dear Editor' reminds one of Wadsworth's 'Cher Maître' to Tawney in 1924 – signposts to a state of mind.

and said it had struck him that this tradition had been broken in the last few years. Would Wadsworth revive it? He replied:

You can be assured that the *Manchester Guardian* will always do the utmost in its power to uphold Liberal principles and to further the Liberal cause. I feel, however, that, in the best interests of the paper in the present state of national affairs, I should not formally accept membership of any political organisation. Any help I can give to Liberalism, nationally and locally, I shall, of course, continue to give gladly, provided that it is without formal ties.'[11]

The draft went to John Scott with the characteristic note, 'Is this too straightforward an answer?' At least Wadsworth used a capital 'L', even if he avoided the word 'party.' In 1948 he refused on the same grounds an invitation to join a national fund-raising committee and in 1949 to attend a dinner of Liberal journalists to meet the Party leader. In 1956 he revised the entry on the *Manchester Guardian* for a new edition of *Everyman's Encyclopaedia* to read 'Since the decline of the Liberal party it has been independent progressive.'

3

'Very sorry. I cannot undertake whirlwind tour. Have had enough whirlwinds for a little while.' With these words Harry Boardman unwittingly put himself out of one job and into another. Wadsworth had decided that Boardman, who had been the M.G.'s Lobby correspondent for fifteen years, should accompany Churchill on his triumphal progress through the country – and it was a personal triumph as truly as the election result was to be a personal defeat. Boardman would have done the tour superbly well, but one is glad that he was recalcitrant. Reporting his refusal to Bone, Wadsworth went on 'I shall not say anything more to him at the moment, but I think it gives us very good grounds for asking him to take the House and give up the Political job. A Political Correspondent who cannot go on a tour with the Prime Minister is not much use.'[12]

The wording makes it clear that the idea was already in Wadsworth's mind. It may seem odd that an editor should feel the need to find grounds such as this for rearranging his staff. But Wadsworth and Boardman had entered the reporters' room within two years of one another and they had served together during the Irish troubles, which *Guardian* reporters looked back on as the heroic age of the Room. The difficulty was that the Lobby, or political correspondent's job, had ranked higher than the Gallery, or parliamentary correspondent's, in the *Guardian* hierarchy. Atkins and Gretton had doubled the London editorship with the Lobby. When Bone became London editor, the Lobby had gone to G. H. Mair who had been paid more than Bone himself.

The last thing Wadsworth wanted was to hurt Boardman's feelings. The move was indeed a positive as well as a negative decision. Boardman belonged to the generation and group of *Guardian* men who thought of themselves essentially as writers. The Gallery job gave better scope for this than the Lobby. During the pre-war years Boardman, consciously or unconsciously, had often strayed deep into no man's land or even across the frontier which separates the two functions.* During the war, apart from the interval between Dunkirk and the North African landings when Evelyn Montague wrote the sketch, Boardman had doubled both jobs. Now the Gallery man, Francis Boyd, would soon be out of the army and they could change over.

But it is doubtful whether Wadsworth would have brought himself to propose it but for Boardman's refusal to accompany Churchill. As it was he took his time. He waited until the new House had met. After all, Francis Boyd was not yet back. Boardman would have to carry on both jobs for a little. When Wadsworth put it to Boardman he could, and no doubt did, wrap it up with compliments on his handling of the silent revolution in the House. 'Wrap it up' – the phrase is quite out of place. 'Give Boardman his chance' would be more like it. It would have been negligence to deny the M.G. more passages such as this on the election of the Speaker. The Tories had greeted Churchill with 'For he's a jolly good fellow,' sung well and in unison. 'But this in the House of Commons!' Labour had then sung two verses of the 'Red Flag.'

' "I wondered a moment ago," said Colonel Clifton Brown later, "whether I was going to be elected Speaker of the House or director of a musical show." In this merry English fashion was the curtain rung up on the new Parliament . . .

Mr Churchill drew the eyes of all the Labour newcomers when he rose to deliver a few firm sentences in congratulation to the Speaker . . . He did not get very much beyond conventional phrases, but his voice was strong as ever. The new Labour men should have known the giant when he "held the heavens suspended."

One will hazard the assertion that many of the old Labour members found it hard not to cheer in retrospective gratitude. Were they not the men

* An example of this is provided by the debate on the Hoare–Laval Pact. See p. 523.

who cheered him in the blackness of 1940 when the Tories were silent?'
(2 August 1945)

Four days later Wadsworth wrote to Bone: 'The trick has worked.
I have a note from Boardman to say that he agrees with the proposal,
which he describes as "congenial work," so the way is clear.'* Boardman continued as the *Guardian*'s Gallery man until his death in 1958. He
had the great gift of conveying both the atmosphere of a debate and
the content of the argument. His sketches provide perhaps the clearest
contemporary evidence of the effect of what was said in Parliament on
the House itself during a period of great and revolutionary change.
In this way they form a lasting supplement to Hansard. Like
James Drysdale he worked to the last. Drysdale died in the Gallery
as he finished the last slip of his copy, Boardman died correcting a
proof.

Bone was at his country cottage in Surrey when he got Wadsworth's
letter about Boardman. His reply began 'First letter to you in the
Atomic Era. What a first-rate leader yesterday.'[13] This was one of two
leaders, written on successive days, by Walter James. The fact that
Wadsworth was willing to allow one of his younger men to write on a
topic of such overwhelming importance is characteristic of the style of
his editorship. There was no careful conference to form a collective
opinion or to determine the paper's line. The writer was expected to
sense what his editor was thinking just as the editor inferred from his
previous knowledge of the leader writer what his line would probably
be. At the most these mutual impressions would be checked by a quick
word, but A.P., like his predecessors, felt that in selecting the writer
he had in fact indicated the paper's line.

Both Crozier and Wadsworth had been 'hard-liners' during the
war. Walter James's first leader showed no moral hesitation. 'In spite of
the horror that must be kindled in all hearts,' he wrote, 'by the very
thought of such a weapon being turned against the human species, its
use against the Japanese is entirely legitimate. It is illogical to judge the
morality of bombing by the size of the bomb used.' If we had not
developed and used it, the Germans would soon have been ready with
one. 'No race was ever more worth winning, and the wisdom of Mr
Churchill and Mr Roosevelt . . . is something to be ever remembered
with gratitude by this country and the United States, and, indeed, by
the world.' James went on to consider briefly the problem of control

* Wadsworth–Bone 6 August 1945. Francis Boyd collected some of Boardman's
work under a title which would have pleased him: *The Glory of Parliament* (Allen
and Unwin 1960).

to which he returned more fully in his second leader. 'Never has man handled a sharper-edged tool. Already one may see the first reaction to the new challenge in the simple division into optimists and pessimists – into those who see in atomic energy the end of war and those who see in it the end of man.' He recognised that the rest of the world, and especially Russia, would never accept a monopoly of 'this shattering power' by America and Britain. The Security Council, based on the sovereign independence of the Great Powers, was 'far from impressive' as an organ of international control. 'The natural consequence of sticking to the present conception of the Security Council would be for each Great Power to maintain its own atomic bomb plants . . . Such an arrangement would invite some final calamity.' James saw us drawn inexorably to some form of world authority.[14] It was perhaps a more plausible forecast than the sustained balance of terror which has actually resulted.

As the summer of 1945 turned to autumn Bone and Wadsworth felt happier about the future of the London office. Just before Bank Holiday Evelyn Montague had written to Wadsworth, 'About my health, I think you can take it as certain that I shall be all right from the end of September; my specialist was completely definite about it, and he is a cautious man – and has had TB himself.'[15] Montague was already working part-time in the London Office and nothing happened that autumn to interfere with the plans that were being made for Bone to retire and hand over to Montague as London editor. This accordingly took place at the New Year.

Bone remained a director for some time and continued to take the closest interest in the paper and above all in 'his' London Letter – 'a model of its kind, often imitated, never excelled, even in Shoe Lane, where the milking pails are brought out daily,' as Wadsworth put it in a farewell speech. J.B. in his retirement continued to be, to quote Wadsworth again, 'the adopted citizen of Baltimore and the magnet for American visitors.'* He became a Companion of Honour in 1947. He lived to see the London printing of the *Guardian* and attended a dinner to mark its start. On his ninetieth birthday there was a small party with messages from Harold Macmillan, Hugh Gaitskell, Jo Grimond, the Queen and President Kennedy. There has never been a more devoted *Guardian* man. More than others, perhaps, he loved it not so much for its views as for itself.

No one man could long do all that Bone had latterly been doing. The position in the London office must at least be restored to its pre-war

* 25 January 1946. Shoe Lane: where the office of the *Evening Standard* is.

state when Evelyn Montague had been Bone's deputy. The right deputy for Montague was found by Wadsworth in Gerard Fay, a young man who had become a *Guardian* reporter in Manchester in April, 1939. In 1940 he had gone into the army, was seriously wounded in July 1944 and invalided out in the spring of 1945. As far as the paper was concerned, he was almost a new hand. He had come up a hard, but by no means the worst way for a journalist to whom no human experience is trash. He had been born in Rochdale, like Leach and Wadsworth. His father and his uncle were responsible with Lady Gregory, Yeats and George Russell for getting the Abbey Theatre, Dublin established. As a child actor he appeared on its stage. It was in Dublin that Gerard Fay went too briefly to school and there that he first met the M.G. which his father took solely for its dramatic criticism. Fay's first job was with a Dublin bookmaker; he moved to a Manchester hire purchase business and then to a Lancashire engineering firm. He acted and produced plays for the Curtain Theatre, Rochdale and in 1935 he persuaded the *Rochdale Observer* to let him write a weekly column on 'The Amateur Stage.' Not long before the war Arthur Wallace began to invite him to do occasional notices for the M.G. Wadsworth and Montague thought that this young man, who still hobbled about on two sticks, was the kind of man who could take up many sides of Bone's work. They were right.

There was still a lack of relatively senior men on the Corridor in Manchester. Wadsworth decided to bring back a former member of the staff. Patrick Monkhouse, A.N.M.'s son, had gone to the *Evening Standard* in 1936 partly because he wanted to widen his experience and partly because Crozier, who had made him news editor, proved unwilling to let it mean much. The war had taken Monkhouse to the Middle East and finally put him in charge of Forces newspapers in that theatre. He came back to the M.G. as news editor and a little later became an assistant editor. Wadsworth had secured in Pringle and Monkhouse two men to whom he could safely delegate responsibility, old enough to have their roots in the M.G. past, young enough to have been in the war and to know what the silent revolution had been about. At last Wadsworth's long period of overwork was at an end. Looking back, Pringle wrote 'I may say it very nearly broke him. His health was very bad in the winter of 1944/45, and only slowly improved. He was often ill and at one time I was seriously alarmed.'[16]

Still, by 1946 Wadsworth had got together both in London and Manchester a staff greatly to his liking. It looked as if the main jobs were settled for some years to come. It was not so. Evelyn Montague's hopes proved vain as so often happens with tuberculosis. Before the end of the year he had to resign. John Beavan, the editor of the *Manchester Evening News*, took his place.

'It's a bit 'ard, guv'nor,' had been Montague's only complaint when he was invalided back from Italy and heard that he must spend three months in bed.[17] He faced what was to come with the same uncomplaining courage. Death kept him waiting until February 1948.

CHAPTER THIRTY-SIX

One World: Divided

I

WADSWORTH'S career ran nearly parallel to Ernest Bevin's. Between the wars Wadsworth, the *Guardian*'s Labour correspondent, had had many dealings with Bevin, the trade union leader. During the war Wadsworth had been responsible for the M.G.'s policy on the vital issue of the use of man-power. He had come to place Bevin as second only to Churchill among the men who saved Britain. As editor, Wadsworth had to turn his attention to what, with the exception of the United States, was virtually a new field to him – foreign politics. For the first five years after victory in Europe Bevin was Foreign Secretary. The two men, journalist and politician, had this in common. They had been brought up in and about the Labour movement and on its trade union side. Bevin was never a real House of Commons man. Similarly Wadsworth knew all, or virtually all, the senior members of Attlee's government, but it was at Union conferences, the TUC or the Labour Party Conference that he had got to know them. Both he and Bevin knew more about Communists than could be learned at Westminster. What they knew stood them in good stead in the disappointing peace. These two amateurs in foreign policy were in some ways better equipped to understand what was happening in Europe than many a career diplomat or foreign correspondent.

One of the ways in which an editor, and especially the editor of the M.G., determined his paper's policy was by writing leaders himself. In the first three years of peace, 1946, 1947, and 1948, Wadsworth wrote nearly a quarter of the first leaders – roughly the same proportion each year. Sixty per cent of them dealt with foreign affairs. Ten per cent of his foreign leaders had Bevin's name in the title. During the same period Wadsworth also wrote frequently on home affairs. Only one other Cabinet Minister's name appeared in the title of any of his first leaders, and that only once. 'Mr Attlee's Task' was a leader on the coal crisis of 1947. It was sandwiched between 'Mr Bevin' and 'Mr Bevin's Triumph.' Wadsworth's admiration for Bevin was genuine but it was not undiscriminating. 'Mr Bevin's Triumph' was followed by

'In the Wrong' – 'Our policy in Palestine is, there is reason to fear, Mr Bevin's personal policy, and Mr Bevin is an obstinate man. But our national credit matters more than Mr Bevin's obsessions.'[1] Wadsworth's policy, though Palestine was not a subject on which he often wrote at this time, was the traditional M.G. policy. To his thinking, Bevin was here utterly in the wrong. More commonly his criticism was that Bevin moved too slowly in the right direction. He thought that Bevin might have hastened total mobilisation during the war. He was certain that he should have responded sooner to the need for free institutions in Western Germany. But he recognised Bevin's rapid response to the first whisper of the Marshall Plan as 'a stroke of genius,' a word he could rarely bring himself to use.

'In the Wrong' was the first leader but it was not in the traditional *Guardian* three paragraph form. In the war years Crozier had occasionally put a short leader first, but Wadsworth carried the practice much further. He quite often gave pride of place to a two-paragraph or a one-paragraph leader. This might, but need not, be followed by a three-paragraph one. When it was, it is a pretty clear indication that the three-paragraph leader had been intended to take first place, but that something more important had come up in the night's news. With the much earlier edition times that were now necessary, it was not uncommon for important news to arrive too late for full-dress treatment, but in time for a short 'first leader.' A.P. liked to be quick in comment. He also valued the flexibility that this licence gave. There might be one or two important points to make on a subject, but not three. This should be recognised in the form of the leader. Moreover, this new flexibility enabled him to write the chief leader himself more frequently than he could otherwise have done as editor. The practice grew on him. Two-thirds of his own first leaders were three-paragraph ones in 1946, half in 1947 and only 37 per cent in 1948. The kind of revolution that Wadsworth favoured in journalism (and changing the pattern of leaders was little less) was the unobtrusive kind that grows unnoticed. In politics, too, he liked to look back and notice how far we had come rather than to take a running jump.

2

Not since the fall of Napoleon had there been such a clean sweep of European Governments. It was this that turned Wadsworth into a prolific foreign leader-writer, though even so he shared the work with others, especially with Pringle in the early years. It also made it necessary not only to restore but to extend the *Guardian*'s own foreign service.

Fortunately it was possible to do so. After the terrifying losses of the thirties, the M.G. had begun to make profits once again. They were small, but increasing. The *Manchester Evening News* was making large ones. It was possible for Wadsworth to choose between undertaking this or that new expenditure whereas Crozier before the war had only been able to choose between making this or that cut.

Wadsworth's growing attention to foreign affairs can be indicated in various ways. He spent much more money on foreign news than Crozier, a career foreign editor, had been able to do. By 1950 it cost the M.G. four times as much as it had done in the year before Munich. Partly, of course, this was because everything cost more than in pre-war days. Increased expenditure might only have meant not letting things get worse. In fact it meant a bigger share of the budget. Twenty years before – in the last year before the 1931 crisis – the *Guardian's* foreign service had accounted for not much over a tenth of the total editorial costs; in 1950–51 the corresponding figure was nearly a quarter.* But again this increased share was partly caused by the way the exchanges had moved against us. Convertibility of sterling had been suspended in 1947 and Stafford Cripps was forced to devalue in 1949.

The *Guardian* was both buying and selling foreign news. It bought foreign news in three ways: from its own staff correspondents, 'stringers,' and contributors; from the agencies, of which the two principal were Reuter's and the United Press; and from other newspapers. In practice, at this period this meant from the *Times*. News from this last source was published with the attribution '*Times* and *Manchester Guardian* Service.' It cost the M.G. £5,200 a year at the end of the war and £2,600 in 1947, which was about the cost of the *Guardian's* own Paris service. The arrangement with the *Times* ended in 1948. Readers of the *Guardian* in 1971 will notice that a good deal of foreign news is attributed in a similar way and under a similar arrangement to the *Washington Post* and the *Los Angeles Times*. But these are foreign newspapers which do not compete with the *Guardian* for readers. Nor, except to a small extent, did the *Times* in 1946.

The *Guardian* sold news not only to its own readers but to other newspapers. Without this the expansion of its own foreign news service would have been severely limited. Some of the news sold was English news, but the great bulk was foreign. The most important customer was the *Glasgow Herald* which had a roughly similar though less 'advanced' political outlook and, of course, a totally different group of readers. In 1950–51 it was buying the *Guardian's* American, French and

* In both cases the cost of foreign sub-editing and leader-writing are excluded. In 1950 there was also a diplomatic correspondent whose salary is excluded.

German correspondence, contributing about a third of their combined cost. Three years before it had also been buying the M.G.'s Moscow service. There was nothing new about the system – similar arrangements had been made in the nineteenth century, usually for covering wars. One of the most successful had been during the First World War when H. W. Nevinson had covered the Gallipoli campaign for a consortium of regional newspapers headed by the M.G. With the whole of England and Wales and to some extent Scotland becoming one common newspaper market, even for 'quality' papers, there is now less room for such co-operation.

Within the increased total expenditure there were significant variations in the proportion spent under various heads. More staff men meant fewer outside contributors and 'stringers.' In 1937–38 30 per cent of the total foreign budget went on this source; ten years later it was only 8 per cent. There had not only been a relative but a small absolute decline in the amount spent. It was money prudently spent. Included in the total for 1947–48, for instance, were modest payments to Philips Price for a series of articles on what until 1939 would have been called the Near East. Philips Price was now a Labour member of parliament. When the House was not sitting he travelled extensively in the Balkans and through the Persian and Turkish borderlands of Russia as he had first done before the 1914 war, describing his journeys in the paper. Wadsworth repeated the invitation which C.P. had given him in 1913. In this way at very little expense to the paper the *Guardian* kept its readers well informed about a sensitive area in world affairs of which few had first-hand knowledge. Certainly the M.G. could never have afforded to send a staff man on such journeys.[2]

Comparisons based on expenditure can be misleading because of the changing value of money and of relative costs. The best measure, perhaps, of the value which Wadsworth put upon foreign news is a negative one which his tortuous mind would have enjoyed. During one of the repeated newsprint crises of the nineteen-forties Wadsworth worked out a comparison between the pre-war and the post-war *Guardian*. In 1948 the total space available for news and comment was less than a third (30 per cent) of the 1938 allowance. But foreign news got nearly two-thirds (65 per cent) of its pre-war amount, home politics only half.

3

News from the Caspian brought by Philips Price might seem an extravagance for a relatively poor paper, if one did not know how little it cost. News from India, one would think, was a necessity. But, in spite of the fact that Lancashire's trade with India had been so important, the *Guardian* had never had a good Indian news service apart from certain special occasions such as Vaughan Nash's investigation into the Great Famine. It was not that the paper ignored India. It commented frequently and in a progressive sense which satisfied Indian Liberals who did not, of course, rely on the paper for their home news. But its Indian news ought not to have satisfied the *Guardian*, and no doubt would not have done but for the need for economy. It left its readers in a position where they too often had to take its views on trust because they were not given the often considerable evidence on which they were based. M.G. readers, unless they took other papers as well, were not really free to make up their own minds.

When Wadsworth became editor the paper's main Indian expert was J. T. Gwynn who was also, oddly enough, its principal contributor on Ireland where he lived and, among other things, kept a preparatory school. He had retired from the I.C.S. twenty-two years before and begun to work for the M.G. He was a sensible man, well informed, level-headed, greatly liked but seriously deaf. It was necessary to look ahead to the time when there would be no Gwynn.

In India Shiva Rao had been a contributor to the paper since before the war, and Crozier had agreed that the regularity and quality of his work entitled him to the style of 'our correspondent' which he desired. His messages throughout the period when independence was being negotiated and partition established were well informed. His private memoranda to Wadsworth sometimes influenced him considerably and led him slightly to change the direction of the paper's policy. The M.G., for instance, had been inclined to support the natural desire of the Dutch to recover their East Indian possessions when the Japanese were driven out. But Wadsworth changed course after Shiva Rao wrote to him, 'I do not think anyone outside India can realise the indirect but powerful effect of the struggle in Indonesia on the national movement in this country . . . There is not a single element in Indian public life on whose support the British Government can rely. Most of the Congress leaders are speaking in terms of a renewed struggle and Nehru has frequently used the term revolution in this connection.'[3]

But Shiva Rao's good work was far from the equivalent of what a staff man could have done for the paper. The cost of a man in India would have been less than that of a man in New York, little more perhaps than that of a man in Paris. But instead of appointing his own man Wadsworth preferred to rely on the *Times* service up to the murder of Gandhi and its aftermath.

Wadsworth also needed first-class help in England over Indian affairs during this difficult time. Fortunately Fry, the City editor, had many influential Indian friends. In the years before independence he himself wrote a good many of the leaders on India. And there was still Gwynn. Soon there was also to be Guy Wint.

Wint had a considerable reputation as an Orientalist when he and Wadsworth first met in the summer of 1947. He had spent fifteen years working in India, China, Malaya and Singapore. He had collaborated with the Finance Member of the Viceroy's Council in a book.[4] He was also a man who inspired young Indian writers and scholars: 'He nagged us to work; he found us patrons and publishers; he gave us praise when others turned their backs on us. He was our friend and our Guru,' as one of them wrote when he died.[5]

Wint came to Manchester, met Wadsworth and wrote, then and there, an article for the paper. Next day they exchanged letters. Wint told Wadsworth how extraordinarily pleasant it had been to discover 'the human element behind the monument of the *Manchester Guardian* which one had revered for so many years' – he was only 35. Wadsworth told him what had happened to his article:

'For your amusement I send you a copy of the leader page in the first two editions. Your manuscript was really a godsend because the leader I had expected from Gwynn did not turn up in time so I adopted your text. When Gwynn's stuff did come in I found that he had a reference to Gandhi which seemed to be useful so I tacked it on to the end. That is how newspapers are produced.'[6]

Certainly someone nearer at hand than Gwynn was needed. Certainly Wint had the knowledge to take his place. He and the editor were almost at once on intimate terms. Travelling to Germany in civilian clothes that December, Wint was taken off a troop train and put in a cage marked 'Deserters.' Wadsworth wrote to him 'I have just had a letter from Freda in which she gives me the good news that you have been put in a cage. You will have more sympathy than ever with cats after that!'* An affection for cats was always a talking point with Wadsworth. Wint at once became a frequent contributor. On the day of Gandhi's murder he wrote:

'While his western opponents were conscious that he was not in all respects as saintly as his own supporters believed . . . they felt that he was enough of a

* Wadsworth–Wint 8 December 1947. Cats have had an affinity with many M.G. men. There were, for instance, the cat which sat on Montague's shoulders while he wrote leaders, and Bone's cat, Potiphar, which appeared in many London Letter paragraphs.

This drawing by Francis Dodd marks a peak in *Guardian* illustration. Scott, Montague and Monkhouse shared an intense admiration for Meredith's work

In the 1920s Sylvia Baker made many animal drawings for the *Guardian*

Manchester United won the Cup
in 1909

1919

saint to be given a saint's privileges. And this prevented, tenuously and precariously enough at times, a sheer violent clash of the forces of nationalism and imperialism. Now imperialism has gone. Gandhi has not long survived it, and the stage is vacant for new events and new leaders.' (31 January 1948)

Wint joined the staff towards the end of 1948 and wrote crisply, knowledgeably and shrewdly about the new events and new leaders in India and the Far East. But Wadsworth had only half solved his problem. He had persuaded Wint not to settle on a Cumberland farm, but after a time he allowed him to live at Hartland Abbey. As Philip Mason remarked 'Even (the *Guardian*), with its deserved reputation for tolerance of eccentric writers, must have found it a little out of the ordinary to have a leader-writer living on a remote clifftop in Devon, four miles from the nearest telephone.'[7]

4

Wadsworth's most important foreign development was the establishment for the first time of an American service of which the *Guardian* could be proud. By 1950 he spent on it alone more than the whole cost of the M.G.'s foreign service in 1930. Cables from America in 1950 came to nearly half the total foreign service bill in 1938. It was indeed the high cost of transmitting news across the Atlantic which had for so long condemned the paper to an American service of which the best that could be said was that it would have done credit to a political weekly. It had been served, and still was, by some of the best American journalists – Walter Lippmann at the end of the First World War; then by Arthur Krock of the *New York World* and since 1927 by Bruce Bliven, editor of the *New Republic*. But they were busy men. The paper could not expect overmuch for the £500 it paid Bliven, especially when he was asked to cable as little as possible. Visiting journalists also helped to give the M.G.'s American service a distinction which made English readers wish for more. For many years S. K. Ratcliffe was a regular occasional contributor, James Bone from time to time proved that he understood American life as well as he understood English, and American politics a good deal better. Denis Brogan was travelling backwards and forwards for the paper at the point in the *Guardian*'s history at which we have now arrived.

While England was undergoing its silent revolution the United Nations were meeting in San Francisco. Bruce Bliven was there. So was Alistair Cooke who helped him with his M.G. work. The process of forming the United Nations Organisation was lengthy; the *New Republic* needed its editor. Cooke took over the whole of the M.G. work. From the start his work was realistic: 'Russia insisted on the veto – reputable and well-documented proof that of Europe's Big Three Russia alone has launched a thorough policy of unilateral security that admits only a passing nod to the principles (of collective security) being established at San Francisco.'[8] A month later the Charter was finally approved. This did not happen without a protest on the day itself from Mr Gromyko about the wording of a committee report: 'He pronounced with unambiguous firmness the words "The Union of Soviet Socialist Republics can in no way agree to this." He walked doggedly from the rostrum through a silence that was heavy with embarrassment, fear and curiosity, a silence that spoke more honestly of the conference feeling towards Russia than any conscious fear the delegates would be at pains to deny . . . (Still at) seven minutes before 11 o'clock on 25 June, the Allied Nations had once again taken the pledge, made 300 years ago in the preamble to the Treaty of Westphalia, to ban war from all their dealings and live together "in all peace and neighbourliness".' John Pringle's leader caught the same anxious note: ' "We, the peoples," as the preamble begins so grandly, are ready and willing, but, as it sadly ends, it is "our respective Governments" which must make it work. In this country we at least are fortunate in being able to choose our Government.'[9]

The following March Cooke came to Manchester. Wadsworth, the devotedly Rochdale man, took Cooke, the man from Blackpool where Rochdale spends its holidays, to lunch at the Midland Hotel. It was a long lunch. A.P. was invariably inquisitive and especially so about the United States. He had never been there though he had been writing most of the leaders about American affairs since the early days of the New Deal. He had made up his mind that he must put New York on the same footing as Paris as far as the *Guardian* was concerned. He was making up his mind that Cooke was the man he needed. His background was right: a Lancashire Grammar school, a First in English at Cambridge, several years dealing with America first for the *Times* and then for the *Daily Herald*. His temperament fitted: an observer rather than a campaigner, neither didactic nor interfering but a man who gave his readers the sense of attending 'theatre in the round.' He enjoyed most of the pleasant things in life from politics to golf. His work in the *Guardian* during the past year had showed that he had 'an eye, an ear, a mind that hustles into place the significant detail,'[10] as John Rosselli put it. Before lunch was over Wadsworth scratched his nose with his pipe and tentatively ventured 'Well, I'm afraid that in the end we shall have to have a full-time man in New York.'

Cooke became that man. Through his writing *Guardian* readers have become familiar with the States – most, if not all of them – and with American life outside the diplomatic set. Two anecdotes illustrate both the range of Cooke's reporting and why men liked working for Wadsworth. In 1951 Cooke was in California describing a hydro-electric scheme for the Central Valley. Randolph Turpin, 'the first British boxer in the USA for a long time who could remain vertical,' was due to fight in New York. Cooke wanted to stay in the West; Wadsworth cabled 'Return New York blood thicker than water.' The other incident had taken place two years before. Cooke and Fry, the *Guardian*'s City editor, were jointly covering the critical conference in Washington after Cripps had devalued the pound. Roger Makins, then the British Minister at Washington, complained to Fry. Cooke, he said, had let the side down by sympathetically reporting American concern about the suffering that would occur in single-crop regions of the West if the British dollar drive was as successful as we hoped. Fry and Cooke passed on the complaint. Next morning Cooke was wakened by a cable from Wadsworth: 'Tell Makins Cooke's job is to let the side down.'

5

It is one of the oddities of a foreign correspondent's life that he knows his rivals much better than his colleagues. Alistair Cooke and Darsie Gillie started work for the *Guardian* about the same time and served it for twenty years together. They have never met. Both have an infectious zest for life and a gift for making their readers feel that for the time being they are honorary naturalised Frenchmen or Americans. Both are, so to speak, commentators at the match, not players in it as Dell and Voigt had been. Both had worked for the *Times* before they came to the *Guardian*. Both, one may say, were natural *Guardian* men, happy in working for the most non-directive paper in the world under its most non-directive editor. Gillie compared it with his original paper, the *Morning Post*, which 'used to ask you for what it wanted. A.P.W. left you alone; never praised or criticised; but somehow you knew you were doing well.' Forty years before, Harold Williams, who moved in the other direction, from the *Guardian* to the *Morning Post*, had found the same contrast.

There is, perhaps, point as well as amusement, in setting a *Guardian* leader on Cooke's thousandth 'Letter from America' to the BBC side by side with a passage on Gillie from Thomas Barman's 'Diplomatic

Correspondent.' They could almost be describing the same man. They are describing a special quality in many *Guardian* men, a quality which imposes a heavy burden on sub-editors, the faceless men on whom newspapers depend more than ever in a period of personalised journalism:

'Cooke is a nuisance. There is no pretending he is not. He telephones his copy at the last moment so that everything else has to be dropped to get it into the paper. He says that he will be in Chicago and turns up in Los Angeles. He discards the agreed subject ("pick that up from the tapes") to write about something which has taken his fancy, news of the moment or not . . . But we think he's worth it and we love him just the same.' (25 March 1968)

'Gillie's nonconformist spirit still haunts the corridors of the B.B.C., and so do the legends of his great battles with authority. The *Guardian* under its brilliant editor, Wadsworth, adapted itself to Gillie's ways, not the other way round. Gillie was not successful in adapting himself to the ways of the *Times* with its fixed routines and rigid time-tables. In matters of this kind Gillie was an anarchist. On the *Guardian* he could select the topics that interested him most and leave the rest to Reuter's and the other news agencies. This arrangement worked to everybody's satisfaction because it was soon discovered that what interested Gillie also interested the paper's readers.'[11]

'What interested Gillie?' – *cet grand sauvage avec un tête intellectuel* according to General Brosset, a man whose 'mind comes down in interesting places' as Edward Murrow recognised. One day it would be the flap of the brief-case from which Laval tugged his papers during his trial. 'It bore the words "Pierre Laval, Président du Conseil, Janvier 1931 – ." The concluding date was missing as if there was still a hope.'[12] Another day he was struck by the continuity of French law in spite of revolutions: he had been reading an official notice in the Métro which cited as authority a decree of the First Consul dated Messidor 12 of the Year VIII.[13] Gillie's writings on the Worker Priests recall Voigt's on the Confessional Church.[14] He contrasted the squabbles of Bourbon and Bonapartist nobles about precedence in receiving communion with the creation about the same time at Marseilles of a range of cheap pottery figures – the maire, the fisherman, the baker's wife, 'full of imaginative taste, vitality, grace and brilliant colour' – which first gave the poorest home a Christmas crib.[15]

Almost every Friday afternoon Gillie used to go to the weekly meeting of the Académie des Inscriptions. He did not vary his routine for a French Cabinet crisis. On 3 February 1950, for instance, he went to hear Daniel Schlumberger on his Afghan excavations although all that day and until late in the evening it was touch and go whether M.

Bidault would be able to hold his Government together. On Saturday Gillie went into the country with Cecilia Reeves of the BBC and Denis Brogan. They left before the English papers had arrived. Gillie would talk of nothing but the discoveries at Kala Bist. His companions teased him about the Cabinet crisis and the first duty of a journalist. When they got back to his flat on the Quai Bourbon the telephone was ringing. It was the *Times* correspondent who had been trying to get Gillie all the afternoon because Printing House Square wanted the Afghan story. While Gillie talked, they opened the M.G. Gillie had, it is true, sent over a column about Mahmud of Ghazir, but he had also sent a long, detailed narrative of the Cabinet crisis: Leon Blum, the socialist, wanted Bidault to remain Prime Minister but wanted also to avoid responsibility for Vietnam since: 'There is no possible intermediary; no hope at any rate of the Viet-Minh Government, which is now enjoying the sun of Moscow's recognition, accepting it.'[16]

A fortnight later Professor Virolleaud lectured at the Académie on the find at Ras Shamra of a Ugaritic alphabet dating from the fourteenth century BC – 'the only one in our letters which has been removed from the place it occupied 3,000 years ago in the ABC of Ugaritic is Z. "Thou whoreson zed, thou unnecessary letter" as Kent observed in King Lear.'[17] That Friday night Gillie sent a column on the oldest known alphabet but also another column on the case of the Chief of the General Staff, whose appreciation of the military situation in Vietnam had fallen into Vietminh hands. He claimed that he had been 'framed' by Gaullists because he had remained in France during the war. Anything was possible in French politics even five years after the war. 'Occupation brought the necessity for duplicity. Resistance exalted the bold spirit . . . Many of the single-minded have had to conceal their purposes. Those who were neither very honest nor very single-minded had to as well, and have learnt some tricks in the process.'[18]

The excursions into archaeology served two purposes. They were good news stories in their own right. They also drew attention to the glory of French scholarship and culture. While most of Gillie's correspondence had to describe the pitifully divided state of France and its shifting, shady politics, these descants took the reader up into the realm of its true greatness which had led Hammond to describe the liberation of Paris as 'an event in the history of man, and not merely in the history of a nation.'[19]

Gillie in France and Sylvia Sprigge in Italy both served in countries where the Communist Party was strong. There were times when it seemed possible that the Iron Curtain might run down the Channel and along the Pyrenees. It was because of this risk that the *Guardian* kept a full-time member of its staff in Rome for ten years after the end of the war. That had not happened since Cecil Sprigge had moved to Berlin in 1929. Although she was only a year older than Gillie, Sylvia Sprigge belonged in spirit and style to an earlier generation of *Guardian* foreign correspondents. She was a participant, almost a partisan. She knew everybody from Togliatti to Croce; she lived in the thick of Italian political life; she openly took sides against Fascists and Communists. When she died the *Guardian* described her writing and herself as

'sparkling, vivid, energetic, full of fun, with a touch of malice, a warm, even headlong play of feeling, and a great appetite for the manifestations of human character. In the same headlong way she could be notably inaccurate and indiscreet. Because of this she made some heroic blunders and a number of enemies. Yet even when her reporting was inaccurate in detail (and Sylvia could be alarmingly cavalier about dates, names, and other mundane facts) it was often penetratingly true in substance; even when it was frankly prejudiced it gave the reader a much truer sense of the emotional pitch of a situation than he could have got from reporters outwardly more balanced and careful.' (13 June 1966)

6

'In these islands we no longer claim or seek equality of power with Russia or the United States.'[20] To recognise this, as the *Guardian* did, was to admit that it needed its own men in the USA and the USSR just as much as Swiss or Dutch papers had long needed their own men in London. Alistair Cooke was half the answer; for a short time Alexander Werth was the other half.

After Hitler's invasion of Russia Werth had left the M.G., without giving proper notice, in order to go to Moscow for the BBC and the *Sunday Times*. He was by the standards of the time impeccably Left, he had been born in St Petersburg of a Russian father and spoke the language perfectly. According to Thomas Barman, he and Stevens of the *Christian Science Monitor* were the most successful foreign correspondents in war-time Russia whereas 'most of us were kept at arm's length.'[21] Towards the end of 1946 Wadsworth got Werth back for the *Guardian*. The way he had left the paper still rankled, but Werth had a name that counted both with old *Guardian* readers, who remembered his Paris correspondence, and with a wider public. It was worth while making it up. Unfortunately soon after this Werth too, like everybody else, began to be kept at arm's length by the Russians. It was not he that had changed but they. He travelled in other Eastern European countries which were becoming Russian satellites and wrote about them.

In the summer of 1947, for instance, he was in Poland. Back in Moscow he thought that the outlook for his work was slightly better, but it did not last. He could write freely and interestingly about the musical life of Moscow, but he could not carry out the main purpose of his mission. An increasing proportion of his work took the form of reviews of Russian writings which could have been done as well in England. In 1948 his Moscow assignment came to an end. He went to Prague.

Early in 1949 he came to Manchester to talk things over with Wadsworth. He had already decided to move to Paris and had arranged to write regularly for the *New Statesman*. He suggested to Wadsworth that for the summer months he should cover Eastern Europe for the *Guardian* from Paris making separate journeys to the various countries and providing leader page articles. After that he hoped Wadsworth would again find him a staff job. Wadsworth turned both proposals down after talking things over with the *Glasgow Herald*. Werth, he felt, 'leans too far backward to put the Communist view of the places he is in.'[22] This was a mirror image of the view that the Communists were beginning to take of him. A little later he was denounced by *Rude Pravo* as 'the notorious British spy.'

Wadsworth's first attempt to redress the balance of the New World by calling in the Old had failed. To keep a man in Moscow was not the answer. It was three years before the solution turned up.

7

Characteristically John Anderson arrived in Berlin in 1945 three days before the British contingent entered the city. For more than a year he was the *Guardian*'s chief correspondent in Germany. His assignment was unlike any other. Providing the M.G. with news of Germany was only half of his job. The other half, or at least another part of it, was helping in what was described as the 're-education' of Germany. When Anderson first reached Berlin he found a situation in which Russian, American and British officers were getting on well together. His early messages described how 'democratic' parties were allowed to function in the Russian zone while all political activity was forbidden in the west. He did not realise how very rapidly the Russian definition of 'democratic' would narrow until it became a synonym for its own antithesis. Of course there could 'be no successful compromise between permitting political activity in Berlin and forbidding it in Hamburg and Hanover.'[23] He did not see that by the time he left Germany the position would have been reversed.

Anderson's, and the M.G.'s, part in the re-education of Germany was in producing a German edition of the *Manchester Guardian Weekly*. It was printed in Hamburg and soon developed an enormous sale. Germany was, of course, news hungry, and hungry for undoctored news. This the *M.G. Weekly* gave it. Its success was flattering and deserved. It was not all due however to its quality as a newspaper. Germans were hungry for paper as well as for news. Paper could more cheaply be brought in the form of the *M.G. Weekly* than by itself, and it was just as good for wrapping goods in.

'Berlin could conceivably be divided into separate cities with national frontiers between them. This would mean a Customs examination of every tram-car, but if the world decides on lunacy it could conceivably be worked.'[24] Anderson's eighteen months in Germany was a period in which the world began to decide on this and other manifestations of lunacy. An increasing number of his messages were concerned with the problem of food shortages. Reluctantly he and Wadsworth found themselves engaged in a campaign for feeding Western Germany and for putting Germany into a position where she could pay for herself. Anderson found himself addressing an all-party meeting of members of the House of Commons on this subject. Something had to be done, too, about a position by which we found ourselves in effect paying reparations to the Russians since Russia took what she wanted and left us to make good the deficiency. It is not surprising that by the autumn of 1946 Anderson asked for a transfer home. He was succeeded by Terence Prittie whom Evelyn Montague had recruited to report on cricket. The Russians do not play cricket. By 1948 the season seemed set for Russian roulette.

8

The first period of Wadsworth's editorship ended in 1948 when his deputy John Pringle joined the *Times*. He had been perhaps the best all round leader-writer the paper had ever had. That at least was what Hammond once told John Beavan. Not long after, he was asked by his successor, Paddy Monkhouse, to write an obituary notice of the editor. He refused, but sent some notes which he hoped would be of use. In them he reviewed their work together and made a tentative assessment of Wadsworth as editor. These notes are valuable just because it is an interim opinion that they give – and interim judgments usually disappear when a man dies and the catch-line 'Not till' is removed from the proof of his obituary. Pringle's half-time assessment ran like this:

A. P. Wadsworth by Birger Lundquist

'His first real test as editor came with the general election and he rose to the occasion. I think you can say he was the first of all the Left wing press to attack Churchill openly at a time when the Labour party was still mesmerised by the huge figure of the old man . . . He put the paper firmly behind Labour with scant respect for the Liberals. And when the results came in – which, by the way, he did not expect – he wrote a magnificent leader headed the "Silent Revolution" (this was the first time the phrase was used?) seeing the thing in its true proportions and welcoming the Government.

His attitude to Russia developed slowly and arose out of his deep dislike of force and humbug rather than out of intellectual considerations. Poland had less effect on his mind than Germany. His visit to Germany in 1947 played a most important part in his development. He came back deeply shocked at conditions and convinced that the Western Powers must get on with restoring their zones without waiting for Russian agreement. This started a lively interest in foreign affairs and especially Germany and he gradually seemed to lose interest in home politics and economics leaving them more and more to Kent. At the same time he got angrier and angrier with the Russians and spent far too much time reading Russian broadcasts which drove him almost to fury! At that time he left the broader issues, with the exception of Germany, to me, but was never so happy as when he was digging at Russia over some trifling example of obstinacy, malignance or stupidity.'

I think it is right to add here that his instinct was often sound. Left to himself, I believe, he would have welcomed Churchill's Fulton speech but he let me criticise it pretty severely.

Another thing worth mentioning in the history of the paper was his marked cooling off towards Zionism. He was really very anti-Zionist but because of the tradition of the paper allowed me to carry on a moderate support for their cause.

The paper played a big part on the Greek rebellion for which Churchill has never forgiven it. Once again I think I was wrong though I never wrote better leaders in my life. Wadsworth fully supported me and wrote one or two himself. Of course we both relied too much on the reports of the *Times* correspondent in Athens whose service we shared.

I must add one important thing. Perhaps his chief achievement as an editor in the first four years was to lead the intellectual Left away from appeasement of Russia to full support of Ernest Bevin's policy. There was a short period – while the *Times* was still queer – when the M.G. was the only responsible paper giving Bevin that help.

Other general points. After a time, a relaxation and enjoyment of office, a broadening of interest, a slightly amusing contempt for local and Lancashire affairs – he was determined to forget the lad from Rochdale, and a wish to be the editor of an international paper or nothing. He travelled more, went to London more often, saw more people . . . He is a great journalist and a brilliant mind but only a second rate thinker and editor. I still like him as well as any man in Britain.'*

A word may perhaps be added about the last two sentences. Wadsworth would have been amused and touched by the precision with which Pringle expressed his liking. As for the apparent contradiction

* Pringle–P. J. Monkhouse 5 May. Year not given but probably 1951 because on 25 January that year Wadsworth sent Monkhouse some notes: 'Having helped in the scratching together of the obits of two editors of the M.G. I think that at the risk of seeming vain I ought to assist posterity! Here are a few things out of which to choose.' Pringle's notes cannot be later than 1952 because he left the *Times* that year for the *Sydney Morning Herald* and he wrote from the *Times*. Kent (M.G. 1945–1950) went to the *Economist* and in 1954 as editor to the *Winnipeg Free Press*. R. H. Fry remembers Kent's time in Manchester as a golden age of *Guardian* economic leader-writing and thought Wadsworth wrong to let him go.

between a brilliant mind and a second rate thinker this can probably be resolved by remembering that Pringle took a First in Greats and that speculative abstract thought was not a Wadsworth activity. But a second rate editor? Surely not? Wadsworth was an editor *sui generis*, who could have been bred only in and for the M.G.; not to be compared, for better or for worse, with editors elsewhere.

CHAPTER THIRTY-SEVEN

Laurence Scott's Programme

I

LAURENCE SCOTT was 35 when he started work in Cross Street as the company secretary. The following year he was made a director. In 1947 he became managing director, but his father kept the position of governing director, and remained the absolute head of the family business. He handed over the management of both papers to his son. The heir presumptive had been recognised as the heir apparent.

But it was not clear what there would be to inherit. Wealth there could not be, but would there be the *Guardian* for the sake of whose integrity John Scott had surrendered not the chance but the certainty of a large fortune? The Scott Trust had been established in 1936 in order to preserve the independence of the *Manchester Guardian* under the guardianship of the Scott family by ensuring that estate duty would not become payable on the death of J.R.S. Counsel who drafted the deed was clear that 'no claim for death duties can arise against anyone by reason of the death of Mr J. R. Scott.'[1] But that had been in 1935. As John Scott grew older the position was not so clear. Lawyers had another look at the terms of the 1936 Trust in the light of the law as it had become a dozen years later. They did not like what they found. A race against time began.

The 1936 Trust had a maximum life of twenty years, but it could be ended by the trustees at any time after the last day of March 1941. This option was now to prove of vital importance. On 31 March 1948 counsel was asked whether it would make any difference to a possible claim for death duties if the option had been exercised. On 3 May he advised that there would be a serious risk of liability if John Scott died while the existing trust was in force, but he thought this risk could be eliminated if a new trust were substituted for the old. John Scott was 68 and a sick man. The trustees acted promptly. On 15 May they resolved to terminate the existing Scott Trust. They now had six months during which they could make up their mind about appointing beneficiaries to receive the Trust Funds. This interval was filled by anxious consultation about what to do next. A private act of parliament was suggested. The Scotts felt that 'there is considerable hope of their obtaining assistance for this purpose in government circles,' for the Royal Commission on the Press under Sir W. D. Ross was paying careful attention to newspaper ownership in its relation to news. But counsel thought this chance 'so small as to be negligible.' It was finally agreed to establish another trust under the general law but with different terms which would avoid the difficulties into which the 1936 Trust had run.

All was ready by the beginning of November. On the ninth the five beneficiaries appointed by the trustees were handed their individual cheques. Four of the five beneficiaries were grandsons of C. P. Scott: the two brothers, Laurence and Charles Scott, J.R.'s sons; Montague's son Laurence and Ted Scott's eldest son, Richard.* All were employed by the company as was the fifth beneficiary, the company secretary, Robert Ebbage. They were informed by a solicitor that they were free to do what they liked with what was now their absolute property, the whole of the ordinary shares in the Manchester Guardian and Evening News, Ltd. They then and there settled the shares on a new Scott Trust of which they and three others became trustees. The other three were Haley, Wadsworth and J. R. Scott, who was too ill to be present at the ceremony. Five months later John Scott died. On the day of his funeral came the news of J. L. Hammond's death. These two were almost the last of the legendary race of C. P. Scott's lieutenants. Only James Bone soldiered on, still for another year a director of the company and for another dozen after that the careful guardian of the paper's tradition.

The new Trust differed from the old in several important ways. It was given, for instance, a much longer currency – not twenty years, but twenty years after the death of the survivor of a number of C.P.'s great-grandsons. This, if the fates are propitious, should see the *Guardian* through into its third century. Particular care was taken to avoid a repetition of the situation which threatened as soon as John Scott died. The new Trust Deed was scrutinised carefully by the Inland Revenue authorities in connection with the work of the Royal Commission, and Laurence Scott heard unofficially that the Board was satisfied that no liability to death duties would arise on the death of any of the five men who established it. The most important change, however, was in the constitution of the Trust itself. The 1936 Trust had

* Laurence Scott and Laurence Montague were both born in 1909, the year after the death of their uncle, C.P.'s eldest son, after whom they were named. 'We are both happy for we had a great wish for a son to call Laurie,' Montague wrote to Francis Dodd four days after the birth.

left John Scott in absolute control of the company through his power to appoint and dismiss trustees. It is true that after his death the remaining trustees would exercise a collective authority in this respect, but that was almost inevitable in 1936 since there was then no member of the family who could safely be identified as next in succession. By 1948 there was a successor designate, but the new deed neither gave John Scott back the powers he had enjoyed under the old nor transferred them to Laurence. The principle of collective authority was established. The trustees as trustees were responsible for their own membership; the trustees as the ordinary shareholders were responsible for electing directors.

Another clause in the new deed prevented the five beneficiaries under the old trust, the men who established the new, from becoming both trustees and directors. The lawyers' advice was that for the same people to appear in all three capacities would create a dangerous tax situation. It was thought that one exception to this rule would be permissible and so Laurence Scott, who was a beneficiary, became a trustee and remained a director. The other four beneficiaries – two Scotts, one Montague and the company secretary – were eligible to be either trustees or directors, but not both. No similar ban on joint office was imposed on other people. Thus Wadsworth was both chairman of the 1948 trustees and a director of the company. He was succeeded as chairman of the trustees by Richard Scott, the *Guardian's* Washington correspondent, who was not a director and could not become one as long as he remained a trustee. Since then membership of the Trust, and indeed of the directorate, has been widened to include people who are neither members of the family nor of the staff. Thus Jo Grimond is now both a trustee and a director. Several non-family trustees are not directors and vice versa.

From 1821 to 1948 the ultimate control of the *Manchester Guardian* had always rested with one single member of the Taylor or Scott families. From 1948 to 1967 ultimate executive power was still exercised by one member of the Scott family, Laurence Scott,* but under a constitution by which he was responsible to a body of trustees which included both members of the family and others. The 1936 trustees were simply preventive men against the Inland Revenue, if one may introduce a meaningful distortion of terms. The 1948 trustees have wider duties.

The establishment of a new Trust could not, of course, affect

---

* For the first four months of 1932, however, J. R. Scott and E. T. Scott were joint governing directors. See p. 492. Since October 1967 Laurence Scott has been the active, but non-executive chairman of the company.

liability to estate duty under the old. If a claim were made, and sustained by the Courts, the *Guardian*'s survival in any form in which the trustees would probably be content to see it survive would be doubtful. Duty was either not payable at all, or payable on an estate of about a million pounds. A claim was made. There followed three years of acute anxiety and careful legal argument. It was not until 1952 that the Inland Revenue withdrew its claim and Laurence Scott was free to go ahead with the plans he had been making ever since he came to help his father.

2

Before Laurence Scott had been a year with the company he put down on paper for his father an appreciation of the situation and a programme for action which was eventually completed in 1961. Up to this time there had only been two directors or senior members of the staff who had ever had experience of London newspapers. L. T. Hobhouse had been for a short and unhappy time editor of the ill-starred *Tribune* and Ted Scott had been for a few years on the *Daily News*. Hobhouse and E.T.S. were journalists. As far as management was concerned there had never been an infusion from Fleet Street.

Laurence Scott, then, was bound to look at things from a different angle to his predecessors. As personal assistant to the general manager of the *News Chronicle* he had watched the inter-war struggle between the mass circulation London dailies from a privileged position. He brought what he had learned in Fleet St to bear on the *Guardian*'s prospects in the post-war world. He concluded that the *Guardian* would have to be printed in London if it was to continue to be run 'in the same spirit as heretofore,' the sacred words first used by Edward Taylor in his will, words which now really meant 'at the same level as in C.P.'s time' i.e. as an independent, progressive paper of international standing. Once or twice in the past, as we have seen, there had been talk of the *Guardian* publishing in London, but this had been canvassed mainly in the spirit in which the great Victorians subscribed to overseas missionary societies. Now Laurence Scott put it forward as something which had to be done to save the *Guardian* itself. His reasoning was simple.

Other newspapers the world over might quote the opinions of the *Manchester Guardian* as freely as they did those of the London *Times*, but this was a journalistic judgment. Advertising men thought differently. To them the *Times* was to the *Guardian* as 'London is to Paddington' simply because Manchester was provincial and London national. They were able to pay less for space in the *Guardian* because they got less from space in the *Guardian*. Their view of the position can be seen in a simple table comparing the cost of display advertising just before the war in the M.G., the *Times* and the *Daily Telegraph* – three newspapers read by people with roughly the same educational background,

	Rate per single column inch	*Cost per 1,000 readers*
Daily Telegraph	£5	1.6d
Times	£3	3.0d
Manchester Guardian	£1	4.7d

The consequences are clear since roughly half the money a paper earns, half what it costs to produce, comes from advertisements.

In spite of the different financial status of these three newspapers each had to provide for their readers a comparable service. Because of this the *Manchester Guardian* was at a disadvantage compared with the other regional morning papers of similar financial standing. Its readers' expectations were higher than theirs because for something like half a century its editors' aspirations had been higher. The object they had set themselves was, put crudely, to live beyond their means – to provide a newspaper of world class on an income which was now insufficient to conduct a profitable provincial paper. They had only been able to do this because the owners had voluntarily surrendered all hope of personal profit, because there was a constant supply of able men willing to work for less than they would have got elsewhere since the M.G. came nearer than any other paper to their ideal of what a paper ought to be, and because behind the *Guardian* there were the profits of the *Manchester Evening News*.

It had been a losing battle for the reasons set out in chapter 29. It would have been a losing battle even if the M.G. had lowered its sights to the range of other regional mornings. In 1939 they were all losing money. Cobbett's Great Wen had grown until England was becoming a London suburb. But the war had given the regional morning papers a respite. This offered, Laurence Scott thought, a fleeting opportunity that had to be taken. During his early years in Manchester he had to argue the matter time and again – with his father, with the trustees, with the directors, with outside financiers. He took pains to find out not only how many *Guardian* readers there were, nor even simply how many in this place or that, but also what kind of people they were. Before his time there had been no such systematic enquiry. When cotton was king one knew that a high proportion of *Guardian* readers were among his courtiers. Later Crozier told a meeting that he thought that the largest single group of *Guardian* readers were teachers, but this was only a guess. Laurence Scott discovered a series of striking and perhaps unexpected contrasts. In 1950 an investigation by random sample was made into M.G. readership in Greater Manchester; in six other northern towns (Blackburn, Chester, Leeds, Sheffield, Derby and Stoke); and in London (Finchley, Highgate, Chelsea, Kensington).[2] The findings are shown in the table overleaf. They throw light on the kind of paper the *Guardian* would have to be according to whether Laurence Scott chose 'Manchesterisation,' wider north country penetration, or nation-wide coverage. There were, of course, far more M.G. readers in Manchester than elsewhere, but people who appreciated the paper for what it was were not thicker on the ground there than in the other places sampled. Outside Manchester only those people bought the M.G. who valued its special characteristics. Notice, for instance the great interest in international politics among London readers. The contrast with Manchester is of course a proportionate, not an absolute one; Manchester's two-fifths with this kind of interest represented more readers than London's four-fifths. All the same the profile of Manchester readers as a whole – their age, their politics, their low proportion of university graduates – suggests a city in which there were few additional readers to be found who would really enjoy the kind of *Guardian* that C.P. had created and that Wadsworth was providing. From the editorial point of view that might well have been sufficient to decide the choice. It probably was not since Wadsworth was a cautious man without affection for sampling techniques.

The business argument as it struck Laurence Scott is summarised in a memorandum that he wrote in 1950. The *Times* with 270,000 readers and the *Telegraph* with 970,000 sold in the same specialised market as the M.G. with its inadequate 140,000. A quarter of a million was the absolute minimum for commercial security. He went on to discuss the position of the paper in the eyes of national advertisers. They had always put the *Guardian* on the provincial side of their budget, the smaller side, and there it had to compete against, for instance, the *Manchester Evening News* which gave five times the coverage in the same area for only a 50 per cent higher charge. 'I am convinced,' he wrote, 'that our future depends largely on acquiring "national" status in the eyes of advertisers.' He linked this with the reading tastes of purchasers. 'Evening papers with necessarily restricted circulation areas must give prominence to local affairs, purchasers of a morning and an evening paper do not want their news duplicated and are likely to demand less local emphasis in the morning. The London papers offer this.'

Between the wars the provincial mornings had lost, absolutely or

SURVEY OF MANCHESTER GUARDIAN READERS 1950

(the most important differences are underlined)

		Manchester % of sample	Six Northern Towns % of sample	London % of sample
AGE	Under 45	42	52	60
SEX	Men	54	60	68
EDUCATION	University Education	11	24	51
	Elementary School only	31	24	5
JOBS	Men employed in education	7	15	5
	Women ,, ,, ,,	9	13	10
	All employed women	26	29	42
	Men in other professions	16	30	31
	Men in textiles	8	2	7
	Retired, etc.	14	12	11
INCOME	Grade A	16	21	45
	B	22	22	18
	C	34	41	22
	DE	28	16	16
MANCHESTER CONNECTIONS		Not Applicable	18	25
POLITICS	Left	23	35	46
	Centre	36	37	34
	Right	35	23	13
RELIGION	Regular churchgoer	40	40	17
	Never or very rarely	34	31	56
INTERESTS	Literature and Books			
	Very interested	59	61	65
	Not at all	6	3	1
	Music: Very	42	39	42
	Not at all	9	8	8
	Theatre: Very	42	42	43
	Not at all	11	10	7
	Education: Very	58	57	33
	Not at all	5	3	9
	Cricket: Very	30	31	17
	Not at all	41	33	57
	International Politics: Very	43	49	79
	Not at all	12	3	2
	Economic and Social: Very	41	49	62
	Not at all	10	3	4

		Manchester % of sample	Six Northern Towns % of sample	London % of sample
NEWSPAPER READING	Mornings: MG only	50	49	29
	MG and Times	1	1	32
	MG and Tel	3	3	24
Sundays:	None	14	24	8
	Observer	15	32	75
	Sunday Times	15	17	44

relatively, readers to the London mornings and advertisements to the provincial evenings. The war, by restricting size, stopping the free gift racket and creating a shortage of advertising space had put them on their feet again, but this would last only as long as newsprint was limited:

'Fortunately for us the special advantages that the newsprint shortage confers on us are likely to last for a few years yet, but it is to my mind essential that we use this period to build up our status and circulation. To wait until we have lost our present special advantages, or worse still until we have begun to slip, would make the task far harder.

The key lies in printing the paper in London as well as in Manchester.'

3

With this memorandum Laurence Scott sent Wadsworth a letter in his own handwriting to read on the voyage to America. It throws a good deal of light on the character of the two men and on the relation between them.

'I am rooting again for news on the front page. I suspect that you dislike the idea, though I have never yet got you to do more than evade the issue.

I am therefore taking the liberty of sending the enclosed memorandum to you on board ship in the hope that you will at least have the time to clear your own mind on the subject. I have taken a great deal of trouble over this memorandum – the subject is of vital importance – and I think I deserve a serious reply . . .'[3]

News on the front page was the essential first step in the plan to print the paper in London as well as in Manchester because the front page was the most purely local part of the paper as well as the most prominent. Nobody outside Lancashire and Cheshire, apart from a few émigrés in retirement, could have any interest in the advertisements that filled it; nobody outside Greater Manchester could find much in it that concerned him. Two out of three readers could, and no doubt did, ignore the small, classified advertisements that filled it without giving the matter a second thought. Advertising agents, however, so Laurence Scott thought, took a different view. It suggested to them a purely local paper and no amount of propaganda could undo that impression. But the *Guardian* in 1946 was in fact much more than a local paper. Only a third of its readers lived in Manchester and its suburbs, using the term to include such commuter districts as Wilmslow and Alderley Edge. It was more even than a regional paper. About a third of its readers lived outside the north western counties of Lancashire, Cheshire, Cumberland and Westmorland. But this last third were few and far between, scattered sporadically among a population amounting to some six-sevenths of the United Kingdom total – less than 40,000 readers out of some forty-eight million people. On the other hand a comparison made in mid-1949 between the sales of morning newspapers in Stockport and in eleven Lancashire towns showed that in only one of them were there more *Daily Telegraph* than *Guardian* readers and then only by 0.2 per cent. In eleven other towns, which excluded Manchester, Salford and Liverpool, the *Guardian* sale was in each case at least double that of the *Telegraph*. In four towns it was three times as great, and in three other towns it was respectively four, five and six times as great. In eight of the twelve towns the Manchester *Daily Dispatch* sold more copies than any other paper and in three others it ran second. In four of the towns it accounted for over 30 per cent of the morning papers sold.

These figures speak clearly of the strength of regional newspapers in the North-West both among readers of 'quality' and 'popular' papers. But there was a significant difference. The *Daily Dispatch* competed with the London popular papers most of which had also been printed in Manchester for many years before the shortage of newsprint imposed a compulsory standstill. When that went the *Dispatch* would, of course, have to face renewed competition, but of a kind with which it was familiar. The *Guardian*'s competitors were other 'quality' papers and not the 'populars' except perhaps, so Laurence Scott thought, to a small extent the *News Chronicle*. The *Telegraph*'s sale in these towns was artificially low because it had not started printing in Manchester until late in 1940. When newsprint rationing was finally lifted the *Guardian* would have to face competition from another 'quality' paper with far greater resources than its own, printed in Manchester and therefore easily accessible throughout the North-West. For the first time since the death of the *Manchester Courier* in 1916 Conservatives in the *Guardian*'s heart-land would have the option of buying a 'quality' paper of their own way of thinking with a late news service as good as the *Guardian*'s.

On the other hand, unless the *Guardian* could print in London, most Liberal and Labour people living south of the Trent who wanted a 'quality' paper to their liking would have to go on wanting.

The small size of newspapers caused by the newsprint shortage had altered the balance of the *Guardian* and put an end to Crozier's policy of 'Manchesterisation' which had caused such heart-burning among reporters during Ted Scott's time as editor.* There simply was no longer room for the trivia of Manchester life. It is probable that Wadsworth gladly consented to its going: he was a whole-hearted Northerner, but not excessively a Manchester man. Rochdale meant more to him than Didsbury, yet he did not want to fill the paper with the doings of his home town. It was, however, one thing to accept and perhaps welcome the new balance of the paper's news and another thing to change the whole format and appearance of the paper by putting news on the front page. Wadsworth was a conservative in matters of taste and a cautious man not inclined to take any irreversible step unless it was absolutely necessary. He could always resume 'Manchesterisation' if more paper became available and it seemed sensible to do so. But, once classified advertisements had been banished to inside pages, they could never be put back. His delaying tactics astonished none of his colleagues. He delayed long after he realised that he would have in the end to give way and probably after he had been intellectually convinced of its necessity.

The story of how in the end the *Guardian* – still, of course, the *Manchester Guardian* – appeared one morning in the autumn of 1952 with the news outside is told by John Anderson, who was by this time an assistant editor. A great deal of preparatory work had been done and a New Model *Guardian* designed as a theoretical exercise. But –

'Wadsworth adopted a masterly policy of approving changes but taking scrupulous care not to commit himself to any date for carrying out change of any sort . . . "Yes, yes," he would say, "but you know, John, I think you'll really have to hit this man Bevan on the head to-night." And we'd find ourselves discussing the night's leader.

Gradually we approached crisis . . . The advertisement people were trying to book advertisements for the New Model paper, and naturally the advertisers wanted to know When? One morning just before lunch, near the beginning of September 1952, a rather worried L.P.S. came to see me. "When," he said, "*are* you going to put news on the front page?" I said, "I'm ready to do whatever you like, but it's not a matter for me. It's a question of getting A.P.W. to fix a date." "Yes," said L.P.S., "but how?"

By this time I was pretty fed up with the endless talk about news on the front page and nothing ever happening. So I said, "Let's make it 29 Septem-

* See p. 450, 452-3.

ber." Laurence was a bit surprised. "Fine," he said, "but what about A.P.?"

I said, "You fix the date, and we'll do it. I'm not quite sure how, but we'll do it." L.P.S. agreed and went off, leaving me considerably worried. We were committed to a date which at that stage the editor didn't even know.

I had a plan of a sort, but I wasn't at all sure that it would work. That year 29 September was the opening day of the Labour Party Conference at Morecambe, and my plan was to try to persuade A.P. that it would be a splendid thing to kick off with the new paper at the conference, where there would be a large gathering every day for a week to see it and to talk about it. I put it to him that afternoon . . . Perhaps by this time A.P. was really as fed up as I was with all the endless talk about the front page, and to my infinite relief he agreed . . .

My Labour Party conference idea . . . had one great lack – what was to be our lead story on the Monday, the first day of the conference? We badly wanted something exclusive. A few days before 29 September we got a Letter to the Editor from an official of the North Western Road Car Company, the company running country and long-distance buses all round Manchester, protesting against a decision of the Ministry of Transport permitting the Liverpool company – Crosvilles – to run unrestricted coach services to London, but denying the same freedom to the North Western company . . . A.P. gave me the letter and asked me to look into it.

As far as I could make out the Liverpool company was being allowed to run coach services as it pleased because it was nationalised . . . whereas the North Western was a private company . . .

This struck me as a wildly improper bureaucratic decision, and also as a jolly good political story . . . I went into the office on Sunday afternoon and said that I'd got a lead story for our first front page with news on it . . . It did lead the paper, with the heading "State Buses Held Above The Law." It caused some stir at the time. I was delighted when a friend in another newspaper office rang me up. "It was a dull night," he said, "and we were all wondering what on earth you'd use to lead your new front page. We ought to have known better. Of course you got clean away with the best story of the night." I liked particularly his "Of course".'

Meanwhile Wadsworth was making his own leisurely enquiries. Towards the end of May Laurence Scott had told him that he wanted to put news on the front page in the second half of September or early in October.[4] A month later Wadsworth wrote to the typographer, Allen Hutt, remarking in the middle of a long letter:

'I suppose we shall have to contemplate sometime putting news on the front page, tho' I don't know when. That, I assume, might affect the choice of title lettering . . . All this is really academic at the moment but something might come of it sometime. I should be most grateful if you could spare a few minutes to cast your expert eye over the problem.'[5]

A fortnight later Hutt wrote making a number of suggestions about the whole front page. On 10 September Wadsworth started another long letter asking for advice on the typography of the whole paper with a characteristic paragraph:

'I hope you have had a good holiday. I am afraid your hints have landed me in a lot of trouble and I shall need a holiday now! When I wrote it was quite an academic speculation but, as you know, once one begins to play about with a thing one gets led on imperceptibly, and now we have got ourselves committed to going the whole hog and putting news on the front page at the end of the month. It's not a thing I like in itself, but it seems to be accepted by all the newspaper pundits that it is preferable to be in the fashion. Certainly there is something in it for us because our front page advertisements are extremely parochial.'

On the Wednesday before the change Wadsworth sent Hutt proof of a 'dummy' of the two main news pages: 'The front page looks pretty well,' Wadsworth wrote. 'Fairish' was Allen Hutt's verdict. But three weeks later, when the paper had settled down, he was more forthcoming: 'I think the paper is looking very good, by and large, and this seems to be the general trade view.'[6] It had taken Laurence Scott seven years to carry out the first stage in his three point plan for the future of the *Guardian*.

4

News on the front page was worth while in its own right. Other journalists thought so, and more people began to buy the M.G. But in Laurence Scott's programme it was also a step towards the larger project of printing in London. Before this could be considered great changes were necessary in the London office. Bone had kept the staff small partly to save expense, partly because he liked it that way. In his time it had something of a family party atmosphere which most of those who worked there remembered with pleasure. The three political specialists – the Lobby and Gallery men and the diplomatic correspondent – worked largely on their own and were responsible directly to the editor in Manchester, a tradition established when C.P. appointed Bone to succeed Gretton and told him in effect to keep out of politics.*

In the post-war situation changes were inevitable. Edition times were earlier. The latest possible time for 'copy' to catch the London edition was 8.30 p.m. Most of it, of course, must be earlier. This produced a regular traffic jam on the private wire which, because it also served the *Manchester Evening News*, was not available for the M.G. until

* See p. 350.

5.30 p.m.* There were also more men working from the London office
so that the private wire was still more over-crowded. Much more
careful organisation and discipline was required. The London editor
and the Manchester end had to know in advance as far as was humanly
possible what 'copy' to expect. Newspapers thrive, of course, on unexpected news, but they choke with unannounced stories which could
have been foreseen. A thick file shows that there was far too much of
this.

On the face of it John Beavan had been a sensible man to appoint
to deal with this and, no doubt in Laurence Scott's mind, to prepare
the way for London printing which they had often discussed as a
possibility. Beavan had had experience as production editor of the
Observer under Ivor Brown. He had been a reporter in the London
office of the *Manchester Evening News* before the war and was its editor
at the time of his appointment. In that capacity he had kept up the high
standard of book reviewing and special political articles that Haley
had set.

But his appointment did not work out as well as might have been
expected. From a technical standpoint his *Manchester Evening News*
connection was an asset; from a psychological angle it was a serious
handicap in dealing with old *Guardian* men. There was tension between
the organisational need for a well-recognised and observed chain of
command and the editor's need for direct personal dealing with his
political specialists who worked in London while he lived in Manchester. There was a concealed difficulty in the fact that, although the London editor was a director, two of the specialists on his staff were
members of the Scott cousinhood and trustees. Added to this was
Wadsworth's incurable reluctance to make firm decisions about organisation a moment before they were needed. John Beavan put this
delicately in one of the most perceptive appreciations written when
A.P. died. 'This attitude sometimes made things difficult for those with
executive responsibilities. "Well, we shall have to see," he would say
when a plan was outlined to him. His consent was usually given in
time – just in time. But he was always forgiven. He probably never
appreciated how much he was loved and admired by his staff.'[7]

In fact Wadsworth never gave the clear directive about the working
of the London office which Beavan wanted. 'What is this about your
canalising all information from the House?' he once wrote to Beavan.
'I don't want to have to resort to direct communication with Boyd
but I do think it unreasonable that he should not be permitted to trans-

* New equipment was installed in 1947 and one of the six channels then available
was open for *Guardian* work after 3 p.m., but there were still difficulties.

mit messages here through Baker (the chief sub-editor in London) as well as yourself. It seems to me a needless formality and we don't want that.'[8] Perhaps Wadsworth's evasiveness was justified. If he had given the directive which Beavan wanted, he might soon have lost some of the best members of his London staff. By refusing to be drawn he kept a kind of uneasy peace which yet worked for ten years. There was no decline in the quality of the work. Indeed in some respects it was better than ever. But it was not a happy office. Looking back Beavan felt he was 'like a teacher from a strictly disciplined elementary school taking a class in A. S. Neill's school without any knowledge of the philosophy.' No one was surprised that he moved on to the Nuffield Foundation when threatened by a palace revolution. It is arguable that no satisfactory and happy solution was possible until the editor himself moved to London.

That was still a long way off, but by November 1952 Wadsworth in an unusual moment of unguarded optimism reported that 'he did not envisage any large sudden increase in editorial costs as a consequence of printing in London.' 'It should be stressed,' he wrote, 'that although the paper is directed from Manchester the most considerable part of it is already written in or supplied through London. Already the main specialist writers work from London: parliamentary, political, industrial, financial, diplomatic, air and science correspondents. There are also staff writers there on music, art, theatre, etc. A good many leaders are also written from London, especially on finance and international affairs.'[9]

5

The dropping of the Estate Duty claim on John Scott's estate had cleared the way for London printing. Preparations had now gone far enough to make it desirable to take the trade union leaders into Laurence Scott's confidence, although London printing was not scheduled to start until 1956. What he had to tell them was a fascinating story with revolutionary implications for one of the most conservatively minded bodies of trade unionists in the country. Caxton had set up his press in a chapel and consequently trade union branches are still called chapels. Moreover technological development in the industry had been slow for many years. Here was something new.

Among Laurence Scott's papers there survive the notes he made for his talk with the general secretaries of the Typographical Association and the Lithographic Printers. They are dated 22 August 1952 – six weeks before the introduction of news on the front page.

His notes start with the *Guardian*'s need to find more readers and its knowledge that a newspaper of its kind could not expect to win more than a small proportion of the readers in any one place. This meant that it must try to sell all over the country. Various methods of distribution had been considered in considerable detail – aeroplane and helicopter services, special trains and so on but because of the unreliability of the weather or for other reasons all had been rejected. The only solution seemed to be to print in London because it was only from London that newspapers were distributed throughout England south of the Trent. The *Guardian*, printed in London, would catch the tide; printed in Manchester it would have to swim against the tide to reach its scattered potential south country readers. The tide was strong and the handicap impossible. But, equally, London printing had always seemed to be beyond the *Guardian*'s means.

Laurence Scott went on to tell the trade union secretaries how in 1949 he had begun to investigate the possibility of facsimile reproduction. The enquiries had taken Charles Markwick, the company's engineer, to the United States and to Denmark. Laurence Scott had been, so to speak, the lay client, and Markwick the professional client to the consultants, Sir Robert Watson Watt and Partners, and the transmission engineers, Muirhead and Co., Ltd. Between them they had reached and tested a solution well adapted to the *Guardian*'s needs and means – it promised to reduce the cost of printing in a second centre by one quarter. What they proposed is most easily understood by laymen from the account in Laurence Scott's notes:

'We shall go to press in Manchester in the normal way, take page proofs of each page, and transmit these page proofs to London by telephoto. In London, we find that it will be more convenient and much more efficient to print by lithographic instead of by letterpress methods. We propose to use the new Aller Bi-metallic plate. That in brief is the method and you will see at once that it is cheaper, for while we have some additional mechanical costs, in transmission from Manchester to London, we start in London with full page proofs and cut out all the earlier processes.'

The saving in cost would be entirely a saving in labour cost. In the second centre there would be no need at all for certain of the printing crafts, especially compositors, the root from whom the whole printing industry stems, and stereo men. But, of course, the M.G. would be employing more men altogether through printing in two centres than it was now employing when it printed only in Manchester. Nobody on the M.G. would lose his job through facsimile printing in London. But might not the process be reversed and London papers already printing in Manchester turn over their existing second plant from conventional printing to facsimile reproduction? In that case, jobs would be lost in the key crafts and there would be a net loss of employment. Laurence Scott's notes go on to deal with this rational anxiety. He argued that the London newspapers were very unlikely to use facsimile reproduction because it was a slower method and therefore, in that all important respect for newspapers, a second best. The London newspapers which already printed in two centres would not choose a second best because with their greater resources they had not to count each thousand pounds as carefully as the *Guardian* had.

'The facts of the delay are these. Because we have to transmit pages from Manchester to London, the time from "going to press" in Manchester . . . to having "papers up" in London . . . is estimated at two and a quarter hours . . . The time between "going to press" and "papers up" by the traditional printing method is just over a quarter of an hour, and we therefore lose two hours. Add to this also the fact that lithographic printing has no technique comparable to the stereotyping process by which plates can be reproduced rapidly. Every plate for a lithographic press has to be individually made and . . . there is going to be a delay between each set of plates. We expect between fifteen and twenty minutes from getting the first machine running to getting the second machine running, but as we shall only use two machines this isn't vital to us. Imagine however an office using ten or twelve machines and a delay of anything up to and over two hours between getting the first machine running and getting the last machine running and you will see why I don't think the method is suitable for national newspapers.'

The confidential conversations with the unions went well. Laurence Scott reported at the end of his round of talks that the secretaries had been 'without exception reasonable and helpful,' but he had to admit that he had not been able to see the secretary of the London Society of Compositors, the metropolitan equivalent of the Typographical Association, and that there might possibly be trouble there. All the men he saw advised him to take the whole staff into his confidence, and this he did that autumn in the company's annual 'working report.'

Characteristically Wadsworth would have liked to continue to play his cards close to his chest for a little longer.[10] Disclosure involved a degree of commitment which he was loath to accept. He was almost certainly wrong, but what happened in 1953 might be thought to prove him right. The increase in price from 2d to 3d in May 1951, the first increase in thirty-one years, had not only checked the steady war and post-war increase in circulation but had caused a serious loss which had not wholly been made good two years later. The loss had been most severe in Lancashire and there it had continued without recovery. The *Guardian* was losing readers to whom it was relatively cheap to supply the paper and gaining readers who lived in districts which it was expensive to reach. It looked, Wadsworth thought – and, though he did not say so, it must have grieved him – that the *Guardian* was losing its working class readers, the survivors of the 25,000 cut price readers who up to 1940 had been able to buy the M.G. for a penny. He wanted the paper to concentrate its circulation drive in the cheap-to-reach North – '5,000 gained here would possibly be worth 10,000 in the South.'[11]

The trading results for 1951–2 were bad; they were worse for 1952–3. Moreover there was, as the Working Report for the year put it, 'a shadow on the horizon . . . the apparent and announced intention of the *Daily Express* organisation to start a third evening newspaper in Manchester.' It might not take place but 'whatever happens one thing is certain and that is that should this newspaper appear we shall have suddenly to give a very high priority to maintaining the status and readership of the *Evening News*.'[12] Work on the London printing project went on, but few members of the staff reading the Working Report can have been surprised to learn that it was 'if anything at a slower rate than was anticipated last year.' Laurence Scott's introduction to the Report, from which these words are taken, was dated 3 September. Two months later he wrote to the merchant bankers through whom London printing was to be financed to say that 'the immediate future is not looking quite so rosy as it did twelve months ago and we think it wiser not to undertake such a major venture at the moment,' and received the reply 'what you say is most interesting and not entirely unexpected.'[13]

Officially the project was still on. And it was still very much alive in Laurence Scott's mind. Nothing had happened to change his diagnosis of the *Guardian*'s needs. But in practice the scheme had had to be put into cold storage. It was not taken up again until after Wadsworth's death, the terminal point of this history.

CHAPTER THIRTY-EIGHT

Wadsworth on Pisgah

I

'What a remarkable position of superiority is that occupied by the editor of the *Manchester Guardian*. (Handclaps) On the one hand are ten million or twelve million or more of reactionary Tories ... On the other are ten million or twelve million of ignorant Socialists ... Meanwhile, around his knees the little Liberal spaniel leaps and plays to whom he gives an affectionate pat, or from time to time a cuff for some unfortunate indiscretion. (Prolonged laughter) ... So long as an unending flow of brilliant articles are produced putting everyone in their place and often stating all the arguments on both sides of every question the editorial duty in the world is done. But I think this is a time when all true Englishmen must choose their side (loud cheers) for, believe me, the very life of this nation as a great Power in the world has quite needlessly been brought into jeopardy. Ponder, please, Mr *Manchester Guardian*, on these words of a fifty years' reader and do not forget them as you sometimes do after a few years have passed.'[1]

Churchill was speaking in Manchester during the 1950 election campaign. Wadsworth took up his challenge the same night: 'It is hard to be convinced that the Conservatives (even led by Mr Churchill with all his virtues) or Labour (with such an incumbrance as Mr Aneurin Bevan) can be whole-heartedly supported. All common political instinct demands that one choose a side – it makes things wonderfully easy – but, sometimes, perhaps, the wisest course is to try to tell all sides their faults – and suffer the brickbats that always afflict the candid friend.' And so Wadsworth left it with the conclusion, two days later in his leader for polling day, that in the current economic crisis the party likely 'to achieve realism and courage first will be the one that is out of office to-morrow.'[2]

Attlee won the election. The Labour Government went downhill. Ernest Bevin died. Herbert Morrison was moved to the Foreign Office. 'No one who looks round at the available timber can doubt that he is the best piece the Prime Minister can use for the job,' was Wadsworth's first opinion.[3] He was soon to retract it. 'It has taken the loss of British oil interests in Persia and the turmoil in Egypt to awaken Mr

Morrison to the importance of the war against poverty in the East.'[4] Nye Bevan resigned: 'If this is really what Mr Bevan and Mr Harold Wilson believe, the country is to be congratulated on having lost their services.'[5] Hugh Dalton made a mess of European unity. He 'must be tethered to a post in one of his National Parks and kept strictly out of European affairs.'[6] Cripps, 'one of the most attractive and able political leaders of our time,' fell ill and resigned. 'Had his life been spared he must have been a future Prime Minister.'[7] These opinions from Wadsworth's leaders written between the 1950 and 1951 elections are a melancholy roll call of the men whom he had known so well during his years as Labour correspondent. He was witnessing the disintegration of a party. It hurt him.

No one who was in the Corridor in the *Guardian* office in Cross Street on the night of Monday 21 October 1951 is likely to forget it. The last week of the general election campaign had begun. Attlee had just finished his final election broadcast. A.P. was writing the leader. He finished it and came out of his room. He handed the slips to Paddy Monkhouse, who had been his deputy since Pringle left – Allan Monkhouse's son had been Paddy to everybody since his first day on the paper a quarter of a century before. Both men were obviously stirred and unhappy. Both no doubt went back in thought to the Crozier leaders at the fall of the second Labour Government Paddy suggested that perhaps A.P. might be able to modify it a little. But, although Wadsworth was unhappy, he was determined. The leader stood as he had written it. He went along to Mary Crozier's room – she had been the M.G.'s radio critic since 1933 – showed her the copy and asked 'Do you think your father would have approved?' He had never done such a thing before. It was indeed quite unlike him and underlines the emotion he felt.

Next morning readers had only to glance at the title to see what had happened. Certainly, it ended with a question mark; but the implication of 'Time for Change?' was clear:

'The Radically minded voter (he wrote) . . . would like to be sympathetic to the Labour Government, which, after all, has been the instrument of a mainly beneficent social revolution . . . But the campaign has strengthened the conviction . . . that the Labour Government has come to the end of its usefulness . . . It has still some men of high ability at the top . . . though fewer now than in 1945 . . . And behind their façade of unity there is Mr Bevan and the hate-gospellers of his entourage . . . Another spell of importance and stumbling like that of the last eighteen months might bring greater catastrophe and a more lasting setback than Labour's loss of office now.' (22 October 1951)

Once again, as in 1950, he clinched the matter with a polling day leader: 'If action and courage are needed what alternative is there at the moment but to look for new men? . . . For the next few years a Churchill Government is, it seems to us, the lesser evil.'[8] Just sufficient men and women voters shared his unenthusiastic support for Churchill to turn the Labour Government out. He could not bring himself to be among them.

2

'Mr Bevan and the hate-gospellers of his entourage': in Wadsworth's opinion they were the main reason why those 'next few years' dragged on and on. Wadsworth had hoped that the Labour party would quickly pull itself together in opposition and provide the country with the Left Centre Government which it needed and which, he thought, it desired. Instead, the party continued to tear itself to pieces in what were 'personal, almost dynastic divisions.'[9] But they were also something more. Bevan's anti-Americanism threatened the whole of Ernest Bevin's work. The M.G. had argued hard to rally the Labour intellectuals to the Western Alliance and had largely succeeded. This had been the main political achievement of the first half of Wadsworth's editorship. Its defence was to be his main pre-occupation in the second period. That meant hitting Bevan and his followers hard. 'Many people of such views were readers of the *Manchester Guardian*. All the more reason to attack them strongly,' as a recent member of the M.G. staff, himself a Bevanite, wrote when A.P. died.[10] What the *Times* or the *Telegraph*, the *Mail* or the *Express* said could be discounted as the work of an enemy, but the M.G. was at least three-quarters within the fold and could not be ignored.

There was, however, more than a purely political difference between Wadsworth and Bevan. Both were men of strong feeling. What Wadsworth found it impossible to forgive was Bevan's bitterness about his fellow countrymen. No one was less of a Tory than Wadsworth but he could never have said, as Bevan did in Manchester: 'no amount of cajolery could eradicate from his heart a deep burning hatred for the Tory party . . . "so far as I am concerned they are lower than vermin".'[11] That kind of bitterness might be explained, as Bevan did in its context in that famous speech, in terms of the depression in which he grew up, but it could not be excused. Wadsworth's rejection of Bevanism was intellectual, his rejection of Bevan was emotional. It expressed itself, therefore, in harsher terms than he would otherwise have used, and the great debate took on some of the quality of a personal feud. Wadsworth

in Manchester and Boardman in Westminster sometimes appeared to be
Bevan's ruthless enemies determined to speak no good of him.

That is the impression that remains in the memory of many who
were actively concerned in politics and journalism in the Bevanite
years. It is not the whole truth. Eighteen months after the 'vermin'
speech when Bevan became Minister of Labour, Wadsworth wrote
that he was 'almost the best choice the Prime Minister could make . . .
he will not be without courage to rebuke unreasonable strikers or to
use that skill in negotiation which is his when he chooses to use it.'[12]
This was the skill that had delighted Boardman during the committee
stage of a bill dealing with the National Health service:

'Those who picture Mr Bevan only as a master of vituperation should . . .
come upon him at midnight or in the early hours of the morning . . . for
ordinary mortals just the moment for impatience and frayed temper. At such
times Mr Bevan is a man transfigured. He is conciliatory without being weak,
firm without being intransigent, and patient beyond belief.'[13]

Boardman, the connoisseur of parliament, admired Bevan the
master of a parliamentary occasion. When Bevan resigned, Boardman
wrote:

'There has never been a personal statement by a resigning Minister like
that of Mr Bevan to-day. But then no one like Mr Bevan has ever resigned.
He is famed as a great virtuoso of speech and here was a moment and a setting
made for the exercise of his rhetorical art and his debating skill: he explored
it to the utmost. But what would you? He was within his rights.

Consider the manner of it. Was there any regret at this breach with old
colleagues? Not a tincture. Was there any sense that the occasion had the
seeds of tragedy in it? That his action may have killed the Government? Not
a hint. Was there any attempt to see the Government's side of the case?
There was not . . . He would raise that quivering index-finger above his
head, or he would draw it, still quivering, in an imaginary line before the
front Opposition bench. At times he would claw the air towards him with
an open palm, or he would pause to pass his hand through his unruly
forelock.

This variety of gesture kept the speech tinglingly alive. From the corner
of the third bench below the gangway he hung like an avenging figure over
the Treasury bench. He talked down to Mr Morrison and Mr Gaitskell
literally and also passionately . . .' (24 April 1951)

It is against this not ungenerous treatment of Bevan that the
following episode should be set. At 3.40 p.m. on a November day in
1952 the chief sub-editor in the London office sent a service message
to Wadsworth which ran: 'This is what Nye Bevan said to me on the

Whitsuntide 1928: the
road to Blackpool

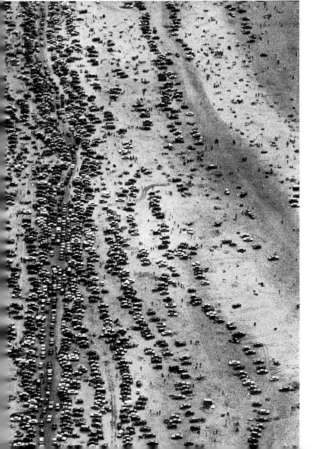

Whitsuntide 1969:
Southport Sands

A. P. Wadsworth,
Editor 1944–1956

1946: Return of the
Trust Deed from the
United States
Left to right: A. P.
Wadsworth, W. J.
Haley, L. P. Scott,
Paul Patterson, (The
Baltimore Sun), J. R.
Scott, James Bone,
J. C. Beavan

phone this afternoon. Though he is used to the M.G.'s venom and illiberality, to-day's parliamentary correspondent's message reached the lowest depths. It is damaging and utterly unfair and he thinks that he will now proceed against us. He demands an immediate withdrawal in the most prominent position. He is not sure that our parliamentary correspondent has not committed a breach of parliamentary privilege but he is quite sure that he was inspired by malignant malice.'[14]

At the beginning of the session Bevan had stood against Morrison for the deputy leadership of the Labour party and been defeated. Since then Bevan had hardly been seen in the House. Three times Boardman had drawn attention to his absence on occasions when he might have been expected to be there. Now Morrison had been moving a vote of censure on the Government and doing so in moderate terms. 'Of course, Mr Bevan was not present to hear Mr Morrison,' Boardman remarked. 'What can Mr Morrison teach him? Besides Mr Bevan is only technically a member of the House of Commons. They have probably noted in Tredegar that he takes no part in the business of the House. He has been seen in the Chamber twice since . . . the House reassembled . . . and then only for a few fleeting moments . . .'[15]

Wadsworth dealt with this complaint by writing the main leader under the title of 'Mr Bevan.' The second paragraph dealt with Boardman's sketch. Wadsworth noted that Bevan had voted in nine out of fifteen divisions, 'by no means a bad record.' 'The member of Parliament,' he went on, 'is happier than the reporter in the Press Gallery in that he is not under compulsion to listen to the dull speeches of others and has much to occupy him in other parts of the House. But Mr Bevan must also be conscious of the interest that his silences, as well as his speeches have for the political observer . . . we are sure that Mr Bevan, with his acute sense of the relative political importance of things, will understand.'[16] No doubt Mr Bevan did. But he did not forgive.

Bevanism continued throughout the 1951 parliament. Towards its end Wadsworth sent out Mark Arnold Forster to see what signs he could discover of 'radical dissent' in the country. He found few. Instead the personal controversies continued. The Labour party was still inward-looking. The cracks were papered over for the purpose of the 1955 election and a manifesto was drawn up 'in the good old Santa Claus manner' which offended Wadsworth's economic orthodoxy.[17] For the second time Wadsworth reluctantly concluded that a Conservative Government would be better for the country, though 'Heaven forbid that, because we do not want a Labour Government just now, every Tory candidate who appears before us should be returned.'[18] Electors ought to use their votes to get rid of the extremists in both parties. In his polling day leader – his thirteenth leader of the campaign – Wadsworth wrote: 'We may grant that the Conservative party of to-day is in some degree a reformed sinner. But we may doubt very much whether its good intentions would survive the prosperity of a majority of much over sixty.'[19] Sixty is just what it got. Even so, next year, not far from Sinai, it fell into more grievous sin in the eyes of the M.G. than any that the Labour Government had committed. The paper could be itself again.

3

'It happens that this paper was the first on this side of the world to publish a Low cartoon – in the days before the First World War when a brilliant young artist was pricking the dignity of the public men of Australia.'[20] So Wadsworth wrote in 1953 when he introduced David Low to his readers as a regular member of the staff – by far the most highly paid in fact, though he did not say so, earning more than the editor or the managing director. The occasional cartoons by Low which the M.G. had published in those early days were accidental in the sense that they were not commissioned. The paper, too poor to afford its own cartoonist, used to make a feature of political cartoons from many countries – and excellent they were. But from 1931 onwards for twenty years the *Guardian* had regularly published the famous series drawn for the London *Evening Standard*, which was still too far away from most *Guardian* readers to fear the risk of competition. But when Low moved to the *Daily Herald*, which printed in Manchester as well as in London, the position changed and *Guardian* readers were cut off from Colonel Blimp and the TUC cart-horse. The benevolent cart-horse, however, soon proved too much of a good thing for the TUC owners of the *Herald* and Low was free to stable it once more in the *Guardian*, this time as its only home.

It was Coronation Year. The Queen was crowned on the first Tuesday in June. Next day Low's cartoon was called 'Morning After.' There does not seem anything very objectionable in the two punch-drunk children, surrounded by the débris of a £100 million spree – empty champagne bottles, fairy princess tales, Snow White and all – looking at a TV screen on which is to be seen an unprepossessing female labelled Reality. But next day the paper was flooded with angry letters – 'lowest taste,' 'unsuitably vulgar,' 'Union Jack in the most insulting possible position on the human frame – that of a romper,' 'an affront to us all,' 'a new low in sheer bad taste,' 'repulsive and scandalous,' 'hot with shame,' 'your so appropriately named cartoonist.' And so it went on. One reader of fifty years' standing gave up the paper. Another recalled how during the Boer War men crumpled the *Guardian* into a ball and threw it away as soon as they had read the market reports from America. 'One hopes,' he added, 'that for a better reason the tram and railway lines in Lancashire have been similarly decorated to-day.'[21]

'The tram and railway lines in Lancashire' – that proved to be a significant phrase. As the days passed those who had enjoyed the cartoon, or at any rate disagreed with the intemperance of the protests, began to write in. An analysis was made, but not published, to show where the letters came from. Obviously an analysis by age was impossible, but it would probably have given a similar result. The final score was:

	No. of Letters	% Hostile
Lancashire, Cheshire	219	79
Rest of North Country	79	69
Midlands and South England	244	55
Elsewhere	33	60
Total	575	66

Among the largely hereditary or customary readers of the M.G. in its own heart-land many more were shocked than in the rest of the country where men took the paper because they agreed with its social and political outlook. But the fact that in every region the objectors exceeded the supporters suggests that the paper had misjudged the mood of the country on the day after the Coronation. A day or two later people might have been more ready to accept Low's feeling, 'as a Radical brought up in the less respectful and more irreverent atmosphere of a young nation, that, unless we are careful, an affair like the Coronation, in which rank and station seem to be elevated, can minister to snobbery.'*

The premature timing of the publication was an easy mistake for Wadsworth to make since, although he was fascinated by the British monarchy, his interest fell short of idolatry – 'there can be no other such mixture with so little harm and so much good in it' was the Coronation Day leader's conclusion. The quasi-religious fervour which was sweeping the country was alien from his temper and his understanding. But his interest was deep and wide. On the Saturday there had been nine special pages beautifully laid out. One two-page spread

---

* M.G. 5 June 1953. The uncharacteristically tortuous style of this leader by Wadsworth suggests that he was unhappy at the storm he had provoked.

dealt with 'The Evolution of the British Monarchy – and the Triumph of Parliamentary Supremacy'; another with 'Constitutional Monarchy in Western Europe – Democracy and the Written Constitution' with among others A. J. P. Taylor on the Nineteenth Century Tradition, G. J. Renier on Holland, and Nancy Crawshaw on 'The Instability of the Crown in Greece.' A Low cartoon showed the empty Coronation Chair and towering behind it a man in plain clothes holding a sceptre labelled Parliament and the orb marked Law. Behind him Oliver Cromwell and Lloyd George could be seen. No other paper approached the Coronation from quite this angle which faithfully reflected the attitude of the editor. The Coronation became, perhaps unconsciously, an occasion for the presentation of the *Guardian*'s own traditional way of looking at British politics and society.

For the eve of the Coronation Low devised a strip which ran across the whole of one page giving his 'cultural addition to the procession,' a picture of the literary and artistic scene as the *Guardian* saw it. The file was led by A. J. Munnings and Gerald Kelly in a bus welded by Reg. Butler, labelled 'Past, Present and Future'; and followed by Epstein 'gone all orthodox' and Sutherland 'off at a tangent.' Then came Gilbert Harding 'demonstrating his line'; Evelyn Waugh, Graham Greene, Bertrand Russell and J. B. Priestley in a hansom, discussing Progress; Olivier, Gielgud and Ralph Richardson soliloquising on British drama; 'Benjy' Britten setting T. S. Eliot to music for Donald (sic) Peers; with Rank and Korda bringing up the end 'lost in the Fourth Dimension.' Wednesday's paper contained besides the much criticised Low cartoon, accounts of the great day from almost every possible vantage point – 'the reporting delightful and with what pleasure one translated well-loved initials into names.' Thus one satisfied reader among the horde of dissenters. That Wednesday, now eighteen years ago, there were thirteen signed articles by past or present members of the staff. Their names illustrate the continuity of *Guardian* history. One joined the staff in 1902; six are still on it. Their names, the dates of their *Guardian* service, and where they were are set out here:

James Bone (1902–1945) in Park Lane
Harry Boardman (1919–1958) in the Abbey
R. H. Chadwick (1926–1954) 'All Quiet and Wet in Manchester'
Francis Boyd (1934–   ) in Parliament Square
Gerard Fay (1939–1966) outside Buckingham Palace
John C. Beavan (1946–1955) in Whitehall
Norman Shrapnel (1947–   ) in East Carriage Drive and among North
   Country villages

Mark Arnold Forster (1948–   ) on the Fly Past in an RAF Meteor
Nesta Roberts (1947–   ) at night outside the Palace
G. S. Gale (1950– 1955) in the Mall
Patrick Keatley (1952–   ) in Hyde Park
Philip Hope-Wallace (1950–   ) in Regent Street
W. F. Weatherby (1952–1963) in an excursion train from Manchester to
    London
John Bowra (1935–1954) in the East End

Bone had already recalled in a leader page article his Coronation Eve
vigils for the *Guardian* in 1902 and 1911. Boardman's *Guardian* memories did not go so far back but he too could recall journalism in 1910.
After returning his top hat to Moss Brothers, he wrote in a letter to
Wadsworth: 'The first topper I owned I bought, together with a frock
coat, in a great hurry to do something or other in Birmingham Town
Hall on King Edward VII's funeral. The *Birmingham Post* was then
paying me £3 a week and they were horrified that I had not a top hat
and a frock coat. Calling myself a "gentleman of the Press," indeed!'[22]
   Early in Wadsworth's editorship there had been the present
Queen's marriage. 'There is no reason,' he wrote, 'why this land of
Victoria Stations and Albert Halls should not one day pay equal
testimony to the lives and service of Elizabeth and Philip.' He followed
this up the next day with a short leader on the throne: 'There is no
royalist party. There is ceasing to be a Court class. We can respond
to and enjoy the royalist emotion without sinning against the light of
reason.'* Then in 1952 George VI died. Many newspapers published
'blown up' pictures of the three queens – the dead king's mother,
wife and daughter – at the door of Westminster Hall. Wadsworth,
always intensely sensitive to suffering, regarded this as an indefensible
intrusion into private grief and said so in a leader which brought in
many letters of congratulation and two critical ones. Both were from
journalists who suggested that the M.G. was taking a 'holier than thou'
attitude. But, as Wadsworth argued, 'if newspapers cannot criticise
each other, whom on earth can they criticise? And is journalism to
have no standards of propriety?'[23]
   The new reign meant a new Civil List. Wadsworth criticised its
amount because it seemed 'to imply a higher scale of living, entertain-
ment, and size of establishment than is really necessary under modern
conditions.'[24] Soon after the Coronation the newspapers were filled
with gossip about Princess Margaret's attachment to an RAF officer,
who had been divorced. The gossip, and the reported pressure on the

* M.G. 20, 21 November 1947. Manchester as well as London has an Albert
Hall and a Victoria Station.

Princess made Wadsworth angry. 'To most people,' he wrote, 'it would seem that this is a private matter . . . It is true that the Princess is not exactly a private person . . . But the succession is already pretty well assured without her . . . And the mass of ordinary people would not care two hoots, when she came to lay a foundation stone or open a town hall, whether her husband had been married before or not.'[25] A few days later it was proposed to leave her out of the regency council. Wadsworth argued strongly against the *Times* that this was a matter for Parliament and not for the Royal Family. The monarchy was a public affair and ought to be publicly controlled.

4

'Though journalism was his life Wadsworth would have preferred to be known as an historian.' This self-judgment appears in some notes for his own obituary which Wadsworth prepared in 1951. It rings true. He went on to tell how in his formative 'teens he fell under 'the magical spell of his friends R. H. Tawney and George Unwin' and later of J. L. Hammond. The history of the *Guardian* should have been his masterpiece. In 1921 Haslam Mills had written his slight but brilliant sketch for the paper's centenary. Hammond's biography was largely a study of C. P. Scott as a politician and dealt only incidentally with his paper. The hundredth anniversary of C.P.'s birth in 1946 provided Wadsworth with the opportunity and the responsibility of taking stock. The fatigue and the overwork of the war years made it impossible to produce more than a volume of collected essays by members of the staff which Wadsworth edited.[26] He included in it Crozier's brilliant sketch of 'C.P.S. in the Office' reprinted from the Hammond book. The result, however, was to show him that there was a chapter of newspaper history and to some extent also of English history still to be written.

The 'peg,' since journalists inevitably think in these sometimes artificial terms, would obviously be the centenary of the *Guardian* as a daily which was due to fall in 1955. It looks as if Wadsworth was deliberately clearing the decks for a major work. In the three years 1946–8 he wrote the first leader on an average seventy-three times each year. In the three years 1951–3 his average fell to thirty-three. In the last of those years he at last brought himself to appoint a literary editor, John Rosselli, and to give up arranging the book reviews himself. This went bitterly against the grain. Books were his passion. His unfortunate London editor was bombarded with notes about interesting items coming up at Sotheby's which would be worth a 'Letter par.'

He ended the notes for his own obituary with the remarks: 'Outside the paper he had few public interests. He enjoyed greatly his membership (since 1944) of the Council of Governors of the John Rylands Library, and of the Committee of the Manchester University Press.'

He set to work to assemble the pieces which he would need for the history. G. S. Whatmore, the *Guardian's* librarian, was set to work. A. E. Musson, the historian of the Typographical Association, was encouraged to use the M.G. as the main thread of a study on 'Newspaper Printing in the Industrial Revolution', although characteristically Wadsworth himself identified all the relevant material in the old account books, copied out the extracts and sent them to Musson who never saw the actual books themselves until this history was in preparation.[27] Alan Dent made an elaborate study of the M.G. and the theatre. Donald Read, who was to build up a fine reputation as a student of newspapers and their influence especially in the first half of the nineteenth century, undertook for Wadsworth a systematic exploration of *Guardian* history.[28] Wadsworth himself undertook an exhaustive study of newspaper circulations. An enormous amount of pioneer work was compressed into a short paper for the Manchester Statistical Society.[29] Though he employed others to help him he could never refrain from mastering their own materials at first hand for himself as well. This he did not out of distrust but from the love of doing it. Besides it might lead him on – who could know? No one who has worked through the *Guardian* records can fail to be impressed by the range of his enquiries. Repeatedly one comes across traces of his knowledge appearing lightly or incidentally in a reference to something else. But unfortunately they remain traces only. There is perhaps no source which has been used in the preparation of this book, possibly no single fact contained in it, which was not known to Wadsworth. His knowledge, however, most of it, remained in his head. He fell ill before he had time to start writing or even to arrange or collect together the material he had discovered. The only consolation to be found for the loss of A.P.'s own history of the Guardian is that it is now possible to carry the story beyond 1939 or 1944, where he would have stopped it, to 1956.

Wadsworth's own first historical work, 'The Cotton Trade and Industrial Lancashire 1600-1780',[30] brought him an honorary MA from Manchester University in 1932. This gave him immense personal pleasure. The boy who left school at fourteen years and two months, and who had crammed much of his research work into visits to the Public Record Office between bouts of industrial newsgathering, was now rather more than academically respectable. In 1955 he received a doctorate. This he rightly regarded as Manchester University's recognition of the worth of the *Manchester Guardian*. For its prosperity and increased circulation during his editorship he would not, to quote his own obituary notes once more, 'have claimed any virtue for himself.' 'He held firmly that a newspaper was a co-operative endeavour giving as much liberty of self-expression to the members of the team as is possible . . . A newspaper, he held, could be over-edited.'

And yet, though perhaps he did not realise it, no paper was ever a more perfect expression of its editor's character, tastes and values than was A.P.'s *Guardian*. The explanation lies partly at least in the conditions of the time. The chronic shortage of newsprint during his editorship meant a smaller paper than in the past. Much had to go. The policy of 'Manchesterisation' came to an end. The women's page disappeared for a time; there was less space for cars and motoring – two features which the *Guardian* had developed as early as any newspaper. For this reason there was less in the M.G. in A.P.'s time which did not interest the editor than there had been in C.P.'s. In the same way what remained automatically gained prominence. Wadsworth kept the traditional *Guardian* strengths – politics at home and abroad, books of all kinds, fine descriptive writing, archaeological discoveries, historical analysis.

There was another more subtle way in which the paper reflected Wadsworth's personality. Men write to be read and, if possible, to be read with appreciation. Established M.G. men knew that the editor would be their first reader and a sympathetic one. Consciously or unconsciously they wrote for him. They wrote differently, each in his own manner, about different things. But, of course, they did not write what they thought he would not like. Fortunately he liked many things and many different ways of saying them. In 1952 the first *Guardian Bedside Book* appeared. It was edited by Ivor Brown, but the pieces from which he made the anthology were chosen personally by Wadsworth. There is certainly nothing in the book which he would have wished away. Individually each article might probably have appeared in some other paper. Collectively they could only have come from the M.G., and from the M.G. in Wadsworth's time.

Wadsworth's own contribution to the paper was shot through and through with his historical interests. 'Only yesterday and to-day were real to him, never to-morrow,' one of his staff once said and there is truth beneath the exaggeration. Sometimes he would use the past seriously to illuminate the present, as in his careful analysis of the comparative balance of Tories and Radicals in Lancashire and in England as a whole at each general election since 1832. This he worked out as part of his contribution to the 1951 election.[31] Sometimes, however, he would use it as a plaything to give pleasure or to catch the attention of a particular reader without thinking that he had proved anything by his excursion into history. The best example, perhaps, is 'Dreadful Old Man.' He wrote it partly because he did not like those who were attacking Churchill – *Punch* with a 'vicious cartoon and a splenetic piece from its editor' (Malcolm Muggeridge*), 'its rakish companion, the *Daily Mirror*,' and 'the voice of the Gallup poll.' He paraded in front of them the warning example of middle-aged Queen Victoria who had called her two most internationally respected Ministers – Palmerston and Russell – 'two dreadful old men.' He enlisted Palmerston who at 80 climbed railings to see if he was losing his agility, and Gladstone who was knocked down by a cow and said nothing about it until someone mentioned a strange cow at dinner. But probably Wadsworth wrote his leader also in the hope of catching the eye of Churchill, that 'fifty years' reader,' and strengthening his resolve to hold on. Wadsworth would have liked to avoid Eden as Prime Minister now in the hope of getting Butler later. 'Why then all the fuss and the yapping? What has Sir Winston done to let down either the country or his party? . . . He can write a better State paper and make a better speech than any of his Ministers . . . There is no pretence among the critics that Mr Eden is not the successor designate. . . . Why the urgency to get the old man out of the way, to replace Charles by James?'[32]

But next day Wadsworth wrote to Boardman about 'the extraordinary old bird.' He thought he was probably reserving himself for his appearances in the House. 'I wonder what his control of his Cabinet is like and how far he keeps anything, except perhaps major foreign affairs, under close review.'[33] The end could not be far off. Next year Churchill resigned. 'He loved England with the passionate enthusiasm which Pericles felt for Athens, and he trusted the House of Commons as no one else.'[34] Those words, first applied to the Long Parliament's Sir John Eliot, were, Boardman felt, fit to use of Churchill on the day he ceased to be Prime Minister. Perhaps it was a recognition of the same qualities in the *Guardian*'s man in the Gallery that caused Churchill to choose that moment to invite Boardman to see him in his private room, something which his fellow political journalists rightly took to be a signal honour.

---

* Wadsworth also reacted adversely to another ex-*Guardian* editor, Kingsley Martin. The New Statesman, for instance, was 'rapidly developing into the *Chicago Tribune* in reverse.' (26 April 1947)

5

At the end of 1955 Wadsworth became seriously ill. In the New Year he went to Italy in the hope that the sunshine would do him good. He came back in the spring, determined to get better; but he came back to die. In the last months he was unable to get down to the office. He was confined first to his home and then to his bed. But each morning, towards noon, members of the staff would drop in to see him in the little suburban house lined everywhere with books – some in proper bookshelves, some in converted packing cases. He was still interested, still alert, still occupied. He reviewed books – his last long review was a notice of Beatrice Webb's autobiography; he wrote occasional leaders. His mind was still preoccupied with the paper and the world.

As far as the paper was concerned all was well. The circulation was getting on for three times what it had been when he took over, which was itself the highest figure recorded up to that time. Its reputation had never been higher. Laurence Scott was beginning to think seriously again about London printing. Wadsworth believed that the paper which he was now producing was editorially fit to go anywhere. But he must have known too that he would not be its editor when, and if, it started printing in a second centre. During his last three months he was able to see his paper edited to other journalists' admiration through a world crisis by the men he had trained up. Wadsworth was consulted and even took a small hand himself but he was not, and could not be, in practice responsible in a full, effective sense. But he could be content. One side of him must have felt privileged as Moses felt when he climbed 'to the top of Pisgah which is opposite Jericho. And the Lord showed him all the land . . . and said to him . . . "I have let you see it with your eyes, but you shall not go over there".'* Another side of Wadsworth must have been relieved; he would have made but a doubting Moses, uncertain whether the Lord would be well advised to send Joshua over Jordan.

But there were more immediate things to think about in that last summer. In Europe there was hope. In Poland, in Czechoslovakia and in Hungary the rigid mental slavery which had marked Stalin's Europe was loosening. Wadsworth had never found a successor for Werth but one had miraculously forced his way into the paper.

Back in 1939 a boy of 14, a Polish Jew, had lain awake at night listening to the tanks go by – German or Russian? They turned out to be Russian and for a short time all seemed well. Then his family was

* Deut. 34, 1–4 (R.S.V.).

deported into Russia. Soon Victor Zorza escaped from a labour camp and for two years he was on the run living from hand to mouth, twice arrested, at first without passport or identity card, then, later, with a forged one. Eventually he came to Kuibyshev, the temporary capital. He saw in a paper an article by Ilya Ehrenburg written from that town. He went to see the great man whose work he admired. Ehrenburg took him for a Polish refugee fleeing before the Germans, which in a sense he was; told him that a Polish air force was being formed for England and advised him to join it. He was to say that he spoke English – nobody would be able to contradict him – and to suppress the fact that he was a Jew. To be convincing he found that he had to build up a Christian past for himself, and become a man with a double identity.

Zorza served with the Polish Air Force in Intelligence until the end of the war. Then he went to the BBC's monitoring service, but his job was purely transcribing and he wanted to interpret. He wanted, oddly enough, to interpret for the *Manchester Guardian*. Even as a boy he had heard of it and had been grateful for the light it let in on that dark corner of the world where he was born. During his war service and with the BBC he had been educating himself, reading widely in history, then turning to contemporary affairs, trying to see how things fitted together, assembling the jig-saw, forging his analytical weapon, a man and a method after Wadsworth's heart.

He bombarded the M.G. with articles. They came back. At last one day in January 1950 he rang the London office and asked for Richard Scott. Zorza was told that he would not be back for a day or so. Zorza then asked to be put through to the copy-takers, and dictated a story which he said had been commissioned by Richard Scott – he had not been on the run for two years for nothing. The story, on nationalism in the Ukraine, duly appeared.[35] It mentioned that a young Ukrainian had been made secretary of the Moscow Communist party. His name was Nikita Khrushchev. From this time Zorza worked regularly for the *Guardian* without the permission of the BBC though no doubt with his colleagues' knowledge since he used to carry round a copy of the M.G. displaying his own anonymous contributions. But somehow he was shy about visiting the *Guardian* office. He did all his work by post or telephone and remained unknown to the staff until the day that Stalin died. He arrived that morning in the office at 9.30 and wrote hard all day.

Throughout the summer of 1956 Zorza wrote much for the paper on Eastern Europe. When the Hungarian rising developed he made his way to the Austrian frontier at Nickersdorf. In no man's land he and other journalists met Hungarian rebels fresh from fighting the Russian tanks. Among them was one woman, a girl of 17. She was asked what she thought she and her friends could achieve.

'They believe that by thus drawing the attention of the world to what is happening they will compel the Russians to get out,' she said, and without pausing asked 'And what is the feeling of the British people?' We all hesitated. No one was anxious to reply. Haltingly one of the reporters began to frame an answer, 'First, amazement.' Then a pause . . . 'Second . . . admiration.' Then, quickly, desperately as if he wanted to withdraw each word as soon as he had uttered it: 'And a great feeling of guilt.' The girl came back like a flash: 'There is much to be guilty for.' (29 October 1956)

6

There was indeed much to feel guilty about, for example, Britain's handling of the Suez crisis. There were three separate elements, which the *Guardian* carefully distinguished. The two local, geographical ones were the position of Israel and the ownership of the canal. The third was world opinion and the United Nations. Back in the days of the Stern gang, before the establishment of the State of Israel, Wadsworth, according to Pringle, had been anti-Zionist although he allowed the paper to continue its traditional policy. Certainly Wadsworth was never a Zionist in the Sidebotham, Crozier succession. But he had visited Israel at the end of 1951 and found it a land of promise in a world where there were far too few. He delighted in its 'extraordinary changes of fascinating sociological interest.'[36] He recognised the need clearly to guarantee her frontiers (and Egypt's) and to see that she could obtain the arms she needed. A.P. did not live to see the *Guardian*'s unmasking of the 'collusion' between Israel and the Western Powers in the Sinai campaign. He would no doubt have endorsed his paper's line. He would no doubt also have insisted that Israel's gamble would have been entirely unnecessary if her security had been properly underwritten long before.

The ownership of the canal was quite another matter. When Egypt nationalised it Wadsworth suffered the longest editorial conference of his career, unable to break it up as he liked to do by moving away. For forty minutes he and his leader-writers discussed whether Nasser's action involved a breach of an international treaty. In the end he was convinced that it did not. The paper's line on the direct issue followed from this. Should Britain use force, if necessary to impose her will?

Put like this it might sound an academic question such as student debating societies discuss. The *Guardian* answer would not be in doubt.

The questions which the paper had to answer were whether England was intending to use force and, if so, what other Powers would think and do. It had to find out quickly and to tell its readers what it found out. At the beginning of the crisis Gaitskell had been more willing than the *Guardian* to give Eden the benefit of the doubt. The other papers of the Left were also hesitant. The *Guardian* almost alone was confident and consistent in its warnings. It could be so because it was well briefed.

Much of the credit for this belongs to the *Guardian*'s Washington correspondent. The decision to double the paper's representation in America had been made in 1953, a courageous decision to take in a bad trading year. It showed its value, indeed its necessity, at once because the man chosen was Max Freedman, then in his fortieth year, a Canadian of Ukrainian–Jewish stock. It was not only his 24,000 books that endeared him to Wadsworth but his intelligent enjoyment of life at so many points. Theatres, cinemas, the White House, the Senate were all places he liked to visit and, visiting, brought alive to his readers. He was a sensitive observer and a deeply committed man, a 'keeper of the *Guardian*'s conscience' as the present editor describes him. He knew almost everybody who counted in the public life of Washington. Many, like Felix Frankfurter of the Supreme Court, a man old enough to be his father, were his intimate friends. When the Candian Prime Minister, Lester Pearson, tried to persuade him to stand for Parliament in 1956 it was Frankfurter who persuaded him that his work for the *Guardian* was more important than any Canadian political career. He had ready access to John Foster Dulles, Eisenhower's Secretary of State. There is something remarkable in a man who can combine this with being acceptable also to both John F. Kennedy and Lyndon Johnson. The year before Suez the United States in its concern over Formosa had trembled on the brink of war with Communist China. The *Guardian*'s young foreign editor, Alastair Hetherington, had written leaders counselling restraint. This went on day after day for three weeks at Wadsworth's insistence, encouraged by Freedman. The leaders were cabled to Washington and each morning were put on Dulles's desk. When the crisis was over Freedman was able to tell Manchester that they had helped to convince Dulles.[37]

Now it was the other way round. Freedman had to tell the *Guardian* how concerned the United States was about Britain's apparent willingness to go to war with Egypt if it could not get its way without. He sent discreet messages for the news columns and much longer frank memoranda for editorial guidance. Near the beginning of August one of these service messages reported that Freedman had heard from the

British ambassador that Dulles had sent through him 'the most urgent warning for Britain to go slow in taking military measures against Egypt.'[38] The *Guardian* continued to tell its readers about the preparations that were being made. Its warnings began to have effect. The national unity which had been expressed in the House by the leaders of the Opposition parties was beginning to wear thin. The Government decided to see whether it could put things in such a way to the *Guardian* that it would stop being awkward. The Minister of Defence asked Hetherington, who was doubling the rôle of foreign editor and defence correspondent, to come and see him. Hetherington went to London and talked with Sir Walter Monckton and with William Clark, the Prime Minister's press adviser. He gathered that Britain was now poised ready to intervene but that the decision to do so had not yet been taken.

On his way back to Manchester Hetherington scribbled a note to Wadsworth: 'Dear A.P., Here are copies of notes on my conversations. . . . Note Eden's estimate of the extent of public support for him. . . . On the intention to use (or not use) force, Richard Scott says that what I've been told is plainly contrary to the FO private briefing ten days ago. That's puzzling . . .' It was; but whatever the truth might be it was necessary to keep on warning the public about the Government's plans and the Government about public opinion since Hetherington had been told 'essential to get solution while country united behind Government and ready for sharp action . . . W.C. (William Clark) admits country perhaps less completely united than Government believed, and has himself put this to Eden; Eden a bit misled by unity of House in debate.'[39]

Sick though he was Wadsworth himself saw that the paper used its influence to disillusion Eden about national unity, if that were still possible. He telephoned to Mark Arnold Forster, then the paper's Labour correspondent, and told him to persuade Gaitskell at all costs to make a statement condemning the use of force. Gaitskell gave Arnold Forster a long interview which provided the main news story on the eve of the TUC meeting. The Government, Gaitskell said, 'should avoid any sabre-rattling; I hope they will go further and declare that their military preparations are really precautionary and for self-defence only . . . In spite of rumours, I cannot believe that after the London conference they can be seriously considering the use of force "to impose a solution" on Egypt.'[40] It was a timely statement by the party leader. At that moment nobody knew where Labour stood. There was considerable debate both in the TUC's International Committee and in the General Council before agreement was reached on a resolution which objected to the use of force except under United Nations' authority. But once drafted, it went through Congress easily. A week later Wadsworth wrote a leader which ended with these words, the last he was to write in the *Guardian*:

We shall probably be told . . . that the fears were all ignoble newspaper errors and that the Prime Minister has been the victim of heartless newspaper misrepresentation . . . That, however, is not the case. The vagueness has been his; it has been deliberate. It frightened Mr Dulles. It frightened the members of the (London) conference. The fears were acute. They are still alive. The onus of proof lies on the Prime Minister. We cannot feel safe until the United Nations is invoked. It is not enough to have peace or war at the mercy of a Prime Minister and his personal policy. (10 September 1956)

The *Guardian* had been instrumental in securing a firm stand by organised Labour. Its leading articles had also been effective in another direction and with unexpected consequences. We now know that they had so angered the Prime Minister that he determined, if he could, to stop the BBC quoting them or continuing to include Richard Scott in its discussion programmes. The troops must believe that the country was united, whether it was or not. Shortly before the actual Suez invasion Eden had a plan prepared to take over control of the BBC The Governors stood firm. An important victory for freedom of opinion had been won by the BBC's insistence on its right to quote whatever paper it liked, even the *Manchester Guardian*.[41]

The world was united in its desire to safeguard the freedom of passage through the Suez Canal. It was united in its rejection of the means Britain and France took to secure this. The attitude of the two world Powers was predictable. The USSR could be guaranteed to be unfriendly to Britain and France; the USA to be suspicious of the walking ghost of the British Empire and apprehensive lest Russia should lay the ghost and occupy the premises. But world opinion counted as well as world force of arms, and, perhaps for the first time, it mattered what India and Pakistan thought. The messages from Delhi of Tanya Zinkin were important in helping both the staff and readers to feel what was in the air. Vernon Bartlett reported regularly from Singapore. What was significant and novel was that other countries, especially Asian countries, seemed to regard Egypt's point of view as every bit as important as Britain's. Egyptian opinion was faithfully reported to the *Guardian*. Since Easter there had been a staff correspondent in Cairo. In 1956 Michael Adams had had just enough journalistic experience to fit him for his very exacting job. His messages showed a grasp of Egypt's military weakness, the strength of her feelings, and the probable long-term effects of flouting them. They were the more effective because they were more detached than his later work.

Compared with other later confrontations there was one piece conspicuously missing both in the diplomatic line-up and in the M.G.'s news service during the Suez crisis. Africa south of the Sahara was still a continent of European dependencies peopled by what Wadsworth teasingly called 'Paddy's Blacks' living a primitive, isolated life. True, there were faint stirrings of political nationalism. There had, for instance, been a Pan-African conference in Manchester as long ago as 1945 at which Joseph Appiah and Jomo Kenyatta were present. It had passed the expected anti-imperialist resolutions couched in traditional Marxist verbiage. They were faithfully reported by R. H. Chadwick, a whimsical Yorkshireman who could always make a good story out of his innumerable misadventures but who on this occasion treated the conference soberly enough as a very minor piece of week-end news.[42] Their studies finished, the delegates went home to Africa. Progress was slow. Twelve months before Suez Patrick Monkhouse had been on a long tour of East Africa for the paper. What he wrote had the general heading of 'Kenya after the Mau Mau,'[43] and was concerned a great deal with economic problems, a certain amount with settler politics, but hardly at all with anything like a nationalist movement. Kenyatta was still in detention. There were still some years to go before Harold Macmillan felt a wind of change. But in 1956 it began to blow steadily south from Suez.

Wadsworth was rapidly losing strength. From the middle of September he could take no more part in editing the paper although until the end he liked to know what was happening. In this last stage he consented to what was done instead of being consulted about what should be done. On 17 October it was announced that he would retire at the end of the month with the title of Editor Emeritus, a pleasantly academic distinction for probably the world's most scholarly newspaper man. His successor, Alaistair Hetherington, may be said to have emerged in the same kind of way that Conservative prime ministers used to do. He was 36 and young enough to take the paper to London when the time came. On 31 October the *Guardian* carried two pages of affectionate tributes to Wadsworth from newspapers all over the world and from many public men. It also carried news of the Anglo-French ultimatum: 'an act of folly without justification.' The *Guardian* was almost alone in its stand. Twenty-four hours later the *Daily Mirror* and the *News Chronicle* joined in.

Wadsworth died on 4 November. The same paper that brought the news of his death reported that British and French troops were embarking in Cyprus for the invasion of Egypt, and that Russian tanks had suppressed the Hungarian revolution. ('Haltingly one of the reporters began to frame an answer . . . "And a great feeling of guilt." The girl came back like a flash: "There is much to feel guilty for".') Low's cartoon next day showed Khrushchev dashing off to a tank and waving cheerfully to Eden who was about to embark in a bomber. He called it 'Me, Too.'

There was a touch of winter in the air. Old *Guardian* men thought of 1899, of 1920, of 1931, of 1938. Once again they were ashamed of the Government, but not of the paper. In the Reporters' Room young men had waited anxiously to know what the M.G. would say now that Wadsworth's hand was gone and it had come to the crunch. Close the ranks, or stick to principle? Older now, they still recall the relief and exhilaration with which they read 'The Anglo-French ultimatum is an act of folly without justification . . . It pours petrol on a growing fire.'[44] Most leading articles are fugitive pieces, but some of the young M.G. men of 1956 can still quote these words verbatim, unrehearsed. Outside the office they often met with hostility as they went about their business during the next few days. Suez divided. It still divides. After all it is a watershed.

An End and a Beginning

There is a shifting but always ill-defined frontier between history and current affairs. The writer of a history does well not to venture into no man's land, and this book halts accordingly at Wadsworth's death. Nevertheless there are a number of loose threads, especially some left over from chapter 37, which ought to be gathered up not only to round off the story which began in 1821 but to link the youthful *Guardian* of to-day with all the yesterdays through which the *Manchester Guardian* had delighted successive generations of readers young in spirit.

Laurence Scott's programme, outlined to his father in 1945, involved three distinct steps—news on the front page; the dropping of Manchester from the masthead; and the printing of the paper in London as well as in Manchester so that it would be available to readers wherever they lived in England or Wales. Only the first step had been taken before Wadsworth died. News appeared on the front page for the first time on 29 September 1952. The circulation was then 130,000, more than three times its pre-war figure.

Seven years later the paper, whose circulation had just reached 180,000 was ready to take the second step. On 24 August 1959 the masthead on the front page read simply *The Guardian* in the same way as the title above the leaders had always done. Readers were warned in the previous issue what to expect:

'It acknowledges an accomplished fact. Nearly two-thirds of the paper's circulation now lies outside the Manchester area. Twenty years ago, although the *Guardian*'s voice was heard and sometimes heeded far from Manchester, only 20,000 copies were sold more than a score of miles from Cross Street. To-day the number is about 118,000 . . . Eventually the best solution (for nationwide distribution) must lie in simultaneously printing in Manchester and London . . .'

From a world point of view the change of title was irrelevant—the French have always been, and still are, happy to talk about '*Le Manchester*' just as we used to refer to the *Frankfurter* without implying that it was thereby of any lower standing than the *Berliner Tageblatt*. From a narrowly English point of view it was no doubt right. But did this carry the necessary implication that a nation-wide newspaper could not effectively be edited outside London? But perhaps the regional capitals of England are so bored with one another that they prefer yet another London product to a Manchester *Guardian*. And perhaps, although there are clearly three nations in Great Britain and many towns and villages, regions now exist only in geography and civil servants' files.

Two years later that third step was taken. The first issue to be printed in Grays Inn Road, London was published on 11 September 1960. Laurence Scott's programme was complete. London printing took a technically traditional form partly because Laurence Scott feared that the trade union side of the industry would not prove sufficiently flexible to adapt itself quickly enough to a new system of production in one isolated newspaper office. Initiative passed from England to Japan. The *Asahi Shimbun* became the first daily newspaper to use the long-distance facsimile reproduction process developed for the *Manchester Guardian*. In June 1959 it began printing five editions each day in Tokyo and Sapporo, 500 miles away.* At the meeting of the Commonwealth Press Union that year delegates were given copies of the Japanese paper. Charles Markwick had the melancholy satisfaction of showing them copies of the 'dummy' run of the *Manchester Guardian* produced in the same way in Copenhagen in February, 1951. One cannot but regret that the *Guardian* which had pioneered the method had not felt able to persist. Readers of the *Guardian Weekly* will have noticed since 1969 the gain in beauty which the introduction of 'offset litho' printing has given it. That gain would have been available to readers of the daily. Letterpress printing in Manchester with only facsimile reproduction in London, the original plan, might well have left more of the weight of the editorial departments in the paper's original home and preserved that distinct extra-metropolitan flavour in its comment and its standpoint to which C.P. and Wadsworth attached importance.

For three years the editor continued to live in Manchester and to visit London. Now the position is reversed. But the paper, born and bred in the North, knows that England is more than just London writ large. It is knowledge worth having and passing on.

In London the *Guardian* is still a lodger with the *Sunday Times* for its landlord. In Manchester it has a home of its own; a new one now, provided on a new pattern of plant co-ownership with another newspaper. On Saturday 29 August 1970 the paper was published for the

---

* A new method developed in 1953 had reduced the processing time to fifteen minutes.

last time from the building in Cross Street, Manchester, which had been its home for 85 years on a site which it had occupied for 130 years. The Corridor is now hardly even a term of art, but the spirit that justified the capital letter it has been given in this book is still there. The last leader written in C.P.'s old room at the head of the Corridor explained the reason for the move to the new site in Deansgate ten minutes walk away:

'Many a family has to decide that, rich in history and associations though its Victorian pile had become, a more modest, modern residence would be cheaper and more convenient to run. We are in something of the same case. The new company set up to print the *Guardian*'s northern editions is jointly owned by us and the *Daily Mail*. The editorial and commercial control of the two remains quite separate and unaffected by the formation of the new company; but by sharing plant and equipment we feel we can reduce some of the enormous and growing overheads of newspaper production. Our sister paper and helpmeet, the *Manchester Evening News,* will use the same plant in the daytime and the *People* has contracted to print there at week-ends. All this is no more than prudent housekeeping. To be frank we do not want to go; to be fair, it is better that we should ...'

On the following Monday the first issue to come from Deansgate contained the last descriptive article written at a desk in the old Reporters' Room beneath the ancestral photographs of Haslam Mills and George Leach:

'There has been scaffolding all the way up the front of the old, smoky red-brick building, and a great hole was made in the wall so that machinery and effects could be taken out and lowered on to wagons in the street. Not much of the Corridor or the Room went out that way. All that was worth taking had to go out in the minds of those who knew them best.'

Surely the shade of Haslam Mills went appraisingly with them as they gathered to see for what engagements they had been marked in the half-filled Diary on that first day of their new life.

Sources

This book is based mainly on two sources – the files of the paper and the paper's own archives. The latter are of two main kinds - business records and memoranda, mainly of a financial character; and letters to and from outside contacts, members of the staff and contributors. There are very few surviving letters from the period before Scott's editorship. There are in the firm's possession about 4,000 letters from the time of C. P. Scott. Nearly all of them are later than 1885 when the *Guardian* moved to the Cross St. offices which it occupied until 1970. Some of C. P. Scott's correspondence, selected on no apparent grounds, and all his interview notes with leading politicians were given to the British Museum after J. L. Hammond had finished his biography. The greater part of the interview notes were published with introductions by Professor Trevor Wilson in 1970 under the title of 'The Political Diaries of C. P. Scott.' Quotations from notes not included in this edition are distinguished by the suffix (MS) in the list of references. Crozier's correspondence with his foreign correspondents is extensive – the telephone had not replaced letter-writing as a means of communication in his time on the *Guardian*. Wadsworth also was a letter-writer though more selectively so than Crozier.

There are, of course, or were, other collections of letters which bear on the *Guardian* history. For the early period there are Scott and Taylor letters printed by Isabella and Catherine Scott in the privately printed 'A Family Biography' (1908) which is cited as I & C Scott. Other Taylor and Allen letters of the early period have kindly been made available by Canon R. R. Allen, a great grandson of the founder of the paper. Three other series which have been freely used are the letters from C. E. Montague to Francis Dodd in the British Museum (all quotations from Montague's letters to Dodd are from this collection and are therefore not otherwise distinguished); letters between C. P. Scott and other members of the *Guardian* circle and Chaim Weizmann and other Zionist leaders in the Weizmann Archives at Rehevoth in Israel; letters from C. P. Scott, E. T. Scott and W. P. Crozier to J. L. Hammond, and occasional letters from him, in the Bodleian.

Unfortunately, although we possess some 630 letters from John Edward Taylor, the younger, to C. P. Scott, Scott's answers have not survived except in a few instances in draft form.

Three other manuscript sources must be mentioned: 'Harland's Annals' of which there is a microfilm in the Manchester Central Library; Leary's manuscript 'History of the Manchester Periodical Press' in the same library; and Crozier's Diary (1940-1942) and Interview Notes (1933-1943).

References both to these sources and to books quoted in the text are given either in footnotes or in the following list of references. Grateful thanks are due to their authors and publishers.

Particular gratitude is due to Mrs. Mary MacManus (Mary Crozier) and Miss Janet Wadsworth for preserving and making available a great deal of material which had been in their fathers' possession.

Books & Papers

This short list excludes books dealing with general political history, general newspaper history and general Manchester history. Books made of articles reprinted from the *Guardian* have also been excluded. It might better be described as 'Suggestions for Further Reading' than as a bibliography. It is confined to books either wholly or largely about the *Guardian* or to books by people closely connected with it and dealing at some length with their connection with the paper.

Agate, James   Ego (1935)
Ego 2 (1936)

Atkins, J. B.   Incidents and Reflections (1947)

Cardus, Neville   Autobiography (1947)

Elton, Oliver   C. E. Montague (1929)

Hammond, J. L.   C. P. Scott of the Manchester Guardian (1934)

Lejeune, C. A.   Thank You for Having Me (1964)

Martin, Kingsley   Father Figures (1966)

Matthews, T. S.   The Sugar Pill (1957)

Mills, Haslam   The Manchester Guardian: A Century of History (1921)

Montague, C. E.
and
Mrs Humphry Ward   W. T. Arnold (1907)

Musson, A. E.   The first Daily Newspapers in Lancashire (Lancs & Cheshire Antiquarian Society 1955)
Newspaper Printing in the Industrial Revolution (Economic History Review 1958)

Prentice, Archibald   Historical Sketches (1851; new edition 1970)
History of the Anti-Corn Law League (1853)

Philips Price, M.	My Three Revolutions (1969)
Read, Donald	Press and People 1790-1850 (1961) Peterloo (1958) John Harland (Manchester Review 1958)
Spring, Howard	In the Meantime (1942)
Tyrkova- Williams, A.	Cheerful Giver (1935)
Wadsworth, A. P.	Newspaper Circulations 1800-1954 (Manchester Statistical Society 1955)
Wadsworth, A. P. (editor)	C. P. Scott and the Making of the Manchester Guardian (1946)
Walmsley, Robert	Peterloo; The Case Reopened (1969)
Wilkinson, H. Spenser	Thirty-Five Years (1933)
Wilson, Trevor	The Political Diaries of C. P. Scott (1970)

References

CHAPTER ONE

1 Prentice: Historical Sketches (1851), p. 145. There is a reprint (Cass & Co. 1970 with an introduction by Donald Read).
2 The account is based on 'A Full and Accurate Report of the Trial . . .' with an introduction by Taylor (Manchester: W. Cowdroy) 1819, and on Prentice: Historical Sketches (1851), pp. 133–144.
3 M.G. 10 January 1844.
4 Taylor's early life is described in I. and C. Scott: A Family Biography, drawing on contemporary letters, in the obituary in the M.G. 10 January 1844 almost certainly by Jeremiah Garnett, and in a memoir in the Christian Reformer March 1844 which was reprinted as a pamphlet.
5 Prentice: Historical Sketches, p. 163.
6 Francis Philips: Exposure of the Calumnies.
7 Manchester Gazette 7 August 1819.
8 Taylor's account of Peterloo is from his 'Notes and Observations'.
9 The Peterloo Massacre No. 2; No. 1, p. 1. See Walmsley; Peterloo: The Case Reopened (Manchester Univ. Press 1969).
10 Prentice Historical Sketches, pp. 202–203.
11 I. and C. Scott, p. 184.
12 I. and C. Scott, p. 184.

CHAPTER TWO

1 Select Committee on Newspaper Stamps (1851). Evidence of W. H. Smith pp. 420–437.
2 For the next six paragraphs see A. E. Musson: Newspaper Printing in the Industrial Revolution (Economic History Review 1958), and The Typographical Association (1954), pp. 25–29.
3 M.G. 3 December 1825.
4 M.G. 14 September 1822.
5 M.G. 28 September 1870.
6 M.G. 7 September 1822.
7 M.G. 1 June 1822.
8 M.G. 25 May 1822. A year before the M.G. had reported that two boys had been knocked down and killed by the Liverpool coach in Manchester (21 July 1821).
9 M.G. 26 May 1821.

10 M.G. 7 July 1821.
11 M.G. 1 June 1822.
12 M.G. 28 September 1822.
13 M.G. 18 November 1822. Wellington was at Verona for the Congress called to deal with the Greek rebellion against Turkey and the constitutional revolt in Spain.
14 M.G. 2 and 9 November 1822.
15 M.G. 17 August 1822.
16 M.G. 12 October and 7 September 1822.
17 M.G. 13, 20 July 1822; M.G. 8 June 1822.
18 e.g. Racing M.G. 2 and 9 June 1821; Walking 28 September 1822; Boxing 23 June 1821; Cockfighting 16 June 1837; Bull-baiting 21 September 1822.
19 M.G. 21 September; 26 October 1822.
20 Prentice: Historical Sketches of Manchester (1851), p. 289.
21 M.G. 10 August 1822.
22 M.G. 15 February, 2 August 1823.
23 I. and C. Scott, p. 198.

CHAPTER THREE

1 The population of Manchester before 1801 is discussed in Wadsworth and Mann: The Cotton Trade and Industrial Lancashire, pp. 509–511.
The census figures in the text (M.G. 9 June 1821) cover Manchester, Salford and adjacent suburbs long since incorporated.
2 Manchester Advertiser (Taylor's new Tuesday paper) No. 1, 30 August 1825.
3 W. E. A. Axon: Annals of Manchester – under 1752, 1764; Cranfield: Development of the English Provincial Newspaper O.U.P. (1962), p. 166; Harland: Collectanea, p. 108.
4 Cranfield: English Provincial Newspaper, p. 152.
5 Harland: Collectanea relating to Manchester (Chetham Society), p. 97.
6 Leary: Manchester Periodical Press, p. 171.
7 J. T. Slugg: Manchester Fifty Years Ago (1881), p. 282.
8 Aspinall: Politics and the Press (Benn 1949), p. 270.
9 Exchange Herald 22 April 1823.
10 Prentice: Historical Sketches, pp. 208, 262.
11 Exchange Herald 28 September 1826.
12 Exchange Herald 14 January 1823.
13 Exchange Herald 22 April; 13 May 1823.
14 Harland: Collectanea, p. 113.
15 Manchester Gazette 19 January 1822.
16 Harland: Collectanea, p. 36.
17 Westminster Review XII.

CHAPTER FOUR

1 M.G. 26 May; 9, 16, 23 June 1821.
2 M.G. 12 April 1823.
3 M.G. 7 September 1822.
4 M.G. 29 March 1823.
5 Prentice: Historical Sketches, pp. 240–241.
6 Prentice: Historical Sketches, p. 246.
7 Prentice: Historical Sketches, p. 361.
8 Cobden to A. W. Paulton 8 January 1858 quoted in N. McCord: The Anti-Corn Law League (Allen & Unwin 1958). Bentham to Place 24 April 1831 (B.M. Add. MSS 35149).
  Absalom Watkin: Extracts from his Journal (1920), pp. 191–192.
9 Prentice: History of the Anti-Corn Law League, p. 8.
10 I. and C. Scott, pp. 151, 202.
11 J. T. Slugg: Manchester Fifty Years Ago, pp. 290, 291.
  W. E. A. Axon: Annals of Manchester.
  Leary: History of the Manchester Periodical Press, p. 162.
12 M.G. 26 August 1826.
13 The Letters between Richard Potter and Taylor are quoted in Meinertzhagen: The Potters of Tadcaster (1908), pp. 227–236.
  Shuttleworth's contributions to the Guardian are in a cuttings book in Manchester Central Reference Library.
14 I. and C. Scott, p. 209.
  I. and C. Scott, p. 459.
15 Exchange Herald 28 September 1826.
16 Prospectus of Manchester Times 1828 quoted in Leary: Manchester Periodical Press, p. 174.

CHAPTER FIVE

1 M.G. 4 December 1830; 1 January 1831.
2 M.G. 28 January 1832; 13 March 1832; Manchester and Salford Advertiser 21 May 1836.
3 Brooke Herford's Preface to Vol. 2 of Harland's edition of Baines's Lancashire; Harland Annals;
4 Richard Oastler: The Law and the Needle quoted from J. T. Ward: The Factory Movement (Macmillan 1962), p. 161. M.G. 28 January 1832.
5 Garnett's obituary in M.G. 28 September 1870; article in D.N.B. by his nephew Richard Garnett; for Thomas Forrest see J. T. Slugg: Manchester Fifty Years Ago (1881), pp. 80, 286. I am indebted to Mr R. K. B. Alridge, Chief Librarian of Huddersfield Public Libraries, for information about the West Yorkshire Gazette.
6 Redford v. Birley and others: Manchester C. Wheeler & Son, Chronicle Office (1822), pp. 13, 100–108.

7 Manchester Courier 13, 20, 27 July 1839.
    M.G. 17, 24, 27 July 1839; 28 March, 1 April 1840.
    Other Manchester papers 27 July 1839.
8 Harland: Annals; T. T. Wilkinson: Memoir of John Harland in Lancashire
    Legends by Harland and Wilkinson (1873), p. xxii.
    James Tait: The Chetham Society: A Retrospect (Chetham Society
    New Series, vol. xii).
9 Harland: Annals; M.G. 4 December 1830.
10 M.G. 3 December 1831; 17 March 1832; 25 April 1868.
11 M.G. 19 May 1832.
12 P.R.O. Home Office Papers 52/37.
13 Prentice: Anti-Corn Law League, p. 30; M.G. 2 January 1842.
14 Prentice: Anti-Corn Law League, p. 368; Hansard 21 July 1842.
15 Prentice: Anti-Corn Law League, p. 117 (28 February 1839).
    Manchester Courier, Advertiser 16 December 1843 quoted from J. T.
    Ward: The Factory Movement, p. 276.

CHAPTER SIX

1 I. and C. Scott, pp. 229, 328.
    Absalom Watkin: Extracts from his Journal (T. Fisher Unwin 1920), p.
    156.
    Harland: Annals.
2 I. and C. Scott, p. 295.
3 Manchester Times 21 December 1839.
4 Leary: Manchester Periodical Press passim.
5 Select Committee on Newspaper Stamps 1851, pp. 420–437.
6 Manchester and Salford Advertiser 14 December 1839.
7 M.G. 27 June 1846.
8 M.G. 27 December 1834. (See Leary: Manchester Periodical Press, pp.
    199, 200.)
9 Manchester and Salford Advertiser 15 September, and 8 December 1832.
    M.G. March 1833. (See Leary: Manchester Periodical Press, p. 194.)
10 Absalom Watkin: Extracts from his Journal, p. 122.

CHAPTER SEVEN

1 I. and C. Scott, pp. 261, 312.
2 I. and C. Scott, p. 328.
3 M.G. 24 November 1947.
    Lord Chilston: W. H. Smith (Routledge & Kegan Paul) 1965), pp. 4, 5.
4 Select Committee on Newspaper Stamps (1851). Evidence of W. H. Smith,
    pp. 420–437; Wadsworth: Newspaper Circulations (Manchester Statistical
    Society 1955).
5 Scott–Hobhouse, 4 January 1900.

6 Select Committee on Newspaper Stamps (1851). Evidence of W. H. Smith.
7 Select Committee on Newspaper Stamps (1851). Evidence of F. K. Hunt.
8 e.g. M.G. 16 October 1847.
9 M.G. 21 August 1847.
10 M.G. 19 February 1848.
11 Manchester Examiner 23 November 1847.
12 M.G. 13 December 1845.
13 Manchester Examiner 2 May 1848; M.G. 3 May 1848.

CHAPTER EIGHT

1 M.G. 20 September 1848 (obituary notice).
2 Liverpool Correspondence 1848: Mexican War 15 March; French Revolution 22 March; California 1 April; New York Herald 10 June; U.S.A. Taxation 5 July; U.S.A. Election 18 November; Emigration 20 December; Gold Rush 23 December.
3 M.G. 1848: West Indian Sugar 5 February; Schleswig–Holstein 18 April; India Board 6 May; Navigation Laws 10 June; Ireland 21 October.
4 Bagehot: Literary Studies, pp. 367 (ff)
5 M.G. 22 November; 13 December; 9 December; 23 December; 30 December, 1948.
6 The Sphinx 29 October 1870.
  Marx-Engels Gesamtausgabe Abt. III, Band 2 (1930), p. 99.
7 e.g. M.G. 1, 26, 29 April; 20 May; 21 June 1848.
8 M.G. 15 April 1848.
9 Sophia Taylor–Russell Scott 12 October 1848.
10 R. S. Taylor–Russell Scott or Robert 11 August 1848.
11 M.G. 30 September; 4 October.
12 M.G. 1 April 1848.
13 Sophia Taylor–Russell Scott 17 June 1848; 21 March 1849.
14 M.G. 29 July; 12 April 1848
15 M.G. 6 May; 15 July 1848.
16 M.G. 20, 27 December 1848.
17 M.G. 25 October; 25 November; 20 December 1848.
18 M.G. 13, 24 November 1848.
19 M.G. 12 January; 15 March; 2 August 1848.
20 M.G. 29 March 1845.
21 M.G. 22 March 1848.
22 M.G. 22 March; 28 June 1848.
23 Manchester Examiner 27 June 1848.
24 M.G. 20 May (Public Health); 19 April 1848 (Education).
25 M.G. 22 December 1847. The debate was on The Jewish Disabilities Removal Bill.
26 M.G. 20 September 1848.

CHAPTER NINE

1 Report of Select Committee on Newspaper Stamps (1851), p. xvii; A. E. Musson: The First Daily Newspapers in Manchester (Lancashire and Cheshire Antiquarian Society 1956).
2 Sophia Taylor–Russell Scott 9 May 1852; 28 May 1854.
3 Engels–Marx 7 February 1856; Marx–Engels 30 October 1856 (Marx-Engels: Gesamtausgabe Abt. III, Band 2 (1930); M.G. 20 October 1856.
4 M.G. 25 April 1868.
5 First special parliamentary report M.G. 12 February 1856; Crimean enquiry, e.g. 14 April 1856.
6 e.g. M.G. 5–10 July 1857; Select Committee on Parliamentary Reporting (1878), Q. 2359.
7 M.G. 22 May 1856.
8 e.g. M.G. 2 April 1856; 11 December 1855 (Roman Catholics); 21 May 1857 (Divorce); 18 May 1857 (capital punishment); 3 July 1855, 21 May 1856 (Sunday Games).
9 M.G. 28 August 1855.
10 Diaries of John Bright ed. Walling (Cassell) (1930) 5 December 1856.
11 M.G. 2 April 1857.
12 M.G. 19 March 1857.

CHAPTER TEN

1 Allen–Boyce 28 February 1858.
2 Allen–Boyce 28 February 1858; Taylor–Hoe 19 December 1858.
3 Taylor, Garnett & Co to Wm. Whitefield & Co, Kendal, 14 August 1858.
4 Taylor–Cobb 3, 4, 10 December 1858.
5 Allen–Boyce 28 February 1858.
6 Engels–Marx 7 December 1858. Marx–Engels Gesamtausgabe III, 2 (1930), p. 250.
7 M.G. 2 July 1855.
8 Allen–Boyce 29 February 1858.
9 Taylor–Feeny 14 December 1858.

CHAPTER ELEVEN

1 Harland: Annals 1842 – the occasion was the British Association meeting in Manchester; Preface to Vol. 2 of Baines's Lancashire (1870).
2 The Sphinx 29 October 1870.
3 M.G. 17, 24 October 1861; 21–25 June 1862; 10 October 1862; Manchester Examiner 26 June 1862.
4 M.G. House Journal December 1920.

5 Select Committee on Electric Telegraphs Bill (1868); Evidence of John Edward Taylor, Francis D. Finlay.
6 See Hugo R. Meyer: The British State Telegraphs (New York 1907); Select Committee on Newspaper Stamps (1851): Evidence of F. K. Hunt, pp. 337f; Whorlow: The Provincial Newspaper Society (1886), p. 55.
7 Taylor–Pender 31 August 1858.
8 On the foundation of the Press Association see George Scott: Reporter Anonymous: Hutchinson (1968).
9 Select Committee on Post Office (Telegraph Dept) 1876. Evidence of J. E. Taylor, John Lovell.
10 Meyer: British State Telegraphs, p. 122.
11 The Sphinx 29 October 1870.
12 Select Committee on House of Commons Arrangements (1868). Evidence of Henry Dunphy.
13 Select Committee on Parliamentary Reporting (1878). Evidence of Charles Ross and R. A. Gosset; Michael Macdonagh: The Reporters' Gallery (Hodder & Stoughton) 1913, pp. 396, 397.

CHAPTER TWELVE

1 M.G. 3, 4 December 1863; 17, 18 March 1865.
2 e.g. M.G. 20 January 1862.
3 M.G. 9 October 1862.
4 M.G. 23 January 1862; 1 February 1862.
5 Boston Courier 16 December 1861; Manchester Examiner 4 January 1862; M.G. 13 January 1862; Times 9, 10 January 1862. See Henry Adams: A Diary in Manchester edited Silver in American Historical Journal October 1945; The Education of Henry Adams (1928 edition), p. 120.
6 M.G. 23 January 1862; 2 January 1863.
7 M.G. 1, 2 January; 11 February 1863.
8 M.G. 22 December 1870.
9 M.G. 12 November 1870; 6 December 1870.
10 M.G. 27 March 1871.
11 M.G. 15 December 1870; 18 January 1871; 1 September 1870.
12 M.G. 7 January 1871; 29 December 1870.
13 M.G. 28, 31 December 1870.
14 The Fall of Metz (Bradbury, Evans & Co. 1871).
15 M.G. 5–27 January 1866 (reprinted as a pamphlet); 26 April 1871.
16 Scott–Mrs Russell Scott 10 February 1871.

CHAPTER THIRTEEN

1 Grant: The Newspaper Press (1871) Vol. 3, p. 360.
2 Furneaux–Enfield 13 June (no year) quoted in I. and C. Scott, p. 397.

3 Taylor–Scott 23 March 1889.

4 C. P. Scott–Russell Scott October 1867 quoted J. L. Hammond: C. P. Scott: Bell (1934), p. 24.

5 Sophia Allen–Russell Scott 31 December (probably 1867).

6 C. P. Scott–Mrs Russell Scott 10 February 1871.

7 Hammond, p. 37; M.G. 29 March 1845; I. and C. Scott, p. 384.

8 (Law Reform) M.G. 1873; 22, 24, 29 January; 1, 7 February.
(Medical Aid) 3, 4, 5, 12 April; 16, 23 May.
(Emigration) 28, 30 May.
(South Wales Strike) 1, 4, 8, 10, 14, 18, 19 March.
(Miners' Parliament) 1, 2, 5 April.
(Collier at Home) 16, 17, 18, 19, 23, 25, 30 April; 2, 9, 21, 23, 30 May.
None of these articles is signed. Some may well be by Richard Whiteing (see p. 182-3).

9 W. Buchanan Taylor–James Agate 6 March 1933 in 'Ego' (Gollancz 1935), p. 274.

10 M.G. 13 October; 15 October 1868.

11 M.G. 2 February 1874.

12 M.G. 4, 5 February 1874; 6 October 1868.

13 M.G. 24, 26 January 1874.

14 M.G. 7 February 1874.

15 M.G. 19–21 February 1874.

CHAPTER FOURTEEN

1 Hammond, pp. 16, 55 (C. P. Scott–Russell Scott 10 November 1865); Russell Scott–Taylor 23 May 1838. I. and C. Scott, p. 310.

2 Haslam Mills: Grey Pastures (Chatto & Windus 1924), pp. 51, 60.

3 M.G. 24 April 1876.

4 Michael Kennedy: The Hallé Tradition (Manchester University Press 1960), p. 20.

5 M.G. 12 March 1873.

6 M.G. 14 and 17 August 1876.

7 M.G. 6 May 1876 et seq.

8 Michael Kennedy: The Hallé Tradition, p. 84.

9 M.G. 20 July 1857.

10 Taylor–Scott 23 August 1872.

11 C. P. Scott–L. P. Scott 19 August 1907.

12 Haslam Mills: Grey Pastures, p. 127.

13 M.G. 17 November 1876.

14 Buxton–Whiteing 15 August 1878.

15 Richard Whiteing: My Harvest (Hodder & Stoughton 1915), p. 123.

16 Richard Whiteing: My Harvest, pp. 131, 132.

17 M.G. 13 January 1882.

18 M.G. 30 January 1933. In Saintsbury's time reviews were still unsigned.

19 M.G. 19 April 1871.
20 M.G. 13 March; 7 April; 11 December; 17 April; 24 March 1876.
21 Mrs Montague–J. L. Hammond 16 December (? 1932).
22 Hammond: p. 41.
23 The first appeared on 29 December 1876.
24 J. B. Atkins: Incidents and Reflections, p. 73.
25 M.G. 17 July 1884; Cape–Scott 13 March 1884.
26 Atkins: Incidents and Reflections, p. 74.
27 M.G. 28 February 1849 (the review was of the third edition); M.G. 29 September 1910.

CHAPTER FIFTEEN

1 Through Bosnia and Herzegovina on Foot during the Insurrection (Longmans 1876), p. 310.
2 Joan Evans: Time and Chance (Longmans 1943), p. 189.
3 M.G. 27 April 1877.
4 See summary in Evans: Illyrian Letters, pp. 84–91 (Longmans 1878).
5 M.G. 16 February 1882.
6 M.G. 27 February 1882.
7 Joan Evans: Time and Chance, p. 249.
8 MS Diary 7 September 1883 (in School of Slavonic Studies).
9 Joan Evans: Time and Chance, pp. 287, 323–335.
10 L'Italie et les Yougo-Slaves: Une Situation Dangereuse (Paris: Long, Blanchong et Cie).
11 Woods: Spunyarn, 2 vols. (Hutchinson) 1924.
12 M.G. 23 September 1889; The Truth about Asia Minor (C. D. Collet) 1890, p. 6.
13 M.G. 29 June 1876.
14 M.G. 20 December 1876.
15 M.G. 20 October 1877.
16 Woods, Spunyarn. II, 39.
17 Woods: Spunyarn, pp. 11, 14.
18 Buxton–Woods September 1878.
19 Orders for these appear in the manager's business letter book.
20 M.G. 4 September 1876.
21 M.G. 8 August; 7, 9 May 1877.

CHAPTER SIXTEEN

1 M.G. 24 June 1886.
2 The quotations from the Guardian in this paragraph come from the issues of 19 January, 17 June and 15 April 1886.
3 Haslam Mills: Grey Pastures, pp. 70, 124.
4 W. T. Arnold–Mrs T. Arnold 15 August 1879.
5 M.G. 2 February 1880.

6 M.G. 10 March 1880.
7 W. Buchanan Taylor quoted in Agate: Ego, p. 274.
8 M.G. 13 May 1882.
9 M.G. 3, 8 May 1882.
10 M.G. 12 May 1882.
11 M.G. 3 April 1882.
12 M.G. 19, 21 August 1882.
13 Fitzgerald–Scott 23 August 1882.
14 H. Spenser Wilkinson: Thirty-five Years (Constable 1933), pp. 33, 36.
15 Fortnightly Review 1 July 1888.
16 Quoted by C. E. Montague in W. T. Arnold: pp. 82, 3.
17 Taubman–Scott 30 December 1884.
18 Scott–Taylor 9 October 1884.
19 Quoted by Mrs Humphry Ward in W. T. Arnold (Manchester Univ. Press 1907), p. 44.
20 M.G. 6 January 1886.
21 Bright–Scott 17 February 1886.
22 M.G. 19 April 1886.

CHAPTER SEVENTEEN

1 Taylor–Scott 29 January 1886.
2 Taylor–Scott 10 April 1886.
3 Taylor–Scott 4 December 1890.
4 Taylor–Scott 7 March 1884; 29 April 1892.
5 Taylor–Scott 21 September and 28 October 1890.
6 Taylor–Scott 2 and 6 June 1891.
7 Buxton–T. P. O'Connor 16 August 1887.
8 Buxton–J. A. Gallighan 3 and 7 February 1879.
9 Buxton's letter is dated 3 November 1879.
10 Taylor–Scott 16 September 1882.
11 Mrs Taylor–Scott 28 September 1883; 18 October 1883.
12 Taylor–Mrs Taylor October 1883.
13 Scott–Taylor 11 October 1883.
14 e.g. Taylor–Scott 18 January 1890.
15 Taylor–Scott 21 and 25 March 1890.
16 Buxton–Thorne & Co 2 June 1886; Buxton–J. W. Riggs 15 July 1886.
17 Taylor–Scott 10 April 1890.
18 Haslam Mills: The Manchester Guardian (Chatto & Windus 1926), p. 117.
19 Taylor–Scott 30 January 1889.
20 Taylor–Scott 12 March 1889.

CHAPTER EIGHTEEN

1 Taylor–Scott 11 March 1884.
2 Taylor–Scott 13 June 1886.
3 Scott–Taylor 9 October 1884.
4 Taylor–Scott 6 January 1895.
5 Taylor–Scott 16 May 1895.
6 Scott–Wilkinson 24 January 1890.
7 Wilkinson–Scott 30 December 1891.
8 Taylor–Scott 19 October 1892; and 29 January 1896.
9 Atkins: Incidents and Reflections, p. 80.
10 Taylor–Scott Easter Sunday 1895.
11 Hobhouse–Scott 21 February 1901.
12 Taylor–Scott 16 October 1896.
13 Taylor–Scott 21 October 1896.
14 Taylor–Scott 17 February 1898.
15 Taylor–Scott 23 August 1899.
16 Scott–Taylor 28 August 1899.
17 Taylor–Scott 22 December 1899.
18 Scott–Taylor 9 January 1900.

CHAPTER NINETEEN

1 M.G. 18 July 1900.
2 Oliver Elton: C. E. Montague (Chatto and Windus 1929), p. 46.
3 M.G. 18 November 1890.
4 M.G. 24 November 1890.
5 St Stephen's December 1901.
6 Yeats: Autobiographies (Macmillan 1955), pp. 98–99 and 213; Joyce: Ulysses, pp. 142, 144 (Penguin).
7 Scott–Montague 10 December 1890.
   Taylor–Scott 9 and 19 December 1890.
8 M.G. 29 November 1890.
9 In a letter of 1914 quoted in Elton: Montague, p. 97. Reports of the Carlow by-election appear on p. 34.
10 Taylor–Montague 7 February 1896. Montague was 28.
11 M.G. 6 September 1889.
12 M.G. 27 August 1889.
13 M.G. 2 September 1889.
14 M.G. 28 August; 4 September 1889.
15 M.G. 16, 17, 19 December 1889; 11 June 1890.
16 M.G. 13, 25 July 1893.
17 M.G. 8, 9, 11 September 1893.
18 Barbara Hammond in Hobson and Ginsberg: L. T. Hobhouse (Allen & Unwin 1931), p. 34.
19 Hobhouse–Sidgwick 18 November 1896.

20 Hobhouse–Scott 12 February 1898.
21 In his Introduction to Hobson & Ginsberg: L. T. Hobhouse.
22 Atkins op. cit., p. 71.
23 Atkins op. cit., p. 10.
24 Atkins op. cit., pp. 76, 80.
25 Taylor–Scott 18 August 1896; 15 October 1897.
26 Taylor–Scott 2 January 1899. Atkins turned his articles into a book, 'The War in Cuba.'
27 Taylor–Scott 9 January 1899.
28 Scott–Sidebotham 10 July 1929.
29 Daily Dispatch 20 March 1940.
30 R. W. Raper–G. B. Diblee 5 November 1895.
31 M.G. 6 April 1897.
32 Taylor–Scott 9, 15, 23 December 1897; M.G. 17 December 1897; Times 17, 20, 21, 22, 23, 24 December 1897.
33 8 March 1899.
34 Taylor–Scott 9 January 1899.

CHAPTER TWENTY

1 Queen Victoria to Kitchener quoted in Philip Magnus: Kitchener: J. Murray (1958), p. 135.
2 M.G. 11 April 1899; Churchill: My Early Life (Thornton Butterworth 1930), p. 242.
3 G. W. Steevens: With Kitchener to Khartoum (Blackwood: 22nd Edition 1900, p. 289). Steevens represented the Daily Mail.
4 Bennett–Scott 22 January 1899.
5 Quoted in M.G. 9 January 1899.
6 E. T. Cook–Scott 26 May 1899; Scott–Hobhouse 3 June 1899.
7 Hobhouse–Scott 7 April 1899.
8 M.G. 6 June 1899.
9 Winston S. Churchill: The River War (1899) Vol. II, pp. 195, 196.
10 The description is by Sir Robert Donald, the editor of the Daily Chronicle. (Robert Donald by H. A. Taylor (Stanley Paul), p. 36).
11 The five articles appeared in the M.G. on 15, 19, 21, 25 and 26 July 1899. The reference to a sixth article is in a letter from Hobson to Scott from RMS Carisbrook Castle, undated.
12 M.G. 19 July 1899.
13 M.G. 17 November and 11 December 1899.
14 M.G. 24 May and 18 June 1900.
15 Dibblee–Scott 21 December 1899.
16 H. W. Nevinson: Fire of Life (Nisbet 1935), pp. 115, 116.
17 Harold Spender: The Fire of Life 1926, p. 105; M.G. 2–6, 11, 13 October 1900; Hobhouse–Scott 26 November 1899; Taylor–Scott 4, 5 January 1901.
18 Curzon–Scott 15 March 1900.

19 M.G. 3 January 1900.
20 C. P. Scott and the Making of the Manchester Guardian: Muller (1946), p. 86.
21 See To-day's News To-day: The Story of the Argus Co, Johannesburg 1956, p. 163; Hobson: War in South Africa, p. 207.
22 M.G. 9 February 1901.
23 Emily Hobhouse in the M.G. 19 February 1902.
24 Taylor–Scott 4 and 6 November 1901; M.G. 5 November 1901.
25 Leipoldt–Scott 7 March 1910.
26 Gibbings & Co 1901.
27 19 and 20 August 1901.
28 Taylor–Scott 29 August 1901.
29 August 1901.
30 Manchester Courier 6 September 1901 (Merriman was J. X. Merriman, later Prime Minister of Cape Colony. He was under police surveillance in 1901).
31 Dibblee–Taylor 9 September 1901.
32 Dibblee–Scott 13 September 1901. The figures are not of purchasers but of readers estimated roughly at three or four per copy sold.
33 M.G. 27 December 1901.

CHAPTER TWENTY-ONE

1 Taylor–Scott 27 November 1889; 25 March 1890.
2 Taylor–Scott 12 February 1891.
3 Scott's letter to Sadler, and Sadler's to his wife are in Michael Ernest Sadler by Michael Sadleir (Constable) 1949, pp. 107–110.
4 Sadler–Scott 28 November 1890.
5 Taylor–Scott 11 March 1891; Spender–Scott 15 March 1891. J. A. Spender was the elder brother of Harold.
6 Dibblee–Scott 15 May 1893.
7 C. P. Scott–E. T. Scott 3 October 1931.
8 M.G. 30 September, 30 August, 6 July 1893.
9 The circulation and profit and loss figures for 1893–1896 are from Dibblee's Notes; Taylor–Scott 20 December 1898; 28 February 1900.
10 Dibblee–Scott 31 January 1900.
11 M.G. 15 October 1900.
12 Dibblee–Scott 20 March 1900.
13 Taylor–Scott 14 June 1893.
14 Taylor–Scott 25 November 1893.
15 In an undated letter.
16 J. H. Buxton–Jacob Bright 20 June 1889.
17 Labour Leader October 1895.
18 Taylor–Scott 27 April; 2 and 9 October; 29 December 1895.
19 Quoted in Robert Blatchford: Portrait of an Englishman by Laurence

Thompson (Gollancz) 1951, p. 100. The Clarion was not part of the
Hulton press, though largely written in their own time by Hulton men.
20 Taylor–Dibblee 23 November 1896; Taylor–Scott 1 December 1896.
21 Taylor–Scott 29 December 1898. Scott was 52 at the time.

CHAPTER TWENTY-TWO

1 Dibblee–Taylor 2 and 4 December 1898.
2 Taylor–Scott 27 December 1898.
3 Taylor–Scott 2 and 4 January 1899.
4 Dibblee–Scott 4 April 1902; Scott–Dibblee 4 April 1902; Taylor–Scott
7 April 1902.
5 Dibblee–Scott 6 May 1902.
6 A. W. Ward–Scott 17 June 1902.
7 Dibblee–Scott 11 September 1902.
8 Young–Scott 30 December 1903.
9 Taylor–Scott 8 January 1904.
10 Taylor–Scott 11 January 1904.
11 Taylor–J. R. Scott 13 January 1904.
12 J. R. Scott–C. P. Scott 13 January 1904.
13 Taylor–Scott 22 September 1905.
14 Scott–Hobhouse 2 November 1905.
15 Scott–Reid 25 October 1905.
16 Montague–Hobhouse 4 December 1905.
17 Montague–Hobhouse 1 November 1905.
18 Montague–Hobhouse 7 December 1905.
19 Montague–Hobhouse 10 December 1905.
20 Montague–Hobhouse 20 December 1905.
21 J. R. Scott–L. P. Scott 10 March 1907.
22 Phillips–Scott 21 May 1906.
23 Taylor–Dibblee 14 February 1895.
24 C. P. Scott–L. P. Scott 10 August 1907.
25 Mrs O'Neill–Scott, Christmas Day (no year, but probably 1905).
26 C. P. Scott–Laurence Scott 19 August 1907.

CHAPTER TWENTY-THREE

1 Arnold Bennett: Journals (Cassell 1932), 4 December 1909.
2 M.G. 3 March 1910.
3 Montague–Dodd 8 December 1909.
4 M.G. 4 December 1909.
5 M.G. 1 March 1911.
6 J. E. Agate: Ego, p. 46. The description of Mills comes from a letter of
W. Buchanan Taylor quoted in Ego, p. 275.
7 Montague–Dodd 5 November 1908.
8 Frank Swinnerton–Swinnerton (Hutchinson 1939) p. 157.

9 Horniman–Scott 6 or 7 February; Award 29 April; Scott–Yeats 23 May 1911. Mair–Yeats 8 February, 1911.
10 M.G. 7 February 1950.
11 Montague–Dodd 3 August 1912.
12 Montague–Dodd 25 December 1909.
13 M.G. 20 October 1908.
14 M.G. 10 July 1912.
15 T. M. Young–Scott 24 May 1899.
16 Memorandum from the Counting House.
17 T. M. Young–Scott 9 December 1903; M.G. 19 November; 3, 4, 5, 7, 9, 11 December 1903; Manchester Courier 3 and 9 December; Daily Dispatch 4, 8, 9 December; Times 5 and 9 December.
18 Walter Greenwood: There was a Time: Cape (1967), p. 125.
19 Agate: Ego, p. 44.
20 M.G. 13 February 1911.
21 A. Yates–Scott 10 August 1912.

CHAPTER TWENTY-FOUR

1 M.G. 6 July 1912, 'A Silver Wedding.'
2 Russell–Scott 2 and 5 December 1896.
3 Taylor–Scott 28 October 1896; 28 December 1896; 3 January 1897.
4 Atkins–Scott 13 October 1904.
5 Russell–Scott 6 July 1912.
6 Russell–Scott 21 March 1901.
7 Montague–Dodd 14 and 20 December 1910.
8 Paton–Scott 16 February 1901.
9 Bone, A. M. Drysdale and E. W. Record quoted in 'Reporter' (Hutchinson & Co 1938), pp. 9, 20, 25.
10 Bone–Scott 26 June 1911.
11 Scott–Bone 31 October 1911.
12 Interview Notes 16 November 1911.
13 Interview Notes 15 January 1914 (MS).
14 Interview Notes 18 January 1914 (MS).
15 Scott–Hobhouse 28 January 1914.
16 Interview notes 27 June 1916 (MS).

CHAPTER TWENTY-FIVE

1 Pares–Oliver Elton 16 April; Pares–Scott 4 November; Williams–Scott 30 September, 3 November 1904.
2 Quoted in 'Cheerful Giver.' Ariadna Tyrkova–Williams (Peter Davies 1935), p. 20. After the 1917 Revolution Williams rejoined the *Times* and became its foreign editor.
3 Williams–Scott 3 November 1904.
4 Tyrkova–Williams op. cit., p. 62.

5 Williams–Scott 15 August 1905.
6 Janet Adam Smith: John Buchan (Hart Davies 1965), pp. 34, 42.
7 M.G. 11 August 1906.
8 Ramsay–Mair 31 March 1910.
9 Ramsay–Scott 1 and 7 October; Scott–Ramsay 9 October 1911; M.G. 10 October 1911.
10 J. B. Atkins: Incidents and Reflections, pp. 44, 46.
11 M.G. 30 October 1911.
12 M.G. 24 July 1911.
13 The World Crisis: Thornton Butterworth 1931 (one vol. edn.), p. 46.
14 M.G. 26 July 1911.
15 Agate: Ego Two, p. 292.
16 He put his conclusions in articles in the Spectator signed Vigilans sed Aequus and republished as 'German Ambitions' (Smith, Elder 1903).
17 Atkins op. cit., pp. 83, 84.

CHAPTER TWENTY-SIX

1 Montague–Scott 31 July 1914.
2 Montague–Dodd 19 December 1911.
3 Montague–Dodd 11 March 1915.
4 Nevinson: Last Changes, Last Chances, p. 140.
5 Hobhouse–Scott 12 December 1914.
6 Scott–Morel 24 August 1914.
7 M.G. 20 August 1914.
8 Emily Hobhouse–Scott 25 December 1914. M.G. 24 December 1914.
9 Nevinson: Fire of Life, p. 349.
10 Quoted by Elton: C. E. Montague, p. 224.
11 Scott–Hobhouse 20 December 1914.
12 Montague–Dodd 11 March 1915.
13 Scott–Hobhouse 25 April 1918.
14 Russell–Scott 6 August 1914; 30 January 1915.
15 Interview Notes 10 August 1917 (MS).
16 Fisher–Scott 19 June 1916; 12 November 1917.
17 People who believe that the British are the Lost Ten Tribes of Israel.
18 22 December 1916 enclosed in Fisher–Scott 24 December 1916.
19 Interview Notes 29 February 1916.
20 Scott–Hobhouse 4 February 1917.
21 M.G. 23 June 1916.
22 M.G. 14 June 1919.
23 M.G. 11 March 1919.
24 M.G. 30 October 1914.
25 Scott–Weizmann 13 December 1914.
26 Weizmann–Scott 16 November 1914.
27 Scott–Weizmann 5 December 1914.

28 Interview Notes 29 June 1917. It seems possible that the frustration which Scott shared with Weizmann may have contributed to his willingness to believe and support Fisher.

29 M.G. 5 November 1917.

30 Scott–Sacher, Sieff and Marks 17 October 1916.

31 Frank O'Connor: My Father's Son (Macmillan 1968), p. 80.

32 The descriptions of Radcliffe and Meakin are from a letter from Howard Spring to the author written shortly before his death.

33 Manchester Guardian House Journal March 1920.

34 C. P. Scott–Isabella Scott 23 March 1917.

CHAPTER TWENTY-SEVEN

1 Montague–Dodd 12 October 1917. Buchan had written the letterpress for a volume of Francis Dodd's drawings.

2 Sunday Times 24 March 1940. He succeeded Col. Repington as military critic.

3 Scott–Sidebotham 10 July 1929.

4 Scott–Hammond 31 October 1918.

5 Brunner–Scott 22 February 1899.

6 Hammond–Scott 31 August 1906.

7 H. W. Nevinson: Fire of Life, pp. 213, 215. 'The Village Labourer' had appeared in 1911 and 'The Town Labourer' in 1917.

8 Scott–Hammond 31 October 1918; Bone–Hammond 11 December 1918.

9 M.G. 2 January 1919.

10 M.G. 20 January 1919.

11 M.G. 1 February 1919.

12 M.G. 10 March 1919.

13 M.G. 8, 14 April 1919.

14 Crozier–Hammond 17 December 1918. Cachin's article appeared on 21 February 1919; the interviews with Feisal on 21 January, Vandervelde 29 January, Painlevé 17 February, Venizélos 1 March, Léon Bourgeois 5 March, and Branting 28 February and 28 March.

15 M.G. 1 and 12 March 1919.

16 Crozier–Hammond 12 December 1918.

17 Dore–Scott 19 November 1918.

18 Hansard 20 February 1919; M.G. 2 April and 20 October 1919.

19 Scott–Labour Monthly 24 February 1924; Reade–Scott 25 May 1924.

20 M.G. 20 March 1917.

21 Scott–Hobhouse 21 and 25 March 1917. The Russian 'of some distinction' was the musician Rosing.

22 M.G. 21 December 1917; 21 October 1967, based on 'My Reminiscences of the Russian Revolution' (Allen & Unwin 1921).

23 Seymour: The Intimate Papers of Colonel House (Benn 1928), Vol. III, pp. 325, 326.

24 M.G. 31 January and 2 February 1918.
25 The account of Philips Price in Russia is based on several conversations, his book 'My Three Revolutions': Allen & Unwin (1969) and the typescript of an earlier version of it.
26 Scott: Interview Notes 20 April 1918 (MS); the descriptive phrase about Farbman is from an obituary paragraph in the London Letter: M.G. 29 May 1933.
27 M.G. 16 December 1918; 2 January; 3, 20 February; 4, 7 April.
28 Goode described his first abortive attempt to reach Moscow in the M.G. 21, 22 August; his second successful visit M.G. 13–25 October 1919.
29 Scott–Curzon 12 October 1919.
30 Times 7 October 1919. The vicious attack 'from a special correspondent, Helsingfors,' was given great prominence on the main news page of the Times on 13 September.
31 Scott–Weizmann 19 November 1918.
32 Interview Notes 23–25 September 1918 (MS); House–Scott 29 September 1918; Scott–Hobhouse 18 October 1918; Interview Notes 25–26 October 1918 (MS).
33 Ratcliffe–Crozier 5 January 1919. Scott's report of his conversation with Wilson is in his Interview Notes.
34 Scott–Lippmann 22 December 1920.
35 Interview Notes 17 August 1918 (MS).
36 Lippmann–Scott 24 February 1919.
37 F. W. Graham–Scott 11 May 1916.
38 Villard–Scott 15 November 1918.

CHAPTER TWENTY-EIGHT

1 Leach–Spring 18 March 1915.
2 The Labour Party's short-lived official newspaper.
3 Cardus: Autobiography (Collins 1947) , pp. 24, 50.
4 Cardus: Autobiography, p. 90.
5 Cardus: Autobiography, p. 95.
6 J. L. Hammond–Barbara Hammond 13 January 1922.
7 M.G. 27, 28 April; 7, 8, 10 May 1920.
8 Interview Notes 15 July 1921.
9 Bone: London Echoing (Cape 1948), p. 48.
10 Interview Notes 28 October 1921 (MS).
11 Scott–Hammond 25 August 1921.
12 M.G. 12 October 1921.
13 M.G. 9 June 1922; Belfast Telegraph 2 June, 25 May 1922.
14 Scott–Hobhouse 30 January 1918.
15 S. G. Hobson: 'Pilgrim to the Left' (1938) p. 219.
16 S. G. Hobson: 'Pilgrim to the Left' (1938) p. 145.
17 Keynes–Scott 20 October 1921.

18 R. F. Harrod: John Maynard Keynes (Macmillan 1951), p. 315.
19 Hewart–Scott 27 April 1921.
20 M.G. 4 May 1921.

CHAPTER TWENTY-NINE

1 M.G. 10 March 1917. The paper in its leading articles strongly supported the protest. The vote was so overwhelming that the majority was only estimated.
2 Benjamin Bowker: Lancashire Under the Hammer (Hogarth Press 1928), pp. 33, 34, 42.
3 Bowker: Lancashire Under the Hammer, pp. 59, 105.
4 Lloyd George–Scott 23 July 1921.
5 J. L. Hammond–Barbara Hammond 29 May 1922.
6 M.G. 27 May 1922.
7 Quoted in M.G. 27 May 1922.
8 Scott–Hugh Chisholm 4 February 1923. Chisholm was editor of the Encyclopaedia Britannica; Scott–Asquith 4 March 1923. Bryce had died before Scott could be elected.
9 M.G. 8 March 1924. Mr MacDonald had been speaking to Free Churchmen.
10 MacDonald–Scott 11 December 1923.
11 Scott–Hobhouse 6 September 1924.
12 M.G. 3 October 1924.
13 Lejeune: Thank You for Having Me, (Hutchinson 1964), p. 36.
14 Quoted in Lejeune: Thank You For Having Me, pp. 123–125.
15 Lejeune: Thank You For Having Me, p. 70.
16 M.G. 16, 19 May 1922.
17 M.G. 9 June 1919.
18 M.G. 12 May 1924.
19 E. T. Scott–Mitrany 27 December 1925. I have omitted the names of the outgoing and incoming Chief Reporters, neither of whom was a success in the job, because they appear nowhere else in this book.
20 Scott–Montague 14 May 1925.
21 Scott–Montague 31 July 1914.
22 M.G. 21 December 1925 at a farewell dinner for Montague.
23 Montague: Disenchantment (Chatto & Windus), p. 89 (1928 edition).
24 Scott–Hobhouse 20 March 1919.
25 Montague–Dodd 26 July 1925.

CHAPTER THIRTY

1 Scott–Crozier 18, 20 January 1926; Crozier–Scott 23 January 1926. The earlier Hobhouse incident is described on p, 243.
2 M.G. 10 and 11 May 1926.

3 M.G. 8 August 1931.

4 M.G. 6 August 1931.

5 E. T. Scott–Hammond 30 August 1931.

6 Francis Williams: A Pattern of Rulers (Longmans 1965), pp. 111, 112.

7 E. T. Scott–Hammond 16 November 1931.

8 Hammond–E. T. Scott 21 November 1931.

9 E. T. Scott–Hammond 25 November 1931.

10 C. P. Scott–E. T. Scott 12 October 1931.

11 E.T.S.–Hammond n.d. probably 1929.

12 Crozier–Hammond 16, 20 February 1933; C. P. Scott by J. L. Hammond (1934), p. 319.

13 Hammond–Crozier 31 December 1933. Hammond's later admission was to Sir William Haley.

CHAPTER THIRTY-ONE

1 Frayman–Ayerst 13 June 1964.

2 M.G. 6 April 1949.

3 See pp. 156-7.

4 See pp. 294-5.

5 Scott–Hobhouse 18 December 1924. The last accounts had shown the M.G. profit as £40,000; the Evening News as £50,000.

6 Scott–Hammond 21 and 28 May 1926.

7 M.G. 9 and 11 June 1917; 28 August–20 September 1920. The reference to 'vexatious restrictions' is from the report of the T.U.C. deputation to the M.G. 30 August 1926.

8 'A Personal Note on the Proposals', 31 May 1926.

9 T.U.C. General Council: Report of Interview with the Manchester Guardian and Evening News Ltd 30 August 1926; Scott–Citrine 20 September 1926.

10 Ramsay MacDonald–Scott 9 September 1927. 'The T.A., who have been aggressive, are feeling that they have been out-generalled again by the other Unions,' was how John Scott had put it to Hammond 17 December 1926.

11 M.G. 4 September 1926.

12 P.E.P.: Report on the British Press (1938), p. 88.

13 P.E.P.: Report on the British Press (1938), p. 123.

14 P.E.P.: Report on the British Press (1938), p. 130.

15 R. F. Scott–L. P. Scott 31 July 1969.

16 J. R. Scott–E. T. Scott 22 April 1932.

17 M.G. 6 April 1949.

CHAPTER THIRTY-TWO

1 Dennis–Crozier 9 June 1933; Crozier–Dennis 24 August 1933. Crozier appears as Mr Rouvier in 'Bloody Mary's' by Geoffrey Dennis.

2 Crozier–Attenborough 25 January 1937.
3 Montague–C. P. Scott 29 May 1921.
4 Interview Notes 20 March 1941.
5 Crozier–Hammond 4 April 1934.
6 J. L. Bugary–Jonathan Cape 9 January 1943: Letters of Pontius Pilate (Cape 1928), p. 79.
7 Crozier–Voigt 13 March 1933.
8 Crozier–Hammond 27 August 1934.
9 Alexander–Scott 14 October 1905.
10 Hamilton–Scott 27 April 1910.
11 Nevinson: Last Changes and Chances, p. 228.
12 Voigt–Crozier 17 March 1933.
13 Jonathan Cape 1920.
14 Hamilton–Crozier n.d.
15 M.G. 7, 9, 12 April 1920; Interview Notes 10 April 1920 (MS); Hansard 14 April 1920.
16 Nevinson: Last Changes and Chances, p. 59.
17 Scott–Dell 29 December 1916.
18 Interview Notes 27 June 1918.
19 Lejeune: Thank You for Having Me, p. 109.

CHAPTER THIRTY-THREE

1 Werth–Crozier 27 January 1933.
2 Crozier–Werth 6 February.
3 Voigt–Crozier 15 March 1933.
4 Wiskemann: The Europe I Saw (Collins 1968), p. 35.
5 Werth–Crozier 21 March 1933.
6 Crozier–Voigt 17 March 1933.
7 Crozier–Werth 20 March 1933.
8 Crozier–Muggeridge 8 March 1933.
9 Muggeridge–Crozier 3 April 1933.
10 Muggeridge–Crozier 22 March 1933.
11 Muggeridge–Crozier 3 April 1933.
12 Voigt–Crozier 9 February 1933.
13 Voigt–Crozier 4 November 1933.
14 Voigt–Crozier 1 December 1933.
15 Voigt–Crozier 18 December 1933.
16 Voigt–Crozier 28 December 1933.
17 Voigt–Crozier 24 July 1935; Voigt–Crozier 12 December 1935.
18 Crozier–Voigt 31 March 1936.
19 See Christopher Sykes: Troubled Loyalty (Collins 1968), pp. 104–111. Voigt's articles appeared in the M.G. on 22 and 23 January 1934. Adam von Trott's first letter on 21 February.
20 Tobias: The Reichstag Fire (Secker and Warburg 1963), p. 105.
21 Voigt–Crozier 20 December 1935.

22 O.U.P. 1964. See especially pp. 10–13, 31, 50, 59.
23 Crozier–Dell 6 October 1935.
24 M.G. 22 August 1935.
25 Crozier–Voigt 4 September 1935.
26 Hammond–E. T. Scott 22 January 1930 on Voigt's return to Berlin.
27 Crozier–Hammond 29 March 1938. Hammond was reviewing 'Unto Caesar.'
28 Voigt–Crozier 16 December 1935.
29 M.G. 22 August 1935; Crozier–Voigt 24 October 1935.
30 M.G. 23 October 1935; Crozier–Dell 3 November 1935.
31 Crozier–Dell 29 October 1935.
32 Dell–Crozier 31 October 1935.
33 Crozier–Werth 31 October 1935.
34 Dell–Crozier 3 November 1935; Werth–Crozier 2 November 1935.
35 M.G. 7 March 1935.
36 M.G. 24 August 1935.
37 M.G. 15, 20, 21 September 1938.
38 M.G. 27 September 1938.
39 M.G. 1 October 1938.

CHAPTER THIRTY-FOUR

1 Hammond–Crozier 27 August 1939.
2 M.G. 6 December 1935: one of two 'turn-overs' on this subject which Crozier supported in leading articles. There was some controversy in the correspondence columns.
3 M.G. 4 February 1948.
4 E. A. Montague–Crozier 7 October 1939.
5 M.G. 6 May 1940.
6 M.G. 1 June 1940.
7 M.G. 11 May 1940.
8 Diary 27 August 1941.
9 Diary 24 October 1940. A.F.S.: Auxiliary Fire Service.
10 Wallace–J. R. Scott 16 October 1940.
11 Diary 27, 28 September 1941.
12 Cape 1945.
13 Diary 24 March 1941.
14 Diary 8, 9 February 1942.
15 Interview Notes 20 March 1941.
16 See (e.g.) Eden in Interview Notes 31 January 1941.
17 M.G. 4 December 1940; Weizmann–Crozier 6 December 1940; Crozier–Weizmann 10 December 1940.
18 Bone–Crozier 10 July 1943.
19 M.G. 2 and 3 February 1948.
20 M.G. 2 February 1948.
21 Manchester: John Sherratt & Son 1946.

CHAPTER THIRTY-FIVE

1 Bone–Wadsworth 5 May 1944.
2 Pringle–Wadsworth 29 April 1944.
3 Pringle–Wadsworth 6 May; Wadsworth–Pringle 8 May 1944.
4 Bone–Crozier 11 April 1944.
5 Bone–Wadsworth 7 May 1944: SCAEF: Supreme Commander, Allied Expeditionary Force.
6 Bone–Wadsworth 21 June 1944.
7 M.G. 3 July 1945.
8 M.G. 26 June 1945.
9 M.G. 4 and 5 July 1945.
10 Hammond–Wadsworth 10 July 1945.
11 Wadsworth–M. Wheatley Jones 10 March 1947.
12 Wadsworth–Bone 24 June 1945.
13 Bone–Wadsworth 9 August 1945.
14 M.G. 7, 8 August 1945.
15 Montague–Wadsworth 3 August 1945.
16 Pringle–P. J. Monkhouse n.d. probably 1951.
17 M.G. 2 February 1948.

CHAPTER THIRTY-SIX

1 Mr Bevin: M.G. 23 December 1946; Mr Attlee's Task: M.G. 15 February 1947; Mr Bevin's Triumph: M.G. 30 May 1947; In the Wrong: M.G. 24 May 1948.
2 e.g. M.G. 30 September; 14, 25 October; 10, 12, 18 November; 4, 27 December 1947.
3 Shiva Rao–Wadsworth 20 November 1945.
4 India and Democracy (1941) by Sir George Schuster and Guy Wint.
5 *Observer* 26 January 1969 (Letter from Khuswart Singh).
6 Wint–Wadsworth 4 June 1947; Wadsworth–Wint same date.
7 Observer January 1969.
8 M.G. 30 May 1945.
9 M.G. 27 June 1945.
10 M.G. 4 October 1968.
11 Thomas Barman: Diplomatic Correspondent (Hamish Hamilton 1968), p. 77.
12 M.G. 9 April 1951.
13 M.G. 6 February 1949.
14 e.g. 17 substantial articles between 24 September 1953 and 20 April 1954.
15 M.G. 1 January 1950.
16 M.G. 3 February 1950.
17 M.G. 17 February, 31 March 1950.
18 M.G. 28 February 1950.

19 M.G. 24 August 1944.
20 M.G. 18 December 1947.
21 Barman: Diplomatic Correspondent, p. 154.
22 Wadsworth–L. P. Scott 19 January 1949.
23 M.G. 14 July 1945.
24 M.G. 10 July 1945.

CHAPTER THIRTY-SEVEN

1 Opinion of Mr Andrew Clark 16 July 1935.
2 Readership Survey: Manchester Guardian Readers, December 1950 (Research Services Ltd).
3 L. P. Scott–Wadsworth 21 April 1950.
4 L. P. Scott–Wadsworth 22 May 1952.
5 Wadsworth–Hutt 24 June 1952. Hutt was editor of The Journalist.
6 Wadsworth–Hutt 10, 24 September 1952; Hutt–Wadsworth 26 September, 17 October 1952.
7 The Times 6 November 1956.
8 Wadsworth–Beavan 8 December 1952.
9 Memorandum by Wadsworth dated 12 November 1952.
10 L. P. Scott–Wadsworth 31 October 1952.
11 Memorandum by Wadsworth on M.G. Circulation, July 1953.
12 Working Report 1952–53.
13 L. P. Scott–Edward de Stein & Co 3 November 1953; Mark Norman–L. P. Scott 4 November 1953.

CHAPTER THIRTY-EIGHT

1 M.G. 21 February 1950. The reference in the last sentence is to a three weeks' old somewhat acrimonious controversy between the M.G. and Mr Churchill about what he had said at Blenheim in 1947.
2 M.G. 23 February 1950.
3 M.G. 2 March 1951.
4 M.G. 18 October 1951.
5 M.G. 10 July 1951.
6 M.G. 16 June 1950.
7 M.G. 22 April 1952.
8 M.G. 25 October 1951.
9 M.G. 18 May 1955.
10 J.C.B. in the Times 6 November 1956.
11 M.G. 5 July 1948.
12 M.G. 18 January 1951.
13 (Quoted by Brome (Longmans 1952): Bevan, p. 10). The passage did not appear in the last edition of the M.G.
14 S. J. Baker–Wadsworth 11 November 1952.

15 M.G. 11 November 1952. Previous references on 15, 24 and 31 October 1952.
16 M.G. 12 November 1952.
17 M.G. 29 April 1955.
18 M.G. 24 May 1955.
19 M.G. 26 May 1955.
20 M.G. 2 February 1953. The first which can be identified appeared in October 1914 and is reproduced between pp. 464 and 465.
21 M.G. 5 June 1953.
22 Boardman–Wadsworth 6 June 1953.
23 M.G. 15 February 1952.
24 M.G. 1 July 1952.
25 M.G. 13 July 1953.
26 C. P. Scott and the Making of the Manchester Guardian with an introduction by Sir William Haley (Muller 1946).
27 His work was eventually published in the Economic History Review in 1958.
28 Though nothing directly came from his enquiries, he has made good use of the material especially in Press and People (Arnold 1961); Peterloo (Manchester 1958); and 'John Harland' in the Manchester Review, Vol. VIII.
29 Newspaper Circulations 1800–1954. Proceedings of the Manchester Statistical Society 1955.
30 With Julia de L. Mann (Manchester University Press 1931).
31 M.G. 25 October 1951.
32 M.G. 2 February 1954.
33 Wadsworth–Boardman 2 February 1954.
34 M.G. 6 April 1955.
35 M.G. 3 January 1950 (not in last edition).
36 M.G. 15 December 1951. One of three Leader Page articles in which he described his visit.
37 M.G. 24 January–14 February 1955.
38 Freedman–Hetherington 6 August 1956.
39 Hetherington–Wadsworth, enclosing interview notes 14 August 1956.
40 M.G. 31 August 1956.
41 See Harman Grisewood: One Thing at a Time (Hutchinson 1968), pp. 197–201.
42 M.G. 15, 16, 17 October 1945.
43 M.G. 31 August; 2, 7, 14 September 1955.
44 M.G. 31 October 1956.

Index

Index of Persons

Members of the M.G. and company staff, correspondents and regular contributors are shown in capitals.